Praise for *OpenGL®* *Programming Guide,*
Eighth Edition

"Wow! This book is basically one-stop shopping for OpenGL information. It is the kind of book that I will be reaching for a lot. Thanks to Dave, Graham, John, and Bill for an amazing effort."

—*Mike Bailey, professor, Oregon State University*

"The most recent Red Book parallels the grand tradition of OpenGL; continuous evolution towards ever-greater power and efficiency. The eighth edition contains up-to-the minute information about the latest standard and new features, along with a solid grounding in modern OpenGL techniques that will work anywhere. The Red Book continues to be an essential reference for all new employees at my simulation company. What else can be said about this essential guide? I laughed, I cried, it was much better than *Cats*—I'll read it again and again."

—*Bob Kuehne, president, Blue Newt Software*

"OpenGL has undergone enormous changes since its inception twenty years ago. This new edition is your practical guide to using the OpenGL of today. Modern OpenGL is centered on the use of shaders, and this edition of the Programming Guide jumps right in, with shaders covered in depth in Chapter 2. It continues in later chapters with even more specifics on everything from texturing to compute shaders. No matter how well you know it or how long you've been doing it, if you are going to write an OpenGL program, you want to have a copy of the *OpenGL®* *Programming Guide* handy."

—*Marc Olano, associate professor, UMBC*

"If you are looking for the definitive guide to programming with the very latest version of OpenGL, look no further. The authors of this book have been deeply involved in the creation of OpenGL 4.3, and everything you need to know about the cutting edge of this industry-leading API is laid out here in a clear, logical, and insightful manner."

—*Neil Trevett, president, Khronos Group*

OpenGL®
Programming Guide
Eighth Edition

OpenGL®
Programming Guide
Eighth Edition

The Official Guide to
Learning OpenGL®, Version 4.3

Dave Shreiner
Graham Sellers
John Kessenich
Bill Licea-Kane

The Khronos OpenGL ARB Working Group

✦ Addison-Wesley

Upper Saddle River, NJ • Boston • Indianapolis • San Francisco
New York • Toronto • Montreal • London • Munich • Paris • Madrid
Capetown • Sydney • Tokyo • Singapore • Mexico City

Many of the designations used by manufacturers and sellers to distinguish their products are claimed as trademarks. Where those designations appear in this book, and the publisher was aware of a trademark claim, the designations have been printed with initial capital letters or in all capitals.

The authors and publisher have taken care in the preparation of this book, but make no expressed or implied warranty of any kind and assume no responsibility for errors or omissions. No liability is assumed for incidental or consequential damages in connection with or arising out of the use of the information or programs contained herein.

The publisher offers excellent discounts on this book when ordered in quantity for bulk purchases or special sales, which may include electronic versions and/or custom covers and content particular to your business, training goals, marketing focus, and branding interests. For more information, please contact:

U.S. Corporate and Government Sales
(800) 382-3419
corpsales@pearsontechgroup.com

For sales outside the United States, please contact:

International Sales
international@pearsoned.com

Visit us on the Web: informit.com/aw

Library of Congress Cataloging-in-Publication Data

OpenGL programming guide : the official guide to learning OpenGL, version 4.3 /
Dave Shreiner, Graham Sellers, John Kessenich, Bill Licea-Kane ; the Khronos OpenGL
ARB Working Group.—Eighth edition.
    pages   cm
  Includes index.
  ISBN 978-0-321-77303-6 (pbk. : alk. paper)
  1. Computer graphics. 2. OpenGL. I. Shreiner, Dave. II. Sellers, Graham.
  III. Kessenich, John M. IV. Licea-Kane, Bill. V. Khronos OpenGL ARB Working Group.
  T385.O635 2013
  006.6'63—dc23   2012043324

ISBN-13: 978-0-321-77303-6
ISBN-10:   0-321-77303-9
Text printed in the United States on recycled paper at Edwards Brothers Malloy in Ann Arbor, Michigan.
First printing, March 2013

For my family—Vicki, Bonnie, Bob, Cookie, Goatee, Phantom, Squiggles, Tuxedo, and Toby.
—DRS

To Emily: welcome, we're so glad you're here! Chris and J.: you still rock!
—GJAS

In memory of Phil Karlton, Celeste Fowler, Joan Eslinger, and Ben Cheatham.

Contents

Figures xxiii

Tables xxix

Examples xxxiii

About This Guide xli
What This Guide Contains xli
What's New in This Edition xliii
What You Should Know Before Reading This Guide xliii
How to Obtain the Sample Code xliv
Errata xlv
Style Conventions xlv

1. **Introduction to OpenGL** 1
   What Is OpenGL? 2
   Your First Look at an OpenGL Program 3
   OpenGL Syntax 8
   OpenGL's Rendering Pipeline 10
      Preparing to Send Data to OpenGL 11
      Sending Data to OpenGL 11
      Vertex Shading 12
      Tessellation Shading 12
      Geometry Shading 12
      Primitive Assembly 12
      Clipping 13
      Rasterization 13
      Fragment Shading 13

Per-Fragment Operations 13
Our First Program: A Detailed Discussion 14
  Entering **main**() 14
  OpenGL Initialization 16
  Our First OpenGL Rendering 28

2.   **Shader Fundamentals** **33**
Shaders and OpenGL 34
OpenGL's Programmable Pipeline 35
An Overview of the OpenGL Shading Language 37
  Creating Shaders with GLSL 37
  Storage Qualifiers 45
  Statements 49
  Computational Invariance 54
  Shader Preprocessor 56
  Compiler Control 58
  Global Shader-Compilation Option 59
Interface Blocks 60
  Uniform Blocks 61
  Specifying Uniform Blocks in Shaders 61
  Accessing Uniform Blocks from Your Application 63
  Buffer Blocks 69
  In/Out Blocks 70
Compiling Shaders 70
  Our **LoadShaders()** Function 76
Shader Subroutines 76
  GLSL Subroutine Setup 77
  Selecting Shader Subroutines 78
Separate Shader Objects 81

3.   **Drawing with OpenGL** **85**
OpenGL Graphics Primitives 86
  Points 87
  Lines, Strips, and Loops 88
  Triangles, Strips, and Fans 89
Data in OpenGL Buffers 92
  Creating and Allocating Buffers 92
  Getting Data into and out of Buffers 95

Accessing the Content of Buffers 100

Discarding Buffer Data 107

Vertex Specification 108

VertexAttribPointer in Depth 108

Static Vertex-Attribute Specification... 112

OpenGL Drawing Commands 115

Restarting Primitives... 124

Instanced Rendering 128

Instanced Vertex Attributes 129

Using the Instance Counter in Shaders...................................... 136

Instancing Redux 139

4. Color, Pixels, and Framebuffers **141**

Basic Color Theory... 142

Buffers and Their Uses 144

Clearing Buffers 146

Masking Buffers 147

Color and OpenGL 148

Color Representation and OpenGL.. 149

Vertex Colors... 150

Rasterization 153

Multisampling.. 153

Sample Shading 155

Testing and Operating on Fragments 156

Scissor Test.. 157

Multisample Fragment Operations 158

Stencil Test... 159

Stencil Examples 161

Depth Test 163

Blending... 166

Blending Factors 167

Controlling Blending Factors... 167

The Blending Equation... 170

Dithering.. 171

Logical Operations 171

Occlusion Query 173

Conditional Rendering... 176

Per-Primitive Antialiasing.. 178

Antialiasing Lines... 179

Antialiasing Polygons.. 180

Framebuffer Objects 180

Renderbuffers 183

Creating Renderbuffer Storage 185

Framebuffer Attachments 187

Framebuffer Completeness.. 190

Invalidating Framebuffers 192

Writing to Multiple Renderbuffers Simultaneously.......................... 193

Selecting Color Buffers for Writing and Reading 195

Dual-Source Blending.. 198

Reading and Copying Pixel Data 200

Copying Pixel Rectangles 203

5. **Viewing Transformations, Clipping, and Feedback**............................**205**

Viewing 206

Viewing Model 207

Camera Model 207

Orthographic Viewing Model 212

User Transformations 212

Matrix Multiply Refresher 214

Homogeneous Coordinates 215

Linear Transformations and Matrices 219

Transforming Normals 231

OpenGL Matrices 232

OpenGL Transformations 236

Advanced: User Clipping.. 238

Transform Feedback 239

Transform Feedback Objects... 239

Transform Feedback Buffers... 241

Configuring Transform Feedback Varyings................................. 244

Starting and Stopping Transform Feedback 250

Transform Feedback Example—Particle System 252

6. **Textures**..**259**

Texture Mapping 261

Basic Texture Types 262

Creating and Initializing Textures.. 263

Texture Formats 270
Proxy Textures.. 276
Specifying Texture Data 277
   Explicitly Setting Texture Data............................ 277
   Using Pixel Unpack Buffers 280
   Copying Data from the Framebuffer 281
   Loading Images from Files 282
   Retrieving Texture Data 287
   Texture Data Layout 288
Sampler Objects.. 292
   Sampler Parameters 294
Using Textures 295
   Texture Coordinates.. 298
   Arranging Texture Data 302
   Using Multiple Textures.................................... 303
Complex Texture Types.. 306
   3D Textures 307
   Array Textures 309
   Cube-Map Textures.. 309
   Shadow Samplers 317
   Depth-Stencil Textures 318
   Buffer Textures.. 319
Texture Views.. 321
Compressed Textures.. 326
Filtering 329
   Linear Filtering 330
   Using and Generating Mipmaps............................... 333
   Calculating the Mipmap Level............................... 338
   Mipmap Level-of-Detail Control 339
Advanced Texture Lookup Functions.................................. 340
   Explicit Level of Detail 340
   Explicit Gradient Specification 340
   Texture Fetch with Offsets 341
   Projective Texturing....................................... 342
   Texture Queries in Shaders 343
   Gathering Texels 345
   Combining Special Functions 345
Point Sprites 346

    Textured Point Sprites 347
    Controlling the Appearance of Points 350
  Rendering to Texture Maps 351
    Discarding Rendered Data 354
  Chapter Summary 356
    Texture Redux 356
    Texture Best Practices 357

7.   Light and Shadow **359**
  Lighting Introduction 360
  Classic Lighting Model 361
    Fragment Shaders for Different Light Styles 362
    Moving Calculations to the Vertex Shader 373
    Multiple Lights and Materials 376
    Lighting Coordinate Systems 383
    Limitations of the Classic Lighting Model 383
  Advanced Lighting Models 384
    Hemisphere Lighting 384
    Image-Based Lighting 389
    Lighting with Spherical Harmonics 395
  Shadow Mapping 400
    Creating a Shadow Map 401

8.   Procedural Texturing **411**
  Procedural Texturing 412
    Regular Patterns 414
    Toy Ball 422
    Lattice 431
    Procedural Shading Summary 432
  Bump Mapping 433
    Application Setup 436
    Vertex Shader 438
    Fragment Shader 439
    Normal Maps 441
  Antialiasing Procedural Textures 442
    Sources of Aliasing 442
    Avoiding Aliasing 444

Increasing Resolution... 445

Antialiasing High Frequencies 447

Frequency Clamping... 457

Procedural Antialiasing Summary...................................... 459

Noise.. 460

Definition of Noise 461

Noise Textures 468

Trade-offs.. 471

A Simple Noise Shader 472

Turbulence.. 475

Marble... 477

Granite.. 478

Wood 478

Noise Summary... 483

Further Information 483

9. **Tessellation Shaders**..**485**

Tessellation Shaders.. 486

Tessellation Patches... 487

Tessellation Control Shaders 488

Generating Output-Patch Vertices 489

Tessellation Control Shader Variables................................ 490

Controlling Tessellation 491

Tessellation Evaluation Shaders 496

Specifying the Primitive Generation Domain 497

Specifying the Face Winding for Generated Primitives 497

Specifying the Spacing of Tessellation Coordinates........................ 498

Additional Tessellation Evaluation Shader `layout` Options 498

Specifying a Vertex's Position 498

Tessellation Evaluation Shader Variables........................... 499

A Tessellation Example: The Teapot 500

Processing Patch Input Vertices.. 501

Evaluating Tessellation Coordinates for the Teapot........................ 501

Additional Tessellation Techniques 504

View-Dependent Tessellation.. 504

Shared Tessellated Edges and Cracking 506

Displacement Mapping 507

10. Geometry Shaders **509**

Creating a Geometry Shader 510

Geometry Shader Inputs and Outputs 514

Geometry Shader Inputs 514

Special Geometry Shader Primitives 517

Geometry Shader Outputs 523

Producing Primitives 525

Culling Geometry 525

Geometry Amplification 527

Advanced Transform Feedback 532

Multiple Output Streams 533

Primitive Queries 537

Using Transform Feedback Results 539

Geometry Shader Instancing 549

Multiple Viewports and Layered Rendering 550

Viewport Index 550

Layered Rendering 556

Chapter Summary 559

Geometry Shader Redux 560

Geometry Shader Best Practices 561

11. Memory **563**

Using Textures for Generic Data Storage 564

Binding Textures to Image Units 569

Reading from and Writing to Images 572

Shader Storage Buffer Objects 576

Writing Structured Data 577

Atomic Operations and Synchronization 578

Atomic Operations on Images 578

Atomic Operations on Buffers 587

Sync Objects 589

Image Qualifiers and Barriers 593

High Performance Atomic Counters 605

Example 609

Order-Independent Transparency 609

12. Compute Shaders...**623**
   Overview.. 624
   Workgroups and Dispatch 625
      Knowing Where You Are 630
   Communication and Synchronization........................... 632
      Communication 633
      Synchronization 634
   Examples.. 636
      Physical Simulation 636
      Image Processing.. 642
   Chapter Summary... 647
      Compute Shader Redux 647
      Compute Shader Best Practices 648

A. Basics of GLUT: The OpenGL Utility Toolkit.................**651**
   Initializing and Creating a Window 652
   Accessing Functions 654
   Handling Window and Input Events 655
   Managing a Background Process 658
   Running the Program 658

B. OpenGL ES and WebGL **659**
   OpenGL ES 660
   WebGL 662
      Setting up WebGL within an HTML5 page 662
      Initializing Shaders in WebGL 664
      Initializing Vertex Data in WebGL.......................... 667
      Using Texture Maps in WebGL.............................. 668

C. Built-in GLSL Variables and Functions **673**
   Built-in Variables 674
      Built-in Variable Declarations 674
      Built-in Variable Descriptions 676
   Built-in Constants.. 684
   Built-in Functions 686
      Angle and Trigonometry Functions 688
      Exponential Functions 690
      Common Functions... 692
      Floating-Point Pack and Unpack Functions 698

Geometric Functions 700

Matrix Functions.. 702

Vector Relational Functions 703

Integer Functions 705

Texture Functions... 708

Atomic-Counter Functions... 722

Atomic Memory Functions 723

Image Functions 725

Fragment Processing Functions.. 729

Noise Functions 731

Geometry Shader Functions 732

Shader Invocation Control Functions 734

Shader Memory Control Functions... 734

D.   State Variables **737**

The Query Commands.. 738

OpenGL State Variables... 745

Current Values and Associated Data... 746

Vertex Array Object State 747

Vertex Array Data 749

Buffer Object State.. 750

Transformation State... 751

Coloring State.. 752

Rasterization State 753

Multisampling 755

Textures.. 756

Textures.. 759

Textures.. 762

Textures.. 764

Texture Environment 766

Pixel Operations... 767

Framebuffer Controls 770

Framebuffer State 771

Framebuffer State 772

Frambuffer State... 773

Renderbuffer State 775

Renderbuffer State 776

Pixel State 778

Shader Object State 781
Shader Program Pipeline Object State 782
Shader Program Object State 783
Program Interface State 793
Program Object Resource State... 794
Vertex and Geometry Shader State 797
Query Object State 797
Image State 798
Transform Feedback State 799
Atomic Counter State... 800
Shader Storage Buffer State... 801
Sync Object State 802
Hints.. 803
Compute Dispatch State 803
Implementation-Dependent Values 804
Tessellation Shader Implementation-Dependent Limits.................. 810
Geometry Shader Implementation-Dependent Limits 813
Fragment Shader Implementation-Dependent Limits..................... 815
Implementation-Dependent Compute Shader Limits..................... 816
Implementation-Dependent Shader Limits 818
Implementation-Dependent Debug Output State 823
Implementation-Dependent Values 824
Internal Format-Dependent Values 826
Implementation-Dependent Transform Feedback Limits 826
Framebuffer-Dependent Values 827
Miscellaneous 827

E. Homogeneous Coordinates and Transformation Matrices **829**
Homogeneous Coordinates.. 830
    Transforming Vertices 830
    Transforming Normals 831
Transformation Matrices 831
    Translation... 832
    Scaling 832
    Rotation 832
    Perspective Projection 834
    Orthographic Projection... 834

F. OpenGL and Window Systems **835**

Accessing New OpenGL Functions 836

   GLEW: The OpenGL Extension Wrangler 837

GLX: OpenGL Extension for the X Window System 838

   Initialization 839

   Controlling Rendering 840

   GLX Prototypes 842

WGL: OpenGL Extensions for Microsoft Windows 845

   Initialization 846

   Controlling Rendering 846

   WGL Prototypes 848

OpenGL in Mac OS X: The Core OpenGL (CGL) API and the NSOpenGL
   Classes 850

Mac OS X's Core OpenGL Library 851

   Initialization 851

   Controlling Rendering 852

   CGL Prototypes 852

The NSOpenGL Classes 854

   Initialization 854

**G. Floating-Point Formats for Textures, Framebuffers, and
Renderbuffers** **857**

Reduced-Precision Floating-Point Values 858

16-bit Floating-Point Values 858

10- and 11-bit Unsigned Floating-Point Values 860

H. Debugging and Profiling OpenGL **865**

Creating a Debug Context 866

Debug Output 868

   Debug Messages 869

   Filtering Messages 872

   Application-Generated Messages 874

Debug Groups 875

   Naming Objects 877

Profiling 879

   Profiling Tools 879

   In-Application Profiling 881

I.   **Buffer Object Layouts** **885**

Using Standard Layout Qualifiers.. 886

The **std140** Layout Rules... 886

The **std430** Layout Rules... 887

Glossary **889**

Index **919**

Figures

Figure 1.1   Image from our first OpenGL program: triangles.cpp 5

Figure 1.2   The OpenGL pipeline 10

Figure 2.1   Shader-compilation command sequence 71

Figure 3.1   Vertex layout for a triangle strip 89

Figure 3.2   Vertex layout for a triangle fan 90

Figure 3.3   Packing of elements in a BGRA-packed vertex
attribute 112

Figure 3.4   Packing of elements in a RGBA-packed vertex
attribute 112

Figure 3.5   Simple example of drawing commands........................ 124

Figure 3.6   Using primitive restart to break a triangle strip............. 125

Figure 3.7   Two triangle strips forming a cube 127

Figure 3.8   Result of rendering with instanced vertex attributes....... 134

Figure 3.9   Result of instanced rendering using gl_InstanceID 139

Figure 4.1   Region occupied by a pixel 144

Figure 4.2   Polygons and their depth slopes 165

Figure 4.3   Aliased and antialiased lines 178

Figure 4.4   Close-up of RGB color elements in an LCD panel 199

Figure 5.1   Steps in configuring and positioning the viewing
frustum 207

Figure 5.2   Coordinate systems required by OpenGL 209

Figure 5.3   User coordinate systems unseen by OpenGL................. 210

Figure 5.4   A view frustum 211

Figure 5.5   Pipeline subset for user/shader part of transforming
coordinates.. 212

Figure 5.6   One-dimensional homogeneous space........................ 217

Figure 5.7	Translating by skewing	218
Figure 5.8	Translating an object 2.5 in the x direction	220
Figure 5.9	Scaling an object to three times its size	221
Figure 5.10	Scaling an object in place	223
Figure 5.11	Rotation	225
Figure 5.12	Rotating in place	225
Figure 5.13	Frustum projection	228
Figure 5.14	Orthographic projection	230
Figure 5.15	z precision	237
Figure 5.16	Transform feedback varyings packed in a single buffer	246
Figure 5.17	Transform feedback varyings packed in separate buffers	246
Figure 5.18	Transform feedback varyings packed into multiple buffers	250
Figure 5.19	Schematic of the particle system simulator	253
Figure 5.20	Result of the particle system simulator	258
Figure 6.1	Byte-swap effect on byte, short, and integer data	289
Figure 6.2	Subimage	290
Figure 6.3	*IMAGE_HEIGHT pixel storage mode	291
Figure 6.4	*SKIP_IMAGES pixel storage mode	292
Figure 6.5	Output of the simple textured quad example	299
Figure 6.6	Effect of different texture wrapping modes	301
Figure 6.7	Two textures used in the multitexture example	306
Figure 6.8	Output of the simple multitexture example	306
Figure 6.9	Output of the volume texture example	308
Figure 6.10	A sky box	312
Figure 6.11	A golden environment mapped torus	315
Figure 6.12	A visible seam in a cube map	316
Figure 6.13	The effect of seamless cube-map filtering	317
Figure 6.14	Effect of texture minification and magnification	330
Figure 6.15	Resampling of a signal in one dimension	330
Figure 6.16	Bilinear resampling	331
Figure 6.17	A pre-filtered mipmap pyramid	334
Figure 6.18	Effects of minification mipmap filters	335
Figure 6.19	Illustration of mipmaps using unrelated colors	336
Figure 6.20	Result of the simple textured point sprite example	348

Figure 6.21   Analytically calculated point sprites 349
Figure 6.22   Smooth edges of circular point sprites 349
Figure 7.1   Elements of the classic lighting model 361
Figure 7.2   A sphere illuminated using the hemisphere lighting
              model 386
Figure 7.3   Analytic hemisphere lighting function 387
Figure 7.4   Lighting model comparison 388
Figure 7.5   Light probe image 391
Figure 7.6   Lat-long map 391
Figure 7.7   Cube map 392
Figure 7.8   Effects of diffuse and specular environment maps 394
Figure 7.9   Spherical harmonics lighting 400
Figure 7.10   Depth rendering 405
Figure 7.11   Final rendering of shadow map 409
Figure 8.1   Procedurally striped torus 415
Figure 8.2   Stripes close-up 419
Figure 8.3   Brick patterns 420
Figure 8.4   Visualizing the results of the half-space distance
              calculations 427
Figure 8.5   Intermediate results from the toy ball shader 428
Figure 8.6   Intermediate results from "in" or "out" computation 429
Figure 8.7   The lattice shader applied to the cow model 432
Figure 8.8   Inconsistently defined tangents leading to large lighting
              errors 437
Figure 8.9   Simple box and torus with procedural bump mapping ... 441
Figure 8.10   Normal mapping 442
Figure 8.11   Aliasing artifacts caused by point sampling 444
Figure 8.12   Supersampling 446
Figure 8.13   Using the s texture coordinate to create stripes on
              a sphere 448
Figure 8.14   Antialiasing the stripe pattern 449
Figure 8.15   Visualizing the gradient 451
Figure 8.16   Effect of adaptive analytical antialiasing on striped
              teapots 452
Figure 8.17   Periodic step function 454
Figure 8.18   Periodic step function (pulse train) and its integral 454

Figure 8.19   Brick shader with and without antialiasing................... 456

Figure 8.20   Checkerboard pattern... 458

Figure 8.21   A discrete 1D noise function..................................... 462

Figure 8.22   A continuous 1D noise function................................. 463

Figure 8.23   Varying the frequency and the amplitude of the noise function.. 464

Figure 8.24   Summing noise functions... 465

Figure 8.25   Basic 2D noise, at frequencies 4, 8, 16, and 32 467

Figure 8.26   Summed noise, at 1, 2, 3, and 4 octaves...................... 467

Figure 8.27   Teapots rendered with noise shaders 475

Figure 8.28   Absolute value noise or "turbulence"........................... 476

Figure 8.29   A bust of Beethoven rendered with the wood shader...... 482

Figure 9.1   Quad tessellation 492

Figure 9.2   Isoline tessellation 494

Figure 9.3   Triangle tessellation 495

Figure 9.4   Even and odd tessellation... 496

Figure 9.5   The tessellated patches of the teapot 502

Figure 9.6   Tessellation cracking 507

Figure 10.1   Lines adjacency sequence... 518

Figure 10.2   Line-strip adjacency sequence................................... 519

Figure 10.3   Triangles adjacency sequence.................................... 520

Figure 10.4   Triangle-strip adjacency layout................................. 521

Figure 10.5   Triangle-strip adjacency sequence 522

Figure 10.6   Texture used to represent hairs in the fur rendering example 530

Figure 10.7   The output of the fur rendering example 531

Figure 10.8   Schematic of geometry shader sorting example............. 546

Figure 10.9   Final output of geometry shader sorting example 548

Figure 10.10 Output of the viewport-array example......................... 555

Figure 11.1   Output of the simple load-store shader 575

Figure 11.2   Timeline exhibited by the naïve overdraw counter shader.. 579

Figure 11.3   Output of the naïve overdraw counter shader 580

Figure 11.4   Output of the atomic overdraw counter shader 582

Figure 11.5   Cache hierarchy of a fictitious GPU 597

Figure 11.6   Data structures used for order-independent transparency 610

Figure 11.7   Inserting an item into the per-pixel linked lists 616

Figure 11.8   Result of order-independent transparency incorrect order on left; correct order on right. 621

Figure 12.1   Schematic of a compute workload 626

Figure 12.2   Relationship of global and local invocation ID.............. 632

Figure 12.3   Output of the physical simulation program as simple points 640

Figure 12.4   Output of the physical simulation program................. 642

Figure 12.5   Image processing 646

Figure 12.6   Image processing artifacts... 647

Figure B.1   Our WebGL demo 671

Figure H.1   AMD's GPUPerfStudio2 profiling Unigine Heaven 3.0 880

Figure H.2   Screenshot of Unigine Heaven 3.0 880

Tables

Table 1.1	Command Suffixes and Argument Data Types	10
Table 1.2	Example of Determining Parameters for **glVertexAttribPointer()**	26
Table 1.3	Clearing Buffers	28
Table 2.1	Basic Data Types in GLSL	38
Table 2.2	Implicit Conversions in GLSL	39
Table 2.3	GLSL Vector and Matrix Types	40
Table 2.4	Vector Component Accessors	43
Table 2.5	GLSL Type Modifiers	46
Table 2.6	GLSL Operators and Their Precedence	50
Table 2.7	GLSL Flow-Control Statements	52
Table 2.8	GLSL Function Parameter Access Modifiers	54
Table 2.9	GLSL Preprocessor Directives	57
Table 2.10	GLSL Preprocessor Predefined Macros	58
Table 2.11	GLSL Extension Directive Modifiers	60
Table 2.12	Layout Qualifiers for Uniform	62
Table 3.1	OpenGL Primitive Mode Tokens	90
Table 3.2	Buffer Binding Targets	93
Table 3.3	Buffer Usage Tokens	96
Table 3.4	Access Modes for **glMapBuffer()**	101
Table 3.5	Flags for Use with **glMapBufferRange()**	104
Table 3.6	Values of *Type* for **glVertexAttribPointer()**	109
Table 4.1	Converting Data Values to Normalized Floating-Point Values	150
Table 4.2	Query Values for the Stencil Test	161
Table 4.3	Source and Destination Blending Factors	169

Table 4.4	Blending Equation Mathematical Operations	171
Table 4.5	Sixteen Logical Operations	172
Table 4.6	Values for Use with **glHint()**	179
Table 4.7	Framebuffer Attachments	187
Table 4.8	Errors Returned by **glCheckFramebufferStatus()**	191
Table 4.9	**glReadPixels()** Data Formats	201
Table 4.10	Data Types for **glReadPixels()**	202
Table 5.1	Drawing Modes Allowed During Transform Feedback	251
Table 6.1	Texture Targets and Corresponding Sampler Types	263
Table 6.2	Sized Internal Formats	271
Table 6.3	External Texture Formats	274
Table 6.4	Example Component Layouts for Packed Pixel Formats	276
Table 6.5	Texture Targets and Corresponding Proxy Targets	276
Table 6.6	Target Compatibility for Texture Views	322
Table 6.7	Internal Format Compatibility for Texture Views	323
Table 7.1	Spherical Harmonic Coefficients for Light Probe Images	397
Table 9.1	Tessellation Control Shader Input Variables	490
Table 9.2	Evaluation Shader Primitive Types	497
Table 9.3	Options for Controlling Tessellation Level Effects	498
Table 9.4	Tessellation Control Shader Input Variables	500
Table 10.1	Geometry Shader Primitive Types and Accepted Drawing Modes	513
Table 10.2	Geometry Shader Primitives and the Vertex Count for Each	515
Table 10.3	Provoking Vertex Selection by Primitive Mode	524
Table 10.4	Ordering of Cube-Map Face Indices	559
Table 11.1	Generic Image Types in GLSL	565
Table 11.2	Image Format Qualifiers	566
Table B.1	Type Strings for WebGL Shaders	664
Table B.2	WebGL Typed Arrays	667
Table C.1	Cube-Map Face Targets	679
Table C.2	Notation for Argument or Return Type	687
Table D.1	Current Values and Associated Data	746
Table D.2	State Variables for Vertex Array Objects	747

Table D.3	State Variables for Vertex Array Data (Not Stored in a Vertex Array Object)	749
Table D.4	State Variables for Buffer Objects	750
Table D.5	Transformation State Variables	751
Table D.6	State Variables for Controlling Coloring	752
Table D.7	State Variables for Controlling Rasterization	753
Table D.8	State Variables for Multisampling	755
Table D.9	State Variables for Texture Units	756
Table D.10	State Variables for Texture Objects	759
Table D.11	State Variables for Texture Images	762
Table D.12	State Variables Per Texture Sampler Object	764
Table D.13	State Variables for Texture Environment and Generation	766
Table D.14	State Variables for Pixel Operations	767
Table D.15	State Variables Controlling Framebuffer Access and Values	770
Table D.16	State Variables for Framebuffers per Target	771
Table D.17	State Variables for Framebuffer Objects	772
Table D.18	State Variables for Framebuffer Attachments	773
Table D.19	Renderbuffer State	775
Table D.20	State Variables per Renderbuffer Object	776
Table D.21	State Variables Controlling Pixel Transfers	778
Table D.22	State Variables for Shader Objects	781
Table D.23	State Variables for Program Pipeline Object State	782
Table D.24	State Variables for Shader Program Objects	783
Table D.25	State Variables for Program Interfaces	793
Table D.26	State Variables for Program Object Resources	794
Table D.27	State Variables for Vertex and Geometry Shader State	797
Table D.28	State Variables for Query Objects	797
Table D.29	State Variables per Image Unit	798
Table D.30	State Variables for Transform Feedback	799
Table D.31	State Variables for Atomic Counters	800
Table D.32	State Variables for Shader Storage Buffers	801
Table D.33	State Variables for Sync Objects	802
Table D.34	Hints	803
Table D.35	State Variables for Compute Shader Dispatch	803

Table D.36   State Variables Based on Implementation-Dependent Values... 804

Table D.37   State Variables for Implementation-Dependent Tessellation Shader Values 810

Table D.38   State Variables for Implementation-Dependent Geometry Shader Values.. 813

Table D.39   State Variables for Implementation-Dependent Fragment Shader Values.. 815

Table D.40   State Variables for Implementation-Dependent Compute Shader Limits 816

Table D.41   State Variables for Implementation-Dependent Shader Limits... 818

Table D.42   State Variables for Debug Output State 823

Table D.43   Implementation-Dependent Values............................. 824

Table D.44   Internal Format-Dependent Values 826

Table D.45   Implementation-Dependent Transform Feedback Limits 826

Table D.46   Framebuffer-Dependent Values 827

Table D.47   Miscellaneous State Values 827

Table G.1   Reduced-Precision Floating-Point Formats.................... 858

Table I.1   `std140` Layout Rules... 886

Table I.2   `std430` Layout Rules... 887

Examples

Example 1.1	triangles.cpp: Our First OpenGL Program	5
Example 1.2	Vertex Shader for triangles.cpp: triangles.vert	23
Example 1.3	Fragment Shader for triangles.cpp: triangles.frag	25
Example 2.1	A Simple Vertex Shader	36
Example 2.2	Obtaining a Uniform Variable's Index and Assigning Values	48
Example 2.3	Declaring a Uniform Block	61
Example 2.4	Initializing Uniform Variables in a Named Uniform Block	65
Example 2.5	Static Shader Control Flow	77
Example 2.6	Declaring a Set of Subroutines	78
Example 3.1	Initializing a Buffer Object with **glBufferSubData()**	98
Example 3.2	Initializing a Buffer Object with **glMapBuffer()**	103
Example 3.3	Declaration of the DrawArraysIndirectCommand Structure	118
Example 3.4	Declaration of the DrawElementsIndirectCommand Structure	119
Example 3.5	Setting up for the Drawing Command Example	122
Example 3.6	Drawing Commands Example	123
Example 3.7	Intializing Data for a Cube Made of Two Triangle Strips	125
Example 3.8	Drawing a Cube Made of Two Triangle Strips Using Primitive Restart	127
Example 3.9	Vertex Shader Attributes for the Instancing Example	130
Example 3.10	Example Setup for Instanced Vertex Attributes	130
Example 3.11	Instanced Attributes Example Vertex Shader	132

Example 3.12 Instancing Example Drawing Code 132

Example 3.13 gl_VertexID Example Vertex Shader 136

Example 3.14 Example Setup for Instanced Vertex Attributes 138

Example 4.1 Specifying Vertex Color and Position Data: gouraud.cpp 150

Example 4.2 A Simple Vertex Shader for Gouraud Shading 152

Example 4.3 A Simple Fragment Shader for Gouraud Shading 152

Example 4.4 A Multisample-Aware Fragment Shader 155

Example 4.5 Using the Stencil Test: stencil.c 161

Example 4.6 Rendering Geometry with Occlusion Query: occquery.c 174

Example 4.7 Retrieving the Results of an Occlusion Query 175

Example 4.8 Rendering Using Conditional Rendering 177

Example 4.9 Setting Up Blending for Antialiasing Lines: antilines.cpp 180

Example 4.10 Creating a 256 × 256 RGBA Color Renderbuffer 187

Example 4.11 Attaching a Renderbuffer for Rendering 188

Example 4.12 Specifying layout Qualifiers for MRT Rendering 194

Example 4.13 Layout Qualifiers Specifying the Index of Fragment Shader Outputs 198

Example 5.1 Multiplying Multiple Matrices in a Vertex Shader 233

Example 5.2 Simple Use of gl_ClipDistance 238

Example 5.3 Example Initialization of a Transform Feedback Buffer 243

Example 5.4 Example Specification of Transform Feedback Varyings 245

Example 5.5 Leaving Gaps in a Transform Feedback Buffer 247

Example 5.6 Assigning Transform Feedback Outputs to Different Buffers 248

Example 5.7 Assigning Transform Feedback Outputs to Different Buffers 249

Example 5.8 Vertex Shader Used in Geometry Pass of Particle System Simulator 254

Example 5.9 Configuring the Geometry Pass of the Particle System Simulator 254

Example 5.10 Vertex Shader Used in Simulation Pass of Particle System Simulator 255

Example 5.11   Configuring the Simulation Pass of the Particle System Simulator.. 257

Example 5.12   Main Rendering Loop of the Particle System Simulator 257

Example 6.1   Direct Specification of Image Data in C 278

Example 6.2   Loading Static Data into Texture Objects 279

Example 6.3   Loading Data into a Texture Using a Buffer Object 280

Example 6.4   Definition of the vglImageData Structure 283

Example 6.5   Simple Image Loading Example 284

Example 6.6   Loading a Texture Using loadImage 285

Example 6.7   Simple Texture Lookup Example (Fragment Shader) 297

Example 6.8   Simple Texture Lookup Example (Vertex Shader)....... 297

Example 6.9   Simple Texturing Example 298

Example 6.10   Setting the Border Color of a Sampler 301

Example 6.11   Texture Swizzle Example....................................... 302

Example 6.12   Simple Multitexture Example (Vertex Shader)........... 304

Example 6.13   Simple Multitexture Example (Fragment Shader)....... 305

Example 6.14   Simple Multitexture Example 305

Example 6.15   Simple Volume Texture Vertex Shader 307

Example 6.16   Simple Volume Texture Fragment Shader................. 308

Example 6.17   Initializing a Cube-Map Texture 310

Example 6.18   Initializing a Cube-Map Array Texture.................... 311

Example 6.19   Simple Skybox Example—Vertex Shader.................. 313

Example 6.20   Simple Skybox Example—Fragment Shader 313

Example 6.21   Cube-Map Environment Mapping Example—Vertex Shader 314

Example 6.22   Cube-Map Environment Mapping Example—Fragment Shader 314

Example 6.23   Creating and Initializing a Buffer Texture 320

Example 6.24   Texel Lookups from a Buffer Texture 321

Example 6.25   Creating a Texture View with a New Format............. 324

Example 6.26   Creating a Texture View with a New Target 325

Example 6.27   Simple Point Sprite Vertex Shader.......................... 347

Example 6.28   Simple Point Sprite Fragment Shader 347

Example 6.29   Analytic Shape Fragment Shader 348

Example 6.30	Attaching a Texture Level as a Framebuffer Attachment: fbotexture.cpp	353
Example 7.1	Setting Final Color Values with No Lighting	363
Example 7.2	Ambient Lighting	364
Example 7.3	Directional Light Source Lighting	366
Example 7.4	Point-Light Source Lighting	369
Example 7.5	Spotlight Lighting	371
Example 7.6	Point-light Source Lighting in the Vertex Shader	374
Example 7.7	Structure for Holding Light Properties	376
Example 7.8	Multiple Mixed Light Sources	377
Example 7.9	Structure to Hold Material Properties	380
Example 7.10	Code Snippets for Using an Array of Material Properties	380
Example 7.11	Front and Back Material Properties	382
Example 7.12	Vertex Shader for Hemisphere Lighting	388
Example 7.13	Shaders for Image-based Lighting	394
Example 7.14	Shaders for Spherical Harmonics Lighting	398
Example 7.15	Creating a Framebuffer Object with a Depth Attachment	401
Example 7.16	Setting up the Matrices for Shadow Map Generation	402
Example 7.17	Simple Shader for Shadow Map Generation	403
Example 7.18	Rendering the Scene From the Light's Point of View	404
Example 7.19	Matrix Calculations for Shadow Map Rendering	406
Example 7.20	Vertex Shader for Rendering from Shadow Maps	406
Example 7.21	Fragment Shader for Rendering from Shadow Maps	407
Example 8.1	Vertex Shader for Drawing Stripes	416
Example 8.2	Fragment Shader for Drawing Stripes	417
Example 8.3	Vertex Shader for Drawing Bricks	420
Example 8.4	Fragment Shader for Drawing Bricks	421
Example 8.5	Values for Uniform Variables Used by the Toy Ball Shader	423
Example 8.6	Vertex Shader for Drawing a Toy Ball	424
Example 8.7	Fragment Shader for Drawing a Toy Ball	429
Example 8.8	Fragment Shader for Procedurally Discarding Part of an Object	431

Example 8.9   Vertex Shader for Doing Procedural Bump
                    Mapping 438

Example 8.10   Fragment Shader for Procedural Bump Mapping 440

Example 8.11   Fragment Shader for Adaptive Analytic
                    Antialiasing 451

Example 8.12   Source Code for an Antialiased Brick Fragment
                    Shader 456

Example 8.13   Source Code for an Antialiased Checkerboard
                    Fragment Shader 458

Example 8.14   C function to Generate a 3D Noise Texture 469

Example 8.15   A Function for Activating the 3D Noise Texture 471

Example 8.16   Cloud Vertex Shader 473

Example 8.17   Fragment Shader for Cloudy Sky Effect 474

Example 8.18   Sun Surface Fragment Shader 477

Example 8.19   Fragment Shader for Marble 477

Example 8.20   Granite Fragment Shader 478

Example 8.21   Fragment Shader for Wood 480

Example 9.1   Specifying Tessellation Patches 488

Example 9.2   Passing Through Tessellation Control Shader Patch
                    Vertices 490

Example 9.3   Tessellation Levels for Quad Domain Tessellation
                    Illustrated in Figure 9.1 492

Example 9.4   Tesslation Levels for an Isoline Domain Tessellation
                    Shown in Figure 9.2 493

Example 9.5   Tesslation Levels for a Triangular Domain
                    Tessellation Shown in Figure 9.3 494

Example 9.6   A Sample Tessellation Evaluation Shader 499

Example 9.7   gl_in Parameters for Tessellation Evaluation
                    Shaders 499

Example 9.8   Tessellation Control Shader for Teapot Example 501

Example 9.9   The Main Routine of the Teapot Tessellation
                    Evaluation Shader 502

Example 9.10   Definition of $B(i, u)$ for the Teapot Tessellation
                    Evaluation Shader 503

Example 9.11   Computing Tessellation Levels Based on
                    View-Dependent Parameters 504

Example 9.12   Specifying Tessellation Level Factors Using Perimeter
                    Edge Centers 506

Example 9.13	Displacement Mapping in main Routine of the Teapot Tessellation Evaluation Shader	508
Example 10.1	A Simple Pass-Through Geometry Shader	511
Example 10.2	Geometry Shader Layout Qualifiers	512
Example 10.3	Implicit Declaration of gl_in[]	514
Example 10.4	Implicit Declaration of Geometry Shader Outputs	523
Example 10.5	A Geometry Shader that Drops Everything	526
Example 10.6	Geometry Shader Passing Only Odd-Numbered Primitives	526
Example 10.7	Fur Rendering Geometry Shader	528
Example 10.8	Fur Rendering Fragment Shader	529
Example 10.9	Global Layout Qualifiers Used to Specify a Stream Map	533
Example 10.10	Example 10.9 Rewritten to Use Interface Blocks	534
Example 10.11	Incorrect Emission of Vertices into Multiple Streams	535
Example 10.12	Corrected Emission of Vertices into Multiple Streams	536
Example 10.13	Assigning Transform Feedback Outputs to Buffers	537
Example 10.14	Simple Vertex Shader for Geometry Sorting	541
Example 10.15	Geometry Shader for Geometry Sorting	542
Example 10.16	Configuring Transform Feedback for Geometry Sorting	543
Example 10.17	Pass-Through Vertex Shader used for Geometry Shader Sorting	544
Example 10.18	OpenGL Setup Code for Geometry Shader Sorting	545
Example 10.19	Rendering Loop for Geometry Shader Sorting	547
Example 10.20	Geometry Amplification Using Nested Instancing	550
Example 10.21	Directing Geometry to Different Viewports with a Geometry Shader	552
Example 10.22	Creation of Matrices for Viewport Array Example	553
Example 10.23	Specifying Four Viewports	554
Example 10.24	Example Code to Create an FBO with an Array Texture Attachment	556
Example 10.25	Geometry Shader for Rendering into an Array Texture	557
Example 11.1	Examples of Image Format Layout Qualifiers	568

Example 11.2   Creating, Allocating, and Binding a Texture to an Image Unit... 571

Example 11.3   Creating and Binding a Buffer Texture to an Image Unit... 572

Example 11.4   Simple Shader Demonstrating Loading and Storing into Images 574

Example 11.5   Simple Declaration of a Buffer Block 576

Example 11.6   Creating a Buffer and Using it for Shader Storage 577

Example 11.7   Declaration of Structured Data................................ 577

Example 11.8   Naïvely Counting Overdraw in a Scene 578

Example 11.9   Counting Overdraw with Atomic Operations 581

Example 11.10   Possible Definitions for IMAGE_PARAMS.................... 583

Example 11.11   Equivalent Code for imageAtomicAdd.................... 584

Example 11.12   Equivalent Code for imageAtomicExchange and imageAtomicComp 585

Example 11.13   Simple Per-Pixel Mutex Using imageAtomicCompSwap....................................... 585

Example 11.14   Example Use of a Sync Object................................ 592

Example 11.15   Basic Spin-Loop Waiting on Memory 594

Example 11.16   Result of Loop-Hoisting on Spin-Loop.................... 594

Example 11.17   Examples of Using the volatile Keyword 595

Example 11.18   Examples of Using the coherent Keyword 598

Example 11.19   Example of Using the memoryBarrier() Function... 599

Example 11.20   Using the early_fragment_tests Layout Qualifier 604

Example 11.21   Counting Red and Green Fragments Using General Atomics 605

Example 11.22   Counting Red and Green Fragments Using Atomic Counters.. 606

Example 11.23   Initializing an Atomic Counter Buffer 608

Example 11.24   Initializing for Order-Independent Transparency 611

Example 11.25   Per-Frame Reset for Order-Independent Transparency 613

Example 11.26   Appending Fragments to Linked List for Later Sorting... 614

Example 11.27   Main Body of Final Order-Independent Sorting Fragment Shader 617

Example 11.28 Traversing Linked-Lists in a Fragment Shader 618

Example 11.29 Sorting Fragments into Depth Order for OIT 619

Example 11.30 Blending Sorted Fragments for OIT 619

Example 12.1 Simple Local Workgroup Declaration 626

Example 12.2 Creating, Compiling, and Linking a Compute Shader 627

Example 12.3 Dispatching Compute Workloads 629

Example 12.4 Declaration of Compute Shader Built-in Variables 630

Example 12.5 Operating on Data 631

Example 12.6 Example of Shared Variable Declarations 633

Example 12.7 Particle Simulation Compute Shader 637

Example 12.8 Initializing Buffers for Particle Simulation 638

Example 12.9 Particle Simulation Fragment Shader 640

Example 12.10 Particle Simulation Rendering Loop 641

Example 12.11 Central Difference Edge Detection Compute Shader 643

Example 12.12 Dispatching the Image Processing Compute Shader ... 644

Example B.1 An Example of Creating an OpenGL ES Version 2.0 Rendering Context 661

Example B.2 Creating an HTML5 Canvas Element 662

Example B.3 Creating an HTML5 Canvas Element that Supports WebGL 663

Example B.4 Our WebGL Applications Main HTML Page 664

Example B.5 Our WebGL Shader Loader: InitShaders.js 666

Example B.6 Loading WebGL Shaders Using **InitShaders()** 667

Example B.7 Initializing Vertex Buffers in WebGL 668

Example B.8 Our demo.js WebGL Application 669

Example H.1 Creating a Debug Context Using WGL 866

Example H.2 Creating a Debug Context Using GLX 867

Example H.3 Prototype for the Debug Message Callback Function 868

Example H.4 Creating Debug Message Filters 873

Example H.5 Sending Application-Generated Debug Messages 875

Example H.6 Using an Elapsed Time Query 882

About This Guide

The OpenGL graphics system is a software interface to graphics hardware. (The GL stands for Graphics Library.) It allows you to create interactive programs that produce color *images* of moving three-dimensional *objects*. With OpenGL, you can control computer-graphics technology to produce realistic pictures, or ones that depart from reality in imaginative ways. This guide explains how to program with the OpenGL graphics system to deliver the visual effect you want.

What This Guide Contains

This guide contains the following chapters:

- Chapter 1, "Introduction to OpenGL", provides a glimpse into what OpenGL can do. It also presents a simple OpenGL program and explains the essential programming details you need to know for the subsequent chapters.

- Chapter 2, "Shader Fundamentals", discusses the major feature of OpenGL, programmable shaders, demonstrating how to initialize and use them within an application.

- Chapter 3, "Drawing with OpenGL", describes the various methods for rendering geometry using OpenGL, as well as some optimization techniques for making rendering more efficient.

- Chapter 4, "Color, Pixels, and Framebuffers", explains OpenGL's processing of color, including how pixels are processed, buffers are managed, and rendering techniques focused on pixel processing.

- Chapter 5, "Viewing Transformations, Clipping, and Feedback", details the operations for presenting a three-dimensional scene on a two-dimensional computer screen, including the mathematics and shader operations for the various types of geometric projection.

- Chapter 6, "Textures", discusses combining *geometric models* and imagery for creating realistic, high-detailed three-dimensional models.

- Chapter 7, "Light and Shadow", describes simulating illumination effects for computer graphics, focusing on implementing those techniques in programmable shaders.

- Chapter 8, "Procedural Texturing", details the generation of textures and other surface effects using programmable shaders for increased realism and other rendering effects.

- Chapter 9, "Tessellation Shaders", explains OpenGL's shader facility for managing and tessellating geometric surfaces.

- Chapter 10, "Geometry Shaders", describe an additional technique for modifying geometric primitives within the OpenGL rendering pipeline using shaders.

- Chapter 11, "Memory", demonstrates techniques using OpenGL's framebuffer and buffer memories for advanced rendering techniques and nongraphical uses.

- Chapter 12, "Compute Shaders", introduces the newest shader stage which integrates general computation into the OpenGL rendering pipeline.

Additionally, a number of appendices are available for reference.

- Appendix A, "Basics of GLUT: The OpenGL Utility Toolkit", discusses the library that handles window system operations. GLUT is portable and it makes code examples shorter and more comprehensible.

- Appendix B, "OpenGL ES and WebGL", details the other APIs in the OpenGL family, including OpenGL ES for embedded and mobile systems, and WebGL for interactive 3D applications within Web browsers.

- Appendix C, "Built-in GLSL Variables and Functions", provides a detailed reference to OpenGL Shading Language.

- Appendix D, "State Variables", lists the state variables that OpenGL maintains and describes how to obtain their values.

- Appendix E, "Homogeneous Coordinates and Transformation Matrices", explains some of the mathematics behind *matrix* transformations.

- Appendix F, "OpenGL and Window Systems", describes the various window–system-specific libraries that provide the binding routines used for allowing OpenGL to render with their native windows.

- Appendix G, "Floating-Point Formats for Textures, Framebuffers, and Renderbuffers", provides an overview of the floating-point formats used within OpenGL.

- Appendix H, "Debugging and Profiling OpenGL", discusses the latest debug features available within OpenGL.

- Appendix I, "Buffer Object Layouts", provides a reference for use with uniform buffers using the standard memory layouts defined in OpenGL.

What's New in This Edition

Virtually everything! For those familiar with previous versions of the *OpenGL Programming Guide*, this edition is a complete rewrite focusing on the latest methods and techniques for OpenGL application development. It combines the function-centric approach of the classic Red Book, with the *shading* techniques found in the *OpenGL Shading Language* (commonly called the "Orange Book").

In this edition, the author team was expanded to include major contributors to OpenGL's evolution, as well as the OpenGL Shading Language specification editor. As such, this edition covers the very latest version of OpenGL, Version 4.3, including compute shaders. It also describes every stage of the programmable rendering pipeline. We sincerely hope you find it useful and educational.

What You Should Know Before Reading This Guide

This guide assumes only that you know how to program in the C language (we do use a little bit of C++, but nothing you won't be able to figure out easily) and that you have some background in mathematics (geometry, trigonometry, linear algebra, calculus, and differential geometry). Even if you have little or no experience with computer graphics technology, you should be able to follow most of the discussions in this book. Of course, computer graphics is an ever-expanding subject, so you may want to enrich your learning experience with supplemental reading:

- *Computer Graphics: Principles and Practice, Third Edition,* by John F. Hughes et al. (Addison-Wesley, forthcoming 2013)—This book is an encyclopedic treatment of the subject of computer graphics. It includes a wealth of information but is probably best read after you have some experience with the subject.

- *3D Computer Graphics by Andrew S. Glassner* (The Lyons Press, 1994)—This book is a nontechnical, gentle introduction to computer graphics. It focuses on the visual effects that can be achieved, rather than on the techniques needed to achieve them.

Another great place for all sorts of general information is the OpenGL Web site. This Web site contains software, sample programs, documentation,

FAQs, discussion boards, and news. It is always a good place to start any search for answers to your OpenGL questions:

http://www.opengl.org/

Additionally, full documentation of all the procedures and shading language syntax that compose the latest OpenGL version are documented and available at the official OpenGL Web site. These Web pages replace the *OpenGL Reference Manual* that was published by the OpenGL Architecture Review Board and Addison-Wesley.

OpenGL is really a hardware-independent specification of a programming interface, and you use a particular implementation of it on a particular kind of hardware. This guide explains how to program with any OpenGL implementation. However, since implementations may vary slightly—in performance and in providing additional, optional features, for example— you might want to investigate whether supplementary documentation is available for the particular implementation you're using. In addition, the provider of your particular implementation might have OpenGL-related utilities, toolkits, programming and debugging support, widgets, sample programs, and demos available at its Web site.

How to Obtain the Sample Code

This guide contains many sample programs to illustrate the use of particular OpenGL programming techniques. As the audience for this guide has a wide range of experience, from novice to seasoned veteran, with both computer graphics and OpenGL, the examples published in these pages usually present the simplest approach to a particular rendering situation, demonstrated using the OpenGL Version 4.3 interface. This is done mainly to make the presentation straightforward and accessible to those readers just starting with OpenGL. For those of you with extensive experience looking for implementations using the latest features of the API, we first thank you for your patience with those following in your footsteps, and ask that you please visit our Web site:

http://www.opengl-redbook.com/

There, you will find the source code for all examples in this text, implementations using the latest features, and additional discussion describing the modifications required in moving from one version of OpenGL to another.

All of the programs contained within this book use the OpenGL Utility Toolkit (GLUT), originally authored by Mark Kilgard. For this edition, we

use the open-source version of the GLUT interface from the folks
developing the freeglut project. They have enhanced Mark's original work
(which is thoroughly documented in his book, *OpenGL Programming for the
X Window System*, Addison-Wesley, 1997). You can find their open-source
project page at the following address:

http://freeglut.sourceforge.net/

You can obtain code and binaries of their implementation at this site.

The section "OpenGL-Related Libraries" in Chapter 1 and Appendix A give
more information about using GLUT. Additional resources to help
accelerate your learning and programming of OpenGL and GLUT can be
found at the OpenGL Web site's resource pages:

http://www.opengl.org/resources/

Many implementations of OpenGL might also include the code samples
as part of the system. This source code is probably the best source for your
implementation, because it might have been optimized for your system.
Read your machine-specific OpenGL documentation to see where those
code samples can be found.

Errata

Unfortunately, it is likely this book will have errors. Additionally, OpenGL
is updated during the publication of this guide: errors are corrected and
clarifications are made to the specification, and new specifications are
released. We keep a list of bugs and updates at our Web site,
http://www.opengl-redbook.com/, where we also offer facilities for
reporting any new bugs you might find. If you find an error, please accept
our apologies, and our thanks in advance for reporting it. We'll get it
corrected as soon as possible.

Style Conventions

These style conventions are used in this guide:

- **Bold**—Command and routine names and matrices

- *Italics*—Variables, arguments, parameter names, spatial dimensions,
  matrix components, and first occurrences of key terms.

- Regular—Enumerated types and defined constants

Code examples are set off from the text in a monospace font, and
command summaries are shaded with gray boxes.

In a command summary, we sometimes use braces to identify options among data types. In the following example, **glCommand()** has four possible suffixes: s, i, f, and d, which stand for the data types GLshort, GLint, GLfloat, and GLdouble. In the function prototype for **glCommand()**, *TYPE* is a wildcard that represents the data type indicated by the suffix.

void **glCommand{sifd}**(TYPE *x1*, TYPE *y1*, TYPE *x2*, TYPE *y2*);

We use this form when the number of permutations of the function becomes unruly.

Chapter 1

Introduction to OpenGL

Chapter Objectives

After reading this chapter, you'll be able to do the following:

- Describe the purpose of OpenGL, what it can and cannot do in creating computer-generated images.

- Identify the common structure of an OpenGL application.

- Enumerate the shading stages that compose the OpenGL rendering pipeline.

This chapter introduces OpenGL. It has the following major sections:

- "What Is OpenGL?" explains what OpenGL is, what it does and doesn't do, and how it works.

- "Your First Look at an OpenGL Program" provides a first look at what an OpenGL program looks like.

- "OpenGL Syntax" describes the format of the command names that OpenGL uses.

- "OpenGL's Rendering Pipeline" discusses the processing pipeline that OpenGL uses in creating images.

- "Our First Program: A Detailed Discussion" dissects the first program presented and provides more detail on the activities of each section of the program.

What Is OpenGL?

OpenGL is an *application programming interface*—"API" for short—which is merely a software library for accessing features in graphics hardware. Version 4.3 of the OpenGL library (which this text covers) contains over 500 distinct commands that you use to specify the objects, images, and operations needed to produce interactive three-dimensional computer-graphics applications.

OpenGL is designed as a streamlined, hardware-independent interface that can be implemented on many different types of graphics hardware systems, or entirely in software (if no graphics hardware is present in the system) independent of a computer's operating or windowing system. As such, OpenGL doesn't include functions for performing windowing tasks or processing user input; instead, your application will need to use the facilities provided by the windowing system where the application will execute. Similarly, OpenGL doesn't provide any functionality for describing models of three-dimensional objects, or operations for reading image files (like JPEG files, for example). Instead, you must construct your three-dimensional objects from a small set of *geometric primitives*—points, lines, triangles, and patches.

Since OpenGL has been around a while—it was first developed at Silicon Graphics Computer Systems with Version 1.0 released in July of 1994— there are both many versions of OpenGL, as well as many software libraries built on OpenGL for simplifying application development, whether you're writing a video game, creating a visualization for scientific or medical purposes, or just showing images. However, the more modern version of OpenGL differs from the original in significant ways. In this book, we describe how to use the most recent versions of OpenGL to create those applications.

The following list briefly describes the major operations that an OpenGL application would perform to render an image. (See "OpenGL's Rendering Pipeline" for detailed information on these operations.)

- Specify the data for constructing shapes from OpenGL's geometric primitives.

- Execute various *shaders* to perform calculations on the input primitives to determine their position, color, and other rendering attributes.

- Convert the mathematical description of the input primitives into their *fragments* associated with locations on the screen. This process is called *rasterization*.

- Finally, execute a *fragment shader* for each of the fragments generated by rasterization, which will determine the fragment's final color and position.

- Possibly perform additional per-fragment operations such as determining if the object that the fragment was generated from is visible, or blending the fragment's color with the current color in that screen location.

OpenGL is implemented as a client-server system, with the application you write being considered the *client*, and the OpenGL implementation provided by the manufacturer of your computer graphics hardware being the *server*. In some implementations of OpenGL (such as those associated with the *X Window System*), the client and server will execute on different machines that are connected by a *network*. In such cases, the client will issue the OpenGL commands, which will be converted into a window-system specific *protocol* that is transmitted to the server via their shared network, where they are executed to produce the final image.

Your First Look at an OpenGL Program

Because you can do so many things with OpenGL, an OpenGL program can potentially be large and complicated. However, the basic structure of all OpenGL applications is usually similar to the following:

- Initialize the *state* associated with how objects should be rendered.

- Specify those objects to be rendered.

Before you look at some code, let's introduce some commonly used graphics terms. *Rendering*, which we've already used without defining previously, is the process by which a computer creates an image from models. OpenGL is just one example of a rendering system; there are many others. OpenGL is a rasterization-based system, but there are other methods for generating images as well, such as *ray tracing*, whose techniques are outside the scope of this book. However, even a system that uses ray tracing may employ OpenGL to display an image, or compute information to be used in creating an image.

Our *models*, or objects—we'll use the terms interchangeably—are constructed from geometric primitives—*points*, lines, and triangles—that are specified by their *vertices*.

Another concept that is essential to using OpenGL is shaders, which are special functions that the graphics hardware executes. The best way to think of shaders is as little programs that are specifically compiled for your *graphics processing unit*—commonly called a graphics processing unit (GPU). OpenGL includes all the compiler tools internally to take the source code of your shader and create the code that the GPU needs to execute. In OpenGL, there are four *shader stages* that you can use. The most common are *vertex shaders*, which process vertex data, and fragment shaders, which operate on the fragments generated by the rasterizer. Both vertex and fragment shaders are required in every OpenGL program.

The final generated image consists of pixels drawn on the screen; a *pixel* is the smallest visible element on your *display*. The pixels in your system are stored in a *framebuffer*, which is a chunk of memory that the graphics hardware manages, and feeds to your display device.

Figure 1.1 shows the output of a simple OpenGL program, which renders two blue triangles into a window. The source code for the entire example is provided in Example 1.1.

Figure 1.1   Image from our first OpenGL program: triangles.cpp

Example 1.1   triangles.cpp: Our First OpenGL Program

```
///////////////////////////////////////////////////////////////////////
//
// triangles.cpp
//
///////////////////////////////////////////////////////////////////////

#include <iostream>
using namespace std;

#include "vgl.h"
#include "LoadShaders.h"

enum VAO_IDs { Triangles, NumVAOs };
enum Buffer_IDs { ArrayBuffer, NumBuffers };
enum Attrib_IDs { vPosition = 0 };

GLuint   VAOs[NumVAOs];
GLuint   Buffers[NumBuffers];

const GLuint   NumVertices = 6;
```

```
//---------------------------------------------------------------
//
// init
//

void
init(void)
{
    glGenVertexArrays(NumVAOs, VAOs);
    glBindVertexArray(VAOs[Triangles]);

    GLfloat  vertices[NumVertices][2] = {
        { -0.90, -0.90 },  // Triangle 1
        {  0.85, -0.90 },
        { -0.90,  0.85 },
        {  0.90, -0.85 },  // Triangle 2
        {  0.90,  0.90 },
        { -0.85,  0.90 }
    };

    glGenBuffers(NumBuffers, Buffers);
    glBindBuffer(GL_ARRAY_BUFFER, Buffers[ArrayBuffer]);
    glBufferData(GL_ARRAY_BUFFER, sizeof(vertices),
                 vertices, GL_STATIC_DRAW);

    ShaderInfo  shaders[] = {
        { GL_VERTEX_SHADER, "triangles.vert" },
        { GL_FRAGMENT_SHADER, "triangles.frag" },
        { GL_NONE, NULL }
    };

    GLuint program = LoadShaders(shaders);
    glUseProgram(program);

    glVertexAttribPointer(vPosition, 2, GL_FLOAT,
                          GL_FALSE, 0, BUFFER_OFFSET(0));
    glEnableVertexAttribArray(vPosition);
}

//---------------------------------------------------------------
//
// display
//

void
display(void)
{
    glClear(GL_COLOR_BUFFER_BIT);

    glBindVertexArray(VAOs[Triangles]);
    glDrawArrays(GL_TRIANGLES, 0, NumVertices);

    glFlush();
}
```

```
//-----------------------------------------------------------------
//
// main
//

int
main(int argc, char** argv)
{
    glutInit(&argc, argv);
    glutInitDisplayMode(GLUT_RGBA);
    glutInitWindowSize(512, 512);
    glutInitContextVersion(4, 3);
    glutInitContextProfile(GLUT_CORE_PROFILE);
    glutCreateWindow(argv[0]);

    if (glewInit()) {
        cerr << "Unable to initialize GLEW ...  exiting" << endl;
        exit(EXIT_FAILURE);
    }

    init();

    glutDisplayFunc(display);

    glutMainLoop();
}
```

While that may be more code than you were expecting, you'll find that this program will be the basis of just about every OpenGL application you write. We use some additional software libraries that aren't officially part of OpenGL to simplify things like creating a window, or receiving mouse or keyboard input—those things that OpenGL doesn't include. We've also created some helper functions and small C++ classes to simplify our examples. While OpenGL is a "C"-language library, all of our examples are in C++, but very simple C++. In fact, most of the C++ we use is to implement the mathematical constructs *vectors* and matrices.

In a nutshell, here's what Example 1.1 does. We'll explain all of these concepts in complete detail later, so don't worry.

- In the preamble of the program, we include the appropriate header files and declare global variables[1] and other useful programming constructs.

- The **init()** routine is used to set up data for use later in the program. This may be vertex information for later use when rendering

---

1. Yes; in general we eschew global variables in large applications, but for the purposes of demonstration, we use them here.

primitives, or image data for use in a technique called *texture mapping*, which we describe in Chapter 6.

In this version of **init**(), we first specify the position information for the two triangles that we render. After that, we specify shaders we're going to use in our program. In this case, we only use the required vertex and fragment shaders. The **LoadShaders**() routine is one that we've written to simplify the process of preparing shaders for a GPU. In Chapter 2 we'll discuss everything it does.

The final part of **init**() is doing what we like to call *shader plumbing*, where you associate the data in your application with variables in *shader program*s. This is also described in detail in Chapter 2.

- The **display**() routine is what really does the rendering. That is, it calls the OpenGL functions that request something be rendered. Almost all **display**() routines will do the same three steps as in our simple example here.

  1. Clear the window by calling **glClear**().

  2. Issue the OpenGL calls required to render your object.

  3. Request that the image is presented to the screen.

- Finally, **main**() does the heavy lifting of creating a window, calling **init**(), and finally entering into the *event loop*. Here you also see functions that begin with "gl" but look different than the other functions in the application. Those, which we'll describe momentarily, are from the libraries we use to make it simple to write OpenGL programs across the different operating and window systems: GLUT, and GLEW.

Before we dive in to describe the routines in detail, let us explain OpenGL labels functions, constants, and other useful programming constructs.

OpenGL Syntax

As you likely picked up on, all the functions in the OpenGL library begin with the letters "gl", immediately followed by one or more capitalized words to name the function (**glBindVertexArray**(), for example). All functions in OpenGL are like that. In the program you also saw the functions that began with "glut", which are from the OpenGL Utility Toolkit (GLUT), a library written by Mark J. Kilgard. It's a popular cross-platform toolkit for opening windows and managing input, among other operations. We use a version of GLUT named *Freeglut*, originally written by Pawel W. Olszta with contributions from Andreas Umbach and Steve Baker (who currently maintains the library), which is a modern variant of the original library. Similarly, you see a single function, **glewInit()**, which comes from the OpenGL Extension Wrangler written by Milan Ikits and Marcelo Magallon. We describe both of those libraries in more detail in Appendix A.

Similar to OpenGL's function-naming convention, constants like GL_COLOR_BUFFER_BIT, which you saw in **display()**, are defined for the OpenGL library. All constant tokens begin with GL_, and use underscores to separate words. Their definitions are merely #defines found in the OpenGL header files: glcorearb.h and glext.h.

To aid in moving OpenGL applications between operating systems, OpenGL also defines various types of data for its functions, such as GLfloat, which is the floating-point value type we used to declare vertices in Example 1.1. OpenGL defines typedefs for all of the data types accepted by its functions, which are listed in Table 1.1. Additionally, since OpenGL is a "C"-language library, it doesn't have function overloading to deal with the different types of data; it uses a function-naming convention to organize the multitude of functions that result from that situation. For example, we'll encounter a function named **glUniform*()** in Chapter 2, "Shader Fundamentals", which comes in numerous forms, such as **glUniform2f()** and **glUniform3fv()**. The suffixes at the end of the "core" part of the function name provide information about the arguments passed to the function. For example, the "2" in **glUniform2f()** represents that two data values will be passed into the function (there are other parameters as well, but they are the same across all 24 versions of the **glUniform*()** * function—In this book, we'll use **glUniform*()** * to represent the collection of all **glUniform*()** functions). Also note the "f" following the "2". This indicates that those two parameters are of type GLfloat. Finally, some versions of the functions' names end with a "v", which is short for *vector*, meaning that the two floating-point values (in the case of **glUniform2fv()**) are passed as a one-dimensional array of GLfloats, instead of two separate parameters.

To decode all of those combinations, the letters used as suffixes are described in Table 1.1, along with their types.

Table 1.1   Command Suffixes and Argument Data Types

Suffix	Data Type	Typical Corresponding C-Language Type	OpenGL Type Definition
b	8-bit integer	signed char	GLbyte
s	16-bit integer	signed short	GLshort
i	32-bit integer	int	GLint, GLsizei
f	32-bit floating-point	float	GLfloat, GLclampf
d	64-bit floating-point	double	GLdouble, GLclampd
ub	8-bit unsigned integer	unsigned char	GLubyte
us	16-bit unsigned integer	unsigned short	GLushort
ui	32-bit unsigned integer	unsigned int	GLuint, GLenum, GLbitfield

Note: Implementations of OpenGL have leeway in selecting which "C" data types to use to represent OpenGL data types. If you resolutely use the OpenGL-defined data types throughout your application, you will avoid mismatched types when porting your code between different implementations.

OpenGL's Rendering Pipeline

OpenGL implements what's commonly called a *rendering pipeline*, which is a sequence of processing stages for converting the data your application provides to OpenGL into a final rendered image. Figure 1.2 shows the OpenGL pipeline associated with Version 4.3. The OpenGL pipeline has evolved considerably since its introduction.

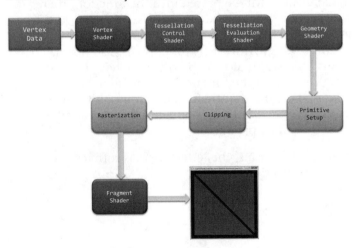

Figure 1.2   The OpenGL pipeline

OpenGL begins with the geometric data you provide (vertices and geometric primitives) and first processes it through a sequence of shader stages: vertex shading, tessellation shading (which itself uses two shaders), and finally geometry shading, before it's passed to the rasterizer. The rasterizer will generate fragments for any primitive that's inside of the *clipping region*, and execute a fragment shader for each of the generated fragments.

As you can see, shaders play an essential role in creating OpenGL applications. You have complete control of which shader stages are used, and what each of them do. Not all stages are required; in fact, only vertex shaders and fragment shaders must be included. Tessellation and geometry shaders are optional.

Now, we'll dive in a little deeper into each stage to provide you a bit more background. We understand that this may be somewhat overwhelming at this point, but please bear with us. It will turn out that understanding just a few concepts will get you very far along with OpenGL.

Preparing to Send Data to OpenGL

OpenGL requires that all data be stored in *buffer objects*, which are just chunks of memory managed by the OpenGL server. Populating these buffers with data can occur in numerous ways, but one of the most common is using the **glBufferData()** command like in Example 1.1. There is some additional setup required with buffers, which we'll cover in Chapter 3.

Sending Data to OpenGL

After we've initialized our buffers, we can request geometric primitives be rendered by calling one of OpenGL's drawing commands, such as **glDrawArrays()**, as we did in Example 1.1.

Drawing in OpenGL usually means transferring vertex data to the OpenGL server. Think of a vertex as a bundle of data values that are processed together. While the data in the bundle can be anything you'd like it to be (i.e., you define all the data that makes up a vertex), it almost always includes positional data. Any other data will be values you'll need to determine the pixel's final color.

Drawing commands are covered in detail in Chapter 3, "Drawing with OpenGL".

Vertex Shading

For each vertex that is issued by a drawing command, a vertex shader will be called to process the data associated with that vertex. Depending on whether any other pre-rasterization shaders are active, vertex shaders may be very simple, perhaps just copying data to pass it through this shading stage—what we'll call a *pass-through shader*—to a very complex shader that's performing many computations to potentially compute the vertex's screen position (usually using *transformation matrices*, described in Chapter 5), determining the vertex's color using lighting computations described in Chapter 7, or any multitude of other techniques.

Typically, an application of any complexity will have multiple vertex shaders, but only one can be active at any one time.

Tessellation Shading

After the vertex shader has processed each vertex's associated data, the tessellation shader stage will continue processing those data, if it's been activated. As we'll see in Chapter 9, tessellation uses *patch*s to describe an object's shape, and allows relatively simple collections of patch geometry to be *tessellated* to increase the number of geometric primitives providing better-looking models. The tessellation shading stage can potentially use two shaders to manipulate the patch data and generate the final shape.

Geometry Shading

The next shader stage—geometry shading—allows additional processing of individual geometric primitives, including creating new ones, before rasterization. This shading stage is also optional, but very powerful as we'll see in Chapter 10.

Primitive Assembly

The previous shading stages all operate on vertices, with the information about how those vertices are organized into geometric primitives being carried along internal to OpenGL. The primitive assembly stage organizes the vertices into their associated geometric primitives in preparation for clipping and rasterization.

Clipping

Occasionally, vertices will be outside of the *viewport*—the region of the window where you're permitted to draw—and cause the primitive associated with that vertex to be modified so none of its pixels are outside of the viewport. This operation is called *clipping* and is handled automatically by OpenGL.

Rasterization

Immediately after clipping, the updated primitives are sent to the rasterizer for fragment generation. Consider a fragment a "candidate pixel", in that pixels have a home in the framebuffer, while a fragment still can be rejected and never update its associated pixel location. Processing of fragments occurs in the next two stages, fragment shading and per-fragment operations.

Fragment Shading

The final stage where you have programmable control over the color of a screen location is during *fragment shading*. In this shader stage, you use a shader to determine the fragment's final color (although the next stage, per-fragment operations can modify the color one last time), and potentially its *depth value*. Fragment shaders are very powerful as they often employ texture mapping to augment the colors provided by the vertex processing stages. A fragment shader may also terminate processing a fragment if it determines the fragment shouldn't be drawn; this process is called *fragment discard*.

A helpful way of thinking about the difference between shaders that deal with vertices and fragment shaders is: vertex shading (including tessellation and geometry shading) determine where on the screen a primitive is, while fragment shading uses that information to determine what color that fragment will be.

Per-Fragment Operations

Additional fragment processing, outside of what you can currently do in a fragment shader is the final processing of individual fragments. During this stage a fragment's visibility is determined using *depth testing* (also commonly known as *z-buffering*) and *stencil testing*.

If a fragment successfully makes it through all of the enabled tests, it may be written directly to the framebuffer, updating the color (and possibly depth value) of its pixel, or if *blending* is enabled, the fragment's color will be combined with the pixel's current color to generate a new color that is written into the framebuffer.

As you saw in Figure 1.2, there's also a path for pixel data. Generally, pixel data comes from an image file, although it may also be created by rendering using OpenGL. Pixel data is usually stored in *texture map* for use with texture mapping, which allows any texture stage to look up data values from one or more texture maps. Texture mapping is covered in depth in Chapter 6.

With that brief introduction to the OpenGL pipeline, we'll dissect Example 1.1 and map the operations back to the rendering pipeline.

Our First Program: A Detailed Discussion

Entering main()

Starting at the beginning, of how our program would execute, we first look at what's going on in **main()**. The first six lines use the OpenGL Utility Toolkit to configure and open window for us. While the details of each of these routines is covered in Appendix A, we'll discuss the flow of the commands here.

```
int
main(int argc, char** argv)
{
    glutInit(&argc, argv);
    glutInitDisplayMode(GLUT_RGBA);
    glutInitWindowSize(512, 512);
    glutInitContextVersion(4, 3);
    glutInitContextProfile(GLUT_CORE_PROFILE);
    glutCreateWindow(argv[0]);

    if (glewInit()) {
        cerr << "Unable to initialize GLEW ... exiting" << endl;
        exit(EXIT_FAILURE);
    }

    init();

    glutDisplayFunc(display);

    glutMainLoop();
}
```

The first function, **glutInit()**, initializes the GLUT library. It processes the command-line arguments provided to the program, and removes any that control how GLUT might operate (such as specifying the size of a window). **glutInit()** needs to be the first GLUT function that your application calls, as it sets up data structures required by subsequent GLUT routines.

glutInitDisplayMode() configures the type of window we want to use with our application. In this case, we only request that the window use the RGBA color space (which we discuss more in Chapter 4). There are other options that we'll add to configure windows with more OpenGL features, such as depth buffers, or to enable animation.

glutInitWindowSize() specifies the size of the window, as you might expect. While we don't do it here, you can also query the size of the display device to dynamically size the window relative to your computer screen.

The next two calls: **glutInitContextVersion()** and **glutInitContextProfile()** specify the type of OpenGL *context*—OpenGL's internal data structure for keeping track of state settings and operations—we want to use. Here, we request an OpenGL Version 4.3 *core profile* for our context. Our profile selection controls whether we're using only the latest features in OpenGL or the features that are compatible with OpenGL versions all the way back to OpenGL Version 1.0.

The last call in this group is **glutCreateWindow()**, which does just what it says. If it's possible to create a window matching the display mode you requested with **glutInitDisplayMode()**, one will be created (by interfacing with your computer's windowing system). Only after GLUT has created a window for you (which includes creating an OpenGL context) can you use OpenGL functions.

Continuing on, the call to **glewInit()** initializes another help library we use: GLEW—the OpenGL Extension Wrangler. GLEW simplifies dealing with accessing functions and other interesting programming phenomena introduced by the various operating systems with OpenGL. Without GLEW, a considerable amount of additional work is required to get an application going.

At this point, we're truly set up to do interesting things with OpenGL. The **init()** routine, which we'll discuss momentarily, initializes all of our relevant OpenGL data so we can use for rendering later.

The next routine, **glutDisplayFunc()**, sets up the *display callback*, which is the routine GLUT will call when it thinks the contents of the window need to be updated. Here, we provide the GLUT library a pointer to a function: **display()**, which we'll also discuss soon. GLUT uses a number of callback functions for processing things like user input, window resizing, and many other operations. GLUT is fully described in Appendix A, "Basics of GLUT: The OpenGL Utility Toolkit".

The final function in **main()** is **glutMainLoop()**, which is an infinite loop that works with the window and operating systems to process user input and other operations like that. It's **glutMainLoop()** that determines that a window needs to be repainted, for example, and will call the function registered with **glutDisplayFunc()**. An important safety tip is that since **glutMainLoop()** is an infinite loop, any commands placed after it aren't executed.

OpenGL Initialization

The next routine that we need to discuss is **init()** from Example 1.1. Once again, here's the code to refresh your memory.

```
void
init (void)
{
    glGenVertexArrays (NumVAOs, VAOs);
    glBindVertexArray (VAOs [Triangles]);

    GLfloat  vertices [NumVertices] [2] = {
        { -0.90, -0.90 },   // Triangle 1
        {  0.85, -0.90 },
        { -0.90,  0.85 },
        {  0.90, -0.85 },   // Triangle 2
        {  0.90,  0.90 },
        { -0.85,  0.90 }
    };

    glGenBuffers (NumBuffers, Buffers);
    glBindBuffer (GL_ARRAY_BUFFER, Buffers [ArrayBuffer]);
    glBufferData (GL_ARRAY_BUFFER, sizeof (vertices),
                  vertices, GL_STATIC_DRAW);

    ShaderInfo  shaders [] = {
        { GL_VERTEX_SHADER, "triangles.vert" },
        { GL_FRAGMENT_SHADER, "triangles.frag" },
        { GL_NONE, NULL }
    };

    GLuint program = LoadShaders (shaders);
    glUseProgram (program);

    glVertexAttribPointer (vPosition, 2, GL_FLOAT,
                      GL_FALSE, 0, BUFFER_OFFSET (0));
    glEnableVertexAttribArray (vPosition);

}
```

Initializing Our Vertex-Array Objects

There's a lot going on in the functions and data of **init()**. Starting at the top, we begin by allocating a *vertex-array object* by calling **glGenVertexArrays()**. This causes OpenGL to allocate some number of vertex array object names for our use; in our case, NumVAOs, which we specified in the global variable section of the code. **glGenVertexArrays()** returns that number of names to us in the array provided, VAOs in this case.

Here's a complete description of **glGenVertexArrays()**:

---

void **glGenVertexArrays**(GLsizei *n*, GLuint **arrays*);

Returns *n* currently unused names for use as vertex-array objects in the array *arrays*. The names returned are marked as used for the purposes of allocating additional buffer objects, and initialized with values representing the default state of the collection of uninitialized vertex arrays.

We'll see numerous OpenGL commands of the form **glGen***, for allocating names to the various types of OpenGL objects. A name is a little like a pointer-type variable in C, in that until you allocate some memory and have the name reference it, the name isn't much help. In OpenGL, the same holds true, and our allocation scheme is called *binding an object*, and is done by a collection of functions in OpenGL that have the form **glBind***. For our example, we create and bind a vertex-array object using **glBindVertexArray()**.

---

void **glBindVertexArray**(GLuint *array*);

glBindVertexArray() does three things. When using the value array that is other than zero and was returned from **glGenVertexArrays()**, a new vertex-array object is created and assigned that name. When binding to a previously created vertex-array object, that vertex array object becomes active, which additionally affects the vertex array state stored in the object. When binding to an array value of zero, OpenGL stops using application-allocated vertex-array objects and returns to the default state for vertex arrays.

A GL_INVALID_OPERATION error is generated if array is not a value previously returned from **glGenVertexArrays()**, or if it is a value that has been released by **glDeleteVertexArrays()**.

In our example, after we generate a vertex-array object name, we bind it with our call to **glBindVertexArray()**. Object binding like this is a very common operation in OpenGL, but it may be immediately intuitive how or why it works. When you bind an object for the first time (e.g., the first time **glBind*()** is called for a particular object name), OpenGL will internally allocate the memory it needs and make that object *current*, which means that any operations relevant to the bound object, like the vertex-array object we're working with, will affect its state from that point on in the program's execution. After the first call to any **glBind*()** function, the newly created object will be initialized to its default state and will usually require some additional initialization to make it useful.

Think of binding an object like setting a track switch in a railroad yard. Once a track switch has been set, all trains go down that set of tracks. When the switch is set to another track, all trains will then travel that new track. It is the same for OpenGL objects. Generally speaking, you will bind an object in two situations: initially when you create and initialize the data it will hold; and then every time you want to use it, and it's not currently bound. We'll see this situation when we discuss the **display()** routine, where **glBindVertexArray()** is called the second time in the program.

Since our example is as minimal as possible, we don't do some operations that you might in larger programs. For example, once you're completed with a vertex-array object, you can delete it by calling **glDeleteVertexArrays()**.

---

void **glDeleteVertexArrays**(GLsizei *n*, GLuint **arrays*);

Deletes the *n* vertex-arrays objects specified in *arrays*, enabling the names for reuse as vertex arrays later. If a bound vertex array is deleted, the bindings for that vertex array become zero (as if you had called **glBindBuffer()** with a value of zero) and the default vertex array becomes the current one. Unused names in arrays are released, but no changes to the current vertex array state are made.

Finally, for completeness, you can also determine if a name is already been reserved as a vertex-array object by calling **glIsVertexArray()**.

GLboolean **glIsVertexArray**(GLuint *array*);

Returns GL_TRUE if *array* is the name of a vertex-array object that was previously generated with **glGenVertexArrays()**, but has not been subsequently deleted. Returns GL_FALSE if *array* is zero or a nonzero value that is not the name of a vertex-array object.

You'll find many similar routines of the form **glDelete*** and **glIs*** for all the different types of object in OpenGL.

Allocating Vertex-Buffer Objects

A vertex-array object holds various data related to a collection of vertices. Those data are stored in buffer objects and managed by the currently bound vertex-array object. While there is only a single type of vertex-array object, there are many types of objects, but not all of them specifically deal with vertex data. As mentioned previously, a buffer object is memory that the OpenGL server allocates and owns, and almost all data passed into OpenGL is done by storing the data in a buffer object.

The sequence of initializing a vertex-buffer object is similar in flow to that of creating a vertex-array object, with an added step to actually populate the buffer with data.

To begin, you need to create some names for your vertex-buffer objects. As you might expect, you'll call a function of the form **glGen***; in this case, **glGenBuffers()**. In our example, we allocate NumVBOs (short for "Vertex-Buffer Objects") into our array buffers. Here is the full description of **glGenBuffers()**.

---

void **glGenBuffers**(GLsizei *n*, GLuint **buffers*);

Returns *n* currently unused names for buffer objects in the array *buffers*. The names returned in buffers do not have to be a contiguous set of integers.

The names returned are marked as used for the purposes of allocating additional buffer objects, but only acquire a valid state once they have been bound.

Zero is a reserved buffer object name and is never returned as a buffer object by **glGenBuffers()**.

Once you have allocated names for your buffers, you bring them into existence by calling **glBindBuffer()**. Since there are many different types of buffer objects in OpenGL, when we bind a buffer, we need to specify which type we'd like it to be. In our example, since we're storing vertex data into the buffer, we use GL_ARRAY_BUFFER. There are currently eight types of buffer objects, which get used for various features in OpenGL. We will discuss each type's operation in the relevant sections later in the book. Here is the full detail for **glBindBuffer()**.

void **glBindBuffer**(GLenum *target*, GLuint *buffer*);

Specifies the current active buffer object. *target* must be set to one of GL_ARRAY_BUFFER, GL_ELEMENT_ARRAY_BUFFER, GL_PIXEL_PACK_BUFFER, GL_PIXEL_UNPACK_BUFFER, GL_COPY_READ_BUFFER, GL_COPY_WRITE_BUFFER, GL_TRANSFORM_FEEDBACK_BUFFER, or GL_UNIFORM_BUFFER. *buffer* specifies the buffer object to be bound to.

glBindBuffer() does three things: 1. When using buffer of an unsigned integer other than zero for the first time, a new buffer object is created and assigned that name. 2. When binding to a previously created buffer object, that buffer object becomes the active buffer object. 3. When binding to a buffer value of zero, OpenGL stops using buffer objects for that *target*.

As with other objects, you can delete buffer objects with **glDeleteBuffers**().

void **glDeleteBuffers**(GLsizei *n*, const GLuint **buffers*);

Deletes *n* buffer objects, named by elements in the array *buffers*. The freed buffer objects may now be reused (for example, by **glGenBuffers**()).

If a buffer object is deleted while bound, all bindings to that object are reset to the default buffer object, as if **glBindBuffer**() had been called with zero as the specified buffer object. Attempts to delete nonexistent buffer objects or the buffer object named zero are ignored without generating an error.

You can query if an integer value is a buffer-object name with **glIsBuffer**().

GLboolean **glIsBuffer**(GLuint *buffer*);

Returns GL_TRUE if *buffer* is the name of a buffer object that has been bound, but has not been subsequently deleted. Returns GL_FALSE if *buffer* is zero or if *buffer* is a nonzero value that is not the name of a buffer object.

Loading Data into a Buffer Object

After initializing our vertex-buffer object, we need to transfer the vertex data from our objects into the buffer object. This is done by the **glBufferData()** routine, which does dual duty: allocating storage for holding the vertex data and copying the data from arrays in the application to the OpenGL server's memory.

As **glBufferData()** will be used many times in many different scenarios, it's worth discussing it in more detail here, although we will revisit its use many times in this book. To begin, here's the full description of **glBufferData()**.

---

void **glBufferData**(GLenum *target*, GLsizeiptr *size*,
                 const GLvoid **data*, GLenum *usage*);

Allocates *size* storage units (usually bytes) of OpenGL server memory for storing data or indices. Any previous data associated with the currently bound object will be deleted.

target may be either GL_ARRAY_BUFFER for vertex attribute data; GL_ELEMENT_ARRAY_BUFFER for index data; GL_PIXEL_UNPACK_BUFFER for pixel data being passed into OpenGL; GL_PIXEL_PACK_BUFFER for pixel data being retrieved from OpenGLGL_COPY_READ_BUFFER and GL_COPY_WRITE_BUFFER for data copied between buffers; GL_TEXTURE_BUFFER for texture data stored as a texture buffer; GL_TRANSFORM_FEEDBACK_BUFFER for results from executing a transform feedback shader; or GL_UNIFORM_BUFFER for uniform variable values.

size is the amount of storage required for storing the respective data. This value is generally number of elements in the data multiplied by their respective storage size.

data is either a pointer to a client memory that is used to initialize the buffer object or NULL. If a valid pointer is passed, size units of storage are copied from the client to the server. If NULL is passed, size units of storage are reserved for use but are left uninitialized.

usage provides a hint as to how the data will be read and written after allocation. Valid values are GL_STREAM_DRAW, GL_STREAM_READ, GL_STREAM_COPY, GL_STATIC_DRAW, GL_STATIC_READ, GL_STATIC_COPY, GL_DYNAMIC_DRAW, GL_DYNAMIC_READ, GL_DYNAMIC_COPY.

glBufferData() will generate a GL_OUT_OF_MEMORY error if the requested *size* exceeds what the server is able to allocate. It will generate a GL_INVALID_VALUE error if usage is not one of the permitted values.

We know that was a lot to see at one time, but you will use this function so much that it's good to make it easy to find at the beginning of the book.

For our example, our call to **glBufferData()** is very straightforward. Our vertex data is stored in the array `vertices`. While we've statically allocated it in our example, you might read these values from a file containing a model, or generate the values algorithmically. Since our data is vertex-attribute data, we'll make this buffer a GL_ARRAY_BUFFER by specifying that value as the first parameter. We also need to specify the size of memory to be allocated (in bytes), so we merely compute `sizeof(vertices)` which does all the heavy lifting. Finally, we need to specify how the data will be used by OpenGL. Since this data will be used for drawing geometry, and won't change for the life of the program, we choose GL_STATIC_DRAW for **glBufferData()**'s *usage* parameter.

There are a lot of options for *usage*, which we describe in detail in Chapter 3.

If you look at the values in the `vertices` array, you'll note they are all in the range $[-1, \ 1]$ in both x and y. In reality, OpenGL only knows how to draw geometric primitives into coordinate space. In fact, that range of coordinates are known as *normalized-device coordinates* (commonly called NDCs). While that may sound like a limitation, it's really none at all. Chapter 5 will discuss all the mathematics required to take the most complex objects in a three-dimensional space, and map them into normalized-device coordinates. We used NDCs here to simplify the example, but in reality, you will almost always use more complex coordinate spaces.

At this point, we've successfully created a vertex-array object and populated its buffer objects. Next, we need to set up the shaders that our application will use.

Initializing Our Vertex and Fragment Shaders

Every OpenGL program that wants to use OpenGL Version 3.1 or greater must provide at least two shaders: a vertex shader and a fragment shader. In our example, we do that by using our helper function **LoadShaders()**, which takes an array of ShaderInfo structures (all of the details for this structure are included in the LoadShaders.h header file).

For an OpenGL programmer (at this point), a shader is a small function written in the OpenGL Shading Language (OpenGL Shading Language (GLSL)), a special language very similar to C++ for constructing OpenGL shaders. GLSL is used for all shaders in OpenGL, although not every feature in GLSL is usable in every OpenGL shader stage. You provide your GLSL shader to OpenGL as a string of characters. To simplify our examples, and to make it easier for you to experiment with shaders, we store our shader strings in files, and use **LoadShaders()** to take care of reading the files and creating our OpenGL shader programs. The gory details of working with OpenGL shaders are discussed in detail in Chapter 2.

To gain an appreciation of shaders, we need to show you some without going into full detail of every nuance. There's the entire rest of the book for all of the GLSL details, so right now, we'll suffice with showing our vertex shader in Example 1.2.

Example 1.2   Vertex Shader for triangles.cpp: triangles.vert

```
#version 430 core

layout(location = 0) in vec4 vPosition;

void
main()
{
    gl_Position = vPosition;
}
```

Yes; that's all there is. In fact, this is an example of a pass-through shader we eluded to earlier. It only copies input data to output data. That said, there is a lot to discuss here.

The first line: "#version 430 core" specifies which version of the OpenGL Shading Language we want to use. The "430" here indicates that we want to use the version of GLSL associated with OpenGL Version 4.3. The naming scheme of GLSL versions based on OpenGL versions works back to Version 3.3. In versions of OpenGL before that, the version numbers incremented differently (the details are in Chapter 2). The "core" relates to wanting to use OpenGL's core profile, which corresponds with our request to GLUT when we called **glutInitContextProfile()**. Every shader should have a "#version" line at its start, otherwise version "110" is assumed, which is incompatible with OpenGL's core profile versions. We're going to stick to shaders declaring version 330 or above, depending on what features the shaders use; you get a bit more portability by not using the most recent version number, unless you need the most recent features.

Next, we allocate a *shader variable*. Shader variables are a shader's connection to the outside world. That is, a shader doesn't know where its data comes from; it merely sees its input variables populated with data every time it executes. It's our responsibility to connect the shader plumbing (this is our term, but you'll see why it makes sense) so that data in your application can flow into and between the various OpenGL shader stages.

In our simple example, we have one input variable named vPosition, which you can determine by the "in" on its declaration line. In fact, there's a lot going on in this one line.

```
layout(location = 0) in vec4 vPosition;
```

It's easier to parse the line from right to left.

- vPosition is, of course, the name of the variable. We'll use the convention of prefixing a vertex attribute with the letter "v". So, in this case, this variable will hold a vertex's positional information.

- Next, you see vec4, which is vPositions type. In this case, it's a GLSL 4-component vector of floating-point values. There are many data types in GLSL, that we'll discuss in Chapter 2.

  You may have noticed that when we specified the data for each vertex in Example 1.1 we only specified two coordinates, but in our vertex shader, we use a vec4. Where do the other two coordinates come from? OpenGL will automatically fill in any missing coordinates with default values. The default value for a vec4 is (0,0,0,1), so if we only specify the x- and y-coordinates, the other values (z and w), are assigned 0 and 1 respectively.

- Preceding the type is the in we mentioned before, which specifies which direction data flows into the shader. If you're wondering if there might be an out; yes, you're right. We don't show that here, but will soon.

- Finally, the layout(location = 0) part is called a *layout qualifier*, and provides meta-data for our variable declaration. There are many options that can be set with a layout qualifier, some of which are shader-stage specific.

  In this case, we just set vPosition attribute location to zero. We'll use that information in conjunction with the last two routines in **init()**.

Finally, the core of the shader is defined in its **main()** routine. Every shader in OpenGL, regardless of which shader stage its used for, will have a **main()** routine. For this shader, all it does is copy the input vertex position to the special vertex-shader output gl_Position. You'll soon see there are several shader variables provided by OpenGL that you'll use, and they all begin with the gl_ prefix.

Similarly, we need a fragment shader to accompany our vertex shader. Here's the one for our example, shown in Example 1.3.

Example 1.3   Fragment Shader for triangles.cpp: triangles.frag

```
#version 430 core

out vec4 fColor;

void
main()
{
    fColor = vec4(0.0, 0.0, 1.0, 1.0);
}
```

Hopefully, much of this looks very familiar, even if it's an entirely different type of shader. We have the version string, a variable declaration, and our **main()** routine. There are a few differences, but as you'll find, almost all shaders will have this structure.

The highlights of our fragment shader are as follows:

- The variable declaration for fColor. If you guessed that there was an out qualifier, you were right! In this case, the shader will output values through fColor, which is the fragment's color (hence the choice of "f" as a prefix).

- Assigning the fragment's color. In this case, each fragment is assigned this vector of four values. In OpenGL, colors are represented in what's called the *RGB color space*, with each color component ("R" for red, "G" for green, and "B" for blue) ranging from [0, 1]. The observant reader is probably asking "Um, but there are four numbers there". Indeed, OpenGL really uses an RGBA color space, with the fourth color not really being a color at all. It's for a value called *alpha*, which is really a measure of translucency. We'll discuss it in detail in Chapter 4, but for now, we'll set it to 1.0, which indicates the color is fully opaque.

Fragment shaders are immensely powerful, and there will be many techniques that we can do with them.

We're almost done with our initialization routine. The final two routines in **init()** deal specifically with associating variables in a vertex shader with data that we've stored in a buffer object. This is exactly what we mean by shader plumbing, in that you need to connect conduits between the application and a shader, and as we'll see, between various shader stages.

To associate data going into our vertex shader, which is the entrance all vertex data take to get processed by OpenGL, we need to connect our

shader "in" variables to a *vertex-attribute array*, and we do that with the
glVertexAttribPointer() routine.

---

void **glVertexAttribPointer**(GLuint *index*, GLint *size*,
                                    GLenum *type*, GLboolean *normalized*,
                                    GLsizei *stride*, const GLvoid **pointer*);

Specifies where the data values for *index* (shader attribute location) can be
accessed. *pointer* is the offset from the start of the buffer object (assuming
zero-based addressing) in basic-machine units (i.e., bytes) for the first set
of values in the array. *size* represents the number of components to be
updated per vertex, and can be either 1, 2, 3, 4, or GL_BGRA. *type*
specifies the data type (GL_BYTE, GL_UNSIGNED_BYTE, GL_SHORT,
GL_UNSIGNED_SHORT, GL_INT, GL_UNSIGNED_INT, GL_FIXED,
GL_HALF_FLOAT, GL_FLOAT, or GL_DOUBLE) of each element in the
array. *normalized* indicates that the vertex data should be normalized
before being stored (in the same manner as **glVertexAttribFourN*()**).
stride is the byte offset between consecutive elements in the array. If *stride*
is zero, the data is assumed to be tightly packed.

While that may seem like a lot of things to figure out, it's because
glVertexAttribPointer() is a very flexible command. As long as your data
is regularly organized in memory (i.e., it's in a contiguous array, and not
in some other node-based container like a linked list), you can use
glVertexAttribPointer() to tell OpenGL how to retrieve data from that
memory. In our case, `vertices` has all the information we need. Table 1.2
works through **glVertexAttribPointer()**'s parameters.

Table 1.2   Example of Determining Parameters for
                    glVertexAttribPointer()

Parameter Name	Value	Explanation
index	0	This is the location value for the respective vertex shader input variable—`vPosition` in our case. This value can be specified by the shader directly using the `layout` qualifier, or determined after compilation of the shader.
size	2	This is the number of values for each vertex in our array. `vertices` was allocated to have `NumVertices` elements, each with two values.
type	GL_FLOAT	The enumerated value for the GLfloat type.

Parameter Name	Value	Explanation
normalized	GL_FALSE	We set this to GL_FALSE for two reasons: First, and most importantly, because positional coordinates values can basically take on any value, so we don't want them constrained to the range $[-1, 1]$; and second, the values are not integer types (e.g., GLint, or GLshort).
stride	0	As our data are "tightly packed", which implies that one set of data values is immediately contiguous in memory to the next, we can use the value zero.
pointer	**BUFFER_OFFSET**(0)	We set this to zero because our data starts at the first byte (address zero) of our buffer object.

Hopefully that explanation of how we arrived at the parameters will help you determine the necessary values for your own data structures. We will have plenty more examples of using **glVertexAttribPointer()**.

One additional technique we use is using our **BUFFER_OFFSET** macro in **glVertexAttribPointer()** to specify the offset. There's nothing special about our macro; here's its definition.

```
#define BUFFER_OFFSET(offset) ((void *)(offset))
```

While there a long history of OpenGL lore on why one might do this,[2] we use this macro to make the point that we're specifying an offset into a buffer object, rather than a pointer to a block of memory as **glVertexAttribPointer()**'s prototype would suggest.

At this point, we have one task left to do in **init()**, which is to enable our vertex-attribute array. We do this by calling **glEnableVertexAttribArray()** and passing the index of the attribute array pointer we initialized by calling **glVertexAttribPointer()**. The full details for **glEnableVertexAttribArray()** are provided below.

---

2. In previous versions of OpenGL (prior to Version 3.1) vertex-attribute data was permitted to be stored in application memory, as compared to GPU buffer objects, so pointers made sense in that respect.

void **glEnableVertexAttribArray**(GLuint *index*);
void **glDisableVertexAttribArray**(GLuint *index*);

Specifies that the vertex array associated with variable *index* be enabled or disabled. *index* must be a value between zero and GL_MAX_VERTEX_ATTRIBS − 1.

Now, all that's left is to draw something.

Our First OpenGL Rendering

With all that setup and data initialization, rendering (for the moment) will be very simple. While our **display()** routine is only four lines long, its sequence of operations is virtually the same in all OpenGL applications. Here it is once again.

```
void
display(void)
{
    glClear(GL_COLOR_BUFFER_BIT);

    glBindVertexArray(VAOs[Triangles]);
    glDrawArrays(GL_TRIANGLES, 0, NumVertices);

    glFlush();
}
```

First, we begin rendering by clearing our framebuffer. This is done by calling **glClear()**.

void **glClear**(GLbitfield *mask*);

Clears the specified buffers to their current clearing values. The *mask* argument is a bitwise logical OR combination of the values listed in Table 1.3.

Table 1.3   Clearing Buffers

Buffer	Name
Color Buffer	GL_COLOR_BUFFER_BIT
Depth Buffer	GL_DEPTH_BUFFER_BIT
Stencil Buffer	GL_STENCIL_BUFFER_BIT

We discuss depth and stencil buffering, as well as an expanded discussion of color in Chapter 4, "Color, Pixels, and Framebuffers".

You may be asking yourself how we set the color that **glClear()** should use. In this first program, we used OpenGL's default clearing color, which is black. To change the clear color, call **glClearColor()**.

---

void **glClearColor**(GLclampf *red*, GLclampf *green*, GLclampf *blue*, GLclampf *alpha*);

Sets the current clear color for use in clearing color buffers in RGBA mode. (See Chapter 4 for more information on *RGBA mode*.) The red, green, blue, and alpha values are clamped if necessary to the range [0, 1]. The default clear color is (0,0,0,0), which is the RGBA representation of black.

The clear color is an example of OpenGL state, which are values that OpenGL retains in its context. OpenGL has a large collection of state variables (which is fully described in Appendix D), all of which is initialized to default values when a context is created. Since OpenGL retains any state changes you update, you can reduce the number of times you set values.

Using the clear color as an example, let's say you always want to clear the background of the viewport to white. You would call `glClearColor(1, 1, 1, 1)`. But where should you make this function call? Of course, you could set the value right before you call **glClear()** in **display()**, but all but the first call would be redundant—OpenGL would be changing the clear color from white to white each time you rendered. A more efficient solution would be to set the clear color in **init()**. In fact, this is the technique we use to minimize redundant state changes; any values that will be constant over the execution of a program are set in **init()**. Of course, there's no harm in making redundant calls; it may just make your application execute slower.

Try This

Add a call to **glClearColor()** into triangles.cpp.

Drawing with OpenGL

Our next two calls select the collection of vertices we want to draw and request that they be rendered. We first call **glBindVertexArray()** to select the vertex array that we want to use as vertex data. As mentioned before, you would do this to switch between different collections of vertex data.

Next, we call **glDrawArrays()**, which actually sends vertex data to the OpenGL pipeline.

---

void **glDrawArrays**(GLenum *mode*, GLint *first*, GLsizei *count*);

Constructs a sequence of geometric primitives using the elements from the currently bound vertex array starting at *first* and ending at *first* + *count* − 1. *mode* specifies what kinds of primitives are constructed and is one of GL_POINTS, GL_LINES, GL_LINE_STRIP, GL_LINE_LOOP, GL_TRIANGLES, GL_TRIANGLE_STRIP, GL_TRIANGLE_FAN, and GL_PATCHES.

In our example, we request that individual triangles are rendered by setting the rendering mode to GL_TRIANGLES, starting at offset zero with respect to the buffer offset we set with **glVertexAttribPointer()**, and continuing for NumVertices (in our case, 6) vertices. We describe all of the rendering shapes in detail in Chapter 3.

Try This

> Modify triangles.cpp to render a different type of geometric primitive, like GL_POINTS or GL_LINES. Any of the above listed primitives can be used, but some of the results may not be what you expect, and for GL_PATCHES, you won't see anything as it requires use of tessellation shaders, which we discuss in Chapter 9.

Finally, the last call in **display()** is **glFlush()**, which requests that any pending OpenGL calls are flushed to the OpenGL server and processed. Very soon, we'll replace **glFlush()** with a command that aids in smooth animation, but that requires a bit more setup than we do in our first example.

---

void **glFlush**(void);

Forces previously issued OpenGL commands to begin execution, thus guaranteeing that they complete in finite time.

Advanced

At some point in your OpenGL programming career, you'll be asked (or ask yourself), "How much time did that take?", where "that" may be the time to render an object, draw a full scene, or any other operations that OpenGL might do. In order to do that accurately, you need to know when OpenGL is completed with whatever operations you want to measure.

While the aforementioned command, **glFlush()**, may sound like the right answer, it's not. In particular, **glFlush()** merely requests all pending commands be sent to the OpenGL server, and then it returns immediately— it doesn't wait until everything pending is completed, which is really what you want. To do that, you need to use the **glFinish()** function, which waits until all OpenGL operations in flight are done, and then returns.

---

void **glFinish**(void);

Forces the completion of all pending OpenGL commands and waits for their completion.

Note: Only use **glFinish()** while you're developing your application— remove calls to it once you've completed development. While it's useful for determining the performance of a set of OpenGL commands, it generally harms the overall performance of your program.

Enabling and Disabling Operations in OpenGL

One important feature that we didn't need to use in our first program, but will use throughout this book, is enabling and disabling modes of operation in OpenGL. Most operational features are turned on and off by the **glEnable()** and **glDisable()** commands.

---

void **glEnable**(GLenum *capability*);
void **glDisable**(GLenum *capability*);

---

glEnable() turns on a capability and **glDisable()** turns it off. There are numerous enumerated values that can be passed as parameters to **glEnable()** or **glDisable()**. Examples include GL_DEPTH_TEST for turning on and off depth testing; GL_BLEND to control blending and GL_RASTERIZER_DISCARD for advanced rendering control while doing transform feedback.

You may often find, particularly if you have to write libraries that use OpenGL that will be used by other programmers, that you need to determine a feature's state before changing for your own needs. **glIsEnabled()** will return if a particular capability is currently enabled.

GLboolean **glIsEnabled**(GLenum *capability*);

Returns GL_TRUE or GL_FALSE, depending on whether or not the queried capability is currently activated.

Chapter 2

Shader Fundamentals

Chapter Objectives

After reading this chapter, you'll be able to do the following:

- Identify the various types of shaders that OpenGL uses to create images.

- Construct and compile shaders using the OpenGL Shading Language.

- Pass data into shaders using a variety of mechanisms available in OpenGL.

- Employ advanced GLSL shading capabilities to make shaders more reusable.

This chapter introduces how to use programmable shaders with OpenGL. Along the way, we describe the OpenGL Shading Language (commonly called GLSL), and detail how shaders will influence your OpenGL applications.

This chapter contains the following major sections:

- "Shaders and OpenGL" discusses programmable graphics shaders in the context of OpenGL applications.

- "OpenGL's Programmable Pipeline" details each stage of the OpenGL programmable pipeline.

- "An Overview of the OpenGL Shading Language" introduces the OpenGL Shading Language.

- "Interface Blocks" shows how to organize shader variables shared with the application or between stages.

- "Compiling Shaders" describes the process of converting GLSL shaders into programmable shader programs usable in your OpenGL application.

- "Shader Subroutines" discusses a method to increase the usability of shaders by allowing them to select execution routines without recompiling shaders.

- "Separate Shader Objects" details how to composite elements from multiple shaders into a single, configurable graphics pipeline.

Shaders and OpenGL

The modern OpenGL rendering pipeline relies very heavily on using shaders to process the data you pass to it. About the only rendering you can do with OpenGL without shaders is clearing a window, which should give you a feel for how important they are when using OpenGL. Versions of OpenGL before (and including) Version 3.0, or those using a compatibility-profile context, include a *fixed-function pipeline* that processes geometric and pixel data for you, without shaders. Starting with Version 3.1, the fixed-function pipeline was removed from the core profile, and shaders became mandatory.

Shaders, whether for OpenGL or any other graphics API, are usually written in a specialized programming language. For OpenGL, we use GLSL, the OpenGL Shading Language, which has been around since OpenGL Version 2.0 (and before as extensions). It has evolved along with OpenGL, usually being updated with each new version of OpenGL. While GLSL is a programming language specially designed for graphics, you'll find it's very similar to the "C" language, with a little C++ mixed in.

In this chapter, we'll describe how to write shaders, gradually introducing GLSL along the way, discuss compiling and integrating shaders into your application, and how data in your application passes between the various shaders.

OpenGL's Programmable Pipeline

While Chapter 1 provided a brief introduction to OpenGL's rendering pipeline, here we'll describe in greater detail the various stages and what operations they carry out. Version 4.3's graphical pipeline contains four processing stages, plus a compute stage, each of which you control by providing a shader.

1. The *Vertex shading stage* receives the vertex data that you specified in your vertex-buffer objects, processing each vertex separately. This stage is mandatory for all OpenGL programs and must have a shader bound to it. We describe vertex shading operation in Chapter 3, "Drawing with OpenGL".

2. The *Tessellation shading stage* is an optional stage that generates additional geometry within the OpenGL pipeline, as compared to having the application specify each geometric primitive explicitly. This stage, if activated, receives the output of the vertex shading stage, and does further processing of the received vertices. We describe the tessellation shading stage in Chapter 9, "Tessellation Shaders".

3. The *Geometry shading stage* is another optional stage that can modify entire geometric primitives within the OpenGL pipeline. This stage operates on individual geometric primitives allowing each to be modified. In this stage, you might generate more geometry from the input primitive, change the type of geometric primitive (e.g., converting triangles to lines), or discarding the geometry altogether. If activated, geometry shading receives its input either after vertex shading has completed processing the vertices of a geometric primitive, or from the primitives generated from the tessellation shading stage, if it's been enabled. The geometry shading stage is described in Chapter 10, "Geometry Shaders".

4. Finally, the last part of the OpenGL shading pipeline is the *Fragment shading stage*. This stage processes the individual fragments (or *samples*, if sample-shading mode is enabled) generated by OpenGL's rasterizer, and also must have a shader bound to it. In this stage, a fragment's color and depth values are computed, and then sent for further

processing in the fragment-testing and blending parts of the pipeline. Fragment shading operation is discussed in many sections of the text.

5. The *Compute shading stage* is not part of the graphical pipeline as the stages above, but rather stands on its own as the only stage in a program. A compute shader processes generic work items, driven by an application-chosen range, rather than by graphical inputs like vertices and fragments. Compute shaders can process buffers created and consumed by other shader programs in your application. This includes framebuffer post-processing effects, or really anything you want. Compute shaders are described in Chapter 12, "Compute Shaders".

An important concept to understand in general is how data flows between the shading stages. Shaders, like you saw in Chapter 1, are like a function call—data are passed in, processed, and passed back out. In "C", for example, this can either be done using global variables, or arguments to the function. GLSL is a little different. Each shader looks a complete "C" program, in that its entry point is a function named **main()**. Unlike "C", GLSL's **main()** doesn't take any arguments, but rather all data going into and out of a shader stage are passed using special global variables in the shader (please don't confuse them with global variables in your application—shader variables are entirely separate than the variables you've declared in your application code). For example, take a look at Example 2.1.

Example 2.1   A Simple Vertex Shader

```
#version 330 core

in vec4   vPosition;
in vec4   vColor;

out vec4   color;

uniform mat4   ModelViewProjectionMatrix;

void
main()
{
    color = vColor;
    gl_Position = ModelViewProjectionMatrix * vPosition;
}
```

Even though that's a very short shader, there're a lot of things to take note of. Regardless of which shading stage you're programming for, shaders will generally have the same structure as this one. This includes starting with a declaration of the version using `#version`.

First, notice the global variables. Those are the inputs and outputs OpenGL uses to pass data through the shader. Aside from each variable having a type (e.g., `vec4`, which we'll get into more momentarily), data is copied into the shader from OpenGL through the `in` variables, and likewise, copied out of the shader through the `out` variables. The values in those variables are updated every time OpenGL executes the shader (e.g., if OpenGL is processing vertices, then new values are passed through those variables for each vertex; when processing fragments, then for each fragment). The other category of variable that's available to receive data from an OpenGL application are `uniform` variables. Uniform values don't change per vertex or fragment, but rather have the same value across geometric primitives, until the application updates them.

An Overview of the OpenGL Shading Language

This section provides an overview of the shading language used within OpenGL. GLSL shares many traits with C++ and Java, and is used for authoring shaders for all the stages supported in OpenGL, although certain features are only available for particular types of shaders. We will first describe GLSL's requirements, types, and other language constructs that are shared between the various shader stages, and then discuss the features unique to each type of shader.

Creating Shaders with GLSL

The Starting Point

A shader program, just like a "C" program, starts execution in **main()**. Every GLSL shader program begins life as follows:

```
#version 330 core

void
main()
{
    // Your code goes here
}
```

The `//` construct is a comment and terminates at the end of the current line, just like in "C". Additionally, "C"-type, multiline comments—the `/*` and `*/` type—are also supported. However, unlike ANSI "C", **main()** does not return an integer value; it is declared void. Also, as with "C" and its derivative languages, statements are terminated with a semicolon. While this is a perfectly legal GLSL program that compiles and even runs, its functionality leaves something to be desired. To add a little more excitement to our shaders, we'll continue by describing variables and their operation.

Declaring Variables

GLSL is a typed language; every variable must be declared and have an associated type. Variable names conform to the same rules as those for "C": you can use letters, numbers, and the underscore character (_) to compose variable names. However, neither a digit nor an underscore can be the first character in a variable name. Similarly, variable names cannot contain consecutive underscores—those names are reserved in GLSL.

Table 2.1 shows the basic types available in GLSL.

Table 2.1   Basic Data Types in GLSL

Type	Description
float	IEEE 32-bit floating-point value
double	IEEE 64-bit floating-point value
int	signed two's-complement 32-bit integer value
uint	unsigned 32-bit integer value
bool	Boolean value

These types (and later, aggregate types composed of these) are all transparent. That is, their internal form is exposed and the shader code gets to assume what they look like internally.

An additional set of types, the opaque types, do not have their internal form exposed. These include sampler types, image types, and atomic counter types. They declare variables used as opaque handles for accessing texture maps, images, and atomic counters as described in Chapter 4, "Color, Pixels, and Framebuffers".

The various types of samplers and their uses are discussed in Chapter 6, "Textures".

Variable Scoping

While all variables must be declared, they may be declared any time before their use (just as in C++, where they must be the first statements in a block of code). The scoping rules of GLSL, which closely parallel those of C++ are as follows:

- Variables declared outside of any function definition have global scope and are visible to all subsequent functions within the shader program.

- Variables declared within a set of curly braces (e.g., function definition, block following a loop or "if" statement, and so on) exist within the scope of those braces only.

- Loop iteration variables, such as i in the loop

```
for (int i = 0; i < 10; ++i) {
    // loop body
}
```

are only scoped for the body of the loop.

Variable Initialization

Variables may also be initialized when declared. For example:

```
int     i, numParticles = 1500;
float   force, g = -9.8;
bool    falling = true;
double  pi = 3.141592653589793238462LF;
```

Integer literal constants may be expressed as octal, decimal, or hexadecimal values. An optional minus sign before a numeric value negates the constant, and a trailing "u" or "U" denotes an unsigned integer value.

Floating-point literals must include a decimal point, unless described in scientific format, e.g., 3E-7. (However, there are many situations where an integer literal will be implicitly converted to a floating-point value.) Additionally, they may optionally include an "f" or "F" suffix as in "C" on a `float` literal. You must include a suffix of "lF" or "LF" to make a literal have the precision of a `double`.

Boolean values are either `true` or `false`, and can be initialized to either of those values or as the result of an operation that resolves to a Boolean expression.

Constructors

As mentioned, GLSL is more type safe than C++; having fewer implicit conversion between values. For example,

```
int f = false;
```

will result in a compilation error due to assigning a Boolean value to an integer variable. Types will be implicitly converted as shown in Table 2.2.

Table 2.2   Implicit Conversions in GLSL

Type Needed	Can Be Implicitly Converted From
uint	int
float	int, uint
double	int, uint, float

The above type conversions work for scalars, vectors, and matrices of these types. Conversions will never change whether something is a vector or a matrix, or how many components they have. Conversions also don't apply to arrays or structures.

Any other conversion of values requires explicit conversion using a conversion *constructor*. A constructor, as in other languages like C++, is a function with the same name as a type, which returns a value of that type. For example,

```
float f = 10.0;
int   ten = int(f);
```

uses an `int` conversion constructor to do the conversion. Likewise, the other types also have conversion constructors: `float`, `double`, `uint`, `bool`, and vectors and matrices of these types. Each accepts multiple other types to explicitly convert from. These functions also illustrate another feature of GLSL: function *overloading*, whereby each function takes various input types, but all use the same base function name. We will discuss more on functions in a bit.

Aggregate Types

GLSL's basic types can be combined to better match core OpenGL's data values and to ease computational operations.

First, GLSL supports vectors of two, three, or four components for each of the basic types of `bool`, `int`, `uint`, `float`, and `double`. Also, matrices of `float` and `double` are available. Table 2.3 lists the valid vector and matrix types.

Table 2.3   GLSL Vector and Matrix Types

Base Type	2D vec	3D vec	4D vec	Matrix Types		
float	vec2	vec3	vec4	mat2 mat2x2 mat3x2 mat4x2	mat3 mat2x3 mat3x3 mat4x3	mat4 mat2x4 mat3x4 mat4x4
double	dvec2	dvec3	dvec4	dmat2 dmat2x2 dmat3x2 dmat4x2	dmat3 dmat2x3 dmat3x3 dmat4x3	dmat4 dmat2x4 dmat3x4 dmat4x4
int	ivec2	ivec3	ivec4	—		
uint	uvec2	uvec3	uvec4	—		
bool	bvec2	bvec3	bvec4	—		

Matrix types that list both dimensions, such as `mat4x3`, use the first value to specify the number of columns, the second the number of rows.

Variables declared with these types can be initialized similar to their scalar counterparts:

```
vec3 velocity = vec3(0.0, 2.0, 3.0);
```

and converting between types is equally accessible:

```
ivec3 steps = ivec3(velocity);
```

Vector constructors can also be used to truncate or lengthen a vector. If a longer vector is passed into the constructor of a smaller vector, the vector is truncated to the appropriate length.

```
vec4 color;
vec3 RGB = vec3(color); // now RGB only has three elements
```

Likewise, vectors are lengthened in somewhat the same manner. Scalar values can be promoted to vectors, as in

```
vec3 white = vec3(1.0);    // white = (1.0, 1.0, 1.0)
vec4 translucent = vec4(white, 0.5);
```

Matrices are constructed in the same manner and can be initialized to either a diagonal matrix or a fully populated matrix. In the case of diagonal matrices, a single value is passed into the constructor, and the diagonal elements of the matrix are set to that value, with all others being set to zero, as in

$$m = \text{mat3}(4.0) = \begin{pmatrix} 4.0 & 0.0 & 0.0 \\ 0.0 & 4.0 & 0.0 \\ 0.0 & 0.0 & 4.0 \end{pmatrix}$$

Matrices can also be created by specifying the value of every element in the matrix in the constructor. Values can be specified by combinations of scalars and vectors, as long as enough values are provided, and each column is specified in the same manner. Additionally, matrices are specified in column-major order, meaning the values are used to populate columns before rows (which is the opposite of how "C" initializes two-dimensional arrays).

For example, we could initialize a 3×3 matrix in any of the following ways:

```
mat3 M = mat3(1.0, 2.0, 3.0,
              4.0, 5.0, 6.0,
              7.0, 8.0, 9.0);
```

```
vec3 column1 = vec3(1.0, 2.0, 3.0);
vec3 column2 = vec3(4.0, 5.0, 6.0);
vec3 column3 = vec3(7.0, 8.0, 9.0);

mat3 M = mat3(column1, column2, column3);
```

or even

```
vec2 column1 = vec2(1.0, 2.0);
vec2 column2 = vec2(4.0, 5.0);
vec2 column3 = vec2(7.0, 8.0);

mat3 M = mat3(column1, 3.0,

column2, 6.0,
column3, 9.0);
```

all yielding the same matrix

$$\begin{pmatrix} 1.0 & 4.0 & 7.0 \\ 2.0 & 5.0 & 8.0 \\ 3.0 & 6.0 & 9.0 \end{pmatrix}$$

Accessing Elements in Vectors and Matrices

The individual elements of vectors and matrices can be accessed and assigned. Vectors support two types of element access: a named-component method and an array-like method. Matrices use a two-dimensional, array-like method.

Components of a vector can be accessed by name, as in

```
float red = color.r;
float v_y = velocity.y;
```

or by using a zero-based index scheme. The following yield identical results to the above:

```
float red = color[0];
float v_y = velocity[1];
```

In fact, as shown in Table 2.4, there are three sets of component names, all of which do the same thing. The multiple sets are useful for clarifying the operations that you're doing.

Table 2.4   Vector Component Accessors

Component Accessors	Description
(x, y, z, w)	components associated with positions
(r, g, b, a)	components associated with colors
(s, t, p, q)	components associated with texture coordinates

A common use for component-wise access to vectors is for swizzling components, as you might do with colors, perhaps for color space conversion. For example, you could do the following to specify a *luminance* value based on the red component of an input color:

```
vec3 luminance = color.rrr;
```

Likewise, if you needed to move components around in a vector, you might do:

```
color = color.abgr; // reverse the components of a color
```

The only restriction is that only one set of components can be used with a variable in one statement. That is, you can't do:

```
vec4 color = otherColor.rgz; // Error:  "z" is from a different group
```

Also, a compile-time error will be raised if you attempt to access an element that's outside the range of the type. For example,

```
vec2 pos;
float zPos = pos.z; // Error:  no "z" component in 2D vectors
```

Matrix elements can be accessed using the array notation. Either a single scalar value or an array of elements can be accessed from a matrix:

```
mat4 m = mat4(2.0);
vec4 zVec = m[2];        // get column 2 of the matrix
float yScale = m[1][1];  // or m[1].y works as well
```

Structures

You can also logically group collections of different types into a structure. Structures are convenient for passing groups of associated data into functions. When a structure is defined, it automatically creates a new type, and implicitly defines a constructor function that takes the types of the elements of the structure as parameters.

```
struct Particle {
    float lifetime;
    vec3 position;
    vec3 velocity;
};

Particle p = Particle(10.0, pos, vel); // pos, vel are vec3s
```

Likewise, to reference elements of a structure, use the familiar "dot" notation as you would in "C".

Arrays

GLSL also supports arrays of any type, including structures. As with "C", arrays are indexed using brackets ([ ]). The range of elements in an array of size n is $0 \ldots n - 1$. Unlike "C", however, neither negative array indices nor positive indices out of range are permitted. As of GLSL 4.3, arrays can be made out of arrays, providing a way to handle multidimensional data. However, GLSL 4.2 and earlier versions do not allow arrays of arrays to be created (that is, you cannot create a multidimensional array).

Arrays can be declared sized or unsized. You might use an unsized array as a forward declaration of an array variable and later redeclare it to the appropriate size. Array declarations use the bracket notation, as in:

```
float      coeff[3]; // an array of 3 floats
float[3]   coeff; // same thing
int        indices[]; // unsized. Redeclare later with a size
```

Arrays are first-class types in GLSL, meaning they have constructors and can be used as function parameters and return types. To statically initialize an array of values, you would use a constructor in the following manner:

```
float coeff[3] = float[3](2.38, 3.14, 42.0);
```

The dimension value on the constructor is optional.

Additionally, similar to Java, GLSL arrays have an implicit method for reporting their number of elements: the **length()** method. If you would like to operate on all the values in an array, here is an example using the **length()** method:

```
for (int i = 0; i < coeff.length(); ++i) {
    coeff[i] *= 2.0;
}
```

The **length()** method also works on vectors and matrices. A vector's length is the number of components it contains, while a matrix's length is the number of columns it contains. This is exactly what you need when using array syntax for indexing vectors and matrices (`m[2]` is the third column of a matrix `m`).

```
mat3x4 m;
int c = m.length();     // number of columns in m:   3
int r = m[0].length(); // number of components in column vector 0:   4
```

When the length is known at compile time, the **length()** method will return a compile-time constant that can be used where compile-time constants are required. For example:

```
mat4 m;
float diagonal[m.length()]; // array of size matching the matrix size
float x[gl_in.length()];    // array of size matching the number of
                            // geometry shader input vertices
```

For all vectors and matrices, and most arrays, **length()** is known at compile time. However for some arrays, **length()** is not known until link time. This happens when relying on the linker to deduce the size from multiple shaders in the same stage. For shader storage buffer objects (declared with `buffer`, as described shortly), **length()** might not be known until render time. If you want a compile-time constant returned from **length()**, just make sure you establish the array size in your shader before using the **length()** method.

Multidimensional arrays are really arrays made from arrays and have a syntax similar to "C":

```
float coeff[3][5];     // an array of size 3 of arrays of size 5
coeff[2][1] *= 2.0;    // inner-dimension index is 1, outer is 2
coeff.length();        // this returns the constant 3
coeff[2];              // a one-dimensional array of size 5
coeff[2].length();     // this returns the constant 5
```

Multidimensional arrays can be formed in this way for virtually any type and resource. When shared with the application, the inner-most (right-most) dimension changes the fastest in the memory layout.

Storage Qualifiers

Types can also have modifiers that affect their behavior. There are four modifiers defined in GLSL, as shown in Table 2.5, with their behaviors at global scope.

Table 2.5 GLSL Type Modifiers

Type Modifier	Description
const	Labels a variable as a read-only. It will also be a compile-time constant if its initializer is a compile-time constant.
in	Specifies that the variable is an input to the shader stage.
out	Specifies that the variable is an output from a shader stage.
uniform	Specifies that the value is passed to the shader from the application and is constant across a given primitive.
buffer	Specifies read-write memory shared with the application. This memory is also referred to as a *shader storage buffer*.
shared	Specifies that the variables are shared within a local work group. This is only used in compute shaders.

const **Storage Qualifier**

Just as with "C", const type modifier indicates that the variable is read-only. For example, the statement

```
const float Pi = 3.141529;
```

sets the variable Pi to an approximation of π. With the addition of the const modifier, it becomes an error to write to a variable after its declaration, so they must be initialized when declared.

in **Storage Qualifier**

The in modifier is used to qualify inputs into a shader stage. Those inputs may be vertex attributes (for vertex shaders), or output variables from the preceding shader stage.

Fragment shaders can further qualify their input values using some additional keywords that we discuss in Chapter 4, "Color, Pixels, and Framebuffers".

out **Storage Qualifier**

The out modifier is used to qualify outputs from a shader stage—for example, the transformed homogeneous coordinates from a vertex shader, or the final fragment color from a fragment shader.

uniform **Storage Qualifier**

The uniform modifier specifies that a variable's value will be specified by the application before the shader's execution and does not change across the primitive being processed. *Uniform variables* are shared between all the shader stages enabled in a program and must be declared as global variables. Any type of variable, including structures and arrays, can be specified as uniform. A shader cannot write to a uniform variable and change its value.

For example, you might want to use a color for shading a primitive. You might declare a uniform variable to pass that information into your shaders. In the shaders, you would make the declaration:

```
uniform vec4 BaseColor;
```

Within your shaders, you can reference BaseColor by name, but to set its value in your application, you need to do a little extra work. The GLSL compiler creates a table of all uniform variables when it links your shader program. To set BaseColor's value from your application, you need to obtain the index of BaseColor in the table, which is done using the **glGetUniformLocation()** routine.

GLint **glGetUniformLocation**(GLuint *program*,
                     const char* *name*);

Returns the index of the uniform variable *name* associated with the shader *program*. *name* is a null-terminated character string with no spaces. A value of minus one (−1) is returned if *name* does not correspond to a uniform variable in the active shader program, or if a reserved shader variable name (those starting with gl_ prefix) is specified.

name can be a single variable name, an element of an array (by including the appropriate index in brackets with the name), or a field of a structure (by specifying *name*, then "." followed by the field name, as you would in the shader program). For arrays of uniform variables, the index of the first element of the array may be queried either by specifying only the array name (for example, "arrayName"), or by specifying the index to the first element of the array (as in "arrayName[0]").

The returned value will not change unless the shader program is relinked (see **glLinkProgram()**).

Once you have the associated index for the uniform variable, you can set the value of the uniform variable using the **glUniform*()** or **glUniformMatrix*()** routines.

Example 2.2 demonstrates obtaining a uniform variable's index and assigning values.

Example 2.2   Obtaining a Uniform Variable's Index and Assigning
Values

```
GLint   timeLoc; /* Uniform index for variable "time" in shader */
GLfloat timeValue; /* Application time */

timeLoc = glGetUniformLocation(program, "time");

glUniform1f(timeLoc, timeValue);
```

---

void **glUniform**{1234}{fdi ui}(GLint *location*, TYPE *value*);
void **glUniform**{1234}{fdi ui}v(GLint *location*, GLsizei *count*,
                     const TYPE * *values*);
void **glUniformMatrix**{234}{fd}v(GLint *location*, GLsizei *count*,
                     GLboolean *transpose*,
                     const GLfloat * *values*);
void **glUniformMatrix**{2x3,2x4,3x2,3x4,4x2,4x3}{fd}v(
                     GLint *location*, GLsizei *count*,
                     GLboolean *transpose*,
                     const GLfloat * *values*);

Sets the value for the uniform variable associated with the index *location*.
The vector form loads *count* sets of values (from one to four values,
depending upon which **glUniform*()** call is used) into the uniform
variable's starting *location*. If *location* is the start of an array, *count*
sequential elements of the array are loaded.

The GLfloat forms can be used to load the single-precision types of float, a
vector of floats, an array of floats, or an array of vectors of floats. Similarly
the GLdouble forms can be used for loading double-precision scalars,
vectors, and arrays. The GLfloat forms can also load Boolean types.

The GLint forms can be used to update a single signed integer, a signed
integer vector, an array of signed integers, or an array of signed integer
vectors. Additionally, individual and arrays of texture samplers and
Boolean scalars, vectors, and arrays can also be loaded. Similarly the
GLuint forms can be used for loading unsigned scalars, vectors, and
arrays.

For **glUniformMatrix**{234}***()**, count sets of 2×2, 3×3, or 4×4
matrices are loaded from *values*.

For **glUniformMatrix**{2x3,2x4,3x2,3x4,4x2,4x3}***()**, *count* sets of
like-dimensioned matrices are loaded from *values*. If *transpose* is
GL_TRUE, *values* are specified in row-major order (like arrays in "C"); or if
GL_FALSE is specified, values are taken to be in column-major order.

`buffer` **Storage Qualifier**

The recommended way to share a large buffer with the application is through use of a `buffer` variable. These are much like `uniform` variables, except that they can be modified by the shader. Typically, you'd use `buffer` variables in a `buffer` block, and blocks in general are described later in this chapter.

The `buffer` modifier specifies that the subsequent block is a memory buffer shared between the shader and the application. This buffer is both readable and writeable by the shader. The size of the buffer can be established after shader compilation and program linking.

`shared` **Storage Qualifier**

The `shared` modifier is only used in compute shaders to establish memory shared within a local work group. This is discussed in more detail in Chapter 12, "Compute Shaders".

Statements

The real work in a shader is done by computing values and making decisions. In the same manner as C++, GLSL has a rich set of operators for constructing arithmetic operations for computing values and a standard set of logical constructs for controlling shader execution.

Arithmetic Operations

No text describing a language is complete without the mandatory table of operator precedence (see Table 2.6). The operators are ordered in decreasing precedence. In general, the types being operated on must be the same, and for vector and matrices, the operands must be of the same dimension. In the table, *integer* types include `int` and `uint` and vectors of them, *floating-point* types include `float` and `double` types and vectors and matrices of them, *arithmetic* types include all integer and floating-point types, and *any* additionally includes structures and arrays.

Overloaded Operators

Most operators in GLSL are overloaded, meaning that they operate on a varied set of types. Specifically, arithmetic operations (including pre- and post-increment and -decrement) for vectors and matrices are well defined in GLSL. For example, to multiply a vector and a matrix (recalling that the

Table 2.6   GLSL Operators and Their Precedence

Precedence	Operators	Accepted types	Description
1	( )	—	Grouping of operations
2	[ ]	arrays, matrices, vectors	Array subscripting
	f( )	functions	Function calls and constructors
	. (period)	structures	Structure field or method access
	++ --	arithmetic	Post-increment and -decrement
3	++ --	arithmetic	Pre-increment and -decrement
	+ -	arithmetic	Unary explicit positive or negation
	~	integer	Unary bit-wise not
	!	bool	Unary logical not
4	* / %	arithmetic	Multiplicative operations
5	+ -	arithmetic	Additive operations
6	<< >>	integer	Bit-wise operations
7	< > <= >=	arithmetic	Relational operations
8	== !=	any	Equality operations
9	&	integer	Bit-wise and
10	^	integer	Bit-wise exclusive or
11	|	integer	Bit-wise inclusive or
12	&&	bool	Logical and operation
13	^^	bool	Logical exclusive-or operation
14	||	bool	Logical or operation
15	a ? b : c	bool ? any : any	Ternary selection operation (inline "if" operation; if (a) then (b) else (c))
16	=	any	Assignment
	+= -=	arithmetic	Arithmetic assignment
	*= /=	arithmetic	
	%= <<= >>=	integer	
	&= ^= |=	integer	
17	, (comma)	any	Sequence of operations

order of operands is important; matrix multiplication is noncommutative, for all you math heads), use the following operation:

```
vec3 v;
mat3 m;
vec3 result = v * m;
```

The normal restrictions apply, that the dimensionality of the matrix and the vector must match. Additionally, scalar multiplication with a vector or matrix will produce the expected result. One notable exception is that the multiplication of two vectors will result in component-wise multiplication of components; however, multiplying two matrices will result in normal matrix multiplication.

```
vec2 a, b, c;
mat2 m, u, v;
c = a * b; //   c = (a.x*b.x, a.y*b.y)
m = u * v; //   m = (u00*v00+u01*v10    u00*v01+u01*v11
           //        u01*v00+u11*v10    u10*v01+u11*v11)
```

Additional common vector operations (e.g., dot and cross products) are supported by function calls, as well as various per-component operations on vectors and matrices.

Flow Control

GLSL's logical control structures are the popular if-else and switch statements. As with the "C" language the else clause is optional, and multiple statements require a block.

```
if (truth) {
    // true clause
}
else {
    // false clause
}
```

Similar to the situation in C, switch statements are available (starting with GLSL 1.30) in their familiar form:

```
switch (int_value) {
    case n:
        // statements
        break;

    case m:
        // statements
        break;

    default:
        // statements
        break;
}
```

GLSL switch statements also support "fall-through" cases; a case statement that does not end with a break statement. Each case does require some statement to execute before the end of the switch (before the closing brace). Also, unlike C++, no statements are allowed before the first case. If no case matches the switch, and a default label is present, then it is executed.

Looping Constructs

GLSL supports the familiar "C" form of for, while, and do ... while loops.

The for loop permits the declaration of the loop iteration variable in the initialization clause of the for loop. The scope of iteration variables declared in this manner is only for the lifetime of the loop.

```
for (int i = 0; i < 10; ++i) {
    ...
}
while (n < 10) {
    ...
}
do {
    ...
} while (n < 10);
```

Flow-Control Statements

Additional control statements beyond conditionals and loops are available in GLSL. Table 2.7 describes available flow-control statements.

The discard statement is available only in fragment programs. The execution of the fragment shader may be terminated at the execution of the discard statement, but this is implementation dependent.

Table 2.7   GLSL Flow-Control Statements

Statement	Description
break	Terminates execution of the block of a loop, and continues execution after the scope of that block.
continue	Terminates the current iteration of the enclosing block of a loop, resuming execution with the next iteration of the loop.
return [result]	Returns from the current subroutine, optionally providing a value to be returned from the function (assuming return value matches the return type of the enclosing function).
discard	Discards the current fragment and ceases shader execution. Discard statements are only valid in fragment shader programs.

Functions

Functions permit you to replace occurrences of common code with a function call. This, of course, allows for smaller code, and less chances for errors. GLSL defines a number of built-in functions, which are listed in

Appendix C as well as support for user-defined functions. User-defined functions can be defined in a single shader object, and reused in multiple shader programs.

Declarations

Function declaration syntax is very similar to "C", with the exception of the access modifiers on variables:

```
returnType functionName([accessModifier] type1 variable1,
                        [accessModifier] type2 varaible2,
                         ...)
{
    // function body
    return returnValue; // unless returnType is void
}
```

Function names can be any combination of letters, numbers, and the underscore character, with the exception that it can neither begin with a digit nor with gl_ nor contain consecutive underscores.

Return types can be any built-in GLSL type or user-defined structure or array type. Arrays as return values must explicitly specify their size. If a function doesn't return a value, its return type is void.

Parameters to functions can also be of any type, including arrays (which must specify their size).

Functions must be either declared with a prototype or defined with a body, before they are called. Just as in C++, the compiler must have seen the function's declaration before its use or an error will be raised. If a function is used in a shader object other than the one where it's defined, a prototype must be declared. A prototype is merely the function's signature without its accompanying body. Here's a simple example:

```
float HornerEvalPolynomial(float coeff[10], float x);
```

Parameter Qualifiers

While functions in GLSL are able to modify and return values after their execution, there's no concept of a pointer or reference, as in "C" or C++. Rather, parameters of functions have associated parameter qualifiers indicating if the value should be copied into, or out of, a function after execution. Table 2.8 describes the available parameter qualifiers in GLSL.

Table 2.8 GLSL Function Parameter Access Modifiers

Access Modifier	Description
in	Value copied into a function (default if not specified)
const in	Read-only value copied into a function
out	Value copied out of a function (undefined upon entrance into the function)
inout	Value copied into and out of a function

The in keyword is optional. If a variable does not include an access modifier, then an in modifier is implicitly added to the parameter's declaration. However, if the variable's value needs to be copied out of a function, it must either be tagged with an out (for copy out-only variables) or an inout (for a variable both copied in and copied out) modifier. Writing to a variable not tagged with one of these modifiers will generate a compile-time error.

Additionally, to verify at compile time that a function doesn't modify an input-only variable, adding a "const in" modifier will cause the compiler to check that the variable is not written to in the function. If you don't do this and do write to an input-only variable, it only modifies the local copy in the function.

Computational Invariance

GLSL does not guarantee that two identical computations in different shaders will result in exactly the same value. The situation is no different than for computational applications executing on the CPU, where the choice of optimizations may result in tiny differences in results. These tiny errors may be an issue for multipass algorithms that expect positions to be computed exactly the same for each shader pass. GLSL has two methods for enforcing this type of invariance between shaders, using the invariant or precise keywords.

Both of these methods will cause computations done by the graphics device to create reproducibility (invariance) in results of the same expression. However, they do not help reproduce the same results between the host and the graphics device. Compile-time constant expressions are computed on the compiler's host and there is no guarantee that the host computes in exactly the same way as the graphics device. For example:

```
uniform float ten;          // application sets this to 10.0
const float f = sin(10.0);  // computed on compiler host
float g = sin(ten);         // computed on graphics device
```

```
void main()
{
    if (f == g)            // f and g might be not equal
        ;
}
```

In this example, it would not matter if `invariant` or `precise` was used on any of the variables involved, as they only effect two computations done on the graphics device.

The `invariant` Qualifier

The invariant qualifier may be applied to any shader output variable. It will guarantee that if two shader *invocation*s each set the output variable with the same expression and the same values for the variables in that expression, then both will compute the same value.

The output variable declared as invariant may be a built-in variable or a user-defined one. For example:

```
invariant gl_Position;
invariant centroid out vec3 Color;
```

As you may recall, output variables are used to pass data from one stage to the next. The `invariant` keyword may be applied at any time before use of the variable in the shader and may be used to modify built-in variables. This is done by declaring the variable only with `invariant`, as was shown above for `gl_Position`.

For debugging, it may be useful to impose invariance on all varying variables in shader. This can be accomplished by using the vertex shader preprocessor pragma.

```
#pragma STDGL invariant(all)
```

Global invariance in this manner is useful for debugging; however, it may likely have an impact on the shader's performance. Guaranteeing invariance usually disables optimizations that may have been performed by the GLSL compiler.

The `precise` Qualifier

The `precise` qualifier may be applied to any computed variable or function return value. Despite its name, its purpose is not to increase precision, but rather to increase reproducibility of a computation. It is mostly used in tessellation shaders to avoid forming cracks in your geometry. Tessellation shading in general is described in Chapter 9, "Tessellation Shaders", and there is additional discussion in that chapter about a use case for `precise` qualification.

Generally, you use `precise` instead of `invariant` when you need to get the same result from an expression, even if values feeding the expression are permuted in a way that should not mathematically affect the result. For example, the following expression should get the same result if the values for *a* and *b* are exchanged. It should also get the same result if the values for *c* and *d* and exchanged, or if both *a* and *c* are exchanged and *b* and *d* are exchanged, etc.

```
Location = a * b + c * d;
```

The `precise` qualifier may be applied to a built-in variable, user variable, or a function return value.

```
precise gl_Position;
precise out vec3 Location;
precise vec3 subdivide(vec3 P1, vec3 P2) { ... }
```

The `precise` keyword may be applied at any time before use of the variable in the shader and may be used to modify previously declared variables.

One practical impact in a compiler of using `precise` is an expression like the one above cannot be evaluated using two different methods of multiplication for the two multiply operations. For example, a multiply instruction for the first multiply and a fused multiply-and-add instruction for the second multiply. This is because these two instructions will get slightly different results for the same values. Since that was disallowed by `precise`, the compiler is prevented from doing this. Because use of fused multipy-and-add instructions is important to performance, it would be unfortunate to completely disallow them. So, there is a built-in function in GLSL, **fma()**, that you can use to explicitly say this is okay.

```
precise out float result;
  ...
float f = c * d;
float result = fma(a, b, f);
```

Of course, you only do that if you weren't going to have the values of *a* and *c* permuted, as you would be defeating the purpose of using `precise`.

Shader Preprocessor

The first step in compilation of a GLSL shader is parsing by the preprocessor. Similar to the "C" preprocessor, there are a number of directives for creating conditional compilation blocks and defining values. However, unlike the "C" preprocessor, there is no file inclusion (#include).

Preprocessor Directives

Table 2.9 lists the preprocessor directives accepted by the GLSL preprocessor and their functions.

Table 2.9   GLSL Preprocessor Directives

Preprocessor Directive	Description
`#define`	Control the definition of constants and
`#undef`	macros similar to the "C" preprocessor
`#if`	Conditional code management similar
`#ifdef`	to the "C" preprocessor, including the `defined` operator.
`#ifndef`	
`#else`	Conditional expressions evaluate integer
`#elif`	expressions and defined values
`#endif`	(as specified by #define) only.
`#error` text	Cause the compiler to insert text (up to the first newline character) into the shader information log
`#pragma` options	Control compiler specific options
`#extension` options	Specify compiler operation with respect to specified GLSL extensions
`#version` number	Mandate a specific version of GLSL version support
`#line` options	Control diagnostic line numbering

Macro Definition

The GLSL preprocessor allows macro definition in much the same manner as the "C" preprocessor, with the exception of the string substitution and concatenation facilities. Macros might define a single value, as in

```
#define NUM_ELEMENTS 10
```

or with parameters like

```
#define LPos(n) gl_LightSource[(n)].position
```

Additionally, there are several predefined macros for aiding in diagnostic messages (that you might issue with the #error directive, for example), as shown in Table 2.10.

Table 2.10   GLSL Preprocessor Predefined Macros

__LINE__	Line number defined by one more than the number of newline characters processed and modified by the #line directive
__FILE__	Source string number currently being processed
__VERSION__	Integer representation of the OpenGL Shading Language version

Likewise, macros (excluding those defined by GLSL) may be undefined by using the #undef directive. For example

```
#undef LPos
```

Preprocessor Conditionals

Identical to the processing by the "C" preprocessor, the GLSL preprocessor provides conditional code inclusion based on macro definition and integer constant evaluation.

Macro definition may be determined in two ways: Either using the #ifdef directive

```
#ifdef NUM_ELEMENTS
  . . .
#endif
```

or using the defined operator with the #if or #elif directives

```
#if defined(NUM_ELEMENTS) && NUM_ELEMENTS > 3
  . . .
#elif NUM_ELEMENTS < 7
  . . .
#endif
```

Compiler Control

The #pragma directive provides the compiler additional information regarding how you would like your shaders compiled.

Optimization Compiler Option

The optimize option instructs the compiler to enable or disable optimization of the shader from the point where the directive resides forward in the shader source. You can enable or disable optimization by issuing either

```
#pragma optimize(on)
```

or

```
#pragma optimize(off)
```

respectively. These options may only be issued outside of a function definition. By default, optimization is enabled for all shaders.

Debug Compiler Option

The debug option enables or disables additional diagnostic output of the shader. You can enable or disable debugging by issuing either

```
#pragma debug(on)
```

or

```
#pragma debug(off)
```

respectively. Similar to the optimize option, these options may only be issued outside of a function definition, and by default, debugging is disabled for all shaders.

Global Shader-Compilation Option

One final #pragma directive that is available is STDGL. This option is currently used to enable invariance in the output of varying values.

Extension Processing in Shaders

GLSL, like OpenGL itself, may be enhanced by extensions. As vendors may include extensions specific to their OpenGL implementation, it's useful to have some control over shader compilation in light of possible extensions that a shader may use.

The GLSL preprocessor uses the #extension directive to provide instructions to the shader compiler regarding how extension availability should be handled during compilation. For any, or all, extensions, you can specify how you would like the compiler to proceed with compilation.

```
#extension extension_name : <directive>
```

where extension_name uses the same extension name returned by calling **glGetString**(GL_EXTENSIONS) or

```
#extension all : <directive>
```

to affect the behavior of all extensions.

The options available are shown in Table 2.11

Table 2.11 GLSL Extension Directive Modifiers

Directive	Description
require	Flag an error if the extension is not supported, or if the all-extension specification is used.
enable	Give a warning if the particular extensions specified are not supported, or flag an error if the all-extension specification is used.
warn	Give a warning if the particular extensions specified are not supported, or give a warning if any extension use is detected during compilation.
disable	Disable support for the particular extensions listed (that is, have the compiler act as if the extension is not supported even if it is) or all extensions if all is present, issuing warnings and errors as if the extension were not present.

Interface Blocks

Shader variables shared with the application or between stages can be, and sometimes must be, organized into *blocks* of variables. Uniform variables can be organized into `uniform` blocks, input and output variables into `in` and `out` blocks, and shader storage buffers into `buffer` blocks.

These all have a similar form. First, we'll use `uniform` to demonstrate.

```
uniform b {        // "uniform" or "in" or "out" or "buffer"
      vec4 v1;     // list of variables
      bool v2;     // ...
};                 // access members as "v1" and "v2"
```

Or:

```
uniform b {        // "uniform" or "in" or "out" or "buffer"
      vec4 v1;     // list of variables
      bool v2;     // ...
} name;            // access members as "name.v1" and "name.v2"
```

Specific interface block details are provided in the sections below. Generally, the block name at the beginning (b above) is used for interface matching or external identification, while the name at the end (name above) is used in the rest of the shader for accessing the members.

Uniform Blocks

As your shader programs become more complex, it's likely that the number of uniform variables they use will increase. Often the same uniform value is used within several shader programs. As uniform locations are generated when a shader is linked (i.e., when **glLinkProgram()** is called), the indices may change, even though (to you) the values of the uniform variables are identical. *Uniform buffer objects* provide a method to optimize both accessing uniform variables and enabling sharing of uniform values across shader programs.

As you might imagine, that given uniform variables can exist both in your application and in a shader, you'll need to both modify your shaders and use OpenGL routines to set up uniform buffer objects.

Specifying Uniform Blocks in Shaders

To access a collection of uniform variables using routines such as **glMapBuffer()** (see Chapter 3, "Drawing with OpenGL" for more details), you need to slightly modify their declaration in your shader. Instead of declaring each uniform variable individually, you group them, just as you would do in a structure, in a uniform block. A uniform block is specified using the uniform keyword. You then enclose all the variables you want in that block within a pair of braces, as demonstrated in Example 2.3.

Example 2.3   Declaring a Uniform Block

```
uniform Matrices {
    mat4 ModelView;
    mat4 Projection;
    mat4 Color;
};
```

Recall types are divided into two categories: opaque and transparent; where the opaque types include samplers, images, and atomic counters. Only the transparent types are permitted to be within a uniform block. Additionally, uniform blocks must be declared at global scope.

Uniform Block Layout Control

A variety of qualifiers are available to specify how to lay out the variables within a uniform block. These qualifiers can be used for each individual uniform block or to specify how all subsequent uniform blocks are arranged (after specifying a layout declaration). The possible qualifiers are detailed in Table 2.12.

Table 2.12   Layout Qualifiers for Uniform

Layout Qualifier	Description
shared	Specify that the uniform block is shared among multiple programs. (This is the default layout and is not to be confused with the shared storage qualifier.)
packed	Lay out the uniform block to minimize its memory use; however, this generally disables sharing across programs.
std140	Use a standard layout for uniform blocks or shader storage buffer blocks, described in Appendix I, "Buffer Object Layouts".
std430	Use a standard layout for buffer blocks, described in Appendix I, "Buffer Object Layouts".
row_major	Cause matrices in the uniform block to be stored in a row-major element ordering.
column_major	Specify matrices should be stored in a column-major element ordering. (This is the default ordering.)

For example, to specify that a single uniform block is shared and has row-major matrix storage, you would declare it in the following manner:

```
layout (shared, row_major) uniform { ... };
```

The multiple qualifying options must be separated by commas within the parentheses. To affect the layout of all subsequent uniform blocks, use the following construct:

```
layout (packed, column_major) uniform;
```

With this specification, all uniform blocks declared after that line will use that layout until the global layout is changed, or unless they include a layout override specific to their declaration.

Accessing Uniform Variables Declared in a Uniform Block

While uniform blocks are named, the uniform variables declared within them are not qualified by that name. That is, a uniform block doesn't scope a uniform variable's name, so declaring two variables of the same name within two uniform blocks of different names will cause an error. Using the block name is not necessary when accessing a uniform variable, however.

Accessing Uniform Blocks from Your Application

Because uniform variables form a bridge to share data between shaders and your application, you need to find the offsets of the various uniform variables inside the named uniform blocks in your shaders. Once you know the location of those variables, you can initialize them with data, just as you would any type of buffer object (using calls such as **glBufferData()**, for example).

To start, let's assume that you already know the names of the uniform blocks used inside the shaders in your application. The first step in initializing the uniform variables in your uniform block is to obtain the index of the block for a given program. Calling **glGetUniformBlockIndex()** returns an essential piece of information required to complete the mapping of uniform variables into your application's address space.

GLuint **glGetUniformBlockIndex**(GLuint *program,*
                              const char * *uniformBlockName*);

Returns the index of the named uniform block specified by *uniformBlockName* associated with *program.* If *uniformBlockName* is not a valid uniform block of program, GL_INVALID_INDEX is returned.

To initialize a buffer object to be associated with your uniform block, you'll need to bind a buffer object to a GL_UNIFORM_BUFFER target using the **glBindBuffer()** routine as shown in the example below (Chapter 3, "Drawing with OpenGL" will add more details).

Once we have a buffer object initialized, we need to determine how large to make it to accommodate the variables in the named uniform block from our shader. To do so, we use the routine **glGetActiveUniformBlockiv()**, requesting the GL_UNIFORM_BLOCK_DATA_SIZE, which returns the size of the block as generated by the compiler (the compiler may decide to eliminate uniform variables that aren't used in the shader, depending on which uniform block layout you've selected).
glGetActiveUniformBlockiv() can be used to obtain other parameters associated with a named uniform block.

After obtaining the index of the uniform block, we need to associate a buffer object with that block. The most common method for doing so is to call either **glBindBufferRange()** or, if all the buffer storage is used for the uniform block, **glBindBufferBase()**.

```
void glBindBufferRange(GLenum target, GLuint index,
                       GLuint buffer, GLintptr offset,
                       GLsizeiptr size);
void glBindBufferBase(GLenum target, GLuint index,
                      GLuint buffer);
```

Associates the buffer object *buffer* with the named uniform block associated with *index*. *target* can either be GL_UNIFORM_BUFFER (for uniform blocks) or GL_TRANSFORM_FEEDBACK_BUFFER (for use with transform feedback; Chapter 5). *index* is the index associated with a uniform block. *offset* and *size* specify the starting index and range of the buffer that is to be mapped to the uniform buffer.

Calling **glBindBufferBase()** is identical to calling **glBindBufferRange()** with *offset* equal to zero and *size* equal to the size of the buffer object.

These calls can generate various OpenGL errors: A GL_INVALID_VALUE is generated if *size* is less than zero; if *offset* + *size* is greater than the size of the buffer; if either *offset* or *size* is not a multiple of 4; or if *index* is less than zero, or greater than or equal to the value returned when querying GL_MAX_UNIFORM_BUFFER_BINDINGS.

Once the association between a named uniform block and a buffer object is made, you can initialize or change values in that block by using any of the commands that affect a buffer's values.

You may also want to specify the binding for a particular named uniform block to a buffer object, as compared to the process of allowing the linker to assign a block binding and then querying the value of that assignment after the fact. You might follow this approach if you have numerous shader programs that will share a uniform block. It avoids having the block be assigned a different index for each program. To explicitly control a uniform block's binding, call **glUniformBlockBinding()** before calling **glLinkProgram()**.

```
GLint glUniformBlockBinding(GLuint program,
                            GLuint uniformBlockIndex,
                            GLuint uniformBlockBinding);
```

Explicitly assigns uniformBlockIndex to uniformBlockBinding for program.

The layout of uniform variables in a named uniform block is controlled by the layout qualifier specified when the block was compiled and linked. If you used the default layout specification, you will need to determine the offset and date-store size of each variable in the uniform block. To do so, you will use the pair of calls: **glGetUniformIndices()**, to retrieve the index of a particular named uniform variable, and **glGetActiveUniformsiv()**, to get the offset and size for that particular index, as demonstrated in Example 2.4.

---

void **glGetUniformIndices**(GLuint *program*,
　　　　　　　　　　　　GLsizei *uniformCount*,
　　　　　　　　　　　　const char ** *uniformNames*,
　　　　　　　　　　　　GLuint * *uniformIndices*);

Returns the indices associated with the *uniformCount* uniform variables specified by name in the array *uniformNames* in the array *uniformIndices* for program. Each name in *uniformNames* is assumed to be NULL terminated, and both *uniformNames* and *uniformIndices* have *uniformCount* elements in each array. If a name listed in *uniformNames* is not the name of an active uniform variables, the value GL_INVALID_INDEX is returned in the corresponding element in *uniformIndices*.

Example 2.4　　Initializing Uniform Variables in a Named Uniform Block

```
/* Vertex and fragment shaders that share a block of uniforms
** named "Uniforms" */
const char* vShader = {
    "#version 330 core\n"
    "uniform Uniforms {"
    "    vec3  translation;"
    "    float scale;"
    "    vec4  rotation;"
    "    bool  enabled;"
    "};"
    "in vec2 vPos;"
    "in vec3 vColor;"
    "out vec4 fColor;"
    "void main()"
    "{"
    "    vec3   pos = vec3(vPos, 0.0);"
    "    float  angle = radians(rotation[0]);"
    "    vec3   axis = normalize(rotation.yzw);"
    "    mat3   I = mat3(1.0);"
    "    mat3   S = mat3(      0, -axis.z,  axis.y, "
    "                    axis.z,       0, -axis.x, "
    "                   -axis.y,  axis.x,       0);"
    "    mat3   uuT = outerProduct(axis, axis);"
```

```
"    mat3   rot = uuT + cos(angle)*(I - uuT)"
"                       + sin(angle)*S;"
"    pos *= scale;"
"    pos *= rot;"
"    pos += translation;"
"    fColor = vec4(scale, scale, scale, 1);"
"    gl_Position = vec4(pos, 1);"
"}"
};

const char* fShader = {
    "#version 330 core\n"
    "uniform Uniforms {"
    "    vec3  translation;"
    "    float scale;"
    "    vec4  rotation;"
    "    bool  enabled;"
    "};"
    "in vec4 fColor;"
    "out vec4 color;"
    "void main()"
    "{"
    "    color = fColor;"
    "}"
};

/* Helper function to convert GLSL types to storage sizes */
size_t
TypeSize(GLenum type)
{
    size_t   size;

    #define CASE(Enum, Count, Type) \
    case Enum: size = Count * sizeof(Type); break

    switch (type) {
      CASE(GL_FLOAT,                1,  GLfloat);
      CASE(GL_FLOAT_VEC2,           2,  GLfloat);
      CASE(GL_FLOAT_VEC3,           3,  GLfloat);
      CASE(GL_FLOAT_VEC4,           4,  GLfloat);
      CASE(GL_INT,                  1,  GLint);
      CASE(GL_INT_VEC2,             2,  GLint);
      CASE(GL_INT_VEC3,             3,  GLint);
      CASE(GL_INT_VEC4,             4,  GLint);
      CASE(GL_UNSIGNED_INT,         1,  GLuint);
      CASE(GL_UNSIGNED_INT_VEC2,    2,  GLuint);
      CASE(GL_UNSIGNED_INT_VEC3,    3,  GLuint);
      CASE(GL_UNSIGNED_INT_VEC4,    4,  GLuint);
      CASE(GL_BOOL,                 1,  GLboolean);
      CASE(GL_BOOL_VEC2,            2,  GLboolean);
      CASE(GL_BOOL_VEC3,            3,  GLboolean);
      CASE(GL_BOOL_VEC4,            4,  GLboolean);
      CASE(GL_FLOAT_MAT2,           4,  GLfloat);
```

```
        CASE(GL_FLOAT_MAT2x3,        6,  GLfloat);
        CASE(GL_FLOAT_MAT2x4,        8,  GLfloat);
        CASE(GL_FLOAT_MAT3,          9,  GLfloat);
        CASE(GL_FLOAT_MAT3x2,        6,  GLfloat);
        CASE(GL_FLOAT_MAT3x4,        12, GLfloat);
        CASE(GL_FLOAT_MAT4,          16, GLfloat);
        CASE(GL_FLOAT_MAT4x2,        8,  GLfloat);
        CASE(GL_FLOAT_MAT4x3,        12, GLfloat);
        #undef CASE

        default:
        fprintf(stderr, "Unknown type:  0x%x\n", type);
        exit(EXIT_FAILURE);
        break;
    }

    return size;
}

void
init()
{
    GLuint program;

    glClearColor(1, 0, 0, 1);

    ShaderInfo shaders[] = {
        { GL_VERTEX_SHADER, vShader },
        { GL_FRAGMENT_SHADER, fShader },
        { GL_NONE, NULL }
    };

    program = LoadShaders(shaders);
    glUseProgram(program);

    /* Initialize uniform values in uniform block "Uniforms" */
    GLuint    uboIndex;
    GLint     uboSize;
    GLuint    ubo;
    GLvoid   *buffer;

    /* Find the uniform buffer index for "Uniforms", and
    ** determine the block's sizes */
    uboIndex = glGetUniformBlockIndex(program, "Uniforms");

    glGetActiveUniformBlockiv(program, uboIndex,
    GL_UNIFORM_BLOCK_DATA_SIZE, &uboSize);

    buffer = malloc(uboSize);

    if (buffer == NULL) {
        fprintf(stderr, "Unable to allocate buffer\n");
        exit(EXIT_FAILURE);
    }
```

```
else {
    enum { Translation, Scale, Rotation, Enabled, NumUniforms };

    /* Values to be stored in the buffer object */
    GLfloat    scale = 0.5;
    GLfloat    translation[] = { 0.1, 0.1, 0.0 };
    GLfloat    rotation[] = { 90, 0.0, 0.0, 1.0 };
    GLboolean enabled = GL_TRUE;

    /* Since we know the names of the uniforms
    ** in our block, make an array of those values */
    const char* names[NumUniforms] = {
        "translation",
        "scale",
        "rotation",
        "enabled"
    };

    /* Query the necessary attributes to determine
    ** where in the buffer we should write
    ** the values */
    GLuint    indices[NumUniforms];
    GLint     size[NumUniforms];
    GLint     offset[NumUniforms];
    GLint     type[NumUniforms];

    glGetUniformIndices(program, NumUniforms, names, indices);
    glGetActiveUniformsiv(program, NumUniforms, indices,
                          GL_UNIFORM_OFFSET, offset);
    glGetActiveUniformsiv(program, NumUniforms, indices,
                          GL_UNIFORM_SIZE, size);
    glGetActiveUniformsiv(program, NumUniforms, indices,
                          GL_UNIFORM_TYPE, type);

    /* Copy the uniform values into the buffer */
    memcpy(buffer + offset[Scale], &scale,
           size[Scale] * TypeSize(type[Scale]));
    memcpy(buffer + offset[Translation], &translation,
           size[Translation] * TypeSize(type[Translation]));
    memcpy(buffer + offset[Rotation], &rotation,
           size[Rotation] * TypeSize(type[Rotation]));
    memcpy(buffer + offset[Enabled], &enabled,
           size[Enabled] * TypeSize(type[Enabled]));

    /* Create the uniform buffer object, initialize
    ** its storage, and associated it with the shader
    ** program */
    glGenBuffers(1, &ubo);
    glBindBuffer(GL_UNIFORM_BUFFER, ubo);
    glBufferData(GL_UNIFORM_BUFFER, uboSize,
                 buffer, GL_STATIC_RAW);
```

```
        glBindBufferBase(GL_UNIFORM_BUFFER, uboIndex, ubo);
    }
    ...
}
```

Buffer Blocks

GLSL buffer blocks, or from the application's perspective *shader storage buffer objects*, operate quite similarly to uniform blocks. Two critical differences give these blocks great power, however. First, the shader can write to them, modifying their content as seen from other shader invocations or the application. Second, their size can be established just before rendering, rather than at compile or link time. For example:

```
buffer BufferObject {  // create a read-writeable buffer
    int mode;          // preamble members
    vec4 points[];     // last member can be unsized array
};
```

If the array above is not provided a size in the shader, then its size can be established by the application before rendering, after compiling and linking. The shader can use the **length()** method to find the render-time size.

The shader may now both read and write the members of the buffer block. Writes modifying the shader storage buffer object will be visible to other shader invocations. This can be particularly valuable in a compute shader, especially when manipulating nongraphical memory rather than an image.

Memory qualifiers (e.g., `coherent`) and atomic operations apply to buffer blocks and are discussed in depth in Chapter 11, "Memory".

You set up a shader storage buffer object similarly to how a uniform buffer was set up, except that **glBindBuffer()** and **glBufferData()** take the target GL_SHADER_STORAGE_BUFFER. A more complete example is given in Chapter 11, "Memory", in section "Shader Storage Buffer Objects" on Page 576.

If you don't need to write to a buffer, use a uniform block, as your device might not have as many resources available for buffer blocks as it does for uniform blocks.

In/Out Blocks

Shader variables output from one stage and input into the next stage can also be organized into interface blocks. These logical groupings can make it easier to visually verify interface matches between stages, as well as to make linking separate programs easier.

For example, a vertex shader might output:

```
out Lighting {
    vec3 normal;
    vec2 bumpCoord;
};
```

This would match a fragment shader input:

```
in Lighting {
    vec3 normal;
    vec2 bumpCoord;
};
```

A vertex shader might output *material* and *lighting* information, each grouped into its own block. The interfaces built into the OpenGL Shading Language are also organized into blocks, like `gl_PerVertex`, which contains the built-in variable `gl_Position`, among others. A complete list of these is available in Appendix C, "Built-in GLSL Variables and Functions".

Compiling Shaders

Writing shaders for use with OpenGL programs is similar to using a compiler-based language like "C". You have a compiler analyze your program, check it for errors, and then translate it into object code. Next, you combine a collection of object files together in a linking phase to generate an executable program. Using GLSL shaders in your program is a similar process, except that the compiler and linker are part of the OpenGL API.

Figure 2.1 illustrates the steps to create GLSL shader objects and link them to create an executable shader program.

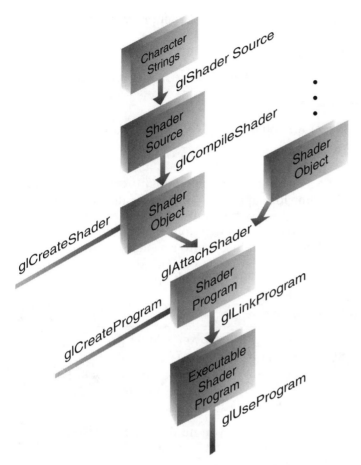

Figure 2.1   Shader-compilation command sequence

For each shader program you want to use in your application, you'll need to do the following sequence of steps:

For each shader object:

1. Create a shader object.

2. Compile your shader source into the object.

3. Verify that your shader compiled successfully.

Then, to link multiple shader objects into a shader program, you'll

1. Create a shader program.

2. Attach the appropriate shader objects to the shader program.

3. Link the shader program.

4. Verify that the shader link phase completed successfully.

5. Use the shader for vertex or fragment processing.

Why create multiple shader objects? Just as you might reuse a function in different programs, the same idea applies to GLSL programs. Common routines that you create might be usable in multiple shaders. Instead of having to compile several large shaders with lots of common code, you'll merely link the appropriate shader objects into a shader program.

To create a shader object, call **glCreateShader()**.

GLuint **glCreateShader**(GLenum *type*);

Allocates a shader object. *type* must be one of GL_VERTEX_SHADER, GL_FRAGMENT_SHADER, GL_TESS_CONTROL_SHADER, GL_TESS_EVALUATION_SHADER, or GL_GEOMETRY_SHADER. The return value is either a nonzero integer or zero if an error occurred.

Once you have created a shader object, you need to associate the source code of the shader with that object created by **glCreateShader()**. This is done by calling **glShaderSource()**.

---

void **glShaderSource**(GLuint *shader*, GLsizei *count*,
                const GLchar **string*, const GLint **length*);

Associates the source of a shader with a shader object *shader*. *string* is an array of *count* GLchar strings that compose the shader's source. The character strings in *string* may be optionally null-terminated. *length* can be one of three values. If *length* is NULL, then it's assumed that each string provided in string is null-terminated. Otherwise, *length* has *count* elements, each of which specifies the length of the corresponding entry in *string*. If the value of an element in the array *length* is a positive integer, the value represents the number of characters in the corresponding *string* element. If the value is negative for particular elements, then that entry in *string* is assumed to be null-terminated.

To compile a shader object's source, use **glCompileShader()**.

---

void **glCompileShader**(GLuint *shader*);

Compiles the source code for *shader*. The results of the compilation can be queried by calling **glGetShaderiv()** with an argument of GL_COMPILE_STATUS.

Similar to when you compile a "C" program, you need to determine if the compilation finished successfully. A call to **glGetShaderiv()**, with an argument of GL_COMPILE_STATUS, will return the status of the compilation phase. If GL_TRUE is returned, the compilation succeeded, and the object can be linked into a shader program. If the compilation failed, you can determine what the error was by retrieving the compilation log. **glGetShaderInfoLog()** will return an implementation-specific set of messages describing the compilation errors. The current size of the error log can be queried by calling **glGetShaderiv()** with an argument of GL_INFO_LOG_LENGTH.

---

void **glGetShaderInfoLog**(GLuint *shader*, GLsizei *bufSize*,
                    GLsizei **length*, char **infoLog*);

Returns the log associated with the last compilation of *shader*. The log is returned as a null-terminated character string of *length* characters in the buffer *infoLog*. The maximum return size of the log is specified in *bufSize*.

If length is NULL, infoLog's length is not returned.

Once you have created and compiled all of the necessary shader objects, you will need to link them to create an executable shader program. This process is similar in nature to creating shader objects. First, you'll need to create a shader program to which you can attach the shader objects. Using **glCreateProgram()**, a shader program will be returned for further processing.

GLuint **glCreateProgram**(void);

Creates an empty shader program. The return value is either a nonzero integer, or zero if an error occurred.

Once you have your shader program, you'll need to populate it with the necessary shader objects to create the executable program. This is

accomplished by attaching a shader object to the program by calling
glAttachShader().

> void **glAttachShader**(GLuint *program*, GLuint *shader*);
>
> Associates the shader object, *shader*, with the shader program, *program*. A
> shader object can be attached to a shader program at any time, although
> its functionality will only be available after a successful link of the shader
> program. A shader object can be attached to multiple shader programs
> simultaneously.

For parity, if you need to remove a shader object from a program to modify
the shader's operation, detach the shader object by calling
glDetachShader() with the appropriate shader object identifier.

> void **glDetachShader**(GLuint *program*, GLuint *shader*);
>
> Removes the association of a shader object, *shader*, from the shader
> program, *program*. If *shader* is detached from *program* and had been
> previously marked for deletion (by calling **glDeleteShader()**), it is deleted
> at that time.

After all the necessary shader objects have been attached to the shader
program, you will need to link the objects for an executable program. This
is accomplished by calling **glLinkProgram()**.

> void **glLinkProgram**(GLuint *program*);
>
> Processes all shader objects attached to *program* to generate a completed
> shader program. The result of the linking operation can be queried by
> calling **glGetProgramiv()** with GL_LINK_STATUS. GL_TRUE is returned
> for a successful link; GL_FALSE is returned otherwise.

As with shader objects, there's a chance that the linking phase may fail due
to errors in the attached shader objects. You can query the result of the
link operation's success by calling **glGetProgramiv()** with an argument of
GL_LINK_STATUS. If GL_TRUE was returned, the link was successful, and
you're able to specify the shader program for use in processing vertices or
fragments. If the link failed, represented by GL_FALSE being returned,

then you can determine the cause of the failure by retrieving the program link information log by calling **glGetProgramInfoLog()**.

---

void **glGetProgramInfoLog**(GLuint *program*, GLsizei *bufSize*,
                      GLsizei **length*, char **infoLog*);

Returns the log associated with the last compilation of *program*. The log is returned as a null-terminated character string of *length* characters in the buffer *infoLog*. The maximum return size of the log is specified in *bufSize*. If length is NULL, *infoLog*'s length is not returned.

After a successful program link, you can engage the vertex or fragment program by calling **glUseProgram()** with the program's object handle.

---

void **glUseProgram**(GLuint *program*);

Use the linked shader program *program*. If *program* is zero, any shaders currently in use are unbound. OpenGL's operation is undefined if no shader is bound, but no error is generated.

While a program is in use, it can have new shader objects attached to it, or detach previously attached objects. It may also be relinked. If the link phase is successful, the newly linked shader program replaces the previously active program. If the link fails, the currently bound shader program remains active and is not replaced until either a new program is specified with **glUseProgram()** or the program is successfully relinked.

When you're done using a shader object, you can delete it using **glDeleteShader()**, even if it's attached to an active program. Just like linking a "C" program, once you have an executable, you don't need the object files until you compile again.

---

void **glDeleteShader**(GLuint *shader*);

Deletes *shader*. If *shader* is currently linked to one or more active shader programs, the object is tagged for deletion and deleted once the shader program is no longer being used by any shader program.

Similarly, if you're done using a shader program, you can delete it by calling **glDeleteProgram()**.

> void **glDeleteProgram**(GLuint *program*);
>
> Deletes *program* immediately if not currently in use in any context, or schedules *program* for deletion when the program is no longer in use by any contexts.

Finally, for completeness, you can also determine if a name is already been reserved as a shader object by calling **glIsShader**(), or a shader program by calling **glIsProgram**():

> GLboolean **glIsShader**(GLuint *shader*);
>
> Returns GL_TRUE if *shader* is the name of a shader object that was previously generated with **glCreateShader**(), but has not been subsequently deleted. Returns GL_FALSE if *shader* is zero or a nonzero value that is not the name of a shader object.

> GLboolean **glIsProgram**(GLuint *program*);
>
> Returns GL_TRUE if *program* is the name of a program object that was previously generated with **glCreateProgram**(), but has not been subsequently deleted. Returns GL_FALSE if *program* is zero or a nonzero value that is not the name of a program object.

Our `LoadShaders()` Function

In order to simplify using shaders in your applications, we created **LoadShaders**() to help in loading and creating shader programs. We used it in our first program in Chapter 1 to load a simple set of shaders.

Shader Subroutines

Advanced

While GLSL allows you to define functions in shaders, the call flow of those functions was always static. To dynamically select between multiple functions, you either created two distinct shaders, or used an if-statement to make a run-time selection, like demonstrated in Example 2.5.

Example 2.5   Static Shader Control Flow

```
#version 330 core

void func_1() { ... }
void func_2() { ... }

uniform int func;

void
main()
{
    if (func == 1)
        func_1();
    else
        func_2();
}
```

Shader subroutines are conceptually similar to function pointers in C for implementing dynamic subroutine selection. In your shader, you specify a subroutine type and use that type when declaring the set of subroutines eligible for dynamic use. Then, you choose which subroutine from the set to execute in the shader by setting a subroutine uniform variable.

GLSL Subroutine Setup

When you want to use subroutine selection inside of a shader, there are three steps required to set up the pool of subroutines:

1. Define the subroutine type using the subroutine keyword

    ```
    subroutine returnType subroutineType(type param, ...);
    ```

    where *returnType* is any valid type that a function can return, and *subroutineType* is any valid name. As with function prototypes, only the parameter types are required; the parameter names are optional. (Hint: Think of this like a typedef in C, with subroutineType as the newly defined type.)

2. Using the *subroutineType* you just defined, define the set of subroutines that you would like to dynamically select from using the subroutine keyword. The prototype for a subroutine function looks like:

    ```
    subroutine (subroutineType) returnType functionName(...);
    ```

3. Finally, specify the subroutine uniform variable that will hold the "function pointer" for the subroutine you've selected in your application:

```
subroutine uniform subroutineType variableName;
```

Demonstrating those steps together, consider the following example where we would like to dynamically select between ambient and diffuse lighting:

Example 2.6   Declaring a Set of Subroutines

```
subroutine vec4 LightFunc(vec3); // Step 1

subroutine (LightFunc) vec4 ambient(vec3 n) // Step 2
{
    return Materials.ambient;
}

subroutine (LightFunc) vec4 diffuse(vec3 n) // Step 2 (again)
{
    return Materials.diffuse *
      max(dot(normalize(n), LightVec.xyz), 0.0);
}

subroutine uniform LightFunc materialShader; // Step 3
```

A subroutine is not restricted to being a single type of subroutine (e.g., LightFunc in Example 2.6). If you have defined multiple types of subroutines, you can associate any number of the types with a subroutine by adding the type to the list when defining the subroutine, as demonstrated,

```
subroutine void Type_1();
subroutine void Type_2();
subroutine void Type_3();

subroutine (Type_1, Type_2) Func_1();
subroutine (Type_1, Type_3) Func_2();

subroutine uniform Type_1 func_1;
subroutine uniform Type_2 func_2;
subroutine uniform Type_3 func_3;
```

For the above example, func_1 could use either Func_1 or Func_2 because of Type_1 appearing in each of their subroutine lines. However, func_2, for example, would be limited to only using Func_1, and similarly, func_3 could only use Func_2.

Selecting Shader Subroutines

Once you have all your subroutine types and functions defined in your shaders, you only need to query a few values from the linked shader program, and then use those values to select the appropriate function.

In step 3 described on page 78, a subroutine uniform value was declared, and we will need its location in order to set its value. As compared to other shader uniforms, subroutine uniforms use **glGetSubroutineUniformLocation()** to retrieve their locations.

GLint **glGetSubroutineUniformLocation**(GLuint *program*,
　　　　　　　　　　　　　　　　　GLenum *shadertype*,
　　　　　　　　　　　　　　　　　const char* *name*);

Returns the location of the subroutine uniform named *name* in *program* for the shading stage specified by *shadertype*. *name* is a null-terminated character string, and *shadertype* must be one of GL_VERTEX_SHADER, GL_TESS_CONTROL_SHADER, GL_TESS_EVALUATION_SHADER, GL_GEOMETRY_SHADER, or GL_FRAGMENT_SHADER.

If *name* is not an active subroutine uniform, minus one (−1) is returned. If *program* is not a successfully linked shader program, a GL_INVALID_OPERATION error will be generated.

Once we have the subroutine uniform to assign values to, we need to determine the indices of the subroutines inside of the shader. For that, we can call **glGetSubroutineIndex()**.

GLuint **glGetSubroutineIndex**(GLuint *program*,
　　　　　　　　　　　　　GLenum *shadertype*,
　　　　　　　　　　　　　const char* *name*);

Returns the index of the shader function associated with *name* from *program* for the shading stage specified by *shadertype*. *name* is a null-terminated character string, and *shadertype* must be one of GL_VERTEX_SHADER, GL_TESS_CONTROL_SHADER, GL_TESS_EVALUATION_SHADER, GL_GEOMETRY_SHADER, or GL_FRAGMENT_SHADER.

If *name* is not an active subroutine for the shader for *shadertype*, GL_INVALID_INDEX is returned.

Once you have both the available subroutine indices, and subroutine uniform location, use **glUniformSubroutinesuiv()** to specify which subroutine should be executed in the shader. All active subroutine uniforms for a shader stage must be initialized.

GLuint **glUniformSubroutinesuiv**(GLenum *shadertype*,
                                  GLsizei *count*,
                                  const GLuint * *indices*);

Sets *count* shader subroutine uniforms using the values in *indices*, for the shader stage *shadertype*. *shadertype* must be one of GL_VERTEX_SHADER, GL_TESS_CONTROL_SHADER, GL_TESS_EVALUATION_SHADER, GL_GEOMETRY_SHADER, or GL_FRAGMENT_SHADER. The ith subroutine uniform will be assigned the value *indices[i]*.

If *count* is not equal to the value of GL_ACTIVE_SUBROUTINE_UNIFORM_LOCATIONS for the shader stage *shadertype* for the currently bound program, a GL_INVALID_VALUE error is generated. All values in indices must be less than GL_ACTIVE_SUBROUTINES, or a GL_INVALID_VALUE error is generated.

Assembling those steps, the following code snippet demonstrates the process for the vertex shader described in Example 2.6.

```
GLint  materialShaderLoc;
GLuint ambientIndex;
GLuint diffuseIndex;

glUseProgram(program);

materialShaderLoc = glGetSubroutineUniformLocation(
    program, GL_VERTEX_SHADER, "materialShader");

if (materialShaderLoc < 0) {
    // Error:  materialShader is not an active subroutine
    // uniform in the shader.
}

ambientIndex = glGetSubroutineIndex(program,
                                    GL_VERTEX_SHADER,
                                    "ambient");
diffuseIndex = glGetSubroutineIndex(program,
                                    GL_VERTEX_SHADER,
                                    "diffuse");
```

```
if (ambientIndex == GL_INVALID_INDEX ||
        diffuseIndex == GL_INVALID_INDEX) {
    // Error:  the specified subroutines are not active in
    //      the currently bound program for the GL_VERTEX_SHADER
    //      stage.
}
else {
    GLsizei n;
    glGetIntegerv(GL_MAX_SUBROUTINE_UNIFORM_LOCATIONS, &n);

    GLuint *indices = new GLuint[n];
    indices[materialShaderLoc] = ambientIndex;

    glUniformSubroutinesuiv(GL_VERTEX_SHADER, n, indices);

    delete [] indices;
}
```

Note: Calling **glUseProgram()** will reset all of the subroutine uniform values to an implementation-dependent ordering.

Separate Shader Objects

Advanced

Previous to OpenGL Version 4.1 (and not considering extensions) only a single shader program could be bound at any one time in an application's execution. This was inconvenient if your application used multiple fragment shaders for a collection of geometry that was all transformed using the same vertex shader. This caused you to need to have multiple programs around that duplicated the same vertex shader, wasting resources and duplicating code.

Separate shader objects allows shader stages (e.g., vertex shading) from various programs to be combined into a program pipeline.

The first step is to create a shader program that's usable in a shader pipeline. This is done by calling **glProgramParameteri()** with the parameter GL_PROGRAM_SEPARABLE before linking the shader program. This marks the shader program as eligible to be used in a program pipeline. To simplify this process, a new command **glCreateShaderProgramv()** was added that encapsulates the shader-compilation process, including marking the program as sharable (as discussed above) and linking it to produce the final object.

Once your collection of shader programs are combined, you need to use the new shader pipeline constructs to combine shader stages from multiple programs into a usable program pipeline. As with most objects in OpenGL, there is a gen-bind-delete sequence of calls to make. A shader pipeline is created by calling **glGenProgramPipelines()**, which will create an unused program pipeline identifier that you pass into **glBindProgramPipeline()**, making that program available for editing (e.g., adding or replacing shader stages), and use. Similar to other generated objects, program pipelines are deleted with **glDeleteProgramPipelines()**.

Once you've bound a program pipeline, you can attach program objects that have been marked as separable to the pipeline by calling **glUseProgramStages()**, which takes a bitfield describing which stages from the provided program should be employed when this pipeline is used to process geometry and shade fragments. The older **glUseProgram()** when called with a program will replace the current program pipeline binding.

The interfaces between shader stages—the in and out variables—must match in order for the pipeline to work. As compared to using a nonseparate shader object, where those interfaces can be verified during program linkage, shader pipelines with separate program objects need to be checked at draw-call issue. If the interfaces don't match correctly, all varying values (out variables) are undefined.

The built-in `gl_PerVertex` block must be redeclared in shaders to explicitly indicate what subset of the fixed pipeline interface will be used. This will be necessary when using multiple programs to complete your pipeline.

For example:

```
out gl_PerVertex {
    vec4 gl_Position;    // makes gl_Position is part of interface
    float gl_PointSize;  // makes gl_PointSize is part of interface
};                       // no more members of gl_PerVertex are used
```

This establishes the output interface the shader will use with the following pipeline stage. It must be a subset of the built-in members of `gl_PerVertex`. If a built-in block interface is formed across shaders in different programs, the shaders must all redeclare the built-in block in the same way.

Since separable shader objects can each have their individual set of program uniforms, two methods are provided for assigning uniform variable values. First, you can select an active shader program with **glActiveShaderProgram**(), which causes calls to glUniform*() and glUniformMatrix*() to assign values to that particular shader program's uniform variables. Alternatively, and more preferred, is to call **glProgramUniform***() and **glProgramUniformMatrix***(), which take an explicit program object in addition to the other parameters used to identify the program's uniform variable.

```
void glProgramUniform{1234}{fdi ui}(GLuint program,
                                    GLint location,
                                    TYPE value);
void glProgramUniform{1234}{fdi ui}v(GLuint program,
                                     GLint location,
                                     GLsizei count,
                                     const TYPE * values);
void glProgramUniformMatrix{234}{fd}v(GLuint program,
                                      GLint location,
                                      GLsizei count,
                                      GLboolean transpose,
                                      const GLfloat * values);
void glProgramUniformMatrix{2x3,2x4,3x2,3x4,4x2,4x3}{fd}v(
                                      GLuint program, GLint location,
                                      GLsizei count,
                                      GLboolean transpose,
                                      const GLfloat * values);
```

glProgramUniform*() and **glProgramUniformMatrix***() routines operate exactly as **glUniform***() and **glUniformMatrix***(), except that *program* specifies the shader program to update the uniform variable for. The advantage of these routines is that *program* need not be the currently bound program (i.e., the last specified shader program to **glUseProgram**()).

Chapter 3

Drawing with OpenGL

Chapter Objectives

After reading this chapter, you will be able to:

- Identify all of the rendering primitives available in OpenGL.

- Initialize and populate data buffers for use in rendering geometry.

- Optimize rendering using advanced techniques like *instanced rendering*.

The primary use of OpenGL is to render graphics into a framebuffer. To accomplish this, complex objects are broken up into *primitives*—points, lines, and triangles that when drawn at high enough density give the appearance of 2D and 3D objects. OpenGL includes many functions for rendering such primitives. These functions allow you to describe the layout of primitives in memory, how many primitives to render, and what form they take, and even to render many copies of the same set of primitives with one function call. These are arguably the most important functions in OpenGL, as without them, you wouldn't be able to do much but clear the screen.

This chapter contains the following major sections:

- "OpenGL Graphics Primitives" describes the available graphics primitives in OpenGL that you can use in your renderings.

- "Data in OpenGL Buffers" explains the mechanics of working with data in OpenGL.

- "Vertex Specification" outlines how to use vertex data for rendering, and processing it using vertex shaders.

- "OpenGL Drawing Commands" introduces the set of functions that cause OpenGL to draw.

- "Instanced Rendering" describes how to render multiple objects using the same vertex data efficiently.

OpenGL Graphics Primitives

OpenGL includes support for many primitive types. Eventually they all get rendered as one of three types—points, lines, or triangles. Line and triangle types can be combined together to form strips, loops (for lines), and fans (for triangles). Points, lines, and triangles are the *native* primitive types supported by most graphics hardware.[1] Other primitive types are supported by OpenGL, including patches, which are used as inputs to the tessellator and the *adjacency primitives* that are designed to be used as inputs to the geometry shader. Tessellation (and tessellation shaders) are introduced in Chapter 9, and geometry shaders are introduced in Chapter 10. The patch and adjacency primitive types will be covered in detail in each of those chapters. In this section, we cover only the point, line, and triangle primitive types.

---

1. In terms of hardware support, this means that the graphics processor likely includes direct hardware support for rasterizing these types of primitives. Other primitive types such as patches and adjacency primitives are never directly rasterized.

Points

Points are represented by a single vertex. The vertex represents a point in four-dimensional *homogeneous coordinates*. As such, a point really has no area, and so in OpenGL it is really an analogue for a square region of the display (or draw buffer). When rendering points, OpenGL determines which pixels are covered by the point using a set of rules called *rasterization rules*. The rules for rasterizing a point in OpenGL are quite straightforward—a sample is considered covered by a point if it falls within a square centered on the point's location in window coordinates. The side length of the square is equal to the point's size, which is fixed state (set with **glPointSize()**), or the value written to the gl_PointSize built-in variable in the vertex, tessellation, or geometry shader. The value written to gl_PointSize in the shader is used only if GL_PROGRAM_POINT_SIZE is enabled, otherwise it is ignored and the fixed state value set with **glPointSize()** is used.

---

void **glPointSize**(GLfloat *size*);

Sets the fixed size, in pixels, that will be used for points when GL_PROGRAM_POINT_SIZE is not enabled.

The default point size is 1.0. Thus, when points are rendered, each vertex essentially becomes a single pixel on the screen (unless it's clipped, of course). If the point size is increased (either with **glPointSize()**, or by writing a value larger than 1.0 to gl_PointSize), then each point vertex may end up lighting more than one pixel. For example, if the point size is 1.2 pixels and the point's vertex lies exactly at a pixel center, then only that pixel will be lit. However, if the point's vertex lies exactly midway between two horizontally or vertically adjacent pixel centers, then both of those pixels will be lit (i.e., two pixels will be lit). If the point's vertex lies at the exact midpoint between four adjacent pixels, then all four pixels will be lit—for a total of four pixels being lit for one point!

Point Sprites

When you render points with OpenGL, the fragment shader is run for every fragment in the point. Each point is essentially a square area of the screen and each pixel can be shaded a different color. You can calculate that color analytically in the fragment shader or use a texture to shade the point. To assist in this, OpenGL fragment shaders include a special *built-in variable* called gl_PointCoord which contains the coordinate within the point where the current fragment is located. gl_PointCoord is available only in the fragment shader (it doesn't make much sense to include it in other shaders) and has a defined value only when rendering points. By simply using `gl_PointCoord` as a source for texture coordinates, bitmaps and textures can be used instead of a simple square block. Combined with alpha blending or with discarding fragments (using the `discard` keyword), it's even possible to create point *sprites* with odd shapes.

We'll revisit point sprites with an example shortly. If you want to skip ahead, the example is shown in "Point Sprites" on Page 346.

Lines, Strips, and Loops

In OpenGL, the term *line* refers to a *line segment*, not the mathematician's version that extends to infinity in both directions. Individual lines are therefore represented by pairs of vertices, one for each endpoint of the line. Lines can also be joined together to represent a connected series of line segments, and optionally closed. The closed sequence is known as a *line loop*, whereas the open sequence (one that is not closed) is known as a *line strip*. As with points, lines technically have no area, and so special rasterization rules are used to determine which pixels should be lit when a line segment is rasterized. The rule for line rasterization is known as the *diamond exit rule*. It is covered in some detail in the OpenGL specification. However, we attempt to paraphrase it here. When rasterizing a line running from point A to point B, a pixel should be lit if the line passes through the imaginary edge of a diamond shape drawn inside the pixel's square area on the screen—unless that diamond contains point B (i.e., the end of the line is inside the diamond). That way, if another, second line is drawn from point B to point C, the pixel in which B resides is lit only once.

The diamond exit rule suffices for thin lines, but OpenGL allows you to specify wider sizes for lines using the **glLineWidth()** function (the equivalent for **glPointSize()** for lines).

void **glLineWidth**(GLfloat *width*);

Sets the fixed width of lines. The default value is 1.0. *width* is the new value of line width and must be greater than 0.0, otherwise an error is generated.

There is no equivalent to `gl_PointSize` for lines—lines are rendered at one fixed width until state is changed in OpenGL. When the line width is greater than 1, the line is simply replicated *width* times either horizontally or vertically. If the line is *y-major* (i.e., it extends further vertically than horizontally), it is replicated horizontally. If it is *x-major* then it is replicated vertically.

The OpenGL specification is somewhat liberal on how ends of lines are represented and how wide lines are rasterized when antialiasing is turned off. When antialiasing is turned on, lines are treated as rectangles aligned along the line, with width equal to the current line width.

Triangles, Strips, and Fans

Triangles are made up of collections of three vertices. When separate triangles are rendered, each triangle is independent of all others. A triangle is rendered by projecting each of the three vertices into screen space and forming three edges running between the edges. A sample is considered covered if it lies on the positive side of all of the *half spaces* formed by the lines between the vertices. If two triangles share an edge (and therefore a pair of vertices), no single sample can be considered inside both triangles. This is important because, although some variation in rasterization algorithm is allowed by the OpenGL specification, the rules governing pixels that lie along a shared edge are quite strict:

- No pixel on a shared edge between two triangles that together would cover the pixel should be left unlit.

- No pixel on a shared edge between two triangles should be lit by more than one of them.

This means that OpenGL will reliably rasterize meshes with shared edges without gaps between the triangles, and without *overdraw*.[2] This is important when rasterizing triangle *strips* or *fans*. When a triangle strip is rendered, the first three vertices form the first triangle, then each subsequent vertex forms another triangle along with the last two vertices of the previous triangle. This is illustrated in Figure 3.1.

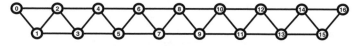

Figure 3.1   Vertex layout for a triangle strip

When rendering a triangle fan, the first vertex forms a shared point that is included in each subsequent triangle. Triangles are then formed using that

---

2. Overdraw is where the same pixel is lit more than once, and can cause artifacts when blending is enabled, for example.

shared point and the next two vertices. An arbitrarily complex *convex* polygon can be rendered as a triangle fan. Figure 3.2 shows the vertex layout of a triangle fan.

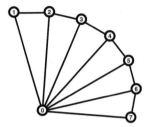

Figure 3.2   Vertex layout for a triangle fan

These primitive types are used by the drawing functions that will be introduced in the next section. They are represented by OpenGL tokens that are passed as arguments to functions used for rendering. Table 3.1 shows the mapping of primitive types to the OpenGL tokens used to represent them.

Table 3.1   OpenGL Primitive Mode Tokens

Primitive Type	OpenGL Token
Points	GL_POINTS
Lines	GL_LINES
Line Strips	GL_LINE_STRIP
Line Loops	GL_LINE_LOOP
Independent Triangles	GL_TRIANGLES
Triangle Strips	GL_TRIANGLE_STRIP
Triangle Fans	GL_TRIANGLE_FAN

Rendering Polygons As Points, Outlines, or Solids

A *polygon* has two sides—front and back—and might be rendered differently depending on which side is facing the viewer. This allows you to have cutaway views of solid objects in which there is an obvious distinction between the parts that are inside and those that are outside. By default, both front and back *faces* are drawn in the same way. To change this, or to draw only outlines or vertices, use **glPolygonMode()**.

void **glPolygonMode**(GLenum *face*, GLenum *mode*);

Controls the drawing mode for a polygon's front and back faces. The parameter *face* must be GL_FRONT_AND_BACK; while *mode* can be GL_POINT, GL_LINE, GL_FILL to indicate whether the polygon should be drawn as points, outlined, or filled. By default, both the front and back faces are drawn filled.

Reversing and Culling Polygon Faces

By convention, polygons whose vertices appear in counterclockwise order on the screen are called *front facing*. You can construct the surface of any "reasonable" solid—a mathematician would call such a surface an orientable manifold (spheres, donuts, and teapots are orientable; Klein bottles and Möbius strips aren't)—from polygons of consistent orientation. In other words, you can use all clockwise polygons or all counterclockwise polygons.

Suppose you've consistently described a model of an orientable surface but happen to have the clockwise orientation on the outside. You can swap what OpenGL considers the back face by using the function **glFrontFace()**, supplying the desired orientation for front-facing polygons.

void **glFrontFace**(GLenum *mode*);

Controls how front-facing polygons are determined. By default, mode is GL_CCW, which corresponds to a counterclockwise orientation of the ordered vertices of a projected polygon in window coordinates. If mode is GL_CW, faces with a clockwise orientation are considered front-facing.

Note: The orientation (clockwise or counterclockwise) of the vertices is also known as its winding.

In a completely enclosed surface constructed from opaque polygons with a consistent orientation, none of the back-facing polygons are ever visible— they're always obscured by the front-facing polygons. If you are outside this surface, you might enable culling to discard polygons that OpenGL determines are back-facing. Similarly, if you are inside the object, only back-facing polygons are visible. To instruct OpenGL to discard front- or back-facing polygons, use the command **glCullFace()** and enable culling with **glEnable()**.

void **glCullFace**(GLenum *mode*);

Indicates which polygons should be discarded (culled) before they're converted to screen coordinates. The mode is either GL_FRONT, GL_BACK, or GL_FRONT_AND_BACK to indicate front-facing, back-facing, or all polygons. To take effect, culling must be enabled using **glEnable**() with GL_CULL_FACE; it can be disabled with **glDisable**() and the same argument.

Advanced

In more technical terms, deciding whether a face of a polygon is front- or back-facing depends on the sign of the polygon's area computed in window coordinates. One way to compute this area is

$$a = \frac{1}{2} \sum_{i=0}^{n-1} x_i y_{i \oplus 1} - x_{i \oplus 1} y_i$$

where x_i and y_i are the x and y window coordinates of the ith vertex of the n-vertex polygon and where $i \oplus 1$ is shorthand for $(i+1) \bmod n$, where mod is the modulus operator.

Assuming that GL_CCW has been specified, if $a > 0$, the polygon corresponding to that vertex is considered to be front-facing; otherwise, it's back-facing. If GL_CW is specified and if $a < 0$, then the corresponding polygon is front-facing; otherwise, it's back-facing.

Data in OpenGL Buffers

Almost everything you will ever do with OpenGL will involve buffers full of data. Buffers in OpenGL are represented as *buffer objects*. You've already had a brief introduction to buffer objects in Chapter 1. However, in this section we'll dig a little deeper into the specifics of how buffer objects are used; ways to create, manage, and destroy them; and the best practices associated with buffer objects.

Creating and Allocating Buffers

As with many things in OpenGL, buffer objects are named using GLuint values. Values are reserved using the **glGenBuffers**() command. This function has already been described in Chapter 1, but we include the prototype here again for handy reference.

void **glGenBuffers**(GLsizei *n*, GLuint **buffers*);
Returns *n* currently unused names for buffer objects in the array *buffers*.

After calling **glGenBuffers()**, you will have an array of buffer object names in *buffers*, but at this time, they're just placeholders. They're not actually buffer objects—yet. The buffer objects themselves are not actually created until the name is first bound to one of the buffer binding points on the context. This is important because OpenGL may make decisions about the best way to allocate memory for the buffer object based on where it is bound. The buffer binding points (called *targets*) are described in Table 3.2.

Table 3.2   Buffer Binding Targets

Target	Uses
GL_ARRAY_BUFFER	This is the binding point that is used to set vertex array data pointers using **glVertexAttribPointer()**. This is the target that you will likely use most often.
GL_COPY_READ_BUFFER and GL_COPY_WRITE_BUFFER	Together, these targets form a pair of binding points that can be used to copy data between buffers without disturbing OpenGL state, or implying usage of any particular kind to OpenGL.
GL_DRAW_INDIRECT_BUFFER	A buffer target used to store the parameters for drawing commands when using *indirect drawing*, which will be explained in detail in the next section.
GL_ELEMENT_ARRAY_BUFFER	Buffers bound to this target can contain vertex indices which are used by *indexed draw commands* such as **glDrawElements()**.
GL_PIXEL_PACK_BUFFER	The pixel pack buffer is used as the destination for OpenGL commands that read data from image objects such as textures or the framebuffer. Examples of such commands include **glGetTexImage()** and **glReadPixels()**.

Table 3.2 (continued)   Buffer Binding Targets

Target	Uses
GL_PIXEL_UNPACK_BUFFER	The pixel unpack buffer is the *opposite* of the pixel pack buffer—it is used as the *source* of data for commands like **glTexImage2D()**.
GL_TEXTURE_BUFFER	Texture buffers are buffers that are bound to texture objects so that their data can be directly read inside shaders. The GL_TEXTURE_BUFFER binding point provides a target for manipulating these buffers, although they must still be attached to textures to make them accessible to shaders.
GL_TRANSFORM_FEEDBACK_ BUFFER	Transform feedback is a facility in OpenGL whereby transformed vertices can be captured as they exit the vertex processing part of the pipeline (after the vertex or geometry shader, if present) and some of their attributes written into buffer objects. This target provides a binding point for buffers that are used to record those attributes. Transform feedback will be covered in some detail in "Transform Feedback" on Page 239.
GL_UNIFORM_BUFFER	This target provides a binding point where buffers that will be used as *uniform buffer objects* may be bound. Uniform buffers are covered in Subsection 2, "Uniform Blocks".

A buffer object actually is created by binding one of the names reserved by a call to **glGenBuffers()** to one of the targets in Table 3.2 using **glBindBuffer()**. As with **glGenBuffers()**, **glBindBuffer()** was introduced in Chapter 1, but we include its prototype here again for completeness.

void **glBindBuffer**(GLenum *target*, GLuint *buffer*);

Binds the buffer object named *buffer* to the buffer-binding point as specified by *target*. *target* must be one of the OpenGL buffer-binding targets, and *buffer* must be a name reserved by a call to **glGenBuffers()**. If this the first time the name *buffer* has been bound, a buffer object is created with that name.

Right, so we now have a buffer object bound to one of the targets listed in Table 3.2, now what? The default state of a newly created buffer object is a buffer with no data in it. Before it can be used productively, we must put some data into it.

Getting Data into and out of Buffers

There are many ways to get data into and out of buffers in OpenGL. These range from explicitly providing the data, to replacing parts of the data in a buffer object with new data, to generating the data with OpenGL and recording it into the buffer object. The simplest way to get data into a buffer object is to load data into the buffer at time of allocation. This is accomplished through the use of the **glBufferData()** function. Here's the prototype of **glBufferData()** again.

---

void **glBufferData**(GLenum *target*, GLsizeiptr *size*,
             const GLvoid **data*, GLenum *usage*);

Allocates *size* bytes of storage for the buffer object bound to *target*. If *data* is non-NULL, that space is initialized with the contents of memory addressed by *data*. *usage* is provided to allow the application to supply OpenGL with a hint as to the intended usage for the data in the buffer.

It's important to note that **glBufferData()** actually allocates (or reallocates) storage for the buffer object. That is, if the size of the new data is greater than the current storage space allocated for the buffer object, the buffer object will be resized to make room. Likewise, if the new data is smaller than what has been allocated for the buffer, the buffer object will shrink to match the new size. The fact that it is possible to specify the initial data to be placed into the buffer object is merely a convenience and is not necessarily the best way to do it (or even the most convenient, for that matter).

The *target* of the initial binding is not the only information OpenGL uses to decide how to best allocate the buffer object's data store. The other important parameter to **glBufferData()** is the *usage* parameter. *usage* must be one of the standard usage tokens such as GL_STATIC_DRAW or GL_DYNAMIC_COPY. Notice how the token name is made of two parts—the first being one of STATIC, DYNAMIC, or STREAM and the second being one of DRAW, READ, or COPY.

The meanings of these "subtokens" are shown in Table 3.3.

Table 3.3   Buffer Usage Tokens

Token Fragment	Meaning
STATIC	The data store contents will be modified once and used many times.
DYNAMIC	The data store contents will be modified repeatedly and used many times.
STREAM	The data store contents will be modified once and used at most a few times.
_DRAW	The data store contents are modified by the application and used as the source for OpenGL drawing and image specification commands.
_READ	The data store contents are modified by reading data from OpenGL and used to return that data when queried by the application.
_COPY	The data store contents are modified by reading data from OpenGL and used as the source for OpenGL drawing and image specification commands.

Accurate specification of the *usage* parameter is important to achieve optimal performance. This parameter conveys useful information to OpenGL about how you plan to use the buffer. Consider the first part of the accepted tokens first. When the token starts with _STATIC_, this indicates that the data will change very rarely, if at all—it is essentially static. This should be used for data that will be specified once and never modified again. When *usage* includes _STATIC_, OpenGL may decide to shuffle the data around internally in order to make it fit in memory better, or be a more optimal data format. This may be an expensive operation, but since the data is static, it needs to be performed only once and so the payoff may be great.

Including _DYNAMIC_ in *usage* indicates that you're going to change the data from time to time but will probably use it many times between modifications. You might use this, for example, in a modeling program where the data is essentially static—until the user edits it. In this case, it'll probably be used for many frames, then be modified, and then used for many more frames, and so on. This is in contrast to the GL_STREAM_ subtoken. This indicates that you're planning on regularly modifying the data in the buffer and using it only a few times (maybe only once) between each modification. In this case, OpenGL might not even copy your data to fast graphics memory if it can access it in place. This should be used for applications such as physical simulations running on the CPU where a new set of data is presented in each frame.

Now turn your attention to the second part of the *usage* tokens. This part of the token indicates *who* is responsible for updating and using the data. When the token includes _DRAW, this infers that the buffer will be used as a source of data during regular OpenGL drawing operations. It will be *read* a lot, compared to data whose *usage* token includes _READ, which is likely to be *written* often. Including _READ indicates that the application will read back from the buffer (see "Accessing the Content of Buffers"), which in turn infers that the data is likely to be written to often by OpenGL. *usage* parameters including _DRAW should be used for buffers containing vertex data, for example, whereas parameters including _READ should be used for pixel buffer objects and other buffers that will be used to retrieve information from OpenGL. Finally, including _COPY in *usage* indicates that the application will use OpenGL to generate data to be placed in the buffer, which will then be used as a source for subsequent drawing operations. An example of an appropriate use of _COPY is transform feedback buffers—buffers that will be written by OpenGL and then be used as vertex buffers in later drawing commands.

Initializing Part of a Buffer

Suppose you have an array containing some vertex data, another containing some color information, and yet another containing texture coordinates or some other data. You'd like to *pack* the data back to back into one big buffer object so that OpenGL can use it. The arrays may or may not be contiguous in memory, so you can't use **glBufferData()** to upload all of it in one go. Further, if you use **glBufferData()** to upload, say, the vertex data first, then the buffer will be sized to exactly match the vertex data and there won't be room for the color or texture coordinate information. That's where **glBufferSubData()** comes in.

---

void **glBufferSubData**(GLenum *target*, GLintptr *offset*,
                    GLsizeiptr *size*, const GLvoid **data*);

Replaces a subset of a buffer object's data store with new data. The section of the buffer object bound to *target* starting at *offset* bytes is updated with the *size* bytes of data addressed by *data*. An error is thrown if *offset* and *size* together specify a range that is beyond the bounds of the buffer object's data store.

By using a combination of **glBufferData()** and **glBufferSubData()**, we can allocate and initialize a buffer object and upload data into several separate sections of it. An example is shown in Example 3.1.

Example 3.1   Initializing a Buffer Object with **glBufferSubData()**

```
// Vertex positions
static const GLfloat positions[] =
{
      -1.0f, -1.0f, 0.0f, 1.0f,
       1.0f, -1.0f, 0.0f, 1.0f,
       1.0f,  1.0f, 0.0f, 1.0f,
      -1.0f,  1.0f, 0.0f, 1.0f
};


// Vertex colors
static const GLfloat colors[] =
{
      1.0f, 0.0f, 0.0f,
      0.0f, 1.0f, 0.0f,
      0.0f, 0.0f, 1.0f,
      1.0f, 1.0f, 1.0f,
};


// The buffer object
GLuint buffer;


// Reserve a name for the buffer object.
glGenBuffers(1, &buffer);
// Bind it to the GL_ARRAY_BUFFER target.
glBindBuffer(GL_ARRAY_BUFFER, buffer);
// Allocate space for it (sizeof(positions) + sizeof(colors)).
glBufferData(GL_ARRAY_BUFFER,                              // target
             sizeof(positions) + sizeof(colors),          // total size
             NULL,                                        // no data
             GL_STATIC_DRAW);                             // usage
// Put "positions" at offset zero in the buffer.
glBufferSubData(GL_ARRAY_BUFFER,                          // target
                0,                                        // offset
                sizeof(positions),                        // size
                positions);                               // data
// Put "colors" at an offset in the buffer equal to the filled size of
// the buffer so far - i.e., sizeof(positions).
glBufferSubData(GL_ARRAY_BUFFER,                          // target
                sizeof(positions),                        // offset
                sizeof(colors),                           // size
                colors);                                  // data
// Now "positions" is at offset 0 and "colors" is directly after it
// in the same buffer.
```

If you simply wish to clear a buffer object's data store to a known value, you can use the **glClearBufferData()** or **glClearBufferSubData()** functions. Their prototypes are as follows:

```
void glClearBufferData(GLenum target, GLenum internalformat,
                       GLenum format, GLenum type,
                       const void * data);
void glClearBufferSubData(GLenum target,
                          GLenum internalformat,
                          GLintptr offset, GLintptr size,
                          GLenum format, GLenum type,
                          const void * data);
```

Clear all or part of a buffer object's data store. The data store of the buffer bound to *target* is filled with the data stored in *data*. *format* and *type* specify the format and type of the data pointed to by *data*, respectively. The data is first converted into the format specified by *internalformat*, and then that data is used to fill the specified range of the buffer's data store. In the case of **glClearBufferData()**, the entire store is filled with the specified data. For **glClearBufferSubData()**, the range is specified by *offset* and *size*, which give the starting offset and size, in bytes of the range, respectively.

Using **glClearBufferData()** or **glClearBufferSubData()** allows you to initialize the data store of a buffer object without necessarily reserving and clearing a region of system memory to do it.

Data can also be copied between buffer objects using the **glCopyBufferSubData()** function. Rather than assembling chunks of data in one large buffer object using **glBufferSubData()**, it is possible to upload the data into separate buffers using **glBufferData()** and then copy from those buffers into the larger buffer using **glCopyBufferSubData()**. Depending on the OpenGL implementation, it may be able to overlap these copies because each time you call **glBufferData()** on a buffer object, it invalidates whatever contents may have been there before. Therefore, OpenGL can sometimes just allocate a whole new data store for your data, even though a copy operation from the previous store has not completed yet. It will then release the old storage at a later opportunity.

The prototype of **glCopyBufferSubData()** is as follows:

```
void glCopyBufferSubData(GLenum readtarget,
                         GLenum writetarget,
                         GLintptr readoffset,
                         GLintprr writeoffset, GLsizeiptr size);
```

Copies part of the data store of the buffer object bound to *readtarget* into the data store of the buffer object bound to *writetarget*. The *size* bytes of data at *readoffset* within *readtarget* are copied into *writetarget* at *writeoffset*. If *readoffset* or *writeoffset* together with *size* would cause either OpenGL to access any area outside the bound buffer objects, a GL_INVALID_VALUE error is generated.

Whilst **glCopyBufferSubData()** can be used to copy data between buffers bound to any two targets, the targets GL_COPY_READ_BUFFER and GL_COPY_WRITE_BUFFER are provided specifically for this purpose. Neither target is used for anything else by OpenGL, and so you can safely bind buffers to them for the purposes of copying or staging data without disturbing OpenGL state or needing to keep track of what was bound to the target before your copy.

Reading the Contents of a Buffer

Data can be read back from a buffer object in a couple of different ways. The first is to use the **glGetBufferSubData()** function. This function reads data from the buffer object bound to one of the targets and places it into a chunk of memory owned by your applications. The prototype of **glGetBufferSubData()** is as follows:

```
void glGetBufferSubData(GLenum target, GLintptr offset,
                        GLsizeiptr size, GLvoid * data);
```

Returns some or all of the data from the buffer object currently bound to *target*. Data starting at byte-offset *offset* and extending for *size* bytes is copied from the data store to the memory pointed to by *data*. An error is thrown if the buffer object is currently mapped, or if *offset* and *size* together define a range beyond the bounds of the buffer object's data store.

glGetBufferSubData() is useful when you have generated data using OpenGL and wish to retrieve it. Examples include using transform feedback to process vertices using a GPU, or reading framebuffer or texture data into a Pixel Buffer Object. Both of these topics will be covered later. Of course, it's also possible to use **glGetBufferSubData()** to simply read back data that you previously put into the buffer object.

Accessing the Content of Buffers

The issue with all of the functions covered in this section so far (**glBufferData()**, **glBufferSubData()**, **glCopyBufferSubData()**, and

glGetBufferSubData()) is that they all cause OpenGL to make a copy of your data. **glBufferData**() and **glBufferSubData**() both copy data from your application's memory into memory owned by OpenGL. Obviously, **glCopyBufferSubData**() causes a copy of previously buffered data to be made. **glGetBufferSubData**() copies data from memory owned by OpenGL into memory provided by your application. Depending on the hardware configuration, it's very possible that the memory owned by OpenGL would be accessible to your application if only you had a pointer to it. Well, you can get that pointer using **glMapBuffer**().

---

void * **glMapBuffer**(GLenum *target*, GLenum *access*);

Maps to the client's address space the entire data store of the buffer object currently bound to *target*. The data can then be directly read or written relative to the returned pointer, depending on the specified *access* policy. If OpenGL is unable to map the buffer object's data store, **glMapBuffer**() generates an error and returns NULL. This may occur for system-specific reasons, such as low virtual memory availability.

When you call **glMapBuffer**(), the function returns a pointer to memory that represents the data store of the buffer object attached to *target*. Note that this memory represents only this buffer—it is not necessarily the memory that the graphics processor will use. The *access* parameter specifies how the application intends to use the memory once it is mapped. It must be one of the tokens shown in Table 3.4.

Table 3.4   Access Modes for **glMapBuffer**()

Token	Meaning
GL_READ_ONLY	The application will only read from the memory mapped by OpenGL.
GL_WRITE_ONLY	The application will only write to the memory mapped by OpenGL.
GL_READ_WRITE	The application may read from or write to the memory mapped by OpenGL.

If **glMapBuffer**() fails to map the buffer object's data store, it returns NULL. The *access* parameter forms a contract between you and OpenGL that specifies how you will access the memory. If you violate that contract, bad things will happen, which may include ignoring writes to the buffer, corrupting your data or even crashing your program.[3]

Note: When you map a buffer whose data store is in memory that will not be accessible to your application, OpenGL may need to move the data around so that when you use the pointer it gives you, you get what you expect. Likewise, when you're done with the data and have modified it, OpenGL may need to move it back to a place where the graphics processor can see it. This can be expensive in terms of performance, so great care should be taken when doing this.

When the buffer is mapped with the GL_READ_ONLY or GL_READ_WRITE *access* mode, the data that was in the buffer object becomes visible to your application. You can read it back, write it to a file, and even modify it in place (so long as you used GL_READ_WRITE as the *access* mode). If *access* is GL_READ_WRITE or GL_WRITE_ONLY, you can write data into memory using the pointer OpenGL gave you. Once you are done using the data or writing data into the buffer object, you must unmap it using **glUnmapBuffer()**, whose prototype is as follows:

GLboolean **glUnmapBuffer**(GLenum *target*);

Releases the mapping created by **glMapBuffer()**. **glUnmapBuffer()** returns GL_TRUE unless the data store contents have become corrupt during the time the data store was mapped. This can occur for system-specific reasons that affect the availability of graphics memory, such as screen mode changes. In such situations, GL_FALSE is returned and the data store contents are undefined. An application must detect this rare condition and reinitialize the data store.

When you unmap the buffer, any data you wrote into the memory given to you by OpenGL becomes visible in the buffer object. This means that you can place data into buffer objects by allocating space for them using **glBufferData()** and passing NULL as the *data* parameter, mapping them, writing data into them directly, and then unmapping them again. Example 3.2 contains an example of loading the contents of a file into a buffer object.

---

3. The unfortunate thing is that so many applications *do* violate this contract that most OpenGL implementations will assume you don't know what you're doing and will treat all calls to **glMapBuffer()** as if you specified GL_READ_WRITE as the *access* parameter, just so these other applications will work.

Example 3.2   Initializing a Buffer Object with **glMapBuffer()**

```
GLuint buffer;
FILE * f;
size_t filesize;

// Open a file and find its size
f = fopen("data.dat", "rb");
fseek(f, 0, SEEK_END);
filesize = ftell(f);
fseek(f, 0, SEEK_SET);

// Create a buffer by generating a name and binding it to a buffer
// binding point - GL_COPY_WRITE_BUFFER here (because the binding means
// nothing in this example).
glGenBuffers(1, &buffer);
glBindBuffer(GL_COPY_WRITE_BUFFER, buffer);

// Allocate the data store for the buffer by passing NULL for the
// data parameter.
glBufferData(GL_COPY_WRITE_BUFFER, (GLsizei)filesize, NULL,
             GL_STATIC_DRAW);
// Map the buffer...
void * data = glMapBuffer(GL_COPY_WRITE_BUFFER, GL_WRITE_ONLY);

// Read the file into the buffer.
fread(data, 1, filesize, f);

// Okay, done, unmap the buffer and close the file.
glUnmapBuffer(GL_COPY_WRITE_BUFFER);
fclose(f);
```

In Example 3.2, the entire contents of a file are read into a buffer object in a single operation. The buffer object is created and allocated to the same size as the file. Once the buffer is mapped, the file can be read directly into the buffer object's data store. No copies are made by the application, and, if the data store is visible to both the application and the graphics processor, no copies will be made by OpenGL.

There may be significant performance advantages to initializing buffer objects in this manner. The logic is this; when you call **glBufferData()** or **glBufferSubData()**, once those functions return, you are free to do whatever you want with the memory you gave them—free it, use it for something else—it doesn't matter. This means that those functions *must* be done with that memory by the time they return, and so they need to make a copy of your data. However, when you call **glMapBuffer()**, the pointer you get points at memory owned by OpenGL. When you call **glUnmapBuffer()**, OpenGL still owns that memory—it's the application that has to be done with it. This means that if the data needs to be moved or copied, OpenGL can start that process when you call **glUnmapBuffer()** and return immediately, content in the knowledge that it can finish the operation at its leisure without your application interfering in any way. Thus the copy that OpenGL needs to perform can overlap whatever your application does next (making more buffers, reading more files, and so on). If it doesn't need to make a copy, then great! The unmap operation essentially becomes free in that case.

Asynchronous and Explicit Mapping

To address many of the issues involved with mapping buffers using **glMapBuffer()** (such as applications incorrectly specifying the *access* parameter or always using GL_READ_WRITE), **glMapBufferRange()** uses flags to specify *access* more precisely. The prototype for **glMapBufferRange()** is as follows:

---

void * **glMapBufferRange**(GLenum *target*, GLintptr *offset*,
  GLsizeiptr *length*, GLbitfield *access*);

Maps all or part of a buffer object's data store into the application's address space. *target* specifies the target to which the buffer object is currently bound. *offset* and *length* together indicate the range of the data (in bytes) that is to be mapped. *access* is a bitfield containing flags that describe the mapping.

For **glMapBufferRange()**, *access* is a bitfield that must contain one or both of the GL_MAP_READ_BIT and the GL_MAP_WRITE_BIT indicating whether the application plans to read from the mapped data store, write to it, or do both. In addition, *access* may contain one or more of the flags shown in Table 3.5.

Table 3.5   Flags for Use with **glMapBufferRange()**

Flag	Meaning
GL_MAP_INVALIDATE_RANGE_BIT	If specified, any data in the specified range of the buffer may be discarded and considered invalid. Any data within the specified range that is not subsequently written by the application becomes undefined. This flag may not be used with GL_MAP_READ_BIT.

Table 3.5   (continued)   Flags for Use with **glMapBufferRange**()

Flag	Meaning
GL_MAP_INVALIDATE_BUFFER_BIT	If specified, the *entire contents* of the buffer may be discarded and considered invalid, regardless of the specified range. Any data lying outside the mapped range of the buffer object becomes undefined, as does data within the range but not subsequently written by the application. This flag may not be used with GL_MAP_READ_BIT.
GL_MAP_FLUSH_EXPLICIT_BIT	The application will take responsibility to signal to OpenGL which parts of the mapped range contain valid data by calling **glFlushMappedBufferRange**() prior to calling **glUnmapBuffer**(). Use this flag if a larger range of the buffer will be mapped and not all of it will be written by the application. This bit must be used in conjunction with GL_MAP_WRITE_BIT. If GL_MAP_FLUSH_EXPLICIT_BIT is not specified, **glUnmapBuffer**() will automatically flush the entirety of the mapped range.
GL_MAP_UNSYNCHRONIZED_BIT	If this bit is not specified, OpenGL will wait until all pending operations that may access the buffer have completed before returning the mapped range. If this flag is set, OpenGL will not attempt to synchronize operations on the buffer.

As you can see from the flags listed in Table 3.5, the command provides a significant level of control over how OpenGL uses the data in the buffer and how it synchronizes operations that may access that data.

When you specify that you want to invalidate the data in the buffer object by specifying either the GL_MAP_INVALIDATE_RANGE_BIT or GL_MAP_INVALIDATE_BUFFER_BIT, this indicates to OpenGL that it is free to dispose of any previously stored data in the buffer object. Either of the flags can be set only if you also specify that you're going to write to the buffer by also setting the GL_MAP_WRITE_BIT flag. If you specify GL_MAP_INVALIDATE_RANGE_BIT, it indicates that you will update the entire range (or at least all the parts of it that you care about). If you set the GL_MAP_INVALIDATE_BUFFER_BIT, it means that you don't care what ends up in the parts of the buffer that you didn't map. Either way, setting the flags indicates that you're planning to update the rest of the buffer with subsequent maps.[4] When OpenGL is allowed to throw away the rest of the buffer's data, it doesn't have to make any effort to merge your modified data back into the rest of the original buffer. It's probably a good idea to use GL_MAP_INVALIDATE_BUFFER_BIT for the first section of the buffer that you map, and then GL_MAP_INVALIDATE_RANGE_BIT for the rest of the buffer.

The GL_MAP_UNSYNCHRONIZED_BIT flag is used to disengage OpenGL's automatic synchronization between data transfer and use. Without this bit, OpenGL will finish up any in-flight commands that might be using the buffer object. This can *stall* the OpenGL pipeline, causing a bubble and a loss of performance. If you can guarantee that all pending commands will be complete before you actually modify the contents of the buffer (but not necessarily before you call **glMapBufferRange()**) through a method such as calling **glFinish()** or using a *sync object* (which are described in "Atomic Operations and Synchronization" on Page 578 in Chapter 11), then OpenGL doesn't need to do this synchronization for you.

Finally, the GL_MAP_FLUSH_EXPLICIT_BIT flag indicates that the application will take on the responsibility of letting OpenGL know which parts of the buffer it has modified before calling **glUnmapBuffer()**. It does this through a call to **glFlushMappedBufferRange()**, whose prototype is as follows:

---

void **glFlushMappedBufferRange**(GLenum *target*, GLintptr *offset*, GLsizeiptr *length*);

Indicates to OpenGL that the range specified by *offset* and *length* in the mapped buffer bound to *target* has been modified and should be incorporated back into the buffer object's data store.

It is possible to call **glFlushMappedBufferRange()** multiple times on separate or even overlapping ranges of a mapped buffer object. The range of the buffer object specified by *offset* and *length* must lie within the range of buffer object that has been mapped, and that range must have been mapped by a call to **glMapBufferRange()** with *access* including the GL_MAP_FLUSH_EXPLICIT_BIT flag set. When this call is made, OpenGL assumes that you're done modifying the specified range of the mapped buffer object, and can begin any operations it needs to perform in order to

---

4. Don't specify the GL_MAP_INVALIDATE_BUFFER_BIT for every section, otherwise only the last section you mapped will have valid data in it!

make that data usable such as copying it to graphics processor visible memory, or flushing, or invalidating data caches. It can do these things even though some or all of the buffer is still mapped. This is a useful way to parallelize OpenGL with other operations that your application might perform. For example, if you need to load a very large piece of data from a file into a buffer, map a range of the buffer large enough to hold the whole file, then read chunks of the file, and after each chunk call **glFlushMappedBufferRange**(). OpenGL will then operate *in parallel* to your application, reading more data from the file for the next chunk.

By combining these flags in various ways, it is possible to optimize data transfer between the application and OpenGL or to use advanced techniques such as *multithreading* or *asynchronous file operations*.

Discarding Buffer Data

Advanced

When you are done with the data in a buffer, it can be advantageous to tell OpenGL that you don't plan to use it any more. For example, consider the case where you write data into a buffer using transform feedback, and then draw using that data. If that drawing command is the last one that is going to access the data, then you can tell OpenGL that it is free to discard the data and use the memory for something else. This allows an OpenGL implementation to make optimizations such as tightly packing memory allocations or avoiding expensive copies in systems with more than one GPU.

To discard some or all of the data in a buffer object, you can call **glInvalidateBufferData**() or **glInvalidateBufferSubData**(), respectively. The prototypes of these functions are as follows:

---

void **glInvalidateBufferData**(GLuint *buffer*);
void **glInvalidateBufferSubData**(GLuint *buffer*, GLintptr *offset*,
                            GLsizeiptr *length*);

Tell OpenGL that the application is done with the contents of the buffer object in the specified range and that it is free to discard the data if it believes it is advantageous to do so. **glInvalidateBufferSubData**() discards the data in the region of the buffer object whose name is *buffer* starting at *offset* bytes and continuing for *length* bytes. **glInvalidateBufferData**() discards the entire contents of the buffer's data store.

Note that semantically, calling **glBufferData()** with a NULL pointer does a very similar thing to calling **glInvalidateBufferData()**. Both methods will tell the OpenGL implementation that it is safe to discard the data in the buffer. However, **glBufferData()** logically recreates the underlying memory allocation, whereas **glInvalidateBufferData()** does not. Depending on the OpenGL implementation, it may be more optimal to call **glInvalidateBufferData()**. Further, **glInvalidateBufferSubData()** is really the only way to discard a *region* of a buffer object's data store.

Vertex Specification

Now that you have data in buffers, and you know how to write a basic vertex shader, it's time to hook the data up to the shader. You've already read about *vertex array objects*, which contain information about where data is located and how it is laid out, and functions like **glVertexAttribPointer()**. It's time to take a deeper dive into vertex specifications, other variants of **glVertexAttribPointer()**, and how to specify data for vertex attributes that aren't floating point or aren't enabled.

VertexAttribPointer in Depth

The **glVertexAttribPointer()** command was briefly introduced in Chapter 1. The prototype is as follows:

```
void glVertexAttribPointer(GLuint index, GLint size,
                           GLenum type, GLboolean normalized,
                           GLsizei stride, const GLvoid *pointer);
```

Specifies where the data values for the vertex attribute with location *index* can be accessed. *pointer* is the offset in basic-machine units (i.e., bytes)from the start of the buffer object currently bound to the GL_ARRAY_BUFFER target for the first set of values in the array. *size* represents the number of components to be updated per vertex. *type* specifies the data type of each element in the array. *normalized* indicates that the vertex data should be normalized before being presented to the vertex shader. *stride* is the byte offset between consecutive elements in the array. If *stride* is zero, the data is assumed to be tightly packed.

The state set by **glVertexAttribPointer()** is stored in the currently bound vertex array object (VAO). *size* is the number of elements in the attribute's vector (1, 2, 3, or 4), or the special token GL_BGRA, which should be specified when *packed* vertex data is used. The *type* parameter is a token that specifies the type of the data that is contained in the buffer object. Table 3.6 describes the token names that may be specified for *type* and the OpenGL data type that they correspond to:

Table 3.6   Values of *Type* for **glVertexAttribPointer()**

Token Value	OpenGL Type
GL_BYTE	GLbyte (signed 8-bit bytes)
GL_UNSIGNED_BYTE	GLubyte (unsigned 8-bit bytes)
GL_SHORT	GLshort (signed 16-bit words)
GL_UNSIGNED_SHORT	GLushort (unsigned 16-bit words)
GL_INT	GLint (signed 32-bit integers)
GL_UNSIGNED_INT	GLuint (unsigned 32-bit integers)
GL_FIXED	GLfixed (16.16 signed fixed point)
GL_FLOAT	GLfloat (32-bit IEEE single-precision floating point)
GL_HALF_FLOAT	GLhalf (16-bit S1E5M10 half-precision floating point)
GL_DOUBLE	GLdouble (64-bit IEEE double-precision floating point)
GL_INT_2_10_10_10_REV	GLuint (packed data)
GL_UNSIGNED_INT_2_10_10_10_REV	GLuint (packed data)

Note that while integer types such as GL_SHORT or GL_UNSIGNED_INT can be passed to the *type* argument, this tells OpenGL only what data type is stored in memory in the buffer object. OpenGL will convert this data to floating point in order to load it into floating-point vertex attributes. The way this conversion is performed is controlled by the *normalize* parameter. When *normalize* is GL_FALSE, integer data is simply typecast into floating-point format before being passed to the vertex shader. This means that if you place the integer value 4 into a buffer and use the GL_INT token for the *type* when *normalize* is GL_FALSE, the value 4.0 will be placed into the shader. When *normalize* is GL_TRUE, the data is normalized before being passed to the vertex shader. To do this, OpenGL divides each element by a fixed constant that depends on the incoming data type. When the data type is signed, the following formula is used:

$$f = \frac{c}{2^b - 1}$$

Whereas, if the data type is unsigned, the following formula is used:

$$f = \frac{2c + 1}{2^b - 1}$$

In both cases, f is the resulting floating-point value, c is the incoming integer component, and b is the number of bits in the data type (i.e., 8 for GL_UNSIGNED_BYTE, 16 for GL_SHORT, and so on). Note that unsigned data types are also scaled and biased before being divided by the type-dependent constant. To return to our example of putting 4 into an integer vertex attribute, we get:

$$f = \frac{4}{2^{32} - 1}$$

which works out to about 0.000000009313—a pretty small number!

Integer Vertex Attributes

If you are familiar with the way floating-point numbers work, you'll also realize that precision is lost as numbers become very large, and so the full range of integer values cannot be passed into a vertex shader using floating-point attributes. For this reason, we have *integer vertex attributes*. These are represented in vertex shaders by the `int`, `ivec2`, `ivec3`, or `ivec4` types or their unsigned counterparts—`uint`, `uvec2`, `uvec3`, and `uvec4`.

A second vertex-attribute function is needed in order to pass raw integers into these vertex attributes—one that doesn't automatically convert everything to floating point. This is **glVertexAttribIPointer()**—the I stands for integer.

---

void **glVertexAttribIPointer**(GLuint *index*, GLint *size*,
                    GLenum *type*, GLsizei *stride*,
                    const GLvoid **pointer*);

Behaves similarly to **glVertexAttribPointer()**, but for vertex attributes declared as integers in the vertex shader. *type* must be one of the integer data type tokens GL_BYTE, GL_UNSIGNED_BYTE, GL_SHORT, GL_UNSIGNED_SHORT, GL_INT, or GL_UNSIGNED_INT.

Notice that the parameters to **glVertexAttribIPointer()** are identical to the parameters to **glVertexAttribPointer()**, except for the omission of the *normalize* parameter. *normalize* is missing because it's not relevant to integer vertex attributes. Only the integer data type tokens, GL_BYTE, GL_UNSIGNED_BYTE, GL_SHORT, GL_UNSIGNED_SHORT, GL_INT, and GL_UNSIGNED_INT may be used for the *type* parameter.

Double-Precision Vertex Attributes

The third variant of **glVertexAttribPointer()** is **glVertexAttribLPointer()**—here the L stands for "long". This version of the function is specifically for loading attribute data into *64-bit double-precision* floating-point vertex attributes.

---

void **glVertexAttribLPointer**(GLuint *index*, GLint *size*,
                     GLenum *type*, GLsizei *stride*,
                     const GLvoid **pointer*);

Behaves similarly to **glVertexAttribPointer()**, but for vertex attributes declared as 64-bit double-precision floating-point types in the vertex shader. *type* must be GL_DOUBLE.

Again, notice the lack of the *normalize* parameter. In **glVertexAttribPointer()**, *normalize* was used only for integer data types that aren't legal here, and so the parameter is not needed. If GL_DOUBLE is used with **glVertexAttribPointer()**, the data is automatically down-converted to 32-bit single-precision floating-point representation before being passed to the vertex shader—even if the target vertex attribute was declared using one of the double-precision types `double`, `dvec2`, `dvec3`, or `dvec4`, or one of the double-precision matrix types such as `dmat4`. However, with **glVertexAttribLPointer()**, the full precision of the input data is kept and passed to the vertex shader.

Packed Data Formats for Vertex Attributes

Going back to the **glVertexAttribPointer()** command, you will notice that the allowed values for the *size* parameter are 1, 2, 3, 4, and the special token GL_BGRA. Also, the *type* parameter may take one of the special values GL_INT_2_10_10_10_REV or GL_UNSIGNED_INT_2_10_10_10_REV, both of which correspond to the GLuint data type. These special tokens are used to represent *packed* data that can be consumed by OpenGL. The GL_INT_2_10_10_10_REV and GL_UNSIGNED_INT_2_10_10_10_REV tokens represent four-component data represented as ten bits for each of the first three components and two for the last, packed in reverse order into a single 32-bit quantity (a GLuint). GL_BGRA could just have easily been called GL_ZYXW.[5] Looking at the data layout within the 32-bit word, you would see the bits divided up as shown in Figure 3.3.

Figure 3.3 Packing of elements in a BGRA-packed vertex attribute

In Figure 3.3, the elements of the vertex are packed into a single 32-bit integer in the order *w*, *x*, *y*, *z*—which when reversed is *z*, *y*, *x*, *w*, or *b*, *g*, *r*, *a* when using color conventions. In Figure 3.4, the coordinates are packed in the order *w*, *z*, *y*, *x*, which reversed and written in color conventions is *r*, *g*, *b*, *a*.

Figure 3.4 Packing of elements in a RGBA-packed vertex attribute

Vertex data may be specified only in the first of these two formats by using the GL_INT_2_10_10_10_REV or GL_UNSIGNED_INT_2_10_10_10_REV tokens. When one of these tokens is used as the *type* parameter to **glVertexAttribPointer()**, each vertex consumes one 32-bit word in the vertex array. The word is unpacked into its components and then optionally normalized (depending on the value of the *normalize* parameter before being loaded into the appropriate vertex attribute. This data arrangement is particularly well suited to normals or other types of attributes that can benefit from the additional precision afforded by the 10-bit components but perhaps don't require the full precision offered by half-float data (which would take 16-bits per component). This allows the conservation of memory space and bandwidth, which helps improve performance.

Static Vertex-Attribute Specification

Remember from Chapter 1 where you were introduced to **glEnableVertexAttribArray()** and **glDisableVertexAttribArray()**.

---

5. Not a valid OpenGL token; just to be clear.

These functions are used to tell OpenGL which vertex attributes are backed by vertex buffers. Before OpenGL will read any data from your vertex buffers, you must enable the corresponding vertex attribute arrays with **glEnableVertexAttribArray()**. You may wonder what happens if you don't enable the attribute array for one of your vertex attributes. In that case, the *static vertex attribute* is used. The static vertex attribute for each vertex is the default value that will be used for the attribute when there is no enabled attribute array for it. For example, imagine you had a vertex shader that would read the vertex color from one of the vertex attributes. Now suppose that all of the vertices in a particular mesh or part of that mesh had the same color. It would be a waste of memory and potentially of performance to fill a buffer full of that constant value for all the vertices in the mesh. Instead, you can just disable the vertex attribute array and use the static vertex attribute to specify color for all of the vertices.

The static vertex attribute for each attribute may be specified using one of **glVertexAttrib*()** functions. When the vertex attribute is declared as a floating-point quantity in the vertex shader (i.e., it is of type `float`, `vec2`, `vec3`, `vec4`, or one of the floating-point matrix types such as `mat4`), the following **glVertexAttrib*()** commands can be used to set its value.

---

void **glVertexAttrib{1234}{fds}**(GLuint *index*, TYPE *values*);
void **glVertexAttrib{1234}{fds}v**(GLuint *index*,
                           const TYPE **values*);
void **glVertexAttrib4{bsifd ub us ui}v**(GLuint *index*,
                           const TYPE **values*);

Specifies the static value for the vertex attribute with index *index*. For the non-**v** versions, up to four values are specified in the *x*, *y*, *z*, and *w* parameters. For the **v** versions, up to four components are sourced from the array whose address is specified in *v* and used in place of the *x*, *y*, *z*, and *w* components in that order.

All of these functions implicitly convert the supplied parameters to floating-point before passing them to the vertex shader (unless they're already floating-point). This conversion is a simple typecast. That is, the values are converted exactly as specified as if they had been specified in a buffer and associated with a vertex attribute by calling **glVertexAttribPointer()** with the *normalize* parameter set to GL_FALSE. For the integer variants of the functions, versions exist that normalize the parameters to the range [0, 1] or [−1, 1] depending on whether the parameters are signed or unsigned. These are:

---

void **glVertexAttrib4Nub**(GLuint *index*, GLubyte *x*, GLubyte *y*,
　　　　　　　　　　　　GLubyte *z*, GLubyte *w*);
void **glVertexAttrib4N**{bsi ub us ui}v(GLuint *index*,
　　　　　　　　　　　　　　　const TYPE **v*);

Specifies a single or multiple vertex-attribute values for attribute *index*, normalizing the parameters to the range [0, 1] during the conversion process for the unsigned variants and to the range [−1, 1] for the signed variants.

Even with these commands, the parameters are still converted to floating-point before being passed to the vertex shader. Thus, they are suitable only for setting the static values of attributes declared with one of the single-precision floating-point data types. If you have vertex attributes that are declared as integers or double-precision floating-point variables, you should use one of the following functions:

---

void **glVertexAttribI**{1234}{i ui}(GLuint *index*, TYPE *values*);
void **glVertexAttribI**{123}{i ui}v(GLuint *index*,
　　　　　　　　　　　　　　const TYPE **values*);
void **glVertexAttribI4**{bsi ub us ui}v(GLuint *index*,
　　　　　　　　　　　　　　const TYPE **values*);

Specifies a single or multiple static integer vertex-attribute values for integer vertex attribute *index*.

Furthermore, if you have vertex attributes that are declared as one of the double-precision floating-point types, you should use one of the **L** variants of **glVertexAttrib*()**, which are:

---

void **glVertexAttribL**{1234}(GLuint *index*, TYPE *values*);
void **glVertexAttribL**{1234}v(GLuint *index*, const TYPE **values*);

Specifies a single or multiple static vertex-attribute values for double-precision vertex attribute *index*.

Both the **glVertexAttribI*()** and **glVertexAttribL*()** variants of **glVertexAttrib*()** pass their parameters through to the underlying vertex attribute just as the **I** versions of **glVertexAttribIPointer()** do.

If you use one of the **glVertexAttrib*()** functions with less components than there are in the underlying vertex attribute (e.g., you use **glVertexAttrib*()** 2f to set the value of a vertex attribute declared as a `vec4`), default values are filled in for the missing components. For *w*, 1.0 is used as the default value, and for *y* and *z*, 0.0 is used.[6] If you use a function that takes more components than are present in the vertex attribute in the shader, the additional components are simply discarded.

Note: The static vertex attribute values are stored in the current VAO, not the program object. That means that if the current vertex shader has, for example, a `vec3` input and you use **glVertexAttrib*()** 4fv to specify a four-component vector for that attribute, the fourth component will be ignored *but still stored*. If you change the vertex shader to one that has a `vec4` input at that attribute location, the fourth component specified earlier will appear in that attribute's *w* component.

OpenGL Drawing Commands

Most OpenGL drawing commands start with the word *Draw*.[7] The drawing commands are roughly broken into two subsets—indexed and nonindexed draws. Indexed draws use an array of indices stored in a buffer object bound to the GL_ELEMENT_ARRAY_BUFFER binding that is used to indirectly index into the enabled vertex arrays. On the other hand, nonindexed draws do not use the GL_ELEMENT_ARRAY_BUFFER at all, and simply read the vertex data sequentially. The most basic, nonindexed drawing command in OpenGL is **glDrawArrays()**.

---

void **glDrawArrays**(GLenum *mode*, GLint *first*, GLsizei *count*);

Constructs a sequence of geometric primitives using array elements starting at *first* and ending at *first* + *count* − 1 of each enabled array. *mode* specifies what kinds of primitives are constructed and is one of the primitive mode tokens such as GL_TRIANGLES, GL_LINE_LOOP, GL_LINES, and GL_POINTS.

Similarly, the most basic *indexed* drawing command is **glDrawElements()**.

---

6. The lack of a default for *x* is intentional—you can't specify values for *y*, *z*, or *w* without also specifying a value for *x*.

7. In fact, the only two commands in OpenGL that start with *Draw* but don't draw anything are **glDrawBuffer()** and **glDrawBuffers()**.

> void **glDrawElements**(GLenum *mode*, GLsizei *count*,
>   GLenum *type*, const GLvoid **indices*);
>
> Defines a sequence of geometric primitives using *count* number of
> elements, whose indices are stored in the buffer bound to the
> GL_ELEMENT_ARRAY_BUFFER buffer binding point (the *element array
> buffer*). *indices* represents an offset, in bytes, into the element array buffer
> where the indices begin. *type* must be one of GL_UNSIGNED_BYTE,
> GL_UNSIGNED_SHORT, or GL_UNSIGNED_INT, indicating the data type
> of the indices the element array buffer. *mode* specifies what kind of
> primitives are constructed and is one of the primitive mode tokens, such
> as GL_TRIANGLES, GL_LINE_LOOP, GL_LINES, and GL_POINTS.

Each of these functions causes vertices to be read from the enabled
vertex-attribute arrays and used to construct primitives of the type
specified by *mode*. Vertex-attribute arrays are enabled using
glEnableVertexAttribArray() as described in Chapter 1. **glDrawArrays()**
just uses the vertices in the buffer objects associated with the enabled
vertex attributes in the order they appear. **glDrawElements()** uses the
indices in the element array buffer to index into the vertex attribute arrays.
Each of the more complex OpenGL drawing functions essentially builds
functionality on top of these two functions. For example,
glDrawElementsBaseVertex() allows the indices in the element array
buffer to be offset by a fixed amount.

> void **glDrawElementsBaseVertex**(GLenum *mode*, GLsizei *count*,
>   GLenum *type*,
>   const GLvoid **indices*,
>   GLint *basevertex*);
>
> Behaves identically to **glDrawElements()** except that the *i*th element
> transferred by the corresponding draw command will be taken from
> element *indices[i]* + *basevertex* of each enabled vertex attribute array.

glDrawElementsBaseVertex() allows the indices in the element array
buffer to be interpreted relative to some base index. For example,
multiple versions of a model (say, frames of an animation) can be stored in
a single set of vertex buffers at different offsets within the buffer.
glDrawElementsBaseVertex() can then be used to draw any frame of that
animation by simply specifying the first index that corresponds to that
frame. The same set of indices can be used to reference every frame.

Another command that behaves similarly to **glDrawElements**() is **glDrawRangeElements**().

---

void **glDrawRangeElements**(GLenum *mode*, GLuint *start*,
　　　　　　　　　　　　　　 GLuint *end*, GLsizei *count*,
　　　　　　　　　　　　　　 GLenum *type*,
　　　　　　　　　　　　　　 const GLvoid **indices*);

This is a restricted form of **glDrawElements**() in that it forms a contract between the application (i.e., *you*) and OpenGL that guarantees that any index contained in the section of the element array buffer referenced by *indices* and *count* will fall within the range specified by *start* and *end*.

Various combinations of functionality are available through even more advanced commands—for example, **glDrawRangeElementsBaseVertex**() combines the features of **glDrawElementsBaseVertex**() with the contractual arrangement of **glDrawRangeElements**().

---

void **glDrawRangeElementsBaseVertex**(GLenum *mode*,
　　　　　　　　　　　　　　　　　　 GLuint *start*, GLuint *end*,
　　　　　　　　　　　　　　　　　　 GLsizei *count*,
　　　　　　　　　　　　　　　　　　 GLenum *type*,
　　　　　　　　　　　　　　　　　　 const GLvoid **indices*,
　　　　　　　　　　　　　　　　　　 GLint *basevertex*);

Forms a contractual agreement between the application similar to that of **glDrawRangeElements**(), while allowing the base vertex to be specified in *basevertex*. In this case, the contract states that the values stored in the element array buffer will fall between *start* and *end* before *basevertex* is added.

Instanced versions of both of these functions are also available. Instancing will be covered in "Instanced Rendering" on Page 128. The instancing commands include **glDrawArraysInstanced**(), **glDrawElementsInstanced**(), and even **glDrawElementsInstancedBaseVertex**(). Finally, there are two commands that take their parameters not from your program directly, but from a *buffer object*. These are the draw-indirect functions, and to use them, a buffer object must be bound to the GL_DRAW_INDIRECT_BUFFER binding. The first is the indirect version of **glDrawArrays**(), **glDrawArraysIndirect**().

void **glDrawArraysIndirect**(GLenum *mode,*
                          const GLvoid **indirect*);

Behaves exactly as **glDrawArraysInstanced()**, except that the parameters for the drawing command are taken from a structure stored in the buffer bound to the GL_DRAW_INDIRECT_BUFFER binding point (the *draw indirect buffer*). *indirect* represents an offset into the draw indirect buffer. *mode* is one of the primitive types that is accepted by **glDrawArrays()**.

In **glDrawArraysIndirect()**, the parameters for the actual draw command are taken from a structure stored at offset *indirect* into the *draw indirect* buffer. The structure's declaration in "C" is presented in Example 3.3:

Example 3.3   Declaration of the DrawArraysIndirectCommand Structure

```
typedef struct DrawArraysIndirectCommand_t
{
    GLuint count;
    GLuint primCount;
    GLuint first;
    GLuint baseInstance;
} DrawArraysIndirectCommand;
```

The fields of the DrawArraysIndirectCommand structure are interpreted as if they were parameters to a call to **glDrawArraysInstanced()**. *first* and *count* are passed directly to the internal function. The *primCount* field is the instance count, and the *baseInstance* field becomes the *baseInstance* offset to any instanced vertex attributes (don't worry, the instanced rendering commands will be described shortly).

The indirect version of **glDrawElements()** is **glDrawElementsIndirect()** and its prototype is as follows:

void **glDrawElementsIndirect**(GLenum *mode,* GLenum *type,*
                          const GLvoid * *indirect*);

Behaves exactly as **glDrawElements()**, except that the parameters for the drawing command are taken from a structure stored in the buffer bound to the GL_DRAW_INDIRECT_BUFFER binding point. *indirect* represents an offset into the draw indirect buffer. *mode* is one of the primitive types that is accepted by **glDrawElements()**, and *type* specifies the type of the indices stored in the element array buffer at the time the draw command is called.

As with **glDrawArraysIndirect()**, the parameters for the draw command in **glDrawElementsIndirect()** come from a structure stored at offset *indirect* stored in the element array buffer. The structure's declaration in "C" is presented in Example 3.4:

Example 3.4   Declaration of the DrawElementsIndirectCommand Structure

```
typedef struct DrawElementsIndirectCommand_t
{
    GLuint   count;
    GLuint   primCount;
    GLuint   firstIndex;
    GLuint   baseVertex;
    GLuint   baseInstance;
} DrawElementsIndirectCommand;
```

As with the `DrawArraysIndirectCommand` structure, the fields of the `DrawElementsIndirectCommand` structure are also interpreted as calls to the **glDrawElementsInstancedBaseVertex()** command. *count* and *baseVertex* are passed directly to the internal function. As in **glDrawArraysIndirect()**, *primCount* is the instance count. *firstVertex* is used, along with the size of the indices implied by the *type* parameter to calculate the value of *indices* that would have been passed to **glDrawElementsInstancedBaseVertex()**. Again, *baseInstance* becomes the instance offset to any instanced vertex attributes used by the resulting drawing commands.

Now, we come to the drawing commands that do not start with *Draw*. These are the multivariants of the drawing commands, **glMultiDrawArrays()**, **glMultiDrawElements()**, and **glMultiDrawElementsBaseVertex()**. Each one takes an array of *first* parameters, and an array of *count* parameters acts as if the nonmultiversion of the function had been called once for each element of the array. For example, look at the prototype for **glMultiDrawArrays()**.

---

void **glMultiDrawArrays**(GLenum *mode*, const GLint * *first*,
                          const GLint * *count*, GLsizei *primcount*);

Draws multiple sets of geometric primitives with a single OpenGL function call. *first* and *count* are arrays of *primcount* parameters that would be valid for a call to **glDrawArrays()**.

Calling **glMultiDrawArrays()** is equivalent to the following OpenGL code sequence:

```
void glMultiDrawArrays(GLenum mode,
                       const GLint * first,
                       const GLint * count,
                       GLsizei primcount)
{
    GLsizei i;

    for (i = 0; i < primcount; i++)
    {
        glDrawArrays(mode, first[i], count[i]);
    }
}
```

Similarly, the multiversion of **glDrawElements()** is **glMultiDrawElements()**, and its prototype is as follows:

---

void **glMultiDrawElements**(GLenum *mode*, const GLint * *count*,
                      GLenum *type*,
                      const GLvoid * const * *indices*,
                      GLsizei *primcount*);

Draws multiple sets of geometric primitives with a single OpenGL function call. *first* and *indices* are arrays of *primcount* parameters that would be valid for a call to **glDrawElements()**.

Calling **glMultiDrawElements()** is equivalent to the following OpenGL code sequence:

```
void glMultiDrawElements(GLenum mode,
                         const GLsizei * count,
                         GLenum type,
                         const GLvoid * const * indices,
                         GLsizei primcount);
{
    GLsizei i;

    for (i = 0; i < primcount; i++)
    {
        glDrawElements(mode, count[i], type, indices[i]);
    }
}
```

An extension of **glMultiDrawElements()** to include a *baseVertex* parameter is **glMultiDrawElementsBaseVertex()**. Its prototype is as follows:

void **glMultiDrawElementsBaseVertex**(GLenum *mode*,
                                   const GLint * *count*,
                                   GLenum *type*,
                                   const GLvoid * const * *indices*,
                                   GLsizei *primcount*,
                                   const GLint * *baseVertex*);

Draws multiple sets of geometric primitives with a single OpenGL function call. *first*, *indices*, and *baseVertex* are arrays of *primcount* parameters that would be valid for a call to **glDrawElementsBaseVertex()**.

As with the previously described OpenGL multidrawing commands, **glMultiDrawElementsBaseVertex()** is equivalent to another code sequence that ends up calling the nonmultiversion of the function.

```
void glMultiDrawElementsBaseVertex(GLenum mode,
                                   const GLsizei * count,
                                   GLenum type,
                                   const GLvoid * const * indices,
                                   GLsizei primcount,
                                   const \GLint * baseVertex);
{
    GLsizei i;

    for (i = 0; i < primcount; i++)
    {
        glDrawElements(mode, count[i], type,
                       indices[i], baseVertex[i]);
    }
}
```

Finally, if you have a large number of draws to perform and the parameters are already in a buffer object suitable for use by **glDrawArraysIndirect()** or **glDrawElementsIndirect()**, it is possible to use the *multi* versions of these two functions, **glMultiDrawArraysIndirect()** and **glMultiDrawElementsIndirect()**.

void **glMultiDrawArraysIndirect**(GLenum *mode*,
                               const void * *indirect*,
                               GLsizei *drawcount*,
                               GLsizei *stride*);

Draws multiple sets of primitives, the parameters for which are stored in a buffer object. *drawcount* independent draw commands are dispatched as a result of a call to **glMultiDrawArraysIndirect()**, and parameters are sourced from these commands as they would be for **glDrawArraysIndirect()**. Each `DrawArraysIndirectCommand` structure is separated by *stride* bytes. If *stride* is zero, then the data structures are assumed to form a tightly packed array.

void **glMultiDrawElementsIndirect**(GLenum *mode*,
                               GLenum *type*,
                               const void * *indirect*,
                               GLsizei *drawcount*,
                               GLsizei *stride*);

Draws multiple sets of primitives, the parameters for which are stored in a buffer object. *drawcount* independent draw commands are dispatched as a result of a call to **glMultiDrawElementsIndirect()**, and parameters are sourced from these commands as they would be for **glDrawElementsIndirect()**. Each `DrawElementsIndirectCommand` structure is separated by *stride* bytes. If *stride* is zero, then the data structures are assumed to form a tightly packed array.

OpenGL Drawing Exercises

This is a relatively simple example of using a few of the OpenGL drawing commands covered so far in this chapter. Example 3.5 shows how the data is loaded into the buffers required to use the draw commands in the example. Example 3.6 shows how the drawing commands are called.

Example 3.5   Setting up for the Drawing Command Example

```
// A four vertices
static const GLfloat vertex_positions[] =
{
    -1.0f, -1.0f, 0.0f, 1.0f,
     1.0f, -1.0f, 0.0f, 1.0f,
    -1.0f,  1.0f, 0.0f, 1.0f,
    -1.0f, -1.0f, 0.0f, 1.0f,
};
```

```
// Color for each vertex
static const GLfloat vertex_colors[] =
{
    1.0f, 1.0f, 1.0f, 1.0f,
    1.0f, 1.0f, 0.0f, 1.0f,
    1.0f, 0.0f, 1.0f, 1.0f,
    0.0f, 1.0f, 1.0f, 1.0f
};

// Three indices (we're going to draw one triangle at a time
static const GLushort vertex_indices[] =
{
    0, 1, 2
};

// Set up the element array buffer
glGenBuffers(1, ebo);
glBindBuffer(GL_ELEMENT_ARRAY_BUFFER, ebo[0]);
glBufferData(GL_ELEMENT_ARRAY_BUFFER,
             sizeof(vertex_indices), vertex_indices, GL_STATIC_DRAW);

// Set up the vertex attributes
glGenVertexArrays(1, vao);
glBindVertexArray(vao[0]);

glGenBuffers(1, vbo);
glBindBuffer(GL_ARRAY_BUFFER, vbo[0]);
glBufferData(GL_ARRAY_BUFFER,
             sizeof(vertex_positions) + sizeof(vertex_colors),
             NULL, GL_STATIC_DRAW);
glBufferSubData(GL_ARRAY_BUFFER, 0,
                sizeof(vertex_positions), vertex_positions);
glBufferSubData(GL_ARRAY_BUFFER,
                sizeof(vertex_positions), sizeof(vertex_colors),
                vertex_colors);
```

Example 3.6   Drawing Commands Example

```
// DrawArrays
model_matrix = vmath::translation(-3.0f, 0.0f, -5.0f);
glUniformMatrix4fv(render_model_matrix_loc, 4, GL_FALSE, model_matrix);
glDrawArrays(GL_TRIANGLES, 0, 3);

// DrawElements
model_matrix = vmath::translation(-1.0f, 0.0f, -5.0f);
glUniformMatrix4fv(render_model_matrix_loc, 4, GL_FALSE, model_matrix);
glDrawElements(GL_TRIANGLES, 3, GL_UNSIGNED_SHORT, NULL);

// DrawElementsBaseVertex
model_matrix = vmath::translation(1.0f, 0.0f, -5.0f);
glUniformMatrix4fv(render_model_matrix_loc, 4, GL_FALSE, model_matrix);
glDrawElementsBaseVertex(GL_TRIANGLES, 3, GL_UNSIGNED_SHORT, NULL, 1);
```

```
// DrawArraysInstanced
model_matrix = vmath::translation(3.0f, 0.0f, -5.0f);
glUniformMatrix4fv(render_model_matrix_loc, 4, GL_FALSE, model_matrix);
glDrawArraysInstanced(GL_TRIANGLES, 0, 3, 1);
```

The result of the program in Examples 3.5 and 3.6 is shown in Figure 3.5.
It's not terribly exciting, but you can see four similar triangles, each
rendered using a different drawing command.

Figure 3.5   Simple example of drawing commands

Restarting Primitives

As you start working with larger sets of vertex data, you are likely to
find that you need to make numerous calls to the OpenGL drawing
routines, usually rendering the same type of primitive (such as
GL_TRIANGLE_STRIP) that you used in the previous drawing call. Of
course, you can use the glMultiDraw*() routines, but they require the
overhead of maintaining the arrays for the starting index and length of
each primitive.

OpenGL has the ability to restart primitives within the same drawing
command by specifying a special value, the *primitive restart index*, which is
specially processed by OpenGL. When the primitive restart index is
encountered in a draw call, a new rendering primitive of the same type is

started with the vertex following the index. The primitive restart index is specified by the **glPrimitiveRestartIndex()** function.

---

void **glPrimitiveRestartIndex**(GLuint *index*);

Specifies the vertex array element index used to indicate that a new primitive should be started during rendering. When processing of vertex-array element indices encounters a value that matches index, no vertex data is processed, the current graphics primitive is terminated, and a new one of the identical type is started from the next vertex.

As vertices are rendered with one of the **glDrawElements()** derived function calls, it can watch for the index specified by **glPrimitiveRestartIndex()** to appear in the element array buffer. However, it watches only for this index to appear if primitive restating is enabled. Primitive restarting is controlled by calling **glEnable()** or **glDisable()** with the GL_PRIMITIVE_RESTART parameter.

To illustrate, consider the layout of vertices in Figure 3.6, which shows how a triangle strip would be broken in two by using primitive restarting. In this figure, the primitive restart index has been set to 8. As the triangles are rendered, OpenGL watches for the index 8 to be read from the element array buffer, and when it sees it go by, rather than creating a vertex, it ends the current triangle strip. The next vertex (vertex 9) becomes the first vertex of a new triangle strip, and so in this case two triangle strips are created.

Figure 3.6   Using primitive restart to break a triangle strip

The following example demonstrates a simple use of primitive restart—it draws a cube as a pair of triangle strips separated by a primitive restart index. Examples 3.7 and 3.8 demonstrate how the data for the cube is specified and then drawn.

Example 3.7   Intializing Data for a Cube Made of Two Triangle Strips

```
// 8 corners of a cube, side length 2, centered on the origin
static const GLfloat cube_positions[] =
{
    -1.0f, -1.0f, -1.0f, 1.0f,
    -1.0f, -1.0f,  1.0f, 1.0f,
    -1.0f,  1.0f, -1.0f, 1.0f,
```

```
    -1.0f,   1.0f,   1.0f,  1.0f,
     1.0f,  -1.0f,  -1.0f,  1.0f,
     1.0f,  -1.0f,   1.0f,  1.0f,
     1.0f,   1.0f,  -1.0f,  1.0f,
     1.0f,   1.0f,   1.0f,  1.0f
};

// Color for each vertex
static const GLfloat cube_colors[] =
{
    1.0f, 1.0f, 1.0f, 1.0f,
    1.0f, 1.0f, 0.0f, 1.0f,
    1.0f, 0.0f, 1.0f, 1.0f,
    1.0f, 0.0f, 0.0f, 1.0f,
    0.0f, 1.0f, 1.0f, 1.0f,
    0.0f, 1.0f, 0.0f, 1.0f,
    0.0f, 0.0f, 1.0f, 1.0f,
    0.5f, 0.5f, 0.5f, 1.0f
};

// Indices for the triangle strips
static const GLushort cube_indices[] =
{
    0, 1, 2, 3, 6, 7, 4, 5,         // First strip
    0xFFFF,                         // <<-- This is the restart index
    2, 6, 0, 4, 1, 5, 3, 7          // Second strip
};

// Set up the element array buffer
glGenBuffers(1, ebo);
glBindBuffer(GL_ELEMENT_ARRAY_BUFFER, ebo[0]);
glBufferData(GL_ELEMENT_ARRAY_BUFFER,
             sizeof(cube_indices),
             cube_indices, GL_STATIC_DRAW);

// Set up the vertex attributes
glGenVertexArrays(1, vao);
glBindVertexArray(vao[0]);

glGenBuffers(1, vbo);
glBindBuffer(GL_ARRAY_BUFFER, vbo[0]);
glBufferData(GL_ARRAY_BUFFER,
             sizeof(cube_positions) + sizeof(cube_colors),
             NULL, GL_STATIC_DRAW);
glBufferSubData(GL_ARRAY_BUFFER, 0,
                sizeof(cube_positions), cube_positions);
glBufferSubData(GL_ARRAY_BUFFER, sizeof(cube_positions),
                sizeof(cube_colors), cube_colors);

glVertexAttribPointer(0, 4, GL_FLOAT,
                      GL_FALSE, 0, NULL);
glVertexAttribPointer(1, 4, GL_FLOAT,
                      GL_FALSE, 0,
```

```
                          (const GLvoid *)sizeof(cube_positions));
glEnableVertexAttribArray(0);
glEnableVertexAttribArray(1);
```

Figure 3.7 shows how the vertex data given in Example 3.7 represents the cube as two independent triangle strips.

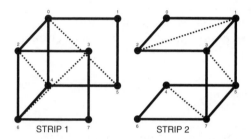

Figure 3.7   Two triangle strips forming a cube

Example 3.8   Drawing a Cube Made of Two Triangle Strips Using Primitive Restart

```
// Set up for a glDrawElements call
glBindVertexArray(vao[0]);
glBindBuffer(GL_ELEMENT_ARRAY_BUFFER, ebo[0]);

#if USE_PRIMITIVE_RESTART
// When primitive restart is on, we can call one draw command
glEnable(GL_PRIMITIVE_RESTART);
glPrimitiveRestartIndex(0xFFFF);
glDrawElements(GL_TRIANGLE_STRIP, 17, GL_UNSIGNED_SHORT, NULL);
#else
// Without primitive restart, we need to call two draw commands
glDrawElements(GL_TRIANGLE_STRIP, 8, GL_UNSIGNED_SHORT, NULL);
glDrawElements(GL_TRIANGLE_STRIP, 8, GL_UNSIGNED_SHORT,
               (const GLvoid *)(9 * sizeof(GLushort)));
#endif
```

Note: OpenGL will restart primitives whenever it comes across the current restart index in the element array buffer. Therefore, it's a good idea to set the restart index to a value that will not be used in your code. The default restart index is zero, which is very likely to appear in your element array buffer. A good value to choose is $2^n - 1$, where n is the number of bits in your indices (i.e., 16 for GL_UNSIGNED_SHORT indices and 32 for GL_UNSIGNED_INT indices). This is very unlikely to be used as a real index. Sticking with such a standard also means that you don't need to figure out the index for every model in your program.

Instanced Rendering

Instancing, or instanced rendering, is a way of executing the same drawing commands many times in a row, with each producing a slightly different result. This can be a very efficient method of rendering a large amount of geometry with very few API calls. Several variants of already-familiar drawing functions exist to instruct OpenGL to execute the command multiple times. Further, various mechanisms are available in OpenGL to allow the shader to use the instance of the draw as an input, and to be given new values for vertex attributes *per-instance* rather than per-vertex. The simplest instanced rendering call is:

void **glDrawArraysInstanced**(GLenum *mode*, GLint *first*,
                               GLsizei *count*, GLsizei *primCount*);

Draws *primCount* instances of the geometric primitives specified by *mode*, *first*, and *count* as if specified by individual calls to **glDrawArrays()**. The built-in variable `gl_InstanceID` is incremented for each instance, and new values are presented to the vertex shader for each *instanced* vertex attribute.

This is the instanced version of **glDrawArrays()**; note similarity of the two functions. The parameters of **glDrawArraysInstanced()** are identical to those of **glDrawArrays()**, with the addition of the *primCount* argument. This parameter specifies the count of the number of instances that are to be rendered. When this function is executed, OpenGL will essentially execute *primCount* copies of **glDrawArrays()**, with the *mode*, *first*, and *count* parameters passed through. There are ***Instanced** versions of several of the OpenGL drawing commands, including **glDrawElementsInstanced()** (for **glDrawElements()**) and **glDrawElementsInstancedBaseVertex()** (for **glDrawElementsBaseVertex()**). The **glDrawElementsInstanced()** function is defined as:

void **glDrawElementsInstanced**(GLenum *mode*, GLsizei *count*,
                               GLenum *type*,
                               const void* *indices*,
                               GLsizei *primCount*);

Draws *primCount* instances of the geometric primitives specified by *mode*, *count* and *indices* as if specified by individual calls to **glDrawElements()**. As with **glDrawArraysInstanced()**, the built-in variable `gl_InstanceID` is incremented for each instance, and new values are presented to the vertex shader for each *instanced* vertex attribute.

Again, note that the parameters to **glDrawElementsInstanced()** are identical to **glDrawElements()**, with the addition of *primCount*. Each time one of the instanced functions is called, OpenGL essentially runs the whole command as many times as is specified by the *primCount* parameter. This on its own is not terribly useful. However, there are two mechanisms provided by OpenGL that allow vertex attributes to be specified as *instanced* and to provide the vertex shader with the index of the current instance.

---

void **glDrawElementsInstancedBaseVertex**(GLenum *mode*,
                                    GLsizei *count*,
                                    GLenum *type*,
                                    const void* *indices*,
                                    GLsizei *instanceCount*,
                                    GLuint *baseVertex*);

Draws *instanceCount* instances of the geometric primitives specified by *mode*, *count*, *indices*, and *baseVertex* as if specified by individual calls to **glDrawElementsBaseVertex()**. As with **glDrawArraysInstanced()**, the built-in variable `gl_InstanceID` is incremented for each instance, and new values are presented to the vertex shader for each *instanced* vertex attribute.

Instanced Vertex Attributes

Instanced vertex attributes behave similarly to regular vertex attributes. They are declared and used in exactly the same way inside the vertex shader. On the application side, they are also configured in the same way as regular vertex attributes. That is, they are backed by buffer objects, can be queried with **glGetAttribLocation()**, set up using **glVertexAttribPointer()**, and enabled and disabled using **glEnableVertexAttribArray()** and **glDisableVertexAttribArray()**. The important new function that allows a vertex attribute to become instanced is as follows:

---

void **glVertexAttribDivisor**(GLuint *index*, GLuint *divisor*);

Specifies the rate at which new values of the instanced the vertex attribute at *index* are presented to the vertex shader during instanced rendering. A *divisor* value of 0 turns off instancing for the specified attribute, whereas any other value of *divisor* indicates that a new value should be presented to the vertex shader each *divisor* instances.

The **glVertexAttribDivisor()** function controls the *rate* at which the vertex attribute is updated. *index* is the index of the vertex attribute whose divisor is to be set, and is the same as you would pass into **glVertexAttribPointer()** or **glEnableVertexAttribArray()**. By default, a new value of each enabled attribute is delivered to each vertex. Setting *divisor* to zero resets the attribute to this behavior and makes it a regular, noninstanced attribute. A nonzero value of *divisor* makes the attribute instanced and causes a new value to be fetched from the attribute array once every *divisor* instances rather than for every vertex. The index within the enabled vertex attribute array from which the attribute is taken is then $\frac{instance}{divisor}$, where *instance* is the current instance number and *divisor* is the value of *divisor* for the current attribute. For each of the instanced vertex attributes, the same value is delivered to the vertex shader for all vertices in the instance. If *divisor* is two, the value of the attribute is updated every second instance; if it is three then the attribute is updated every third instance, and so on. Consider the vertex attributes declared in Example 3.9, some of which will be configured as instanced.

Example 3.9   Vertex Shader Attributes for the Instancing Example

```
#version 410 core

// "position" and "normal" are regular vertex attributes
layout (location = 0) in vec4 position;
layout (location = 1) in vec3 normal;

// Color is a per-instance attribute
layout (location = 2) in vec4 color;

// model_matrix will be used as a per-instance transformation
// matrix. Note that a mat4 consumes 4 consecutive locations, so
// this will actually sit in locations, 3, 4, 5, and 6.
layout (location = 3) in mat4 model_matrix;
```

Note that in Example 3.9, there is nothing special about the declaration of the instanced vertex attributes `color` and `model_matrix`. Now consider the code shown in Example 3.10, which configures a subset of vertex attributes declared in Example 3.9 as instanced.

Example 3.10   Example Setup for Instanced Vertex Attributes

```
// Get the locations of the vertex attributes in "prog", which is
// the (linked) program object that we're going to be rendering
// with. Note that this isn't really necessary because we specified
// locations for all the attributes in our vertex shader. This code
// could be made more concise by assuming the vertex attributes are
// where we asked the compiler to put them.
int position_loc   = glGetAttribLocation(prog, "position");
int normal_loc     = glGetAttribLocation(prog, "normal");
int color_loc      = glGetAttribLocation(prog, "color");
```

```
int matrix_loc        = glGetAttribLocation(prog, "model_matrix");

// Configure the regular vertex attribute arrays -
// position and normal.
glBindBuffer(GL_ARRAY_BUFFER, position_buffer);
glVertexAttribPointer(position_loc, 4, GL_FLOAT, GL_FALSE, 0, NULL);
glEnableVertexAttribArray(position_loc);
glBindBuffer(GL_ARRAY_BUFFER, normal_buffer);
glVertexAttribPointer(normal_loc, 3, GL_FLOAT, GL_FALSE, 0, NULL);
glEnableVertexAttribArray(normal_loc);

// Now we set up the color array. We want each instance of our
// geometry to assume a different color, so we'll just pack colors
// into a buffer object and make an instanced vertex attribute out
// of it.
glBindBuffer(GL_ARRAY_BUFFER, color_buffer);
glVertexAttribPointer(color_loc, 4, GL_FLOAT, GL_FALSE, 0, NULL);
glEnableVertexAttribArray(color_loc);
// This is the important bit... set the divisor for the color array
// to 1 to get OpenGL to give us a new value of "color" per-instance
// rather than per-vertex.
glVertexAttribDivisor(color_loc, 1);

// Likewise, we can do the same with the model matrix. Note that a
// matrix input to the vertex shader consumes N consecutive input
// locations, where N is the number of columns in the matrix. So...
// we have four vertex attributes to set up.
glBindBuffer(GL_ARRAY_BUFFER, model_matrix_buffer);
// Loop over each column of the matrix...
for (int i = 0; i < 4; i++)
{
    // Set up the vertex attribute
    glVertexAttribPointer(matrix_loc + i,              // Location
                          4, GL_FLOAT, GL_FALSE,       // vec4
                          sizeof(mat4),                // Stride
                          (void *)(sizeof(vec4) * i)); // Start offset
    // Enable it
    glEnableVertexAttribArray(matrix_loc + i);
    // Make it instanced
    glVertexAttribDivisor(matrix_loc + i, 1);
}
```

In Example 3.10, `position` and `normal` are regular, noninstanced vertex attributes. However, `color` is configured as an instanced vertex attribute with a divisor of one. This means that each instance will have a new value for the `color` attribute (which will be constant across all vertices in the instance). Further, the `model_matrix` attribute will also be made instanced to provide a new model transformation matrix for each instance. A `mat4` attribute is consuming a consecutive location. Therefore, we loop over each column in the matrix and configure it separately. The remainder of the vertex shader is shown in Example 3.11.

Example 3.11   Instanced Attributes Example Vertex Shader

```
// The view matrix and the projection matrix are constant
// across a draw
uniform mat4 view_matrix;
uniform mat4 projection_matrix;

// The output of the vertex shader (matched to the
// fragment shader)
out VERTEX
{
    vec3    normal;
    vec4    color;
} vertex;

// Ok, go!
void main(void)
{
    // Construct a model-view matrix from the uniform view matrix
    // and the per-instance model matrix.
    mat4 model_view_matrix = view_matrix * model_matrix;

    // Transform position by the model-view matrix, then by the
    // projection matrix.
    gl_Position = projection_matrix * (model_view_matrix *
                                       position);
    // Transform the normal by the upper-left-3x3-submatrix of the
    // model-view matrix
    vertex.normal = mat3(model_view_matrix) * normal;
    // Pass the per-instance color through to the fragment shader.
    vertex.color = color;
}
```

The code to set the model matrices for the instances and then draw the instanced geometry using these shaders is shown in Example 3.12. Each instance has its own model matrix, whereas the view matrix (consisting of a rotation around the y axis followed by a translation in z) is common to all instances. The model matrices are written directly into the buffer by mapping it using **glMapBuffer()**. Each model matrix translates the object away from the origin and then rotates the translated model around the origin. The view and projection matrices are simply placed in uniform variables. Then, a single call to **glDrawArraysInstanced()** is used to draw all instances of the model.

Example 3.12   Instancing Example Drawing Code

```
// Map the buffer
mat4 * matrices = (mat4 *)glMapBuffer(GL_ARRAY_BUFFER,
                                      GL_WRITE_ONLY);

// Set model matrices for each instance
```

```
for (n = 0; n < INSTANCE_COUNT; n++)
{
    float a = 50.0f * float(n) / 4.0f;
    float b = 50.0f * float(n) / 5.0f;
    float c = 50.0f * float(n) / 6.0f;

    matrices[n] = rotation(a + t * 360.0f, 1.0f, 0.0f, 0.0f) *
                  rotation(b + t * 360.0f, 0.0f, 1.0f, 0.0f) *
                  rotation(c + t * 360.0f, 0.0f, 0.0f, 1.0f) *
                  translation(10.0f + a, 40.0f + b, 50.0f + c);
}

// Done. Unmap the buffer.
glUnmapBuffer(GL_ARRAY_BUFFER);

// Activate instancing program
glUseProgram(render_prog);

// Set up the view and projection matrices
mat4 view_matrix(translation(0.0f, 0.0f, -1500.0f) *
                 rotation(t * 360.0f * 2.0f, 0.0f, 1.0f, 0.0f));
mat4 projection_matrix(frustum(-1.0f, 1.0f,
                              -aspect, aspect, 1.0f, 5000.0f));

glUniformMatrix4fv(view_matrix_loc, 1,
                   GL_FALSE, view_matrix);
glUniformMatrix4fv(projection_matrix_loc, 1,
                   GL_FALSE, projection_matrix);

// Render INSTANCE_COUNT objects
glDrawArraysInstanced(GL_TRIANGLES, 0, object_size, INSTANCE_COUNT);
```

The result of the program is shown in Figure 3.8. In this example, the constant INSTANCE_COUNT (which is referenced in the code of Examples 3.10 and 3.12) is 100. One hundred copies of the model are drawn, each with a different position and a different color. These models could very easily be trees in a forest, space ships in a fleet, or buildings in a city.

Figure 3.8   Result of rendering with instanced vertex attributes

There are some inefficiencies in the example shown in Examples 3.9 through 3.12. Work that will produce the same result across all of the vertices in an instance will still be performed per-vertex. Sometimes there are ways to get around this. For example, the computation of `model_view_matrix` will evaluate to the same matrix for all vertices within a single instance. Here, we could avoid this work by using a second instanced `mat4` attribute to carry the per-instance model-view matrix. In other cases, it may not be possible to avoid this work, but it may be possible to move it into a geometry shader so that work is performed once per-primitive rather than once per-vertex, or perhaps use geometry shader instancing instead. Both of these techniques will be explained in Chapter 10.

Note: Remember that calling an instanced drawing command is mostly equivalent to calling its noninstanced counterpart many times before executing any other OpenGL commands. Therefore, converting a sequence of OpenGL functions called inside a loop to a sequence of instanced draw calls will not produce identical results.

Another example of a way to use instanced vertex attributes is to pack a set of textures into a 2D array texture and then pass the array slice to be used for each instance in an instanced vertex attribute. The vertex shader can then pass the instance's slice into the fragment shader, which can then render each instance of the geometry with a different texture.

It is possible to internally add an offset to the indices used to fetch instanced vertex attributes from vertex buffers. Similar to the *baseVertex* parameter that is available through **glDrawElementsBaseVertex()**, the instance offset is exposed through an additional *baseInstance* parameter in some versions of the instanced drawing functions. The functions that take a *baseInstance* parameter are **glDrawArraysInstancedBaseInstance()**, **glDrawElementsInstancedBaseInstance()**, and **glDrawElementsInstancedBaseVertexBaseInstance()**. Their prototypes are as follows:

---

void **glDrawArraysInstancedBaseInstance**(GLenum *mode,*
                                    GLint *first,*
                                    GLsizei *count,*
                                    GLsizei *instanceCount,*
                                    GLuint *baseInstance*);

Draws *primCount* instances of the geometric primitives specified by *mode,* *first,* and *count* as if specified by individual calls to **glDrawArrays()**. The built-in variable `gl_InstanceID` is incremented for each instance, and new values are presented to the vertex shader for each *instanced* vertex attribute. Furthermore, the implied index used to fetch any instanced vertex attributes is offset by the value of *baseInstance* by OpenGL.

---

void **glDrawElementsInstancedBaseInstance**(GLenum *mode,*
                                      GLsizei *count,*
                                      GLenum *type,*
                                      const GLvoid * *indices,*
                                      GLsizei *instanceCount,*
                                      GLuint *baseInstance*);

Draws *primCount* instances of the geometric primitives specified by *mode,* *count,* and *indices* as if specified by individual calls to **glDrawElements()**. As with **glDrawArraysInstanced()**, the built-in variable `gl_InstanceID` is incremented for each instance, and new values are presented to the vertex shader for each *instanced* vertex attribute. Furthermore, the implied index used to fetch any instanced vertex attributes is offset by the value of *baseInstance* by OpenGL.

```
void glDrawElementsInstancedBaseVertexBaseInstance(GLenum mode,
                                                    GLsizei count,
                                                    GLenum type,
                                                    const GLvoid * indices,
                                                    GLsizei instanceCount,
                                                    GLuint baseVertex,
                                                    GLuint baseInstance);
```

Draws *instanceCount* instances of the geometric primitives specified by
mode, count, indices, and *baseVertex* as if specified by individual calls to
glDrawElementsBaseVertex(). As with **glDrawArraysInstanced()**, the built-in
variable gl_InstanceID is incremented for each instance, and new values are
presented to the vertex shader for each *instanced* vertex attribute. Furthermore,
the implied index used to fetch any instanced vertex attributes is offset by the
value of *baseInstance* by OpenGL.

Using the Instance Counter in Shaders

In addition to instanced vertex attributes, the index of the current instance
is available to the vertex shader in the built-in variable gl_InstanceID.
This variable is implicitly declared as an integer. It starts counting from
zero and counts up one each time an instance is rendered.
gl_InstanceID is always present in the vertex shader, even when the
current drawing command is not one of the instanced ones. In those cases,
it will just be zero. The value in gl_InstanceID may be used to index
into uniform arrays, perform texture lookups, as the input to an analytic
function, or for any other purpose.

In the following example, the functionality of Examples 3.9 through 3.12
is replicated by using gl_InstanceID to index into texture buffer objects
(TBOs) rather than through the use of instanced vertex attributes. Here,
the vertex attributes of Example 3.9 are replaced with TBO lookups, and so
are removed from the vertex attribute setup code. Instead, a first TBO
containing color of each instance, and a second TBO containing the model
matrices are created. The vertex attribute declaration and setup code are
the same as in Examples 3.9 and 3.10 (with the omission of the color and
model_matrix attributes, of course). As the instance's color and model
matrix is now explicitly fetched in the vertex shader, more code is added to
the body of the vertex shader, which is shown in Example 3.13.

Example 3.13   gl_VertexID Example Vertex Shader

```
// The view matrix and the projection matrix are constant across a draw
uniform mat4 view_matrix;
uniform mat4 projection_matrix;
```

```
// These are the TBOs that hold per-instance colors and per-instance
// model matrices
uniform samplerBuffer color_tbo;
uniform samplerBuffer model_matrix_tbo;

// The output of the vertex shader (matched to the fragment shader)
out VERTEX
{
    vec3     normal;
    vec4     color;
} vertex;

// Ok, go!
void main(void)
{
    // Use gl_InstanceID to obtain the instance color from the color TBO
    vec4 color = texelFetch(color_tbo, gl_InstanceID);

    // Generating the model matrix is more complex because you can't
    // store mat4 data in a TBO. Instead, we need to store each
    // matrix as four vec4 variables and assemble the matrix in the
    // shader. First, fetch the four columns of the matrix
    // (remember, matrices are stored in memory in column-major
    // order).
    vec4 col1 = texelFetch(model_matrix_tbo, gl_InstanceID * 4);
    vec4 col2 = texelFetch(model_matrix_tbo, gl_InstanceID * 4 + 1);
    vec4 col3 = texelFetch(model_matrix_tbo, gl_InstanceID * 4 + 2);
    vec4 col4 = texelFetch(model_matrix_tbo, gl_InstanceID * 4 + 3);

    // Now assemble the four columns into a matrix.
    mat4 model_matrix = mat4(col1, col2, col3, col4);

    // Construct a model-view matrix from the uniform view matrix
    // and the per-instance model matrix.
    mat4 model_view_matrix = view_matrix * model_matrix;

    // Transform position by the model-view matrix, then by the
    // projection matrix.
    gl_Position = projection_matrix * (model_view_matrix *
                                       position);
    // Transform the normal by the upper-left-3x3-submatrix of the
    // model-view matrix
    vertex.normal = mat3(model_view_matrix) * normal;
    // Pass the per-instance color through to the fragment shader.
    vertex.color = color;
}
```

To drive the shader of Example 3.13, we need to create and initialize TBOs
to back the color_tbo and model_matrix_tbo samplers rather than
initializing the instanced vertex attributes. However, aside from the
differences in setup code, the program is essentially unchanged.

Example 3.14 contains the code to set up the TBOs for use with the shader of Example 3.13.

Example 3.14 Example Setup for Instanced Vertex Attributes

```
// Get the locations of the vertex attributes in "prog", which is
// the (linked) program object that we're going to be rendering
// with. Note that this isn't really necessary because we specified
// locations for all the attributes in our vertex shader. This code
// could be made more concise by assuming the vertex attributes are
// where we asked the compiler to put them.
int position_loc    = glGetAttribLocation(prog, "position");
int normal_loc      = glGetAttribLocation(prog, "normal");

// Configure the regular vertex attribute arrays - position and normal.
glBindBuffer(GL_ARRAY_BUFFER, position_buffer);
glVertexAttribPointer(position_loc, 4, GL_FLOAT, GL_FALSE, 0, NULL);
glEnableVertexAttribArray(position_loc);
glBindBuffer(GL_ARRAY_BUFFER, normal_buffer);
glVertexAttribPointer(normal_loc, 3, GL_FLOAT, GL_FALSE, 0, NULL);
glEnableVertexAttribArray(normal_loc);

// Now set up the TBOs for the instance colors and model matrices...

// First, create the TBO to store colors, bind a buffer to it and
// initialize its format. The buffer has previously been created
// and sized to store one vec4 per-instance.
glGenTextures(1, &color_tbo);
glBindTexture(GL_TEXTURE_BUFFER, color_tbo);
glTexBuffer(GL_TEXTURE_BUFFER, GL_RGBA32F, color_buffer);

// Now do the same thing with a TBO for the model matrices. The
// buffer object (model_matrix_buffer) has been created and sized
// to store one mat4 per-instance.
glGenTextures(1, &model_matrix_tbo);
glActiveTexture(GL_TEXTURE1);
glBindTexture(GL_TEXTURE_BUFFER, model_matrix_tbo);
glTexBuffer(GL_TEXTURE_BUFFER, GL_RGBA32F, model_matrix_buffer);
```

Note that the code in Example 3.14 is actually shorter and simpler than that in Example 3.10. This is because we have shifted the responsibility for fetching per-instance data from built-in OpenGL functionality to the shader writer. This can be seen in the increased complexity of Example 3.13 relative to Example 3.11. With this responsibility comes additional power and flexibility. For example, if the number of instances is small, it may be preferable to use a uniform array rather than a TBO for data storage, which may increase performance. Regardless, there are very few other changes that need to be made to the original example to move to using explicit fetches driven by gl_InstanceID. In fact, the rendering code of Example 3.12 is used intact to produce an identical result to the original program. The proof is in the screenshot (Figure 3.9).

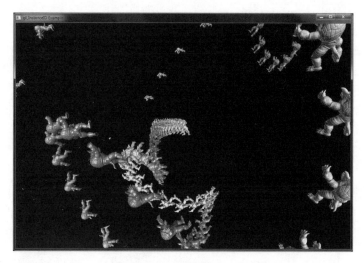

Figure 3.9   Result of instanced rendering using `gl_InstanceID`

Instancing Redux

To use a instancing in your program

- Create some vertex shader inputs that you intend to be instanced.

- Set the vertex attribute divisors with **glVertexAttribDivisor()**.

- Use the `gl_InstanceID` built-in variable in the vertex shader.

- Use the instanced versions of the rendering functions such as **glDrawArraysInstanced()glDrawElementsInstanced()**, or **glDrawElementsInstancedBaseVertex()**.

Chapter 4

Color, Pixels, and Framebuffers

Chapter Objectives

After reading this chapter, you'll be able to do the following:

- Understand how OpenGL processes and represents the colors in your generated images.

- Identify the types of buffers available in OpenGL, and be able to clear and control writing to them.

- List the various tests and operations on fragments that occur after fragment shading.

- Use alpha blending to render translucent objects realistically.

- Use multisampling and antialiasing to remove aliasing artifacts.

- Employ occlusion queries and conditional rendering to optimize rendering.

- Create and use framebuffer objects for advanced techniques, and to minimizing copying of data between buffers.

- Retrieve rendered images, and copy pixels from one place to another, or one framebuffer to another.

The goal of computer graphics, generally speaking, is to determine the colors that make up an image. For OpenGL, that image is usually shown in a window on a computer screen, which itself is made up of a rectangular array of pixels, each of which can display its own color. This chapter further develops how you can use shaders in OpenGL to generate the colors of the pixels in the framebuffer. We discuss how colors set in an application directly contribute to a fragment's color, the processing that occurs after the completion of the fragment shader, and other techniques used for improving the generated image. This chapter contains the following major sections:

- "Basic Color Theory", which briefly describes the physics of light, and how colors are represented in OpenGL.

- "Buffers and Their Uses" presents different kinds of buffers, how to clear them, when to use them, and how OpenGL operates on them.

- "Color and OpenGL" explains how OpenGL processes color in its pipeline.

- "Multisampling" introduces one of OpenGL's antialiasing techniques, and describes how it modfies rasterization.

- "Testing and Operating on Fragments" describes the tests and additional operations that can be applied to individual fragments after the fragment shader has completed, including alpha blending.

- "Per-Primitive Antialiasing" presents how blending can be used to smooth the appearance of individual primitives.

- "Framebuffer Objects" explains how to create and render to your own framebuffers.

- "Writing to Multiple Renderbuffers Simultaneously" describes rendering to multiple buffers simultaneously.

- "Reading and Copying Pixel Data" explains how OpenGL represents pixel data and the operations you can use to process is.

- "Copying Pixel Rectangles" discusses how to copy a block of pixels from one section of the framebuffer to another in OpenGL.

Basic Color Theory

In the physical world, light is composed of photons—in simplest terms, tiny particles traveling along a straight path[1] each with their own "color",

---

1. Ignoring gravitational effects, of course.

which in terms of physical quantities, is represented by their wavelength (or frequency).[2] Photons that we can see have wavelengths in the visible spectrum, which ranges from about 390 nanometers (the color violet) to 720 nanometers (the color red). The colors in between form the dominant colors of the rainbow: violet, indigo, blue, green, yellow, orange, and red.

Your eye is capable of seeing many more colors than the seven that compose the colors of the rainbow. In fact, what we really see is a mixture of photons of different wavelengths that combine to form a unique color. For example, ideal white light is composed of a equal quantities of photons at all visible wavelengths. By comparison, laser light is monochromatic, with all the photons having an identical frequency.

So what does this have to do with computer graphics and OpenGL, you may ask? Modern display devices have a much more restricted range of colors they can display—only a small portion of the entire visible spectrum. In fact, the set of colors a device can display is often represented as its *gamut*. Most display devices you'll work with while using OpenGL create their colors using a combination of three primary colors—red, green, and blue—which form the spectrum of colors that the device can display. We'll call that the RGB color space, and use a set of three values for each color. In OpenGL, we'll often pack those three components with a fourth component alpha (which we discuss later in "Blending"), which we'll predictably call the *RGBA* color space. In addition to RGB, OpenGL also supports the *sRGB color space*. We'll encounter more about sRGB when we discuss framebuffer objects and texture maps.

Note: There are many color spaces, like HSV (Hue-Saturation-Value), or CMYK (Cyan-Magenta-Yellow-Black) . If your data is in a color space different than RGB, you'll need to convert it from that space into RGB (or sRGB) to process it with OpenGL.

Unlike light in the physical world, where frequencies and intensities range continuously, computer framebuffers can only represent a comparatively small number of discrete values (although usually numbering in the millions of colors). This quantization of intensities limits the number of colors we can display. Normally, each component's intensity is stored using a certain number of bits (usually called its *bit depth*), and the sum of each component's bit depth (excluding alpha) determines the color buffer's depth, which also determines the total number of display colors.

---

2. A photon's frequency and wavelength are related by the equation $c = \nu\lambda$, where c is the speed of light (3×10^8 meters/second), ν is the photon's frequency, and λ its wavelength. And for those who want to debate the wave-particle duality of light, we're always open to that discussion over a beer.

For example, a common format for the color buffer is eight bits for each red, green, and blue. This yields a 24-bit deep color buffer, which is capable of displaying 2^{24} unique colors. "Data in OpenGL Buffers" in Chapter 3 expanded on the types of buffers that OpenGL makes available and describes how to control interactions with those buffers.

Buffers and Their Uses

An important goal of almost every graphics program is to draw pictures on the screen (or into an off-screen buffer). The framebuffer (which is most often the screen) is composed of a rectangular array of pixels, each capable of displaying a tiny square of color at that point in the image. After the rasterization stage, which is where the fragment shader was executed, the data are not pixels yet—just fragments. Each fragment has coordinate data that corresponds to a pixel, as well as color and depth values.

As shown in Figure 4.1, the lower-left pixel in an OpenGL window is pixel $(0,0)$, corresponding to the window coordinates of the lower-left corner of the 1×1 region occupied by this pixel. In general, pixel (x, y) fills the region bounded by x on the left, $x + 1$ on the right, y on the bottom, and $y + 1$ on the top.

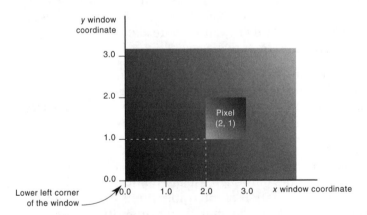

Figure 4.1   Region occupied by a pixel

As an example of a buffer, let's look more closely at the color buffer, which holds the color information that's to be displayed on the screen. Let's say that the screen is 1920 pixels wide and 1080 pixels high and that it's a full 24-bit color screen—in other words, that there are 2^{24} (or 16,777,216) different colors that can be displayed. Since 24 bits translate to 3 bytes (8 bits per byte), the color buffer in this example has to store at least 3 bytes of data for each of the 2,073,600 (1920 × 1080) pixels on the screen. A particular hardware system might have more or fewer pixels on the physical screen, as well as more or less color data per pixel. Any particular color buffer, however, has the same amount of data for each pixel on the screen.

The color buffer is only one of several buffers that hold information about a pixel. In fact, a pixel may have many color buffers associated with it, which are called *renderbuffers*, which we'll discuss more in "Framebuffer Objects" on Page 180. The framebuffer on a system comprises all of these buffers, and you can use multiple framebuffers within your application. With the exception of the primary color buffer, you don't view these other buffers directly; instead, you use them to perform such tasks as *hidden-surface removal*, stenciling, dynamic texture generation, and other operations.

Within an OpenGL system the following types of buffers are available:

- Color buffers, of which there might be one or several active

- Depth buffer

- Stencil buffer

All of those buffers collectively form the framebuffer, although it's up to you to decide which of those buffers you need to use. When your application starts, you're using the *default framebuffer*, which is the one related to the windows of your application. The default framebuffer will always contain a double-buffered, color buffer. You can create additional *framebuffer object*s for doing off-screen rendering.

Your particular OpenGL implementation determines which buffers are available and how many bits per pixel each buffer holds. Additionally, you can have multiple visuals, or window types, that also may have different buffers available. As we describe each of the types of buffers, we'll also cover ways you can query their capabilities, in terms of data storage and precision.

We now briefly describe the type of data that each buffer type stores, and then move to discussing operations that you do with each type of buffer.

Color Buffers

The color buffers are the ones to which you usually draw. They contain the RGB or sRGB color data, and may also contain alpha values for each pixel in the framebuffer. There may be multiple color buffers in a framebuffer. The "main" color buffer of the default framebuffer is special because it's the one associated with your window on the screen and where you will draw to have your image shown on the screen (assuming you want to display an image there)—all other color buffers are off screen.

The pixels in a color buffer may store a single color per pixel, or may logically divide the pixel into *subpixels*, which enables an antialiasing technique called *multisampling*. We discuss multisampling in detail in "Multisampling" on Page 153.

You've already used *double buffering* for animation. Double buffering is done by making the main color buffer have two parts: a front buffer that's displayed in your window; and a back buffer, which is where you render the new image. When you swap the buffers (by calling **glutSwapBuffers()**, for example), the front and back buffers are exchanged. Only the main color buffer of the default framebuffer is double buffered.

Additionally, an OpenGL implementation might support stereoscopic viewing, in which case the color buffer (even if it's double buffered) will have left and right color buffers for the respective *stereo* images.

Depth Buffer

The *depth buffer* stores a depth value for each pixel, and is used for determining the visibility of objects in a three-dimensional scene. Depth is measured in terms of distance to the eye, so pixels with larger depth-buffer values are overwritten by pixels with smaller values. This is just a useful convention, however, and the depth buffer's behavior can be modified as described in "Depth Test" on Page 163. The depth buffer is sometimes called the *z-buffer* (the *z* comes from the fact that *x*- and *y*-values measure horizontal and vertical displacement on the screen, and the *z*-value measures distance perpendicular to the screen).

Stencil Buffer

Finally, the *stencil buffer* is used to restrict drawing to certain portions of the screen. Think of it like a cardboard stencil that can be used with a can of spray paint to make fairly precise painted images. For example, a classic use is to simulate the view of a rear-view mirror in a car. You render the shape of the mirror to the stencil buffer, and then draw the entire scene. The stencil buffer prevents anything that wouldn't be visible in the mirror from being drawn. We discuss the stencil buffer in "Stencil Buffer" on Page 146.

Clearing Buffers

Probably the most common graphics activity after rendering is clearing buffers. You will probably do it once per frame (at least), and as such, OpenGL tries to optimize that operation by clearing all of the active buffers at the same time. As you've seen in our examples, we set the value that each type of buffer should be initialized to in **init()** (if we don't use the default values), and then clear all the buffers we need.

The following commands set the clearing values for each buffer:

---

void **glClearColor**(GLclampf *red*, GLclampf *green*,
                 GLclampf *blue*, GLclampf *alpha*);
void **glClearDepth**(GLclampd *depth*);
void **glClearDepthf**(GLclampf *depth*);
void **glClearStencil**(GLint *s*);

Specifies the current clearing values for the active color buffers, the depth buffer, and the stencil buffer. The GLclampf and GLclampd types (clamped GLfloat and clamped GLdouble) are clamped to be between 0.0 and 1.0. The default depth-clearing value is 1.0; all the other default clearing values are 0. The values set with the clear commands remain in effect until they're changed by another call to the same command.

After you've selected your clearing values and you're ready to clear the buffers, use **glClear()**.

---

void **glClear**(GLbitfield *mask*);

Clears the specified buffers. The value of mask is the bitwise logical OR of some combination of GL_COLOR_BUFFER_BIT, GL_DEPTH_BUFFER_BIT, and GL_STENCIL_BUFFER_BIT to identify which buffers are to be cleared. GL_COLOR_BUFFER_BIT clears the RGBA color buffer, and all the color buffers that are enabled for writing (see "Selecting Color Buffers for Writing and Reading" on Page 195). The pixel ownership test, scissor test, and dithering, if enabled, are applied to the clearing operation, as are masking operations as specified by **glColorMask()**. The depth and stencil tests, however, do not affect the operation of **glClear()**.

Masking Buffers

Before OpenGL writes data into the enabled color, depth, or stencil buffers, a masking operation is applied to the data, as specified with one of the following commands:

```
void glColorMask(GLboolean red, GLboolean green,
                 GLboolean blue, GLboolean alpha);
void glColorMaski(GLuint buffer, GLboolean red,
                  GLboolean green, GLboolean blue,
                  GLboolean alpha);
void glDepthMask(GLboolean flag);
void glStencilMask(GLboolean mask);
void glStencilMaskSeparate(GLenum face, GLuint mask);
```

Sets the masks used to control writing into the indicated buffers.

If *flag* is GL_TRUE for **glDepthMask()**, the depth buffer is enabled for writing; otherwise, it's disabled. The *mask* for **glStencilMask()** is used for stencil data with a one in a bit in the mask indicating that writing to bit in a pixel's stencil value is enabled; a zero indicated that writing is disabled.

The default values of all the GLboolean masks are GL_TRUE, and the default values for the GLuint masks are all ones.

glStencilMaskSeparate() provides different stencil mask values for front- and back-facing polygons.

glColorMaski() allows setting of the color mask for an individual buffer specified by *buffer* when rendering to multiple color buffers.

Note: The mask specified by **glStencilMask()** controls which stencil bitplanes are written. This mask isn't related to the *mask* that's specified as the third parameter of **glStencilFunc()**, which specifies which bitplanes are considered by the stencil function.

Color and OpenGL

How do we use color in OpenGL? As you've seen, it's the job of the fragment shader to assign a fragment's color. There are many ways this can be done.

- The fragment shader can generate the fragment's color without using any "external" data (i.e., data passed into the fragment shader). A very limited example of this was done in our shaders from Chapter 1 where we assigned a constant color to each fragment.

- Additional color data could be provided with each input vertex, potentially modified by another shading stage (e.g., vertex shading), and passed to the fragment shader, which uses that data to determine a color. We'll demonstrate that in "Vertex Colors" on Page 150 in this chapter.

- Supplemental data—but not specifically colors—could be provided to the fragment shader and used in a computation that generates a color (we'll use this technique in Chapter 7, "Light and Shadow").

- External data, like a digital image, can be referenced in a fragment shader, which can look up colors (or other data values as well). Such data are stored in a texture map, yielding a technique called texture mapping, which we describe in Chapter 6, "Textures".

Color Representation and OpenGL

Before we analyze those techniques in depth, let's discuss how OpenGL internally works with colors. We know that the framebuffer requires red, green, and blue values to specify a color for a pixel, so hopefully it's clear that we'll need to provide enough information to the fragment shader to generate those values.

In the most common cases, OpenGL internally represents a color component as a floating-point value and maintains its precision until that value is stored in the framebuffer. Put another way, unless you specify otherwise, a fragment shader will receive its inputs as floating-point values, which it assigns to its fragment's color, and those values are expected to be in the range [0.0, 1.0]—what we'll called a *normalized value*.[3] That color, as it's written into the framebuffer, will be mapped into the range of values the framebuffer can support. For instance, if the framebuffer once again has eight bits for each of red, green, and blue, the possible range for any color component is [0, 255].

Your application can provide data into OpenGL in almost any basic "C" data type (e.g., `int`, or `float`). You have the choice of requesting OpenGL automatically convert nonfloating-point values into normalized floating-point values. You do this with the **glVertexAttribPointer()** or **glVertexAttribN*()** routines, where OpenGL will convert the values from the input data type into the suitable normalized-value range (depending on whether the input data type was signed or unsigned). Table 4.1 describes how those data values are converted.

---

3. Signed normalized values are clamped to the range [−1.0, 1.0].

Table 4.1   Converting Data Values to Normalized Floating-Point Values

OpenGL Type	OpenGL Enum	Minimum Value	Min Value Maps to	Maximum Value	Max Value Maps to
GLbyte	GL_BYTE	−128	−1.0	127	1.0
GLshort	GL_SHORT	−32,768	−1.0	32,767	1.0
GLint	GL_INT	−2,147,483,648	−1.0	2,147,483,647	1.0
GLubyte	GL_UNSIGNED_BYTE	0	0.0	255	1.0
GLushort	GL_UNSIGNED_SHORT	0	0.0	65,535	1.0
GLint	GL_UNSIGNED_INT	0	0.0	4,294,967,295	1.0
GLfixed	GL_FIXED	−32,767	−1.0	32,767	1.0

Vertex Colors

Let's take a closer look at specifying color data with a vertex. Recall from Chapter 1 that vertices can have multiple data values associated with them, and colors can be among them. As with any other vertex data, the color data must be stored in a vertex-buffer object. In Example 4.1, we interleave the vertices' color and position data, and use an integer-valued type to illustrate having OpenGL normalize our values.

Example 4.1   Specifying Vertex Color and Position Data: gouraud.cpp

```
//////////////////////////////////////////////////////////////////////
//
// Gouraud.cpp
//
//////////////////////////////////////////////////////////////////////

#include <iostream>
using namespace std;

#include "vgl.h"
#include "LoadShaders.h"

enum VAO_IDs { Triangles, NumVAOs };
enum Buffer_IDs { ArrayBuffer, NumBuffers };
enum Attrib_IDs { vPosition = 0, vColor = 1 };

GLuint VAOs[NumVAOs];
GLuint Buffers[NumBuffers];

const GLuint  NumVertices = 6;

//--------------------------------------------------------------------
//
```

```
// init
//

void
init(void)
{
    glGenVertexArrays(NumVAOs, VAOs);
    glBindVertexArray(VAOs[Triangles]);

    struct VertexData {
        GLubyte color[4];
        GLfloat position[4];
    };

    VertexData vertices[NumVertices] = {
        {{ 255,   0,   0, 255 }, { -0.90, -0.90 }},  // Triangle 1
        {{   0, 255,   0, 255 }, {  0.85, -0.90 }},
        {{   0,   0, 255, 255 }, { -0.90,  0.85 }},
        {{  10,  10,  10, 255 }, {  0.90, -0.85 }},  // Triangle 2
        {{ 100, 100, 100, 255 }, {  0.90,  0.90 }},
        {{ 255, 255, 255, 255 }, { -0.85,  0.90 }}
    };

    glGenBuffers(NumBuffers, Buffers);
    glBindBuffer(GL_ARRAY_BUFFER, Buffers[ArrayBuffer]);
    glBufferData(GL_ARRAY_BUFFER, sizeof(vertices),
                 vertices, GL_STATIC_DRAW);

    ShaderInfo shaders[] = {
        { GL_VERTEX_SHADER, "gouraud.vert" },
        { GL_FRAGMENT_SHADER, "gouraud.frag" },
        { GL_NONE, NULL }
    };

    GLuint program = LoadShaders(shaders);
    glUseProgram(program);

    glVertexAttribPointer(vColor, 4, GL_UNSIGNED_BYTE,
                          GL_TRUE, sizeof(VertexData),
                          BUFFER_OFFSET(0));
    glVertexAttribPointer(vPosition, 2, GL_FLOAT,
                          GL_FALSE, sizeof(VertexData),
                          BUFFER_OFFSET(sizeof(vertices[0].color)));

    glEnableVertexAttribArray(vColor);
    glEnableVertexAttribArray(vPosition);
}
```

Example 4.1 is only a slight modification of our example from Chapter 1, triangles.cpp. First, we created a simple structure VertexData that encapsulates all of the data for a single vertex: an RGBA color for the vertex, and its spatial position. Like before, we packed all the data into an array that we'll load into our vertex buffer object. As there are now two vertex attributes for our vertex data, we needed to add a second vertex attribute pointer to address the new vertex colors so we can work with that data in our shaders. For the vertex colors, we also ask OpenGL to normalize our colors by setting the fourth parameter to GL_TRUE.

To use our vertex colors, we need to modify our shaders to take the new data into account. First, let's look at the vertex shader:

Example 4.2   A Simple Vertex Shader for Gouraud Shading

```
#version 330 core

layout(location = 0) in vec4 vPosition;
layout(location = 1) in vec4 vColor;

out vec4 color;

void
main()
{
    color = vColor;
    gl_Position = vPosition;
}
```

Modifying our vertex shader in Example 4.2 to use the new vertex colors is straightforward. We added new input and output variables: vColor, and color to complete the plumbing for getting our vertex colors into and out of our vertex shader. In this case, we'll simply pass through our color data for use in the fragment shader.

Example 4.3   A Simple Fragment Shader for Gouraud Shading

```
#version 330 core

in vec4 color;

out vec4 fColor;

void
main()
{
    fColor = color;
}
```

The fragment shader in Example 4.3, looks pretty simple as well; just assigning the shader's input color to the fragment's output color. However, what's different is that the colors passed into the fragment shader don't come directly from the immediately preceding shader stage (i.e., the vertex shader), but from the *rasterizer*.

Rasterization

Within the OpenGL pipeline, between the vertex shading stages (vertex, tessellation, and geometry shading) and fragment shading, is the rasterizer. Its job is to determine which screen locations are covered by a particular piece of geometry (point, line, or triangle). Knowing those locations, along with the input vertex data, the rasterizer linearly interpolates the data values for each varying variable in the fragment shader and sends those values as inputs into your fragment shader. This process of linear *interpolation* when applied to color values has a special name in computer graphics: *Gouraud shading*.[4] Colors are not the only values that are interpolated across a geometric primitive. We'll see in Chapter 7, "Light and Shadow" that a quantity called the *surface normal* can also be interpolated, as are *texture coordinates* used with texture mapping (described in Chapter 6, "Textures").

Note: How an OpenGL implementation rasterizes and interpolates values is platform-dependent; you should not expect that different platforms will interpolate values identically.

While rasterization starts a fragment's life, and the computations done in the fragment shader are essential in computing the fragment's final color, it's by no means all the processing that can be applied to a fragment. In the next sections, we'll describe the tests and operations that are applied to each fragment in its travels to becoming a pixel in the framebuffer.

Multisampling

Multisampling is a technique for smoothing the edges of geometric primitives—commonly known as *antialiasing*. There are many ways to do antialiasing, and OpenGL supports different methods for supporting antialiasing. Other methods require some techniques we haven't discussed yet, so we'll defer that conversation until "Per-Primitive Antialiasing" on Page 178.

Multisampling works by sampling each geometric primitive multiple times per pixel. Instead of keeping a single color (and depth and stencil values, if present) for each pixel, multisampling uses multiple *samples*, which are like mini-pixels, to store color, depth, and stencil values at each sample location. When it comes time to present the final image, all of the samples

---

4. When all of the color values for a primitive's vertices are the same, each fragment will receive the same color value. This is called *flat shading*.

for the pixel are *resolved* to determine the final pixel's color. Aside from a little initialization work, and turning on the feature, multisampling requires very little modification to an application.

Your application begins by requesting a multisampled buffer (which is done when creating your window). You can determine if the request was successful (as not all implementations support multisampling) by querying GL_SAMPLE_BUFFERS using **glGetIntegerv**(). If the value is one, then multisampled rasterization can be used; if not, then single-sample rasterization just like normal will be used. To engage multisampling during rendering, call **glEnable**() with GL_MULTISAMPLE. Since multisampling takes additional time in rendering each primitive, you may not always want to multisample all of your scene's geometry.

Next, it's useful to know how many samples per pixel will be used when multisampling, which you can determine by calling **glGetIntegerv**() with GL_SAMPLES. This value is useful if you wish to know the sample locations within a pixel, which you can find using the **glGetMultisamplefv**() function.

---

void **glGetMultisamplefv**(GLenum *pname*, GLuint *index*,
                  GLfloat **val*);

With *pname* set to GL_SAMPLE_POSITION, **glGetMultisamplefv**() will return the location of sample *index* as a pair of floating-point values in *val*. The locations will be in the range [0, 1], representing the sample's offset from the pixel's lower-left corner.

A GL_INVALID_VALUE error is generated if *index* is greater than or equal to the number of samples supported (as returned by a call to **glGetIntegerv**() when passed GL_SAMPLES).

From within a fragment, you can get the same information by reading the value of gl_SamplePosition. Additionally, you can determine which sample your fragment shader is processing by using the gl_SampleID variable.

With multisampling only enabled, the fragment shader will be executed as normal, and the resulting color will be distributed to all samples for the pixels. That is, the color value will be the same, but each sample will receive individual depth and stencil values from the rasterizer. However, if your fragment shader uses either of the previously mentioned gl_Sample* variables, or modifies any of its shader input variables with the sample keyword, the fragment shader will be executed multiple times for that pixel, once for each active sample location.

Example 4.4 A Multisample-Aware Fragment Shader

```
#version 430 core

sample in vec4 color;

out vec4   fColor;

void main()
{
    fColor = color;
}
```

The simple addition of the `sample` keyword in Example 4.4 causes each instance of the *sample shader* (which is the terminology used when a fragment shader is executed per sample) to receive slightly different values based on the sample's location. Using these, particularly when sampling a texture map, will provide better results.

Sample Shading

If you can't modify a fragment shader to use the `sample` keyword (e.g., you're creating a library that accepts shaders created by another programmer), you can have OpenGL do sample shading by passing GL_SAMPLE_SHADING to **glEnable()**. This will cause unmodified fragment shader `in` variables to be interpolated to sample locations automatically.

In order to control the number of samples that receive unique sample-based interpolated values to be evaluated in a fragment shader, you can specify the minimum-sample-shading ratio with **glMinSampleShading()**.

---

void **glMinSampleShading**(GLfloat *value*);

Specifies the fraction of samples per pixels that should be individually shaded. *value* specifies the ratio of samples to be shaded over total samples, and is clamped to the range [0, 1], with 1.0 representing each sample receives a unique set of sample data.

You might ask why specify a fraction, as compared to an absolute number of samples? Various OpenGL implementations may have differing numbers of samples per pixel. Using a fraction-based approach reduces the need to test multiple sample configurations.

Additionally, multisampling using sample shading can add a lot more work in computing the color of a pixel. If your system has four samples per pixels, you've quadrupled the work per pixel in rasterizing primitives, which can potentially hinder your application's performance. **glMinSampleShading()** controls how many samples per pixel receive individually shaded values (i.e., each executing its own version of the bound fragment shader at the sample location). Reducing the minimum-sample-shading ratio can help improve performance in applications bound by the speed at which it can shade fragments.

We'll visit multisampling again in "Testing and Operating on Fragments" on Page 156, because a fragment's alpha value can be modified by the results of shading at sample locations.

Testing and Operating on Fragments

When you draw geometry on the screen, OpenGL starts processing it by executing the currently bound vertex shader; then the tessellation, and geometry shaders, if they're bound; and then assembles the final geometry into primitives that get sent to the rasterizer, which figures out which pixels in the window are affected. After OpenGL determines that an individual fragment should be generated, its fragment shader is executed, and then several processing stages, which control how and whether the fragment is drawn as a pixel into the framebuffer, remain. For example, if the fragment is outside a rectangular region or if it's farther from the *viewpoint* than the pixel that's already in the framebuffer, its processing is stopped, and it's not drawn. In another stage, the fragment's color is blended with the color of the pixel already in the framebuffer.

This section describes both the complete set of tests that a fragment must pass before it goes into the framebuffer and the possible final operations that can be performed on the fragment as it's written. Most of these tests and operations are enabled and disabled using **glEnable()** and **glDisable()**, respectively. The tests and operations occur in the following order—if a fragment is eliminated in an enabled earlier test, none of the later enabled tests or operations are executed:

1. Scissor test

2. Multisample fragment operations

3. Stencil test

4. Depth test

5. Blending

6. Dithering

7. Logical operations

All of these tests and operations are described in detail in the following subsections.

Note: As we'll see in "Framebuffer Objects" on Page 180, we can render into multiple buffers at the same time. For many of the fragment tests and operations, they can be controlled on a per-buffer basis, as well as for all of the buffers collectively. In many cases, we describe both the OpenGL function that will set the operation for all buffers, as well as the routine for affecting a single buffer. In most cases, the single buffer version of a function will have an 'i' appended to the function's name.

Scissor Test

The first additional test you can enable to control fragment visibility is the scissor test. The *scissor box* is a rectangular portion of your window and restricts all drawing to its region. You specify the scissor box using the **glScissor()** command, and enable the test by specifying GL_SCISSOR_TEST with **glEnable()**. If a fragment lies inside the rectangle, it passes the scissor test.

---

void **glScissor**(GLint *x*, GLint *y*, GLsizei *width*, GLsizei *height*);

Sets the location and size of the scissor rectangle (also known as the scissor box). The parameters define the lower left corner (x, y) and the *width* and *height* of the rectangle. Pixels that lie inside the rectangle pass the scissor test. *Scissoring* is enabled and disabled by passing GL_SCISSOR_TEST to **glEnable()** and **glDisable()**. By default, the rectangle matches the size of the window and scissoring is disabled.

All rendering—including clearing the window—is restricted to the scissor box if the test is enabled (as compared to the viewport, which doesn't limit screen clears). To determine whether scissoring is enabled and to obtain the values that define the scissor rectangle, you can use GL_SCISSOR_TEST with **glIsEnabled()** and GL_SCISSOR_BOX with **glGetIntegerv()**.

Multisample Fragment Operations

By default, multisampling calculates fragment coverage values that are independent of alpha. However, if you **glEnable()** one of the following special modes, then a fragment's alpha value is taken into consideration when calculating the coverage, assuming that multisampling itself is enabled and that there is a multisample buffer associated with the framebuffer. The special modes are as follows:

- GL_SAMPLE_ALPHA_TO_COVERAGE uses the alpha value of the fragment in an implementation-dependent manner to compute the final coverage value.

- GL_SAMPLE_ALPHA_TO_ONE sets the fragment's alpha value the maximum alpha value, and then uses that value in the coverage calculation.

- GL_SAMPLE_COVERAGE uses the value set with the **glSampleCoverage()** routine, which is combined (ANDed) with the calculated coverage value. Additionally, the generated sample mask can be inverted by setting the invert flag with the **glSampleCoverage()** routine.

---

void **glSampleCoverage**(GLfloat *value*, GLboolean *invert*);

Sets parameters to be used to interpret alpha values while computing multisampling coverage. *value* is a temporary coverage value that is used if GL_SAMPLE_COVERAGE or GL_SAMPLE_ALPHA_TO_COVERAGE has been enabled. *invert* is a Boolean that indicates whether the temporary coverage value ought to be bitwise inverted before it is used (ANDed) with the fragment coverage.

- GL_SAMPLE_MASK specifies an exact bit-representation for the coverage mask (as compared to it being generated by the OpenGL implementation). This mask is once again ANDed with the sample coverage for the fragment. The sample mask is specified using the **glSampleMaski()** function.

void **glSampleMaski**(GLuint *index*, GLbitfield *mask*);

Sets one 32-bit word of the sample mask, *mask*. The word to set is specified by *index* and the new value of that word is specified by *mask*. As samples are written to the framebuffer, only those whose corresponding bits in the current sample mask will be updated and the rest will be discarded.

The sample mask can also be specified in a fragment shader by writing to the `gl_SampleMask` variable. Details of using `gl_SampleMask` are covered in "Built-in GLSL Variables and Functions".

Stencil Test

The stencil test takes place only if there is a stencil buffer, which you need to request when your window is created. (If there is no stencil buffer, the stencil test always passes.) Stenciling applies a test that compares a reference value with the value stored at a pixel in the stencil buffer. Depending on the result of the test, the value in the stencil buffer can be modified. You can choose the particular comparison function used, the reference value, and the modification performed with the **glStencilFunc()** and **glStencilOp()** commands.

void **glStencilFunc**(GLenum *func*, GLint *ref*, GLuint *mask*);
void **glStencilFuncSeparate**(GLenum *face*, GLenum *func*,
                               GLint *ref*, GLuint *mask*);

Sets the comparison function (*func*), the reference value (*ref*), and a mask (*mask*) for use with the stencil test. The reference value is compared with the value in the stencil buffer using the comparison function, but the comparison applies only to those bits for which the corresponding bits of the mask are 1. The function can be GL_NEVER, GL_ALWAYS, GL_LESS, GL_LEQUAL, GL_EQUAL, GL_GEQUAL, GL_GREATER, or GL_NOTEQUAL.

If it's GL_LESS, for example, then the fragment passes if *ref* is less than the value in the stencil buffer. If the stencil buffer contains *s* bitplanes, the low-order *s* bits of *mask* are bitwise ANDed with the value in the stencil buffer and with the reference value before the comparison is performed.

The masked values are all interpreted as nonnegative values. The stencil test is enabled and disabled by passing GL_STENCIL_TEST to **glEnable()** and **glDisable()**. By default, *func* is GL_ALWAYS, *ref* is zero, *mask* is all ones, and stenciling is disabled.

glStencilFuncSeparate() allows separate stencil function parameters to be specified for front- and back-facing polygons (as set with **glCullFace()**).

---

void **glStencilOp**(GLenum *fail*, GLenum *zfail*, GLenum *zpass*);
void **glStencilOpSeparate**(GLenum *face*, GLenum *fail*,
                    GLenum *zfail*, GLenum *zpass*);

Specifies how the data in the stencil buffer is modified when a fragment passes or fails the stencil test. The three functions *fail*, *zfail*, and *zpass* can be GL_KEEP, GL_ZERO, GL_REPLACE, GL_INCR, GL_INCR_WRAP, GL_DECR, GL_DECR_WRAP, or GL_INVERT. They correspond to keeping the current value, replacing it with zero, replacing it with the reference value, incrementing it with saturation, incrementing it without saturation, decrementing it with saturation, decrementing it without saturation, and bitwise-inverting it. The result of the increment and decrement functions is clamped to lie between zero and the maximum unsigned integer value ($2^s - 1$ if the stencil buffer holds *s* bits).

The *fail* function is applied if the fragment fails the stencil test; if it passes, then *zfail* is applied if the depth test fails and *zpass* is applied if the depth test passes, or if no depth test is performed. By default, all three stencil operations are GL_KEEP.

glStencilOpSeparate() allows separate stencil tests to be specified for front- and back-facing polygons (as set with **glCullFace()**).

"With saturation" means that the stencil value will clamp to extreme values. If you try to decrement zero with saturation, the stencil value remains zero. "Without saturation" means that going outside the indicated range wraps around. If you try to decrement zero without saturation, the stencil value becomes the maximum unsigned integer value (quite large!).

Stencil Queries

You can obtain the values for all six stencil-related parameters by using the query function **glGetIntegerv()** and one of the values shown in Table 4.2.

You can also determine whether the stencil test is enabled by passing GL_STENCIL_TEST to **glIsEnabled()**.

Table 4.2   Query Values for the Stencil Test

Query Value	Meaning
GL_STENCIL_FUNC	stencil function
GL_STENCIL_REF	stencil reference value
GL_STENCIL_VALUE_MASK	stencil mask
GL_STENCIL_FAIL	stencil fail action
GL_STENCIL_PASS_DEPTH_FAIL	stencil pass and depth buffer fail action
GL_STENCIL_PASS_DEPTH_PASS	stencil pass and depth buffer pass action

Stencil Examples

Probably the most typical use of the stencil test is to mask out an irregularly shaped region of the screen to prevent drawing from occurring within it. To do this, fill the stencil mask with zeros, and then draw the desired shape in the stencil buffer with ones. You can't draw geometry directly into the stencil buffer, but you can achieve the same result by drawing into the color buffer and choosing a suitable value for the zpass function (such as GL_REPLACE). Whenever drawing occurs, a value is also written into the stencil buffer (in this case, the reference value). To prevent the stencil-buffer drawing from affecting the contents of the color buffer, set the color mask to zero (or GL_FALSE). You might also want to disable writing into the depth buffer. After you've defined the stencil area, set the reference value to one, and set the comparison function such that the fragment passes if the reference value is equal to the stencil-plane value. During drawing, don't modify the contents of the stencil planes.

Example 4.5   Using the Stencil Test: stencil.c

```
void
init(void)
{
    ...// Set up our vertex arrays and such

    // Set the stencil's clear value
    glClearStencil(0x0);

    glEnable(GL_DEPTH_TEST);
    glEnable(GL_STENCIL_TEST);
}
```

```
// Draw a sphere in a diamond-shaped section in the
// middle of a window with 2 tori.

void
display(void)
{
    glClear(GL_COLOR_BUFFER_BIT | GL_DEPTH_BUFFER_BIT);

    // draw sphere where the stencil is 1
    glStencilFunc(GL_EQUAL, 0x1, 0x1);
    glStencilOp(GL_KEEP, GL_KEEP, GL_KEEP);
    drawSphere();

    // draw the tori where the stencil is not 1
    glStencilFunc(GL_NOTEQUAL, 0x1, 0x1);
    drawTori();
}

// Whenever the window is reshaped, redefine the
// coordinate system and redraw the stencil area.

void
reshape(int width, int height)
{
    glViewport(0, 0, width, height);

    // create a diamond shaped stencil area
    glClear(GL_STENCIL_BUFFER_BIT);
    glStencilFunc(GL_ALWAYS, 0x1, 0x1);
    glStencilOp(GL_REPLACE, GL_REPLACE, GL_REPLACE);
    drawMask();
}
```

Example 4.5 demonstrates how to use the stencil test in this way. Two tori are drawn, with a diamond-shaped cutout in the center of the scene. Within the diamond-shaped stencil mask, a sphere is drawn. In this example, drawing into the stencil buffer takes place only when the window is redrawn, so the color buffer is cleared after the stencil mask has been created.

The following examples illustrate other uses of the stencil test.

1. Capping—Suppose you're drawing a closed convex object (or several of them, as long as they don't intersect or enclose each other) made up of several polygons, and you have a clipping plane that may or may not slice off a piece of it. Suppose that if the plane does intersect the object, you want to cap the object with some constant-colored surface, rather than see the inside of it. To do this, clear the stencil buffer to zeros, and begin drawing with stenciling enabled and the stencil comparison function set always to accept fragments. Invert the value in the stencil planes each time a fragment is accepted.

After all the objects are drawn, regions of the screen where no capping is required have zeros in the stencil planes, and regions requiring capping are nonzero. Reset the stencil function so that it draws only where the stencil value is nonzero, and draw a large polygon of the capping color across the entire screen.

2. Stippling—Suppose you want to draw an image with a *stipple* pattern. You can do this by writing the stipple pattern into the stencil buffer and then drawing conditionally on the contents of the stencil buffer. After the original stipple pattern is drawn, the stencil buffer isn't altered while drawing the image, so the object is stippled by the pattern in the stencil planes.

Depth Test

For each pixel on the screen, the depth buffer keeps track of the distance between the viewpoint and the object occupying that pixel. Then, if the specified depth test passes, the incoming depth value replaces the value already in the depth buffer.

The depth buffer is generally used for hidden-surface elimination. If a new candidate color for that pixel appears, it's drawn only if the corresponding object is closer than the previous object. In this way, after the entire scene has been rendered, only objects that aren't obscured by other items remain. Initially, the clearing value for the depth buffer is a value that's as far from the viewpoint as possible, so the depth of any object is nearer than that value. If this is how you want to use the depth buffer, you simply have to enable it by passing GL_DEPTH_TEST to **glEnable()** and remember to clear the depth buffer before you redraw each frame. (See "Clearing Buffers" on Page 146.) You can also choose a different comparison function for the depth test with **glDepthFunc()**.

void **glDepthFunc**(GLenum *func*);

Sets the comparison fun for the depth test. The value for *func* must be GL_NEVER, GL_ALWAYS, GL_LESS, GL_LEQUAL, GL_EQUAL, GL_GEQUAL, GL_GREATER, or GL_NOTEQUAL. An incoming fragment passes the depth test if its z-value has the specified relation to the value already stored in the depth buffer. The default is GL_LESS, which means that an incoming fragment passes the test if its z-value is less than that already stored in the depth buffer. In this case, the z-value represents the distance from the object to the viewpoint, and smaller values mean that the corresponding objects are closer to the viewpoint.

More context is provided in "OpenGL Transformations" in Chapter 5 for setting a depth range.

Polygon Offset

If you want to highlight the edges of a solid object, you might draw the object with polygon mode set to GL_FILL, and then draw it again, but in a different color and with the polygon mode set to GL_LINE. However, because lines and filled polygons are not rasterized in exactly the same way, the depth values generated for the line and polygon edge are usually not the same, even between the same two vertices. The highlighting lines may fade in and out of the coincident polygons, which is sometimes called "stitching" and is visually unpleasant.

This undesirable effect can be eliminated by using polygon offset, which adds an appropriate offset to force coincident *z*-values apart, separating a polygon edge from its highlighting line. (The stencil buffer, can also be used to eliminate stitching. However, polygon offset is almost always faster than stenciling.) Polygon offset is also useful for applying decals to surfaces by rendering images with *hidden-line removal*. In addition to lines and filled polygons, this technique can also be used with points.

There are three different ways to turn on polygon offset, one for each type of polygon rasterization mode: GL_FILL, GL_LINE, and GL_POINT. You enable the polygon offset by passing the appropriate parameter to **glEnable()**—either GL_POLYGON_OFFSET_FILL, GL_POLYGON_OFFSET_LINE, or GL_POLYGON_OFFSET_POINT. You must also call **glPolygonMode()** to set the current polygon rasterization method.

---

void **glPolygonOffset**(GLfloat *factor*, GLfloat *units*);

When enabled, the depth value of each fragment is modified by adding a calculated offset value before the depth test is performed. The offset value is calculated by

$$offset = m \cdot factor + r \cdot units$$

where *m* is the maximum depth slope of the polygon (computed during rasterization), and *r* is the smallest value guaranteed to produce a resolvable difference in depth values and is an implementation-specific constant. Both *factor* and *units* may be negative.

To achieve a nice rendering of the highlighted solid object without visual artifacts, you can add either a positive offset to the solid object (push it away from you) or a negative offset to the *wireframe* (pull it toward you). The big question is: How much offset is enough? Unfortunately, the offset required depends on various factors, including the depth slope of each polygon and the width of the lines in the wireframe.

OpenGL calculates the depth slope, as illustrated in Figure 4.2, which is the z (depth) value divided by the change in either the x- or y-coordinates as you traverse the polygon. The depth values are clamped to the range [0, 1], and the x- and y-coordinates are in window coordinates. To estimate the maximum depth slope of a polygon (*m* in the offset equation above), use the formula

$$m = \sqrt{\left(\frac{\partial z}{\partial x}\right)^2 + \left(\frac{\partial z}{\partial y}\right)^2}$$

or an implementation may use the approximation

$$m = \max\left(\frac{\partial z}{\partial x}, \frac{\partial z}{\partial y}\right)$$

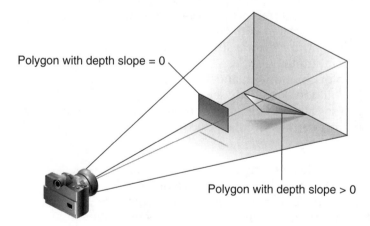

Polygon with depth slope = 0

Polygon with depth slope > 0

Figure 4.2   Polygons and their depth slopes

For polygons that are parallel to the near and far clipping planes, the depth slope is zero. Those polygons can use a small constant offset, which you can specify by setting *factor* = 0.0 and *units* = 1.0 in your call to **glPolygonOffset()**.

For polygons that are at a great angle to the clipping planes, the depth slope can be significantly greater than zero, and a larger offset may be needed. A small, nonzero value for *factor*, such as 0.75 or 1.0, is probably enough to generate distinct depth values and eliminate the unpleasant visual artifacts.

In some situations, the simplest values for *factor* and *units* (1.0 and 1.0) aren't the answer. For instance, if the widths of the lines that are highlighting the edges are greater than 1, then increasing the value of *factor* may be necessary. Also, since depth values while using a perspective projection are unevenly transformed into window coordinates, less offset is needed for polygons that are closer to the near clipping plane, and more offset is needed for polygons that are farther away. You may need to experiment with the values you pass to **glPolygonOffset()** to get the result you're looking for.

Blending

Once an incoming fragment has passed all of the enabled fragment tests, it can be combined with the current contents of the color buffer in one of several ways. The simplest way, which is also the default, is to overwrite the existing values, which admittedly isn't much of a combination. Alternatively, you might want to combine the color present in the framebuffer with the incoming fragment color—a process called blending. Most often, blending is associated with the fragment's *alpha value* (or commonly just alpha), but that's not a strict requirement. We've mentioned alpha several times but haven't given it a proper description. Alpha is the fourth color component, and all colors in OpenGL have an alpha value (even if you don't explicitly set one). However, you don't see alpha, but rather you see alpha's effect: it's a measure of translucency, and is what's used when you want to simulate translucent objects, like colored glass for example.

However, unless you enable blending by calling **glEnable()** with GL_BLEND, or employ advanced techniques like order-independent transparency (discussed in "Order-Independent Transparency" in Chapter 11), alpha is pretty much ignored by the OpenGL pipeline. You see, just like the real world, where color of a translucent object is a combination of that object's color with the colors of all the objects you see behind it. For OpenGL to do something useful with alpha, the pipeline needs more information than the current primitive's color (which is the color output from the fragment shader); it needs to know what color is already present for that pixel in the framebuffer.

Blending Factors

In basic blending mode, the incoming fragment's color is linearly combined with the current pixel's color. As with any linear combination, *coefficients* control the contributions of each term. For blending in OpenGL, those coefficients are called the *source-* and *destination-blending factors*. The source-blending factor is associated with the color output from the fragment shader, and similarly, the destination-blending factor is associated with the color in the framebuffer.

If we let (S_r, S_g, S_b, S_a) represent the source-blending factors, and likewise let (D_r, D_g, D_b, D_a) represent the destination factors, and use (R_s, G_s, B_s, A_s), and (R_d, G_d, B_d, A_d) represent the colors of the source fragment and destination pixel respectively, the blending equation yields a final color of

$$(S_r R_s + D_r R_d, \; S_g G_s + D_g G_d, \; S_b B_s + D_b B_d, \; S_a A_s + D_a A_d)$$

The default blending operation is addition, but we'll see in "The Blending Equation" on Page 170 that we can also control the blending operator.

Controlling Blending Factors

You have two different ways to choose the source and destination blending factors. You may call **glBlendFunc()** and choose two blending factors: the first factor for the source RGBA and the second for the destination RGBA. Or, you may use **glBlendFuncSeparate()** and choose four blending factors, which allows you to use one blending operation for RGB and a different one for its corresponding alpha.

Note: We also list the functions **glBlendFunci()** and **glBlendFuncSeparatei()**, which are used when you're drawing to multiple buffers simultaneously. This is an advanced topic that we describe in "Framebuffer Objects" on Page 180, but since the functions are virtually identical actions to **glBlendFunc()** and **glBlendFuncSeparate()**, we include them here.

---

void **glBlendFunc**(GLenum *srcfactor*, GLenum *destfactor*);
void **glBlendFunci**(GLuint *buffer*, GLenum *srcfactor*,
                 GLenum *destfactor*);

Controls how color values in the fragment being processed (the source) are combined with those already stored in the framebuffer (the destination). The possible values for these arguments are explained in

Table 4.3. The argument *srcfactor* indicates how to compute a source blending factor; *destfactor* indicates how to compute a destination blending factor.

glBlendFunc() specifies the blending factors for all drawable buffers, while **glBlendFunci()** specifies the blending factors only for buffer *buffer*.

The blending factors are clamped to either the range $[0, 1]$ or $[-1, 1]$ for unsigned-normalized or signed-normalized framebuffer formats respectively. If the framebuffer format is floating point, then no clamping of factors occurs.

---

void **glBlendFuncSeparate**(GLenum *srcRGB*, GLenum *destRGB*,
                GLenum *srcAlpha*,
                GLenum *destAlpha*);
void **glBlendFuncSeparatei**(GLuint *buffer*, GLenum *srcRGB*,
                GLenum *destRGB*, GLenum *srcAlpha*,
                GLenum *destAlpha*);

Similar to **glBlendFunc()**, **glBlendFuncSeparate()** also controls how source color values (fragment) are combined with destination values (in the framebuffer). **glBlendFuncSeparate()** also accepts the same arguments (shown in Table 4.3) as **glBlendFunc()**. The argument *srcRGB* indicates the source-blending factor for color values; *destRGB* is the destination-blending factor for color values. The argument *srcAlpha* indicates the source-blending factor for alpha values; *destAlpha* is the destination-blending factor for alpha values.

glBlendFuncSeparatei() specifies the blending factors for all drawable buffers, while **glBlendFuncSeparatei()** specifies the blending factors only for buffer *buffer*.

Note: In Table 4.3, the values with the subscript $_{s1}$ are for dual-source blending factors, which are described in "Dual-Source Blending" on Page 198.

If you use one of the GL_CONSTANT blending functions, you need to use **glBlendColor()** to specify the constant color.

Table 4.3   Source and Destination Blending Factors

Constant	RGB Blend Factor	Alpha Blend Factor
GL_ZERO	$(0, 0, 0)$	0
GL_ONE	$(1, 1, 1)$	1
GL_SRC_COLOR	(R_s, G_s, B_s)	A_s
GL_ONE_MINUS_SRC_COLOR	$(1, 1, 1) - (R_s, G_s, B_s)$	$1 - A_s$
GL_DST_COLOR	(R_d, G_d, B_d)	A_d
GL_ONE_MINUS_DST_COLOR	$(1, 1, 1) - (R_d, G_d, B_d)$	$1 - A_d$
GL_SRC_ALPHA	(A_s, A_s, A_s)	A_s
GL_ONE_MINUS_SRC_ALPHA	$(1, 1, 1) - (A_s, A_s, A_s)$	$1 - A_s$
GL_DST_ALPHA	(A_d, A_d, A_d)	A_d
GL_ONE_MINUS_DST_ALPHA	$(1, 1, 1) - (A_d, A_d, A_d)$	$1 - A_d$
GL_CONSTANT_COLOR	(R_c, G_c, B_c)	A_c
GL_ONE_MINUS_CONSTANT_COLOR	$(1, 1, 1) - (R_c, G_c, B_c)$	$1 - A_c$
GL_CONSTANT_ALPHA	(A_c, A_c, A_c)	A_c
GL_ONE_MINUS_CONSTANT_ALPHA	$(1, 1, 1) - (A_c, A_c, A_c)$	$1 - A_c$
GL_SRC_ALPHA_SATURATE	$(f, f, f), f = \min(A_s, 1 - A_d)$	1
GL_SRC1_COLOR	(R_{s1}, G_{s1}, B_{s1})	A_{s1}
GL_ONE_MINUS_SRC1_COLOR	$(1, 1, 1) - (R_{s1}, G_{s1}, B_{s1})$	$1 - A_{s1}$
GL_SRC1_ALPHA	(A_{s1}, A_{s1}, A_{s1})	A_{s1}
GL_ONE_MINUS_SRC1_ALPHA	$(1, 1, 1) - (A_{s1}, A_{s1}, A_{s1})$	$1 - A_{s1}$

---

void **glBlendColor**(GLclampf *red*, GLclampf *green*, GLclampf *blue*, GLclampf *alpha*);

Sets the current *red*, *blue*, *green*, and *alpha* values for use as the constant color (R_c, G_c, B_c, A_c) in blending operations.

Similarly, use **glDisable()** with GL_BLEND to disable blending. Note that using the constants GL_ONE (as the source factor) and GL_ZERO (for the destination factor) gives the same results as when blending is disabled; these values are the default.

Advanced

OpenGL has the ability to render into multiple buffers simultaneously (see "Writing to Multiple Renderbuffers Simultaneously" on Page 193 for details). All buffers can have blending enabled and disabled simultaneously (using **glEnable()** and **glDisable()**). Blending settings can be managed on a per-buffer basis using **glEnablei()** and **glDisablei()**.

The Blending Equation

With standard blending, colors in the framebuffer are combined (using addition) with incoming fragment colors to produce the new framebuffer color. Either **glBlendEquation()** or **glBlendEquationSeparate()** may be used to select other mathematical operations to compute the difference, minimum, or maximum between color fragments and framebuffer pixels.

---

void **glBlendEquation**(GLenum *mode*);
void **glBlendEquationi**(GLuint *buffer*, GLenum *mode*);

Specifies how framebuffer and source colors are blended together. The allowable values for *mode* are GL_FUNC_ADD (the default), GL_FUNC_SUBTRACT, GL_FUNC_REVERSE_SUBTRACT, GL_MIN, and GL_MAX. The possible modes are described in Table 4.4.

glBlendEquation() specifies the blending mode for all buffers, while **glBlendEquationi()** sets the mode for the buffer specified by the *buffer* argument, which is the integer index of the buffer.

---

void **glBlendEquationSeparate**(GLenum *modeRGB*,
                                 GLenum *modeAlpha*);
void **glBlendEquationSeparatei**(GLuint *buffer*,
                                  GLenum *modeRGB*,
                                  GLenum *modeAlpha*);

Specifies how framebuffer and source colors are blended together, but allows for different blending modes for the rgb and alpha color components. The allowable values for *modeRGB* and *modeAlpha* are identical for the modes accepted by **glBlendEquation()**.

Again, **glBlendEquationSeparate()** sets the blending modes for all buffers, while **glBlendEquationSeparatei()** sets the modes for the buffer whose index is specified in *buffer*.

In Table 4.4, C_s and C_d represent the source and destination colors. The S and D parameters in the table represent the source- and destination-blending factors as specified with **glBlendFunc()** or **glBlendFuncSeparate()**.

Table 4.4   Blending Equation Mathematical Operations

Blending Mode Parameter	Mathematical Operation
GL_FUNC_ADD	$C_s S + C_d D$
GL_FUNC_SUBTRACT	$C_s S - C_d D$
GL_FUNC_REVERSE_SUBTRACT	$C_d D - C_s S$
GL_MIN	$\min(C_s S, C_d D)$
GL_MAX	$\max(C_s S, C_d D)$

Dithering

On systems with a small number of color bitplanes, you can improve the color resolution at the expense of spatial resolution by *dithering* the color in the image. Dithering is like half-toning in newspapers. Although *The New York Times* has only two colors—black and white—it can show photographs by representing the shades of gray with combinations of black and white dots. Comparing a newspaper image of a photo (having no shades of gray) with the original photo (with grayscale) makes the loss of spatial resolution obvious. Similarly, systems with a small number of color bitplanes may dither values of red, green, and blue on neighboring pixels for the appearance of a wider range of colors.

The dithering operation that takes place is hardware-dependent; all OpenGL allows you to do is to turn it on and off. In fact, on some machines, enabling dithering might do nothing at all, which makes sense if the machine already has high color resolution. To enable and disable dithering, pass GL_DITHER to **glEnable()** and **glDisable()**. Dithering is enabled by default.

Logical Operations

The final operation on a fragment is the *logical operation,* such as an OR, XOR, or INVERT, which is applied to the incoming fragment values (source) and/or those currently in the color buffer (destination). Such fragment operations are especially useful on bit-blt-type machines, on which the primary graphics operation is copying a rectangle of data from one place in the window to another, from the window to processor memory, or from memory to the window. Typically, the copy doesn't write the data directly into memory but instead allows you to perform an arbitrary logical operation on the incoming data and the data already present; then it replaces the existing data with the results of the operation.

Since this process can be implemented fairly cheaply in hardware, many such machines are available. As an examplese of using a logical operation, XOR can be used to draw on an image in a revertible way; simply XOR the same drawing again, and the original image is restored.

You enable and disable logical operations by passing GL_COLOR_LOGIC_OP to **glEnable**() and **glDisable**(). You also must choose among the 16 logical operations with **glLogicOp**(), or you'll just get the effect of the default value, GL_COPY.

void **glLogicOp**(GLenum *opcode*);

Selects the logical operation to be performed, given an incoming (source) fragment and the pixel currently stored in the color buffer (destination). Table 4.5 shows the possible values for opcode and their meaning (s represents source and d destination). The default value is GL_COPY.

Table 4.5   Sixteen Logical Operations

Parameter	Operation	Parameter	Operation
GL_CLEAR	0	GL_AND	$s \wedge d$
GL_COPY	s	GL_OR	$s \vee d$
GL_NOOP	d	GL_NAND	$\neg(s \wedge d)$
GL_SET	1	GL_NOR	$\neg(s \vee d)$
GL_COPY_INVERTED	$\neg s$	GL_XOR	$s \, XOR \, d$
GL_INVERT	$\neg d$	GL_EQUIV	$\neg(s \, XOR \, d)$
GL_AND_REVERSE	$s \wedge \neg d$	GL_AND_INVERTED	$\neg s \wedge d$
GL_OR_REVERSE	$s \vee \neg d$	GL_OR_INVERTED	$\neg s \vee d$

For floating-point buffers, or those in sRGB format, logical operations are ignored.

Occlusion Query

Advanced

The depth buffer determines visibility on a per-pixel basis. For performance reasons, it would be nice to be able to determine if a *geometric object* is visible before sending all of its (perhaps complex) geometry for rendering. *Occlusion querys* enable you to determine if a representative set of geometry will be visible after depth testing.

This is particularly useful for complex geometric objects with many polygons. Instead of rendering all of the geometry for a complex object, you might render its bounding box or another simplified representation that require less rendering resources. If OpenGL returns that no fragments or samples would have been modified by rendering that piece of geometry, you know that none of your complex object will be visible for that frame, and you can skip rendering that object for the frame.

The following steps are required to utilize occlusion queries:

1. Generate a query id for each occlusion query that you need.

2. Specify the start of an occlusion query by calling **glBeginQuery()**.

3. Render the geometry for the occlusion test.

4. Specify that you've completed the occlusion query by calling **glEndQuery()**.

5. Retrieve the number of, or if any, samples passed the depth tests.

In order to make the occlusion query process as efficient as possible, you'll want to disable all rendering modes that will increase the rendering time but won't change the visibility of a pixel.

Generating Query Objects

In order to use queries, you'll first need to request identifiers for your query tests. **glGenQueries()** will generate the requested number of unused query ids for your subsequent use.

> void **glGenQueries**(GLsizei *n*, GLuint **ids*);
>
> Returns *n* currently unused names for occlusion query objects in the array *ids* The names returned in *ids* do not have to be a contiguous set of integers.
>
> The names returned are marked as used for the purposes of allocating additional query objects, but only acquire valid state once they have been specified in a call to **glBeginQuery()**.
>
> Zero is a reserved occlusion query object name and is never returned as a valid value by **glGenQueries()**.

You can also determine if an identifier is currently being used as an occlusion query by calling **glIsQuery()**.

> GLboolean **glIsQuery**(GLuint *id*);
>
> Returns GL_TRUE if *id* is the name of an occlusion query object. Returns GL_FALSE if *id* is zero or if *id* is a nonzero value that is not the name of a buffer object.

Initiating an Occlusion Query Test

To specify geometry that's to be used in an occlusion query, merely bracket the rendering operations between calls to **glBeginQuery()** and **glEndQuery()**, as demonstrated in Example 4.6

Example 4.6   Rendering Geometry with Occlusion Query: occquery.c

```
glBeginQuery(GL_SAMPLES_PASSED, Query);
glDrawArrays(GL_TRIANGLES, 0, 3);
glEndQuery(GL_SAMPLES_PASSED);
```

All OpenGL operations are available while an occlusion query is active, with the exception of **glGenQueries()** and **glDeleteQueries()**, which will raise a GL_INVALID_OPERATION error.

> void **glBeginQuery**(GLenum *target*, GLuint *id*);
>
> Specifies the start of an occlusion query operation. *target* must be GL_SAMPLES_PASSED, GL_ANY_SAMPLES_PASSED, or GL_ANY_SAMPLES_PASSED_CONSERVATIVE. *id* is an unsigned integer identifier for this occlusion query operation.

void **glEndQuery**(GLenum *target*);

Ends an occlusion query. *target* must be GL_SAMPLES_PASSED, or
GL_ANY_SAMPLES_PASSED.

Determining the Results of an Occlusion Query

Once you've completed rendering the geometry for the occlusion query,
you need to retrieve the results. This is done with a call to
glGetQueryObjectiv() or **glGetQueryObjectuiv()**, as shown in
Example 4.7, which will return the number of fragments, or samples, if
you're using multisampling.

void **glGetQueryObjectiv**(GLenum *id*, GLenum *pname*,
                                         GLint **params*);
void **glGetQueryObjectuiv**(GLenum *id*, GLenum *pname*,
                                         GLuint **params*);

Queries the state of an occlusion query object. *id* is the name of a query
object. If *pname* is GL_QUERY_RESULT, then *params* will contain the
number of fragments or samples (if multisampling is enabled) that passed
the depth test, with a value of zero representing the object being entirely
occluded.

There may be a delay in completing the occlusion query operation. If
pname is GL_QUERY_RESULT_AVAILABLE, *params* will contain GL_TRUE
if the results for query *id* are available, or GL_FALSE otherwise.

Example 4.7   Retrieving the Results of an Occlusion Query

```
count = 1000; /* counter to avoid a possible infinite loop */

while (!queryReady && count-) {
    glGetQueryObjectiv(Query, GL_QUERY_RESULT_AVAILABLE, &queryReady);
}

if (queryReady) {
    glGetQueryObjectiv(Query, GL_QUERY_RESULT, &samples);
    cerr << "Samples rendered: " << samples << endl;
}
else {
    cerr << " Result not ready ... rendering anyways" << endl;
    samples = 1; /* make sure we render */
}
```

```
if (samples > 0) {
    glDrawArrays(GL_TRIANGLE_FAN}, 0, NumVertices);
}
```

Cleaning Up Occlusion Query Objects

After you've completed your occlusion query tests, you can release the resources related to those queries by calling **glDeleteQueries()**.

---

void **glDeleteQueries**(GLsizei *n*, const GLuint **ids*);

Deletes *n* occlusion query objects, named by elements in the array *ids*. The freed query objects may now be reused (for example, by **glGenQueries()**).

Conditional Rendering

Advanced

One of the issues with occlusion queries is that they require OpenGL to pause processing geometry and fragments, count the number of affected samples in the depth buffer, and return the value to your application. Stopping modern graphics hardware in this manner usually catastrophically affects performance in performance-sensitive applications. To eliminate the need to pause OpenGL's operation, *conditional rendering* allows the graphics server (hardware) to decide if an occlusion query yielded any fragments, and to render the intervening commands. Conditional rendering is enabled by surrounding the rendering operations you would have conditionally executed using the results of **glGetQuery*()**.

---

void **glBeginConditionalRender**(GLuint *id*, GLenum *mode*);
void **glEndConditionalRender**(void);

Delineates a sequence of OpenGL rendering commands that may be discarded based on the results of the occlusion query object *id*. *mode* specifies how the OpenGL implementation uses the results of the occlusion query, and must be one of: GL_QUERY_WAIT, GL_QUERY_NO_WAIT, GL_QUERY_BY_REGION_WAIT, or GL_QUERY_BY_REGION_NO_WAIT.

A GL_INVALID_VALUE is set if *id* is not an existing occlusion query. A GL_INVALID_OPERATION is generated if **glBeginConditionalRender()** is called while a conditional-rendering sequence is in operation;

if **glEndConditionalRender()** is called when no conditional render is underway; if *id* is the name of an occlusion query object with a target different than GL_SAMPLES_PASSED; or if *id* is the name of an occlusion query in progress.

The code shown in Example 4.8 completely replaces the sequence of code in Example 4.7. Not only is it the code more compact, it is far more efficient as it completely removes the results query to the OpenGL server, which is a major performance inhibitor.

Example 4.8   Rendering Using Conditional Rendering

```
glBeginConditionalRender(Query, GL_QUERY_WAIT);
glDrawArrays(GL_TRIANGLE_FAN, 0, NumVertices);
glEndConditionalRender();
```

You may have noticed that there is a *mode* parameter to **glBeginConditionalRender()**, which may be one of GL_QUERY_WAIT, GL_QUERY_NO_WAIT, GL_QUERY_BY_REGION_WAIT, or GL_QUERY_BY_REGION_NO_WAIT. These modes control whether the GPU will wait for the results of a query to be ready before continuing to render, and whether it will consider global results or results only pertaining to the region of the screen that contributed to the original occlusion query result.

- If *mode* is GL_QUERY_WAIT then the GPU will wait for the result of the occlusion query to be ready before determining whether it will continue with rendering.

- If *mode* is GL_QUERY_NO_WAIT then the GPU may not wait for the result of the occlusion query to be ready before continuing to render. If the result is not ready, then it may choose to render the part of the scene contained in the conditional rendering section anyway.

- If *mode* is GL_QUERY_BY_REGION_WAIT then the GPU will wait for anything that contributes to the region covered by the controled rendering to be completed. It may still wait for the complete occlusion query result to be ready.

- If *mode* is GL_QUERY_BY_REGION_NO_WAIT, then the GPU will discard any rendering in regions of the framebuffer that contributed no samples to the occlusion query, but may choose to render into other regions if the result was not available in time.

By using these modes wisely, you can improve performance of the system. For example, waiting for the results of an occlusion query may actually take more time than just rendering the conditional part of the scene. In particular, if it is expected that most results will mean that some rendering should take place, then on aggregate, it may be faster to always use one of the NO_WAIT modes even if it means more rendering will take place overall.

Per-Primitive Antialiasing

You might have noticed in some of your OpenGL images that lines, especially nearly horizontal and nearly vertical ones, appear jagged. These *jaggies* appear because the ideal line is approximated by a series of pixels that must lie on the pixel grid. The jaggedness is called *aliasing*, and this section describes one antialiasing technique for reducing it. Figure 4.3 shows two intersecting lines, both aliased and antialiased. The pictures have been magnified to show the effect.

Figure 4.3   Aliased and antialiased lines

Figure 4.3 shows how a diagonal line 1 pixel wide covers more of some pixel squares than others. In fact, when performing antialiasing, OpenGL calculates a coverage value for each fragment based on the fraction of the pixel square on the screen that it would cover. OpenGL multiplies the fragment's alpha value by its coverage. You can then use the resulting alpha value to blend the fragment with the corresponding pixel already in the framebuffer.

The details of calculating coverage values are complex, and difficult to specify in general. In fact, computations may vary slightly depending on your particular implementation of OpenGL. You can use the **glHint()** command to exercise some control over the trade-off between image quality and speed, but not all implementations will take the hint.

> void **glHint**(GLenum *target*, GLenum *hint*);
>
> Controls certain aspects of OpenGL behavior. The *target* parameter
> indicates which behavior is to be controlled; its possible values are shown
> in Table 4.6. The *hint* parameter can be GL_FASTEST to indicate that the
> most efficient option should be chosen, GL_NICEST to indicate the
> highest-quality option, or GL_DONT_CARE to indicate no preference.
> The interpretation of hints is implementation-dependent; an OpenGL
> implementation can ignore them entirely.

Table 4.6   Values for Use with **glHint()**

Parameter	Specifies
GL_LINE_SMOOTH_HINT	Line antialiasing quality
GL_POLYGON_SMOOTH_HINT	Polygon edge antialiasing quality
GL_TEXTURE_COMPRESSION_HINT	Quality and performance of texture-image *compression* (See Chapter 6, "Textures" for more detail)
GL_FRAGMENT_SHADER_DERIVATIVE_HINT	Derivative accuracy for fragment processing built-in functions dFdx, dFdy, and fwidth (See Appendix C for more details)

We've discussed multisampling before as a technique for antialiasing;
however, it's not usually the best solution for lines. Another way to
antialias lines, and polygons if the multisample results are quite what you
want, is to turn on antialiasing with **glEnable()**, and passing in
GL_LINE_SMOOTH or GL_POLYGON_SMOOTH, as appropriate. You
might also want to provide a quality hint with **glHint()**. We'll describe the
steps for each type of primitive that can be antialiased in the next sections.

Antialiasing Lines

First, you need to enable blending. The blending factors you most likely
want to use are GL_SRC_ALPHA (source) and
GL_ONE_MINUS_SRC_ALPHA (destination). Alternatively, you can use
GL_ONE for the destination factor to make lines a little brighter where
they intersect. Now you're ready to draw whatever points or lines you want
antialiased. The antialiased effect is most noticeable if you use a fairly high
alpha value. Remember that since you're performing blending, you might
need to consider the rendering order. However, in most cases, the ordering
can be ignored without significant adverse effects.

Example 4.9 shows the initialization for line antialiasing.

Example 4.9   Setting Up Blending for Antialiasing Lines: antilines.cpp

```
glEnable (GL_LINE_SMOOTH);
glEnable (GL_BLEND);
glBlendFunc (GL_SRC_ALPHA, GL_ONE_MINUS_SRC_ALPHA);
glHint (GL_LINE_SMOOTH_HINT, GL_DONT_CARE);
```

Antialiasing Polygons

Antialiasing the edges of filled polygons is similar to antialiasing lines. When different polygons have overlapping edges, you need to blend the color values appropriately.

To antialias polygons, you use the alpha value to represent coverage values of polygon edges. You need to enable polygon antialiasing by passing GL_POLYGON_SMOOTH to **glEnable()**. This causes pixels on the edges of the polygon to be assigned fractional alpha values based on their coverage, as though they were lines being antialiased. Also, if you desire, you can supply a value for GL_POLYGON_SMOOTH_HINT.

In order to have edges blend appropriately, set the blending factors to GL_SRC_ALPHA_SATURATE (source) and GL_ONE (destination). With this specialized blending function, the final color is the sum of the destination color and the scaled source color; the scale factor is the smaller of either the incoming source alpha value or one minus the destination alpha value. This means that for a pixel with a large alpha value, successive incoming pixels have little effect on the final color because one minus the destination alpha is almost zero. With this method, a pixel on the edge of a polygon might be blended eventually with the colors from another polygon that's drawn later. Finally, you need to sort all the polygons in your scene so that they're ordered from front to back before drawing them.

Note: Antialiasing can be adversely affected when using the depth buffer, in that pixels may be discarded when they should have been blended. To ensure proper blending and antialiasing, you'll need to disable the depth buffer.

Framebuffer Objects

Advanced

Up to this point, all of our discussion regarding buffers has focused on the buffers provided by the windowing system, as you requested when you

called **glutCreateWindow()** (and configured by your call to
glutInitDisplayMode()). Although you can quite successfully use any
technique with just those buffers, quite often various operations require
moving data between buffers superfluously. This is where framebuffer
objects enter the picture. Using framebuffer objects, you can create our
own framebuffers and use their attached renderbuffers to minimize data
copies and optimize performance.

Framebuffer objects are quite useful for performing off-screen-rendering,
updating texture maps, and engaging in *buffer ping-ponging* (a data-transfer
techniques used in *GPGPU*).

The framebuffer that is provided by the windowing system is the only
framebuffer that is available to the display system of your graphics
server—that is, it is the only one you can see on your screen. It also places
restrictions on the use of the buffers that were created when your window
opened. By comparison, the framebuffers that your application creates
cannot be displayed on your *monitor*; they support only *off-screen rendering*.

Another difference between window-system-provided framebuffers and
framebuffers you create is that those managed by the window system
allocate their buffers—color, depth, and stencil—when your window is
created. When you create an application-managed framebuffer object, you
need to create additional renderbuffers that you associate with the
framebuffer objects you created. The buffers with the window-system-
provided buffers can never be associated with an application-created
framebuffer object, and vice versa.

To allocate an application-generated framebuffer object name, you need to
call **glGenFramebuffers()**, which will allocate an unused identifier for the
framebuffer object.

---

void **glGenFramebuffers**(GLsizei *n*, GLuint **ids*);

Allocate *n* unused framebuffer object names, and return those names in
ids.

A GL_INVALID_VALUE error will be generated if *n* is negative.

Allocating a framebuffer object name doesn't actually create the
framebuffer object or allocate any storage for it. Those tasks are handled
through a call to **glBindFramebuffer()**. **glBindFramebuffer()** operates in a
similar manner to many of the other **glBind*()** routines you've seen in
OpenGL. The first time it is called for a particular framebuffer, it causes

storage for the object to be allocated and initialized. Any subsequent calls will bind the provided framebuffer object name as the active one.

---

void **glBindFramebuffer**(GLenum *target*, GLuint *framebuffer*);

Specifies a framebuffer for either reading or writing. When target is GL_DRAW_FRAMEBUFFER, *framebuffer* specifies the destination framebuffer for rendering. Similarly, when *target* is set to GL_READ_FRAMEBUFFER, *framebuffer* specifies the source of read operations. Passing GL_FRAMEBUFFER for target sets both the read and write framebuffer bindings to *framebuffer*.

framebuffer must either be zero, which binds *target* to the default window-system-provided framebuffer, or a framebuffer object generated by a call to **glGenFramebuffers()**.

A GL_INVALID_OPERATION error is generated if *framebuffer* is neither zero nor a valid framebuffer object previously generated by calling **glGenFramebuffers()** but not deleted by calling **glDeleteFramebuffers()**.

As with all of the other objects you have encountered in OpenGL, you can release an application-allocated framebuffer by calling **glDeleteFramebuffers()**. That function will mark the framebuffer object's name as unallocated and release any resources associated with the framebuffer object.

---

void **glDeleteFramebuffers**(GLsizei *n*, const GLuint **ids*);

Deallocates the *n* framebuffer objects associated with the names provided in *ids*. If a framebuffer object is currently bound (i.e., its name was passed to the most recent call to **glBindFramebuffer()**) and is deleted, the framebuffer target is immediately bound to *id* zero (the window-system provided framebuffer), and the framebuffer object is released.

A GL_INVALID_VALUE error is generated by **glDeleteFramebuffers()** if *n* is negative. Passing unused names or zero does not generate any errors; they are simply ignored.

For completeness, you can determine whether a particular unsigned integer is an application-allocated framebuffer object by calling **glIsFramebuffer()**:

GLboolean **glIsFramebuffer**(GLuint *framebuffer*);

Returns GL_TRUE if *framebuffer* is the name of a framebuffer returned from **glGenFramebuffers**(). Returns GL_FALSE if *framebuffer* is zero (the window-system default framebuffer) or a value that's either unallocated or been deleted by a call to **glDeleteFramebuffers**().

void **glFramebufferParameteri**(GLenum *target*, GLenum *pname*,
GLint *param*);

Sets parameters of a framebuffer object, when the framebuffer object has no attachments, otherwise the values for these parameters are specified by the framebuffer attachments.

target must be DRAW_FRAMEBUFFER, READ_FRAMEBUFFER, or FRAMEBUFFER. FRAMEBUFFER is equivalent to DRAW_FRAMEBUFFER. *pname* specifies the parameter of the framebuffer object bound to target to set, and must be one of GL_FRAMEBUFFER_DEFAULT_WIDTH, GL_FRAMEBUFFER_DEFAULT_HEIGHT, GL_FRAMEBUFFER_DEFAULT_LAYERS, GL_FRAMEBUFFER_DEFAULT_SAMPLES, or GL_FRAMEBUFFER_DEFAULT_FIXED_SAMPLE_LOCATIONS.

Once a framebuffer object is created, you still can't do much with it, generally speaking. You need to provide a place for drawing to go and reading to come from; those places are called *framebuffer attachments*. We'll discuss those in more detail after we examine renderbuffers, which are one type of buffer you can attach to a framebuffer object.

Renderbuffers

Renderbuffers are effectively memory managed by OpenGL that contains formatted image data. The data that a renderbuffer holds takes meaning once it is attached to a framebuffer object, assuming that the format of the image buffer matches what OpenGL is expecting to render into (e.g., you can't render colors into the depth buffer).

As with many other buffers in OpenGL, the process of allocating and deleting buffers is similar to what you've seen before. To create a new renderbuffer, you would call **glGenRenderbuffers**().

void **glGenRenderbuffers**(GLsizei *n*, GLuint **ids*);

Allocate *n* unused renderbuffer object names, and return those names in *ids*. Names are unused until bound with a call to **glBindRenderbuffer**().

Likewise, a call to **glDeleteRenderbuffers**() will release the storage associated with a renderbuffer.

void **glDeleteRenderbuffers**(GLsizei *n*, const GLuint **ids*);

Deallocates the *n* renderbuffer objects associated with the names provided in *ids*. If one of the renderbuffers is currently bound and passed to **glDeleteRenderbuffers**(), a binding of zero replaces the binding at the current framebuffer attachment point, in addition to the renderbuffer being released.

No errors are generated by **glDeleteRenderbuffers**(). Unused names or zero are simply ignored.

Likewise, you can determine whether a name represents a valid renderbuffer by calling **glIsRenderbuffer**().

void **glIsRenderbuffer**(GLuint *renderbuffer*);

Returns GL_TRUE if *renderbuffer* is the name of a renderbuffer returned from **glGenRenderbuffers**(). Returns GL_FALSE if *framebuffer* is zero (the window-system default framebuffer) or a value that's either unallocated or deleted by a call to **glDeleteRenderbuffers**().

Similar to the process of binding a framebuffer object so that you can modify its state, you call **glBindRenderbuffer**() to affect a renderbuffer's creation and to modify the state associated with it, which includes the format of the image data that it contains.

void **glBindRenderbuffer**(GLenum *target*, GLuint *renderbuffer*);

Creates a renderbuffer and associates it with the name *renderbuffer*. *target* must be GL_RENDERBUFFER. *renderbuffer* must either be zero, which removes any renderbuffer binding, or a name that was generated by a call to **glGenRenderbuffers**(); otherwise, a GL_INVALID_OPERATION error will be generated.

Creating Renderbuffer Storage

When you first call **glBindRenderbuffer**() with an unused renderbuffer name, the OpenGL server creates a renderbuffer with all its state information set to the default values. In this configuration, no storage has been allocated to store image data. Before you can attach a renderbuffer to a framebuffer and render into it, you need to allocate storage and specify its image format. This is done by calling either **glRenderbufferStorage**() or **glRenderbufferStorageMultisample**().

---

void **glRenderbufferStorage**(GLenum *target*,
                               GLenum *internalformat*,
                               GLsizei *width*, GLsizei *height*);
void **glRenderbufferStorageMultisample**(GLenum *target*,
                               GLsizei *samples*,
                               GLenum *internalformat*,
                               GLsizei *width*,
                               GLsizei *height*);

Allocates storage for image data for the bound renderbuffer. *target* must be GL_RENDERBUFFER. For a color-renderable buffer, *internalformat* must be one of:

GL_RED	GL_R8	GL_R16
GL_RG	GL_RG8	GL_RG16
GL_RGB	GL_R3_G3_B2	GL_RGB4
GL_RGB5	GL_RGB8	GL_RGB10
GL_RGB12	GL_RGB16	GL_RGBA
GL_RGBA2	GL_RGBA4	GL_RGB5_A1
GL_RGBA8	GL_RGB10_A2	GL_RGBA12
GL_RGBA16	GL_SRGB	GL_SRGB8
GL_SRGB_ALPHA	GL_SRGB8_ALPHA8	GL_R16F

GL_R32F	GL_RG16F	GL_RG32F
GL_RGB16F	GL_RGB32F	GL_RGBA16F
GL_RGBA32F	GL_R11F_G11F_B10F	GL_RGB9_E5
GL_R8I	GL_R8UI	GL_R16I
GL_R16UI	GL_R32I	GL_R32UI
GL_RG8I	GL_RG8UI	GL_RG16I
GL_RG16UI	GL_RG32I	GL_RG32UI
GL_RGB8I	GL_RGB8UI	GL_RGB16I
GL_RGB16UI	GL_RGB32I	GL_RGB32UI
GL_RGBA8I	GL_RGBA8UI	GL_RGBA16I
GL_RGBA16UI	GL_RGBA32I	GL_R8_SNORM
GL_R16_SNORM	GL_RG8_SNORM	GL_RG16_SNORM
GL_RGB8_SNORM	GL_RGB16_SNORM	GL_RGBA8_SNORM
GL_RGBA16_SNORM		

To use a renderbuffer as a depth buffer, it must be depth-renderable, which is specified by setting internalformat to either GL_DEPTH_COMPONENT, GL_DEPTH_COMPONENT16, GL_DEPTH_COMPONENT32, GL_DEPTH_COMPONENT32, or GL_DEPTH_COMPONENT32F.

For use exclusively as a stencil buffer, internalformat should be specified as either GL_STENCIL_INDEX, GL_STENCIL_INDEX1, GL_STENCIL_INDEX4, GL_STENCIL_INDEX8, or GL_STENCIL_INDEX16.

For packed depth-stencil storage, internalformat must be GL_DEPTH_STENCIL, which allows the renderbuffer to be attached as the depth buffer, stencil buffer, or at the combined depth-stencil attachment point.

width and *height* specify the size of the renderbuffer in pixels, and samples specifies the number of multisample samples per pixel. Setting samples to zero in a call to **glRenderbufferStorageMultisample()** is identical to calling **glRenderbufferStorage()**.

A GL_INVALID_VALUE is generated if width or height is greater than the value returned when querying GL_MAX_RENDERBUFFER_SIZE, or if *samples* is greater than the value returned when querying GL_MAX_SAMPLES. A GL_INVALID_OPERATION is generated if internalformat is a signed- or unsigned-integer format (e.g., a format containing a "I", or "UI" in its token), and *samples* is not zero, and the implementation doesn't support multisampled integer buffers. Finally, if the renderbuffer size and format combined exceed the available memory able to be allocated, then a GL_OUT_OF_MEMORY error is generated.

Example 4.10   Creating a 256 × 256 RGBA Color Renderbuffer

```
glGenRenderbuffers(1, &color);
glBindRenderbuffer(GL_RENDERBUFFER, color);
glRenderbufferStorage(GL_RENDERBUFFER, GL_RGBA, 256, 256);
```

Once you have created storage for your renderbuffer as shown in
Example 4.10, you need to attach it to a framebuffer object before you can
render into it.

Framebuffer Attachments

When you render, you can send the results of that rendering to a number
of places:

- The color buffer to create an image, or even multiple color buffers if
  you're using multiple render targets (see "Writing to Multiple
  Renderbuffers Simultaneously" on Page 193).

- The depth buffer to store occlusion information.

- The stencil buffer for storing per-pixel masks to control rendering. Each
  of those buffers represents a framebuffer attachment, to which you can
  attach suitable image buffers that you later render into, or read from.
  The possible framebuffer attachment points are listed in Table 4.7.

Table 4.7   Framebuffer Attachments

Attachment Name	Description
GL_COLOR_ATTACHMENTi	The ith color buffer. i can range from zero (the default color buffer) to GL_MAX_COLOR_ATTACHMENTS - 1
GL_DEPTH_ATTACHMENT	The depth buffer
GL_STENCIL_ATTACHMENT	The stencil buffer
GL_DEPTH_STENCIL_ATTACHMENT	A special attachment for packed depth-stencil buffers (which require the renderbuffer to have been allocated as a GL_DEPTH_STENCIL pixel format)

Currently, there are two types of rendering surfaces you can associate with
one of those attachments: renderbuffers and a level of a texture image.

We'll first discuss attaching a renderbuffer to a framebuffer object, which is
done by calling **glFramebufferRenderbuffer()**.

---

void **glFramebufferRenderbuffer**(GLenum *target*,
                                   GLenum *attachment*,
                                   GLenum *renderbuffertarget*,
                                   GLuint *renderbuffer*);

Attaches *renderbuffer* to attachment of the currently bound framebuffer object. *target* must either be GL_READ_FRAMEBUFFER, GL_DRAW_FRAMEBUFFER, or GL_FRAMEBUFFER (which is equivalent to GL_DRAW_FRAMEBUFFER).

attachment is one of GL_COLOR_ATTACHMENT*i*, GL_DEPTH_ATTACHMENT, GL_STENCIL_ATTACHMENT, or GL_DEPTH_STENCIL_ATTACHMENT.

renderbuffertarget must be GL_RENDERBUFFER, and *renderbuffer* must either be zero, which removes any renderbuffer attachment at *attachment*, or a renderbuffer name returned from **glGenRenderbuffers()**, or a GL_INVALID_OPERATION error is generated.

In Example 4.11, we create and attach two renderbuffers: one for color, and the other for depth. We then proceed to render, and finally copy the results back to the window-system-provided framebuffer to display the results. You might use this technique to generate frames for a movie rendering off-screen, where you don't have to worry about the visible framebuffer being corrupted by overlapping windows or someone resizing the window and interrupting rendering.

One important point to remember is that you might need to reset the viewport for each framebuffer before rendering, particularly if the size of your application-defined framebuffers differs from the window-system provided framebuffer.

Example 4.11   Attaching a Renderbuffer for Rendering

```
enum { Color, Depth, NumRenderbuffers };

GLuint framebuffer, renderbuffer[NumRenderbuffers]

void
init()
{
    glGenRenderbuffers(NumRenderbuffers, renderbuffer);
    glBindRenderbuffer(GL_RENDERBUFFER, renderbuffer[Color]);
    glRenderbufferStorage(GL_RENDERBUFFER, GL_RGBA, 256, 256);

    glBindRenderbuffer(GL_RENDERBUFFER, renderbuffer[Depth]);
```

```
        glRenderbufferStorage(GL_RENDERBUFFER, GL_DEPTH_COMPONENT24, 256, 256);

        glGenFramebuffers(1, &framebuffer);
        glBindFramebuffer(GL_DRAW_FRAMEBUFFER, framebuffer);

        glFramebufferRenderbuffer(GL_DRAW_FRAMEBUFFER, GL_COLOR_ATTACHMENT0,
                                  GL_RENDERBUFFER, renderbuffer[Color]);

        glFramebufferRenderbuffer(GL_DRAW_FRAMEBUFFER, GL_DEPTH_ATTACHMENT,
                                  GL_RENDERBUFFER, renderbuffer[Depth]);

        glEnable(GL_DEPTH_TEST);
}

void
display()
{
        // Prepare to render into the renderbuffer

        glBindFramebuffer(GL_DRAW_FRAMEBUFFER, framebuffer);

        glViewport(0, 0, 256, 256);

        // Render into renderbuffer

        glClearColor(1.0, 0.0, 0.0, 1.0);
        glClear(GL_COLOR_BUFFER_BIT | GL_DEPTH_BUFFER_BIT);

        ...

        // Set up to read from the renderbuffer and draw to
        //   window-system framebuffer

        glBindFramebuffer(GL_READ_FRAMEBUFFER, framebuffer);
        glBindFramebuffer(GL_DRAW_FRAMEBUFFER, 0);

        glViewport(0, 0, windowWidth, windowHeight);
        glClearColor(0.0, 0.0, 1.0, 1.0);

        glClear(GL_COLOR_BUFFER_BIT | GL_DEPTH_BUFFER_BIT);

        /* Do the copy */

        glBlitFramebuffer(0, 0, 255, 255, 0, 0, 255, 255,
                          GL_COLOR_BUFFER_BIT, GL_NEAREST);
        glutSwapBuffers();
}
```

Framebuffer Completeness

Given the myriad of combinations between texture and buffer formats, and between framebuffer attachments, various situations can arise that prevent the completion of rendering when you are using application-defined framebuffer objects. After modifying the attachments to a framebuffer object, it's best to check the framebuffer's status by calling **glCheckFramebufferStatus()**.

GLenum **glCheckFramebufferStatus**(GLenum *target*);

Returns one of the framebuffer completeness status enums listed in Table 4.8. *target* must be one of GL_READ_FRAMEBUFFER, GL_DRAW_FRAMEBUFFER, or GL_FRAMEBUFFER (which is equivalent to GL_DRAW_FRAMEBUFFER).

If **glCheckFramebufferStatus()** generates an error, zero is returned.

The errors representing the various violations of framebuffer configurations are listed in Table 4.8.

Of the listed errors, GL_FRAMEBUFFER_UNSUPPORTED is very implementation dependent, and may be the most complicated to debug.

Advanced

glClear(GL_COLOR_BUFFER_BIT) will clear all of the bound color buffers (we have see in "Framebuffer Objects" on Page 180 how to configure multiple color buffers). You can use the **glClearBuffer*()** commands to clear individual buffers.

If you're using multiple draw buffers—particularly those that have floating-point or nonnormalized integer pixel formats—you can clear each individually bound buffer using **glClearBuffer*()** functions. Unlike functions such as **glClearColor()** and **glClearDepth()**, which set a clear value within OpenGL that's used when **glClear()** is called, **glClearBuffer*()** uses the values passed to it to immediately clear the bound drawing buffers. Additionally, to reduce the number of function calls associated with using multiple draw buffers, you can call **glClearBufferfi()** to simultaneously clear the depth and stencil buffers (which is effectively equivalent to calling **glClearBuffer*()** twice—once for the depth buffer and once for the stencil buffer).

Table 4.8   Errors Returned by **glCheckFramebufferStatus()**

Framebuffer Completeness Status Enum	Description
GL_FRAMEBUFFER_COMPLETE	The framebuffer and its attachments match the rendering or reading state required.
GL_FRAMEBUFFER_UNDEFINED	The bound framebuffer is specified to be the default framebuffer (i.e., **glBindFramebuffer()** with zero specified as the framebuffer), and the default framebuffer doesn't exist.
GL_FRAMEBUFFER_INCOMPLETE_ATTACHMENT	A necessary attachment to the bound framebuffer is uninitialized
GL_FRAMEBUFFER_INCOMPLETE_MISSING_ATTACHMENT	There are no images (e.g., texture layers or renderbuffers) attached to the framebuffer.
GL_FRAMEBUFFER_INCOMPLETE_DRAW_BUFFER	Every drawing buffer (e.g., GL_DRAW_BUFFER*i* as specified by **glDrawBuffers()**) has an attachment.
GL_FRAMEBUFFER_INCOMPLETE_READ_BUFFER	An attachment exists for the buffer specified for the buffer specified by **glReadBuffer()**.
GL_FRAMEBUFFER_UNSUPPORTED	The combination of images attached to the framebuffer object is incompatible with the requirements of the OpenGL implementation.
GL_FRAMEBUFFER_INCOMPLETE_MULTISAMPLE	The number of samples for all images across the framebuffer's attachments do not match.

Clears the buffer indexed by *drawbuffer* associated with *buffer* to *value*.
buffer must be one of GL_COLOR, GL_DEPTH, or GL_STENCIL.

If *buffer* is GL_COLOR, *drawbuffer* specifies an index to a particular draw
buffer, and *value* is a four-element array containing the clear color. If the
buffer indexed by *drawbuffer* has multiple draw buffers (as specified by a
call the **glDrawBuffers**()), all draw buffers are cleared to *value*.

If *buffer* is GL_DEPTH or GL_STENCIL, *drawbuffer* must be zero, and *value*
is a single-element array containing an appropriate clear value (subject to
clamping and type conversion for depth values, and masking and type
conversion for stencil values). Use only **glClearBufferfv**() for clearing the
depth buffer, and **glClearBufferiv**() for clearing the stencil buffer.

glClearBufferfi() can be used to clear both the depth and stencil buffers
simultaneously. *buffer* in this case must be GL_DEPTH_STENCIL.

GL_INVALID_ENUM is generated by **glClearbuffer**{if ui}**v** if *buffer* is not
one of the accepted values listed above. GL_INVALID_ENUM is generated
by **glClearBufferfi**() if *buffer* is not GL_DEPTH_STENCIL.
GL_INVALID_VALUE is generated if *buffer* is GL_COLOR, and *drawbuffer*
is less than zero, or greater than or equal to GL_MAX_DRAW_BUFFERS;
or if *buffer* is GL_DEPTH, GL_STENCIL, or GL_DEPTH_STENCIL and
drawbuffer is not zero.

Invalidating Framebuffers

Implementations of OpenGL (including OpenGL ES on mobile or
embedded devices, most often) may work in limited memory
environments. Framebuffers have the potential of taking up considerable
memory resources (particularly for multiple, multisampled color
attachments and textures). OpenGL provides a mechanism to state that a
region or all of a framebuffer is no longer needed and can be released. This
operation is done with either **glInvalidateSubFramebuffer**() or
glInvalidateFramebuffer().

```
void glInvalidateFramebuffer(GLenum target,
                              GLsizei numAttachments,
                              const GLenum *attachments);
void glInvalidateSubFramebuffer(GLenum target,
                                 GLsizei numAttachmens,
                                 const GLenum *attachments,
                                 GLint x, GLint y,
                                 GLsizei width, GLsizei height);
```

Specifies that a portion, or the entirety, of the bound framebuffer object are not necessary to preserve. For either function, *target* must be either GL_DRAW_FRAMEBUFFER, GL_READ_FRAMEBUFFER, or GL_FRAMEBUFFER specifying both the draw and read targets at the same time. *attachments* provides a list of attachment tokens: GL_COLOR_ATTACHMENT*i*, GL_DEPTH_ATTACHMENT, or GL_STENCIL_ATTACHMENT; and *numAttachments* specifies how many entries are in the *attachments* list.

For **glInvalidateSubFramebuffer()**, the region specified by lower-left corner (x, y) with width *width*, and height *height* (measured from (x, y)), is marked as invalid for all attachments in *attachments*.

Various errors are returned from the calls: A GL_INVALID_ENUM is generated if any tokens are not from those listed above; A GL_INVALID_OPERATION is generated if an index of an attachment (e.g., *i* from GL_COLOR_ATTACHMENT*i*) is greater than or equal to the maximum number of color attachments; A GL_INVALID_VALUE is generated if any of *numAttachments*, *width*, or *height* are negative.

Writing to Multiple Renderbuffers Simultaneously

Advanced

One feature of using framebuffer objects with multiple renderbuffer (or textures, as described in Chapter 6, "Textures") is the ability to write to multiple buffers from a fragment shader simultaneously, often called *MRT* (for *multiple-render target*) rendering. This is mostly a performance optimization, saving processing the same list of vertices multiple times and rasterizing the same primitives multiple times.

While this technique is used often in GPGPU, it can also be used when generating geometry and other information (like textures or normal map) which is written to different buffers during the same rendering pass. Enabling this technique requires setting up a framebuffer object with multiple color (and potentially depth and stencil) attachments, and modification of the fragment shader. Having just discussed setting up multiple attachments, we'll focus on the fragment shader here.

As we've discussed, fragment shaders output values through their `out` variables. In order to specify the correspondence between `out` variables and framebuffer attachments, we simply need to use the `layout` qualifier to direct values to the right places. For instance, Example 4.12 demonstrates associating two variables with color attachment locations zero and one.

Example 4.12   Specifying `layout` Qualifiers for MRT Rendering

```
layout (location = 0) out vec4 color;
layout (location = 1) out vec4 normal;
```

If the attachments of the currently bound framebuffer don't match those of the currently bound fragment shader, misdirected data (i.e., fragment shader data written to an attachment with nothing attached) accumulates in dark corners of the universe, but is otherwise ignored.

Additionally, if you're using dual-source blending (see "Dual-Source Blending" on Page 198), with MRT rendering, you merely specify both the `location` and `index` options to the `layout` directive.

Using the `layout` qualifier within a shader is the preferred way to associate fragment shader outputs with framebuffer attachments, but if they are not specified, then OpenGL will do the assignments during shader linking. You can direct the linker to make the appropriate associations by using the **glBindFragDataLocation()**, or **glBindFragDataLocationIndexed()** if you need to also specify the fragment `index`. Fragment shader bindings specified in the shader source will be used if specified, regardless of whether a location was specified using one of these functions.

```
void glBindFragDataLocation(GLuint program,
                            GLuint colorNumber,
                            const GLchar *name);
void glBindFragDataLocationIndexed(GLuint program,
                                   GLuint colorNumber,
                                   GLuint index,
                                   const GLchar *name);
```

Uses the value in *color* for fragment shader variable *name* to specify the output location associated with shader *program*. For the indexed case, *index* specifies the output index as well as the location.

A GL_INVALID_VALUE is generated if *program* is not a shader program, or if either *index* is greater than one, or if *colorNumber* is greater than or equal to the maximum number of color attachments.

After a program is linked, you can retrieve a fragment shader variable's output location, and source index, if applicable, by calling either **glGetFragDataLocation()**, or **glGetFragDataIndex()**.

```
GLint glGetFragDataLocation(GLuint program,
                            const GLchar *name);
GLint glGetFragDataIndex(GLuint program,
                         const GLchar *name);
```

Returns either the location or index of a fragment shader variable *name* associated with the linked shader program *program*.

A −1 is returned if: *name* is not the name of applicable variable for *program*; if *program* successfully linked, but doesn't have an associated fragment shader; or if *program* has not yet been, or failed, linking. In the last case, a GL_INVALID_OPERATION error is also generated.

Selecting Color Buffers for Writing and Reading

The results of a drawing or reading operation can go into or come from any of the color buffers:

- front, back, front-left, back-left, front-right, or back-right for the default framebuffer, or

- front, or any renderbuffer attachment for a user-defined framebuffer object.

You can choose an individual buffer to be the drawing or reading target. For drawing, you can also set the target to draw into more than one buffer at the same time. You use **glDrawBuffer()**, or **glDrawBuffers()** to select the buffers to be written and **glReadBuffer()** to select the buffer as the source for **glReadPixels()**, **glCopyTexImage*()**, and **glCopyTexSubImage*()**.

---

void **glDrawBuffer**(GLenum *mode*);
void **glDrawBuffers**(GLsizei *n*, const GLenum **buffers*);

Selects the color buffers enabled for writing or clearing and disables buffers enabled by previous calls to **glDrawBuffer()** or **glDrawBuffers()**. More than one buffer may be enabled at one time. The value of *mode* can be one of the following:

GL_FRONT	GL_FRONT_LEFT	GL_NONE
GL_BACK	GL_FRONT_RIGHT	GL_FRONT_AND_BACK
GL_LEFT	GL_BACK_LEFT	GL_COLOR_ATTACHMENT*i*
GL_RIGHT	GL_BACK_RIGHT	

If *mode*, or the entries in *buffers* is not one of the above, a GL_INVALID_ENUM error is generated. Additionally, if a framebuffer object is bound that is not the default framebuffer, then only GL_NONE and GL_COLOR_ATTACHMENT*i* are accepted, otherwise a GL_INVALID_ENUM error is generated.

Arguments that omit LEFT or RIGHT refer to both the left and right stereo buffers; similarly, arguments that omit FRONT or BACK refer to both.

By default, mode is GL_BACK for double-buffered contexts.

The **glDrawBuffers()** routine specifies multiple color buffers capable of receiving color values. *buffers* is an array of buffer enumerates. Only GL_NONE, GL_FRONT_LEFT, GL_FRONT_RIGHT, GL_BACK_LEFT, and GL_BACK_RIGHT are accepted.

When you are using double-buffering, you usually want to draw only in the back buffer (and swap the buffers when you're finished drawing). In some situations, you might want to treat a double-buffered window as though it were single-buffered by calling **glDrawBuffer(GL_FRONT_AND_BACK)** to enable you to draw to both front and back buffers at the same time.

For selecting the read buffer, use **glReadBuffer()**.

void **glReadBuffer**(GLenum *mode*);

Selects the color buffer enabled as the source for reading pixels for subsequent calls to **glReadPixels()**, **glCopyTexImage*()**, **glCopyTexSubImage*()**, and disables buffers enabled by previous calls to **glReadBuffer()**. The value of *mode* can be one of the following:

GL_FRONT	GL_FRONT_LEFT	GL_NONE
GL_BACK	GL_FRONT_RIGHT	GL_FRONT_AND_BACK
GL_LEFT	GL_BACK_LEFT	GL_COLOR_ATTACHMENT*i*
GL_RIGHT	GL_BACK_RIGHT	

If *mode* is not one of the above tokens, a GL_INVALID_ENUM is generated.

As we've seen, when a framebuffer object has multiple attachments, you can control various aspects of what happens with the renderbuffer at an attachment, like controlling the scissors box, or blending. You use the commands **glEnablei()** and **glDisablei()** to control capabilities on a per-attachment granularity.

void **glEnablei**(GLenum *capability*, GLuint *index*);
void **glDisablei**(GLenum *capability*, GLuint *index*);

Enables or disables *capability* for buffer *index*.

A GL_INVALID_VALUE is generated if *index* is greater than or equal to GL_MAX_DRAW_BUFFERS.

GLboolean **glIsEnabledi**(GLenum *capability*, GLuint *index*);

Specifies whether *target* is enabled for buffer *index*.

A GL_INVALID_VALUE is generated if *index* is outside of the range supported for *target*.

Dual-Source Blending

Advanced

Two of the blend factors already described in this chapters are the *second source* blending factors and are special in that they are driven by a second output in the fragment shader. These factors, GL_SRC1_COLOR and GL_SRC1_ALPHA, are produced in the fragment shader by writing to an output whose index is 1 (rather than the default 0). To create such an output we use the `index` *layout qualifier* when declaring it in the fragment shader. Example 4.13 shows an example of such a declaration.

Example 4.13   Layout Qualifiers Specifying the Index of Fragment
                     Shader Outputs

```
layout (location = 0, index = 0) out vec4 first_output;
layout (location = 0, index = 1) out vec4 second_output;
```

When calling **glBlendFunc()**, **glBlendFunci()**, **glBlendFuncSeparate()**, or **glBlendFuncSeparatei()**, the GL_SRC_COLOR, GL_SRC_ALPHA, GL_ONE_MINUS_SRC_COLOR, or GL_ONE_MINUS_SRC_ALPHA factors will cause the blending equation's input to be taken from `first_input`. However, passing GL_SRC1_COLOR, GL_SRC1_ALPHA GL_ONE_MINUS_SRC1_COLOR, or GL_ONE_MINUS_SRC1_ALPHA to these functions will cause the input to be taken from `second_output`. This allows some interesting blending equations to be built up by using combinations of the first and second sources in each of the source and destination blend factors.

For example, setting the source factor to GL_SRC1_COLOR and the destination factor to GL_ONE_MINUS_SRC1_COLOR using one of the blending functions essentially allows a *per-channel alpha* to be created in the fragment shader. This type of functionality is especially useful when implementing subpixel accurate antialiasing techniques in the fragment shader. By taking the location of the red, green, and blue color elements in the pixels on the screen into account, coverage for each element can be generated in the fragment shader and be used to selectively light each color by a function of its coverage. Figure 4.4 shows a close-up picture of the red, green and blue picture elements in a liquid crystal computer monitor. The subpixels are clearly visible, although when viewed at normal distance, the display appears white. By lighting each of the red, green, and blue elements separately, very high-quality antialiasing can be implemented.

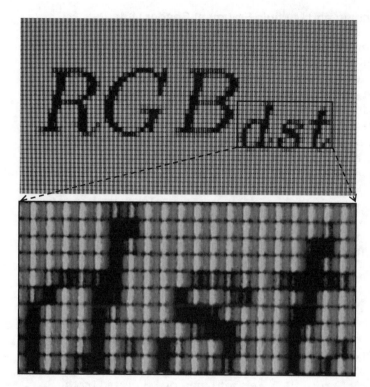

Figure 4.4   Close-up of RGB color elements in an LCD panel

Another possible use is to set the source and destination factors in the blending equation to GL_ONE and GL_SRC1_COLOR. In this configuration, the first color output is added to the framebuffer's content, while the second color output is used to attenuate the framebuffer's content. The equation becomes:

$$RGB_{dst} = RGB_{src0} + RGB_{src1} * RGB_{dst}$$

This is a classic multiply-add operation and can be used for many purposes. For example, if you want to render a translucent object with a colored specular highlight, write the color of the object to second_output and the highlight color to first_output.

Dual-Source Blending and Multiple Fragment Shader Outputs

Because the second output from the fragment shader that
is required to implement dual source blending may take from the resources
available to produce outputs for multiple framebuffer attachments (draw
buffers), there are special counting rules for dual-source blending. When
dual-source blending is enabled—that is, when any of the factors specified
to one of the **glBlendFunc()** functions is one of the tokens that includes
SRC1, the total number of outputs available in the fragment shader may be
reduced. To determine how many outputs may be used (and consequently,
how many framebuffer attachments may be active), query for the value
of GL_MAX_DUAL_SOURCE_DRAW_BUFFERS. Note that the OpenGL
specification only requires that GL_MAX_DUAL_SOURCE_DRAW_BUFFERS
be at least one. If GL_MAX_DUAL_SOURCE_DRAW_BUFFERS
is exactly one, this means that dual source blending and
multiple draw buffers are mutually exclusive and cannot be used together.

Reading and Copying Pixel Data

Once your rendering is complete, you may want to retrieve the rendered
image for posterity. In that case, you can use the **glReadPixels()** function
to read pixels from the read framebuffer and return the pixels to your
application. You can return the pixels into memory allocated by the
application, or into a pixel pack buffer, if one's currently bound.

---

void **glReadPixels**(GLint *x*, GLint *y*, GLsizei *width*, GLsizei *height*,
GLenum *format*, GLenum *type*, void **pixels*);

Reads pixel data from the read framebuffer rectangle whose lower-left
corner is at (x, y) in window coordinates and whose dimensions are *width*
and *height*, and then stores the data in the array pointed to by *pixels*.
format indicates the kind of pixel data elements that are read (color,
depth, or stencil value as listed in Table 4.9), and *type* indicates the data
type of each element (see Table 4.10.)

glReadPixels() can generate a few OpenGL errors. A
GL_INVALID_OPERATION error will be generated if format is set to
GL_DEPTH and there is no depth buffer; or if format is GL_STENCIL and
there is no stencil buffer; or if format is set to GL_DEPTH_STENCIL and
there are not both a depth and a stencil buffer associated with the
framebuffer, or if type is neither GL_UNSIGNED_INT_24_8 nor
GL_FLOAT_32_UNSIGNED_INT_24_8_REV, then GL_INVALID_ENUM is
set.

Table 4.9   glReadPixels() Data Formats

Format Value	**Pixel Format**
GL_RED or GL_RED_INTEGER	a single red color component
GL_GREEN or GL_GREEN_INTEGER	a single green color component
GL_BLUE or GL_BLUE_INTEGER	a single blue color component
GL_ALPHA or GL_ALPHA_INTEGER	a single alpha color component
GL_RG or GL_RG_INTEGER	a red color component, followed by a green component
GL_RGB or GL_RGB_INTEGER	a red color component, followed by green and blue components
GL_RGBA or GL_RGBA_INTEGER	a red color component, followed by green, blue, and alpha components
GL_BGR or GL_BGR_INTEGER	a blue color component, followed by green and red components
GL_BGRA or GL_BGRA_INTEGER	a blue color component, followed by green, red, and alpha components
GL_STENCIL_INDEX	a single stencil index
GL_DEPTH_COMPONENT	a single depth component
GL_DEPTH_STENCIL	combined depth and stencil components

You may need to specify which buffer you want to retrieve pixel values from. For example, in a double-buffered window, you could read the pixels from the front buffer or the back buffer. You can use the **glReadBuffer()** routine to specify which buffer to retrieve the pixels from.

Table 4.10   Data Types for **glReadPixels()**

Type Value	Data Type	Packed
GL_UNSIGNED_BYTE	GLubyte	No
GL_BYTE	GLbyte	No
GL_UNSIGNED_SHORT	GLushort	No
GL_SHORT	GLshort	No
GL_UNSIGNED_INT	GLuint	No
GL_INT	GLint	No
GL_HALF_FLOAT	GLhalf	
GL_FLOAT	GLfloat	No
GL_UNSIGNED_BYTE_3_3_2	GLubyte	Yes
GL_UNSIGNED_BYTE_2_3_3_REV	GLubyte	Yes
GL_UNSIGNED_SHORT_5_6_5	GLushort	Yes
GL_UNSIGNED_SHORT_5_6_5_REV	GLushort	Yes
GL_UNSIGNED_SHORT_4_4_4_4	GLushort	Yes
GL_UNSIGNED_SHORT_4_4_4_4_REV	GLushort	Yes
GL_UNSIGNED_SHORT_5_5_5_1	GLushort	Yes
GL_UNSIGNED_SHORT_1_5_5_5_REV	GLushort	Yes
GL_UNSIGNED_INT_8_8_8_8	GLuint	Yes
GL_UNSIGNED_INT_8_8_8_8_REV	GLuint	Yes
GL_UNSIGNED_INT_10_10_10_2	GLuint	Yes
GL_UNSIGNED_INT_2_10_10_10_REV	GLuint	Yes
GL_UNSIGNED_INT_24_8	GLuint	Yes
GL_UNSIGNED_INT_10F_11F_11F_REV	GLuint	Yes
GL_UNSIGNED_INT_5_9_9_9_REV	GLuint	Yes
GL_FLOAT_32_UNSIGNED_INT_24_8_REV	GLfloat	Yes

Clamping Returned Values

Various types of buffers within OpenGL—most notably floating-point
buffers—can store values with ranges outside of the normal [0, 1] range of
colors in OpenGL. When you read those values back using **glReadPixels()**,

you can control whether the values should be clamped to the normalized range or left at their full range using **glClampColor()**.

---

void **glClampColor**(GLenum *target*, GLenum *clamp*);

Controls the clamping of color values for floating- and fixed-point buffers, when *target* is GL_CLAMP_READ_COLOR. If *clamp* is set to GL_TRUE, color values read from buffers are clamped to the range [0, 1]; conversely, if *clamp* is GL_FALSE, no clamping is engaged. If your application uses a combination of fixed- and floating-point buffers, set *clamp* to GL_FIXED_ONLY to clamp only the fixed-point values; floating-point values are returned with their full range.

Copying Pixel Rectangles

To copy pixels between regions of a buffer, or even different framebuffers, use **glBlitFramebuffer()**. It uses greater pixel *filtering* during the copy operation, much in the same manner as texture mapping (in fact, the same filtering operations, GL_NEAREST and GL_LINEAR are used during the copy). Additionally, this routine is aware of multisampled buffers and supports copying between different framebuffers (as controlled by framebuffer objects).

---

void **glBlitFramebuffer**(GLint *srcX0*, GLint *srcY0*, GLint *srcX1*,
                  GLint *srcY1*, GLint *dstX0*, GLint *dstY0*,
                  GLint *dstX1*, GLint *dstY1*,
                  GLbitfield *buffers*, GLenum *filter*);

Copies a rectangle of pixel values from one region of the read framebuffer to another region of the draw framebuffer, potentially resizing, reversing, converting, and filtering the pixels in the process. *srcX0*, *srcY0*, *srcX1*, *srcY1* represent the source region where pixels are sourced from, and written to the rectangular region specified by *dstX0*, *dstY0*, *dstX1*, and *dstY1*. *buffers* is the bitwise-or of GL_COLOR_BUFFER_BIT, GL_DEPTH_BUFFER_BIT, and GL_STENCIL_BUFFER_BIT, which represent the buffers in which the copy should occur. Finally, *filter* specifies the method of interpolation done if the two rectangular regions are of different sizes, and must be one of GL_NEAREST or GL_LINEAR; no filtering is applied if the regions are of the same size.

If there are multiple-color draw buffers, each buffer receives a copy of the source region.

If *srcX1* < *srcX0*, or *dstX1* < *dstX0*, the image is reversed in the horizontal direction. Likewise, if *srcY1* < *srcY0* or *dstY1* < *dstY0*, the image is reversed in the vertical direction. However, If both the source and destination sizes are negative in the same direction, no reversal is done.

If the source and destination buffers are of different formats, conversion of the pixel values is done in most situations. However, if the read color buffer is a floating-point format, and any of the write color buffers are not, or vice versa; and if the read-color buffer is a signed (unsigned) integer format and not all of the draw buffers are signed (unsigned) integer values, the call will generate a GL_INVALID_OPERATION, and no pixels will be copied.

Multisampled buffers also have an effect on the copying of pixels. If the source buffer is multisampled, and the destination is not, the samples are resolved to a single pixel value for the destination buffer. Conversely, if the source buffer is not multisampled, and the destination is, the source pixel's data is replicated for each sample. Finally, if both buffers are multisampled and the number of samples for each buffer is the same, the samples are copied without modification. However, if the buffers have a different number of samples, no pixels are copied, and a GL_INVALID_OPERATION error is generated.

A GL_INVALID_VALUE error is generated if buffers have other bits set than those permitted, or if *filter* is other than GL_LINEAR or GL_NEAREST.

Chapter 5

Viewing Transformations, Clipping, and Feedback

Chapter Objectives

After reading this chapter, you'll be able to do the following:

- View a three-dimensional geometric model by transforming it to have any size, orientation, and perspective.

- Understand a variety of useful *coordinate systems*, which ones are required by OpenGL, and how to transform from one to the next.

- Transform surface normals.

- Clip your geometric model against arbitrary planes.

- Capture the geometric result of these transforms, before displaying them.

Previous chapters hinted at how to manipulate your geometry to fit into the viewing area on the screen, but we'll give a complete treatment in this chapter. This includes *feedback*, the ability to send it back to the application, as well as clipping, the intersection of your geometry with planes either by OpenGL or by you.

Typically, you'll have many objects with independently specified geometric coordinates. These need to be transformed (moved, scaled, and oriented) into the scene. Then, the scene itself needs to be viewed from a particular location, direction, scaling, and orientation.

This chapter contains the following major sections:

- "Viewing" provides an overview of how computer graphics simulates the three-dimensional world on a two-dimensional display.

- "User Transformations" characterize the various types of transformations that you can employ in shaders to manipulate vertex data.

- "OpenGL Transformations" are the transformations OpenGL implements.

- "Transform Feedback" describes processing and storing vertex data using vertex-transforming shaders to optimize rendering performance.

Viewing

If we display a typical geometric model's coordinates directly onto the display device, we probably won't see much. The range of coordinates in the model (e.g., -100 to $+100$ meters) will not match the range of coordinates consumed by the display device (e.g., 0 to 1919 pixels) and it is cumbersome to restrict ourselves to coordinates that would match. In addition, we want to view the model from different locations, directions, and perspectives. How do we compensate for this?

Fundamentally, the display is a flat, fixed, two-dimensional rectangle while our model contains extended three-dimensional geometry. This chapter will show how to project our model's three-dimensional coordinates onto the fixed two-dimensional screen coordinates.

The key tools for projecting three dimensions down to two are a *viewing model*, use of *homogeneous coordinates*, application of linear *transformations* by matrix multiplication, and setting up a viewportmapping. These tools are each discussed in detail below.

Viewing Model

For the time being, it is important to keep thinking in terms of three-dimensional coordinates while making many of the decisions that determine what is drawn on the screen. It is too early to start thinking about which pixels need to be drawn. Instead, try to visualize three-dimensional space. It is later, after the viewing transformations are completed, after the subjects of this chapter, that pixels will enter the discussion.

Camera Model

The common transformation process for producing the desired view is analogous to taking a photograph with a camera. As shown in Figure 5.1 the steps with a camera (or a computer) might be the following:

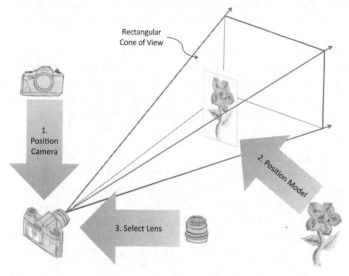

Figure 5.1   Steps in configuring and positioning the viewing frustum

1. Move your camera to the location you want to shoot from and point the camera the desired direction (viewing transformation).

2. Move the subject to be photographed into the desired location in the scene (modeling transformation).

3. Choose a camera lens or adjust the zoom (projection transformation).

4. Take the picture (apply the transformations).

5. Stretch or shrink the resulting image to the desired picture size (viewport transformation). For 3D graphics, this also includes stretching or shrinking the depth (depth-range scaling). This is not to be confused with Step 3, which selected *how much of the scene* to capture, not *how much to stretch* the result.

Notice that Steps 1 and 2 can be considered doing the same thing, but in opposite directions. You can leave the camera where you found it and bring the subject in front of it, or leave the subject where it is and move the camera toward the subject. Moving the camera to the left is the same as moving the subject to the right. Twisting the camera clockwise is the same as twisting the subject counterclockwise. It is really up to you which movements you perform as part of Step 1, with the remainder belonging to Step 2. Because of this, these two steps are normally lumped together as the model-view transform. It will, though, always consist of some sequence of movements (translations), rotations, and scalings. The defining characteristic of this combination is in making a single, unified space for all the objects assembled into one scene to view, or *eye space*.

In OpenGL, you are responsible for doing Steps 1 through 3 above in your shaders. That is, you'll be required to hand OpenGL coordinates with the model-view and projective transformations already done. You are also responsible for telling OpenGL how to do the viewport transformation for Step 5, but the fixed rendering pipeline will do that transformation for you, as described in "OpenGL Transformations" on Page 236.

Figure 5.2 summarizes the coordinate systems required by OpenGL for the full process. So far, we have discussed the second box (user transforms) but are showing the rest to set the context for the whole viewing stack, finishing with how you specify your viewport and *depth range* to OpenGL. The final coordinates handed to OpenGL for clipping and rasterization are *normalized* homogeneous coordinates. That is, the coordinates to be drawn will be in the range $[-1.0, 1.0]$ until OpenGL scales them to fit the viewport.

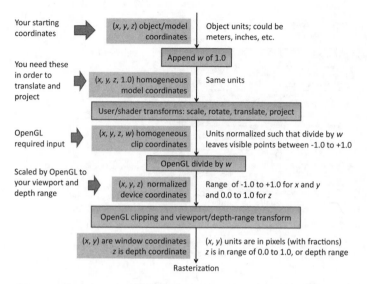

Figure 5.2   Coordinate systems required by OpenGL
(The coordinate systems are the boxes on the left. The central boxes transform from one coordinate system to the next. Units are described to the right.)

It will be useful to name additional coordinate systems lying within the view, model, and projection transforms. These are no longer part of the OpenGL model, but still highly useful and conventional when using shaders to assemble a scene or calculate lighting. Figure 5.3 shows an expansion of the user transforms box from Figure 5.2. In particular, most lighting calculations done in shaders will be done in eye space. Examples making full use of eye space are provided in Chapter 7, "Light and Shadow".

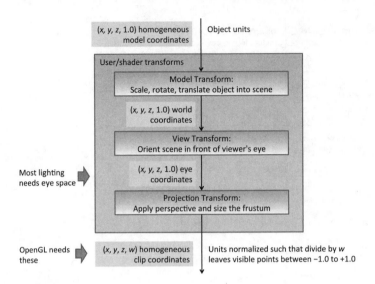

Figure 5.3   User coordinate systems unseen by OpenGL
(These coordinate systems, while not used by OpenGL, are still vital for lighting and other shader operations.)

Viewing Frustum

Step 3 in our camera analogy chose a lens, or zoom amount. This selects how narrow or wide of a rectangular cone through the scene the camera will capture. Only geometry falling within this cone will be in the final picture. At the same time, Step 3 will also produce the information needed (in the homogeneous fourth coordinate, w) to later create the foreshortening effect of perspective.

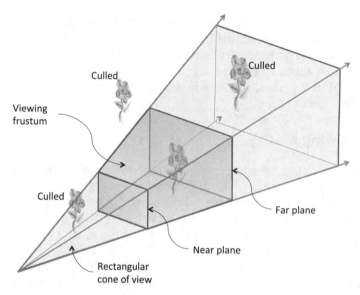

Figure 5.4 A view frustum

OpenGL will additionally exclude geometry that is too close or too far away; that is, those in front of a *near plane* or those behind a *far plane*. There is no counterpart to this in the camera analogy (other than cleaning foreign objects from inside your lens), but is helpful in a variety of ways. Most importantly, objects approaching the cone's apex appear infinitely large, which causes problems, especially if they should reach the apex. At the other end of this spectrum, objects too far away to be drawn in the scene are best excluded for performance reasons and some depth precision reasons as well, if depth must span too large a distance.

Thus, we have two additional planes intersecting the four planes of the rectangular viewing cone. As shown in Figure 5.4, these six planes define a frustum-shaped viewing volume.

Frustum Clipping

Any primitive falling outside the four planes forming the rectangular viewing cone will not get drawn (culled), as it would fall outside our rectangular display. Further, anything in front of the near plane or behind the far plane will also be culled. What about a primitive that spans both sides of one of these planes? OpenGL will *clip* such primitives. That is, it will compute the intersection of their geometry with the plane and form new geometry for just the shape that falls within the frustum.

Because OpenGL has to perform this clipping to draw correctly, the application must tell OpenGL where this frustum is. This is part of Step 3 of the camera analogy, where the shader must apply the transformations, but OpenGL must know about it for clipping. There are ways shaders can clip against additional user planes, discussed later, but the six frustum planes are an intrinsic part of OpenGL.

Orthographic Viewing Model

Sometimes, a perspective view is not desired, and an *orthographic* view is used instead. This type of projection is used by applications for architectural blueprints and computer-aided design, where it's crucial to maintain the actual sizes of objects and the angles between them as they're projected. This could be done simply by ignoring one of the x, y, or z coordinates, letting the other two coordinates give two-dimensional locations. You would do that, of course, after orienting the objects and the scene with model-view transformations, as with the camera model. But, in the end, you will still need to locate and scale the resulting model for display in normalized device coordinates. The transformation for this is the last one given in the next section.

User Transformations

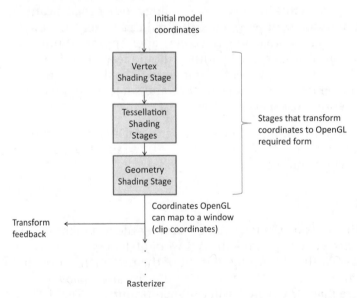

Figure 5.5   Pipeline subset for user/shader part of transforming coordinates

The stages of the rendering pipeline that transform three-dimensional coordinates for OpenGL viewing are shown in Figure 5.5. Essentially, they are the programmable stages appearing before rasterization. Because these stages are programmable, you have a lot of flexibility in the initial form of your coordinates and in how you transform them. However, you are constrained to end with the form the subsequent fixed (nonprogrammable) stages need. That is, we'll need to make homogeneous coordinates that are ready for *perspective division* (also referred to as *clip coordinates*). What that means and how to do it are the subjects of the following sections.

Each of the viewing model steps above was called out as a transformation. They are all linear transformations that can be accomplished through matrix multiplication on homogeneous coordinates. The upcoming matrix multiplication and homogenous coordinate sections give refreshers on these topics. Understanding them is the key to truly understanding how OpenGL transformations work.

In a shader, transforming a vertex by a matrix looks like this:

```
#version 330 core

uniform mat4 Transform; // stays the same for many vertices
                        // (primitive granularity)
in vec4 Vertex;         // per-vertex data sent each time this
                        // shader is run

void main()
{
    gl_Position = Transform * Vertex;
}
```

Linear transformations are composable; so just because our camera analogy needed four transformation steps does not mean we have to transform our data four times. Rather, all those transformations can be composed into a single transformation. If we want to transform our model first by transformation matrix A followed by transformation matrix B, we will see we can do so with transformation matrix C, where

$$C = BA$$

(Because we are showing examples of matrix multiplication with the vertex on the right and the matrix on the left, composing transforms show up in reverse order: B is applied to the result of applying A to a vertex. The details behind this are explained in the upcoming refresher.)

So, the good news is we can collapse any number of linear transformations into a single matrix multiply, allowing the freedom to think in terms of whatever steps are most convenient.

Matrix Multiply Refresher

For our use, matrices and matrix multiplication are nothing more than a convenient mechanism for expressing linear transformations, which in turn are a useful way to do the coordinate manipulations needed for displaying models. The vital matrix mechanism is explained here, while interesting uses for it will come up in numerous places in subsequent discussions.

First, a definition. A 4×4 matrix takes a four-component vector to another four-component vector through multiplication by the following rule:

$$\begin{bmatrix} a & b & c & d \\ e & f & g & h \\ i & j & k & l \\ m & n & o & p \end{bmatrix} \begin{pmatrix} x \\ y \\ z \\ w \end{pmatrix} \rightarrow \begin{pmatrix} ax & + & by & + & cz & + & dw \\ ex & + & fy & + & gz & + & hw \\ ix & + & jy & + & kz & + & lw \\ mx & + & ny & + & oz & + & pw \end{pmatrix}$$

Now, some observations.

- Each component of the new vector is a linear function of all the components of the old vector, hence the need for 16 values in the matrix.

- The multiplication always takes the vector $(0, 0, 0, 0)$ to $(0, 0, 0, 0)$. This is characteristic of linear transformations and shows that if this was a 3×3 matrix times a three-component vector, why translation (moving) can't be done with a matrix multiply. We'll see how translating a three-component vector becomes possible with a 4×4 matrix and homogeneous coordinates.

In our viewing models, we will want to take a vector through multiple transformations, here expressed as matrix multiplications by matrices A and then B:

$$v' = Av \qquad (5.1)$$
$$v'' = Bv' = B(Av) = (BA)v \qquad (5.2)$$

and we'll want to do this efficiently by finding a matrix C such that

$$v'' = Cv$$

where

$$C = BA$$

Being able to compose the B transform and the A transform into a single transform C is a benefit we get by sticking to linear transformations. The following definition of matrix multiplication makes all of this work out.

$$
\begin{bmatrix}
b_{11} & b_{12} & b_{13} & b_{14} \\
b_{21} & b_{22} & b_{23} & b_{24} \\
b_{31} & b_{32} & b_{33} & b_{34} \\
b_{41} & b_{42} & b_{43} & b_{44}
\end{bmatrix}
\begin{bmatrix}
a_{11} & a_{12} & a_{13} & a_{14} \\
a_{21} & a_{22} & a_{23} & a_{24} \\
a_{31} & a_{32} & a_{33} & a_{34} \\
a_{41} & a_{42} & a_{43} & a_{44}
\end{bmatrix}
\rightarrow
\begin{bmatrix}
c_{11} & c_{12} & c_{13} & c_{14} \\
c_{21} & c_{22} & c_{23} & c_{24} \\
c_{31} & c_{32} & c_{33} & c_{34} \\
c_{41} & c_{42} & c_{43} & c_{44}
\end{bmatrix}
$$

where

$$c_{ij} = b_{i1}a_{1j} + b_{i2}a_{2j} + b_{i3}a_{3j} + b_{i4}a_{4j}$$

that is

$$
\begin{aligned}
c_{11} &= b_{11}a_{11} + b_{12}a_{21} + b_{13}a_{31} + b_{14}a_{41} \\
c_{12} &= b_{11}a_{12} + b_{12}a_{22} + b_{13}a_{32} + b_{14}a_{42} \\
c_{13} &= b_{11}a_{13} + b_{12}a_{23} + b_{13}a_{33} + b_{14}a_{43} \\
c_{14} &= b_{11}a_{14} + b_{12}a_{24} + b_{13}a_{34} + b_{14}a_{44}
\end{aligned}
$$

$$
\begin{aligned}
c_{21} &= b_{21}a_{11} + b_{12}a_{21} + b_{13}a_{31} + b_{14}a_{41} \\
c_{22} &= b_{21}a_{12} + b_{22}a_{22} + b_{23}a_{32} + b_{24}a_{42} \\
&\;\;\vdots \qquad \vdots \\
c_{44} &= b_{41}a_{14} + b_{42}a_{24} + b_{43}a_{34} + b_{44}a_{44}
\end{aligned}
$$

Matrix multiplication is noncommutative: generally speaking, when multiplying matrices and A and B

$$AB \neq BA$$

and, generally, when multiplying matrix A and vector v

$$Av \neq vA$$

so care is needed to multiply in the correct order. Matrix multiplication is, fortunately, associative:

$$C(BA) = (CB)A = CBA$$

That's useful, as accumulated matrix multiplies on a vector can be re-associated.

$$C(B(Av)) = (CBA)v$$

This is a key result we will take advantage of to improve performance.

Homogeneous Coordinates

The geometry we want to transform is innately three-dimensional. However, we will gain two key advantages by moving from three-component Cartesian coordinates to four-component homogeneous coordinates. These are 1) the ability to apply perspective and 2) the ability to translate (move) the model using only a linear transform. That is, we will be able to get all the rotations, translations, scaling, and projective transformations we need by doing matrix multiplication if we first move to a four-coordinate system. More accurately, the projective transformation is a key step in creating perspective, and it is the step we must perform in our shaders. (The final step is performed by the system when it eliminates this new fourth coordinate.)

If you want to understand this and homogeneous coordinates more deeply, read the next section. If you just want to go on some faith and grab 4×4 matrices that will get the job done, you can skip to the next section.

Advanced: What Are Homogeneous Coordinates?

Three-dimensional data can be scaled and rotated with linear transformations of three-component vectors by multiplying by 3×3 matrices.

Unfortunately, translating (moving/sliding over) three-dimensional Cartesian coordinates *cannot* be done by multiplying with a 3×3 matrix. It requires an extra vector addition to move the point $(0, 0, 0)$ somewhere else. This is called an *affine transformation*, which is not a linear transformation. (Recall that any linear transformation maps $(0, 0, 0)$ to $(0, 0, 0)$.) Including that addition means the loss of the benefits of linear transformations, like the ability to compose multiple transformations into a single transformation. So, we want to find a way to translate with a linear transformation. Fortunately, by embedding our data in a four-coordinate space, affine transformations turn back into a simple linear transform (meaning you can move your model laterally using only multiplication by a 4×4 matrix).

For example, to move data by 0.3 in the y direction, assuming a fourth vector coordinate of 1.0:

$$\begin{bmatrix} 1.0 & 0.0 & 0.0 & 0.0 \\ 0.0 & 1.0 & 0.0 & 0.3 \\ 0.0 & 0.0 & 1.0 & 0.0 \\ 0.0 & 0.0 & 0.0 & 1.0 \end{bmatrix} \begin{pmatrix} x \\ y \\ z \\ 1.0 \end{pmatrix} \rightarrow \begin{pmatrix} x \\ y + 0.3 \\ z \\ 1.0 \end{pmatrix}$$

At the same time, we acquire the extra component needed to do perspective.

A homogeneous coordinate has one extra component and does not change the point it represents when all its components are scaled by the same amount.

For example, all these coordinates represent the same point:

$$(2.0, 3.0, 5.0, 1.0)$$
$$(4.0, 6.0, 10.0, 2.0)$$
$$(0.2, 0.3, 0.5, 0.1)$$

In this way, homogeneous coordinates act as directions instead of locations; scaling a direction leaves it pointing in the same direction. This is shown in Figure 5.6. Standing at $(0, 0)$, the homogeneous points $(1, 2)$, $(2, 4)$, and others along that line appear in the same place. When projected onto the 1D space, they all become the point 2.

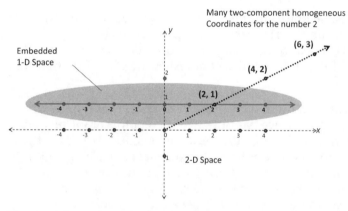

Figure 5.6   One-dimensional homogeneous space
(Shows how to embed the 1D space into two dimensions, at the location $y = 1$, to get homogeneous coordinates.)

Skewing is a linear transformation. Skewing Figure 5.6 can translate the embedded 1D space, as show in Figure 5.7, while preserving the location of $(0, 0)$ in the 2D space (all linear transforms keep $(0, 0)$ fixed).

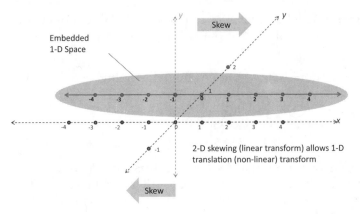

Embedded
1-D Space

Skew

2-D skewing (linear transform) allows 1-D
translation (non-linear) transform

Skew

Figure 5.7   Translating by skewing

The desire is to translate points in the 1D space with a linear transform. This is impossible within the 1D space, as the point 0 needs to move—something 1D linear transformations cannot do. However, the 2D skewing transformation is linear and accomplishes the goal of translating the 1D space.

If the last component of an homogeneous coordinate is 0, it implies a "point at infinity". The 1D space has only two such points at infinity, one in the positive direction and one in the negative direction. However, the 3D space, embedded in a four-coordinate homogeneous space, has a point at infinity for any direction you can point. These points can model the perspective point where two parallel lines (e.g., sides of a building or railroad tracks) would appear to meet. The perspective effects we care about, though, will become visible without needing to specifically think about this.

We will move to homogeneous coordinates by adding a fourth w component of 1.0.

$$(2.0, 3.0, 5.0) \rightarrow (2.0, 3.0, 5.0, 1.0)$$

and later go back to Cartesian coordinates by dividing all components by the fourth component and dropping the fourth component.

$$(4.0, 6.0, 10.0, 2.0) \xrightarrow{\text{divide by } w} (2.0, 3.0, 5.0, 1.0) \xrightarrow{\text{drop } w} (2.0, 3.0, 5.0)$$

Perspective transforms modify w components to values other than 1.0. Making w larger can make coordinates appear further away. When it's time to display geometry, OpenGL will transform homogeneous coordinates back to the three-dimensional Cartesian coordinates by dividing their first three components by the last component. This will make the objects farther away (now having a larger w) have smaller Cartesian coordinates, hence getting drawn on a smaller scale. A w of 0.0 implies (x, y) coordinates at infinity (the object got so close to the viewpoint that its perspective view got infinitely large). This can lead to undefined results. There is nothing fundamentally wrong with a negative w; the following coordinates represent the same point.

$$(2.0, 3.0, 5.0, 1.0)$$
$$(-2.0, -3.0, -5.0, -1.0)$$

But negative w can stir up trouble in some parts of the graphics pipeline, especially if it ever gets interpolated toward a positive w, as that can make it land on or very near 0.0. The simplest way to avoid problems is to keep your w components positive.

Linear Transformations and Matrices

We start our task of mapping into device coordinates by adding a fourth component to our three-dimensional Cartesian coordinates, with a value of 1.0, to make homogeneous coordinates. These coordinates are then ready to be multiplied by one or more 4×4 matrices that rotate, scale, translate, and apply perspective. Examples of how to use each of these transforms are given below. The summary is that each of these transformations can be made through multiplication by a 4×4 matrix, and a series of such transformations can be composed into a single 4×4 matrix, once, that can then be used on multiple vertices.

Translation

Translating an object takes advantage of the fourth component we just added to our model coordinates and of the fourth column of a 4×4 transformation matrix. We want a matrix T to multiply all our object's vertices v by to get translated vertices v'.

$$v' = Tv$$

Each component can be translated by a different amount by putting those amounts in the fourth column of T. For example, to translate by 2.5 in the positive x direction, and not at all in the y or z directions:

$$T = \begin{bmatrix} 1.0 & 0.0 & 0.0 & 2.5 \\ 0.0 & 1.0 & 0.0 & 0.0 \\ 0.0 & 0.0 & 1.0 & 0.0 \\ 0.0 & 0.0 & 0.0 & 1.0 \end{bmatrix}$$

and multiplying by a vector $v = (x, y, z, 1)$ gives

$$\begin{pmatrix} x + 2.5 \\ y \\ z \\ 1.0 \end{pmatrix} = \begin{bmatrix} 1.0 & 0.0 & 0.0 & 2.5 \\ 0.0 & 1.0 & 0.0 & 0.0 \\ 0.0 & 0.0 & 1.0 & 0.0 \\ 0.0 & 0.0 & 0.0 & 1.0 \end{bmatrix} \begin{pmatrix} x \\ y \\ z \\ 1.0 \end{pmatrix}$$

This is demonstrated in Figure 5.8.

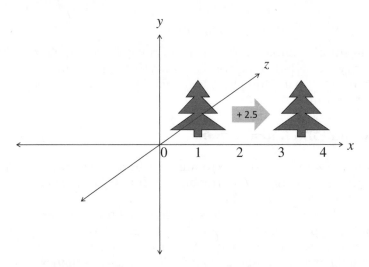

Figure 5.8   Translating an object 2.5 in the x direction

Of course, you'll want such matrix operations encapsulated. There are numerous utilities available for this and one is included in the accompanying vmath.h. We already used it in Chapter 3, "Drawing with OpenGL". To create a translation matrix using this utility, call:

---

vmath::mat4 **vmath::translate**(float x, float y, float z);

Returns a transformation matrix for translating an amount (x, y, z).

The following listing shows a use of this.

```
// Application (C++) code
#include "vmath.h"
    .
    .
    .
// Make a transformation matrix that translates coordinates by (1, 2, 3)
```

```
vmath::mat4 translationMatrix = vmath::translate(1.0, 2.0, 3,0);

// Set this matrix into the current program.
glUniformMatrix4fv(matrix_loc, 1, GL_FALSE, translationMatrix);
        .
        .
        .
```

After going through the next type of transformation, we'll show a code example for combining transformations with this utility.

Scaling

Grow or shrink an object, as in Figure 5.9, by putting the desired scaling factor on the first three diagonal components of the matrix. Making a scaling matrix S, which applied to all vertices v in an object, would change its size.

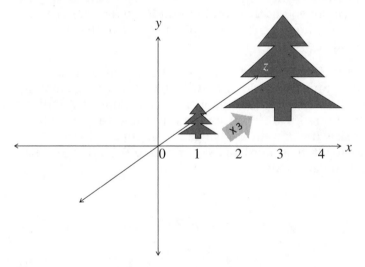

Figure 5.9   Scaling an object to three times its size
(Note that if the object is off center, this also moves its center three times further from $(0, 0, 0)$.)

The following example makes geometry 3 times larger.

$$S = \begin{bmatrix} 3.0 & 0.0 & 0.0 & 0.0 \\ 0.0 & 3.0 & 0.0 & 0.0 \\ 0.0 & 0.0 & 3.0 & 0.0 \\ 0.0 & 0.0 & 0.0 & 1.0 \end{bmatrix}$$

$$\begin{pmatrix} 3x \\ 3y \\ 3z \\ 1 \end{pmatrix} = \begin{bmatrix} 3.0 & 0.0 & 0.0 & 0.0 \\ 0.0 & 3.0 & 0.0 & 0.0 \\ 0.0 & 0.0 & 3.0 & 0.0 \\ 0.0 & 0.0 & 0.0 & 1.0 \end{bmatrix} \begin{pmatrix} x \\ y \\ z \\ 1.0 \end{pmatrix}$$

Note that nonisomorphic scaling is easily done, as the scaling is per component, but it would be rare to do so when setting up your view and model transforms. (If you want to stretch results vertically or horizontally, do that at the end with the viewport transformation. Doing it too early would make shapes change when they rotate.) Note that when scaling, we didn't scale the w component, as that would result in no net change to the point represented by the homogeneous coordinate (since in the end, all components are divided by w).

If the object being scaled is not centered at $(0,0,0)$, the simple matrix above will also move it further or closer to $(0,0,0)$ by the scaling amount. Usually, it is easier to understand what happens when scaling if you first center the object around $(0,0,0)$. Then scaling leaves it in the same place while changing its size. If you want to change the size of an off-center object without moving it, first translate its center to $(0,0,0)$, then scale it, and finally translate it back. This is shown in Figure 5.10.

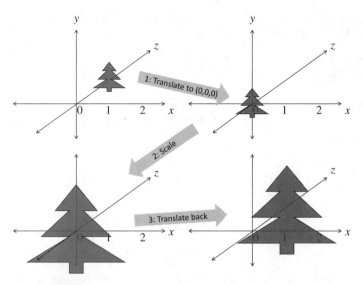

Figure 5.10   Scaling an object in place
(Scale in place by moving to $(0, 0, 0)$, scaling, and then moving it back.)

This would use three matrices, T, S, and T^{-1}, for translate to $(0, 0, 0)$, scale, and translate back, respectively. When each vertex v of the object is multiplied by each of these matrices in turn, the final effect is that the object would change size in place, yielding a new set of vertices v':

$$v' = T^{-1}(S(Tv))$$

or

$$v' = (T^{-1}ST)v$$

which allows for pre-multiplication of the three matrices into a single matrix.

$$M = T^{-1}ST$$

$$v' = Mv$$

M now does the complete job of scaling an off-center object.

To create a scaling transformation with the included utility, you can use

> vmath::mat4 **vmath::scale**(float *s*);
>
> Returns a transformation matrix for scaling an amount *s*.

The resulting matrix can be directly multiplied by another such transformation matrix to compose them into a single matrix that performs both transformations.

```
// Application (C++) code
#include "vmath.h"
        .
        .
        .
// Compose translation and scaling transforms

vmath::mat4 translateMatrix = vmath::translate(1.0, 2.0, 3,0);
vmath::mat4 scaleMatrix = vmath::scale(5.0);
vmath::mat4 scaleTranslateMatrix = scaleMatrix * translateMatrix;
        .
        .
        .
```

Any sequence of transformations can be combined into a single matrix this way.

Rotation

Rotating an object follows a similar scheme. We want a matrix *R* that when applied to all vertices *v* in an object will rotate it. The following example, shown in Figure 5.11 rotates 50 degrees counterclockwise around the *z* axis. Figure 5.12 shows how to rotate an object without moving its center, instead of also revolving it around the *z* axis.

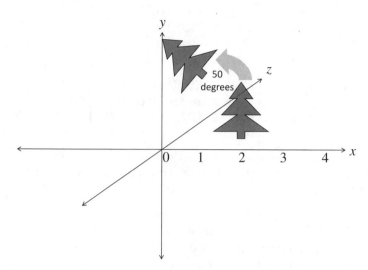

Figure 5.11   Rotation
(Rotating an object 50 degrees in the xy plane, around the z axis. Note if the object is off center, it also revolves the object around the point $(0, 0, 0)$.)

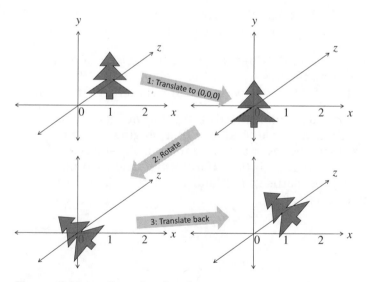

Figure 5.12   Rotating in place
(Rotating an object in place by moving it to $(0, 0, 0)$, rotating, and then moving it back.)

$$R = \begin{bmatrix} \cos 50 & -\sin 50 & 0.0 & 0.0 \\ \sin 50 & \cos 50 & 0.0 & 0.0 \\ 0.0 & 0.0 & 1.0 & 0.0 \\ 0.0 & 0.0 & 0.0 & 1.0 \end{bmatrix}$$

$$\begin{pmatrix} \cos 50 \cdot x - \sin 50 \cdot y \\ \sin 50 \cdot x + \cos 50 \cdot y \\ z \\ 1.0 \end{pmatrix} = \begin{bmatrix} \cos 50 & -\sin 50 & 0.0 & 0.0 \\ \sin 50 & \cos 50 & 0.0 & 0.0 \\ 0.0 & 0.0 & 1.0 & 0.0 \\ 0.0 & 0.0 & 0.0 & 1.0 \end{bmatrix} \begin{pmatrix} x \\ y \\ z \\ 1.0 \end{pmatrix}$$

When rotating around the z axis above, the vertices in the object keep their z values the same, rotating in the xy plane. To rotate instead around the x axis by an amount θ:

$$R_x = \begin{bmatrix} 1.0 & 0.0 & 0.0 & 0.0 \\ 0.0 & \cos \theta & -\sin \theta & 0.0 \\ 0.0 & \sin \theta & \cos \theta & 0.0 \\ 0.0 & 0.0 & 1.0 & 0.0 \\ 0.0 & 0.0 & 0.0 & 1.0 \end{bmatrix}$$

and around the y axis:

$$R_y = \begin{bmatrix} \cos \theta & 0.0 & -\sin \theta & 0.0 \\ 0.0 & 1.0 & 0.0 & 0.0 \\ \sin \theta & 0.0 & \cos \theta & 0.0 \\ 0.0 & 0.0 & 0.0 & 1.0 \end{bmatrix}$$

In all cases, the rotation is in the direction of the first axis toward the second axis. That is, from the row with the $cos -sin$ pattern to the row with the $sin\ cos$ pattern, for the positive axes corresponding to these rows.

If the object being rotated is not centered at $(0,0,0)$, the matrices above will also rotate the whole object around $(0,0,0)$, changing its location. Again, as with scaling, it'll be easier to first center the object around $(0,0,0)$. So, again, translate it to $(0,0,0)$, transform it, and then translate it back. This could use three matrices, T, R, and T^{-1}, to translate to $(0,0,0)$, rotate, and translate back.

$$v' = T^{-1}(R(Tv))$$

or

$$v' = (T^{-1}RT)v$$

which again allows for the pre-multiplication into a single matrix.

To create a rotation transformation with the included utility, you can use

Perspective Projection

This one is a bit tougher. We now assume viewing and modeling transformations are completed, with larger *z* values meaning objects are further away.

We will consider the following two cases:

1. Symmetric, centered frustum, where the *z*-axis is centered in the cone.

2. Asymmetric frustum, like seeing what's through a window when you looking near it, but not toward its middle.

For all, the viewpoint is now at $(0, 0, 0)$, looking generally toward the positive *z* direction.

First, however, let's consider an over-simplified (hypothetical) perspective projection.

$$\begin{bmatrix} 1.0 & 0.0 & 0.0 & 0.0 \\ 0.0 & 1.0 & 0.0 & 0.0 \\ 0.0 & 0.0 & 1.0 & 0.0 \\ 0.0 & 0.0 & 1.0 & 0.0 \end{bmatrix} \begin{pmatrix} x \\ y \\ z \\ 1.0 \end{pmatrix} \rightarrow \begin{pmatrix} x \\ y \\ z \\ z \end{pmatrix}$$

Note the last matrix row replaces the *w* (fourth) coordinate with the *z* coordinate. This will make objects with a larger *z* (further away) appear smaller when the division by *w* occurs, creating a perspective effect. However, this particular method has some shortcomings. For one, all *z* values will end up at 1.0, losing information about depth. We also didn't have much control over the cone we are projecting and the rectangle we are projecting onto. Finally, we didn't scale the result to the $[-1.0, 1.0]$ range expected by the viewport transform. The remaining examples take all this into account.

So, we consider now a fuller example for OpenGL, using a symmetric centered frustum. We refer back to our view frustum, shown again with the size of the near plane labeled in Figure 5.13.

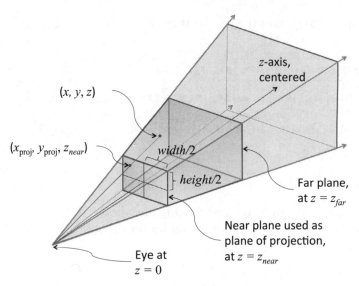

Figure 5.13 Frustum projection
(Frustum with the near plane and half its width and height labeled.)

We want to project points in the frustum onto the near plane, directed along straight lines going toward $(0, 0, 0)$. Any straight line emanating from $(0, 0, 0)$ keeps the ratio if z to x the same for all its points, and similarly for the ratio of z to y. Thus, the (x_{proj}, y_{proj}) value of the projection on the near plane will keep the ratios of $\frac{z_{near}}{z} = \frac{x_{proj}}{x}$ and $\frac{z_{near}}{z} = \frac{y_{proj}}{y}$. We know there is an upcoming division by depth to eliminate homogeneous coordinates, so solving for x_{proj} while still in the homogeneous space simply gives $x_{proj} = x \cdot z_{near}$. Similarly, $y_{proj} = y \cdot z_{near}$. If we then include a divide by the size of the near plane to scale the near plane to the range of $[-1.0, 1.0]$, we end up with the requisite first two diagonal elements shown in the projection transformation matrix.

$$\begin{bmatrix} \frac{z_{near}}{width/2} & 0.0 & 0.0 & 0.0 \\ 0.0 & \frac{z_{near}}{height/2} & 0.0 & 0.0 \\ 0.0 & 0.0 & -\frac{z_{far}+z_{near}}{z_{far}-z_{near}} & \frac{2z_{far}z_{near}}{z_{far}-z_{near}} \\ 0.0 & 0.0 & -1.0 & 0.0 \end{bmatrix}$$

(This could also be computed from the angle of the viewing cone, if so desired.)

Finally, we consider the second perspective projection case: the asymmetric frustum. This is the fully general frustum, when the near plane might not be centered on the z axis. The z axis could even be completely outside it, as mentioned earlier when looking at an interior wall next to a window. Your direction of view is the positive z axis, which is not going through the window. You see the window off to the side, with an asymmetric perspective view of what's outside the window. In this case, points on the near plane are already in the correct location, but those further away need to be adjusted for the fact that the projection in the near plane is off center. You can see this adjustment in the third column of the matrix, which moves the points an amount based on how off-center the near-plane projection is, scaled by how far away the points are (because this column multiplies by z).

$$\begin{bmatrix} \frac{z_{near}}{width/2} & 0.0 & \frac{left+right}{width/2} & 0.0 \\ 0.0 & \frac{z_{near}}{height/2} & \frac{top+bottom}{height/2} & 0.0 \\ 0.0 & 0.0 & -\frac{z_{far}+z_{near}}{z_{far}-z_{near}} & \frac{2z_{far}z_{near}}{z_{far}-z_{near}} \\ 0.0 & 0.0 & -1.0 & 0.0 \end{bmatrix}$$

All the above steps, rotate, scale, translate, project, and possibly others, will make matrices that can be multiplied together into a single matrix. Now with one multiplication by this new matrix, we can simultaneously scale, translate, rotate, and apply the perspective projection.

To create a perspective projection transformation with the included utility, there are a couple of choices. You can have full control, as above, using a **frustum** call or you can more casually and intuitively create one with the **lookat** call.

vmath::mat4 **vmath::frustum**(float *left*, float *right*, float *bottom*, float *top*, float *near*, float *far*);

Returns a perspective projection matrix based on the described frustum. The rectangle of the near plane is defined by the *left*, *right*, *bottom*, and *top*. The distances of the near and far planes are defined by *near* and *far*.

vmath::mat4 **vmath::lookAt**(vmath::vec3 *eye*, vmath::vec3 *center*, vmath::vec3 *up*);

Returns a perspective projection matrix based on looking toward *center* from *eye* with *up* defining what direction is up.

The resulting vectors, still having four coordinates, are the homogeneous coordinates expected by the OpenGL pipeline.

The final step in projecting the perspective view onto the screen is to divide the (x, y, z) coordinates in v' by the w coordinate in v', for every vertex. However, this is done internally by OpenGL; it is not something you do in your shaders.

Orthographic Projection

With an orthographic projection, the viewing volume is a rectangular parallelpiped, or, more informally, a box (see Figure 5.14). Unlike perspective projection, the size of the viewing volume doesn't change from one end to the other, so distance from the camera doesn't affect how large an object appears.

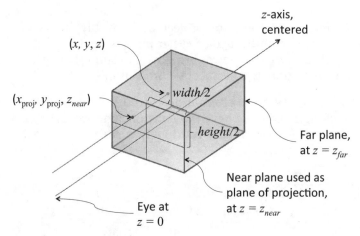

Figure 5.14   Orthographic projection
(Starts with straightforward projection of the parallelpiped onto the front plane. x, y, and z will need to be scaled to fit into $[-1, 1]$, $[-1, 1]$, and $[0, 1]$, respectively. This will be done by dividing by the sizes of the width, height, and depth in the model.)

This is done after all the translation, scaling, and rotation is done to look in the positive z direction to see the model to view. With no perspective, we will keep the w as it is (1.0), accomplished by making the bottom row of the transformation matrix $(0, 0, 0, 1)$. We will still scale z to lie within $[0, 1]$ so z-buffering can hide obscured objects, but neither z nor w will have any effect on the screen location. That leaves scaling x from the width of the model to $[-1, 1]$ and similarly for y. For a symmetric volume (positive z going down the middle of the parallelpiped) this can be done with the following matrix:

$$\begin{bmatrix} \frac{1}{width/2} & 0.0 & 0.0 & 0.0 \\ 0.0 & \frac{1}{height/2} & 0.0 & 0.0 \\ 0.0 & 0.0 & -\frac{1}{(z_{far}-z_{near})/2} & -\frac{z_{far}+z_{near}}{z_{far}-z_{near}} \\ 0.0 & 0.0 & 0.0 & 1.0 \end{bmatrix}$$

For the case of the positive z not going down the middle of the view (but still looking parallel to the z axis to see the model), the matrix is just slightly more complex. We use the diagonal to scale and the fourth column to center.

$$\begin{bmatrix} \frac{1}{(right-left)/2} & 0.0 & 0.0 & -\frac{right+left}{right-left} \\ 0.0 & \frac{1}{(top-bottom)/2} & 0.0 & -\frac{top+bottom}{top-bottom} \\ 0.0 & 0.0 & -\frac{1}{(z_{far}-z_{near})/2} & -\frac{z_{far}+z_{near}}{z_{far}-z_{near}} \\ 0.0 & 0.0 & 0.0 & 1.0 \end{bmatrix}$$

To create an orthographic projection transformation with the included utility, you can use the following:

---

vmath::mat4 **vmath::ortho**(vmath::vec3 *eye*, vmath::vec3 *center*, vmath::vec3 *up*);

Returns an orthographic projection transformation based on looking toward *center* from *eye* with *up* defining which direction is up.

Transforming Normals

In addition to transforming vertices, we will have need to transform surface *normals*, that is, vectors that point in the direction perpendicular to a surface at some point. In perhaps one of the most confusing twists of terminology, normals are often required to be *normalized*, that is, of length 1.0. However, the "normal" meaning perpendicular and the "normal" in normalize are completely unrelated, and we will come upon needs for normalized normals when computing lighting.

Typically, when computing lighting, a vertex will have a normal associated with it, so the lighting calculation knows what direction the surface reflects light. Shaders doing these calculations appear in Chapter 7, "Light and Shadow". Here, though, we will discuss the fundamantals of transforming them by taking them through rotations, scaling, and so on, along with the vertices in a model.

Normal vectors are typically only three-component vectors; not using homogeneous coordinates. For one thing, translating a surface does not change its normal, so normals don't care about translation, removing one of the reasons we used homogeneous coordinates. Since normals are mostly used for lighting, which we complete in a pre-perspective space, we remove the other reason we use homogeneous coordinates (projection).

Perhaps counterintuitively, normal vectors aren't transformed in the same way as vertices or position vectors are. Imagine a surface at an angle that gets stretched by a transformation. Stretching makes the angle of the surface shallower, which changes the perpendicular direction *in the opposite way* than applying the same stretching to the normal would. This would happen, for example, if you stretch a sphere to make an ellipse. We need to come up with a *different* transformation matrix to transform normals than the one we used for vertices.

So, how do we transform normals? To start, let M be the 3×3 matrix that has all the rotations and scaling needed to transform your object from model coordinates to *eye coordinates*, before transforming for perspective. This would be the upper 3×3 block in your 4×4 transformation matrix, before compounding translation or projection transformations into it. Then, to transform normals, use the following equation.

$$n' = {M^{-1}}^T n$$

That is, take the transpose of the inverse of M and use that to transform your normals. If all you did was rotation and isometric (nonshape changing) scaling, you could transform directions with just M. They'd be scaled by a different amount, but will no doubt have a normalize call in their future that will even that out.

OpenGL Matrices

While shaders know how to multiply matrices, the API in the OpenGL core profile does not manipulate matrices beyond setting them, possibly transposed, into uniform and per-vertex data to be used by your shaders. It is up to you to build up the matrices you want to use in your shader, which you can do with the included helper routines as described in the previous section.

You will want to be multiplying matrices in your application, before sending them to your shaders, for a performance benefit. For example, let's say you need matrices to do the following transformations:

1. Move the camera to the right view: Translate and rotate.

2. Move the model into view: Translate, rotate, and scale.

3. Apply perspective projection.

That's a total of six matrices. You can use a vertex shader to do all this math, as in Example 5.1.

Example 5.1   Multiplying Multiple Matrices in a Vertex Shader

```
#version 330 core

uniform mat4 ViewT, ViewR, ModelT, ModelR, ModelS, Project;
in vec4 Vertex;

void main()
{
    gl_Position = Project
                * ModelS * ModelR * ModelT
                * ViewR * ViewT
                * Vertex;
}
```

However, that's a lot of arithmetic to do for each vertex. Fortunately, the intermediate results for many vertices will be the same each time. To the extent consecutive transforms (matrices) are staying the same for a large number of vertices, you'll want to instead pre-compute their composition (product) in your application and send the single resulting matrix to your shader.

```
// Application (C++) code
#include "vmath.h"
    .
    .
    .
vmath::mat4 ViewT = vmath::rotate(...)
vmath::mat4 ViewR = vmath::translate(...);
vmath::mat4 View = ViewR * ViewT;
vmath::mat4 ModelS = vmath::scale(...);
vmath::mat4 ModelR = vmath::rotate(...);
vmath::mat4 ModelT = vmath::translate(...);
vmath::mat4 Model = ModelS * ModelR * ModelT;
vmath::mat4 Project = vmath::frustum(...);
vmath::mat4 ModelViewProject = Project * Model * View;
```

An intermediate situation might be to have a single-view transformation and a single-perspective projection, but multiple-model transformations. You might do this if you reuse the same model to make many instances of an object in the same view.

```
#version 330 core

uniform mat4 View, Model, Project;
in vec4 Vertex;

void main()
{
    gl_Position = View * Model * Project * Vertex;
}
```

In this situation, the application would change the model matrix more frequently than the others. This will be economical if enough vertices are drawn per change of the matrix *Model*. If only a few vertices are drawn per instance, it will be faster to send the model matrix as a vertex attribute.

```
#version 330 core

uniform mat4 View, Project;

in vec4 Vertex;
in mat4 Model;    // a transform sent per vertex

void main()
{
    gl_Position = View * Model * Project * Vertex;
}
```

(Another alternative for creating multiple instances is to construct the model transformation within the vertex shader based on the built-in variable gl_InstanceID. This was described in detail in Chapter 3, "Drawing with OpenGL".)

Of course, when you can draw a large number of vertices all with the same cumulative transformation, you'll want to do only one multiply in your shader.

```
#version 330 core

uniform mat4 ModelViewProject;
in vec4 Vertex;

void main()
{
    gl_Position = ModelViewProject * Vertex;
}
```

Matrix Rows and Columns in OpenGL

The notation used in this book corresponds to the broadly used traditional matrix notation. We stay true to this notation, regardless of how data is set into a matrix. A column will always mean a vertical slice of a matrix when written in this traditional notation.

Beyond notation, matrices have semantics for setting and accessing parts of a matrix, and these semantics are always column oriented. In a shader, using array syntax on a matrix yields a vector with values coming from a column of the matrix

```
mat3x4 m; // 3 columns, 4 rows
vec4 v = m[1]; // v is initialized to the second column of m
```

Note: Neither the notation we use nor these column-oriented semantics are to be confused with column-major order and row-major order, which refer strictly to memory layout of the data behind a matrix. The memory layout has nothing to do with our notation in this book and nothing to do with the language semantics of GLSL: You will probably not know whether internally a matrix is stored in column-major or row-major order.

Caring about column-major or row-major memory order will only come up when you are, in fact, laying out the memory backing a GLSL matrix yourself. This is done when setting matrices in a `uniform` block. As was shown in Chapter 2, "Shader Fundamentals", when discussing uniform blocks, you use layout qualifiers `row_major` and `column_major` to control how GLSL will load the matrix from this memory.

Since OpenGL is not creating or interpreting your matrices, you can treat them as you wish. If you want to transform a vertex by matrix multiplication with the matrix on the right

```
#version 330 core

uniform mat4 M;
in vec4 Vertex;

void main()
{
    gl_Position = Vertex * M; // nontraditional order of multiplication
}
```

then, as expected, `gl_Position.x` will be formed by the dot product of Vertex and the first column of matrix M, and so on for `gl_Position` y, z, and w components transformed by the second, third, and fourth columns. However, we'll stick to the tradition of keeping the matrix on the left and the vertices on the right.

Note: GLSL vectors automatically adapt to being either row vectors or column vectors, depending on whether they are on the left side or right side of a matrix multiply, respectively. In this way, they are different than a one-column or one-row matrix.

OpenGL Transformations

To tell OpenGL where you want the near and far planes, use the **glDepthRange()** commands.

void **glDepthRange**(GLclampd *near*, GLclampd *far*);
void **glDepthRangef**(GLclampf *near*, GLclampf *far*);

Sets the near plane to be *near* on the z axis and the far plane to *far* on the z axis. This defines an encoding for z-coordinates that's performed during the viewport transformation. The *near* and *far* values represent adjustments to the minimum and maximum values that can be stored in the depth buffer. By default, they're 0.0 and 1.0, respectively, which work for most applications. These parameters are clamped to lie within [0, 1].

Viewport

To tell OpenGL where to display the rectangular viewing cone, use:

void **glViewport**(GLint *x*, GLint *y*, GLint *width*, GLint *height*);

Defines a pixel rectangle in the window into which the final image is mapped. The *x* and *y* parameters specify the lower-left corner of the viewport, and *width* and *height* are the size of the viewport rectangle, in pixels. By default, the initial viewport values are (0, 0, *winWidth*, *winHeight*), where *winWidth* and *winHeight* specify the size of the window.

The underlying windowing system of your platform, not OpenGL, is responsible for opening a window on the screen. However, by default, the viewport is set to the entire pixel rectangle of the window that's opened. You use **glViewport()** to choose a smaller drawing region; for example, you can subdivide the window to create a split-screen effect for multiple views in the same window.

Multiple Viewports

You will sometimes want to render a scene through multiple viewports. OpenGL has commands to support doing this, and the geometry shading stage can select which viewport subsequent rendering will target. More details and an example are given in "Multiple Viewports and Layered Rendering" on Page 550.

Advanced: z Precision

One bizarre effect of these transformations is z *fighting*. The hardware's floating-point numbers used to do the computation have limited precision. Hence, depth coordinates that are mathematically distinct end up having the same (or even reversed) actual floating-point z values. This in turn causes incorrectly hidden objects in the depth buffer. The effect varies per pixel and can cause disturbing flickering intersections of nearby objects. Precision of z is made even worse with perspective division, which is applied to the depth coordinate along with all the other coordinates: As the transformed depth coordinate moves farther away from the near clipping plane, its location becomes increasingly less precise, as shown in Figure 5.15.

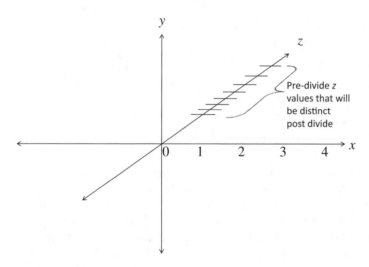

Figure 5.15   z precision
(An exaggerated showing of adjacent, distinctly representable depths, assuming an upcoming perspective division.)

Even without perspective division, there is a finite granularity to floating-point numbers, but the divide makes it worse and nonlinear, resulting in more severe problems at greater depths. The bottom line is it is possible to ask for too much of too small a range of z values. To avoid this, take care to keep the far plane as close to the near plane as possible, and don't compress the z values into a narrower range than necessary.

Advanced: User Clipping

OpenGL automatically clips geometry against the near and far planes as well as the viewport. *User clipping* refers to adding additional clip planes at arbitrary orientations, intersecting your geometry, such that the display sees the geometry on one side of the plane, but not on the other side. You might use one, for example, to show a cut away of a complex object.

OpenGL user clipping is a joint effort between OpenGL and a special built-in vertex shader array, `gl_ClipDistance`, which you are responsible for setting. This variable lets you control where vertices are in relation to a plane. Normal interpolation then assigns distances to the fragments between the vertices. Example 5.2 shows a straight-forward use of this built-in variable.

Example 5.2   Simple Use of `gl_ClipDistance`

```
#version 330 core

uniform vec4 Plane;   // A, B, C, and D for Ax + By + Cz + D = 0
in vec4 Vertex;       // w == 1.0

float gl_ClipDistance[1]; // declare use of 1 clip plane.

void main()
{
    // evaluate plane equation
    gl_ClipDistance[0] = dot(Vertex, Plane);
}
```

The convention is that a distance of 0 means the vertex is on the plane, a positive distance means the vertex is inside (the keep it side) of the clip plane, and a negative distance means the point is outside (the cull it side) of the clip plane. The clip distances will be linearly interpolated across the primitive, and OpenGL will cull fragments whose interpolated distance is less than 0.

Each element of the `gl_ClipDistance` array is set up to represent one plane. There are a limited number of clip planes, likely around eight or more. The built-in, `gl_ClipDistance[]` is declared with no size. You either need to redeclare it with a specific size or only access it with compile-time constants.

All shaders in all stages that declare or use `gl_ClipDistance[]` should make the array the same size. (The constant `gl_MaxClipDistances` lets your shader know the maximum array size on the current OpenGL implementation.) This size needs to include all the clip planes that are enabled via the OpenGL API; if the size does not include all enabled planes, results are undefined. To enable OpenGL clipping of the clip plane written to in Example 5.2, enable the following enumerant in your application:

```
glEnable(GL_CLIP_PLANE0);
```

There are also other enumerates like GL_CLIP_PLANE1, GL_CLIP_PLANE2. These enumerants are organized sequentially, so that GL_CLIP_PLANE*i* is equal to GL_CLIP_PLANE0 + *i*. This allows programmatic selection of which and how many user clip planes to use. Your shaders should write to all the enabled planes, or you'll end up with odd system clipping behavior.

The built-in `gl_ClipDistance` is also available in a fragment shader, allowing nonclipped fragments to read their interpolated distances from each clip plane.

Transform Feedback

Transform feedback can be considered a stage of the OpenGL pipeline that sits after all of the vertex-processing stages and directly before primitive assembly and rasterization.[1] Transform feedback captures vertices as they are assembled into primitives (points, lines, or triangles) and allows some or all of their attributes to be recorded into buffer objects. In fact, the minimal OpenGL pipeline that produces useful work is a vertex shader with transform feedback enabled—no fragment shader is necessary. Each time a vertex passes through primitive assembly, those attributes that have been marked for capture are recorded into one or more buffer objects. Those buffer objects can then be read back by the application, or their contents used in subsequent rendering passes by OpenGL.

Transform Feedback Objects

The state required to represent transform feedback is encapsulated into a *transform feedback object*. This state includes the buffer objects that will be used for recording the captured vertex data, counters indicating how full each buffer object is, and state indicating whether transform feedback is currently active. A transform feedback object is created by reserving a transform feedback object name and then binding it to the transform feedback object binding point on the current context. To reserve transform feedback object names, call:

---

1. To be more exact, transform feedback is tightly integrated into the primitive assembly process as whole primitives are captured into buffer objects. This is seen as buffers run out of space and partial primitives are discarded. For this to occur, some knowledge of the current primitive type is required in the transform feedback stage.

> void **glGenTransformFeedbacks**(GLsizei *n*, GLuint * *ids*);
>
> Reserves *n* names for transform feedback objects and places the reserved names in the array *ids*.

The parameter *n* specifies how many transform feedback object names are to be reserved, and *ids* specifies the address of an array where the reserved names will be placed. If you want only one name, you can set *n* to one and pass the address of a GLuint variable in *ids*. Once you have reserved a name for a transform feedback object, the object doesn't actually exist until the first time it is bound, at which point it is created. To bind a transform feedback object to the context, call:

> void **glBindTransformFeedback**(GLenum *target*, GLuint *id*);
>
> Binds a transform feedback object specified by *id* to the target *target*, which must be GL_TRANSFORM_FEEDBACK.

This binds the transform feedback object named *id* to the binding on the context indicated by *target*, which in this case must be GL_TRANSFORM_FEEDBACK. If this is the first time this name has been bound, a new transform feedback object is created and initialized with the default state, otherwise, the existing state of that object again becomes current. To determine whether a particular value is the name of a transform feedback object, you can call **glIsTransformFeedback**(), whose prototype is as follows:

> GLboolean **glIsTransformFeedback**(GLenum *id*);
>
> Returns GL_TRUE if *id* is the name of an existing transform feedback object and GL_FALSE otherwise.

Once a transform feedback object is bound, all commands affecting transform feedback state affect that transform feedback object. It's not necessary to have a transform feedback object bound in order to use transform feedback functionality as there is a default transform feedback object. The default transform feedback object assumes the *id* zero and so passing zero as the *id* parameter to **glBindTransformFeedback**() returns the context to use the default transform feedback object (unbinding any previously bound transform feedback object in the process). However, as more complex uses of transform feedback are introduced, it becomes convenient to encapsulate the state of transform feedback into transform feedback objects. Therefore, it's good practice to create and bind a transform feedback object even if you intend to use only one.

Once a transform feedback object is no longer needed, it should be deleted by calling:

---

void **glDeleteTransformFeedbacks**(GLsizei *n*, const GLuint *ids*);

Deletes *n* transform feedback objects whose names are stored in the array *ids*. Elements of *ids* that are not names of transform feedback objects are silently ignored, as is the name zero.

This function deletes the *n* transform feedback objects whose names are stored in the array whose address is passed in *ids*. Deletion of the object is deferred until it is no longer in use. That is, if the transform feedback object is active when **glDeleteTransformFeedbacks()** is called, it is not deleted until transform feedback is ended.

Transform Feedback Buffers

Transform feedback objects are primarily responsible for managing the state representing capture of vertices into buffer objects. This state includes which buffers are bound to the transform feedback buffer binding points. Multiple buffers can be bound simultaneously for transform feedback and subsections of buffer objects can also be bound. It is even possible to bind different subsections of the same buffer object to different transform feedback buffer binding points simultaneously. To bind an entire buffer object to one of the transform feedback buffer binding points, call:

---

void **glBindBufferBase**(GLenum *target*, GLuint *index*,
                    GLuint *buffer*);

Binds the buffer object with name *buffer* to the indexed binding point on target *target* at index *index*, and to the generic buffer binding point specified by *target*.

The *target* parameter should be set to
GL_TRANSFORM_FEEDBACK_BUFFER and *index* should be set to the index
of the transform feedback buffer binding point in the currently bound
transform feedback object. The name of the buffer to bind is passed in
buffer. The total number of binding points is an implementation-dependent
constant that can be discovered by querying the value of
GL_MAX_TRANSFORM_FEEDBACK_BUFFERS, and *index* must be less than
this value. All OpenGL implementations must support at least 64 transform
feedback buffer binding points. It's also possible to bind a range of a buffer
object to one of the transform feedback buffer binding points by calling:

---

void **glBindBufferRange**(GLenum *target*, GLuint *index*,
                       GLuint *buffer*, GLintptr *offset*,
                       GLsizeiptr *size*);

Binds a range of a buffer object to the indexed buffer binding point on
target *target* specified by *index*. *offset* and *size*, both in bytes, indicate the
range of the buffer object to bind. **glBindBufferRange()** also binds the
buffer *buffer* to the generic buffer binding point specified by *target*.

Again, *target* should be GL_TRANSFORM_FEEDBACK_BUFFER, *index*
should be between zero and one less than the value of
GL_MAX_TRANSFORM_FEEDBACK_BUFFERS, and *buffer* contains the
name of the buffer object to bind. The *offset* and *size* parameters define
which section of the buffer object to bind. This functionality can be used
to bind different ranges of the same buffer object to different transform
feedback buffer binding points. Care should be taken that the ranges do
not overlap. Attempting to perform transform feedback into multiple,
overlapping sections of the same buffer object will result in undefined
behavior, possibly including data corruption or worse.

In addition to binding buffers (or sections of buffers) to the indexed
binding points, **glBindBufferBase()** and **glBindBufferRange()** also bind
the buffer object to the generic buffer binding point indicated by *target*.
This is useful because it allows other commands that operate on buffer
objects such as **glBufferData()**, **glBufferSubData()**, and
glGetBufferSubData() to operate on the buffer object most recently bound
to one of the indexed buffer binding points. Note though, that neither
glBindBufferBase() nor **glBindBufferRange()** *create* buffer objects (unlike
glBindBuffer()), and so you can't use a **glBindBufferBase()**,
glBufferData() sequence to create and allocate space for a transform
feedback buffer. In order to allocate a transform feedback buffer, code such
as in that shown in Example 5.3 should be used.

Example 5.3   Example Initialization of a Transform Feedback Buffer

```
// Generate the name of a buffer object
GLuint buffer;
glGenBuffers(1, &buffer);

// Bind it to the TRANSFORM_FEEDBACK binding to create it
glBindBuffer(GL_TRANSFORM_FEEDBACK_BUFFER, buffer);

// Call glBufferData to allocate 1MB of space
glBufferData(GL_TRANSFORM_FEEDBACK_BUFFER,      // target
             1024 * 1024,                       // 1 MB
             NULL,                              // no initial data
             GL_DYNAMIC_COPY);                  // usage

// Now we can bind it to indexed buffer binding points.
glBindBufferRange(GL_TRANSFORM_FEEDBACK_BUFFER, // target
                  0,                            // index 0
                  buffer,                       // buffer name
                  0,                            // start of range
                  512 * 1024);                  // first half of buffer

glBindBufferRange(GL_TRANSFORM_FEEDBACK_BUFFER, // target
                  1,                            // index 1
                  buffer,                       // same buffer
                  512 * 1024,                   // start half way
                  512 * 1024);                  // second half
```

Notice how in Example 5.3, the newly reserved buffer object name is first bound to the GL_TRANSFORM_FEEDBACK_BUFFER target, and then **glBufferData()** is called to allocate space. The *data* parameter to **glBufferData()** is set to NULL to indicate that we wish to simply allocate space but do not wish to provide initial data for the buffer. In this case, the buffer's contents will initially be undefined. Also, GL_DYNAMIC_COPY is used as the *usage* parameter. This provides a hint to the OpenGL implementation of the intended use for the buffer object. The DYNAMIC part of the token implies that the data in the buffer will be changed often, and the COPY part of the token indicates that we will be using OpenGL (normally a GPU) to produce data to be written into the buffer. This, together with the fact that the buffer is bound to the GL_TRANSFORM_FEEDBACK_BUFFER binding point should give the implementation enough information to intelligently allocate memory for the buffer object in an optimal manner for it to be used for transform feedback.

Once the buffer has been bound to the generic GL_TRANSFORM_FEEDBACK_BUFFER target and space has been allocated for it, sections of it are then bound to the indexed transform feedback buffer binding points by calling **glBindBufferRange()** twice—once to bind the first half of the buffer to the first binding point, and again to bind the second half of the buffer to the second binding point. This demonstrates why the buffer needs to be created and allocated first before using it with **glBindBufferRange()**. **glBindBufferRange()** takes an *offset*, *size* parameters describing a range of the buffer object that must lie within the buffer object. This cannot be determined if the object does not yet exist.

Configuring Transform Feedback Varyings

While the buffer bindings used for transform feedback are associated with a transform feedback object, the configuration of which outputs of the vertex (or geometry) shader are to be recorded into those buffers is stored in the active program object. To specify which varyings will be recorded during transform feedback, call:

---

void **glTransformFeedbackVaryings**(GLuint *program*,
                             GLsizei *count*,
                             const GLchar ** *varyings*,
                             GLenum *bufferMode*);

Sets the varyings to be recorded by transform feedback for the program specified by *program*. *count* specifies the number of strings contained in the array *varyings*, which contains the names of the varyings to be captured. *buferMode* is the mode in which the varyings will be captured—either separate mode (specified by GL_SEPARATE_ATTRIBS) or interleaved mode (specified by GL_INTERLEAVED_ATTRIBS).

In this function, *program* specifies the program object that will be used for transform feedback. *varyings* contains an array of strings that represent the names of varying variables that are outputs of the fragment (or geometry) shader that are to be captured by transform feedback. *count* is the number of strings in *varyings*. *bufferMode* is a token indicating how the captured varyings should be allocated to transform feedback buffers. If *bufferMode* is set to GL_INTERLEAVED_ATTRIBS, all of the varyings will be recorded one after another into the buffer object bound to the first transform feedback buffer binding point on the current transform feedback object. If *bufferMode* is GL_SEPARATE_ATTRIBS, each varying will be captured into its own buffer object.

An example of the use of **glTransformFeedbackVaryings()** is shown in Example 5.4 below.

Example 5.4   Example Specification of Transform Feedback Varyings

```
// Create an array containing the names of varyings to record
static const char * const vars[] =
{
    "foo", "bar", "baz"
};

// Call glTransformFeedbackVaryings
glTransformFeedbackVaryings(prog,
                            sizeof(vars) / sizeof(vars[0]),
                            varyings,
                            GL_INTERLEAVED_ATTRIBS);

// Now the program object is set up to record varyings squashed
// together in the same buffer object. Alternatively, we could call...
glTransformFeedbackVaryings(prog,
                            sizeof(vars) / sizeof(vars[0]),
                            varyings,
                            GL_SEPARATE_ATTRIBS);
// This sets up the varyings to be recorded into separate buffers.
// Now (this is important), link the program object...
// ... even if it's already been linked before.
glLinkProgram(prog);
```

Notice in Example 5.4 that there is a call to **glLinkProgram()** directly after the call to **glTransformFeedbackVaryings()**. This is because the selection of varyings specified in the call to **glTransformFeedbackVaryings()** *does not take effect until the next time the program object is linked.* If the program has previously been linked and is then used without being re-linked, no errors will occur, but nothing will be captured during transform feedback.[2]

After the code in Example 5.4 has been executed, whenever prog is in use while transform feedback is active, the values written to foo, bar, and baz will be recorded into the transform feedback buffers bound to the current transform feedback object. In the case where the *bufferMode* parameter is set to GL_INTERLEAVED_ATTRIBS, the values of foo, bar, and baz will be tightly packed into the buffer bound to the first transform feedback buffer binding point as shown in Figure 5.16.

---

2. Calling **glTransformFeedbackVaryings()** after a program object has already been linked and then not linking it again is a common error made even by experienced OpenGL programmers.

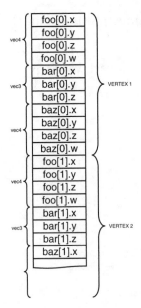

Figure 5.16   Transform feedback varyings packed in a single buffer

However, if *bufferMode* is GL_SEPARATE_ATTRIBS then each of foo, bar, and baz will be packed tightly into its own buffer object as shown in Figure 5.17.

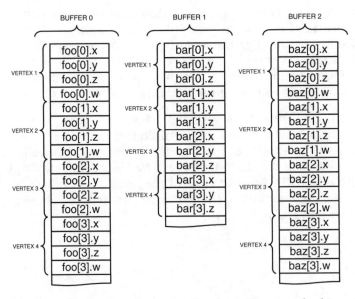

Figure 5.17   Transform feedback varyings packed in separate buffers

In both cases, the attributes will be tightly packed together. The amount of space in the buffer object that each varying consumes is determined by its type in the vertex shader. That is, if foo is declared as a vec3 in the vertex shader, it will consume exactly three floats in the buffer object. In the case where *bufferMode* is GL_INTERLEAVED_ATTRIBS, the value of bar will be written immediately after the value of foo. In the case where *bufferMode* is GL_SEPARATE_ATTRIBS, the values of foo will be tightly packed into one buffer with no gaps between them (as will the values of bar and baz).

This seems rather rigid. There are cases where you may wish to align the data written into the transform feedback buffer differently from default (leaving unwritten gaps in the buffer). There may also be cases where you would want to record more than one variable into one buffer, but record other variables into another. For example, you may wish to record foo and bar into one buffer while recording baz into another. In order to increase the flexibility of transform feedback varying setup and allow this kind of usage, there are some special variable names reserved by OpenGL that signal to the transform feedback subsystem that you wish to leave gaps in the output buffer, or to move between buffers. These are gl_SkipComponents1, gl_SkipComponents2, gl_SkipComponents3, gl_SkipComponents4, and gl_NextBuffer. When any of the gl_SkipComponents variants is encountered, OpenGL will leave a gap for the number of components specified (1, 2, 3, or 4) in the transform feedback buffer. These variable names can only be used when *bufferMode* is GL_INTERLEAVED_ATTRIBS. An example of using this is shown in Example 5.5.

Example 5.5   Leaving Gaps in a Transform Feedback Buffer

```
// Declare the transform feedback varying names
static const char * const vars[] =
{
    "foo",
    "gl_SkipComponents2",
    "bar",
    "gl_SkipComponents3",
    "baz"
};

// Set the varyings
glTransformFeedbackVaryings(prog,
                            sizeof(vars) / sizeof(vars[0]),
                            varyings,
                            GL_INTERLEAVED_ATTRIBS);
// Remember to link the program object
glLinkProgram(prog);
```

When the other special variable name, gl_NextBuffer name is encountered, OpenGL will start allocating varyings into the buffer bound to the next transform feedback buffer. This allows multiple varyings to be recorded into a single buffer object. Additionally, if gl_NextBuffer is encountered when *bufferMode* is GL_SEPARATE_ATTRIBS, or if two or more instances of gl_NextBuffer are encountered in a row in GL_INTERLEAVED_ATTRIBS, it allows a whole binding point to be skipped and nothing recorded into the buffer bound there. An example of gl_NextBuffer is shown in Example 5.6.

Example 5.6   Assigning Transform Feedback Outputs to Different Buffers

```
// Declare the transform feedback varying names
static const char * const vars[] =
{
    "foo", "bar" // Variables to record into buffer 0
    "gl_NextBuffer", // Move to binding point 1
    "baz" // Variable to record into buffer 1
};

// Set the varyings
glTransformFeedbackVaryings(prog,
                            sizeof(vars) /
sizeof(vars[0]),
                            varyings,
                            GL_INTERLEAVED_ATTRIBS);
// Remember to link the program object
glLinkProgram(prog);
```

The special variables names gl_SkipComponentsN and gl_NextBuffer can be combined to allow very flexible vertex layouts to be created. If it is necessary to skip over more than four components, multiple instances of gl_SkipComponents may be used back to back. Care should be taken with aggressive use of gl_SkipComponents, though, because skipped components still contribute toward the count of the count of the number of components captured during transform feedback, even though no data is actually written. This may cause a reduction in performance, or even a failure to link a program. If there is a lot of unchanged, static data in a buffer, it may be preferable to separate the data into static and dynamic parts and leave the static data in its own buffer object(s), allowing the dynamic data to be more tightly packed.

Finally, Example 5.7 shows an (albeit rather contrived) example of the combined use of gl_SkipComponents and gl_NextBuffer, and Figure 5.18 shows how the data ends up laid out in the transform feedback buffers.

Example 5.7   Assigning Transform Feedback Outputs to Different Buffers

```
// Declare the transform feedback varying names
static const char * const vars[] =
{
    // Record foo, a gap of 1 float, bar, and then two floats
    "foo", "gl_SkipComponents1", "bar", "gl_SkipComponents2"
    // Move to binding point 1
    "gl_NextBuffer",
    // Leave a gap of 4 floats, then record baz, then leave
    // another gap of 2 floats
    "gl_SkipComponents4" "baz", "gl_SkipComponents2"
    // Move to binding point 2
    "gl_NextBuffer",
    // Move directly to binding point 3 without directing anything
    // to binding point 2
    "gl_NextBuffer",
    // Record iron and copper with a 3 component gap between them
    "iron", "gl_SkipComponents3", "copper"
};

// Set the varyings
glTransformFeedbackVaryings(prog,
                            sizeof(vars) / sizeof(vars[0]),
                            varyings,
                            GL_INTERLEAVED_ATTRIBS);
// Remember to link the program object
glLinkProgram(prog);
```

As you can see in Example 5.7, gl_SkipComponents can come between varyings, or at the start or end of the list of varyings to record into a single buffer. Putting a gl_SkipComponents variant-first in the list of varyings to capture will result in OpenGL leaving a gap at the front of the buffer before it records data (and then a gap between each sequence of varyings). Also, multiple gl_NextBuffer variables can come back to back, causing a buffer binding point to be entirely passed over and nothing recorded into that buffer. The resulting output layout is shown in Figure 5.18.

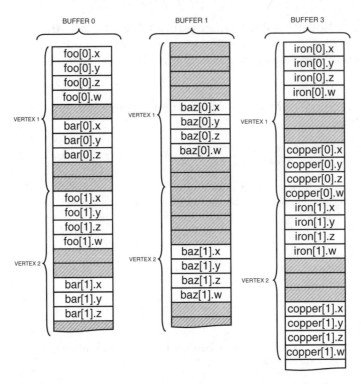

Figure 5.18   Transform feedback varyings packed into multiple buffers

Starting and Stopping Transform Feedback

Transform feedback can be started and stopped, and even paused. As might be expected starting transform feedback when it is not paused causes it to start recording into the bound transform feedback buffers from the beginning. However, starting transform feedback when it is already paused causes it to continue recording from wherever it left off. This is useful to allow multiple components of a scene to be recorded into transform feedback buffers with other components rendered in between that are not to be recorded.

To start transform feedback, call **glBeginTransformFeedback()**.

void **glBeginTransformFeedback**(GLenum *primitiveMode*);

Sets the primitive type expected to be recorded by transform feedback. *primitiveMode* must be GL_POINTS, GL_LINES, or GL_TRIANGLES. The primitive mode specified in subsequent drawing commands must match *primitiveMode*, or (if present) the output of the geometry shader must match *primitiveMode*.

The **glBeginTransformFeedback()** function starts transform feedback on the currently bound transform feedback object. The *primitiveMode* parameter must be GL_POINTS, GL_LINES, or GL_TRIANGLES, and must match the primitive type *expected to arrive at primitive assembly*. Note that it does not need to match the primitive mode used in subsequent draw commands if tessellation or a geometry shader is active because those stages might change the primitive type mid-pipeline. That will be covered in Chapters 9 and 10. For the moment, just set the *primitiveMode* to match the primitive type you plan to draw with. Table 5.1 shows the allowed combinations of *primitiveMode* and draw command modes.

Table 5.1   Drawing Modes Allowed During Transform Feedback

Transform Feedback *primitiveMode*	Allowed Drawing types
GL_POINTS	GL_POINTS
GL_LINES	GL_LINES GL_LINE_STRIP GL_LINE_LOOP GL_LINES_ADJACENCY GL_LINE_STRIP_ADJACENCY
GL_TRIANGLES	GL_TRIANGLES GL_TRIANGLE_STRIP GL_TRIANGLE_FAN GL_TRIANGLES_ADJACENCY GL_TRIANGLE_STRIP_ADJACENCY

Once transform feedback is started, it is considered to be active. It may be paused by calling **glPauseTransformFeedback()**. When transform feedback is paused, it is still considered active, but will not record any data into the transform feedback buffers. There are also several restrictions about changing state related to transform feedback while transform feedback is active but paused.

- The currently bound transform feedback object may not be changed.

- It is not possible to bind different buffers to the GL_TRANSFORM_FEEDBACK_BUFFER binding points.

- The current program object cannot be changed.[3]

---

3. Actually, it is possible to change the current program object, but an error will be generated by **glResumeTransformFeedback()** if the program object that was current when **glBeginTransformFeedback()** was called is no longer current. So, be sure to put the original program object back before calling **glResumeTransformFeedback()**.

void **glPauseTransformFeedback**(void);

Pauses the recording of varyings in transform feedback mode. Transform feedback may be resumed by calling **glResumeTransformFeedback()**.

glPauseTransformFeedback() will generate an error if transform feedback is not active, or if it is already paused. To restart transform feedback while it is paused, **glResumeTransformFeedback()** must be used (not **glBeginTransformFeedback()**). Likewise, **glResumeTransformFeedback()** will generate an error if it is called when transform feedback is not active or if it is active but not paused.

void **glResumeTransformFeedback**(void);

Resumes transform feedback that has previously been paused by a call to **glPauseTransformFeedback()**.

When you've completed rendering all of the primitives for transform feedback, you change back to normal rendering mode by calling **glEndTransformFeedback()**.

void **glEndTransformFeedback**(void);

Completes the recording of varyings in transform feedback mode.

Transform Feedback Example—Particle System

This section contains the description of a moderately complex use of transform feedback. The application uses transform feedback in two ways to implement a particle system. On a first pass, transform feedback is used to capture geometry as it passes through the OpenGL pipeline. The captured geometry is then used in a second pass along with another instance of transform feedback in order to implement a particle system that uses the vertex shader to perform collision detection between particles and the rendered geometry. A schematic of the system is shown in Figure 5.19.

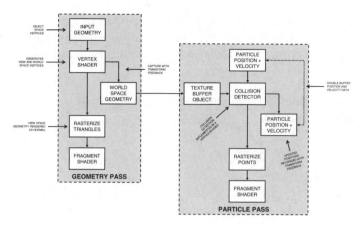

Figure 5.19   Schematic of the particle system simulator

In this application, the particle system is simulated in world space. In a first pass, a vertex shader is used to transform object space geometry into both world space (for later use in the particle system simulation), and into eye space for rendering. The world space results are captured into a buffer using transform feedback, while the eye space geometry is passed through to the rasterizer. The buffer containing the captured world space geometry is attached to a *texture buffer object* (TBO) so that it can be randomly accessed in the vertex shader that is used to implement collision detection in the second, simulation pass. Using this mechanism, any object that would normally be rendered can be captured, so long as the vertex (or geometry) shader produces world space vertices in addition to eye space vertices. This allows the particle system to interact with multiple objects, potentially with each rendered using a different set of shaders—perhaps even with tessellation enabled or other procedurally generated geometry.[4]

The second pass is where the particle system simulation occurs. Particle position and velocity vectors are stored in a pair of buffers. Two buffers are used so that data can be double-buffered as it's not possible to update vertex data in place. Each vertex in the buffer represents a single particle in the system. Each instance of the vertex shader performs collision detection between the particle (using its velocity to compute where it will move to during the time-step) and all of the geometry captured during the first pass. It calculates new position and velocity vectors, which are captured using transform feedback, and written into a buffer object ready for the next step in the simulation.

---

4. Care should be taken here—tessellation can generate a very large amount of geometry, all of which the simulated particles must be tested against, which could severely affect performance and increase storage requirements for the intermediate geometry.

Example 5.8 contains the source of the vertex shader used to transform the incoming geometry into both world and eye space, and Example 5.9 shows how transform feedback is configured to capture the resulting world space geometry.

Example 5.8   Vertex Shader Used in Geometry Pass of Particle System Simulator

```
#version 420 core

uniform mat4 model_matrix;
uniform mat4 projection_matrix;

layout (location = 0) in vec4 position;
layout (location = 1) in vec3 normal;

out vec4 world_space_position;

out vec3 vs_fs_normal;

void main(void)
{
    vec4 pos = (model_matrix * (position * vec4(1.0, 1.0, 1.0, 1.0)));
    world_space_position = pos;
    vs_fs_normal = normalize((model_matrix * vec4(normal, 0.0)).xyz);
    gl_Position = projection_matrix * pos;
};
```

Example 5.9   Configuring the Geometry Pass of the Particle System Simulator

```
static const char * varyings2[] =
{
    "world_space_position"
};

glTransformFeedbackVaryings(render_prog, 1, varyings2,
                            GL_INTERLEAVED_ATTRIBS);
glLinkProgram(render_prog);
```

During the first geometry pass, the code in Exaples 5.8 and 5.9 will cause the world space geometry to be captured into a buffer object. Each triangle in the buffer is represented by three vertices[5] that are read (three at a time) during the second pass into the vertex shader and used to perform line segment against triangle intersection test. A TBO is used to access the data in the intermediate buffer so that the three vertices can be read in a simple

---

5. Only triangles are used here. It's not possible to perform a meaningful physical collision detection between a line segment and another line segment or a point. Also, individual triangles are required for this to work. If strips or fans are present in the input geometry, it may be necessary to include a geometry shader in order to convert the connected triangles into independent triangles.

for loop. The line segment is formed by taking the particle's current position and using its velocity to calculate where it *will be* at the end of the time step. This is performed for every captured triangle. If a collision is found, the point's new position is reflected about the plane of the triangle to make it "bounce" off the geometry.

Example 5.10 contains the code of the vertex shader used to perform collision detection in the simulation pass.

Example 5.10   Vertex Shader Used in Simulation Pass of Particle System Simulator

```
#version 420 core

uniform mat4 model_matrix;
uniform mat4 projection_matrix;
uniform int triangle_count;

layout (location = 0) in vec4 position;
layout (location = 1) in vec3 velocity;

out vec4 position_out;
out vec3 velocity_out;

uniform samplerBuffer geometry_tbo;
uniform float time_step = 0.02;

bool intersect(vec3 origin, vec3 direction, vec3 v0, vec3 v1, vec3 v2,
               out vec3 point)
{
    vec3 u, v, n;
    vec3 w0, w;
    float r, a, b;

    u = (v1 - v0);
    v = (v2 - v0);
    n = cross(u, v);

    w0 = origin - v0;
    a = -dot(n, w0);
    b = dot(n, direction);

    r = a / b;
    if (r < 0.0 || r > 1.0)
        return false;

    point = origin + r * direction;

    float uu, uv, vv, wu, wv, D;

    uu = dot(u, u);
    uv = dot(u, v);
    vv = dot(v, v);
    w = point - v0;
```

```
        wu = dot(w, u);
        wv = dot(w, v);
        D = uv * uv - uu * vv;

        float s, t;

        s = (uv * wv - vv * wu) / D;
        if (s < 0.0 || s > 1.0)
            return false;
        t = (uv * wu - uu * wv) / D;
        if (t < 0.0 || (s + t) > 1.0)
            return false;

        return true;
}

vec3 reflect_vector(vec3 v, vec3 n)
{
        return v - 2.0 * dot(v, n) * n;
}

void main(void)
{
        vec3 acceleration = vec3(0.0, -0.3, 0.0);
        vec3 new_velocity = velocity + acceleration * time_step;
        vec4 new_position = position + vec4(new_velocity * time_step, 0.0);
        vec3 v0, v1, v2;
        vec3 point;
        int i;
        for (i = 0; i < triangle_count; i++)
        {
            v0 = texelFetch(geometry_tbo, i * 3).xyz;
            v1 = texelFetch(geometry_tbo, i * 3 + 1).xyz;
            v2 = texelFetch(geometry_tbo, i * 3 + 2).xyz;
            if (intersect(position.xyz, position.xyz - new_position.xyz,
                        v0, v1, v2, point))
            {
                vec3 n = normalize(cross(v1 - v0, v2 - v0));
                new_position = vec4(point
                                  + reflect_vector(new_position.xyz -
                                    point, n), 1.0);
                new_velocity = 0.8 * reflect_vector(new_velocity, n);
            }
        }
        if (new_position.y < -40.0)
        {
            new_position = vec4(-new_position.x * 0.3, position.y + 80.0,
                        0.0, 1.0);
            new_velocity *= vec3(0.2, 0.1, -0.3);
        }
        velocity_out = new_velocity * 0.9999;
        position_out = new_position;
        gl_Position = projection_matrix * (model_matrix * position);
};
```

The code to set up transform feedback to capture the updated particle position and velocity vectors is shown in Example 5.11.

Example 5.11   Configuring the Simulation Pass of the Particle System Simulator

```
static const char * varyings[] =
{
    "position_out", "velocity_out"
};

glTransformFeedbackVaryings(update_prog, 2, varyings,
                            GL_INTERLEAVED_ATTRIBS);

glLinkProgram(update_prog);
```

The inner rendering loop of the application is quite simple. First, the program object used for rendering the geometry is bound, as is a transform feedback object representing the state required to capture the world space geometry. Then, all of the solid objects in the scene are rendered, causing the intermediate buffer to be filled with world space geometry. Next, the program object used for updating particle positions is made current, as is the transform feedback object used for capturing position and velocity data for the particle system. Finally, the particles are rendered. The code for this inner loop is shown in Example 5.12.

Example 5.12   Main Rendering Loop of the Particle System Simulator

```
glUseProgram(render_prog);
glUniformMatrix4fv(render_model_matrix_loc, 1, GL_FALSE, model_matrix);
glUniformMatrix4fv(render_projection_matrix_loc, 1, GL_FALSE,
                   projection_matrix);

glBindVertexArray(render_vao);

glBindBufferBase(GL_TRANSFORM_FEEDBACK_BUFFER, 0, geometry_vbo);
glBeginTransformFeedback(GL_TRIANGLES);
object.Render();
glEndTransformFeedback();

glUseProgram(update_prog);
glUniformMatrix4fv(model_matrix_loc, 1, GL_FALSE, model_matrix);
glUniformMatrix4fv(projection_matrix_loc, 1, GL_FALSE,
                   projection_matrix);
glUniform1i(triangle_count_loc, object.GetVertexCount() / 3);

if ((frame_count & 1) != 0)
{
    glBindVertexArray(vao[1]);
    glBindBufferBase(GL_TRANSFORM_FEEDBACK_BUFFER, 0, vbo[0]);
}
```

```
else
{
    glBindVertexArray(vao[0]);
    glBindBufferBase(GL_TRANSFORM_FEEDBACK_BUFFER, 0, vbo[1]);
}

glBeginTransformFeedback(GL_POINTS);
glDrawArrays(GL_POINTS, 0, min(point_count, (frame_count >> 3)));
glEndTransformFeedback();

glBindVertexArray(0);

frame_count++;
```

The result of the program is shown in Figure 5.20.

Figure 5.20   Result of the particle system simulator

Chapter 6

Textures

Chapter Objectives

After reading this chapter, you'll be able to do the following:

- Understand what texture mapping can add to your scene.

- Supply texture images in compressed and uncompressed formats.

- Control how a texture image is filtered as it is applied to a fragment.

- Create and manage texture images in texture objects.

- Supply texture coordinates describing what part of the texture image should be mapped onto objects in your scene.

- Perform complex texture operations using multiple textures in a single shader.

- Specify textures to be used for processing point sprites.

The goal of computer graphics, generally speaking, is to determine the colors that make up each part of an image. While it is possible to calculate the color of a pixel using an advanced shading algorithm, often the complexity of such a shader is so great that it is not practical to implement such approaches. Instead, we rely on *textures*—large chunks of image data that can be used to paint the surfaces of objects to make them appear more realistic. This chapter discusses various approaches and techniques to apply textures using shaders in your application.

This chapter has the following major sections:

- "Texture Mapping" provides an overview the the process of texture mapping.

- "Basic Texture Types" provides an outline of the types of texture that are available in OpenGL.

- "Creating and Initializing Textures" explains how to create and set up a texture for use in your application.

- "Proxy Textures" introduces the *proxy texture* targets, which provide a mechanism to probe the capabilities of the OpenGL implementation.

- "Specifying Texture Data" provides a description of the formatting of texture data in OpenGL and how you get that data into your texture objects.

- "Sampler Objects" shows how *sampler objects* can be used to control the way that OpenGL reads data from textures into your shaders.

- "Using Textures" delves into the ways that you can make best use of textures in your shaders.

- "Complex Texture Types" describes some of the more advanced texture types that are available in OpenGL, including array textures, cube maps, depth, and buffer textures.

- "Texture Views" describes how to share one texture's data with one or more other textures, and to interpret it in different ways.

- "Compressed Textures" explores methods to use *compressed texture* data in your application in order to save memory and bandwidth, which are both important performance considerations.

- "Filtering" outlines the various ways in which multiple texels may be combined in order to reduce artifacts and to improve the quality of your rendered images.

- "Advanced Texture Lookup Functions" takes a closer look at some of the more advanced functions available in GLSL that can be used to read data from textures with more control.

- "Point Sprites" describes a feature of OpenGL that provides texture coordinates automatically for geometry rendered as points, allowing your application to very quickly render small bitmaps to the display.

- "Rendering to Texture Maps" explains how to render directly into a texture map by using framebuffer objects.

Texture Mapping

In the physical world, colors within your field of view can change rapidly. Odds are you're reading this book inside of a building.[1] Look at the walls, ceiling, floors, and objects in the room. Unless you've furnished your home entirely at Ikea, it's likely some surface in the room will have detail where the colors change rapidly across a small area. Capturing color changes with that amount of detail is both toilsome and data-intensive (effectively, you need to specify a triangle for each region of linear color change). It would be much simpler to be able to use a picture and "glue" it onto the surface like wallpaper. Enter *texture mapping*. This technique allows you to look up values, like colors, from a shader in a special type of table. While texture mapping is available in all of OpenGL's shading stages, we'll first discuss it in the context of processing fragments, because that's where it's used most often.

Often a *texture map* (or just "texture" for short) is an image captured by a camera or painted by an artist, but there's no requirement that be the case—it's possible that the image is procedurally generated (see Chapter 8, "Procedural Texturing") or even rendered by OpenGL targeting a texture instead of the display device. Textures of this nature would be two-dimensional, but OpenGL supports many other types of textures as well: one-, and three-dimensional textures, cube-map textures, and buffer textures. Array textures are also supported, which are treated as a set of *slice*s of similar dimension and format, wrapped up in a single texture object. All of these will be discussed in detail below.

Textures are composed of *texels*, which will often contain color values. However, there's a lot of utility in merely considering a texture as a table of values that you can query in a shader and use for any purpose you desire.

In order to use texture mapping in your application, you will need to do the following steps:

- Create a *texture object* and load texel data into it.

- Include texture coordinates with your vertices.

---

1. We applaud you if that's not true, except if you're currently operating a moving vehicle.

- Associate a *texture sampler* with each texture map you intend to use in your shader.

- Retrieve the texel values through the texture sampler from your shader.

We'll discuss each of those steps in the following sections.

Basic Texture Types

OpenGL supports many types of texture object of varying dimensionalities and layout. Each texture object represents a set of images that make up the complete texture. Each image is a 1D, 2D, or 3D array of texels and many images may be "stacked" one on top of another to form what is known as a *mipmap* pyramid. More information about mipmaps, how they affect texturing, and how to create them is covered in "Using and Generating Mipmaps" on Page 333. Furthermore, textures may contain arrays of 1D or 2D slices—such textures are known as *array textures*, and each element of the array is known as a slice. A *cube map* is a special case of an array texture that has a multiple of six slices. A single cube-map texture has exactly six faces, whereas a cube-map array represents an array of cube-map textures, always having an integer multiple of six faces. Textures may be used to represent multisampled surfaces by using the multisampled texture types for 2D and 2D-array textures. Multisampling is a term that refers to an implementation of antialiasing where each texel (or pixel) is assigned multiple independent colors and those colors may be merged together later in the rendering process to produce the final output color. A multisampled texture has several samples (typically between two and eight) for each texel.

Textures are bound to the OpenGL context via *texture units*, which are represented as binding points named GL_TEXTURE0 through GL_TEXTUREi where i is one less than the number of texture units supported by the implementation. Many textures may be bound to the same context concurrently as the context supports many texture units. Once a texture has been bound to a context, it may be accessed in shaders using *sampler variables*, which were declared with dimensionality that matches the texture. Table 6.1 gives a list of the available texture dimensionalities (known as *texture targets*) and the corresponding sampler type that must be used in shaders to access the texels in the texture.

Table 6.1 Texture Targets and Corresponding Sampler Types

Target (GL_TEXTURE*	Sampler Type	Dimensionality
1D	`sampler1D`	1D
1D_ARRAY	`sampler1DArray`	1D array
2D	`sampler2D`	2D
2D_ARRAY	`sampler2DArray`	2D array
2D_MULTISAMPLE	`sampler2DMS`	2D multisample
2D_MULTISAMPLE_ARRAY	`sampler2DMSArray`	2D multisample array
3D	`sampler3D`	3D
CUBE	`samplerCube`	cube-map texture
ARRAY	`samplerCubeArray`	cube-map array
RECTANGLE	`samplerRect`	2D rectangle
BUFFER	`samplerBuffer`	1D buffer

In Table 6.1, a number of special texture targets are listed. First, the rectangle texture target (GL_TEXTURE_RECTANGLE) is a special case of 2D texture that represents a simple rectangle of texels—it cannot have mipmaps and it cannot be used to represent a texture array. Also, some of the texture wrapping modes are not supported for rectangle textures. Second, the buffer texture (GL_TEXTURE_BUFFER), which represents arbitrary 1D arrays of texels. Like rectangle textures, they do not have mipmaps and cannot be aggregated into arrays. Furthermore, the storage (i.e., memory) for buffer textures is actually represented using a buffer object. Because of this, the upper bound on the size of a buffer texture is much larger than a normal one-dimensional texture. Buffer textures make it possible to access things like vertex data from any shader stage without needing to copy it into a texture image. In the first few sections of this chapter, we will cover basic texturing using single 2D textures, which will be sufficient to describe how to create, initialize, and access textures in shaders. Later in the chapter, beginning in "Complex Texture Types" on Page 306, we will discuss more advanced texture types such as volume textures, buffer textures, and texture arrays. First, we will continue our introduction to texturing using 2D textures, and then return to each of the special types in detail once the basics have been covered.

Creating and Initializing Textures

The first step in using textures in OpenGL is to reserve names for texture objects and bind them to the context's texture units. To create a texture, as with many other objects in OpenGL, names are reserved and then bound to their appropriate target. To reserve names for texture objects, call **glGenTextures()**, specifying the number of names to reserve and the address of an array into which to deposit the names.

---

void **glGenTextures**(GLsizei *n*, GLuint **textures*);

Returns *n* currently unused names for texture objects in the array *textures*. The names returned in *textures* will not necessarily be a contiguous set of integers.

The names in *textures* are marked as used, but they acquire texture state and dimensionality (1D, 2D, or 3D, for example) only when they are first bound.

Zero is a reserved texture name and is never returned by **glGenTextures()**.

After texture object names have first been reserved, they don't yet represent textures and so they don't have any dimensionality or type. A texture object is created with the reserved name the first time it is bound to a texture target using **glBindTexture()**. The target used for this initial binding determines what type of texture is created. From then on, the texture may only be bound to that target[2] until it is destroyed.

---

void **glBindTexture**(GLenum *target*, GLuint *texture*);

glBindTexture() does three things. First, when using an unsigned integer value of *texture* other than zero for the first time, a new texture object is created and assigned that name. Next, when binding a previously created texture object, that texture object becomes active. Finally, when binding a *texture* value of zero, OpenGL removes any binding previously associated with the specified target of the active texture unit, leaving no texture bound there.

When a texture object is initially bound (i.e., created), it assumes the dimensionality of *target*, which must be one of GL_TEXTURE_1D, GL_TEXTURE_2D, GL_TEXTURE_3D, GL_TEXTURE_1D_ARRAY, GL_TEXTURE_2D_ARRAY, GL_TEXTURE_RECTANGLE, GL_TEXTURE_BUFFER, GL_TEXTURE_CUBE_MAP, GL_TEXTURE_CUBE_MAP_ARRAY, GL_TEXTURE_2D_MULTISAMPLE, GL_TEXTURE_2D_MULTISAMPLE_ARRAY

---

2. Or targets that are compatible with that type of texture.

Immediately on its initial binding, the state of the texture object is reset to the default state for the specified target. In this initial state, texture and sampler properties such as coordinate wrapping modes, and minification and magnification filters are set to their default values, which may be found in the state tables contained in the OpenGL specification.

An GL_INVALID_OPERATION error is generated if *texture* is not zero, or the name previously generated by **glGenTextures()**. If *texture* is the name of an existing texture object (i.e., it has previously been bound to any target), then an GL_INVALID_OPERATION error is generated if the dimensionality of *texture* does not match the dimensionality of *target*.

As already described, the OpenGL context supports multiple texture units. Calling **glBindTexture()** binds a texture object to the active texture unit with the dimensionality specified by *target*. The active texture unit is inferred from a *selector* which may be changed by calling the **glActiveTexture()** function. A single texture may be bound to multiple texture units simultaneously. This causes the same texture data to be read through different samplers representing the texture units to which the texture is bound.

void **glActiveTexture**(GLenum *texture*);

Selects the texture unit that is currently modified by texturing functions. *texture* is a symbolic constant of the form GL_TEXTURE*i*, where *i* is in the range from 0 to $k - 1$, where k is the maximum number of texture units. The value of GL_TEXTURE*i* is equal to the value of *GL_TEXTURE0 + i*.

The maximum number of texture units supported by OpenGL can be determined by retrieving the value of the GL_MAX_COMBINED_TEXTURE_IMAGE_UNITS constant, which is guaranteed to be at least 80 as of OpenGL 4.0. Once a texture has been bound to a texture unit for the first time, it is initialized with default state[3] and *becomes* a texture object. Until this point, the reserved name is really just a placeholder and is not yet a texture object. To determine whether a reserved name refers to a texture object, you may call **glIsTexture()**.

---

3. The default state of texture objects may be found in the state tables in the OpenGL specification.

GLboolean **glIsTexture**(GLuint *texture*);

Returns GL_TRUE if *texture* is the name of a texture that has been bound and has not been subsequently deleted, and returns GL_FALSE if *texture* is zero or is a nonzero value that is not the name of an existing texture.

Once a texture object has reached the end of its useful life, it should be deleted. The function for deleting textures is **glDeleteTextures()**, and it works similarly to **glGenTextures()** in that it takes a number of texture objects to delete and the address of an array containing the names of those textures. Any reference to the underlying storage associated with the textures is removed, and that storage will eventually be released by OpenGL when it is no longer needed.

void **glDeleteTextures**(GLsizei *n*, const GLuint **textures*);

Deletes *n* texture objects, named by the elements of the array *textures*. The freed texture names may now be reused (e.g., by **glGenTextures()**).

If a texture that is currently bound is deleted, the binding reverts to the default texture, as if **glBindTexture()** were called with zero for the value of *texture*. Attempts to delete nonexistent texture names or the texture name of zero are ignored without generating an error.

Once a texture object has been deleted using **glDeleteTextures()**, its name becomes unused again and may be returned from a subsequent call to **glGenTextures()**.

Once we have created some texture objects, we must specify storage and ultimately data for them. Each dimensionality of texture object has an associated storage function that defines the bounds of the texture. These are **glTexStorage1D()**, **glTexStorage2D()**, and **glTexStorage3D()**, which define the storage for 1D, 2D, and 3D textures, respectively. For array textures, the next higher dimension is used to specify the size of the array. For example, **glTexStorage2D()** is used to initialize storage for 1D-array textures, and **glTexStorage3D()** is used to initialize storage for 2D-array textures and cube-map array textures. Array textures will be covered in more detail in "Array Textures" on Page 309.

void **glTexStorage1D**(GLenum *target*, GLsizei *levels*,
  GLenum *internalFormat*, GLsizei *width*);
void **glTexStorage2D**(GLenum *target*, GLsizei *levels*,
  GLenum *internalFormat*, GLsizei *width*,
  GLsizei *height*);
void **glTexStorage3D**(GLenum *target*, GLsizei *levels*,
  GLenum *internalFormat*, GLsizei *width*,
  GLsizei *height*, GLsizei *depth*);

Specify *immutable* texture storage for the texture object currently bound to *target*. **glTexStorage1D()** may be used to specify storage for 1D textures, and for this function, *target* must be GL_TEXTURE_1D. **glTexStorage2D()** is used to specify storage for 1D array textures when *target* is GL_TEXTURE_1D_ARRAY, and for 2D textures when *target* is GL_TEXTURE_2D. For 1D array textures, *width* specifies the extent of the texture and *height* specifies the number of slices in the array. For 2D textures, *width* and *height* specify the dimensions of the texture. **glTexStorage3D()** is used to specify storage for 2D array textures when *target* is GL_TEXTURE_2D_ARRAY and for 3D textures when *target* is GL_TEXTURE_3D. For 2D array textures, *width* and *height* specify the dimensions of each slice, and *depth* specifies the number of slices in the array. For 3D textures, *width*, *height*, and *depth* specify the dimensions of the texel array.

The **glTexStorage1D()** through **glTexStorage3D()** are used to create immutable storage for textures. The attributes of the storage for the texture include the amount of memory required to store all of the texels in all of the mipmap levels for the texture in the chosen *internal format* at the specified resolution. Once allocated with one of these functions, the storage may not be redefined. This is generally considered best practice in OpenGL as once defined, the OpenGL implementation can make assumptions that the dimensions and format of the texture object will not change over its lifetime and thus can stop tracking certain aspects of the texture object. Note that it's only the attributes of the storage that cannot change once a texture has been designated as immutable—the *contents* of the texture may be changed using functions such as **glTexSubImage2D()** as explained in "Specifying Texture Data" on Page 277.

The functions **glTexStorage1D()**, **glTexStorage2D()**, and **glTexStorage3D()** only allow the creation of storage for single-sampled textures. If a multisampled texture is being used, you may call **glTexStorage2DMultisample()** or **glTexStorage3DMultisample()** to create storage for the textures.

```
void glTexStorage2DMultisample(GLenum target,
                               GLsizei samples,
                               GLenum internalFormat,
                               GLsizei width, GLsizei height,
                               GLboolean fixedsamplelocations);
void glTexStorage3DMultisample(GLenum target,
                               GLsizei samples,
                               GLenum internalFormat,
                               GLsizei width, GLsizei height,
                               GLsizei depth,
                               GLboolean fixedsamplelocations);
```

Specify immutable texture storage for the multisample texture object currently bound to *target*. For **glTexStorage2DMultisample()**, *target* must be GL_TEXTURE_2D_MULTISAMPLE, and it is used to specify storage 2D multisample textures. *width* and *height* specify the dimensions of the texture. **glTexStorage3D()** is used to specify storage for 2D multisample array textures. *target* must be GL_TEXTURE_2D_MULTISAMPLE_ARRAY. For 2D multisample array textures, *width* and *height* specify the dimensions of each slice, and *depth* specifies the number of slices in the array. In both functions, *samples* specifies the number of samples represented by the texture. If *fixedsamplelocations* is GL_TRUE then OpenGL will use the same sub-texel position for the same sample in each texel of the texture. If *fixedsamplelocations* is GL_FALSE, then OpenGL may choose a spatially varying location for a given sample in each texel.

Although it is best practice to declare texture storage as immutable, it may be desirable to allow texture objects to be redefined (to be resized, or have their format changed, for example). If immutable storage is not desired, one of the mutable texture allocation functions may be used. The *mutable* texture image specification commands include, **glTexImage1D()**, **glTexImage2D()**, and **glTexImage3D()**, or their multisample variants, **glTexImage2DMultisample()** and **glTexImage3DMultisample()**.

```
void glTexImage1D(GLenum target, GLint level,
                  GLint internalFormat, GLsizei width,
                  GLint border, GLenum format, GLenum type,
                  const void *data);
void glTexImage2D(GLenum target, GLint level,
                  GLint internalFormat, GLsizei width,
                  GLsizei height, GLint border, GLenum format,
                  GLenum type, const void *data);
```

void **glTexImage3D**(GLenum *target*, GLint *level*,
                    GLint *internalFormat*, GLsizei *width*,
                    GLsizei *height*, GLsizei *depth*, GLint *border*,
                    GLenum *format*, GLenum *type*,
                    const void **data*);

The functions **glTexImage1D()**, **glTexImage2D()**, and **glTexImage3D()** are used to specify mutable storage and to optionally provide initial image data for a single mipmap level of a 1D, 2D, or 3D texture, respectively. In addition, **glTexImage2D()** and **glTexImage3D()** may be used to specify storage and image data for a single mipmap level of a 1D- or 2D-array texture.

The parameters *width*, *height*, and *depth* (if present) specify the width, height, and depth of the resulting texel array in texels. For array texture specification, *height* specifies the number of slices in a 1D array texture and *depth* specifies the number of slices in a 2D array texture.

internalFormat specifies the format with which OpenGL should store the texels in the texture. *data* specifies the location of the initial texel data in memory. If a buffer is bound to the GL_PIXEL_UNPACK_BUFFER binding point, texel data is read from that buffer object, and *data* is interpreted as an offset into that buffer object from which to read the data. If no buffer is bound to GL_PIXEL_UNPACK_BUFFER then *data* is interpreted as a direct pointer to the data in application memory, unless it is NULL, in which case the initial contents of the texture are undefined. The format of the initial texel data is given by the combination of *format* and *type*. OpenGL will convert the specified data from this format into the internal format specified by *internalFormat*.

---

void **glTexImage3DMultisample**(GLenum *target*,
                                GLenum *samples*,
                                GLint *internalFormat*,
                                GLsizei *width*, GLsizei *height*,
                                GLsizei *depth*,
                                GLboolean *fixedsamplelocations*);
void **glTexImage2DMultisample**(GLenum *target*,
                                GLenum *samples*,
                                GLint *internalFormat*,
                                GLsizei *width*, GLsizei *height*,
                                GLboolean *fixedsamplelocations*);

The **glTexImage2DMultisample()** and **glTexImage3DMultisample()** functions specify storage for 2D and 2D-array multisample textures, respectively. For **glTexImage2DMultisample()**, *target* must be GL_TEXTURE_2D_MULTISAMPLE, and for **glTexImage3DMultisample()**, *target* must be GL_TEXTURE_2D_MULTISAMPLE_ARRAY. Unlike nonmultisampled textures, no initial data may be specified for multisample textures, and multisample textures may not have mipmaps. *width* and *height* specify the width and height of the texture. For 2D-array textures specified by **glTexImage3DMultisample()**, *depth* specifies the number of slices in the array.

If *fixedsamplelocations* is GL_TRUE then the locations of the samples within each texel are always the same for a given sample count and are invariant with respect to position in the texel array. If *fixedsamplelocations* is GL_FALSE then OpenGL may use a different set of locations for the samples in each texel based on its position within the array or on some other criteria.

Because initial data cannot be specified for multisample textures, and functions such as **glTexSubImage2D()** cannot be used to update the contents of multisample textures, the only way to place data into a multisample texture is to attach it to a framebuffer object and render into it. Rendering into textures using framebuffer objects is discussed in more detail in Chapter 4, "Color, Pixels, and Framebuffers".

Texture Formats

The functions **glTexStorage1D()**, **glTexStorage2D()**, **glTexStorage3D()**, **glTexImage1D()**, **glTexImage2D()**, and **glTexImage3D()** and their corresponding multisample variants all take an *internalformat* parameter, which determines the format that OpenGL will use to store the internal texture data. They also take a *format* and *type* parameter indicating the format and type of the data supplied by the application.

Internal Formats

The *internal format* of a texture is the format that OpenGL will use to internally store the texture data you give it. Your data will be converted (if necessary) into this format at image specification time. There are a large number of internal formats that OpenGL can store image data in, and each comes with a size, performance, and quality tradeoff. It is up to you, the application writer, to determine the appropriate format for your needs. Table 6.2 lists all of the internal formats supported by OpenGL, along with their bit sizes for each component.

Table 6.2   Sized Internal Formats

Sized Internal Format	Base Internal Format	R Bits	G Bits	B Bits	A Bits	Shared Bits
GL_R8	GL_RED	8				
GL_R8_SNORM	GL_RED	s8				
GL_R16	GL_RED	16				
GL_R16_SNORM	GL_RED	s16				
GL_RG8	GL_RG	8	8			
GL_RG8_SNORM	GL_RG	s8	s8			
GL_RG16	GL_RG	16	16			
GL_RG16_SNORM	GL_RG	s16	s16			
GL_R3_G3_B2	GL_RGB	3	3	2		
GL_RGB4	GL_RGB	4	4	4		
GL_RGB5	GL_RGB	5	5	5		
GL_RGB565	GL_RGB	5	6	5		
GL_RGB8	GL_RGB	8	8	8		
GL_RGB8_SNORM	GL_RGB	s8	s8	s8		
GL_RGB10	GL_RGB	10	10	10		
GL_RGB12	GL_RGB	12	12	12		
GL_RGB16	GL_RGB	16	16	16		
GL_RGB16_SNORM	GL_RGB	s16	s16	s16		
GL_RGBA2	GL_RGBA	2	2	2	2	
GL_RGBA4	GL_RGBA	4	4	4	4	
GL_RGB5_A1	GL_RGBA	5	5	5	1	
GL_RGBA8	GL_RGBA	8	8	8	8	
GL_RGBA8_SNORM	GL_RGBA	s8	s8	s8	s8	
GL_RGB10_A2	GL_RGBA	10	10	10	2	
GL_RGB10_A2UI	GL_RGBA	ui10	ui10	ui10	ui2	
GL_RGBA12	GL_RGBA	12	12	12	12	
GL_RGBA16	GL_RGBA	16	16	16	16	
GL_RGBA16_SNORM	GL_RGBA	s16	s16	s16	s16	
GL_SRGB8	GL_RGB	8	8	8		
GL_SRGB8_ALPHA8	GL_RGBA	8	8	8	8	

Table 6.2　(continued)　Sized Internal Formats

Sized Internal Format	Base Internal Format	R Bits	G Bits	B Bits	A Bits	Shared Bits
GL_R16F	GL_RED	f16				
GL_RG16F	GL_RG	f16	f16			
GL_RGB16F	GL_RGB	f16	f16	f16		
GL_RGBA16F	GL_RGBA	f16	f16	f16	f16	
GL_R32F	GL_RED	f32				
GL_RG32F	GL_RG	f32	f32			
GL_RGB32F	GL_RGB	f32	f32	f32		
GL_RGBA32F	GL_RGBA	f32	f32	f32	f32	
GL_R11F_G11F_B10F	GL_RGB	f11	f11	f10		
GL_RGB9_E5	GL_RGB	9	9	9		5
GL_R8I	GL_RED	i8				
GL_R8UI	GL_RED	ui8				
GL_R16I	GL_RED	i16				
GL_R16UI	GL_RED	ui16				
GL_R32I	GL_RED	i32				
GL_R32UI	GL_RED	ui32				
GL_RG8I	GL_RG	i8	i8			
GL_RG8UI	GL_RG	ui8	ui8			
GL_RG16I	GL_RG	i16	i16			
GL_RG16UI	GL_RG	ui16	ui16			
GL_RG32I	GL_RG	i32	i32			
GL_RG32UI	GL_RG	ui32	ui32			
GL_RGB8I	GL_RGB	i8	i8	i8		
GL_RGB8UI	GL_RGB	ui8	ui8	ui8		
GL_RGB16I	GL_RGB	i16	i16	i16		
GL_RGB16UI	GL_RGB	ui16	ui16	ui16		
GL_RGB32I	GL_RGB	i32	i32	i32		
GL_RGB32UI	GL_RGB	ui32	ui32	ui32		
GL_RGBA8I	GL_RGBA	i8	i8	i8	i8	
GL_RGBA8UI	GL_RGBA	ui8	ui8	ui8	ui8	
GL_RGBA16I	GL_RGBA	i16	i16	i16	i16	
GL_RGBA16UI	GL_RGBA	ui16	ui16	ui16	ui16	
GL_RGBA32I	GL_RGBA	i32	i32	i32	i32	
GL_RGBA32UI	GL_RGBA	ui32	ui32	ui32	ui32	

For each format listed in Table 6.2 the full format is made up of an identifier representing the *base format*, one or more size indicators, and an optional type. The base format essentially determines which components of the texture are present. Formats starting with GL_R have only the red component present, GL_RG formats have both red and green, GL_RGB formats contain red, green, and blue, and finally, GL_RGBA contain red, green, blue, and alpha.

The subsequent size indicator determines the number of bits that are used to store the texture data. In many cases, only a single size parameter is included. In such cases, all components present receive the same number of bits. By default, OpenGL stores textures in *unsigned normalized* format. When data is stored in unsigned normalized format, the values of the texels are stored in memory as an integer which when read into a shader is converted to floating point and divided by the maximum representable value for the corresponding size of integer. This results in data in the range 0.0 to 1.0 (i.e., normalized data) being presented to the shader. If the _SNORM modifier is present (as in GL_RGBA8_SNORM, for example) then the data is *signed normalized*. In this case, the data in memory is treated as a signed integer, and before it is returned to the shader, it is converted to floating point and divided by the maximum representable signed integer value, resulting in floating-point values in the range −1.0 to 1.0 being returned to the shader.

Type specifiers may be present in the internal format name. These type specifiers are I, UI, and F, indicating signed integer, unsigned integer, and floating-point data, respectively. The signed and unsigned integer internal formats are designed to be used with signed or unsigned integer sampler types in your shader (`isampler2D` or `usampler2D`, for example). The floating point internal formats are true floating-point formats in that the data is stored in memory in a floating-point representation and returned to the shader with the full precision supported by the OpenGL implementation. In such cases, the texels can represent floating-point values outside the range −1.0 to 1.0.

In some cases, a different size specifier is used for some or each of the channels. In these cases, OpenGL will use a different number of bits for each of the channels. For example, GL_RGB10_A2 textures are stored using a 32-bit quantity per texel with 10 bits allocated to each of the red, green, and blue channels, but only 2 bits allocated to the alpha channel. This format of texture is useful for representing higher dynamic range textures with only a few levels of opacity (or with the alpha channel used to store something other than traditional opacity). The GL_R11F_G11F_B10F uses 11 bits for each of red and green, and 10 bits for blue, but stores each channel in a special reduced-precision floating point format. The 11-bit components have no sign bit, a 5-bit *exponent* and a 6-bit *mantissa*.

The format GL_RGB9_E5 is special in that it is a *shared exponent* format. Each component is stored as an independent 9-bit mantissa but shares a single 5-bit exponent between all of the components. This allows textures to be stored with a fairly high dynamic range but to only consume 16 bits per texel.

The GL_SRGB8 and GL_SRGB8_ALPHA8 formats are RGB textures in the sRGB color space, the former without alpha and the latter including an alpha channel. The alpha channel in GL_SRGB8_ALPHA8 is represented separately because it is not part of the sRGB color space and is not subject to the (de)gamma calculations affecting the other components.

External Formats

The *external format* is the format that you use to supply data through the OpenGL API and is represented by the *format* and *type* parameters to functions such as **glTexSubImage2D()**. The *format* is made up of a part indicating which channels are present and an optional INTEGER format specifier. Additionally, there are a handful of *packed integer* formats that are used to represent prepacked texture data. Ideally, there would be no conversion required to take your texture data and place it into the texture with the requested internal format.

The possible values for the *format* parameter are given in Table 6.3, which lists the external format identifier, the components present, their order, and whether the data is comprised of integer values.

Table 6.3   External Texture Formats

Format	Components Present
GL_RED	Red
GL_GREEN	Green
GL_BLUE	Blue
GL_RG	Red, Green
GL_RGB	Red, Green, Blue
GL_RGBA	Red, Green, Blue, Alpha
GL_BGR	Blue, Green, Red
GL_BGRA	Blue, Green, Red, Alpha
GL_RED_INTEGER	Red (Integer)
GL_GREEN_INTEGER	Green (Integer)

Table 6.3   (continued)   External Texture Formats

Format	Components Present
GL_BLUE_INTEGER	Blue (Integer)
GL_RG_INTEGER	Red, Green (Integer)
GL_RGB_INTEGER	Red, Green, Blue (Integer)
GL_RGBA_INTEGER	Red, Green, Blue, Alpha (Integer)
GL_BGR_INTEGER	Blue, Green, Red (Integer)
GL_BGRA_INTEGER	Blue, Green, Red, Alpha (Integer)

Again, notice that the format specifiers listed in Table 6.3 indicate which components are present (red, green, blue, and alpha), their order, and an optional _INTEGER suffix. If this suffix is present, then the values passed to OpenGL are treated as unnormalized integer data and used verbatim. If the internal format of the texture is a floating-point format, then the data is converted to floating point directly—that is, an integer value of 100 becomes 100.0 in floating point, regardless of the incoming data type. If you wish to receive integers in your shader, then you should use an integer sampler type, an integer internal format (e.g., GL_RGBA32UI), and an integer external format and type (e.g., GL_RGBA_INTEGER and GL_UNSIGNED_INT).

The *format* parameter is used in conjunction with a *type* parameter to describe the texture data in memory. *type* is normally one of GL_BYTE, GL_UNSIGNED_BYTE, GL_SHORT, GL_UNSIGNED_SHORT, GL_INT, GL_UNSIGNED_INT, GL_HALF_FLOAT, or GL_FLOAT to indicate signed or unsigned bytes, signed or unsigned shorts, signed or unsigned integers, or half-precision, or full-precision floating-point quantities. GL_DOUBLE may also be used to indicate double-precision quantities. These tokens correspond to the GLbyte, GLubyte, GLshort, GLushort, GLint, GLuint, GLhalf, GLfloat, and GLdouble types, respectively.

In addition to the tokens representing the native types, several special tokens are used to specify packed or mixed-type formats. These are used when data is packed into larger native types with the boundaries between components not necessarily lining up nicely on native byte, short, or integer boundaries. These type names are generally made up of a standard type specifier (such as GL_UNSIGNED_INT) followed by a suffix indicating how the data is laid out in memory. Table 6.4 shows a few examples of how components may be packed into native data types using packed format tokens.

Table 6.4   Example Component Layouts for Packed Pixel Formats

Format Token	Component Layout
GL_UNSIGNED_BYTE_3_3_2	RED GREEN BLUE
GL_UNSIGNED_BYTE_2_3_2_REV	BLUE GREEN RED
GL_UNSIGNED_SHORT_5_6_5	RED GREEN BLUE
GL_UNSIGNED_SHORT_5_6_5_REV	BLUE GREEN RED
GL_UNSIGNED_SHORT_4_4_4_4	RED GREEN BLUE ALPHA
GL_UNSIGNED_SHORT_4_4_4_4_REV	ALPHA BLUE GREEN RED
GL_UNSIGNED_SHORT_5_5_5_1	RED GREEN BLUE A
GL_UNSIGNED_SHORT_1_5_5_5_REV	A BLUE GREEN RED
GL_UNSIGNED_INT_10_10_10_2	RED GREEN BLUE A
GL_UNSIGNED_INT_2_10_10_10_REV	A BLUE GREEN RED
GL_UNSIGNED_INT_10F_11F_11F_REV	BLUE GREEN RED
GL_UNSIGNED_INT_5_9_9_9_REV	ALPHA BLUE GREEN RED

Proxy Textures

In addition to the texture targets listed in Table 6.1, OpenGL supports what are known as proxy texture targets. Each standard texture target[4] has a corresponding proxy texture target. Table 6.5 lists the standard texture targets and their corresponding proxy texture targets.

Table 6.5   Texture Targets and Corresponding Proxy Targets

Texture Target (GL_TEXTURE*)	Proxy Texture Target (GL_PROXY_TEXTURE*)
1D	1D
1D_ARRAY	1D_ARRAY
2D	2D
2D_ARRAY	2D_ARRAY
2D_MULTISAMPLE	2D_MULTISAMPLE
2D_MULTISAMPLE_ARRAY	2D_MULTISAMPLE_ARRAY
3D	3D
CUBE	CUBE
CUBE_ARRAY	CUBE_ARRAY
RECTANGLE	RECTANGLE
BUFFER	n/a

---

4. All targets except for GL_TEXTURE_BUFFER have a corresponding proxy texture target.

Proxy texture targets may be used to test the capabilities of the OpenGL implementation when certain limits are used in combination with each other. For example, consider an OpenGL implementation that reports a maximum texture size of 16384 texels (which is the minimum requirement for OpenGL 4). If one were to create a texture of 16384 × 16384 texels with an internal format of GL_RGBA8 (which requires four bytes of storage per texel), then the total storage requirement for such a texture would be at least a gigabyte—more if mipmaps or other internal storage is required. Therefore, such a request would fail on an OpenGL implementation with less than a gigabyte of available storage for textures. By requesting such a texture allocation on a proxy texture target, the implementation can tell you whether the request might[5] succeed on a normal target, or whether it is destined to fail. If an allocation of a texture on a proxy texture target fails, the texture on the virtual proxy target will have a width and height of zero. Querying the dimensions of the proxy target will tell you whether the call was successful and whether such a request on a real target might succeed.

Specifying Texture Data

In this section, we describe the method in which image data is loaded into texture objects. Two methods are covered—first, we show how to load images directly into the texture object either from data stored in arrays in your program or from buffer objects. This illustrates the storage and data formats used for texture objects. Next, we show how to use the **vglLoadImage()** function that is supplied as part of the sample code for this book and how it allows you to load images from files.

Explicitly Setting Texture Data

In order to describe the process in which texture data is specified to OpenGL, it's possibly easiest to be able to see the image data directly in your program. Texture data is laid out[6] as you might expect it to be—left to right, top to bottom. In Example 6.1, texture data is stored in a constant array declared in C.

---

5. Just because an allocation appears to succeed on a proxy texture target, it does not mean that it will definitely succeed on a real target. It may fail for a variety of other reasons such as the total amount of other textures allocated, or memory fragmentation, for example. However, if it fails on a proxy texture target, it will certainly fail on a real texture target.

6. There are several parameters supported by OpenGL that allow you to change the layout of image data in memory. These are discussed later in this chapter, but the defaults are sufficient for this example.

Example 6.1   Direct Specification of Image Data in C

```c
// The following is an 8x8 checkerboard pattern using
// GL_RED, GL_UNSIGNED_BYTE data.
static const GLubyte tex_checkerboard_data[] =
{
    0xFF, 0x00, 0xFF, 0x00, 0xFF, 0x00, 0xFF, 0x00,
    0x00, 0xFF, 0x00, 0xFF, 0x00, 0xFF, 0x00, 0xFF,
    0xFF, 0x00, 0xFF, 0x00, 0xFF, 0x00, 0xFF, 0x00,
    0x00, 0xFF, 0x00, 0xFF, 0x00, 0xFF, 0x00, 0xFF,
    0xFF, 0x00, 0xFF, 0x00, 0xFF, 0x00, 0xFF, 0x00,
    0x00, 0xFF, 0x00, 0xFF, 0x00, 0xFF, 0x00, 0xFF,
    0xFF, 0x00, 0xFF, 0x00, 0xFF, 0x00, 0xFF, 0x00,
    0x00, 0xFF, 0x00, 0xFF, 0x00, 0xFF, 0x00, 0xFF
};

// The following data represents a 2x2 texture with red,
// green, blue, and yellow texels represented as GL_RGBA,
// GL_FLOAT data.
static const GLfloat tex_color_data[] =
{
    // Red texel              Green texel
    1.0f, 0.0f, 0.0f, 1.0f,   0.0f, 1.0f, 0.0f, 1.0f,
    // Blue texel             Yellow texel
    0.0f, 0.0f, 1.0f, 1.0f,   1.0f, 1.0f, 0.0f, 1.0f
};
```

Of course, specifying texture data by hand directly in your code is not the most efficient way of creating textures. For simple cases such as solid colors or basic checkerboard patterns, it will suffice though. You can load the data into a texture object using one of the **glTexSubImage1D**(), **glTexSubImage2D**(), or **glTexSubImage3D**() functions listed below.

---

void **glTexSubImage1D**(GLenum *target*, GLint *level*, GLint *xoffset*,
                GLsizei *width*, GLenum *format*,
                GLenum *type*, const void **data*);

void **glTexSubImage2D**(GLenum *target*, GLint *level*, GLint *xoffset*,
                GLint *yoffset*, GLsizei *width*,
                GLsizei *height*, GLenum *format*,
                GLenum *type*, const void **data*);

void **glTexSubImage3D**(GLenum *target*, GLint *level*, GLint *xoffset*,
                GLint *yoffset*, GLint *zoffset*,
                GLsizei *width*, GLsizei *height*,
                GLsizei *depth*, GLenum *format*,
                GLenum *type*, const void **data*);

Replace a region of a texture with new data specified in *data*. The *level*, *format*, and *type* parameters have the same meaning as in **glTexImage1D()** through **glTexImage3D()**. *level* is the mipmap level number. *format* and *type* describe the format and data type of the texture image data pointed to by *data*.

data contains the texture data for the subimage. *width*, *height*, and *depth* (if present) are the dimensions of the region that is to replace all or part of the current texture image. *xoffset*, *yoffset*, and *zoffset* (if present) specify the texel offset in the *x*, *y*, and *z* dimensions, respectively. *target* represents the texture target to which the texture object to be modified is bound. If *target* represents a 1D array texture, then *yoffset* and *height* specify the first layer and number of layers to be updated, respectively, otherwise they are treated as texel coordinates. If *target* is a 2D array texture, cube map, or cube-map array texture, *zoffset* and *depth* represent the first layer and number of layers to be updated, otherwise they are treated as texel coordinates.

The specified region may not include any texels outside the range of the originally defined texture array.

The data shown in Example 6.1 shows two simple textures directly coded into constant arrays. The first, `tex_checkerboard_data`, specifies a simple 8 × 8 region of texels of alternating full intensity (`0xFF`) and zero intensity (`0x00`) represented as single unsigned bytes. The second array in Example 6.1 shows color data, this time represented as floating-point data with four channels—the channels representing the amount of red, green, blue, and alpha[7] in each texel. Example 6.2 shows how to load this data into texture objects using **glTexSubImage2D()**.

Example 6.2   Loading Static Data into Texture Objects

```
// First, the black-and-white checkerboard texture...
// Bind the texture (possibly creating it)
glBindTexture(GL_TEXTURE_2D, tex_checkerboard);
// Allocate storage for the texture data
glTexStorage2D(GL_TEXTURE_2D, 4, GL_R8, 8, 8);
// Specify the data for the texture
glTexSubImage2D(GL_TEXTURE_2D,                // target
                0,                            // First mipmap level
                0, 0,                         // x and y offset
                8, 8,                         // width and height
                GL_RED, GL_UNSIGNED_BYTE,     // format and type
                tex_checkerboard_data);       // data
```

---

7. Alpha is normally used to represent *opacity*, but in this case we have set the alpha channel to its maximum value to represent fully opaque texels.

```
// Next, the color, floating-point data.
// Bind the next texture
glBindTexture(GL_TEXTURE_2D, tex_color);
// Allocate storage
glTexStorage2D(GL_TEXTURE_2D, 2, GL_RGBA32F, 2, 2);
// Specify the data
glTexSubImage2D(GL_TEXTURE_2D,                      // target
                0,                                  // First mipmap level
                0, 0,                               // x and y offset
                2, 2,                               // width and height
                GL_RGBA, GL_FLOAT,                  // format and type
                tex_color_data);                    // data
```

Notice how, in Example 6.2, we specify an internal format for the texture that somewhat matches our supplied texture data. For the array of unsigned bytes, we used the internal format GL_R8, which indicates a single channel, 8-bit format. For the color data, we used GL_RGBA32F, which is a four-channel, 32-bit floating-point format. There is no requirement that we use an internal format that matches the data we'll supply. There are well-defined rules as to how OpenGL converts the data you supply into each internal format and these are explained in detail in the OpenGL specification.

Using Pixel Unpack Buffers

The *data* parameter to **glTexSubImage2D()** may be interpreted in one of two ways. The first is as a natural pointer to data stored in the application's memory. This is the use case shown in Example 6.2. *data* is interpreted this way if no buffer object is bound to the GL_PIXEL_UNPACK_BUFFER target. The second interpretation of *data*, which is used when there is a buffer bound to the GL_PIXEL_UNPACK_BUFFER target, is as an offset into that buffer object. This allows the application to stage data into a buffer object and transfer it from there into a texture object at a later time.

Example 6.3   Loading Data into a Texture Using a Buffer Object

```
// First, bind a buffer to the GL_PIXEL_UNPACK_BUFFER binding
glBindBuffer(GL_PIXEL_UNPACK_BUFFER, buf);
// Place our source data into the buffer
glBufferData(GL_PIXEL_UNPACK_BUFFER,
             sizeof(tex_checkerboard_data),
             tex_checkerboard_data,
             GL_STATIC_DRAW);
// Bind the texture (possibly creating it)
glBindTexture(GL_TEXTURE_2D, tex_checkerboard);
// Allocate storage for the texture data
glTexStorage2D(GL_TEXTURE_2D, 4, GL_R8, 8, 8);
// Specify the data for the texture
```

```
glTexSubImage2D(GL_TEXTURE_2D,      // target
                0,                  // First mipmap level
                0, 0,               // x and y offset
                8, 8,               // width and height
                GL_RED,             // Format
                GL_UNSIGNED_BYTE,   // Type
                NULL);              // data(an offset into buffer)
```

In Example 6.3, we first place our source data (`tex_checkerboard_data`) into a buffer object bound to the GL_PIXEL_UNPACK_BUFFER binding point, and then call **glTexSubImage2D()** as we did before. However, this time *data* is interpreted as an offset into the buffer object rather than a raw pointer because we left the buffer bound. This causes OpenGL to take the data from the buffer object, but not necessarily immediately. The primary advantage of using a buffer object to stage texture data is that the transfer from the buffer object into the texture need not occur immediately, so long as it occurs by the time the data is required by a shader. This allows the transfer to occur in parallel with the application running. If instead the data is located in application memory, then the semantics of **glTexSubImage2D()** require that a copy of the data is made before the function returns, preventing a parallel transfer. The advantage of this method is that the application is free to modify the data it passed to the function as soon as the function returns.

Copying Data from the Framebuffer

It is possible to read part of the framebuffer into a texture object, and then use it in subsequent rendering. To do this, use either the **glCopyTexImage1D()** or **glCopyTexImage2D()** functions whose prototypes are as follows:

---

void **glCopyTexImage1D**(GLenum *target*, GLint *level*,
                    GLint *internalFormat*, GLint *x*, GLint *y*,
                    GLsizei *width*, GLint *border*);
void **glCopyTexImage2D**(GLenum *target*, GLint *level*,
                    GLint *internalFormat*, GLint *x*, GLint *y*,
                    GLsizei *width*, GLsizei *height*,
                    GLint *border*);

Copy pixels from the current read framebuffer into the texture currently bound to *target* of the active texture unit. *x* and *y* specify the horizontal and vertical offset of the source region to copy from the framebuffer. *width* and *height* (if present) specify the width and height of the region, respectively. *internalFormat* specifies the format with which the resulting texels should be stored. *border* is reserved and must be zero.

When **glCopyTexImage1D()** or **glCopyTexImage2D()** is called, it is essentially equivalent to calling **glReadPixels()**, and then immediately calling either **glTexImage1D()** or **glTexImage2D()** to re-upload the image data into the texture.

---

void **glCopyTexSubImage1D**(GLenum *target*, GLint *level*,
                              GLint *xoffset*, GLint *x*, GLint *y*,
                              GLsizei *width*);

void **glCopyTexSubImage2D**(GLenum *target*, GLint *level*,
                              GLint *xoffset*, GLint *yoffset*,
                              GLint *x*, GLint *y*, GLsizei *width*,
                              GLsizei *height*);

void **glCopyTexSubImage3D**(GLenum *target*, GLint *level*,
                              GLint *xoffset*, GLint *yoffset*,
                              GLint *zoffset*, GLint *x*, GLint *y*,
                              GLsizei *width*, GLsizei *height*);

Use image data from the framebuffer to replace all or part of a contiguous subregion of the current, existing texture image in the texture object bound to *target* of the active texture unit. *x* and *y* specify the *x* and *y* offset of the region in the framebuffer to copy. *width* and *height* (if present) specify the width and height of the region to copy, respectively. *xoffset*, *yoffset*, and *zoffset* (if present) specify the origin of the destination region in the target texture. If *target* is a 1D array texture, then *yoffset* is the layer of the texture into which the 1D region of texels will be written, otherwise it is the *y* coordinate of the origin of the destination region. If *target* is a 2D array, cube map, or cube-map array texture, then *zoffset* is the index of the layer of the texture containing the destination region, otherwise it is the *z* coordinate of the destination region in a 3D texture.

Although it is possible to read from the framebuffer into a texture, this involves making a copy of the image data, and may also involve format conversions or other work being conducted by the graphics hardware. In general, it is more efficient to draw directly into the texture wherever possible. This is covered in detail in Chapter 4, "Color, Pixels, and Framebuffers".

Loading Images from Files

The simple example of directly storing image data in arrays in your "C" code (or from buffer objects) isn't very practical if you have large images stored on disk. In most applications, you'll store your texture data in a formatted image file—a JPEG, PNG, GIF, or other type for image format—OpenGL works either with raw pixels or with textures compressed with specific algorithms. As such, your application will need to decode the image file into memory that OpenGL can read to initialize its internal texture store. To simplify that process for our examples, we wrote a function, **vglLoadImage()**, which will read an image file,[8] and return the texels in memory, along with other information you'll need to help OpenGL to decode the its pixel data:

- Width (measured in pixels)
- Height (measured in pixels)
- OpenGL's pixel format (e.g., GL_RGB for RGB pixels)
- A recommended internal format to use for the texture
- The number of mipmap levels present in the texture
- Data type for each component in a pixel
- Image data

All of that data is stored in structure of type vglImageData, which is defined in LoadImage.h. The definition of vglImageData is shown in Example 6.4 below.

Example 6.4   Definition of the vglImageData Structure

```
// Enough mips for 16K x 16K, which is the minimum required for
// OpenGL 4.x and higher
#define MAX_TEXTURE_MIPS   14

// Each texture image data structure contains an array of
// MAX_TEXTURE_MIPS of these mipmap structures. The structure
// represents the mipmap data for all slices at that level.
struct vglImageMipData
{
    GLsizei width;             // Width of this mipmap level
    GLsizei height;            // Height of this mipmap level
    GLsizei depth;             // Depth pof mipmap level
    GLsizeiptr mipStride;      // Distance between mip levels
                               //    in memory
    GLvoid* data;              // Pointer to data
};

// This is the main image data structure. It contains all
// the parameters needed to place texture data into a texture
// object using OpenGL.
```

---

8. Currently, DDS files are supported by **vglLoadImage()**.

```
struct vglImageData
{
    GLenum target;                  // Texture target (2D, cube map, etc.)
    GLenum internalFormat;          // Recommended internal format
    GLenum format;                  // Format in memory
    GLenum type;                    // Type in memory (GL_RGB, etc.)
    GLenum swizzle[4];              // Swizzle for RGBA
    GLsizei mipLevels;             // Number of present mipmap levels
    GLsizei slices;                // Number of slices (for arrays)
    GLsizeiptr sliceStride;        // Distance between slices of an
                                    //    array texture
    GLsizeiptr totalDataSize;       // Total data allocated for texture
    vglImageMipData mip[MAX_TEXTURE_MIPS];   // Actual mipmap data
};
```

In order to create, initialize, manipulate, and destroy images in memory, we have defined two functions—**vglLoadImage()** and **vglUnloadImage()**. Each takes a pointer to a vglImageData structure. **vglLoadImage()** fills it in and **vglUnloadImage()** releases any resources that were allocated by a previous call to **vglLoadImage()**. The prototypes of **vglLoadImage()** and **vglUnloadImage()** are as follows:

void **vglLoadImage**(const char* *filename*, vglImageData* *image*);
void **vglUnloadImage**(vglImageData* *image*);

vglLoadImage() loads an image from a file on disk. *filename* specifies the name of the file to load. *image* is the address of a vglImageData structure that will be filled with the parameters of the image on success. On failure, *image* will be cleared. **vglUnloadImage()** should be used to release any resources consumed by a previous, successful call to **vglLoadImage()**.

To load an image file, simply use code such as that shown in Example 6.5 in your application.

Example 6.5   Simple Image Loading Example

```
vglImageData image;
vglLoadImage(filename, &image);
// Use image data here
vglUnloadImage(&image);
```

The result of calling **vglLoadImage()** is that the texture data from the specified image file is loaded into memory, and information about that image data is stored in the vglImageData structure given to the function.

Once the image data has been loaded from the file, you may use it to establish the texels for your texture object. To do this, pass the data pointer and texture dimensions to the appropriate texture image function. If the texture is allocated as an immutable object (using **glTexStorage2D()**, for example), then the image data is specified using a texture subimage command such as **glTexSubImage2D()**. The `vglImageData` structure contains all of the parameters required to initialize the image.

Example 6.6 shows a simple but complete example of using the **vglLoadImage()** function to load an image from disk, the **glTexStorage2D()** function to allocate storage in texture object, and **glTexSubImage2D()** to load the image data into the texture object.

Example 6.6   . Loading a Texture Using loadImage

```
GLuint LoadTexture(const char* filename,
                   GLuint texture,
                   GLboolean generateMips)
{
    vglImageData image;
    int level;

    vglLoadImage(filename, &image);

    if (texture == 0)
    {
        glGenTextures(1, &texture);
    }

    glBindTexture(image.target, texture);

    switch (image.target)
    {
        case GL_TEXTURE_2D:
            glTexStorage2D(image.target,
                           image.mipLevels,
                           image.internalFormat,
                           image.mip[0].width,
                           image.mip[0].height);
        // Handle other texture targets here.
        default:
            break;
    }

    // Assume this is a 2D texture.
    for (level = 0; level < image.mipLevels; ++level)
    {
        glTexSubImage2D(GL_TEXTURE_2D,
                        level,
                        0, 0,
                        image.mip[level].width,
                        image.mip[level].height,
                        image.format, image.type,
                        image.mip[level].data);
    }
}
```

```
    // Unload the image here as glTexSubImage2D has consumed
    // the data and we don't need it any more.
    vglUnloadImage(&image);

        return texture;
}
```

As you can see, this code could become quite complex depending on how generic your texture-loading function might be and how many types of texture you might want to load. To make things easier for you, we have included the function **vglLoadTexture()**, which internally uses **vglLoadImage()** to load an image file, and then place its contents into a texture object for you. The listing shows a simplified version of the **vglLoadTexture()** function, which will take an image file and load it into a texture object for you. It will handle any dimensional image, array textures, cube maps, compressed textures, and anything else that's supported by the **vglLoadImage()** function. The complete implementation of **vglLoadTexture()** is included in this book's accompanying source code.

GLuint **vglLoadTexture**(const char* *filename*, GLuint *texture*,
                          vglImageData* *image*);

Loads a texture from disk and places it into an OpenGL texture object. *filename* is the name of the file to load. *texture* is the name of a texture object into which to load the data. If *texture* is zero, then **vglLoadTexture()** will create a new texture object into which to place the data. *image* is the address of a vglImageData structure that may be used to return the parameters of the loaded image. If *image* is not NULL, then it will be used to return information about the image, and the image data will not be freed. The application should use **vglUnloadImage()** to release any resources associated with the image. If *image* is NULL then internal data structures will be used to load the image, and the resulting image data will be freed automatically. Upon success, **vglLoadTexture()** returns the texture object into which the texture image was loaded. If *texture* is not zero, then the return value will be equal to *texture*, otherwise it is a newly created texture object. Upon failure, **vglLoadTexture()** returns zero.

Note: It's not possible to directly specify the image data for a multisampled texture. The only way to place data into a multisampled texture is to attach it to a framebuffer object and render into it. Framebuffers and multisampling is explained in some detail in Chapter 4, "Color, Pixels, and Framebuffers".

Retrieving Texture Data

Once you have a texture containing data, it is possible to read that data either back into your application's memory or back into a buffer object. The function for reading image data from a texture is **glGetTexImage()**, whose prototype is as follows:

---

void **glGetTexImage**(GLenum *target*, GLint *lod*, GLenum *format*,
GLenum *type*, GLvoid* *image*);

Retrieves a texture image from the texture bound to *target*. *target* must be one of GL_TEXTURE_1D, GL_TEXTURE_2D, GL_TEXTURE_3D, GL_TEXTURE_1D_ARRAY, GL_TEXTURE_2D_ARRAY, GL_TEXTURE_CUBE_MAP_ARRAY, or GL_TEXTURE_RECTANGLE. Additionally, the targets GL_TEXTURE_CUBE_MAP_POSITIVE_X, GL_TEXTURE_CUBE_MAP_NEGATIVE_X, GL_TEXTURE_CUBE_MAP_POSITIVE_Y, GL_TEXTURE_CUBE_MAP_NEGATIVE_Y, GL_TEXTURE_CUBE_MAP_POSITIVE_Z, and GL_TEXTURE_CUBE_MAP_NEGATIVE_Z may be used to indicate the corresponding face of a single cube-map texture. *lod* is the level-of-detail number. *format* and *type* are the pixel format and type of the desired data. *image* is interpreted either as an address in client memory where the image data will be placed or, if a buffer is bound to the GL_PIXEL_PACK_BUFFER target as an offset into that buffer at which the image data will be placed.

Great care should be exercised when using this function. The number of bytes written into *image* is determined by the dimensions of the texture currently bound to *target*, and by *format* and *type*. Potentially, a great deal of data could be returned and no bound checks are performed by OpenGL on the memory area you supply. Therefore, incorrect usage of this function could lead to buffer overruns and bad things happening.

Furthermore, reading pixel data back from textures is generally not a high-performance operation. Doing so should be a sparingly invoked operation and should certainly not be in a performance critical path of your application. If you must read data back from textures, we strongly recommend that you bind a buffer to the GL_PIXEL_PACK_BUFFER buffer target, read the texels into that, and subsequently map the buffer in order to transfer the pixel data into your application.

Texture Data Layout

So far, our descriptions of the texture image specification commands have not addressed the physical layout of image data in memory. In many cases, image data is laid out left-to-right, top-to-bottom[9] in memory with texels closely following each other. However, this is not always the case, and so OpenGL provides several controls that allow you to describe how the data is laid out in your application.

These parameters are set using the **glPixelStorei()** and **glPixelStoref()** commands, whose prototypes are as follows:

---

void **glPixelStorei**(GLenum *pname*, GLint *param*);
void **glPixelStoref**(GLenum *pname*, GLfloat *param*);

Set the pixel storage parameter *pname* to the value specified by *param*. *pname* must be one of the pixel unpacking parameter names (GL_UNPACK_ROW_LENGTH, GL_UNPACK_SWAP_BYTES, GL_UNPACK_SKIP_PIXELS, GL_UNPACK_SKIP_ROWS, GL_UNPACK_SKIP_IMAGES, GL_UNPACK_ALIGNMENT, GL_UNPACK_IMAGE_HEIGHT, or GL_UNPACK_LSB_FIRST) or one of the pixel packing parameter names (GL_PACK_ROW_LENGTH, GL_PACK_SWAP_BYTES, GL_PACK_SKIP_PIXELS, GL_PACK_SKIP_ROWS, GL_PACK_SKIP_IMAGES, GL_PACK_ALIGNMENT, GL_PACK_IMAGE_HEIGHT, or GL_PACK_LSB_FIRST).

The unpack parameters set by **glPixelStorei()** and **glPixelStoref()** (those beginning with GL_UNPACK_) specify how OpenGL will read data from client memory or the buffer bound to the GL_PIXEL_UNPACK_BUFFER binding in functions such as **glTexSubImage2D()**. The packing parameters specify how OpenGL will write texture data into memory during functions such as **glGetTexImage()**.

Since the corresponding parameters for packing and unpacking have the same meanings, they're discussed together in the rest of this section and referred to without the GL_PACK_ or GL_UNPACK_ prefix. For example, *SWAP_BYTES refers to GL_PACK_SWAP_BYTES and GL_UNPACK_SWAP_BYTES. If the *SWAP_BYTES parameter is GL_FALSE (the default), the ordering of the bytes in memory is whatever is native for the OpenGL client; otherwise, the bytes are reversed. The byte reversal

---

9. It's important to understand that textures don't really have a *top* and a *bottom*, but rather they have an origin and a direction of increasing of texture coordinates. What appears to be rendered at the top of a frame in window coordinates depends entirely on the texture coordinates used.

applies to any size element, but has a meaningful effect only for multibyte elements.

The effect of *byte swapping* may differ among OpenGL implementations. If on an implementation, GLubyte has 8 bits, GLushort has 16 bits, and GLuint has 32 bits, then Figure 6.1 illustrates how bytes are swapped for different data types. Note that byte swapping has no effect on single-byte data.

Note: As long as your OpenGL application doesn't share images with other machines, you can ignore the issue of byte ordering. If your application must render an OpenGL image that was created on a different machine, and the two machines have different byte orders, byte ordering can be swapped using *SWAP_BYTES. However, *SWAP_BYTES does not allow you to reorder elements (e.g., to swap red and green).

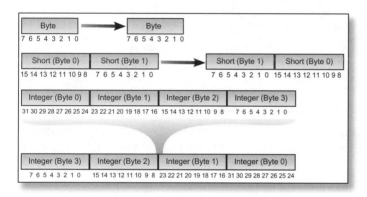

Figure 6.1   Byte-swap effect on byte, short, and integer data

The *LSB_FIRST parameter applies only when drawing or reading 1-bit images or bitmaps for which a single bit of data is saved or restored for each pixel. If *LSB_FIRST is GL_FALSE (the default), the bits are taken from the bytes starting with the most significant bit; otherwise, they're taken in the opposite order. For example, if *LSB_FIRST is GL_FALSE, and the byte in question is 0x31, the bits, in order, are {0, 0, 1, 1, 0, 0, 0, 1}. If *LSB_FIRST is GL_TRUE, the order is {1, 0, 0, 0, 1, 1, 0, 0}.

Sometimes you want to draw or read only a subrectangle of the entire rectangle of image data stored in memory. If the rectangle in memory is larger than the subrectangle that's being drawn or read, you need to specify the actual length (measured in pixels) of the larger rectangle with *ROW_LENGTH. If *ROW_LENGTH is zero (which it is by default), the row length is understood to be the same as the width that's implied by the parameters to **glTexSubImage2D()**, for example. You also need to specify the number of rows and pixels to skip before starting to copy the data for the subrectangle. These numbers are set using the parameters *SKIP_ROWS and *SKIP_PIXELS, as shown in Figure 6.2. By default, both parameters are 0, so you start at the lower left corner.

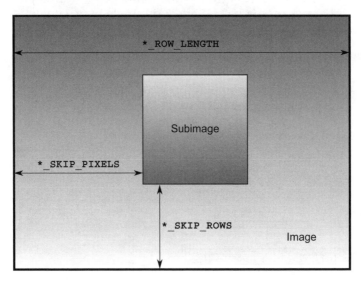

Figure 6.2   Subimage
(A subimage identified by *SKIP_ROWS, *SKIP_PIXELS, and *ROW_LENGTH parameters.)

Often, a particular machine's hardware is optimized for a particular byte alignment when moving pixel data to and from memory. For example, in a machine with 32-bit words, hardware can often retrieve data much faster if it's initially aligned on a 32-bit boundary, which typically has an address that is a multiple of 4. Likewise, 64-bit architectures might work better when the data is aligned to 8-byte boundaries. On some machines, however, byte alignment makes no difference.

As an example, suppose your machine works better with pixel data aligned to a 4-byte boundary. Images are most efficiently saved by forcing the data for each row of the image to begin on a 4-byte boundary. If the image is 5 pixels wide and each pixel consists of 1 byte each of red, green, and blue information, a row requires $5 \times 3 = 15$ bytes of data. Maximum display efficiency can be achieved if the first row, and each successive row, begins on a 4-byte boundary, so there is 1 byte of waste in the memory storage for each row. If your data is stored in this way, set the *ALIGNMENT parameter appropriately (to 4, in this case).

If *ALIGNMENT is set to 1, the next available byte is used. If it's 2, a byte is skipped if necessary at the end of each row so that the first byte of the next row has an address that's a multiple of 2. In the case of bitmaps (or 1-bit images), where a single bit is saved for each pixel, the same byte alignment works, although you have to count individual bits. For example, if you're saving a single bit per pixel, if the row length is 75, and if the alignment is 4, then each row requires 75/8, or 93/8 bytes. Since 12 is the smallest multiple of 4 that is bigger than 93/8, 12 bytes of memory are used for each row. If the alignment is 1, then 10 bytes are used for each row, as 9 3/8 is rounded up to the next byte.

Note: The default value for *ALIGNMENT is 4. A common programming mistake is to assume that image data is tightly packed and byte aligned (which assumes that *ALIGNMENT is set to 1).

The parameters *IMAGE_HEIGHT and *SKIP_IMAGES affect only the defining and querying of three-dimensional textures and two-dimensional texture arrays. These pixel-storage parameters allow the routines **glTexImage3D()**, **glTexSubImage3D()**, and **glGetTexImage()** to delimit and access any desired subvolume or subset of slices of an array texture.

If the three-dimensional texture in memory is larger than the subvolume that is defined, you need to specify the height of a single subimage with the *IMAGE_HEIGHT parameter. Also, if the subvolume does not start with the very first layer, the *SKIP_IMAGES parameter needs to be set.

*IMAGE_HEIGHT is a pixel-storage parameter that defines the height (number of rows) of a single layer of a three-dimensional texture image, as shown in Figure 6.3. If the *IMAGE_HEIGHT value is zero (a negative number is invalid), then the number of rows in each two-dimensional rectangle is the value of height, which is the parameter passed to **glTexImage3D()** or **glTexSubImage3D()**. (This is commonplace because *IMAGE_HEIGHT is zero, by default.) Otherwise, the height of a single layer is the *IMAGE_HEIGHT value.

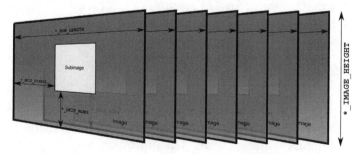

Figure 6.3   *IMAGE_HEIGHT pixel storage mode

*SKIP_IMAGES defines how many layers to bypass before accessing the first data of the subvolume. If the *SKIP_IMAGES value is a positive integer (call the value n), then the pointer in the texture image data is advanced that many layers (n * the size of one layer of texels). The resulting subvolume starts at layer n and is several layers deep—how many layers deep is determined by the depth parameter passed to **glTexImage3D()** or **glTexSubImage3D()**. If the *SKIP_IMAGES value is zero (the default), then accessing the texel data begins with the very first layer described in the texel array.

Figure 6.4 shows how the *SKIP_IMAGES parameter can bypass several layers to get to where the subvolume is actually located. In this example, *SKIP_IMAGES is 4 and the subvolume begins at layer 4.

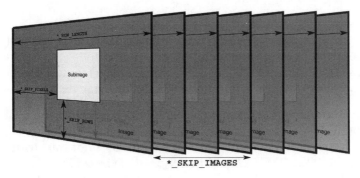

Figure 6.4   *SKIP_IMAGES pixel storage mode

Sampler Objects

Textures may be read by a shader by associating a sampler variable with a texture unit and using GLSL's built-in functions to fetch texels from the texture's image. The way in which the texels are fetched depends on a number of parameters that are contained in another object called a sampler object. Sampler objects are bound to sampler units much as texture objects are bound to texture units. For convenience, a texture object may be considered to contain a built-in sampler object of its own that will be used by default to read from it, if no sampler object is bound to the corresponding sampler unit.

To create a sampler object, as with most other object types in OpenGL, we reserve a name for the new object and bind it to a binding point—in this case, one of the GL_SAMPLER binding points. The prototype of **glGenSamplers()** is as follows:

---

void **glGenSamplers**(GLsizei *count*, GLuint **samplers*);

Returns *count* currently unused names for sampler objects in the array *samplers*. The names returned in *samplers* will not necessarily be a contiguous set of integers.

The names in *samplers* are marked as used, but they acquire sampler state only when they are first bound.

The value zero is reserved and is never returned by **glGenSamplers()**.

glGenSamplers() will return a set of unused sampler object names. Once the names have been generated, they are reserved for use as sampler objects and may be bound to the sampler binding points using the **glBindSampler()** function, whose prototype is shown below.

---

void **glBindSampler**(GLuint *unit*, GLuint *sampler*);

Binds the sampler object named *sampler* to the sampler unit whose index is given in *unit*. If *sampler* is zero, any sampler object currently bound to sampler unit *unit* is unbound and no object is bound in its place.

Until a name has been bound to a sampler unit, it is not yet considered a sampler object. To determine if a given value is the name of an existing sampler object, you can call **glIsSampler()**, whose prototype is as follows:

GLboolean **glIsSampler**(GLenum *id*);

Returns GL_TRUE if *id* is the name of an existing sampler object and GL_FALSE otherwise.

Notice that there are a couple of subtle differences[10] between the **glBindSampler()** function and the **glBindTexture()** function. First, there is no *target* parameter for samplers. This is because the target is implied by

---

10. These differences may seem to introduce inconsistency into the OpenGL API. That is a fair observation. However, it is a byproduct of the way that OpenGL evolves. The API takes small, incremental steps, each striking a balance among introduction of new functionality, enablement of innovation, and maintenance of backwards compatibility. It has been recognized that modern OpenGL implementations can support a huge number of textures and samplers, and reserving tokens from GL_SAMPLER0 through GL_SAMPLER79 is simply not practical, and is not forward-looking. Thus, the decision to sacrifice some consistency in order to achieve some forward compatibility was made.

the function. As sampler objects have no inherent dimensionality, there is no reason to distinguish among multiple sampler object types. Secondly, the *unit* parameter is present here, and there is no selector for sampler objects—that is, there is no **glActiveSampler()** function. Furthermore, in contrast to the parameter to **glActiveTexture()**, which is a token between GL_TEXTURE0 and GL_TEXTURE*i*, where *i* is an arbitrarily large implementation-defined maximum, *unit* is a zero-based unsigned integer, allowing any number of sampler units to be supported by an OpenGL implementation without reserving a large number of OpenGL tokens.

Sampler Parameters

Each sampler object represents a number of parameter that controls the way texels will ultimately be read from a texture object. The parameters of the sampler object are set using the **glSamplerParameteri()** and **glSamplerParameterf()** functions (for integer and floating-point parameters), and **glSamplerParameteriv()** and **glSamplerParameterfv()** functions (for vectors of integer and floating-point parameters). Their prototypes are given below.

---

void **glSamplerParameter{fi}**(GLuint *sampler*, GLenum *pname*,
                                Type *param*);
void **glSamplerParameter{fi}v**(GLuint *sampler*, GLenum *pname*,
                              const Type* *param*);
void **glSamplerParameterI{i ui}v**(GLuint *sampler*,
                              GLenum *pname*,
                              const Type* *param*);

Set the parameter given by *pname* on the sampler object whose name is passed in *sampler* to the value or values given in *param*. For **glSamplerParameteri()**, *param* is a single integer value, and for **glSamplerParameterf()**, *param* is a single floating-point value. For **glSamplerParameteriv()**, *param* is the address of an array of integer values, and for **glSamplerParameterfv()**, *param* is the address of an array of floating-point values.

The **glSamplerParameteri()** and similar functions set the parameters of a sampler object directly. The *sampler* argument of the functions is the *name* of the sampler object that is being modified. However, as noted, there is a default sampler object *contained* in each texture object that will be used to read from the texture when no sampler object is bound to the corresponding sampler unit. To modify the parameters of this object, similar glTexParameter functions are provided.

void **glTexParameter{fi}**(GLenum *target*, GLenum *pname*,
                            Type *param*);
void **glTexParameter{fi}v**(GLenum *target*, GLenum *pname*,
                             const Type **param*);
void **glTexParameterI{i ui}v**(GLenum *target*, GLenum *pname*,
                                const Type **param*);

Set the parameter *pname* on the texture object currently bound to *target* of the active texture unit to the value or values given by *param*. For **glTexParameteri()**, *param* is a single integer, and for **glTexParameterf()**, *param* is a single floating-point value. For **glTexParameteriv()** and **glTexParameterIiv()**, *param* is the address of an array of integer values. For **glTexParameterfv()**, *param* is the address of an array of floating-point values. Finally, for **glTexParameterIuiv()**, *param* is the address of an array of unsigned integer values. If *pname* represents one of the parameters of a sampler object, then the textures internal default sampler object is accessed.

For both the `glSamplerParameter` and `glTexParameter` functions, there are a multitude of values that may be used for the *pname* parameters. Each controls a different aspect of sampling, and for the `glTexParameter` functions, there are some values for *pname* that are not related to sampling at all. Rather than introduce each and every legal value for *pname* here, we introduce each in the following subsections as the topics to which they pertain are covered.

Once you are done using a sampler object, as with any other type of object in OpenGL, it is good practice to clean up after yourself and delete any unused objects. To delete sampler objects, use the **glDeleteSamplers()** function.

void **glDeleteSamplers**(GLsizei *count*, const GLuint **samplers*);

Deletes *count* samplers whose names are stored in the array *samplers*. After deletion, the names in *samplers* are no longer used, and may again be returned from a subsequent call to **glGenSamplers()**.

Using Textures

Once you have created and initialized a texture object and have placed image data into it, you may read from it using shaders in your application. As already noted, textures in shaders are represented as sampler variables of dimensioned sampler types. Each sampler variable is a combination of a set of image data represented by the texture object and a set of sampling parameters that are represented by a sampler object (or the texture's own, internal sampler object). A texture is bound to a texture unit and a sampler object is bound to the corresponding sampler unit, and together they are used to read data from the texture's images. This process is called *sampling*, and is performed using the `texture` built-in function in GLSL or one of its many variants.

The usual way to read data from a texture in GLSL is to use one of the built-in functions. GLSL supports *function overloading*, which is a term that should be familiar to C++ programmers, among others. Function overloading is the process where a single function name can represent several different functions with different parameter types. At compile time, the compiler can determine which version of the function should be called based on the types of the parameter used to call it. The basic overloaded variants of the `texture` lookup functions are given below. (All texture functions are listed in Appendix C, "Built-in GLSL Variables and Functions".)

gvec4 **texture**(gsampler1D *tex*, float *P*[, float *bias*]);
gvec4 **texture**(gsampler2D *tex*, vec2 *P*[, float *bias*]);
gvec4 **texture**(gsampler3D *tex*, vec3 *P*[, float *bias*]);
gvec4 **texture**(gsamplerCube *tex*, vec3 *P*[, float *bias*]);
gvec4 **texture**(gsampler1DArray *tex*, vec2 *P*[, float *bias*]);
gvec4 **texture**(gsampler2DArray *tex*, vec3 *P*[, float *bias*]);
gvec4 **texture**(gsampler2DRect *tex*, vec2 *P*);
gvec4 **texture**(gsamplerCubeArray *tex*, vec4 *P*[, float *bias*]);

Sample a texel from the sampler given by *tex* at the texture coordinates given by *P*. If mipmapping is enabled and if *bias* is present, it is used to offset the level-of-detail calculation that determines the mipmap from which to sample. The return value is a vector containing the sampled texture data.

Note: A note on terminology: In many of the GLSL function prototypes, you will see the term `gvec4` (or other dimensional vectors). This is a *placeholder* type that means a vector of any type. It could stand for `vec4`, `ivec4`, or `uvec4`. Likewise, `gsampler2D`, for example, is a placeholder that may stand for `sampler2D`, `isampler2D`, or `usampler2D`. Also, if you see a parameter surrounded in square brackets (i.e., [and]), that means that the parameter is *optional* and may be omitted if desired.

The texture functions in GLSL each take a sampler variable and a set of texture coordinates. The return value from the functions is the result of sampling from the texture represented by the sampler.

The sampler argument passed into the texture function can be an element of a sampler array, or a parameter in a function. In all cases the argument must be *dynamically uniform*. That is, the argument must be the result of an expression involving uniforms, constants, or variables otherwise known to have the same value for all the instances of the shader (such as loop counters).

An example of using a `texture` function to read texels from a texture is given in Example 6.7.

Example 6.7   Simple Texture Lookup Example (Fragment Shader)

```
#version 330 core

uniform sampler2D tex;

in vec2 vs_tex_coord;

layout (location = 0) out vec4 color;

void main(void)
{
    color = texture(tex, vs_tex_coord);
}
```

In Example 6.7, a fragment shader that reads from a texture is given. Textures may be used from any shader stage, but the effects of texturing are easiest to demonstrate in a fragment shader. At the top of the shader, a 2D uniform sampler, `tex`, is declared. The single input to the fragment shader is the texture coordinate (`vs_tex_coord`), which is declared as a `vec2` and the output from the fragment shader is a single color output `color`.

The corresponding vertex shader is shown in Example 6.8.

Example 6.8   Simple Texture Lookup Example (Vertex Shader)

```
#version 330 core

layout (location = 0) in vec4 in_position;
layout (location = 1) in vec2 in_tex_coord;

out vec2 vs_tex_coord;

void main(void)
{
    gl_Position = in_position;
    vs_tex_coord = in_tex_coord;
}
```

In Example 6.8, the two inputs are the vertex position and the input texture coordinate, which is passed directly to the shader's outputs. In this case, these are the built-in `gl_Position` output and the `vs_tex_coord` user-defined output that will be passed to the similarly named input in the fragment shader given in Example 6.7.

Texture Coordinates

Texture coordinates are the coordinates within the texture at which to sample the image. These are often supplied per vertex, and then interpolated over the area of the resulting geometry to provide a per-fragment coordinate. This coordinate is used in the fragment shader to read from the texture and retrieve a color from the texture for the resulting fragment. The texture coordinates in the example of Examples 6.7 and 6.8 is supplied by the application, passed to the vertex shader in `in_tex_coord`, interpolated by OpenGL, and then passed to the fragment shader in `vs_tex_coord` before being used to read from the texture.

The application side code to set up a simple set of texture coordinates is shown in Example 6.9.

Example 6.9   Simple Texturing Example

```
// prog is the name of a linked program containing our
// example vertex and fragment shaders
glUseProgram(prog);

// tex is the name of a texture object that has been
// initialized with some texture data
glBindTexture(GL_TEXTURE_2D, tex);

// Simple quad with texture coordinates
static const GLfloat quad_data[] =
{
    // Vertex positions
    -1.0f, -1.0f, 0.0f, 1.0f,
     1.0f, -1.0f, 0.0f, 1.0f,
     1.0f,  1.0f, 0.0f, 1.0f,
    -1.0f,  1.0f, 0.0f, 1.0f,
    // Texture coordinates
    0.0f, 0.0f,
    1.0f, 0.0f,
    1.0f, 0.0f,
    0.0f, 0.0f
};

// Create and initialize a buffer object
GLuint buf;
```

```
glGenBuffers(1, &buf);
glBindBuffer(GL_ARRAY_BUFFER, buf);
glBufferData(GL_ARRAY_BUFFER, quad_data,
             sizeof(quad_data), GL_STATIC_DRAW);

// Setup vertex attributes
GLuint vao;

glGenVertexArrays(1, &vao);
glBindVertexArray(vao);
glVertexAttribPointer(0, 4, GL_FLOAT, GL_FALSE, 0, (GLvoid*)0);
glEnableVertexAttribArray(0);
glVertexAttribPointer(1, 2, GL_FLOAT, GL_FALSE, 0,
                      (GLvoid*)(16 * sizeof(float)));
glEnableVertexAttribArray(1);

// Ready. Draw.
glDrawArrays(GL_TRIANGLE_FAN, 0, 4);
```

In Example 6.9, the geometry for a simple *quadrilateral* is placed into a
buffer object along with texture coordinates for each of its four vertices.
The position data is sent to vertex attribute 0 and the texture coordinates
are sent to vertex attribute 1. In the example, prog is the name of a
program object that has previously had the shaders of Examples 6.7 and
6.8 compiled and linked into it, and tex is a texture object with texture
data already loaded into it. The result of rendering with this program is
shown in Figure 6.5.

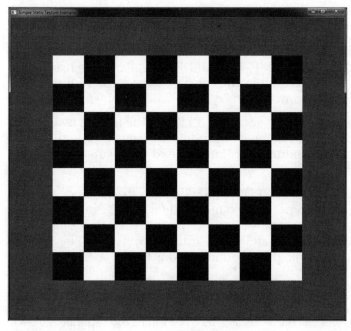

Figure 6.5   Output of the simple textured quad example

Each of the texture lookup functions in GLSL takes a set of coordinates from which to sample the texel. A texture is considered to occupy a domain spanning from 0.0 to 1.0 along each axis (remember, you may use one-, two-, or even three-dimensional textures). It is the responsibility of the application to generate or supply texture coordinates for these functions to use, as we have done in Example 6.9. Normally, these would be passed into your vertex shader in the form of a vertex input and then interpolated across the face of each polygon by OpenGL before being sent to the fragment shader. In Example 6.9 the texture coordinates used range from 0.0 to 1.0, so all of the resulting interpolated coordinates lie within this range. If texture coordinates passed to a texture lookup function end up outside the range 0.0 to 1.0, they must be modified to bring them back into this range. There are several ways in which OpenGL will do this for you, controlled by the GL_TEXTURE_WRAP_S, GL_TEXTURE_WRAP_T, and GL_TEXTURE_WRAP_R sampler parameters.

The GL_TEXTURE_WRAP_S, GL_TEXTURE_WRAP_T, and GL_TEXTURE_WRAP_R parameters control the way that texture coordinates outside the range 0.0 to 1.0 are handled by OpenGL for the S, T, and R[11] axes of the texture's domain respectively. The clamping mode in each dimension may be set to one of GL_CLAMP_TO_EDGE, GL_CLAMP_TO_BORDER, GL_REPEAT, or GL_MIRRORED_REPEAT. The clamping modes work as follows:

- If the mode is GL_CLAMP_TO_EDGE, whenever a texture coordinate is outside the range 0.0 to 1.0, texels on the very edge of the texture are used to form the value returned to the shader.

- When the mode is GL_CLAMP_TO_BORDER, an attempt to read outside the texture will result in the constant border color for the texture being used to form the final value.

- When the clamping mode is set to GL_REPEAT, the texture is simply wrapped and considered to repeat infinitely. In essence, only the fractional part of the texture coordinate is used to lookup texels, and the integer part is discarded.

- The clamping mode GL_MIRRORED_REPEAT is a special mode that allows a texture to be repeated in a mirrored fashion. Texture coordinates whose integer part is even have only their fractional part considered. Texture coordinates whose integer part is odd (i.e., 1.3, 3.8, etc.) have their fractional part subtracted from 1.0 in order to form the

---

11. Texture coordinates are traditionally referred to as s, t, r, and q, to distinguish them from spatial coordinates (x, y, z, and w) and color coordinates (r, g, b, and a). One caveat is that in GLSL, r is already used for *red*, so the four components of a texture coordinate are referred to as s, t, p, and q.

final coordinate. This mode can help to eliminate tiling artifacts from repeating textures.

Figure 6.6 shows each of the texture modes used to handle texture coordinates ranging from 0.0 to 4.0. All of these modes, except for GL_CLAMP_TO_BORDER eventually take texels from somewhere in the texture's data store. In the case of GL_CLAMP_TO_BORDER, the returned texels come from the texture's virtual border, which is a constant color. By default, this color is transparent black (i.e., 0.0 in each component of the texture). However, you may change this color by setting the value of the GL_TEXTURE_BORDER_COLOR sampler parameter. The snippet of Example 6.10 shows how to set the texture border color to red.

Example 6.10   Setting the Border Color of a Sampler

```
GLuint sampler; // This variable holds the name of our sampler.
GLuint texture; // This variable holds the name of a texture.
const GLfloat red[] = { 1.0f, 0.0f, 0.0f, 1.0f }; // Opaque red.
// Set the GL_TEXTURE_BORDER_COLOR for the sampler object
glSamplerParameterfv(sampler, GL_TEXTURE_BORDER_COLOR, red);
// Or alternatively, set the border color for a texture object.
// This will be used when a texture is bound to a texture unit
// without a corresponding sampler object.
glBindTexture(GL_TEXTURE_2D, texture);
glTexParameterfv(GL_TEXTURE_2D, GL_TEXTURE_BORDER_COLOR, red);
```

Figure 6.6   Effect of different texture wrapping modes (GL_CLAMP_TO_EDGE (top left), GL_CLAMP_TO_BORDER (top right), GL_REPEAT (bottom left), and GL_MIRRORED_REPEAT (bottom right).)

Arranging Texture Data

Suppose you have an external source of texture data—say an image editing program or another component of your application, perhaps written in another language or using another API over which you have no control. It is possible that the texture data is stored using a component order other than red, green, blue, alpha (RGBA). For example, ABGR is fairly common (i.e., RGBA bytes stored in little-endian order), as is ARGB and even RGBx (RGB data packed into a 32-bit word with one byte left unused). OpenGL is quite capable of consuming this data and making it appear as nicely formatted RGBA data to your shader. To do this, we use *texture swizzle*, which is a mechanism that allows you to rearrange the component order of texture data on-the-fly as it is read by the graphics hardware.

Texture swizzle is a set of texture parameters—one for each channel of the texture—that can be set using the **glTexParameteri()** function by passing one of the texture swizzle parameter names and the desired source for the data. The swizzle texture parameters are GL_TEXTURE_SWIZZLE_R, GL_TEXTURE_SWIZZLE_G, GL_TEXTURE_SWIZZLE_B, and GL_TEXTURE_SWIZZLE_A, which specify the outgoing texture channels in the order red, green, blue, and alpha, respectively. Furthermore, the token name GL_TEXTURE_SWIZZLE_RGBA is provided to allow all four channels to be configured using a single call to **glTexParameteriv()**. Each one specifies what the source of data should be for the corresponding channel of the texture and may be set to one of the source selectors GL_RED, GL_GREEN, GL_BLUE, GL_ALPHA, GL_ONE, or GL_ZERO. These indicate the values of the red, green, blue, or alpha channels of the incoming texture, or the constant values one and zero, respectively.

By default, the swizzle settings are configured to pass the data directly through unmodified. That is, GL_TEXTURE_SWIZZLE_R, GL_TEXTURE_SWIZZLE_G, GL_TEXTURE_SWIZZLE_B, and GL_TEXTURE_SWIZZLE_A are set to GL_RED, GL_GREEN, GL_BLUE, and GL_ALPHA, respectively.

Example 6.11 shows how to configure a texture to read from ABGR and RGBx data. In the case of RGBx, we specify that the constant value 1.0 be returned for the missing alpha channel.

Example 6.11   Texture Swizzle Example

```
// The name of a texture whose data is in ABGR format.
GLuint abgr_texture;
// The name of a texture whose data is in RGBx format.
GLyint rgbx_texture;
```

```
// An array of tokens to set ABGR swizzle in one function call.
static const GLenum abgr_swizzle[] =
{
    GL_ALPHA, GL_RED, GL_GREEN, GL_BLUE
};

// Bind the ABGR texture
glBindTexture(GL_TEXTURE_2D, abgr_texture);
// Set all four swizzle parameters in one call to glTexParameteriv
glTexParameteriv(GL_TEXTURE_2D,
                 GL_TEXTURE_SWIZZLE_RGBA,
                 abgr_swizzle);

// Now bind the RGBx texture
glBindTexture(GL_TEXTURE_2D, rgbx_texture);
// We're only setting the GL_TEXTURE_SWIZZLE_A parameter here
// because the R, G, and B swizzles can be left as their default values.
glTexParameteri(GL_TEXTURE_2D,
                GL_TEXTURE_SWIZZLE_A,
                GL_ONE);
```

Using Multiple Textures

Now that you have seen a simple application of texture to rendering, you may have noticed some omissions from the sample above. For example, in Example 6.9, we did not set a value for the sampler in the fragment shader. This is because we are only using a single texture. In fact, OpenGL can support many textures simultaneously—a minimum of 16 textures per shader stage are supported, which when multiplied by the number of shader stages supported by OpenGL comes out to 80 textures! In fact, OpenGL has 80 texture units, referred to by tokens named GL_TEXTURE0 through GL_TEXTURE79. Whenever one of the texture functions, such as **glBindTexture()** is called, it operates on the texture bound to the *active texture unit*, which is implied by what is known as a *selector*. By default, the active texture selector is 0. However, it may be changed (and will need to be if you want to use more than one texture). The function to change the active texture selector is **glActiveTexture()**, which was introduced above.

In order to use multiple textures in your shader, you will need to declare multiple uniform sampler variables. Each will refer to a different[12] texture unit. From the application side, uniform samplers appear much like uniform integers. They are enumerated using the normal

---

12. Technically, they don't need to be associated with different texture units. If two or more samplers refer to the same texture unit, then they will both end up sampling from the same texture.

glGetActiveUniform() function and may have their values modified using the **glUniform1i()** function. The integer value assigned to a uniform sampler is the index of the texture unit to which it refers.

The steps to use multiple textures in a single shader (or program) are therefore as follows: first, we need to select the first texture unit using **glActiveTexture()** and bind a texture to one of its targets using **glBindTexture()**. We repeat this process for each texture unit. Then, we set the values of the uniform sampler variables to the indices of the texture units that we wish to use by calling the **glUniform1i()** function.

To illustrate this, we will modify our example from the previous section to use two textures. We will first change the vertex shader of Example 6.8 to produce two sets of texture coordinates. The updated vertex shader is shown in Example 6.12.

Example 6.12   Simple Multitexture Example (Vertex Shader)

```
#version 330 core

layout (location = 0) in vec2 in_position;
layout (location = 1) in vec2 in_tex_coord;

out vec2 tex_coord0;
out vec2 tex_coord1;

uniform float time;

void main(void)
{
    const mat2 m = mat2(vec2(cos(time), sin(time)),
                        vec2(-sin(time), cos(time)));
    tex_coord0 = in_tex_coord * m;
    tex_coord1 = in_tex_coord * transpose(m);
    gl_Position = vec4(in_position, 0.5, 1.0);
}
```

The new vertex shader performs simple animation by using a `time` uniform variable to construct a rotation matrix, and uses that to rotate the incoming texture coordinates in opposite directions. Next, we modify the original fragment shader from Example 6.7 to include two uniform sampler variables, read a texel from each, and sum them together. This new shader is shown in Example 6.13.

Example 6.13   Simple Multitexture Example (Fragment Shader)

```
#version 330 core

in vec2 tex_coord0;
in vec2 tex_coord1;

layout (location = 0) out vec4 color;

uniform sampler2D tex1;
uniform sampler2D tex2;

void main(void)
{
    color = texture(tex1, tex_coord0) + texture(tex2, tex_coord1);
}
```

In Example 6.13 we are using a different texture coordinate to sample from the two textures. However, it is perfectly reasonable to use the same set of texture coordinates for both textures. In order to make this shader do something useful, we need to set values for the two uniform samplers, tex1 and tex2 and bind textures to the corresponding texture units. We do this using the **glUniform1i()**, **glActiveTexture()**, and **glBindTexture()** functions as shown in Example 6.14.

Example 6.14   Simple Multitexture Example

```
// prog is the name of a linked program containing our example
// vertex and fragment shaders
glUseProgram(prog);

// For the first texture, we will use texture unit 0...
// Get the uniform location
GLint tex1_uniform_loc = glGetUniformLocation(prog, "tex1");
// Set it to 0
glUniform1i(tex1_uniform_loc, 0);
// Select texture unit 0
glActiveTexture(GL_TEXTURE0);
// Bind a texture to it
glBindTexture(GL_TEXTURE_2D, tex1);

// Repeat the above process for texture unit 1
GLint tex2_uniform_loc = glGetUniformLocation(prog, "tex2");
glUniform1i(tex2_uniform_loc, 1);
glActiveTexture(GL_TEXTURE1);
glBindTexture(GL_TEXTURE_2D, tex2);
```

The two source textures used in this example are shown in Figure 6.7 and the result of rendering with our updated fragment shader with two textures bound is shown in Figure 6.8.

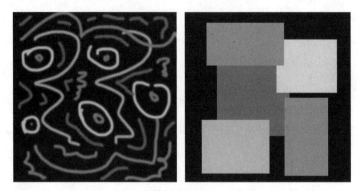

Figure 6.7   Two textures used in the multitexture example

Figure 6.8   Output of the simple multitexture example

Complex Texture Types

Textures are often considered only as one- or two-dimensional images that may be read from. However, there are several types of textures, including 3D textures, texture arrays, and cube maps, shadows, depth-stencil, and buffer textures. This section describes the types of texture and outlines their potential use cases.

3D Textures

A 3D texture can be thought of as a volume of texels arranged in a 3D grid. To create a 3D texture, generate a texture object name and bind it initially to the GL_TEXTURE_3D target. Once bound, you may use **glTexStorage3D()** or **glTexImage3D()** to create the storage for the texture object. The 3D texture has not only a width and a height but also a depth. The maximum width and height of a 3D texture is the same as that of a 2D texture and may be found by retrieving the value of GL_MAX_TEXTURE_SIZE. The maximum depth of a 3D texture supported by your OpenGL implementation is found by retrieving the value of GL_MAX_3D_TEXTURE_SIZE, and this may be different than the maximum width and height of the texture.

3D textures are read in shaders using three-dimensional texture coordinates. Otherwise, they work very similarly to other textures types. A typical use case for a 3D texture is for volume rendering in fields such as medical imaging or fluid simulation. In this type of application, the content of the texture is usually a density map where each *voxel*[13] represents the density of a medium at that point.

A simple way to render a volume is to render planes cutting through the volume as a textured quadrilateral with a 3D texture coordinate at each vertex. The vertex shader in Example 6.15 shows how a set of two-dimensional texture coordinates are transformed into three-dimensional space using a transformation matrix. These coordinates are then interpolated by OpenGL and used in the fragment shader of Example 6.16.

Example 6.15   Simple Volume Texture Vertex Shader

```
#version 330 core

// Position and 2D texture coordinate from application
layout (location = 0) in vec2 in_position;
layout (location = 1) in vec2 in_tex_coord;

// Output 3D texture coordinate after transformation
out vec3 tex_coord;

// Matrix to transform the texture coordinates into 3D space
uniform mat4 tc_rotate;

void main(void)
{
```

---

13. A voxel is a term that refers to an element of a volume, just as pixel refers to an element of a picture and texel refers to an element of a texture.

```
    // Multiply the texture coordinate by the transformation
    // matrix to place it into 3D space
    tex_coord = (vec4(in_tex_coord, 0.0, 1.0) * tc_rotate).stp;
    // Pass position through unchanged.
    gl_Position = vec4(in_position, 0.5, 1.0);
}
```

Example 6.16   Simple Volume Texture Fragment Shader

```
#version 330 core

// Incoming texture coordinate from vertex shader
in vec3 tex_coord;

// Final color
layout (location = 0) out vec4 color;


// Volume texture
uniform sampler3D tex;

void main(void)
{
    // Simply read from the texture at the 3D texture coordinate
    // and replicate the single channel across R, G, B, and A
    color = texture(tex, tex_coord).rrrr;
}
```

The result of rendering with the vertex and fragment shaders of Examples 6.15 and 6.16 is shown in Figure 6.9. In this example, the volume texture contains a density field of a cloud. The example animates the cloud by moving a cutting plane through the volume and sampling the 3D texture at each point on the plane.

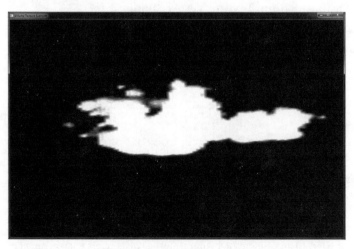

Figure 6.9   Output of the volume texture example

Array Textures

For certain applications, you may have a number of one- or two-dimensional textures that you might like to access simultaneously within the confines of a single draw call. For instance, suppose you're authoring a game that features multiple characters of basically the same geometry, but each of which has its own costume. Or you might want to use multiple layers of texture for the character (diffuse color, a normal map, a specular intensity map, and a number of other attributes).

When using many textures like this, you would need to bind all of the required textures before the draw command. The calls to **glBindTexture()** for each draw call could have performance implications for the application if the texture objects needed to be updated by OpenGL.

Texture arrays allow you to combine a collection of one- or two-dimensional textures, all of the same size and format, into a texture of the next higher dimension (e.g., an array of two-dimensional textures becomes something like a three-dimensional texture). If you were to try to use a three-dimensional texture to store a collection of two-dimensional textures, you would encounter a few inconveniences: The indexing texture coordinate—r in this case—is normalized to the range [0,1]. To access the third texture in a stack of seven, you would need to pass 0.35714 (or thereabouts) to access what you would probably like to access as "2". Texture arrays permit this type of texture selection. Additionally, texture arrays allow suitable mipmap filtering within the texture accessed by the index. In comparison, a three-dimensional texture would filter between the texture "slices", likely in a way that doesn't return the results you were hoping for.

```
gvec4 texture(gsampler2D tex, vec2 P[, float bias]);
gvec4 texture(gsampler2DArray tex, vec3 P[, float bias]);
```

Compare the prototypes of the `texture` function for 2D textures and for 2D array textures. The second function takes a `sampler2DArray` sampler type and its texture coordinate, P, has an additional dimension. This third component of P is the array index, or *slice*.

Cube-Map Textures

Cube-map textures are a special type of texture, useful for *environment mapping*, that takes a set of images and treats them as the faces of a cube. The six faces of the cube are represented by six subtextures that must be square and of the same size. When you sample from a cube map, the texture coordinate used is three dimensional and is treated as a direction from the origin. This direction essentially points at the location on the surface of the cube from where to read the texture. Imagine you were standing in the middle of a square room with a laser pointer. You could point the laser in any direction and hit part of the wall, floor, or ceiling of the room. The spot where the pointer shines is the point from which you would sample the texture map. Cube maps are ideal for representing surrounding environments, lighting, and reflection effects, and can also be used to wrap complex objects with textures.

Allocating storage for cube-map textures is achieved by binding a new texture name to the GL_TEXTURE_CUBE_MAP texture target and calling **glTexStorage2D()** on the GL_TEXTURE_CUBE_MAP target. This single call will allocate the storage for all six faces of the cube map. However, once allocated, the cube map is represented by a set of six special targets, which can be thought of as subtargets of the GL_TEXTURE_CUBE_MAP target. These are GL_TEXTURE_CUBE_MAP_POSITIVE_X, GL_TEXTURE_CUBE_MAP_NEGATIVE_X, GL_TEXTURE_CUBE_MAP_POSITIVE_Y, GL_TEXTURE_CUBE_MAP_NEGATIVE_Y, GL_TEXTURE_CUBE_MAP_POSITIVE_Z, and GL_TEXTURE_CUBE_MAP_NEGATIVE_Z[14]. Each face has its own complete set of mipmaps. These special targets may be passed to the **glTexSubImage2D()** command in order to specify image data for the cube map's faces. Example 6.17 gives an example of how to create and initialize a cube-map texture.

Example 6.17   Initializing a Cube-Map Texture

```
GLuint tex; // Texture to be created

extern const GLvoid* texture_data[6]; // Data for the faces

// Generate, bind, and initialize a texture object using
// the GL_TEXTURE_CUBE_MAP target.
glGenTextures(1, &tex);
glBindTexture(GL_TEXTURE_CUBE_MAP, tex);
glTexStorage2D(GL_TEXTURE_CUBE_MAP, 10, GL_RGBA8, 1024, 1024);
```

---

14. Note that the tokens GL_TEXTURE_CUBE_MAP_POSITIVE_X, GL_TEXTURE_CUBE_MAP_NEGATIVE_X, GL_TEXTURE_CUBE_MAP_POSITIVE_Y, GL_TEXTURE_CUBE_MAP_NEGATIVE_Y, GL_TEXTURE_CUBE_MAP_POSITIVE_Z, and GL_TEXTURE_CUBE_MAP_NEGATIVE_Z have contiguous numeric values defined in that order. Thus, it's possible to index into the faces of the cube map by simply adding a face index to GL_TEXTURE_CUBE_MAP_POSITIVE_X so long as the index is consistent with the defined ordering.

```
// Now that storage is allocated for the texture object,
// we can place the texture data into its texel array.
for (int face = 0; face < 6; face++)
{
    GLenum target = GL_TEXTURE_CUBE_MAP_POSITIVE_X + face;
    glTexSubImage2D(target,                          // Face
                    0,                               // Level
                    0, 0,                            // X, Y offset
                    1024, 1024,                      // Size of face
                    GL_RGBA,                         // Format
                    GL_UNSIGNED_BYTE,                // Type
                    texture_data[face]);             // Data
}

// Now, optionally, we could specify the data for the
// lower mipmap levels of each of the faces.
```

Cube-map textures may also be aggregated into arrays. The
GL_TEXTURE_CUBE_MAP_ARRAY texture target may be used to create
and modify cube-map array textures. Each cube in the cube-map array
consumes six contiguous slices of the underlying array texture. Thus, an
array with five cube-map textures in it will have a total of 30 slices. The
example shown in Example 6.17 is modified below in Example 6.18 to
create a cube-map array of five cubes in a single texture.

Example 6.18   Initializing a Cube-Map Array Texture

```
GLuint tex; // Texture to be created

extern const GLvoid* texture_data[6][5]; // Data for the faces

// Generate, bind, and initialize a texture object using the
// GL_TEXTURE_CUBE_MAP_ARRAY target.
glGenTextures(1, &tex);
glBindTexture(GL_TEXTURE_CUBE_MAP_ARRAY, tex);
glTexStorage3D(GL_TEXTURE_CUBE_MAP_ARRAY, 10,
               GL_RGBA8, 1024, 1024, 5);

// Now that storage is allocated for the texture object, we can
// place the texture data into its texel array.
for (int cube_index = 0; cube_index < 5; cube_index++)
{
    for (int face = 0; face < 6; face++)
    {
        GLenum target = GL_TEXTURE_CUBE_MAP_POSITIVE_X + face;
        glTexSubImage3D(target,                      // Face
                        0,                           // Level
                        0, 0,                        // Offset
                        cube_index,                  // Cube index
                        1024, 1024,                  // Width, Height
                        1,                           // Face count
```

```
                    GL_RGBA,                          // Format
                    GL_UNSIGNED_BYTE,                 // Type
                    texture_data[face][cube_index]); // Data
        }
    }
```

Cube-Map Example—Sky Boxes

A common use for cube-map texture is as *sky box*s. A sky box is an application of texturing where the entire scene is effectively wrapped in a large cube with the viewer placed in the center. As the scene is rendered anything not covered by objects within the scene is displayed as the inside of the cube. With an appropriate texture, it appears as if the viewer is located in the environment represented by the cube map.

Figure 6.10 (a) shows a cube map[15] viewed from the outside, illustrating that a sky box really is just a cube with a texture applied to it. In Figure 6.10 (b), we have zoomed in until the sky box cuts the near plane and we can now see inside it. Finally, in Figure 6.10 (c), we have placed the viewer at the very center of the cube, making it appear as if we are in the environment represented by the cube map.

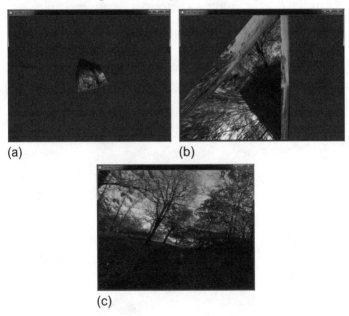

(a)   (b)

(c)

Figure 6.10   A sky box
(Shown as seen from the outside, from close up, and from the center.)

---

15. The cube-map images shown in this example were taken, with permission, from http://humus.name.

To render the images shown in Figure 6.10, we simply render a unit cube centered at the origin and use the object space position as a texture coordinate from which to sample the cube map. The vertex shader for this example is shown in Example 6.19 and the corresponding fragment shader is shown in Example 6.20.

Example 6.19   Simple Skybox Example—Vertex Shader

```
#version 330 core
layout (location = 0) in vec3 in_position;
out vec3 tex_coord;
uniform mat4 tc_rotate;
void main(void)
{
    tex_coord = in_position;
    gl_Position = tc_rotate * vec4(in_position, 1.0);
}
```

Example 6.20   Simple Skybox Example—Fragment Shader

```
#version 330 core
in vec3 tex_coord;
layout (location = 0) out vec4 color;
uniform samplerCube tex;
void main(void)
{
    color = texture(tex, tex_coord);
}
```

Using Cube Maps for Environment Mapping

Now that we have created an environment into which we can place the components of our scene, we can make the objects appear to be part of the environment. This is known as *environment mapping*, and is another common use for cube-map textures. Here, the cube map is employed as an *environment map* and is used to texture objects in the scene. To implement environment mapping, we must calculate the texture coordinate from which to sample the cube map by reflecting the incoming view vector around the surface normal at the point to be textured.

The vertex shader shown in Example 6.21 transforms the object space position into view space by multiplying it by a concatenated model-view-projection matrix. It also rotates the surface normal into view space by multiplying it by a concatenated model-view matrix.

Example 6.21   Cube-Map Environment Mapping Example—Vertex
Shader

```
#version 330 core
// Incoming position and normal
layout (location = 0) in vec4 in_position;
layout (location = 1) in vec3 in_normal;

// Outgoing surface normal and view-space position
out vec3 vs_fs_normal;
out vec3 vs_fs_position;

// Model-view-projection and model-view matrices
uniform mat4 mat_mvp;
uniform mat4 mat_mv;

void main(void)
{
    // Clip-space position
    gl_Position = mat_mvp * in_position;
    // View-space normal and position
    vs_fs_normal = mat3(mat_mv) * in_normal;
    vs_fs_position = (mat_mv * in_position).xyz;
}
```

Once the view-space normal and position of the surface point have been
passed into the fragment shader, we can use the GLSL `reflect` function to
reflect the fragment's view-space position around the surface normal at
each point. This effectively *bounces* the view vector off the surface and into
the cube map. We use this reflected vector as a texture coordinate to
sample from the cube map, using the resulting texel to color the surface.
The result of this is that the environment appears to be reflected in the
object's surface. The fragment shader performing these operations is
shown in Example 6.22.

Example 6.22   Cube-Map Environment Mapping Example—Fragment
Shader

```
#version 330 core

// Incoming surface normal and view-space position
in vec3 vs_fs_normal;
in vec3 vs_fs_position;

// Final fragment color
layout (location = 0) out vec4 color;

// The cube-map texture
uniform samplerCube tex;

void main(void)
{
    // Calculate the texture coordinate by reflecting the
```

```
      // view-space position around the surface normal.
      vec3 tc = reflect(-vs_fs_position, normalize(vs_fs_normal));
      // Sample the texture and color the resulting fragment
      // a golden color.
      color = vec4(0.3, 0.2, 0.1, 1.0) +
              vec4(0.97, 0.83, 0.79, 0.0) *
              texture(tex, tc);
}
```

The fragment shader also slightly modifies the sampled texture value
retrieved from the cube map in order to make it appear to be slightly
golden in color. The result of rendering with the vertex and fragment
shaders of Examples 6.21 and 6.22 is shown in Figure 6.11 below.

Figure 6.11   A golden environment mapped torus

Seamless Cube-Map Sampling

A cube map is a collection of six independent faces, possibly aggregated
into arrays of cubes with an integer multiple of six faces in total. When
OpenGL samples from a cube map, as a first step, it uses the dominant
component of the three-dimensional texture coordinate to determine
which of the six faces of the cube to sample from. Once this face has been
determined, it is effectively treated as a two-dimensional texture and used
to look up texel values. By default, at the edges of the texture, normal
texture coordinate wrapping modes are used. At first thought, this would
seem logical, and as the generated two-dimensional texture coordinates
always lie within a face, we don't expect to see any issues with this.

However, if the texture filtering mode is linear, toward the edges of the cube's faces, the adjoining faces' texels are not considered when calculating the final filtered texel values. This can cause a noticeable seam to appear in the filtered texture. Even worse, if the texture coordinate wrapping mode is left at one of the repeating modes, then texels from the opposite side of the face may be used, causing quite incorrect results.

Figure 6.12 shows the result of sampling from a cube-map texture across the join between two faces. Inset is a close-up view of the seam that is visible between the adjacent faces of the cube map.

Figure 6.12   A visible seam in a cube map

To avoid the visible seams between adjacent faces of a cube map, we can enable seamless cube-map filtering. To do this, call **glEnable()** with *cap* set to GL_TEXTURE_CUBE_MAP_SEAMLESS. When seamless cube-map filtering is enabled, OpenGL will use texels from adjacent cube-map faces to retrieve texels for use in filtering. This will eliminate artifacts, especially when there is an abrupt change in color from one face to another, or when the cube map is a particularly low resolution. Figure 6.13 shows the result of enabling seamless cube-map filtering. Notice that the bright line of pixels has been eliminated.

Figure 6.13   The effect of seamless cube-map filtering

Shadow Samplers

A special type of sampler is provided in GLSL called a *shadow sampler*.
A shadow sampler takes an additional component in the texture
coordinate that is used as a reference against which to compare the fetched
texel values. When using a shadow sampler, the value returned from the
texture function is a floating-point value between 0.0 and 1.0, indicating
the fraction of fetched texel values that passed the comparison operator.
For texture accesses that sample only a single texel value (using the
GL_NEAREST filtering mode, no mipmaps, and one sample per texel), the
returned value will be either 0.0 or 1.0, depending on whether the texel
passes the comparison or not. If more than one texel would normally be
used to construct the value returned to the shader (such as when the filter
mode is linear, or if a multisample texture is used), then the value may be
anything between 0.0 and 1.0, depending on how many of those texels
pass the comparison operator. The shadow texturing functions are as
follows:

```
float texture(gsampler1DShadow tex, vec3 P[, float bias]);
float texture(gsampler2DShadow tex, vec3 P[, float bias]);
float texture(gsamplerCubeShadow tex, vec4 P[, float bias]);
float texture(gsampler1DArrayShadow tex, vec3 P[, float bias]);
```

float **texture**(gsampler2DArrayShadow *tex*, vec4 *P*[, float *bias*]);
float **texture**(gsampler2DRectShadow *tex*, vec3 *P*);
float **texture**(gsamplerCubeArrayShadow *tex*, vecP *P*, float
        compare);

Sample the shadow texture bound to the texture unit referenced by *tex* at the texture coordinates specified by *P*. The return value is a floating-point quantity representing the fraction of samples that passed the shadow comparison operator with the fetched texel data.

To enable the comparison function for a sampler, call **glSamplerParameteri()** (or **glTexParameteri()** if you are not using a sampler object) with *pname* set to GL_TEXTURE_COMPARE_MODE and *param* set to GL_COMPARE_REF_TO_TEXTURE, and to disable it, set *param* to GL_NONE. When the texture comparison mode is set to GL_COMPARE_REF_TO_TEXTURE, the comparison is carried out with the mode specified by the sampler. This is set by calling **glSamplerParameteri()** with *pname* set to GL_TEXTURE_COMPARE_FUNC and *param* set to one of the comparison functions, GL_LEQUAL, GL_GEQUAL, GL_LESS, GL_GREATER, GL_EQUAL, GL_NOTEQUAL, GL_ALWAYS, or GL_NEVER. These comparison functions have the same meanings as they do for depth testing.

A comprehensive example of using a shadow sampler is shown in "Shadow Mapping" on Page 400 of Chapter 7, "Light and Shadow".

Depth-Stencil Textures

Instead of an image, a texture can hold depth and stencil values, one of each per texel, using the texture format GL_DEPTH_STENCIL. This is the typical way a framebuffer will store the rendered *z* component for depth and the stencil value, as discussed in detail in Chapter 4, "Color, Pixels, and Framebuffers". When texturing from a depth-stencil texture, by default a shader will read the depth. However, as of version 4.3, a shader can also read the stencil value. To do so, the application must set GL_DEPTH_STENCIL_TEXTURE_MODE to GL_STENCIL_COMPONENTS and the shader must use an integer sampler type.

Buffer Textures

Buffer textures are a special class of texture that allow a buffer object to be accessed from a shader as if it were a large, one-dimensional texture. Buffer textures have certain restrictions and differences from normal one-dimensional textures but otherwise appear similar to them in your code. You create them as normal texture objects, bind them to texture units, control their parameters[16] with **glTexParameteri()**. However, the storage for the texture's data is actually owned and controlled by a buffer object (hence the name buffer texture). Also, buffer textures have no internal sampler and sampler objects have no effect on buffer textures. The main differences between buffer textures and one-dimensional textures are as follows:

- One-dimensional textures have sizes limited to the value of GL_MAX_TEXTURE_SIZE, but buffer textures are limited to the value of GL_MAX_TEXTURE_BUFFER_SIZE, which is often two gigabytes or more.

- One-dimensional textures support filtering, mipmaps, texture coordinate wrapping and other sampler parameters, buffer textures do not.

- Texture coordinates for one-dimensional textures are normalized floating-point values, but buffer textures use unnormalized integer texture coordinates.

Whether you decide to use a buffer texture or a one-dimensional texture for a particular application will depend on your needs. In order to create a buffer texture, you need to generate a name for your new texture using **glGenTextures()**, bind it to the GL_TEXTURE_BUFFER texture target, and then associate a buffer object with the texture using the **glTexBuffer()** function.

---

void **glTexBuffer**(GLenum *target*, GLenum *internalFormat*,
           GLuint *buffer*);

Attaches the storage for the buffer object named *buffer* to the buffer texture bound to the *target* target of the active texture unit. *target* must be GL_TEXTURE_BUFFER. The data store of *buffer* is then interpreted as an array of elements whose type is determined by *internalFormat*, which must be a sized internal format. If *buffer* is zero, than any existing association between the active buffer texture and its data store is broken.

---

16. Not all texture parameters are relevant for buffer textures, and as no sampler is used with buffer textures, sampler parameters are essentially ignored.

The code shown in Example 6.23 shows an example of creating a buffer, initializing its data store, and then associating it with a buffer texture.

Example 6.23   Creating and Initializing a Buffer Texture

```
// Buffer to be used as the data store
GLuint buf;
// Texture to be used as a buffer texture
GLuint tex;

// Data is located somewhere else in this program
extern const GLvoid* data;

// Generate, bind, and initialize a buffer object
// using the GL_TEXTURE_BUFFER binding. Assume we're
// going to use one megabyte of data here.
glGenBuffers(1, &buf);
glBindBuffer(GL_TEXTURE_BUFFER,  buf);
glBufferData(GL_TEXTURE_BUFFER,  1024 * 1024,
             data, GL_STATIC_DRAW);

// Now create the buffer texture and associate it
// with the buffer object.
glGenTextures(1, &tex);
glBindTexture(GL_TEXTURE_BUFFER, tex);
glTexBuffer(GL_TEXTURE_BUFFER, GL_R32F, buf);
```

To attach only a range of a buffer object to a buffer texture, you may use the **glTexBufferRange()** function, whose prototype is as follows:

void **glTexBufferRange**(GLenum *target*, GLenum *internalFormat*,
                          GLuint *buffer*, GLintptr *offset*,
                          GLsizeiptr *size*);

Attaches a section of the storage for the buffer object named *buffer* starting at *offset* and reaching for *size* bytes to the buffer texture bound to the *target* target of the active texture unit. *target* must be GL_TEXTURE_BUFFER. The data store of *buffer* is then interpreted as an array of elements whose type is determined by *internalFormat*, which must be a sized internal format. If *buffer* is zero, than any existing association between the active buffer texture and its data store is broken. *offset* must be an integer multiple of the implementation-defined constant GL_TEXTURE_BUFFER_OFFSET_ALIGNMENT.

To access a buffer texture in a shader, you must create a uniform `samplerBuffer` (or one of its signed- or unsigned-integer variants, `isamplerBuffer` or `usamplerBuffer`), and use it with the `texelFetch` function[17] to read individual samples from it. The `texelFetch` function for buffer textures is defined as follows:

vec4 **texelFetch**(samplerBuffer *s*, int *coord*);
ivec4 **texelFetch**(isamplerBuffer *s*, int *coord*);
uvec4 **texelFetch**(usamplerBuffer *s*, int *coord*);

Perform a lookup of a single texel from texture coordinate *coord* in the texture bound to *s*.

An example of the declaration of a buffer sampler and fetching from it using `texelFetch` is shown in Example 6.24.

Example 6.24   Texel Lookups from a Buffer Texture

```
#version 330 core

uniform samplerBuffer buf

in int buf_tex_coord;

layout (location = 0) out vec4 color;

void main(void)
{
    color = texelFetch(buf, tex_coord);
}
```

Texture Views

So far, we have considered textures to be large buffers of data that have a specified format and consume a fixed amount of storage space. The amount of space depends on the format and on other parameters such as the texture's dimensions and whether it has mipmaps or not. However, conceptually, the format and to some extent the dimensions can be separated from the size of the underlying storage requirements of a texture. For example, many texture internal formats will consume the same number of bits per texel, and in some cases it is possible to interpret

---

17. The `texelFetch` function may be used with regular textures as well as buffer textures. When it is used to sample from a nonbuffer texture, the texture's sampler parameters are ignored, and the texture coordinate is still interpreted as a nonnormalized integer value as it is with buffer textures. We introduce this function here solely because its most common use is with buffer textures.

textures with various different dimensionalities—perhaps taking a single slice of an array texture and treating it as a single 2D texture, say.

OpenGL allows you to share a single data store between multiple textures, each with its own format and dimensions. First, a texture is created and its data store initialized with one of the immutable data storage functions (such as **glTexStorage2D()**). Next, we create a *texture view* of the "parent" texture. In effect, this increments a reference count to the underlying storage allocated for the first texture, giving each view a reference to it. To create a texture view, call **glTextureView()**, whose prototype is as follows:

---

void **glTextureView**(GLuint *texture*, GLenum *target*,
                    GLuint *origTexture*, GLenum *internalFormat*,
                    GLuint *minLevel*, GLuint *numLevels*,
                    GLuint *minLayer*, GLuint *numLayers*);

Creates a new view of the texture named by *origTexture*, which must be the name of an existing texture whose data store has been initialized and is immutable. *texture* is attached to the data store of *origTexture* and becomes an immutable texture with a target specified by *target*. The internal format of *texture* is specified by *internalFormat*, which must be *compatible* with the internal format of *origTexture*. *minLevel* and *numLevels* specify the first mipmap level and number of mipmap levels to use for the new texture, respectively. Likewise, *minLayer* and *numLayers* specify the first layer and number of layers of an array texture to attach to *texture*.

When creating views of existing textures, the target for the new texture must be compatible with the target of the original texture. The compatible targets are given in Table 6.6.

Table 6.6   Target Compatibility for Texture Views

Original Target (GL_TEXTURE*)	Compatible Targets (GL_TEXTURE*)
1D	1D, 1D_ARRAY
2D	2D, 2D_ARRAY
3D	3D
CUBE_MAP	CUBE_MAP, 2D, 2D_ARRAY, CUBE_MAP_ARRAY
RECTANGLE	RECTANGLE
BUFFER	*none*

Table 6.6 (continued) Target Compatibility for Texture Views

Original Target (GL_TEXTURE*)	Compatible Targets (GL_TEXTURE*)
1D_ARRAY	1D, 1D_ARRAY
2D_ARRAY	2D, 2D_ARRAY
CUBE_MAP_ARRAY	CUBE_MAP, 2D, 2D_ARRAY, CUBE_MAP_ARRAY
2D_MULTISAMPLE	2D_MULTISAMPLE, 2D_MULTISAMPLE_ARRAY
2D_MULTISAMPLE_ARRAY	2D_MULTISAMPLE, 2D_MULTISAMPLE_ARRAY

In addition to target compatibility, the internal format of the new view must be of the same format class (i.e., bits-per-texel) of the original parent texture. Table 6.7 lists the texture format classes and their compatible specific internal formats.

Table 6.7 Internal Format Compatibility for Texture Views

Original Target	Compatible Targets
128-bit	GL_RGBA32F, GL_RGBA32UI, GL_RGBA32I
96-bit	GL_RGB32F, GL_RGB32UI, GL_RGB32I
64-bit	GL_RGBA16F, GL_RG32F, GL_RGBA16UI, GL_RG32UI, GL_RGBA16I, GL_RG32I, GL_RGBA16, GL_RGBA16_SNORM
48-bit	GL_RGB16, GL_RGB16_SNORM, GL_RGB16F, GL_RGB16UI, GL_RGB16I
32-bit	GL_RG16F, GL_R11F_G11F_B10F, GL_R32F, GL_RGB10_A2UI, GL_RGBA8UI, GL_RG16UI, GL_R32UI, GL_RGBA8I, GL_RG16I, GL_R32I, GL_RGB10_A2, GL_RGBA8, GL_RG16, GL_RGBA8_SNORM, GL_RG16_SNORM, GL_SRGB8_ALPHA8, GL_RGB9_E5
24-bit	GL_RGB8, GL_RGB8_SNORM, GL_SRGB8, GL_RGB8UI, GL_RGB8I
16-bit	GL_R16F, GL_RG8UI, GL_R16UI, GL_RG8I, GL_R16I, GL_RG8, GL_R16, GL_RG8_SNORM, GL_R16_SNORM
8-bit	GL_R8UI, GL_R8I, GL_R8, GL_R8_SNORM

Table 6.7 (continued) Internal Format Compatibility for Texture Views

Original Target	Compatible Targets
GL_RGTC1_RED	GL_COMPRESSED_RED_RGTC1, GL_COMPRESSED_SIGNED_RED_RGTC1
GL_RGTC2_RG	GL_COMPRESSED_RG_RGTC2, GL_COMPRESSED_SIGNED_RG_RGTC2
GL_BPTC_UNORM	GL_COMPRESSED_RGBA_BPTC_UNORM, GL_COMPRESSED_SRGB_ALPHA_BPTC_UNORM
GL_BPTC_FLOAT	GL_COMPRESSED_RGB_BPTC_SIGNED_FLOAT, GL_COMPRESSED_RGB_BPTC_UNSIGNED_FLOAT

Given the format and target compatibility matrices above, it is possible to reinterpret data in a texture in multiple ways simultaneously. For example, it is possible to create two views of an RGB8 texture, one as unsigned normalized (returning floating-point data to the shader) and another as an unsigned integer texture (which will return the underlying integer data to the shader). Example 6.25 shows an example of how to achieve this.

Example 6.25 Creating a Texture View with a New Format

```
// Create two texture names - one will be our parent,
// one will be the view
GLuint tex[2];
glGenTextures(2, &tex);

// Bind the first texture and initialize its data store
// Here, the store will be 1024 x 1024 2D texture with
// mipmaps and the format will be GL_RGB8 - 8-bits per
// component RGB, unsigned normalized
glBindTexture(GL_TEXTURE_2D, tex[0]);
glTexStorage2D(GL_TEXTURE_2D, 10, GL_RGB8, 1024, 1024);

// Now,.create a view of the texture, this time using
// GL_RGB8UI so as to receive the raw data from the texture
glTextureView(tex[1],              // New texture view
              GL_TEXTURE_2D,       // Target for the new view
              tex[0],              // Original texture
              GL_RGB8UI,           // New format
              0, 10,               // All mipmaps
              0, 1);               // Only one layer
```

As a second example, consider a case where you have a large 2D array texture and wish to take a single slice of the array and use it as an independent 2D texture. To do this, we can create a view of the target

GL_TEXTURE_2D even though the original texture is
GL_TEXTURE_2D_ARRAY. Example 6.26 shows an example of this.

Example 6.26   Creating a Texture View with a New Target

```
// Create two texture names - one will be our parent,
// one will be the view
GLuint tex[2];
glGenTextures(2, &tex);

// Bind the first texture and initialize its data store
// We are going to create a 2D array texture with a layer
// size of 256x256 texels and 100 layers.
glBindTexture(GL_TEXTURE_2D_ARRAY, tex[0]);
glTexStorage3D(GL_TEXTURE_2D_ARRAY, 8, GL_RGAB32F, 256, 256, 100);

// Now, create a GL_TEXTURE_2D view of the texture,
// extracting a single slice from the middle of the array
glTextureView(tex[1],             // New texture view
              GL_TEXTURE_2D,      // Target for the new view
              tex[0],             // Original texture
              GL_RGBA32F,         // Same format as original texture
              0, 8,               // All mipmaps
              50, 1);             // Only one layer
```

Once a view of a texture has been created, it can be used in any place that
you can use a texture, including image loads and stores or framebuffer
attachments. It is also possible to create views of views (and views of those
views, etc.), with each view holding a reference to the original data store. It
is even legal to delete the original parent texture. So long as at least one
view of the data exists, it will not be deleted.

Other use cases for texture views include aliasing data of various formats—
for example, bit casting floating-point and integer data to enable atomic
operations and OpenGL's logic-op to be performed on floating-point data,
which would normally not be allowed. Aliasing a single data store as both
sRGB and linear data allows a single shader to simultaneously access the
same data with and without sRGB conversion applied. A single-array
texture may effectively have different format data stored in its slices by
creating multiple array views of the texture and rendering different
outputs to different slices of the texture. With some lateral thinking
applied, texture views become a very powerful way to access and manage
texture data.

Compressed Textures

Compression is a mechanism by which the amount of data required to store or transmit information is reduced. Because texture data can consume a very large amount of memory (and consequently, memory bandwidth), OpenGL supports storing textures in compressed forms in order to reduce their size. Compression algorithms fall into two general categories—*lossless* and *lossy*. *Lossless compression* algorithms will not discard any information and an exact copy of the original is retrievable after decompression. However, *lossy compression* sacrifices some of the original information during the process in order to make the remaining information more suited to the compression algorithm and reduce its size. This will reduce quality some but normally provides much greater reduction in memory cost. Obviously for some content, such as computer executables, text documents, and the like, it is imperative that no information is lost. You may be familiar with lossless compression in the form of zip-type algorithms used to compress file archives.

For other content, though, some loss in quality is acceptable. For example, common audio and video compression algorithms such as MPEG are lossy. They throw out some information in order to improve the *compression ratio*. A trade-off is made between the acceptable loss in quality and reduced file sizes. Without lossy compression, MP3 players and streaming video would be almost impractical.

For the most part, the loss in fidelity is not perceptible to most audiences[18]— think, when was the last time you noticed that the music you were listening to was compressed? Most texture compression schemes in use today are based on lossy algorithms designed to be easy to decompress, even at the expense of additional complexity in the compression side of the algorithm.

There are two ways to get compressed texture data into OpenGL. The first is to ask OpenGL to compress it for you. In this case, you supply uncompressed data but specify a compressed internal format. The OpenGL implementation will take the uncompressed, raw texture data, and attempt to compress it. Because this is a real-time process, the compressor in the OpenGL implementation will often implement a rather naive algorithm in order to compress the data quickly resulting in a poor quality compressed texture. The other way to bring compressed texture data into OpenGL is to compress it offline (i.e., before your program runs) and pass the

---

18. Lossless compressors such as FLAC are popular for archival of digital music. These algorithms normally reach compression ratios of the order of 30% to 50% of the original file size. However, for day-to-day use, lossy algorithms such as MP3 and AC3 can reach compression ratios of 10% or less and provide satisfactory experience to most users.

compressed data to OpenGL directly. This way, you can spend as much time as is necessary to achieve the desired quality level in the resulting texture without sacrificing run-time performance.

Under either mechanism, the first step is to choose a compressed internal format. There are a myriad of texture-compression algorithms and formats, and different hardware and implementations of OpenGL will support different sets of formats—many of which are documented in extensions. To determine which formats your OpenGL implementation supports, you can examine the implementation's list of extensions.

Although the set of formats supported by a particular implementation of OpenGL may well contain several proprietary and possibly undocumented compression formats, two format families are guaranteed to be supported by OpenGL. These are RGTC (Red-Green Texture Compression) and BPTC (Block Partitioned Texture Compression). Both formats are block-based and store texels in units of 4×4 texel blocks. This means that they store the image in blocks of 4×4 texels, each independently compressed. Such blocks can be easily decompressed by hardware as they are brought from main memory into the graphics processor's texture caches.

If you have chosen to ask the OpenGL implementation to compress your texture for you, all you need to do is choose the appropriate compressed internal format and specify the texel data as normal. OpenGL will take that data and compress it as its read. However, if you have texel data that has been processed offline and is already in its compressed form, you need to call one of the compressed texture image specification functions. To establish immutable storage for the texture using a compressed format, you may use the **glTexStorage1D()**, **glTexStorage2D()** or **glTexStorage3D()** functions described earlier. You may also create a mutable store for the texture using **glCompressedTexImage1D()**, **glCompressedTexImage2D()**, **glCompressedTexImage3D()**, whose prototypes are shown below.

```
void glCompressedTexImage1D(GLenum target, GLint level,
                            GLenum internalFormat,
                            GLsizei width, GLint border,
                            GLsizei imageSize,
                            const void *data);
void glCompressedTexImage2D(GLenum target, GLint level,
                            GLenum internalFormat,
                            GLsizei width, GLsizei height,
                            GLint border, GLsizei imageSize,
                            const void *data);
```

void **glCompressedTexImage3D**(GLenum *target*, GLint *level*,
GLenum *internalFormat*,
GLsizei *width*, GLsizei *height*,
GLsizei *depth*, GLint *border*,
GLsizei *imageSize*,
const void **data*);

Establish storage for textures using a compressed internal format. Any existing data store for level *level* of the texture bound to *target* of the active texture unit is released and a new store is established in its place. *internalFormat* specifies the format of the texture data, which must be a supported compressed internal texture format. *width* specifies the width of the new store, in texels. For 2D and 3D textures, *height*, if present specifies the height of the texture and for 1D array textures, it specifies the number of slices in the array. *depth*, if present, specifies the depth of a 3D texture and the number of slices in a 2D array texture. *data* specifies the address in memory of the compressed image data to be used in the texture, and *imageSize* is the size of that data in memory. *border* is reserved and must be zero.

When you specify compressed data, the absolute size of the data is determined by the compression format. Therefore, all of the compressed image data functions take a parameter that specifies this size, in bytes. It is your application's responsibility to make sure that this size is correct and that the data you give to OpenGL is of a valid form for the compression format that you have chosen. Once storage for a texture object has been established, it is also possible to update parts of that texture using the following functions.

void **glCompressedTexSubImage1D**(GLenum *target*, GLint *level*,
GLint *xoffset*, GLsizei *width*,
GLenum *format*,
GLsizei *imageSize*,
const void **data*);
void **glCompressedTexSubImage2D**(GLenum *target*, GLint *level*,
GLint *xoffset*, GLint *yoffset*,
GLsizei *width*,
GLsizei *height*,
GLenum *format*,
GLsizei *imageSize*,
const void **data*);

| void **glCompressedTexSubImage3D**(GLenum *target*, GLint *level*, |
| GLint *xoffset*, GLint *yoffset*, |
| GLint *zoffset*, GLsizei *width*, |
| GLsizei *height*, GLsizei *depth*, |
| GLenum *format*, |
| GLsizei *imageSize*, |
| const void **data*); |

Update the compressed texture data in *level* of the texture bound to *target* of the active texture unit. *xoffset* and *width* specify the offset in the *x*-axis and the width of the texture data, in texels. For 2D and 3D textures, *yoffset* and *height* specify offset in the *y*-axis and the height of the texture data, respectively. For 1D array textures, *yoffset* and *height* specify the starting slice and number of slices to update. For 3D textures, *zoffset* and *depth* specify the offset in the *z*-axis and depth of the texture data. For 2D array textures, they specify the starting slice and number of slices to update. *format* specifies the format of the compressed image data and must match the internal format of the texture. *imageSize* and *data* specify the size and location of the data to be used to update the texture.

Filtering

Texture maps may be linear, square, or rectangular, or even 3D, but after being mapped to a polygon or surface and transformed into screen coordinates, the individual texels of a texture rarely correspond directly to individual pixels of the final screen image. Depending on the transformations used and the texture mapping applied, a single pixel on the screen can correspond to anything from a tiny portion of a single texel (magnification) to a large collection of texels (minification), as shown in Figure 6.14. In either case, it's unclear exactly which texel values should be used and how they should be averaged or interpolated. Consequently, OpenGL allows you to specify any of several filtering options to determine these calculations. The options provide different trade-offs between speed and image quality. Also, you can specify the filtering methods to be used for magnification and minification independently.

In some cases, it isn't obvious whether magnification or minification is called for. If the texture map needs to be stretched (or shrunk) in both the *x* and *y* directions, then magnification (or minification) is needed. If

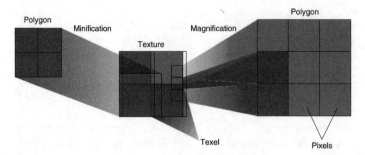

Figure 6.14   Effect of texture minification and magnification

the texture map needs to be stretched in one direction and shrunk in the other, OpenGL makes a choice between magnification and minification[19] that in most cases gives the best result possible. It's best to try to avoid these situations by using texture coordinates that map without such distortion.

Linear Filtering

Linear filtering is a technique in which a coordinate is used to select adjacent samples from a discretely sampled signal and replace that signal with a linear approximation of the original. Consider the signal shown in Figure 6.15.

Figure 6.15   Resampling of a signal in one dimension

In Figure 6.15, the signal represented by the solid line has been discretely sampled at the points shown by the large dots. The original signal cannot be reconstructed by placing a straight line between each of the dots. In some areas of the signal, the linear reconstruction matches the original signal reasonably well. However, in other areas, the reconstruction is not faithful to the original and sharp peaks that were present before resampling are lost.

---

19. When a texture is enlarged by different amounts in the horizontal and vertical axes, this is referred to as *anisotropic filtering*. This is exposed by some OpenGL implementations in the form of an extension. However, this is not part of core OpenGL.

For image data, the same technique can be applied. So long as the sampling rate (resolution) of the texture is high enough relative to the sharp peaks in the image data (details), a linear reconstruction of the image will appear to have reasonably high quality. The translation from a signal as shown in Figure 6.15 into a texture is easy to conceive when a 1D texture is considered. Simply place the samples into a 1D texture and reconstruct the original 1D image from those samples as needed.

To do this, OpenGL takes the texture coordinate that you pass it as a floating-point number and finds the two samples that lie closest to it. It uses the distance to each of those two points to create weights for each of the samples and then uses those weights to create a weighted average of them. Because linear resampling is *separable*[20], OpenGL can apply this technique first in one dimension, and then again in a second dimension in order to reconstruct 2D images and even a third time for 3D textures. Figure 6.16 illustrates the process as applied to a 2D image.

GL_NEAREST

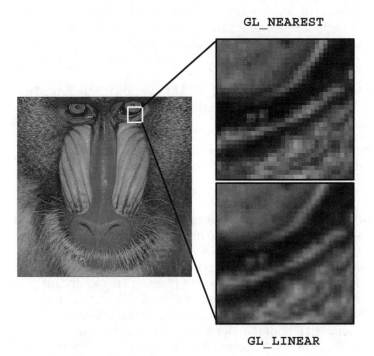

GL_LINEAR

Figure 6.16   Bilinear resampling

20. A separable operation is one that can be deconstructed into two or more, usually similar passes over the data. In this case, we can apply one pass per dimension of the image data.

Not only can linear filtering be used to smoothly transition from one sample to the adjacent ones in 1D, 2D, and 3D textures, it can also be used to blend texels sampled from adjacent mipmap levels in a texture. This works in a very similar manner to that described above. OpenGL calculates the mipmap level from which it needs to select samples and the result of this calculation will often be a floating-point value with a fractional component. This is used just as a fractional texture coordinate is used to filter spatially adjacent texels. The two closest mipmaps are used to construct a pair of samples and the fractional part of the level-of-detail calculation is used to weight the two samples into an average.

All of these filtering options are controlled by the *texture filter* modes in OpenGL's sampler objects. As explained in "Sampler Objects" on Page 292, the sampler object represents a collection of parameters that control how texels are read from textures. Two of those parameters, GL_TEXTURE_MAG_FILTER and GL_TEXTURE_MIN_FILTER, control how OpenGL filters textures. The first is used when the texture is *magnified*—that is, when the level-of-detail required is of a higher resolution than the highest resolution mipmip level (by default, level 0) and represents cases where the mipmip calculation produces a level less than or equal to zero. Because, under magnification, only one mipmap level is used, only two choices are available for GL_TEXTURE_MAG_FILTER. These are GL_NEAREST and GL_LINEAR. The first disables filtering and returns the nearest texel to the sample location. The second enables linear filtering.

Texture minification is where mipmapping takes effect, and this is explained in some detail in the following sections.

Advanced

From a signaling-theory perspective, a texture needs to sample the original signal at at least twice the frequency of the highest frequency data present. The original should be low-pass filtered to some frequency, then sampled at greater than twice that frequency. This gives enough samples to exactly reconstruct the original image. However, linear filtering fails to do this reconstruction and can lead to aliasing. Also, if the original filtering and 2X sampling are not done, aliasing and other artifacts can occur. This is discussed in more detail in Chapter 8, "Procedural Texturing", and mipmapping as one technique for dealing with it is described below. You can also do custom filtering using texture gathers to improve over the artifacts of linear filtering. Gathering texels is discussed later in this chapter.

Using and Generating Mipmaps

Textured objects can be viewed, like any other objects in a scene, at different distances from the viewpoint. In a dynamic scene, as a textured object moves farther from the viewpoint, the ratio of pixels to texels in the texture becomes very low and the texture ends up being sampled at a very low rate. This has the effect of producing artifacts in the rendered image due to undersampling of the texture data. For example, to render a brick wall, you may use a large texture image (say 1024×1024 texels) when the wall is close to the viewer. But if the wall is moved farther away from the viewer until it appears on the screen as a single pixel, then the sampled texture may appear to change abruptly at certain transition points.

To reduce this effect, we can pre-filter the texture map and store the pre-filtered images as successively lower and lower-resolution versions of the full resolution image. These are called mipmaps, and are shown in Figure 6.17. The term mipmap was coined by Lance Williams, when he introduced the idea in his paper "Pyramidal Parametrics" (SIGGRAPH 1983 Proceedings). Mip stands for the Latin *multum in parvo*, meaning "many things in a small place." Mipmapping uses some clever methods to pack image data into memory.

When using mipmapping, OpenGL automatically determines which resolution level of the texture map to use based on the size (in pixels) of the object being mapped. With this approach, the *level of detail* in the texture map is appropriate for the image that's drawn on the screen; as the image of the object gets smaller, the size of the texture map decreases. Mipmapping requires some extra computation and texture storage area. However, when it's not used, textures that are mapped onto smaller objects might shimmer and flash as the objects move.

This description of OpenGL mipmapping avoids detailed discussion of the scale factor (known as λ) between texel size and polygon size. This description also assumes default values for parameters related to mipmapping. To see an explanation of λ and the effects of mipmapping parameters, see "Calculating the Mipmap Level" on Page 338. Additional details on controlling λ from your application can be found in "Mipmap Level-of-Detail Control" on Page 339.

Original texture

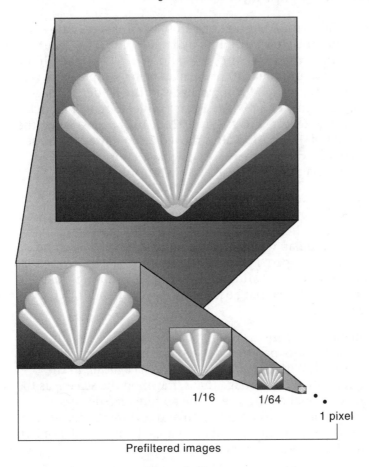

1/16   1/64

1 pixel

Prefiltered images

Figure 6.17   A pre-filtered mipmap pyramid

The parameter GL_TEXTURE_MIN_FILTER controls how texels are constructed when the mipmap level is greater than zero. There are a total of six settings available for this parameter. The first two are the same as for magnification—GL_NEAREST and GL_LINEAR. Choosing one of these two modes disables mipmapping and causes OpenGL to only use the base level (level 0) of the texture. The other four modes enable mipmapping and control how the mipmaps are used. The four values are GL_NEAREST_MIPMAP_NEAREST, GL_NEAREST_MIPMAP_LINEAR, GL_LINEAR_MIPMAP_NEAREST, and GL_LINEAR_MIPMAP_LINEAR. Notice how each mode is made up of two parts and the token names are structured as GL_{A}_MIPMAP_{B}. Here, {A} and {B} may both be either

NEAREST or LINEAR. The first part, {A}, controls how the texels from each of the mipmap levels is constructed and works the same way as the GL_TEXTURE_MAG_FILTER setting. The second, {B}, controls how these samples are blended between the mipmap levels. When it's NEAREST, only the closest mipmap level is used. When it's LINEAR, the two closest mipmaps are linearly interpolated.

To illustrate the effect of the GL_TEXTURE_MIN_FILTER parameter on a mipmapped texture, Figure 6.18 shows how each affects a simple checker type pattern at different resolutions in a mipmap pyramid. Notice how with the intra-mipmap filter specified as NEAREST (as in GL_NEAREST_ MIPMAP_NEAREST and GL_NEAREST_MIPMAP_LINEAR), the checkerboard pattern becomes quite evident, whereas when it is LINEAR (as in GL_LINEAR_MIPMAP_NEAREST and GL_LINEAR_MIPMAP_LINEAR), it is less well defined and the texture appears blurred. Likewise, when the inter-mipmap filter mode is NEAREST (as in GL_NEAREST_MIPMAP_ NEAREST and GL_LINEAR_MIPMAP_NEAREST), the boundary between the mipmap levels is visible. However, when the inter-mipmap filter is LINEAR (as in GL_NEAREST_MIPMAP_LINEAR and GL_LINEAR_MIPMAP_LINEAR), that boundary is hidden by filtering.

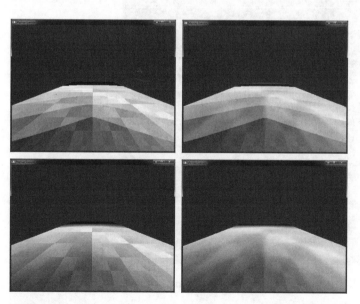

Figure 6.18   Effects of minification mipmap filters
(GL_NEAREST_MIPMAP_NEAREST (top left), GL_LINEAR_MIPMAP_
NEAREST (top right), GL_NEAREST_MIPMAP_LINEAR (bottom left), and
GL_LINEAR_MIPMAP_LINEAR (bottom right).)

To use mipmapping, you must provide all sizes of your texture in powers of 2 between the largest size and a 1 × 1 map. If you don't intend to use mipmapping to go all the way to a 1 × 1 texture, you can set the value of GL_TEXTURE_MAX_LEVEL to the maximum level you have supplied, and OpenGL will not consider any further levels in its evaluation of texture completeness. If the highest resolution level of the texture is not square, one dimension will reach one texel in size before the other. In this case, continue making new levels with that dimension sized to one texel until the level becomes 1 × 1 texel in size. For example, if your highest resolution map is 64 × 16, you must also provide maps of size 32 × 8, 16 × 4, 8 × 2, 4 × 1, 2 × 1, and 1 × 1. The smaller maps are typically filtered, and down-sampled versions of the largest map in which each texel in a smaller texture is a weighted average of the corresponding 4 texels in the higher-resolution texture. (Since OpenGL doesn't require any particular method for calculating the lower-resolution maps, the differently sized textures could be totally unrelated. In practice, unrelated textures would make the transitions between mipmaps extremely noticeable, as in Figure 6.19.)

Figure 6.19   Illustration of mipmaps using unrelated colors

The image in Figure 6.19 was generated by creating a 64 × 64 texture and filling each of its 7 mipmap levels with a different color. The highest resolution level was filled with red, then green, blue, yellow, and so on down the mipmap pyramid. This texture was applied to a large plane extending into the distance. The further the plane gets from the viewer, the narrower it becomes in screen space and the more compressed the texture becomes. OpenGL chooses successively higher mipmap levels (lower resolution levels) from the texture. To further illustrate the effect, the example sets the mipmap filtering mode to nearest and applies a bias to the calculated mipmap level.

To specify these textures, allocate the texture using **glTexStorage2D()** and then call **glTexSubImage2D()** once for each resolution of the texture map, with different values for the level, width, height, and image parameters. Starting with zero, *level* identifies which texture in the series is specified; with the previous example, the highest-resolution texture of size 64×64 would be declared with *level* = 0, the 32×32 texture with *level* = 1, and so on. In addition, for the mipmapped textures to take effect, you need to choose one of the mipmapped minification filters as described earlier.

OpenGL provides a function to automatically generate all of the mipmaps for a texture under application control. This function is called **glGenerateMipmap()**, and it is up to the OpenGL implementation to provide a mechanism to downsample the high resolution images to produce the lower resolution mipmaps. This will often be implemented internally by using a shader or perhaps the texture-filtering hardware. The technique used will generally be designed for performance over quality and will vary from implementation to implementation. If you want high-quality, well-defined results, it is best to generate and supply the mipmap images yourself. However, if you need to quickly generate a mipmap chain and are satisfied with whatever results you get, you can rely on **glGenerateMipmap()** for this purpose.

---

void **glGenerateMipmap**(GLenum *target*);

Generates a complete set of mipmaps for the texture image associated with *target*, which must be one of GL_TEXTURE_1D, GL_TEXTURE_2D, GL_TEXTURE_3D, GL_TEXTURE_1D_ARRAY, GL_TEXTURE_2D_ARRAY, or GL_TEXTURE_CUBE_MAP. The mipmap levels constructed are controlled by the GL_TEXTURE_BASE_LEVEL and GL_TEXTURE_MAX_LEVEL. If those values are left to their defaults, an entire mipmap stack down to a single-texel texture map is created. The filtering method used in creating each successive level is implementation dependent. A GL_INVALID_OPERATION error will be generated if target is GL_TEXTURE_CUBE_MAP, and not all cube-map faces are initialized and consistent.

Calculating the Mipmap Level

The computation of which mipmap level of a texture to use for a particular pixel depends on the scale factor between the texture image and the size of the polygon to be textured (in pixels). Let's call this scale factor ρ, and also define a second value, λ, where $\lambda = \log_2 \rho + lod_{bias}$. (Since texture images can be multidimensional, it is important to clarify that ρ is the maximum scale factor of all dimensions.)

lod_{bias} is the level-of-detail bias for the sampler, a constant value set by calling **glSamplerParameteri()** with the *pname* parameter set to GL_TEXTURE_LOD_BIAS and is used to adjust λ. By default, $lod_{bias} = 0.0$, which has no effect. It's best to start with this default value and adjust in small amounts, if needed. If $\lambda \leq 0.0$, then the texel is smaller than the pixel, and so a magnification filter is used. If $\lambda > 0.0$, then a minification filter is used. If the minification filter selected uses mipmapping, then λ indicates the mipmap level. (The minification-to-magnification switchover point is usually at $\lambda = 0.0$, but not always. The choice of mipmapping filter may shift the switchover point.)

For example, if the texture image is 64×64 texels and the polygon size is 32×32 pixels, then $\rho = 2.0$ (not 4.0), and therefore $\lambda = 1.0$. If the texture image is 64×32 texels and the polygon size is 8×16 pixels, then $\rho = 8.0$ (*x* scales by 8.0, *y* by 2.0; use the maximum value), and therefore $\lambda = 3.0$.

The equations for the calculation of λ and ρ are as follows:

$$\lambda_{base}(x, y) = \log_2 [\rho(x, y)] \tag{6.1}$$

$$\lambda'(x, y) = \lambda_{base} + clamp(bias_{texobj} + bias_{shader}) \tag{6.2}$$

The calculation of mipmap level can be further controlled by a number of sampler parameters. In particular, the GL_TEXTURE_LOD_BIAS parameter may be used to bias λ. Once λ has been calculated, it may be clamped into a user-specified range, which is given by the parameters GL_TEXTURE_MIN_LOD and GL_TEXTURE_MAX_LOD, which are specified by passing those token values to **glSamplerParameterf()** (or to **glTexParameterf()** if sampler objects are not in use). The default values for GL_TEXTURE_MIN_LOD and GL_TEXTURE_MAX_LOD are -1000.0 and 1000.0, respectively, allowing them to effectively pass through any value. The values of GL_TEXTURE_MIN_LOD and GL_TEXTURE_MAX_LOD are represented by lod_{min} and lod_{max} in the following equation.

$$\lambda = \begin{cases} lod_{max}, & \lambda' > lod_{max} \\ \lambda', & lod_{min} \leq \lambda' \leq lod_{max} \\ lod_{min}, & \lambda' < lod_{min} \\ undefined, & lod_{min} > lod_{max} \end{cases} \tag{6.3}$$

The default parameters for GL_TEXTURE_MAG_FILTER and GL_TEXTURE_MIN_FILTER are GL_LINEAR and GL_LINEAR_MIPMAP_LINEAR, respectively. Notice that the default minification filter enables mipmapping. This is important because in order to use mipmapping, the texture must have a complete set of mipmap levels and they must have a consistent set of resolutions as described in "Using and Generating Mipmaps" on Page 333; otherwise, the texture is considered *incomplete* and will not return useful data to the shader. Textures allocated using the **glTexStorage2D()** function are always complete, so you don't need to worry about that; but these textures will still contain no data when they are newly created. This is a common source of errors for new OpenGL programmers—they forget to either change the filtering mode or fill in the mipmaps for newly created textures resulting in their texturing code not working.

Mipmap Level-of-Detail Control

In addition to the parameters controlling lod_{min}, lod_{max}, and λ_{base} during the calculation of λ, further control over the selected level of the mipmap pyramid is provided through the GL_TEXTURE_BASE_LEVEL and GL_TEXTURE_MAX_LEVEL parameters, which may be set using **glSamplerParameteri()**. GL_TEXTURE_BASE_LEVEL specifies the *lowest* mipmap level (i.e., highest resolution) that will be sampled, regardless of the value of λ, whereas GL_TEXTURE_MAX_LEVEL specifies the *highest* mipmap level (i.e., lowest resolution) that will be sampled. This can be used to constrain sampling to a subset of the mipmap pyramid.

One potential use for GL_TEXTURE_BASE_LEVEL is *texture streaming*. When using texture streaming, storage for the complete texture object is allocated using a function such as **glTexStorage2D()** but the initial data is not loaded. As the application runs and new objects come into view, their texture data is loaded from lowest to highest resolution mipmap. To ensure that something meaningful is displayed to the user even when the complete texture has not yet been loaded, the value of GL_TEXTURE_BASE_LEVEL can be set to the highest resolution mipmap level that has been loaded so far. That way, as more and more texture data is loaded, objects on the screen achieve higher and higher fidelity.

Advanced Texture Lookup Functions

In addition to simple texturing functions such as `texture` and `texelFetch`, several more variants of the texture fetch functions are supported by the shading language. These are covered in this subsection.

Explicit Level of Detail

Normally, when using mipmaps, OpenGL will calculate the level of detail and the resulting mipmap levels from which to sample for you (see "Calculating the Mipmap Level" on Page 338 for more details on how OpenGL calculates mipmap levels). However, it is possible to override this calculation and specify the level of detail explicitly as an argument to the texture fetch function. The `textureLod` function takes this `lod` parameter in place of the `bias` parameter that would normally be optionally supplied to the `texture` function. Like other texture functions supported by GLSL, `textureLod` has many overloaded prototypes for the various types and dimensionalities of the supported sampler types. Some key prototypes of `textureLod` are as follows: (A full list is in Appendix C, "Built-in GLSL Variables and Functions".)

```
gvec4 textureLod(gsampler1D tex, float P, float lod);
gvec4 textureLod(gsampler2D tex, vec2 P, float lod);
gvec4 textureLod(gsampler3D tex, vec3 P, float lod);
gvec4 textureLod(gsamplerCube tex, vec3 P, float lod);
gvec4 textureLod(gsampler1DArray tex, vec2 P, float lod);
gvec4 textureLod(gsampler2DArray tex, vec3 P, float lod);
gvec4 textureLod(gsampler2DRect tex, vec2 P, float lod);
gvec4 textureLod(gsamplerCubeArray tex, vec4 P, float lod);
```

Sample a texel from the sampler given by *tex* at the texture coordinates given by *P* with explicit level of detail given by *lod*.

Notice that because they don't support mipmaps, `samplerBuffer` and `samplerRect` are missing from the supported sampler types for `textureLod`.

Explicit Gradient Specification

It is also possible to override the level-of-detail calculation for mipmapping at an earlier part of the process rather than explicitly giving the level-of-detail parameter directly. When the gradient texture functions are used, the partial derivative of the texture coordinates is given as a parameter. Some key prototypes are listed below. (A full list is in Appendix C, "Built-in GLSL Variables and Functions".)

---

gvec4 **textureGrad**(gsampler1D *tex*, float *P*,float *dPdx*, float *dPdy*);
gvec4 **textureGrad**(gsampler2D *tex*, vec2 *P*,vec2 *dPdx*, vec2 *dPdy*);
gvec4 **textureGrad**(gsampler3D *tex*, vec3 *P*,vec3 *dPdx*, vec3 *dPdy*);
gvec4 **textureGrad**(gsamplerCube *tex*, vec3 *P*,vec3 *dPdx*,
                 vec3 *dPdy*);
gvec4 **textureGrad**(gsampler1DArray *tex*, vec2 *P*,float *dPdx*,
                 float *dPdy*);
gvec4 **textureGrad**(gsampler2DArray *tex*, vec3 *P*,vec2 *dPdx*,
                 vec2 *dPdy*);
gvec4 **textureGrad**(gsamplerCubeArray *tex*, vec4 *P*,vec3 *dPdx*,
                 vec3 *dPdy*);

Sample a texel from the sampler given by *tex* at the texture coordinates given by *P* using the partial derivatives for *P* in *x* and *y* as specified by *dPdx* and *dPdy*, respectively.

In the `textureGrad` functions, the variable ρ as described in "Calculating the Mipmap Level" on Page 338 is essentially passed in using *dPdx* and *dPdy*. This can be useful when an analytic function for the derivative of a texture coordinate may be known, or when a function that is not the derivative of the texture coordinate is required.

Texture Fetch with Offsets

Some applications require a number of texels around a region of interest, or may need to offset the texture coordinates slightly during sampling. GLSL includes functions for doing this that will likely be more efficient than physically offsetting the texture coordinates in the shader. This functionality is exposed through an overloaded set of texture lookup functions called `textureOffset` with some example prototypes as follows: (A full list is in Appendix C, "Built-in GLSL Variables and Functions".)

---

gvec4 **textureOffset**(gsampler1D *tex*, float *P*, int offset,
               [float *bias*]);
gvec4 **textureOffset**(gsampler2D *tex*, vec2 *P*, ivec2 offset,
               [float *bias*]);
gvec4 **textureOffset**(gsampler3D *tex*, vec3 *P*, ivec3 offset,
               [float *bias*]);

```
gvec4 textureOffset(gsampler1DArray tex, vec2 P, int offset,
                    [float bias]);
gvec4 textureOffset(gsampler2DArray tex, vec3 P, ivec2 offset,
                    [float bias]);
gvec4 textureOffset(gsampler2DRect tex, vec2 P, ivec2 offset,
                    [float bias]);
```

Sample a texel from the sampler given by *tex* at the texture coordinates given by *P*. After the floating-point texture coordinate *P* has been suitably scaled and converted to absolute texel coordinates, *offset* is added to the texel coordinates before the fetch is performed.

Notice that for the `textureOffset` function, the `offset` parameter is an integer value. In fact, this must be a constant expression and must be with a limited range. This range is given by the built-in GLSL constants `gl_MinProgramTexelOffset` and `gl_MaxProgramTexelOffset`.

Projective Texturing

Projective texturing is employed when a perspective transformation matrix has been used to transform texture coordinates. The input to the transform is a set of homogeneous coordinates and the resulting output of this transform is a vector whose last component is unlikely to be 1. The `textureProj` function can be used to divide through by this final component, projecting the resulting texture coordinate into the coordinate space of the texture. This is useful for techniques such as projecting decals onto flat surfaces (e.g., the halo projected by a flashlight) or in shadow mapping[21]. Some example prototypes are given below. (A full list is in Appendix C, "Built-in GLSL Variables and Functions".)

```
gvec4 textureProj(gsampler1D tex, vec2 P[, float bias]);
gvec4 textureProj(gsampler1D tex, vec4 P[, float bias]);
gvec4 textureProj(gsampler2D tex, vec3 P[, float bias]);
gvec4 textureProj(gsampler2D tex, vec4 P[, float bias]);
gvec4 txtureProj(gsampler3D tex, vec4 P[, float bias]);
```

---

21. An in-depth example of shadow mapping is given in "Shadow Mapping" on Page 400.

gvec4 **textureProj**(gsamplerRect *tex*, vec3 *P*);
gvec4 **textureProj**(gsamplerRect *tex*, vec4 *P*);

Perform a texture lookup with projection by dividing the texture coordinate specified in *P* by the last component of *P* and using the resulting values to perform a texture lookup as would be executed by the normal `texture`.

Texture Queries in Shaders

The following two built-in GLSL functions don't actually read from the texture, but return information about the texture or about how it will be processed. The first function, `textureQueryLod` retrieves mipmap information calculated by the fixed-function texture lookup hardware.

vec2 **textureQueryLod**(gsampler1D *tex*, float *P*);
vec2 **textureQueryLod**(gsampler2D *tex*, vec2 *P*);
vec2 **textureQueryLod**(gsampler3D *tex*, vec3 *P*);
vec2 **textureQueryLod**(gsamplerCube *tex*, vec3 *P*);
vec2 **textureQueryLod**(gsampler1DArray *tex*, float *P*);
vec2 **textureQueryLod**(gsampler2DArray *tex*, vec2 *P*);
vec2 **textureQueryLod**(gsamplerCubeArray *tex*, vec3 *P*);
vec2 **textureQueryLod**(sampler1DShadow *tex*, float *P*);
vec2 **textureQueryLod**(sampler2DShadow *tex*, vec2 *P*);
vec2 **textureQueryLod**(samplerCubeShadow *tex*, vec3 *P*);
vec2 **textureQueryLod**(sampler1DArrayShadow *tex*, float *P*);
vec2 **textureQueryLod**(sampler2DArrayShadow *tex*, vec2 *P*);
vec2 **textureQueryLod**(samplerCubeArrayShadow *tex*, vec3 *P*);

Return the mipmap array(s) that would be accessed in the *x* component of the return value and the computed level of detail relative to the base level of the texture in the *y* component.

For each of these `textureQueryLod()` functions, there is a corresponding query, `textureQueryLevels()`, that returns the number of mipmap levels present.

```
int textureQueryLevels(gsampler1D tex);
int textureQueryLevels(gsampler2D tex);
int textureQueryLevels(gsampler3D tex);
int textureQueryLevels(gsamplerCube tex);
int textureQueryLevels(gsampler1DArray tex);
int textureQueryLevels(gsampler2DArray tex);
int textureQueryLevels(gsamplerCubeArray tex);
int textureQueryLevels(sampler1DShadow tex);
int textureQueryLevels(sampler2DShadow tex);
int textureQueryLevels(samplerCubeShadow tex);
int textureQueryLevels(sampler1DArrayShadow tex);
int textureQueryLevels(sampler2DArrayShadow tex);
int textureQueryLevels(samplerCubeArrayShadow tex);
```

Return the number of mipmap levels the provided sampler contains.

Sometimes, it may be necessary to know the dimensions of a texture from which you are about to sample. For example, you may need to scale an integer texture coordinate representing an absolute texel location into a floating-point range suitable for sampling from the texture, or to iterate over all the samples in a texture. The `textureSize` function will return the dimensions of the texture at a specified level of detail. Its prototype is as follows: (A full list is in Appendix C, "Built-in GLSL Variables and Functions".)

```
int textureSize(gsampler1D tex, int lod);
ivec2 textureSize(gsampler2D tex, int lod);
ivec3 textureSize(gsampler3D tex, int lod);
ivec2 textureSize(gsamplerCube tex, int lod);
ivec2 textureSize(gsamplerRect tex, int lod);
ivec3 textureSize(gsamplerCubeRect tex);
ivec2 textureSize(gsampler1DArray tex, int lod);
ivec3 textureSize(gsampler2DArray tex, int lod);
int textureSize(gsamplerBuffer tex);
```

Return the dimensions of the level-of-detail lod (if present) of the texture bound to sampler tex. The components of the return value are filled in order with the width, height, and depth of the texture. For array forms, the last component of the return value is the number of slices in the array.

Gathering Texels

The `textureGather` function is a special function that allows your shader to read the four samples that would have been used to create a bilinearly filtered texel from a 2D texture (or cube map, rectangle texture, or array of these types). Typically used with single-channel textures, the optional *comp* component of the function allows you to select a channel other than the *x* or *r* component of the underlying data. This function can provide significant performance advantages when you need to sample many times from a single channel of a texture because, depending on the desired access pattern, it is possible to use this function to cut the number of texture lookups by three quarters.

gvec4 **textureGather**(gsampler2D *tex*, vec2 *P*[, int *comp*]);
gvec4 **textureGather**(gsampler2DArray *tex*, vec3 *P*[, int *comp*]);
gvec4 **textureGather**(gsamplerCube *tex*, vec3 *P*[, int *comp*]);
gvec4 **textureGather**(gsamplerCubeArray *tex*, vec4 *P*[, int *comp*]);
gvec4 **textureGather**(gsamplerRect *tex*, vec2 *P*[, int *comp*]);

Gather the four texels from the underlying rectangle, two-dimensional (array), or cube-map (array) texture bound to the sampler *tex* that would normally have been used to create a bilinearly filtered texel value and return a selected component of the four texels in the four components of the return value. If specified, *comp* specifies the component to fetch with 0, 1, 2, and 3 representing the *x*, *y*, *z*, and *w* components, respectively. If *comp* is not specified, then the *x* component is returned.

Combining Special Functions

In addition to all of the special texturing functions, several more variants of these functions exist that combine features from multiple variants. For example, if you want to do projective texturing with an explicit level-of-detail or gradients (each is described in "Explicit Gradient Specification" on Page 340), then you can use the combined functions `textureProjLod` or `textureProjGrad`, respectively. The combined functions using a 2D sampler are shown below. Variants of almost all of these functions exist for other dimensionalities and types of sampler, and a full list is in Appendix C, "Built-in GLSL Variables and Functions".

gvec4 **textureProjLod**(gsampler2D *tex*, vec2 *P*, float *lod*);
gvec4 **textureProjGrad**(gsampler2D *tex*, vec3 *P*, vec2 *dPdx*,
                vec2 *dPdy*);
gvec4 **textureProjOffset**(gsampler2D *tex*, vec3 *P*, ivec2 *offset*[,
                float *bias*);
gvec4 **textureGradOffset**(gsampler2D *tex*, vec2 *P*, vec2 *dPdx*,
                vec2 *dPdy*, ivec2 *offset*);
gvec4 **textureProjLodOffset**(gsampler2D *tex*, vec3 *P*, float *lod*,
                ivec2 *offset*);
gvec4 **textureProjGradOffset**(gsampler2D *tex*, vec3 *P*, vec2 *dPdx*,
                vec2 *dPdy*, ivec2 *offset*);

Advanced texture lookup functions may be combined to perform more than one special function in a single call. `textureProjLod` performs projective texturing from the texture bound to the unit represented by *tex* as would be performed by `textureProj`, but with explicit level of detail specified in *lod*, as accepted by `textureLod`. Similarly, `textureProjGrad` executes a projective texture lookup as performed by `textureProj`, but with explicit gradients passed in *dPdx* and *dPdy* as would be accepted by `textureGrad`. `textureProjOffset` performs a projective texture lookup with texel offsets applied to the *post projected* texture coordinates. `textureProjLodOffset` and `textureProjGradOffset` further combine two special functions—the first performs a projective texture fetch with explicit level of detail and texel offsets (as accepted by `textureOffset`) and the second performs a projective texture lookup with explicit gradients and texel offsets.

Point Sprites

Point sprites are essentially OpenGL points rendered using a fragment shader that takes the fragment's coordinates within the point into account when running. The coordinate within the point is available in the two-dimensional vector `gl_PointCoord`. This variable can be used in any number of ways. Two common uses are to use it as a texture coordinate (this is the classic origin of the term point sprite), or to use it to analytically compute color or coverage. The following are a few examples of how to use the `gl_PointCoord` vector to produce interesting effects in the fragment shader.

Textured Point Sprites

By using gl_PointCoord to lookup texels in a texture in the fragment shader, simple point sprites can be generated. Each point sprite simply shows the texture as a square. Example 6.27 is the vertex shader used in the example. Notice that we're writing to gl_PointSize in the vertex shader. This is to control the size of the point sprites—they're scaled relative to their distance from the near plane. Here we've used a simple linear mapping, but more complex logarithmic mappings can be used.

Example 6.27   Simple Point Sprite Vertex Shader

```
uniform mat4 model_matrix;
uniform mat4 projection_matrix;

layout (location = 0) in vec4 position;

void main(void)
{
    vec4 pos = projection_matrix * (model_matrix * position);
    gl_PointSize = (1.0 - pos.z / pos.w) * 64.0;
    gl_Position = pos;
}
```

Example 6.28 shows the fragment shader used in this example. Not including the declaration of the texture and the output vector, it's a single line of real code! We simply look up into the texture using gl_PointCoord as a texture coordinate.

Example 6.28   Simple Point Sprite Fragment Shader

```
uniform sampler2D sprite_texture;

out vec4 color;

void main(void)
{
    color = texture(sprite_texture, gl_PointCoord);
}
```

When we render 400 points randomly placed in a two-unit cube centered on the origin, we get the result shown in Figure 6.20.

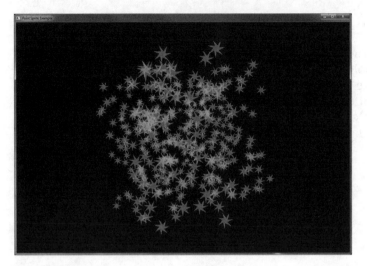

Figure 6.20   Result of the simple textured point sprite example

Analytic Color and Shape

You are not limited to sourcing your point sprite data from a texture.
Textures have a limited resolution, but gl_PointCoord can be quite
precise. The shader shown in Example 6.29 demonstrates how you can
analytically determine coverage in the fragment shader. This shader
centers gl_PointCoord around the origin and then calculates the squared
distance of the fragment from the center of the point sprite. If it's greater
than 0.25 (the square root of half the width of the sprite—or the radius of
a circle that just fits inside it) then the fragment is rejected using the
discard keyword. Otherwise, we interpolate between two colors to
produce the final output. This produces a perfect circle. Note that the
same vertex shown in Example 6.27 is used for this example as well.

Example 6.29   Analytic Shape Fragment Shader

```
out vec4 color;

void main(void)
{
    const vec4 color1 = vec4(0.6, 0.0, 0.0, 1.0);
    const vec4 color2 = vec4(0.9, 0.7, 1.0, 0.0);

    vec2 temp = gl_PointCoord - vec2(0.5);
    float f = dot(temp, temp);

    if (f > 0.25)
        discard;

    color = mix(color1, color2, smoothstep(0.1, 0.25, f));
}
```

Figure 6.21 shows the output of this example.

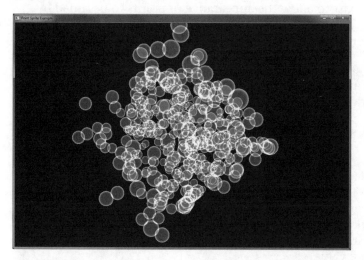

Figure 6.21   Analytically calculated point sprites

By increasing the size of the point sprite and reducing the number of points in the scene, it is possible to see the extremely smooth edges of the discs formed by the fragment shader as shown in Figure 6.22.

Figure 6.22   Smooth edges of circular point sprites

Controlling the Appearance of Points

Various controls exist to allow the appearance of points to be tuned by your application. These parameters are set using **glPointParameterf()** or **glPointParameteri()**.

---

void **glPointParameter**{if}(GLenum *pname*, TYPE *param*);
void **glPointParameter**{if}v(GLenum *pname*, const TYPE **param*);

Set the point parameter specified by *pname* to the value(s) specified by *param*. *pname* must be GL_POINT_SPRITE_COORD_ORIGIN or GL_POINT_FADE_THRESHOLD_SIZE. If *pname* is GL_POINT_SPRITE_COORD_ORIGIN, *param* must be one of GL_LOWER_LEFT or GL_UPPER_LEFT (or the address of a variable containing one of these values). If *pname* is GL_POINT_FADE_THRESHOLD_SIZE, *param* must be a floating point quantity greater than or equal to zero (or the address of a variable containing such a value).

The two parameters that you can change with **glPointParameteri()** or **glPointParameterf()** are the origin for gl_PointCoord (using GL_POINT_SPRITE_COORD_ORIGIN) the *point fade threshold* (using GL_POINT_FADE_THRESHOLD_SIZE). The point sprite coordinate origin controls whether gl_PointCoord.y increases from top down or bottom up in the fragment shader as points are rasterized. By default, the value of GL_POINT_SPRITE_COORD_ORIGIN is GL_UPPER_LEFT, meaning that it increases from top down. Note that this goes in the *opposite direction to window coordinates*, which have their origin in the lower right. By specifying GL_LOWER_LEFT for GL_POINT_SPRITE_COORD_ORIGIN you can make gl_PointCoord.y increase in the same direction as gl_FragCoord.y, which represents the fragment's window coordinate.

The other parameter that can be changed, GL_POINT_FADE_THRESHOLD controls how points (and point sprites) are antialiased. When the size of a point falls below this threshold, OpenGL has the option to stop performing true antialiasing and instead fade the point into the background using blending. The default value of this parameter is 1.0, which means that if a point whose size is less than 1.0 is rasterized, rather than only lighting a single sample within each fragment, it may light all the fragments in that sample but end up having its alpha component attenuated by the point *fade factor*, which is computed as follows:

$$fade = \begin{cases} 1 & \text{if } (derived\_size \geq threshold) \\ \left(\frac{derived\_size}{threshold}\right)^2 & \text{otherwise} \end{cases}$$

Rendering to Texture Maps

In addition to using framebuffer objects (as described in "Framebuffer Objects" on Page 180 in Chapter 4) for offscreen rendering, you can also use FBOs to update texture maps. You might do this to indicate changes in the texture for a surface (such as damage to a wall in a game) or to update values in a lookup table, if you're doing GPGPU-like computations. In these cases, you bind a level of a texture map as a framebuffer attachment. After rendering, the texture map can be detached from the framebuffer object, and used for subsequent rendering.

Note: Nothing prevents you from reading from a texture that is simultaneously bound as a framebuffer attachment for writing. In this scenario, called a framebuffer rendering loop, the results are undefined for both operations. That is, the values returned from sampling the bound texture map, as well as the values written into the texture level while bound, are undefined, and likely incorrect.

```
void glFramebufferTexture(GLenum target, GLenum attachment,
                          GLuint texture, GLint level);
void glFramebufferTexture1D(GLenum target,
                            GLenum attachment,
                            GLenum texturetarget,
                            GLuint texture, GLint level);
void glFramebufferTexture2D(GLenum target,
                            GLenum attachment,
                            GLenum texturetarget,
                            GLuint texture, GLint level);
void glFramebufferTexture3D(GLenum target,
                            GLenum attachment,
                            GLenum texturetarget,
                            GLuint texture, GLint level,
                            GLint layer);
```

The **glFramebufferTexture*** family of routines attaches levels of a texture map as a framebuffer attachment. **glFramebufferTexture()** attaches *level* of texture object *texture* (assuming *texture* is not zero) to *attachment*. **glFramebufferTexture1D()**, **glFramebufferTexture2D()**, and **glFramebufferTexture3D()** each attach a specified texture image of a texture object as a rendering attachment to a framebuffer object. *target* must be either GL_READ_FRAMEBUFFER, GL_DRAW_FRAMEBUFFER, or GL_FRAMEBUFFER (which is equivalent to GL_DRAW_FRAMEBUFFER). *attachment* must be one of the framebuffer attachment points: GL_COLOR_ATTACHMENT*i*, GL_DEPTH_ATTACHMENT, GL_STENCIL_ATTACHMENT, or GL_DEPTH_STENCIL_ATTACHMENT (in which case, the internal format of the texture must be GL_DEPTH_STENCIL). For **glFramebufferTexture1D()**, *texturetarget* must be GL_TEXTURE_1D, if *texture* is not zero. For **glFramebufferTexture2D()**, *texturetarget* must be GL_TEXTURE_2D, GL_TEXTURE_RECTANGLE, GL_TEXTURE_CUBE_MAP_POSITIVE_X, GL_TEXTURE_CUBE_MAP_POSITIVE_Y, GL_TEXTURE_CUBE_MAP_POSITIVE_Z, GL_TEXTURE_CUBE_MAP_NEGATIVE_X, GL_TEXTURE_CUBE_MAP_NEGATIVE_Y, GL_TEXTURE_CUBE_MAP_NEGATIVE_Z, and for **glFramebufferTexture3D()** *texturetarget* must be GL_TEXTURE_3D.

If *texture* is zero, indicating that any texture bound to *attachment* is released, no subsequent bind to *attachment* is made. In this case, *texturetarget*, *level*, and *layer* are ignored.

If *texture* is not zero, it must be the name of an existing texture object (created with **glGenTextures()**), with *texturetarget* matching the texture type (e.g., GL_TEXTURE_1D, etc.) associated with the texture object, or if *texture* is a cube map, then *texturetarget* must be one of the cube-map face targets, otherwise, a GL_INVALID_OPERATION error is generated.

level represents the mipmap level of the associated texture image to be attached as a render target, and for three-dimensional textures or two-dimensional texture arrays, *layer* represents the layer of the texture to be used. If *texturetarget* is GL_TEXTURE_RECTANGLE, or GL_TEXTURE_2D_MULTISAMPLE, then *level* must be zero.

Example 6.30   Attaching a Texture Level as a Framebuffer
                    Attachment: fbotexture.cpp

```cpp
GLsizei  TexWidth, TexHeight;
GLuint   framebuffer, texture;

void init() {
    GLuint renderbuffer;

    // Create an empty texture
    glGenTextures(1, &texture);
    glBindTexture(GL_TEXTURE_2D, texture);
    glTexImage2D(GL_TEXTURE_2D, 0, GL_RGBA8, TexWidth,
        TexHeight, 0, GL_RGBA, GL_UNSIGNED_BYTE, NULL);

    // Create a depth buffer for our framebuffer
    glGenRenderbuffers(1, &renderbuffer);
    glBindRenderbuffer(GL_RENDERBUFFER, renderbuffer);
    glRenderbufferStorage(GL_RENDERBUFFER, GL_DEPTH_COMPONENT24,
                          TexWidth, TexHeight);

    // Attach the texture and depth buffer to the framebuffer
    glGenFramebuffers(1, &framebuffer);
    glBindFramebuffer(GL_DRAW_FRAMEBUFFER, framebuffer);
    glFramebufferTexture2D(GL_DRAW_FRAMEBUFFER,
        GL_COLOR_ATTACHMENT0, GL_TEXTURE_2D, texture, 0);
    glFramebufferRenderbuffer(GL_DRAW_FRAMEBUFFER,
        GL_DEPTH_ATTACHMENT, GL_RENDERBUFFER, renderbuffer);
    glEnable(GL_DEPTH_TEST);
}

void
display()
{
    // Render into the renderbuffer
    glBindFramebuffer(GL_DRAW_FRAMEBUFFER, framebuffer);
    glViewport(0, 0, TexWidth, TexHeight);
    glClearColor(1.0, 0.0, 1.0, 1.0);
    glClear(GL_COLOR_BUFFER_BIT | GL_DEPTH_BUFFER_BIT);
    ...

    //Generate mipmaps of our texture
    glGenerateMipmap(GL_TEXTURE_2D);

    // Bind to the window-system framebuffer, unbinding from
    //  the texture, which we can use to texture other objects
    glBindFramebuffer(GL_FRAMEBUFFER, 0);
    glViewport(0, 0, windowWidth, windowHeight);
    glClearColor(0.0, 0.0, 1.0, 1.0);
    glClear(GL_COLOR_BUFFER_BIT | GL_DEPTH_BUFFER_BIT);

    // Render using the texture
    glEnable(GL_TEXTURE_2D);
    ...

    glutSwapBuffers();
}
```

For three-dimensional, or one- and two-dimensional texture arrays, you can also attach a single layer of the texture as a framebuffer attachment.

---

void **glFramebufferTextureLayer**(GLenum *target*,
                                   GLenum *attachment*,
                                   GLuint *texture*, GLint *level*,
                                   GLint *layer*);

Attaches a layer of a three-dimensional texture, or a one- or two-dimensional array texture as a framebuffer attachment, in a similar manner to **glFramebufferTexture3D()**.

target must be one of GL_READ_FRAMEBUFFER, GL_DRAW_FRAMEBUFFER, or GL_FRAMEBUFFER (which is equivalent to GL_DRAW_FRAMEBUFFER). *attachment* must be one of GL_COLOR_ATTACHMENT*i*, GL_DEPTH_ATTACHMENT, GL_STENCIL_ATTACHMENT, or GL_DEPTH_STENCIL_ATTACHMENT.

texture must be either zero, indicating that the current binding for the attachment should be released, or a texture object name (as returned from **glGenTextures()**). *level* indicates the mipmap level of the texture object, and layer represents which layer of the texture (or array element) should be bound as an attachment.

Discarding Rendered Data

Advanced

As a rule of thumb, you should always clear the framebuffer before you begin rendering a frame. Modern GPUs implement compression and other techniques to improve performance, memory bandwidth requirements, and so on. When you clear a framebuffer, the OpenGL implementation knows that it can discard any rendered data in the framebuffer and return it to a clean, compressed state if possible. However, what happens if you're sure that you're about to render over the whole framebuffer? It seems that clearing it would be a waste as you are about to draw all over the cleared area. If you are certain that you are going to completely replace the contents of the framebuffer with new rendering, you can *discard* it with a call to **glInvalidateFramebuffer()** or **glInvalidateSubFramebuffer()**. Their prototypes are as follows:

```
void glInvalidateFramebuffer(GLenum target,
                          GLsizei numAttachments,
                          const GLenum * attachments);
void glInvalidateSubFramebuffer(GLenum target,
                          GLsizei numAttachments,
                          const GLenum * attachments,
                          GLint x, GLint y, GLint width,
                          GLint height);
```

Instruct OpenGL that it may discard the contents of the specified framebuffer attachments within the region delimited by *x, y, width,* and *height*. **glInvalidateFramebuffer()** discards the entire contents of the specified attachments. The number of attachments is given by *numAttachments* and *attachments* is the address of an array of that many tokens. For the nondefault framebuffer, the tokens stored in the *attachments* arary must be selected from GL_DEPTH_ATTACHMENT, GL_STENCIL_ATTACHMENT, GL_DEPTH_STENCIL_ATTACHMENT, and GL_COLOR_ATTACHMENT*i* where *i* is the index of a color attachment.

Discarding the content of a framebuffer can be far more efficient than clearing it, depending on the OpenGL implementation. Furthermore, this can eliminate some expensive data copies in systems with more than one GPU. If, rather than discarding the content of the attachments of a framebuffer object you wish to discard the content of a texture directly, you can call **glInvalidateTexImage()** or **glInvalidateTexSubImage()**. The prototypes for **glInvalidateTexImage()** and **glInvalidateTexSubImage()** are as follows:

```
void glInvalidateTexImage(GLuint texture, GLint level);
void glInvalidateTexSubImage(GLuint texture, GLint level,
                          GLint xoffset, GLint yoffset,
                          GLint zoffset, GLint width,
                          GLint height, GLint depth);
```

Instruct OpenGL that it may discard the contents of the specified *level* of the texture whose name is given in *texture*. **glInvalidateTexImage()** discards the entire image level of the texture object, whereas **glInvalidateTexSubImage()** discards only the region encompassed by the *width* by *height* by *depth* region whose origin is given by *xoffset*, *yoffset*, and *zoffset*.

Chapter Summary

In this chapter, we have given an overview of texturing in OpenGL. Applications of textures in computer graphics are wide ranging and surprisingly complex. The best that can be done in a single chapter of a book is to scratch the surface and hopefully convey to the reader the depth and usefulness of textures. Entire books could be written on advanced uses of textures. More information about textures can be found in subsequent chapters—including examples of how to draw into textures, use buffer textures, and store nonimage data in textures.

Texture Redux

To use a texture in your program:

- Create a texture by
    - Reserving a name for a texture using **glGenTextures()**.
    - How about: Binding its name to the appropriate binding point using **glBindTexture()**.
    - Specifying the dimensions and format of the texture using **glTexStorage2D()** or the appropriate function for the specified texture target.
    - Placing data into the texture using **glTexSubImage2D()**, or the appropriate function for the specified texture target.
- Access the texture in your shader by
    - Declaring a uniform sampler in your shader to represent the texture.
    - Associating the sampler with the desired texture unit using **glUniform1i()**.
    - Binding the texture object and optionally a sampler object to the correct texture unit.
    - Reading from the texture in the shader using `texture` or one of other the built-in texture functions.

To use a buffer object as a texture:

- Create a buffer texture by
    - Generating a texture name using **glGenTextures()**.
    - Binding that name to the GL_TEXTURE_BUFFER texture target.
- Create and initialize a buffer texture by
    - Generating a buffer name using **glGenBuffers()**.

- Binding the buffer to a target, preferably the GL_TEXTURE_BUFFER target.
- Defining the storage for the buffer object using **glBufferData()**.
- Attach the buffer object's data store to the texture by
  - Binding the texture to the GL_TEXTURE_BUFFER target and,
  - Calling **glTexBuffer()** with the name of the initialized buffer object.

Texture Best Practices

Here are some tips to ensure that you allow OpenGL to use your textures most efficiently, ensuring the best possible performance for your application. Some common pitfalls are enumerated here with some advice on how to avoid them.

Immutable Texture Storage

Use immutable texture storage for textures wherever possible. Immutable storage for textures is created using the **glTexStorage2D()** function or the appropriate one for your chosen texture target. Mutable storage is created by calling **glTexImage2D()**. When a texture is marked as immutable, the OpenGL implementation can make certain assumptions about the validity of a texture object. For example, the texture will always be *complete*.

Mipmaps

Create and initialize the mipmap chain for textures unless you have a good reason not to. Allowing the graphics hardware to use a lower resolution mipmap when it needs to will not only improve the image quality of your program's rendering, but it will also make more efficient use of the caches in the graphics processor. The texture cache is a small piece of memory that is used to store recently accessed texture data. The smaller the textures your application uses, the more of them will fit into the cache, and the faster your application will run.

Integer Format Textures

Don't forget to use an integer sampler (`isampler2D`, `usampler3D`, etc.) in your shader when your texture data is an unnormalized integer and you intend to use the integer values it contains directly in the shader. A common mistake is to create a floating-point sampler and use an integer internal format for the sampler, such as GL_RED_INTEGER. In this case, you may get undesired or even undefined results.

Chapter 7

Light and Shadow

Chapter Objectives

After reading this chapter, you'll be able to do the following:

- Code a spectrum of fragment shaders to light surfaces with ambient, diffuse, and specular lighting from multiple light sources.

- Migrate lighting code between fragment and vertex shaders, based on quality and performance trade-offs.

- Use a single shader to apply a collection of lights to a variety of materials.

- Select from a variety of alternative lighting models.

- Have the objects in your scene cast shadows onto other objects.

In the real world, we see things because they reflect light from a light source or because they are light sources themselves. In computer graphics, just as in real life, we won't be able to see an object unless it is illuminated by or emits light. We will explore how the OpenGL Shading Language can help us implement such models so that they can execute at interactive rates on programmable graphics hardware.

This chapter contains the following major sections:

- "Classic Lighting Model" shows lighting fundamentals, first based on doing light computations in a fragment shader, then in both the vertex and fragment shaders. This section also shows how to handle multiple lights and materials in a single shader.

- "Advanced Lighting Models" introduces a sampling of advanced methods for lighting a scene including hemisphere lighting, image-based lighting, and spherical harmonics. These can be layered on top of the classic lighting model to create hybrid models.

- "Shadow Mapping" shows a key technique for adding shadows to a scene.

Lighting Introduction

The programmability of OpenGL shaders allows virtually limitless possibilities for lighting a scene. Old-school fixed-functionality lighting models were comparatively constraining, lacking in some realism and in performance-quality trade-offs. Programmable shaders can provide far superior results, especially in the area of realism. Nevertheless, it is still important to start with an understanding of the classic lighting model that was embodied by old fixed functionality, though we will be more flexible on which shader stages do which part. This lighting model still provides the fundamentals on which most rasterization lighting techniques are based, and is a springboard for grasping the more advanced techniques.

In that light, we will first show a number of simple shaders that each perform some aspect of the classic lighting model, with the goal being that you may pick and choose the techniques you want in your scene, combine them, and incorporate them into your shaders. Viewing transformations and other aspects of rendering are absent from these shaders so that we may focus just on lighting.

In the later examples in this chapter, we explore a variety of more complex shaders that provide more flexible results. But even with these more flexible shaders, we are limited only by our imaginations. Keep exploring new lighting methods on your own.

Classic Lighting Model

The classic lighting model adds up a set of independently computed lighting components to get a total lighting effect for a particular spot on a material surface. These components are *ambient, diffuse,* and *specular.* Each is described below, and Figure 7.1 shows them visually.

Figure 7.1   Elements of the classic lighting model
(Ambient (top left) plus diffuse (top right) plus specular (bottom) light adding to an overall realistic effect.)

Ambient light is light not coming from any specific direction. The classic lighting model considers it a constant throughout the scene, forming a decent first approximation to the scattered light present in a scene. Computing it does not involve any analysis of the direction of light sources or the direction of the eye observing the scene. It could either be accumulated as a base contribution per light source or be pre-computed as a single global effect.

Diffuse light is light scattered by the surface equally in all directions for a particular light source. Diffuse light is responsible for being able to see a surface lit by a light even if the surface is not oriented to reflect the light source directly toward your eye. It doesn't matter which direction the eye is, but it does matter which direction the light is. It is brighter when the surface is more directly facing the light source, simply because that orientation collects more light than an oblique orientation. Diffuse light computation depends on the direction of the surface *normal* and the direction of the light source, but not the direction of the eye. It also depends on the color of the surface.

Specular highlighting is light reflected directly by the surface. This highlighting refers to how much the surface material acts like a mirror. A highly polished metal ball reflects a very sharp bright specular highlight, while a duller polish reflects a larger, dimmer specular highlight, and a cloth ball would reflect virtually none at all. The strength of this angle-specific effect is referred to as *shininess*. Computing specular highlights requires knowing how close the surface's orientation is to the needed direct reflection between the light source and the eye, hence it requires knowing the surface normal, the direction of the light source, and the direction of the eye. Specular highlights might or might not incorporate the color of the surface. As a first approximation, it is more realistic to *not* involve any surface color, making it purely reflective. The underlying color will be present anyway from the diffuse term, giving it the proper tinge.

Fragment Shaders for Different Light Styles

We'll next discuss how fragment shaders compute the ambient, diffuse, and speculative amounts for several types of light, including *directional* lighting, *point* lighting, and *spotlight* lighting. These will be complete with a vertex and fragment shader pair built up as we go from simplest to more complex. The later shaders may seem long, but if you start with the simplest and follow the incremental additions, it will be easy to understand.

Note: The comments in each example highlight the change or difference from the previous step, making it easy to look and identify the new concepts.

No Lighting

We'll start with the simplest lighting—no lighting! By this, we don't mean everything will be black, but rather that we'll just draw objects with color unmodulated by any lighting effects. This is inexpensive, occasionally useful, and is the base we'll build on. Unless your object is a perfect mirror, you'll need this color as the basis for upcoming lighting calculations; all lighting calculations will somehow *modulate* this base color. It is a simple matter to set a per-vertex color in the vertex shader that will be interpolated and displayed by the fragment shader, as shown in Example 7.1.

Example 7.1 Setting Final Color Values with No Lighting

```
---------------------- Vertex Shader -----------------------
// Vertex shader with no lighting

#version 330 core

uniform mat4 MVPMatrix; // model-view-projection transform

in vec4 VertexColor;    // sent from the application, includes alpha
in vec4 VertexPosition; // pre-transformed position

out vec4 Color;         // sent to the rasterizer for interpolation

void main()
{
    Color = VertexColor;
    gl_Position = MVPMatrix * VertexPosition;
}

---------------------- Fragment Shader ----------------------
// Fragment shader with no lighting

#version 330 core

in vec4 Color;       // interpolated between vertices

out vec4 FragColor;  // color result for this fragment

void main()
{
    FragColor = Color;
}
```

In the cases of texture mapping or procedural texturing, the base color will come from sending texture coordinates instead of a color, using those coordinates to manifest the color in the fragment shader. Or, if you set up material properties, the color will come from an indexed material lookup. Either way, we start with an unlit base color.

Ambient Light

The ambient light doesn't change across primitives, so we will pass it in from the application as a `uniform` variable.

It's a good time to mention that light itself has color, not just intensity. The color of the light interacts with the color of the surface being lit. This interaction of the surface color by the light color is modeled well by multiplication. Using 0.0 to represent black and 1.0 to represent full intensity enables multiplication to model expected interaction. This is demonstrated for ambient light in Example 7.2.

It is okay for light colors to go above 1.0 though, especially as we start adding up multiple sources of light. We will start now using the `min()` function to saturate the light at white. This is important if the output color is the final value for display in a framebuffer. However, if it is an intermediate result, skip the saturation step now, and save it for application to a final color when that time comes.

Example 7.2   Ambient Lighting

```
------------------------- Vertex Shader ----------------------------
// Vertex shader for ambient light

#version 330 core

uniform mat4 MVPMatrix;

in vec4 VertexColor;
in vec4 VertexPosition;

out vec4 Color;

void main()
{
    Color = VertexColor;
    gl_Position = MVPMatrix * VertexPosition;
}


------------------------- Fragment Shader --------------------------
// Fragment shader for global ambient lighting

#version 330 core

uniform vec4 Ambient; // sets lighting level, same across many vertices

in vec4 Color;

out vec4 FragColor;

void main()
{
    vec4 scatteredLight = Ambient; // this is the only light
    // modulate surface color with light, but saturate at white
    FragColor = min(Color * scatteredLight, vec4(1.0));
}
```

You probably have an alpha (fourth component) value in your color that you care about, and don't want it modified by lighting. So, unless you're after specific transparency effects, make sure your ambient color has as an alpha of 1.0, or just include only the *r*, *g*, and *b* components in the computation. For example, the two lines of code in the fragment shader could read

```
vec3 scatteredLight = vec3(Ambient); // this is the only light
vec3 rgb = min(Color.rgb * scatteredLight, vec3(1.0));
FragColor = vec4(rgb, Color.a);
```

which passes the `Color` alpha component straight through to the output `FragColor` alpha component, modifying only the *r*, *g*, and *b* components. We will generally do this in the subsequent examples.

A keen observer might notice that `scatteredLight` could have been multiplied by `Color` in the vertex shader instead of the fragment shader. For this case, the interpolated result would be the same. Since the vertex shader usually processes fewer vertices than the number of fragments processed by the fragment shader, it would probably run faster too. However, for many lighting techniques, the interpolated results will not be the same. Higher quality will be obtained by computing per fragment rather than per vertex. It is up to you to make this performance vs. quality trade-off, probably by experimenting with what is best for a particular situation. We will first show the computation in the fragment shader, and then discuss optimizations (approximations) that involve moving computations up into the vertex shader, or even to the application. Feel free to put them whereever is best for your situation.

Directional Light

If a light is far, far away, it can be approximated as having the same direction from every point on our surface. We refer to such a light as *directional*. Similarly, if a viewer is far, far away, the viewer (eye) can also be approximated as having the same direction from every point on our surface. These assumptions simplify the math, so the code to implement a directional light is simple and runs faster than the code for other types of lights. This type of light source is useful for mimicking the effects of a light source like the sun.

We'll start with the ambient light computation from the previous example, and add on the effects for diffuse scattering and specular highlighting. We compute these effects for each fragment of the surface we are lighting. Again, just like with ambient light, the directional light will have its own color and we will modulate the surface color with this light color for the diffuse scattering. The specular contribution will be computed separately to allow the specular highlights to be the color of the light source, not modulated by the color of the surface.

The scattered and reflected amounts we need to compute vary with the cosine of the angles involved. Two vectors in the same direction form an angle of 0° with a cosine of 1.0. This indicates a completely direct reflection. As the angle widens, the cosine moves toward 0.0, indicating less reflected light. Fortunately, if our vectors are normalized (having a length of 1.0), these cosines are computed with a simple dot product, as shown in Example 7.3. The surface normal will be interpolated between vertices, though it could also come from a texture map or an analytic computation. The far away light-source assumption lets us pass in the light direction as the `uniform` variable `LightDirection`. For a far-away light and eye, the specular highlights all peak for the same surface-normal direction. We compute this direction once in the application and pass it in through the `uniform` variable `HalfVector`. Then, cosines of this direction with the actual surface normal are used to start specular highlighting.

Shininess for specular highlighting is measured with an exponent used to sharpen the angular fall off from a direct reflection. Squaring a number less than 1.0 but near to 1.0 makes it closer to 0.0. Higher exponents sharpen the effect even more. That is, leaving only angles near 0°, whose cosine is near 1.0, with a final specular value near 1.0. The other angles decay quickly to a specular value of 0.0. Hence, we see the desired effect of a shiny spot on the surface. Overall, higher exponents dim the amount of computed reflection, so in practice you'll probably want to use either a brighter light color or an extra multiplication factor to compensate. We pass such defining specular values as `uniform` variables, because they are surface properties that are constant across the surface.

The only way either a diffuse reflection component or a specular reflection component can be present is if the angle between the light source direction and the surface normal is in the range $[-90.0°, 90.0°]$: a normal at 90° means the surface itself is edge on to the light. Tip it a bit further, and no light will hit it. As soon as the angle grows beyond 90°, the cosine goes below 0. We determine the angle by examining the variable `diffuse`. This is set to the greater of 0.0 and the cosine of the angle between the light source direction and the surface normal. If this value ends up being 0.0, the value that determines the amount of specular reflection is set to 0.0 as well. Recall we assume that the direction vectors and surface normal vector are normalized, so the dot product between them yields the cosine of the angle between them.

Example 7.3   Directional Light Source Lighting

```
--------------------------- Vertex Shader ---------------------------
// Vertex shader for a directional light computed in the fragment shader

#version 330 core

uniform mat4 MVPMatrix;
uniform mat3 NormalMatrix; // to transform normals, pre-perspective
```

```
in vec4 VertexColor;
in vec3 VertexNormal;        // we now need a surface normal
in vec4 VertexPosition;

out vec4 Color;
out vec3 Normal;             // interpolate the normalized surface normal

void main()
{
    Color = VertexColor;

    // transform the normal, without perspective, and normalize it
    Normal = normalize(NormalMatrix * VertexNormal);

    gl_Position = MVPMatrix * VertexPosition;
}

------------------------ Fragment Shader ---------------------------
// Fragment shader computing lighting for a directional light

#version 330 core

uniform vec3 Ambient;
uniform vec3 LightColor;
uniform vec3 LightDirection; // direction toward the light
uniform vec3 HalfVector;     // surface orientation for shiniest spots
uniform float Shininess;     // exponent for sharping highlights
uniform float Strength;      // extra factor to adjust shininess

in vec4 Color;
in vec3 Normal;       // surface normal, interpolated between vertices

out vec4 FragColor;

void main()
{
    // compute cosine of the directions, using dot products,
    // to see how much light would be reflected

    float diffuse = max(0.0, dot(Normal, LightDirection));
    float specular = max(0.0, dot(Normal, HalfVector));

    // surfaces facing away from the light (negative dot products)
    // won't be lit by the directional light
    if (diffuse == 0.0)
        specular = 0.0;
    else
        specular = pow(specular, Shininess);  // sharpen the highlight

    vec3 scatteredLight = Ambient + LightColor * diffuse;
    vec3 reflectedLight = LightColor * specular * Strength;
```

```
// don't modulate the underlying color with reflected light,
// only with scattered light

vec3 rgb = min(Color.rgb * scatteredLight + reflectedLight, vec3(1.0));
FragColor = vec4(rgb, Color.a);
}
```

A couple more notes about this example. First, in this example, we used a scalar Strength to allow independent adjustment of the brightness of the specular reflection relative to the scattered light. This could potentially be a separate light color, allowing per-channel (red, green, or blue) control, as will be done with material-properties a bit later in Example 7.9. Second, near the end of Example 7.3, it is easy for these lighting effects to add up to color components greater than 1.0. Again, usually, you'll want to keep the brightest final color to 1.0, so we use the min() function. Also note that we already took care to not get negative values, as in this example we caught that case when we found the surface facing away from the light, unable to reflect any of it. However, if negative values do come into play, you'll want to use the clamp() function to keep the color components in the range [0.0, 1.0]. Finally, some interesting starting values would be a Shininess of around 20 for a pretty tight specular reflection, with a Strength of around 10 to make it bright enough to stand out, and with Ambient colors around 0.2 and LightColor colors near 1.0. That should make something interesting and visible for a material with color near 1.0 as well, and then you can fine tune the effect you want from there.

Point Lights

Point lights mimic lights that are near the scene or within the scene, such as lamps or ceiling lights or street lights. There are two main differences between point lights and directional lights. First, with a point-light source, the direction of the light is different for each point on the surface, so cannot be represented by a uniform direction. Second, light received at the surface is expected to decrease as the surface gets farther and farther from the light.

This fading of reflected light based on increasing distance is called *attenuation*. Reality and physics will state that light attenuates as the square of the distance. However, this attenuation normally fades too fast, unless you are adding on light from all the scattering of surrounding objects and otherwise completely modeling everything physically happening with light. In the classic model, the ambient light helps fill in the gap from not doing a full modeling, and attenuating linearly fills it in some more. So, we will show an attenuation model that includes coefficients for constant, linear, and quadratic functions of the distance.

The additional calculations needed for a point light over a directional light show up in the first few lines of the fragment shader in Example 7.4. The first step is to compute the light direction vector from the surface to the light position. We then compute light distance by using the `length()` function. Next, we normalize the light direction vector so we can use it in a dot product to compute a proper cosine. We then compute the attenuation factor and the direction of maximum highlights. The remaining code is the same as for our directional-light shader except that the diffuse and specular terms are multiplied by the attenuation factor.

Example 7.4   Point-Light Source Lighting

```
------------------------- Vertex Shader ----------------------------
// Vertex shader for a point-light (local) source, with computation
// done in the fragment shader.

#version 330 core

uniform mat4 MVPMatrix;
uniform mat4 MVMatrix;      // now need the transform, minus perspective
uniform mat3 NormalMatrix;

in vec4 VertexColor;
in vec3 VertexNormal;
in vec4 VertexPosition;

out vec4 Color;
out vec3 Normal;
out vec4 Position;    // adding position, so we know where we are

void main()
{
    Color = VertexColor;
    Normal = normalize(NormalMatrix * VertexNormal);
    Position = MVMatrix * VertexPosition;     // pre-perspective space
    gl_Position = MVPMatrix * VertexPosition; // includes perspective
}

------------------------- Fragment Shader --------------------------
// Fragment shader computing a point-light (local) source lighting.

#version 330 core

uniform vec3 Ambient;
uniform vec3 LightColor;
uniform vec3 LightPosition;          // location of the light, eye space
uniform float Shininess;
uniform float Strength;

uniform vec3 EyeDirection;
uniform float ConstantAttenuation; // attenuation coefficients
```

```
uniform float LinearAttenuation;
uniform float QuadraticAttenuation;

in vec4 Color;
in vec3 Normal;
in vec4 Position;

out vec4 FragColor;

void main()
{
    // find the direction and distance of the light,
    // which changes fragment to fragment for a local light
    vec3 lightDirection = LightPosition - vec3(Position);
    float lightDistance = length(lightDirection);

    // normalize the light direction vector, so
    // that a dot products give cosines
    lightDirection = lightDirection / lightDistance;

    // model how much light is available for this fragment
    float attenuation = 1.0 /
                (ConstantAttenuation +
                    LinearAttenuation * lightDistance +
                QuadraticAttenuation * lightDistance * lightDistance);

    // the direction of maximum highlight also changes per fragment
    vec3 halfVector = normalize(lightDirection + EyeDirection);

    float diffuse = max(0.0, dot(Normal, lightDirection));
    float specular = max(0.0, dot(Normal, halfVector));

    if (diffuse == 0.0)
        specular = 0.0;
    else
        specular = pow(specular, Shininess) * Strength;

    vec3 scatteredLight = Ambient + LightColor * diffuse * attenuation;
    vec3 reflectedLight = LightColor * specular * attenuation;
    vec3 rgb = min(Color.rgb * scatteredLight + reflectedLight,
                    vec3(1.0));
    FragColor = vec4(rgb, Color.a);
}
```

Depending on what specific effects you are after, you can leave out one or two of the constant, linear, or quadratic terms. Or, you can attenuate the Ambient term. Attenuating ambient light will depend on whether you have a global ambient color, or per-light ambient colors, or both. It would be the per-light ambient colors for point lights that you'd want to attenuate. You could also put the constant attenuation in your Ambient and leave it out of the attenuation expression.

Spotlights

In stage and cinema, spotlights project a strong beam of light that illuminates a well-defined area. The illuminated area can be further shaped through the use of flaps or shutters on the sides of the light. OpenGL includes light attributes that simulate a simple type of spotlight. Whereas point lights are modeled as sending light equally in all directions, OpenGL models spotlights as restricted to producing a cone of light in a particular direction.

The direction to the spotlight is not the same as the focus direction of the cone from the spotlight, unless you are looking from the middle of the "spot" (Well, technically, they'd be opposite directions; nothing a minus sign can't clear up). Once again our friend the cosine, computed as a dot product, will tell us to what extent these two directions are in alignment. This is precisely what we need to know to deduce if we are inside or outside the cone of illumination. A real spotlight has an angle whose cosine is very near 1.0, so you might want to start with cosines around 0.99 to see an actual spot.

Just as with specular highlighting, we can sharpen (or not) the light falling within the cone by raising the cosine of the angle to higher powers. This allows control over how much the light fades as it gets near the edge of the cutoff.

The vertex shader and the first and last parts of our spotlight fragment shader (see Example 7.5) look the same as our point-light shader (shown earlier in Example 7.4). The differences occur in the middle of the shader. We take the dot product of the spotlight's focus direction with the light direction, and compare it to a pre-computed cosine cutoff value SpotCosCutoff to determine whether the position on the surface is inside or outside the spotlight. If it is outside, the spotlight attenuation is set to 0; otherwise, this value is raised to a power specified by SpotExponent. The resulting spotlight attenuation factor is multiplied by the previously computed attenuation factor to give the overall attenuation factor. The remaining lines of code are the same as they were for point lights.

Example 7.5   Spotlight Lighting

```
------------------------- Vertex Shader -------------------------
// Vertex shader for spotlight computed in the fragment shader

#version 330 core

uniform mat4 MVPMatrix;
uniform mat4 MVMatrix;
uniform mat3 NormalMatrix;
```

```
in vec4 VertexColor;
in vec3 VertexNormal;
in vec4 VertexPosition;

out vec4 Color;
out vec3 Normal;
out vec4 Position;

void main()
{
    Color = VertexColor;
    Normal = normalize(NormalMatrix * VertexNormal);
    Position = MVMatrix * VertexPosition;
    gl_Position = MVPMatrix * VertexPosition;
}

------------------------ Fragment Shader ----------------------------
// Fragment shader computing a spotlight's effect

#version 330 core

uniform vec3 Ambient;
uniform vec3 LightColor;
uniform vec3 LightPosition;
uniform float Shininess;
uniform float Strength;

uniform vec3 EyeDirection;
uniform float ConstantAttenuation;
uniform float LinearAttenuation;
uniform float QuadraticAttenuation;

uniform vec3 ConeDirection;        // adding spotlight attributes
uniform float SpotCosCutoff;       // how wide the spot is, as a cosine
uniform float SpotExponent;        // control light fall-off in the spot

in vec4 Color;
in vec3 Normal;
in vec4 Position;

out vec4 FragColor;

void main()
{
    vec3 lightDirection = LightPosition - vec3(Position);
    float lightDistance = length(lightDirection);
    lightDirection = lightDirection / lightDistance;

    float attenuation = 1.0 /
                (ConstantAttenuation +
                    LinearAttenuation * lightDistance +
                QuadraticAttenuation * lightDistance * lightDistance);
```

```
// how close are we to being in the spot?
float spotCos = dot(lightDirection, -ConeDirection);

// attenuate more, based on spot-relative position
if (spotCos < SpotCosCutoff)
    attenuation = 0.0;
else
    attenuation *= pow(spotCos, SpotExponent);

vec3 halfVector = normalize(lightDirection + EyeDirection);

float diffuse = max(0.0, dot(Normal, lightDirection));
float specular = max(0.0, dot(Normal, halfVector));

if (diffuse == 0.0)
    specular = 0.0;
else
    specular = pow(specular, Shininess) * Strength;

vec3 scatteredLight = Ambient + LightColor * diffuse * attenuation;
vec3 reflectedLight = LightColor * specular * attenuation;
vec3 rgb = min(Color.rgb * scatteredLight + reflectedLight,
               vec3(1.0));
FragColor = vec4(rgb, Color.a);
}
```

Moving Calculations to the Vertex Shader

We've been doing all these calculations per fragment. For example, Position is interpolated and then the lightDistance is computed per fragment. This gives pretty high-quality lighting, at the cost of doing an expensive square-root computation (hidden in the length() built-in function) per fragment. Sometimes, we can swap these steps: perform the light distance calculation per vertex in the vertex shader and interpolate the result. That is, rather than interpolating all the terms in the calculation and calculating per fragment, calculate per vertex and interpolate the result. The fragment shader then gets the result as an input and directly uses it.

Interpolating vectors between two normalized vectors (vectors of length 1.0) does not typically yield normalized vectors. (It's easy to imagine two vectors pointing notably different directions; the vector that's the average of them comes out quite a bit shorter.) However, when the two vectors are nearly the same, the interpolated vectors between them all have length quite close to 1.0. Close enough, in fact, to finish doing decent lighting calculations in the fragment shader. So, there is a balance between having vertices far enough apart that you can improve performance by computing in the vertex shader, but not too far apart that the lighting vectors (surface normal, light direction, etc.) point in notably different directions.

Example 7.6 goes back to the point-light code (from Example 7.4) and moves some lighting calculations to the vertex shader.

Example 7.6   Point-light Source Lighting in the Vertex Shader

```
------------------------- Vertex Shader --------------------------
// Vertex shader pulling point-light calculations up from the
// fragment shader.

#version 330 core

uniform mat4 MVPMatrix;
uniform mat3 NormalMatrix;

uniform vec3 LightPosition;    // consume in the vertex shader now
uniform vec3 EyeDirection;
uniform float ConstantAttenuation;
uniform float LinearAttenuation;
uniform float QuadraticAttenuation;

in vec4 VertexColor;
in vec3 VertexNormal;
in vec4 VertexPosition;

out vec4 Color;
out vec3 Normal;
// out vec4 Position; // no longer need to interpolate this

out vec3 LightDirection;    // send the results instead
out vec3 HalfVector;
out float Attenuation;

void main()
{
    Color = VertexColor;
    Normal = normalize(NormalMatrix * VertexNormal);

    // Compute these in the vertex shader instead of the fragment shader

    LightDirection = LightPosition - vec3(VertexPosition);
    float lightDistance = length(LightDirection);

    LightDirection = LightDirection / lightDistance;

    Attenuation = 1.0 /
                (ConstantAttenuation +
                    LinearAttenuation * lightDistance +
                QuadraticAttenuation * lightDistance * lightDistance);

    HalfVector = normalize(LightDirection + EyeDirection);
```

```
        gl_Position = MVPMatrix * VertexPosition;
}


------------------------- Fragment Shader -------------------------
// Fragment shader with point-light calculations done in vertex shader

#version 330 core

uniform vec3 Ambient;
uniform vec3 LightColor;
// uniform vec3 LightPosition; // no longer need this
uniform float Shininess;
uniform float Strength;

in vec4 Color;
in vec3 Normal;
// in vec4 Position;        // no longer need this

in vec3 LightDirection;      // get these from vertex shader instead
in vec3 HalfVector;
in float Attenuation;

out vec4 FragColor;

void main()
{
    // LightDirection, HalfVector, and Attenuation are interpolated
    // now, from vertex shader calculations

    float diffuse = max(0.0, dot(Normal, LightDirection));
    float specular = max(0.0, dot(Normal, HalfVector));

    if (diffuse == 0.0)
        specular = 0.0;
    else
        specular = pow(specular, Shininess) * Strength;

    vec3 scatteredLight = Ambient + LightColor * diffuse * Attenuation;
    vec3 reflectedLight = LightColor * specular * Attenuation;
    vec3 rgb = min(Color.rgb * scatteredLight + reflectedLight,
                vec3(1.0));
    FragColor = vec4(rgb, Color.a);
}
```

There are no rules about where to do each calculation. Pick one, or experiment to find what is best for your surfaces.

In the extreme, the color can be completely computed in the vertex shader, just at the vertex, and then interpolated. The fragment shader then has little to no lighting computation left to do. This is the essence of *Gouraud shading*. While cheap from a computational perspective, it leaves lighting artifacts that betray a surface's tessellation to the viewer. This is especially obvious for coarse tessellations and specular highlights.

When surface normals are interpolated and then consumed in the fragment shader, we get variants of *Phong shading*. This is not to be confused with the *Phong reflection model*, which is essentially what this entire section on classic lighting has been describing.

Multiple Lights and Materials

Typically, a scene has many light sources and many surface materials. Normally, you shade one material at a time, but many lights will light that material. We'll show a shading model where each invocation of the shader selects a material and then applies all of, or a subset of, the lights to light it.

Multiple Lights

Normally, we need to light with multiple lights, while we've been writing example shaders for just one. A scene might have a street light, a flashlight, and the moon, for example, with each surface fragment getting a share of light from all three. You'd likely model these three lights as a point light, a spotlight, and a directional light, respectively, and have a single shader invocation perform all three.

Group a light's characteristics into structure, as shown in Example 7.7, and then create an array of them for the shader to process.

Example 7.7   Structure for Holding Light Properties

```
// Structure for holding light properties

struct LightProperties {
    bool isEnabled;    // true to apply this light in this invocation
    bool isLocal;      // true for a point light or a spotlight,
                       // false for a positional light
    bool isSpot;       // true if the light is a spotlight
    vec3 ambient;      // light's contribution to ambient light
    vec3 color;        // color of light
    vec3 position;     // location of light, if is Local is true,
                       // otherwise the direction toward the light
    vec3 halfVector;   // direction of highlights for directional light
    vec3 coneDirection;        // spotlight attributes
    float spotCosCutoff;
    float spotExponent;
    float constantAttenuation; // local light attenuation coefficients
    float linearAttenuation;
    float quadraticAttenuation;
    // other properties you may desire
};
```

In this example, we are using a couple of Booleans, `isLocal` and `isSpot` to select what kind of light is represented. If you end up with lots of different light types to choose from, this would be better done as an `int` going through a switch statement.

This structure also includes an ambient color contribution. Earlier, we used a global `Ambient` assumed to represent all ambient light, but we can also have each light making its own contribution. For directional lights, it doesn't make any difference, but for local lights it helps to have their ambient contribution attenuated. You could also add separate diffuse and specular colors to get richer effects.

The first member, `isEnabled`, can be used to selectively turn lights on and off. If a light were truly off while rendering a whole scene, it would be faster to not include it in the set of lights to begin with. However, sometimes we want one surface lit with a different subset of lights than another, and so might be enabling and disabling a light at a faster rate. Depending on how frequently you enable/disable, it might be better as a separate array, or even as a per-vertex input.

All the pieces are put together in Example 7.8. We now need all the lighting forms together in a single shader, so we can loop over different kinds of lights and do the right calculations for each one. It is based on the shaders that did all lighting in the fragment shader, but again, performance/quality trade-offs can be made by moving some of it into the vertex shader.

Example 7.8   Multiple Mixed Light Sources

```
-------------------------- Vertex Shader ----------------------------
// Vertex shader for multiple lights stays the same with all lighting
// done in the fragment shader.

#version 330 core

uniform mat4 MVPMatrix;
uniform mat4 MVMatrix;
uniform mat3 NormalMatrix;

in vec4 VertexColor;
in vec3 VertexNormal;
in vec4 VertexPosition;

out vec4 Color;
out vec3 Normal;
out vec4 Position;

void main()
{
    Color = VertexColor;
    Normal = normalize(NormalMatrix * VertexNormal);
```

```
        Position = MVMatrix * VertexPosition;
        gl_Position = MVPMatrix * VertexPosition;
}

------------------------ Fragment Shader ----------------------------
// Fragment shader for multiple lights.

#version 330 core

struct LightProperties {
    bool isEnabled;
    bool isLocal;
    bool isSpot;
    vec3 ambient;
    vec3 color;
    vec3 position;
    vec3 halfVector;
    vec3 coneDirection;
    float spotCosCutoff;
    float spotExponent;
    float constantAttenuation;
    float linearAttenuation;
    float quadraticAttenuation;
};

// the set of lights to apply, per invocation of this shader
const int MaxLights = 10;
uniform LightProperties Lights[MaxLights];

uniform float Shininess;
uniform float Strength;
uniform vec3 EyeDirection;

in vec4 Color;
in vec3 Normal;
in vec4 Position;

out vec4 FragColor;

void main()
{
    vec3 scatteredLight = vec3(0.0); // or, to a global ambient light
    vec3 reflectedLight = vec3(0.0);

    // loop over all the lights
    for (int light = 0; light < MaxLights; ++light) {
        if (! Lights[light].isEnabled)
            continue;

        vec3 halfVector;
        vec3 lightDirection = Lights[light].position;
        float attenuation = 1.0;

        // for local lights, compute per-fragment direction,
        // halfVector, and attenuation
```

```
if (Lights[light].isLocal) {
    lightDirection = lightDirection - vec3(Position);
    float lightDistance = length(lightDirection);
    lightDirection = lightDirection / lightDistance;

    attenuation = 1.0 /
        (Lights[light].constantAttenuation
         + Lights[light].linearAttenuation    * lightDistance
         + Lights[light].quadraticAttenuation * lightDistance
                                              * lightDistance);

    if (Lights[light].isSpot) {
        float spotCos = dot(lightDirection,
                            -Lights[light].coneDirection);
        if (spotCos < Lights[light].spotCosCutoff)
            attenuation = 0.0;
        else
            attenuation *= pow(spotCos,
                               Lights[light].spotExponent);
    }

    halfVector = normalize(lightDirection + EyeDirection);
} else {
    halfVector = Lights[light].halfVector;
}

float diffuse = max(0.0, dot(Normal, lightDirection));
float specular = max(0.0, dot(Normal, halfVector));

if (diffuse == 0.0)
    specular = 0.0;
else
    specular = pow(specular, Shininess) * Strength;

// Accumulate all the lights' effects
scatteredLight += Lights[light].ambient * attenuation +
                  Lights[light].color * diffuse * attenuation;
reflectedLight += Lights[light].color * specular * attenuation;
}

vec3 rgb = min(Color.rgb * scatteredLight + reflectedLight,
               vec3(1.0));
FragColor = vec4(rgb, Color.a);
}
```

Material Properties

One material property we came across above was shininess. We use
shininess to control how sharply defined specular highlights are. Different
materials have differently sized specular highlights, and seeing this is key
to your viewer recognizing a material once rendered on the screen. We can
also have material-specific modulation of the color of ambient, diffuse,
and specular lighting. This is an easy new addition to our computations:

Some metals and clothes display cool-looking properties as having different underlying colors for scattered light and reflected light. It's your choice how many of these independent colors you mix together for the effect you want to create. For example, in the method below, setting the material's `specular` value to $(1.0, 1.0, 1.0, 1.0)$ would make the model degenerate to the model used in the examples above.

Materials can also have their own real or apparent light source. For example, something glowing will emit its own light. This light could easily include colors not present in the any of the light sources; so light won't be visible unless it is added on the light calculation we've done so far.

It is natural to use a structure to store a material's properties, as shown in Example 7.9.

Example 7.9   Structure to Hold Material Properties

```
struct MaterialProperties {
    vec3 emission;    // light produced by the material
    vec3 ambient;     // what part of ambient light is reflected
    vec3 diffuse;     // what part of diffuse light is scattered
    vec3 specular;    // what part of specular light is scattered
    float shininess;  // exponent for sharpening specular reflection
    // other properties you may desire
};
```

These material properties (and others you may wish to add) are not specific to surface location; so they can be passed into the shader as a `uniform` structure.

Scenes have multiple materials with different properties. If your application switches between materials frequently, consider using the same fragment shader to shade several different materials without having to change shaders or update uniforms. To do this, make an array of `MaterialProperties`, each element holding the description of a different material. Pass the material index into a vertex shader input, which it will pass on to the fragment shader. Then the fragment shader will index into the material array and render properly for that material. For example, see Example 7.10. We've modified snippets of the multilight shader to make a multilight–selected-material shader.

Example 7.10   Code Snippets for Using an Array of Material Properties

```
------------------------- Fragment Shader -------------------------
// Snippets of fragment shader selecting what material to shade
// with multiple lights.

#version 330 core
```

```
struct MaterialProperties {
    vec3 emission;
    vec3 ambient;
    vec3 diffuse;
    vec3 specular;
    float shininess;
};

// a set of materials to select between, per shader invocation
const int NumMaterials = 14;
uniform MaterialProperties Material[NumMaterials];

flat in int MatIndex; // input material index from vertex shader
.
.
.
void main()
{
    .
    .
    .
        // Accumulate all the lights' effects
        scatteredLight +=
                Lights[light].ambient * Material[MatIndex].ambient *
                attenuation +
                Lights[light].color * Material[MatIndex].diffuse *
                diffuse * attenuation;
        reflectedLight +=
                Lights[light].color * Material[MatIndex].specular *
                specular * attenuation;
    }

    vec3 rgb = min(Material[MatIndex].emission
                    + Color.rgb * scatteredLight + reflectedLight,
                vec3(1.0));
    FragColor = vec4(rgb, Color.a);
}
```

Two-Sided Lighting

You might want to render a surface differently if the eye is looking at the
"back" of the surface than if looking at the front of the surface. OpenGL
Shading Language has a built-in Boolean variable gl_FrontFacing
allowing you to do so. The gl_FrontFacing variable is set for each
fragment to true if the fragment is part of a front-facing primitive; the
gl_FrontFacing variable is set to false otherwise. It is only available in
fragment shaders.

If the backs have properties quite different than the fronts, just make two
sets of MaterialProperties, as in Example 7.11. There are lots of ways

to do this. Here we chose to double the array and use even indexes for the front and odd indexes for the back. This is likely faster than having two separate arrays. If the properties are extensive and mostly the same, it might be more efficient to just expand `MaterialProperties` with the one or two differing properties.

Example 7.11   Front and Back Material Properties

```
struct MaterialProperties {
    vec3 emission;
    vec3 ambient;
    vec3 diffuse;
    vec3 specular;
    float shininess;
};

// a set of materials to select between, per shader invocation
// use even indexes for front-facing surfaces and odd indexes
// for back facing
const int NumMaterials = 14;
uniform MaterialProperties Material[2 * NumMaterials];

flat in int MatIndex; // input material index from vertex shader
    .
    .
    .
void main()
{
    int mat;
    if (gl_FrontFacing)
        mat = MatIndex;
    else
        mat = MatIndex + 1;
        .
        .
        .
        // Accumulate all the lights' effects
        scatteredLight +=
                Lights[light].ambient * Material[mat].ambient *
                attenuation +
                Lights[light].color * Material[mat].diffuse *
                diffuse * attenuation;
        reflectedLight +=
                Lights[light].color * Material[mat].specular *
                specular * attenuation;
    }

    vec3 rgb = min(Material[mat].emission
                    + Color.rgb * scatteredLight + reflectedLight,
                vec3(1.0));
    FragColor = vec4(rgb, Color.a);
}
```

Lighting Coordinate Systems

To make any sense, all the normal, direction, and position coordinates used in a lighting calculation must come from the same coordinate system. If light-position coordinates come after model-view transforms but before perspective projection, so should the surface coordinates that will be compared against them. In this typical case, both are in eye space. That is, the eye is at $(0, 0, 0)$ looking in the negative z direction. This is a regular 3D-coordinate system, not the 4-component homogeneous space needed for perspective. (See the first block diagrams in Chapter 5, "Viewing Transformations, Clipping, and Feedback" to see where in the stack of transformations eye space resides.) This is why, in the examples above, we sent `Position` separately with its own transform and the types involved are `vec3` and `mat3` rather than `vec4` and `mat4`. Generally, we used eye space for all the directions and locations feeding light equations, while alongside, homogeneous coordinates were fed to the rasterizer.

OpenGL lighting calculations require knowing the eye direction in order to compute specular reflection terms. For eye space, the view direction is parallel to and in the direction of the $-z$ axis. In the examples above, we could have replaced the `EyeDirection` with the vector $(0, 0, 1)$, knowing our coordinates were in eye space. But for clarity and potential flexibility, we used a variable. This could be generalized a bit to allow a *local viewer*, much like we had local lights, rather than only directional lights. With a local viewer, specular highlights on multiple objects will tend toward the eye location rather than all being in the same parallel direction.

Limitations of the Classic Lighting Model

The classic lighting model works pretty well at what it tries to do: modeling the surface reflection properties, modeling each light, combining them together to modulate an underlying color, and getting a pretty realistic approximation of what color is scattered and reflected. Yet, there are some important things missing.

Shadows are a big item. We lit each surface as if it was the only surface present, with no other objects blocking the path of the lights to the surface. We will provide techniques for shadowing later in this chapter.

Another big missing item is accurate ambient lighting. If you look around a room, you won't see a constant level of ambient lighting. Corners, for example, are darker than other areas. As another example, consider a bright red ball resting near other objects. You'll probably see that the ambient light around the other objects has a reddish tint, created by the red ball. These nearby objects then reflect a redder ambient light than objects further from the ball. We look at some techniques for addressing this in "Advanced Lighting Models" on Page 384. Other techniques for adding in this realism, loosely referred to as *global illumination*, are outside the scope of this book.

A glowing object or very bright object might also have both a *halo* around it as well as *lens flare*. We used an *emission* value earlier to model a glowing object, but that effect is limited to the actual geometric extent of the object, whereas haloing and lens flare extend beyond the object. In real life, these effects are apparent not only when taking videos or photographs; the lens and fluid in our eye also make them occur. Multiple techniques have been developed for rendering this effect.

A textured surface usually is not perfectly smooth. The bumps on the surface must individually be affected by lighting, or the surface ends up looking artificially flat. *Bump mapping* techniques for doing this are described in Chapter 8, "Procedural Texturing".

Advanced Lighting Models

The classic lighting model lacks some realism. To generate more realistic images, we need to have more realistic models for illumination, shadows, and reflection than those we've discussed so far. In this section, we explore how OpenGL Shading Language can help us implement some of these models. Much has been written on the topic of lighting in computer graphics. We examine only a few methods now. Ideally, you'll be inspired to try implementing some others on your own.

Hemisphere Lighting

Earlier we looked carefully at the classic lighting model. However, this model has a number of flaws, and these flaws become more apparent as we strive for more realistic rendering effects. One problem is that objects in a scene do not typically receive all their illumination from a small number of specific light sources. Interreflections between objects often have noticeable and important contributions to objects in the scene. The traditional computer graphics illumination model attempts to account for this phenomena through an ambient light term. However, this ambient light term is usually applied equally across an object or an entire scene. The result is a flat and unrealistic look for areas of the scene that are not affected by direct illumination.

Another problem with the traditional illumination model is that light sources in real scenes are not point lights or even spotlights—they are area lights. Consider the indirect light coming in from the window and illuminating the floor and the long fluorescent light bulbs behind a rectangular translucent panel. For an even more common case, consider the illumination outdoors on a cloudy day. In this case, the entire visible hemisphere is acting like an area light source. In several presentations and tutorials, Chas Boyd, Dan Baker, and Philip Taylor of Microsoft described this situation as hemisphere lighting. Let's look at how we might create an OpenGL shader to simulate this type of lighting environment.

The idea behind hemisphere lighting is that we model the illumination as two hemispheres. The upper hemisphere represents the sky and the lower hemisphere represents the ground. A location on an object with a surface normal that points straight up gets all of its illumination from the upper hemisphere, and a location with a surface normal pointing straight down gets all of its illumination from the lower hemisphere (see Figure 7.2). By picking appropriate colors for the two hemispheres, we can make the sphere look as though locations with normals pointing up are illuminated and those with surface normals pointing down are in shadow.

To compute the illumination at any point on the surface, we compute the linear interpolation for the illumination received at that point:

$$Color = a \cdot SkyColor + (1 - a) \cdot GroundColor$$

where

$$a = 1.0 - (0.5 \cdot sin(\theta)) \text{ for } \theta \leq 90°,$$

$$a = 0.5 \cdot sin(\theta) \text{ for } \theta > 90°,$$

with θ being the angle between the surface normal and the north pole direction.

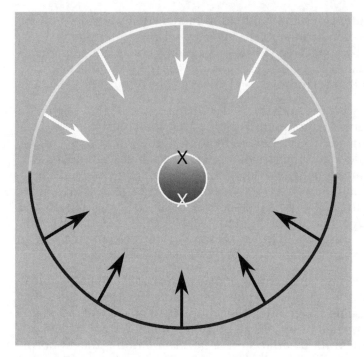

Figure 7.2   A sphere illuminated using the hemisphere lighting model

In Figure 7.2, a point on the top of the sphere (the black "x") receives illumination only from the upper hemisphere (i.e., the sky color). A point on the bottom of the sphere (the white "x") receives illumination only from the lower hemisphere (i.e., the ground color). A point right on the equator would receive half of its illumination from the upper hemisphere and half from the lower hemisphere (e.g., 50% sky color and 50% ground color).

But we can actually calculate a in another way that is simpler but roughly equivalent:

$$a = 0.5 + (0.5 \cdot cos(\theta))$$

This approach eliminates the need for a conditional. Furthermore, we can easily compute the cosine of the angle between two unit vectors by taking the dot product of the two vectors. This is an example of what Jim Blinn likes to call "the ancient Chinese art of Chi Ting." In computer graphics, if it looks good enough, it is good enough. It doesn't really matter whether your calculations are physically correct or a bit of a cheat. The difference between the two functions is shown in Figure 7.3. The shape of the two curves is similar. One is the mirror of the other, but the area under the curves is the same. This general equivalency is good enough for the effect we're after, and the shader is simpler and will execute faster as well.

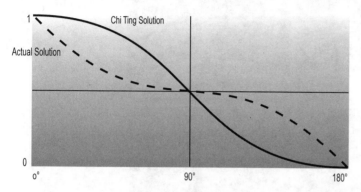

Figure 7.3   Analytic hemisphere lighting function
(Compares the actual analytic function for hemisphere lighting to a similar but higher-performance function.)

For the hemisphere shader, we need to pass in uniform variables for the sky color and the ground color. We can also consider the "north pole" to be our light position. If we pass this in as a uniform variable, we can light the model from different directions.

Example 7.12 shows a vertex shader that implements hemisphere lighting. As you can see, the shader is quite simple. The main purpose of the shader is to compute the diffuse color value and leave it in the user-defined out variable `Color`, as with the chapter's earlier examples. Results for this shader are shown in Figure 7.4. Compare the hemisphere lighting (D) with a single directional light source (A and B). Not only is the hemisphere shader simpler and more efficient, it produces a much more realistic lighting effect too! This lighting model can be used for tasks like model preview, where it is important to examine all the details of a model. It can also be used in conjunction with the traditional computer graphics illumination model. Point, directional, or spotlights can be added on top of the hemisphere lighting model to provide more illumination to important parts of the scene. And, as always, if you want to move some or all these computations to the fragment shader, you may do so.

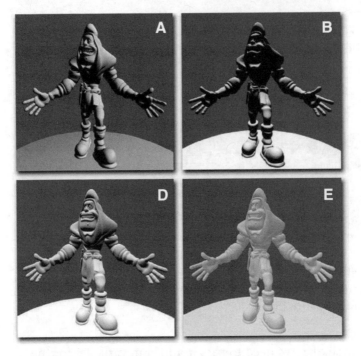

Figure 7.4 Lighting model comparison
(A comparison of some of the lighting models discussed in this chapter. The model uses a base color of white, $RGB = (1.0, 1.0, 1.0)$, to emphasize areas of light and shadow. (A) uses a directional light above and to the right of the model. (B) uses a directional light directly above the model. These two images illustrate the difficulties with the traditional lighting model. Detail is lost in areas of shadow. (D) illustrates hemisphere lighting. (E) illustrates spherical harmonic lighting using the Old Town Square coefficients. (3Dlabs, Inc.))

Example 7.12 Vertex Shader for Hemisphere Lighting

```
#version 330 core

uniform vec3 LightPosition;
uniform vec3 SkyColor;
uniform vec3 GroundColor;

uniform mat4 MVMatrix;
uniform mat4 MVPMatrix;
uniform mat3 NormalMatrix;

in vec4 VertexPosition;
in vec3 VertexNormal;
```

```
out vec3 Color;

void main()
{
    vec3 position = vec3(MVMatrix * VertexPosition);
    vec3 tnorm = normalize(NormalMatrix * VertexNormal);
    vec3 lightVec = normalize(LightPosition - position);
    float costheta = dot(tnorm, lightVec);
    float a = costheta * 0.5 + 0.5;
    Color = mix(GroundColor, SkyColor, a);
    gl_Position = MVPMatrix * VertexPosition;
}
```

One of the issues with this model is that it doesn't account for self-occlusion. Regions that should really be in shadow because of the geometry of the model will appear too bright. We will remedy this later.

Image-Based Lighting

If we're trying to achieve realistic lighting in a computer graphics scene, why not just use an environment map for the lighting? This approach to illumination is called *image-based lighting*; it has been popularized in recent years by researcher Paul Debevec at the University of Southern California. Churches and auditoriums may have dozens of light sources on the ceiling. Rooms with many windows also have complex lighting environments. It is often easier and much more efficient to sample the lighting in such environments and store the results in one or more environment maps than it is to simulate numerous individual light sources.

The steps involved in image-based lighting are as follows:

1. Use a *light probe* (e.g., a reflective sphere) to capture (e.g., photograph) the illumination that occurs in a real-world scene. The captured omnidirectional, high-dynamic range image is called a *light probe image*.

2. Use the light probe image to create a representation of the environment (e.g., an environment map).

3. Place the synthetic objects to be rendered inside the environment.

4. Render the synthetic objects by using the representation of the environment created in Step 2.

On his Web site (www.debevec.org), Debevec offers a number of useful things to developers. For one, he has made available a number of images that can be used as high-quality environment maps to provide realistic lighting in a scene. These images are high dynamic range (HDR) images that represent each color component with a 32-bit floating-point value. Such images can represent a much greater range of intensity values than can 8-bit-per-component images. For another, he makes available a tool called HDRShop that manipulates and transforms these environment maps. Through links to his various publications and tutorials, he also provides step-by-step instructions on creating your own environment maps and using them to add realistic lighting effects to computer graphics scenes.

Following Debevec's guidance, we purchased a 2-inch chrome steel ball from McMaster-Carr Supply Company (www.mcmaster.com). We used this ball to capture a light probe image from the center of the square outside our office building in downtown Fort Collins, Colorado, shown in Figure 7.5. We then used HDRShop to create a lat-long environment map, shown in Figure 7.6, and a cube map, shown in Figure 7.7. The cube map and lat-long map can be used to perform environment mapping. That shader simulated a surface with an underlying base color and diffuse reflection characteristics that was covered by a transparent mirror-like layer that reflected the environment flawlessly.

Figure 7.5   Light probe image
(A light-probe image of Old Town Square, Fort Collins, Colorado. (3Dlabs, Inc.))

Figure 7.6   Lat-long map
(An equirectangular (or lat-long) texture map of Old Town Square, Fort Collins, Colorado. (3Dlabs, Inc.))

Figure 7.7   Cube map
(A cube-map version of the Old Town Square light probe image. (3Dlabs, Inc.))

We can simulate other types of objects if we modify the environment maps before they are used. A point on the surface that reflects light in a diffuse fashion reflects light from all the light sources that are in the hemisphere in the direction of the surface normal at that point. We can't really afford to access the environment map a large number of times in our shader. What we can do instead is similar to what we discussed for hemisphere lighting. Starting from our light probe image, we can construct an environment map for diffuse lighting. Each texel in this environment map will contain the weighted average (i.e., the convolution) of other texels in the visible hemisphere as defined by the surface normal that would be used to access that texel in the environment.

Again, HDRShop has exactly what we need. We can use HDRShop to create a lat-long image from our original light probe image. We can then use a command built into HDRShop that performs the necessary convolution. This operation can be time consuming, because at each texel in the image, the contributions from half of the other texels in the image must be considered. Luckily, we don't need a very large image for this purpose. The effect is essentially the same as creating a very blurry image of the original light probe image. Since there is no high-frequency content in the computed image, a cube map with faces that are 64×64 or 128×128 works just fine.

A single texture access into this diffuse environment map provides us with the value needed for our diffuse reflection calculation. What about the specular contribution? A surface that is very shiny will reflect the illumination from a light source just like a mirror. A single point on the surface reflects a single point in the environment. For surfaces that are rougher, the highlight defocuses and spreads out. In this case, a single point on the surface reflects several points in the environment, though not the whole visible hemisphere like a diffuse surface. HDRShop lets us blur an environment map by providing a Phong exponent—a degree of shininess. A value of 1.0 convolves the environment map to simulate diffuse reflection, and a value of 50 or more convolves the environment map to simulate a somewhat shiny surface.

The shaders that implement these concepts end up being quite simple and quite fast. In the vertex shader, all that is needed is to compute the reflection direction at each vertex. This value and the surface normal are sent to the fragment shader as out variables. They are interpolated across each polygon, and the interpolated values are used in the fragment shader to access the two environment maps in order to obtain the diffuse and the specular components. The values obtained from the environment maps are combined with the object's base color to arrive at the final color for the fragment. The shaders are shown in Example 7.13. Examples of images created with this technique are shown in Figure 7.8.

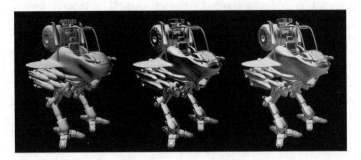

Figure 7.8   Effects of diffuse and specular environment maps
(A variety of effects using the Old Town Square diffuse and specular en-
vironment maps shown in Figure 7.6. Left: BaseColor set to $(1.0, 1.0, 1.0)$,
SpecularPercent is 0, and DiffusePercent is 1.0. Middle: BaseColor is set to
$(0, 0, 0)$, SpecularPercent is set to 1.0, and DiffusePercent is set to 0. Right:
BaseColor is set to $(0.35, 0.29, 0.09)$, SpecularPercent is set to 0.75, and Dif-
fusePercent is set to 0.5. (3Dlabs, Inc.))

Example 7.13   Shaders for Image-based Lighting

```
-------------------- Vertex Shader --------------------
// Vertex shader for image-based lighting

#version 330 core

uniform mat4 MVMatrix;
uniform mat4 MVPMatrix;
uniform mat3 NormalMatrix;

in vec4 VertexPosition;
in vec3 VertexNormal;

out vec3 ReflectDir;
out vec3 Normal;

void main()
{
    Normal = normalize(NormalMatrix * VertexNormal);
    vec4 pos = MVMatrix * VertexPosition;
    vec3 eyeDir = pos.xyz;
    ReflectDir = reflect(eyeDir, Normal);
    gl_Position = MVPMatrix * VertexPosition;
}

-------------------- Fragment Shader --------------------
// Fragment shader for image-based lighting

#version 330 core
```

```
uniform vec3 BaseColor;
uniform float SpecularPercent;
uniform float DiffusePercent;
uniform samplerCube SpecularEnvMap;
uniform samplerCube DiffuseEnvMap;

in vec3 ReflectDir;
in vec3 Normal;

out vec4 FragColor;

void main()
{
    // Look up environment map values in cube maps
    vec3 diffuseColor =
    vec3(texture(DiffuseEnvMap, normalize(Normal)));
    vec3 specularColor =
    vec3(texture(SpecularEnvMap, normalize(ReflectDir)));

    // Add lighting to base color and mix
    vec3color=mix(BaseColor,diffuseColor*BaseColor,DiffusePercent);
    color = mix(color, specularColor + color, SpecularPercent);
    FragColor = vec4(color, 1.0);
}
```

The environment maps that are used can reproduce the light from the whole scene. Of course, objects with different specular reflection properties require different specular environment maps. And producing these environment maps requires some manual effort and lengthy pre-processing. But the resulting quality and performance make image-based lighting a great choice in many situations.

Lighting with Spherical Harmonics

In 2001, Ravi Ramamoorthi and Pat Hanrahan presented a method that uses spherical harmonics for computing the diffuse lighting term. This method reproduces accurate diffuse reflection, based on the content of a light probe image, without accessing the light probe image at runtime. The light probe image is pre-processed to produce coefficients that are used in a mathematical representation of the image at runtime. The mathematics behind this approach is beyond the scope of this book. Instead, we lay the necessary groundwork for this shader by describing the underlying mathematics in an intuitive fashion. The result is remarkably simple, accurate, and realistic, and it can easily be codified in an OpenGL shader. This technique has already been used successfully to provide real-time illumination for games and has applications in computer vision and other areas as well.

Spherical harmonics provides a frequency space representation of an image over a sphere. It is analogous to the Fourier transform on the line or circle. This representation of the image is continuous and rotationally invariant. Using this representation for a light probe image, Ramamoorthi and Hanrahan showed that you could accurately reproduce the diffuse reflection from a surface with just nine spherical harmonic basis functions. These nine spherical harmonics are obtained with constant, linear, and quadratic polynomials of the normalized surface normal.

Intuitively, we can see that it is plausible to accurately simulate the diffuse reflection with a small number of basis functions in frequency space since diffuse reflection varies slowly across a surface. With just nine terms used, the average error over all surface orientations is less than 3 percent for any physical input lighting distribution. With Debevec's light probe images, the average error was shown to be less than 1 percent, and the maximum error for any pixel was less than 5 percent.

Each spherical harmonic basis function has a coefficient that depends on the light probe image being used. The coefficients are different for each color channel, so you can think of each coefficient as an RGB value. A pre-processing step is required to compute the nine RGB coefficients for the light probe image to be used. Ramamoorthi makes the code for this pre-processing step available for free on his Web site. We used this program to compute the coefficients for all the light probe images in Debevec's light probe gallery as well as the Old Town Square light probe image and summarized the results in Table 7.1.

Table 7.1   Spherical Harmonic Coefficients for Light Probe Images

Coefficient	Old Town square	Grace cathedral	Eucalyptus grove	St. Peter's basilica	Uffizi gallery
L_{00}	.87 .88 .86	.79 .44 .54	.38 .43 .45	.36 .26 .23	.32 .31 .35
$L_{1}m_{1}$	.18 .25 .31	.39 .35 .60	.29 .36 .41	.18 .14 .13	.37 .37 .43
L_{10}	.03 .04 .04	$-.34$ $-.18$ $-.27$	.04 .03 .01	$-.02$ $-.01$ .00	.00 .00 .00
L_{11}	$-.00$ $-.03$ $-.05$	$-.29$ $-.06$ .01	$-.10$ $-.10$ $-.09$	.03 .02 .00	$-.01$ $-.01$ $-.01$
$L_{2}m_{1}$	.00 .00 .01	$-.26$ $-.22$ $-.47$	.01 $-.01$ $-.05$	$-.05$ $-.03$ $-.01$	$-.01$ $-.01$ $-.01$
$L_{2}m_{2}$	$-.12$ $-.12$ $-.12$	$-.11$ $-.05$ $-.12$	$-.06$ $-.06$ $-.04$	.02 .01 .00	$-.02$ $-.02$ $-.03$
L_{20}	$-.03$ $-.02$ $-.02$	$-.16$ $-.09$ $-.15$	$-.09$ $-.13$ $-.15$	$-.09$ $-.08$ $-.07$	$-.28$ $-.28$ $-.32$
L_{21}	$-.08$ $-.09$ $-.09$	.56 .21 .14	$-.06$ $-.05$ $-.04$	.01 .00 .00	.00 .00 .00
L_{22}	$-.16$ $-.19$ $-.22$	.21 $-.05$ $-.30$	.02 .00 $-.05$	$-.08$ $-.03$ .00	$-.24$ $-.24$ $-.28$

Coefficient	Galileo's tomb	Vine street kitchen	Breezeway	Campus sunset	Funston Beach sunset
L_{00}	1.04 .76 .71	.64 .67 .73	.32 .36 .38	.79 .94 .98	.68 .69 .70
$L_{1}m_{1}$	.44 .34 .34	.28 .32 .33	.37 .41 .45	.44 .56 .70	.32 .37 .44
L_{10}	$-.22$ $-.18$ $-.17$	.42 .60 .77	$-.01$ $-.01$ $-.01$	$-.10$ $-.18$ $-.27$	$-.17$ $-.17$ $-.17$
L_{11}	.71 .54 .56	$-.05$ $-.04$ $-.02$	$-.10$ $-.12$ $-.12$	.45 .38 .20	$-.45$ $-.42$ $-.34$
$L_{2}m_{1}$	$-.12$ $-.09$ $-.08$	.25 .39 .53	$-.01$ $-.02$ .02	$-.14$ $-.22$ $-.31$	$-.08$ $-.09$ $-.10$
$L_{2}m_{2}$	.64 .50 .52	$-.10$ $-.08$ $-.05$	$-.13$ $-.15$ $-.17$	.18 .14 .05	$-.17$ $-.17$ $-.15$
L_{20}	$-.37$ $-.28$ $-.29$	.38 .54 .71	$-.07$ $-.08$ $-.09$	$-.39$ $-.40$ $-.36$	$-.03$ $-.02$ $-.01$
L_{21}	$-.17$ $-.13$ $-.13$	.06 .01 $-.02$	.02 .03 .03	.09 .07 .04	.16 .14 .10
L_{22}	.55 .42 .42	$-.03$ $-.02$ $-.03$	$-.29$ $-.32$ $-.36$	.67 .67 .52	.37 .31 .20

The formula for diffuse reflection using spherical harmonics is

$$\text{diffuse} = c_1 L_{22}(x^2 - y^2) + c_3 L_{20}z^2 + c_4 L_{00} - c_5 L_{20} + \qquad (7.1)$$
$$2c_1(L_{2}m_{2}xy + L_{21}xz + L_{2}m_{1}yz) + 2c_2(L_{11}x + L_{1}m_{1}y + L_{10}z)$$

The constants c_1–c_5 result from the derivation of this formula and are shown in the vertex shader code in Example 7.14. The L coefficients are the nine basis function coefficients computed for a specific light probe image in the pre-processing phase. The *x*, *y*, and *z* values are the coordinates of the normalized surface normal at the point that is to be shaded. Unlike low dynamic range images (e.g., 8 bits per color component) that have an implicit minimum value of 0 and an implicit maximum value of 255, HDR images represented with a floating-point value for each color component don't contain well-defined minimum and maximum values. The minimum and maximum values for two HDR images may be quite different from each other, unless the same calibration or creation process was used to create both images. It is even possible to have an HDR image that contains negative values. For this reason, the vertex shader contains an overall scaling factor to make the final effect look right.

The vertex shader that encodes the formula for the nine spherical harmonic basis functions is actually quite simple. When the compiler gets hold of it, it becomes simpler still. An optimizing compiler typically reduces all the operations involving constants. The resulting code is quite efficient because it contains a relatively small number of addition and multiplication operations that involve the components of the surface normal.

Example 7.14   Shaders for Spherical Harmonics Lighting

```
-------------------- Vertex Shader --------------------
// Vertex shader for computing spherical harmonics

#version 330 core

uniform mat4 MVMatrix;
uniform mat4 MVPMatrix;
uniform mat3 NormalMatrix;
uniform float ScaleFactor;

const float C1 = 0.429043;
const float C2 = 0.511664;
const float C3 = 0.743125;
const float C4 = 0.886227;
const float C5 = 0.247708;

// Constants for Old Town Square lighting
const vec3 L00  = vec3( 0.871297,  0.875222,  0.864470);
const vec3 L1m1 = vec3( 0.175058,  0.245335,  0.312891);
const vec3 L10  = vec3( 0.034675,  0.036107,  0.037362);
const vec3 L11  = vec3(-0.004629, -0.029448, -0.048028);
const vec3 L2m2 = vec3(-0.120535, -0.121160, -0.117507);
const vec3 L2m1 = vec3( 0.003242,  0.003624,  0.007511);
const vec3 L20  = vec3(-0.028667, -0.024926, -0.020998);
const vec3 L21  = vec3(-0.077539, -0.086325, -0.091591);
const vec3 L22  = vec3(-0.161784, -0.191783, -0.219152);
```

```glsl
in vec4 VertexPosition;
in vec3 VertexNormal;

out vec3 DiffuseColor;

void main()
{
    vec3 tnorm = normalize(NormalMatrix * VertexNormal);
    DiffuseColor = C1 * L22 *(tnorm.x * tnorm.x - tnorm.y * tnorm.y) +
                   C3 * L20 * tnorm.z * tnorm.z +
                   C4 * L00 -
                   C5 * L20 +
                   2.0 * C1 * L2m2 * tnorm.x * tnorm.y +
                   2.0 * C1 * L21 * tnorm.x * tnorm.z +
                   2.0 * C1 * L2m1 * tnorm.y * tnorm.z +
                   2.0 * C2 * L11 * tnorm.x +
                   2.0 * C2 * L1m1 * tnorm.y +
                   2.0 * C2 * L10 * tnorm.z;

    DiffuseColor *= ScaleFactor;

    gl_Position = MVPMatrix * VertexPosition;
}

------------------- Fragment Shader --------------------
// Fragment shader for lighting with spherical harmonics

#version 330 core

in vec3 DiffuseColor;

out vec4 FragColor;

void main()
{
    FragColor = vec4(DiffuseColor, 1.0);
}
```

Our fragment shader, shown in Example 7.14, has very little work to do. Because the diffuse reflection typically changes slowly, for scenes without large polygons we can reasonably compute it in the vertex shader and interpolate it during rasterization. As with hemispherical lighting, we can add procedurally defined point, directional, or spotlights on top of the spherical harmonics lighting to provide more illumination to important parts of the scene. Results of the spherical harmonics shader are shown in Figure 7.9. We could make the diffuse lighting from the spherical harmonics computation more subtle by blending it with the object's base color.

Figure 7.9   Spherical harmonics lighting
(Lighting using the coefficients from Table 7.1. From the left: Old Town Square, Grace Cathedral, Galileo's Tomb, Campus Sunset, and St. Peter's Basilica. (3Dlabs, Inc.))

The trade-offs in using image-based lighting versus procedurally defined lights are similar to the trade-offs between using stored textures versus procedural textures. Image-based lighting techniques can capture and re-create complex lighting environments relatively easily. It would be exceedingly difficult to simulate such an environment with a large number of procedural light sources. On the other hand, procedurally defined light sources do not use up texture memory and can easily be modified and animated.

Shadow Mapping

Recent advances in computer graphics have produced a plethora of techniques for rendering realistic lighting and shadows. OpenGL can be used to implement almost any of them. In this section, we will cover one technique known as *shadow mapping*, which uses a *depth texture* to determine whether a point is lit or not.

Shadow mapping is a multipass technique that uses depth textures to provide a solution to rendering shadows. A key pass is to view the scene from the shadow-casting light source rather than from the final viewpoint. By moving the viewpoint to the position of the light source, you will notice that everything seen from that location is lit—there are no shadows from the perspective of the light. By rendering the scene's depth from the point of view of the light into a depth buffer, we can obtain a map of the shadowed and unshadowed points in the scene—a *shadow map*. Those points visible to the light will be rendered, and those points hidden from the light (those in shadow) will be culled away by the depth test. The resulting depth buffer then contains the distance from the light to the closest point to the light for each pixel. It contains nothing for anything in shadow.

The condensed two-pass description is as follows:

- Render the scene from the point of view of the light source. It doesn't matter what the scene looks like; you only want the depth values. Create a shadow map by attaching a depth texture to a framebuffer object and rendering depth directly into it.

- Render the scene from the point of view of the viewer. Project the surface coordinates into the light's reference frame and compare their depths to the depth recorded into the light's depth texture. Fragments that are further from the light than the recorded depth value were not visible to the light, and hence in shadow.

The following sections provide a more detailed discussion, along with sample code illustrating each of the steps.

Creating a Shadow Map

The first step is to create a texture map of depth values as seen from the light's point of view. You create this by rendering the scene with the viewpoint located at the light's position. Before we can render depth into a depth texture, we need to create the depth texture and attach it to a framebuffer object. Example 7.15 shows how to do this. This code is included in the initialization sequence for the application.

Example 7.15 Creating a Framebuffer Object with a Depth Attachment

```
// Create a depth texture
glGenTextures(1, &depth_texture);
glBindTexture(GL_TEXTURE_2D, depth_texture);
// Allocate storage for the texture data
glTexImage2D(GL_TEXTURE_2D, 0, GL_DEPTH_COMPONENT32,
             DEPTH_TEXTURE_SIZE, DEPTH_TEXTURE_SIZE,
             0, GL_DEPTH_COMPONENT, GL_FLOAT, NULL);
// Set the default filtering modes
glTexParameteri(GL_TEXTURE_2D, GL_TEXTURE_MIN_FILTER, GL_LINEAR);
glTexParameteri(GL_TEXTURE_2D, GL_TEXTURE_MAG_FILTER, GL_LINEAR);
// Set up depth comparison mode
glTexParameteri(GL_TEXTURE_2D, GL_TEXTURE_COMPARE_MODE,
                GL_COMPARE_REF_TO_TEXTURE);
glTexParameteri(GL_TEXTURE_2D, GL_TEXTURE_COMPARE_FUNC, GL_LEQUAL);
// Set up wrapping modes
glTexParameteri(GL_TEXTURE_2D, GL_TEXTURE_WRAP_S, GL_CLAMP_TO_EDGE);
glTexParameteri(GL_TEXTURE_2D, GL_TEXTURE_WRAP_T, GL_CLAMP_TO_EDGE);
glBindTexture(GL_TEXTURE_2D, 0);

// Create FBO to render depth into
glGenFramebuffers(1, &depth_fbo);
glBindFramebuffer(GL_FRAMEBUFFER, depth_fbo);
```

```
// Attach the depth texture to it
glFramebufferTexture(GL_FRAMEBUFFER, GL_DEPTH_STENCIL_ATTACHMENT,
                     depth_texture, 0);
// Disable color rendering as there are no color attachments
glDrawBuffer(GL_NONE);
```

In Example 7.15, the depth texture is created and allocated using the GL_DEPTH_COMPONENT32 internal format. This creates a texture that is capable of being used as the depth buffer for rendering and as a texture that can be used later for reading from. Notice also how we set the *texture comparison mode*. This allows us to leverage *shadow textures*—a feature of OpenGL that allows the comparison between a reference value and a value stored in the texture to be performed by the texture hardware rather than explicitly in the shader. In the example, DEPTH_TEXTURE_SIZE has previously been defined to be the desired size for the shadow map. This should generally be at least as big as the default framebuffer (your OpenGL window); otherwise, aliasing and sampling artifacts could be present in the resulting images. However, making the depth texture unnecessarily large will waste lots of memory and bandwidth and adversely affect the performance of your program.

The next step is to render the scene from the point of view of the light. To do this, we create a view-transformation matrix for the light source using the provided lookat function. We also need to set the light's projection matrix. As world and eye coordinates for the light's viewpoint, we can multiply these matrices together to provide a single view-projection matrix. In this simple example we can also bake the scene's model matrix into the same matrix (providing a model-view-projection matrix to the light shader). The code to perform these steps is shown in Example 7.16.

Example 7.16   Setting up the Matrices for Shadow Map Generation

```
// Time varying light position
vec3 light_position = vec3(
    sinf(t * 6.0f * 3.141592f) * 300.0f,
    200.0f,
    cosf(t * 4.0f * 3.141592f) * 100.0f + 250.0f);

// Matrices for rendering the scene
mat4 scene_model_matrix = rotate(t * 720.0f, Y);

// Matrices used when rendering from the light's position
mat4 light_view_matrix = lookat(light_position, vec3(0.0f), Y);
mat4 light_projection_matrix(frustum(-1.0f, 1.0f, -1.0f, 1.0f,
                                     1.0f, FRUSTUM_DEPTH));

// Now we render from the light's position into the depth buffer.
// Select the appropriate program
glUseProgram(render_light_prog);
```

```
glUniformMatrix4fv(render_light_uniforms.MVPMatrix,
                   1, GL_FALSE,
                   light_projection_matrix *
                   light_view_matrix *
                   scene_model_matrix);
```

In Example 7.16, we set the light's position using a function of time (t) and point it towards the origin. This will cause the shadows to move around. FRUSTUM_DEPTH is set to the maximum depth over which the light will influence and represents the far plan of the light's frustum. The near plane is set to 1.0f, but ideally the ratio of far plane to near plane distance should be as small as possible (i.e., the near plane should be as far as possible from the light and the far plane should be as close as possible to the light) to maximize the precision of the depth buffer.

The shaders used to generate the depth buffer from the light's position are trivial. The vertex shader simply transforms the incoming position by the provided model-view-projection matrix. The fragment shader writes a constant into a dummy output and is only present because OpenGL requires it.[1] The vertex and fragment shaders used to render depth from the light's point of view are shown in Example 7.17.

Example 7.17   Simple Shader for Shadow Map Generation

```
------------------- Vertex Shader --------------------
// Vertex shader for shadow map generation

#version 330 core

uniform mat4 MVPMatrix;

layout (location = 0) in vec4 position;

void main(void)
{
    gl_Position = MVPMatrix * position;
}

------------------- Fragment Shader --------------------
// Fragment shader for shadow map generation

#version 330 core

layout (location = 0) out vec4 color;

void main(void)
{
    color = vec4(1.0);
}
```

---

1. The results of rasterization are undefined in OpenGL if no fragment shader is present. It is legal to have no fragment shader when rasterization is turned off, but here we *do* want to rasterize so that we can generate depth values for the scene.

At this point we are ready to render the scene into the depth texture we created earlier. We need to bind the framebuffer object with the depth texture attachment and set the viewport to the depth texture size. Then we clear the depth buffer (which is actually our depth texture now) and draw the scene. Example 7.18 contains the code to do this.

Example 7.18   Rendering the Scene From the Light's Point of View

```
// Bind the "depth only" FBO and set the viewport to the size
// of the depth texture
glBindFramebuffer(GL_FRAMEBUFFER, depth_fbo);
glViewport(0, 0, DEPTH_TEXTURE_SIZE, DEPTH_TEXTURE_SIZE);

// Clear
glClearDepth(1.0f);
glClear(GL_DEPTH_BUFFER_BIT);

// Enable polygon offset to resolve depth-fighting isuses
glEnable(GL_POLYGON_OFFSET_FILL);
glPolygonOffset(2.0f, 4.0f);
// Draw from the light's point of view
DrawScene(true);
glDisable(GL_POLYGON_OFFSET_FILL);
```

Notice that we're using *polygon offset* here. This pushes the generated depth values away from the viewer (the light, in this case) by a small amount. In this application, we want the depth test to be conservative, insofar as when there is doubt about whether a point is in shadow or not, we want to light it. If we did not do this, we would end up with *depth fighting* in the rendered image due to precision issues with the floating-point depth buffer. Figure 7.10 shows the resulting depth map of our scene as seen from the light's position.

Figure 7.10   Depth rendering
(Depths are rendered from the light's position. Within rendered objects, closer points have smaller depths and show up darker.)

Using a Shadow Map

Now that we have the depth for the scene rendered from the light's point of view we can render the scene with our regular shaders and use the resulting depth texture to produce shadows as part of our lighting calculations. This is where the meat of the algorithm is. First, we need to set up the matrices for rendering the scene from the viewer's position. The matrices we'll need are the *model matrix*, *view matrix* (which transforms vertices for classic lighting), and the *projection matrix* (which transforms coordinates to projective space for rasterization). Also, we'll need a *shadow matrix*. This matrix transforms world coordinates into the light's projective space and simultaneously applies a scale and bias to the resulting depth values. The transformation to the light's eye space is performed by transforming the world space vertex coordinates through the light's view matrix followed by the light's projection matrix (which we calculated earlier). The scale and bias matrix maps depth values in projection space (which lie between -1.0 and $+1.0$) into the range 0.0 to 1.0.

The code to set all these matrices up is given in Example 7.19.

Example 7.19   Matrix Calculations for Shadow Map Rendering

```
mat4 scene_model_matrix = rotate(t * 720.0f, Y);
mat4 scene_view_matrix = translate(0.0f, 0.0f, -300.0f);
mat4 scene_projection_matrix = frustum(-1.0f, 1.0f, -aspect, aspect,
                                        1.0f, FRUSTUM_DEPTH);
mat4 scale_bias_matrix = mat4(vec4(0.5f, 0.0f, 0.0f, 0.0f),
                              vec4(0.0f, 0.5f, 0.0f, 0.0f),
                              vec4(0.0f, 0.0f, 0.5f, 0.0f),
                              vec4(0.5f, 0.5f, 0.5f, 1.0f));
mat4 shadow_matrix = scale_bias_matrix *
                     light_projection_matrix *
                     light_view_matrix;
```

The vertex shader used for the final render transforms the incoming vertex coordinates through all of these matrices and provides world coordinates, eye coordinates, and *shadow coordinates* to the fragment shader, which will perform the actual lighting calculations. This vertex shader is given in Example 7.20.

Example 7.20   Vertex Shader for Rendering from Shadow Maps

```
#version 330 core

uniform mat4 model_matrix;
uniform mat4 view_matrix;
uniform mat4 projection_matrix;

uniform mat4 shadow_matrix;

layout (location = 0) in vec4 position;
layout (location = 1) in vec3 normal;

out VS_FS_INTERFACE
{
    vec4 shadow_coord;
    vec3 world_coord;
    vec3 eye_coord;
    vec3 normal;
} vertex;

void main(void)
{
    vec4 world_pos = model_matrix * position;
    vec4 eye_pos = view_matrix * world_pos;
    vec4 clip_pos = projection_matrix * eye_pos;

    vertex.world_coord = world_pos.xyz;
    vertex.eye_coord = eye_pos.xyz;
    vertex.shadow_coord = shadow_matrix * world_pos;
```

```
vertex.normal = mat3(view_matrix * model_matrix) * normal;

    gl_Position = clip_pos;
}
```

Finally, the fragment shader performs lighting calculations for the scene. If the point is considered to be illuminated by the light, the light's contribution is included in the final lighting calculation, otherwise only ambient light is applied. The shader given in Example 7.21 performs these calculations.

Example 7.21   Fragment Shader for Rendering from Shadow Maps

```
#version 330 core

uniform sampler2DShadow depth_texture;
uniform vec3 light_position;

uniform vec3 material_ambient;
uniform vec3 material_diffuse;
uniform vec3 material_specular;
uniform float material_specular_power;

layout (location = 0) out vec4 color;

in VS_FS_INTERFACE
{
    vec4 shadow_coord;
    vec3 world_coord;
    vec3 eye_coord;
    vec3 normal;
} fragment;

void main(void)
{
    vec3 N = fragment.normal;
    vec3 L = normalize(light_position - fragment.world_coord);
    vec3 R = reflect(-L, N);
    vec3 E = normalize(fragment.eye_coord);
    float NdotL = dot(N, L);
    float EdotR = dot(-E, R);

    float diffuse = max(NdotL, 0.0);
    float specular = max(pow(EdotR, material_specular_power), 0.0);

    float f = textureProj(depth_texture, fragment.shadow_coord);

    color = vec4(material_ambient +
                f * (material_diffuse * diffuse +
                    material_specular * specular), 1.0);
}
```

Don't worry about the complexity of the lighting calculations in this shader. The important part of the algorithm is the use of the `sampler2DShadow` sampler type and the `textureProj` function. The `sampler2DShadow` sampler is a special type of 2D texture that, when sampled, will return either 1.0 if the sampled texture satisfies the comparison test for the texture, and 0.0 if it does not. The texture comparison mode for the depth texture was set earlier in Example 7.15 by calling **glTexParameteri**() with the GL_TEXTURE_COMPARE_MODE parameter name and GL_COMPARE_REF_TO_TEXTURE parameter value. When the depth comparison mode for the texture is configured like this, the texel values will be compared against the reference value that is supplied in the third component of `fragment.shadow_coord`—which is the z component of the scaled and biased projective-space coordinate of the fragment as viewed from the light. The depth comparison function is set to GL_LEQUAL, which causes the test to pass if the reference value is less than or equal to the value in the texture. When multiple texels are sampled (e.g., when the texture mode is linear), the result of reading from the texture is the average of all the 0.0s and 1.0s for the samples making up the final texel. That is, near the edge of a shadow, the returned value might be 0.25, or 0.5, and so on, rather than just 0.0 or 1.0. We scale the lighting calculations by this result to take light visibility into account during shading.

The `textureProj` function is a *projective texturing* function. It divides the incoming texture coordinate (in this case `fragment.shadow_coord` by its own last component (`fragment.shadow_coord.w`) to transform it into normalized device coordinates, which is exactly what the perspective transformation performed by OpenGL before rasterization does.

The result of rendering our scene with this shader is shown in Figure 7.11.

Figure 7.11   Final rendering of shadow map

That wraps up *shadow mapping*. There are many other techniques, including enhancements to shadow mapping, and we encourage you to explore on your own.

Chapter 8

Procedural Texturing

Chapter Objectives

After reading this chapter, you'll be able to do the following:

- Texture a surface without using texture look-ups; instead texture a surface using a shader that computes the texture procedurally.

- Antialias a procedurally generated texture.

- Light a surface using a bump map.

- Use *noise* to modulate shapes and textures to get quite realistic surfaces and shapes.

- Generate your own *noise* texture map for storing multiple octaves of portable noise.

Generally, this chapter will cover using computation in shaders to supply quality versions of what might normally come from large texture maps, complex geometry, or expensive multisampling. However, accessing textures won't be forbidden. We'll still occasionally use them as side tables to drive the calculations performed in the shaders.

This chapter contains the following major sections:

- "Procedural Texturing" shows several techniques for using computation to create patterns, rather than accessing images stored in memory.

- "Bump Mapping" presents a key method to give the appearance of a bumpy surface without having to construct geometry to represent it.

- "Antialiasing Procedural Textures" explains how to compute amount of color for each pixel such that aliasing does not occur, especially for edges and patterns created procedurally.

- "Noise" will explain what noise is and how to use it to improve realism.

Procedural Texturing

The fact that we have a full-featured, high-level programming language to express the processing at each fragment means that we can algorithmically compute a pattern on an object's surface. We can use this freedom to create a wide variety of rendering effects that wouldn't be possible otherwise. We can also algorithmically compute the content of a volume from which a surface is cut away, as in a wood object made from a tree. This can lead to a result superior to texture mapping the surface.

In previous chapters, we discussed shaders that achieve their primary effect by reading values from texture memory. This chapter focuses on shaders that do interesting things primarily by means of an algorithm defined by the shader. The results from such a shader are synthesized according to the algorithm rather than being based primarily on precomputed values such as a digitized painting or photograph. This type of shader is sometimes called a *procedural texture shader*, and the process of applying such a shader is called *procedural texturing* or *procedural shading*. Often the texture coordinate or the object coordinate position at each point on the object is the only piece of information needed to shade the object with a shader that is entirely procedural.

In principle, procedural texture shaders can accomplish many of the same tasks as shaders that access stored textures. In practice, there are times when it is more convenient or feasible to use a procedural texture shader and times when it is more convenient or feasible to use a stored texture shader. When deciding whether to write a procedural texture shader or one that uses stored textures, keep in mind some of the main advantages of procedural texture shaders.

- Textures generated procedurally have very low memory requirements compared with stored textures. The only primary representation of the texture is in the algorithm defined by the code in the procedural texture shader. This representation is extremely compact compared with the size of stored 2D textures. Typically, it is a couple of orders of magnitude smaller (e.g., a few kilobytes for the code in a procedural shader versus a few hundred kilobytes or more for a high-quality 2D texture). This means procedural texture shaders require far less memory on the graphics accelerator. Procedural texture shaders have an even greater advantage when the desire is to have a 3D (solid) texture applied to an object (a few kilobytes versus tens of megabytes or more for a stored 3D texture).

- Textures generated by procedural texture shaders have no fixed area or resolution. They can be applied to objects of any scale with precise results because they are defined algorithmically rather than with sampled data, as in the case of stored textures. There are no decisions to be made about how to map a 2D image onto a 3D surface patch that is larger or smaller than the texture, and there are no seams or unwanted replication. As your viewpoint gets closer and closer to a surface rendered with a procedural texture shader, you won't see reduced detail or sampling artifacts like you might with a shader that uses a stored texture.

- Procedural texture shaders can be written to parameterize key aspects of the algorithm. These parameters can easily be changed, allowing a single shader to produce an interesting variety of effects. Very little can be done to alter the shape of the pattern in a stored texture after it has been created.

- When a volume is computed by a procedural texture, rather than a surface, surface cutaways of that volume can be far more realistic than any method of pasting a 2D texture onto the surface. And while a 3D texture could be used, getting high resolution with a 3D texture can take a prohibitive amount of memory.

Some of the disadvantages of using procedural shaders rather than stored textures are as follows:

- Procedural texture shaders require the algorithm to be encoded in a program. Not everyone has the technical skills needed to write such a program, whereas it is fairly straightforward to create a 2D or 3D texture with limited technical skills.

- Performing the algorithm embodied by a procedural texture shader at each location on an object can take longer than accessing a stored texture.

- Procedural texture shaders can have serious aliasing artifacts that can be difficult to overcome. Today's graphics hardware has built-in capabilities for antialiasing stored textures (e.g., filtering methods and mipmaps).

- Because of differences in arithmetic precision and differences in implementations of built-in functions such as noise, procedural texture shaders could produce somewhat different results on different platforms.

The ultimate choice of whether to use a procedural shader or a stored texture shader should be made pragmatically. Things that would be artwork in the real world (paintings, billboards, anything with writing, etc.) are good candidates for rendering with stored textures. Objects that are extremely important to the final "look" of the image (character faces, costumes, important props) can also be rendered with stored textures because this presents the easiest route for an artist to be involved. Things that are relatively unimportant to the final image and yet cover a lot of area are good candidates for rendering with a procedural shader (walls, floors, ground).

Often, a hybrid approach is the right answer. A golf ball might be rendered with a base color, a hand-painted texture map that contains scuff marks, a texture map containing a logo, and a procedurally generated dimple pattern. Stored textures can also control or constrain procedural effects. If our golf ball needs grass stains on certain parts of its surface and it is important to achieve and reproduce just the right look, an artist could paint a grayscale map that would direct the shader to locations where grass smudges should be applied on the surface (for instance, black portions of the grayscale map), and where they should not be applied (white portions of the grayscale map). The shader can read this *control texture* and use it to blend between a grass-smudged representation of the surface and a pristine surface.

All that said, let's turn our attention to a few examples of shaders that are entirely procedural.

Regular Patterns

For our first example, we construct a shader that renders stripes on an object. A variety of man-made objects can be rendered with such a shader: children's toys, wallpaper, wrapping paper, flags, fabrics, and so on.

The object in Figure 8.1 is a partial torus rendered with a stripe shader. The stripe shader and the application in which it is shown were both developed in 2002 by LightWork Design, a company that develops software to provide photorealistic views of objects created with commercial CAD/CAM packages. The application developed by LightWork Design contains a graphical user interface that allows the user to interactively modify the shader's parameters. The various shaders that are available are accessible on the upper-right portion of the user interface, and the modifiable parameters for the current shader are accessible in the lower-right portion of the user interface. In this case, you can see that the parameters for the stripe shader include the stripe color (blue), the background color (orange), the stripe scale (how many stripes there will be), and the stripe width (the ratio of stripe to background; in this case, it is 0.5 to make blue and orange stripes of equal width).

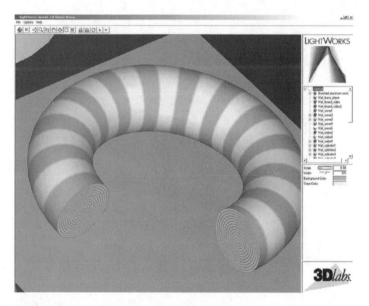

Figure 8.1   Procedurally striped torus
(Close-up of a partial torus rendered with the stripe shader described in "Regular Patterns" (courtesy of LightWork Design).)

For our stripe shader to work properly, the application needs to send down only the geometry (vertex values) and the texture coordinate at each vertex. The key to drawing the stripe color or the background color is the *t* texture coordinate at each fragment (the *s* texture coordinate is not used at all). The application must also supply values that the vertex shader uses to perform a lighting computation. And the aforementioned stripe color, background color, scale, and stripe width must be passed to the fragment shader so that our procedural stripe computation can be performed at each fragment.

Stripes Vertex Shader

The vertex shader for our stripe effect is shown in Example 8.1.

Example 8.1   Vertex Shader for Drawing Stripes

```
#version 330 core

uniform vec3 LightPosition;
uniform vec3 LightColor;
uniform vec3 EyePosition;
uniform vec3 Specular;
uniform vec3 Ambient;

uniform float Kd;
uniform mat4 MVMatrix;
uniform mat4 MVPMatrix;
uniform mat3 NormalMatrix;

in vec4     MCVertex;
in vec3     MCNormal;
in vec2     TexCoord0;

out vec3    DiffuseColor;
out vec3    SpecularColor;
out float   TexCoord;

void main()
{
    vec3 ecPosition = vec3(MVMatrix * MCVertex);
    vec3 tnorm      = normalize(NormalMatrix * MCNormal);
    vec3 lightVec   = normalize(LightPosition - ecPosition);
    vec3 viewVec    = normalize(EyePosition - ecPosition);
    vec3 hvec       = normalize(viewVec + lightVec);

    float spec = clamp(dot(hvec, tnorm), 0.0, 1.0);
    spec = pow(spec, 16.0);

    DiffuseColor    = LightColor * vec3(Kd * dot(lightVec, tnorm));
    DiffuseColor    = clamp(Ambient + DiffuseColor, 0.0, 1.0);
    SpecularColor   = clamp((LightColor * Specular * spec), 0.0, 1.0);
    TexCoord        = TexCoord0.t;
    gl_Position     = MVPMatrix * MCVertex;
}
```

There are some nice features to this particular shader. Nothing in it really makes it specific to drawing stripes. It provides a good example of how we might do the lighting calculation in a general way that would be compatible with a variety of fragment shaders.

As we mentioned, the values for doing the lighting computation (LightPosition, LightColor, EyePosition, Specular, Ambient, and Kd) are all passed in by the application as uniform variables. The purpose of this shader is to compute DiffuseColor and SpecularColor, two out variables that will be interpolated across each primitive and made available to the fragment shader at each fragment location. These values are computed in the typical way. A small optimization is that Ambient is added to the value computed for the diffuse reflection so that we send one less value to the fragment shader as an out variable. The incoming texture coordinate is passed down to the fragment shader as the out variable TexCoord, and the vertex position is transformed in the usual way.

Stripes Fragment Shader

The fragment shader contains the algorithm for drawing procedural stripes. It is shown in Example 8.2.

Example 8.2   Fragment Shader for Drawing Stripes

```
#version 330 core

uniform vec3   StripeColor;
uniform vec3   BackColor;

uniform float Width;
uniform float Fuzz;
uniform float Scale;

in vec3   DiffuseColor;
in vec3   SpecularColor;
in float TexCoord;

out vec4 FragColor;

void main()
{
        float scaledT = fract(TexCoord * Scale);
        float frac1 = clamp(scaledT / Fuzz, 0.0, 1.0);
        float frac2 = clamp((scaledT - Width) / Fuzz, 0.0, 1.0);

        frac1 = frac1 * (1.0 - frac2);
        frac1 = frac1 * frac1 * (3.0 - (2.0 * frac1));

        vec3 finalColor = mix(BackColor, StripeColor, frac1);

        finalColor = finalColor * DiffuseColor + SpecularColor;
        FragColor = vec4(finalColor, 1.0);
}
```

The application provides one other uniform variable, called Fuzz. This value controls the smooth transitions (i.e., antialiasing) between stripe color and background color. With a Scale value of 10.0, a reasonable value for Fuzz is 0.1. It can be adjusted as the object changes size to prevent excessive blurriness at high magnification levels or aliasing at low magnification levels. It shouldn't really be set to a value higher than 0.5 (maximum blurriness of stripe edges).

The first step in this shader is to multiply the incoming *t* texture coordinate by the stripe scale factor and take the fractional part. This computation gives the position of the fragment within the stripe pattern. The larger the value of Scale, the more stripes we have as a result of this calculation. The resulting value for the local variable scaledT is in the range from [0, 1].

We'd like to have nicely antialiased transitions between the stripe colors. One way to do this would be to use **smoothstep()** in the transition from StripeColor to BackColor and use it again in the transition from BackColor to StripeColor. But this shader uses the fact that these transitions are symmetric to combine the two transitions into one.

So, to get our desired transition, we use scaledT to compute two other values, frac1 and frac2. These two values tell us where we are in relation to the two transitions between BackColor and StripeColor. For frac1, if scaledT/Fuzz is greater than 1, that indicates that this point is not in the transition zone, so we clamp the value to 1. If scaledT is less than Fuzz, scaledT/Fuzz specifies the fragment's relative distance into the transition zone for one side of the stripe. We compute a similar value for the other edge of the stripe by subtracting Width from scaledT, dividing by Fuzz, clamping the result, and storing it in frac2.

These values represent the amount of fuzz (blurriness) to be applied. At one edge of the stripe, frac2 is 0 and frac1 is the relative distance into the transition zone. At the other edge of the stripe, frac1 is 1 and frac2 is the relative distance into the transition zone. Our next line of code (frac1 = frac1 * (1.0 - frac2)) produces a value that can be used to do a proper linear blend between BackColor and StripeColor. But we'd actually like to perform a transition that is smoother than a linear blend. The next line of code performs a Hermite interpolation in the same way as the **smoothstep()** function. The final value for frac1 performs the blend between BackColor and StripeColor.

The result of this effort is a smoothly "fuzzed" boundary in the transition region between the stripe colors. Without this fuzzing effect, we would have aliasing; abrupt transitions between the stripe colors that would flash and pop as the object is moved on the screen. The fuzzing of the transition region eliminates those artifacts. A close-up view of the fuzzed boundary is shown in Figure 8.2. (More information about antialiasing procedural shaders can be found in "Antialiasing Procedural Textures" on Page 442.)

Now all that remains to be done is to apply the diffuse and specular lighting effects computed by the vertex shader and supply an alpha value of 1.0 to produce our final fragment color. By modifying the five basic parameters of our fragment shader, we can create a fairly interesting number of variations of our stripe pattern, using the same shader.

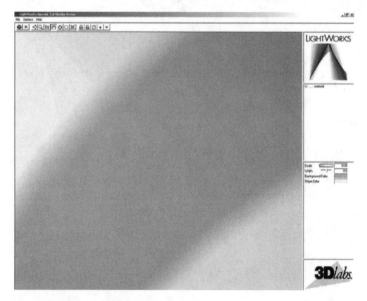

Figure 8.2 Stripes close-up
(Extreme close-up view of one of the stripes that shows the effect of the "fuzz" calculation from the stripe shader (courtesy of LightWork Design).)

Brick

As a second example of a regular pattern, we will look at a shader that draws brick with a slightly different method of lighting than the stripes example. Again, the vertex shader here is somewhat generic and could be used with multiple different fragment shaders. To see the effect they will produce, see Figure 8.3.

Our brick example will also clearly display aliasing, which we will come back and visit in the upcoming antialiasing section. There is a close-up of this aliasing in the left picture in Figure 8.19.

Figure 8.3   Brick patterns
(A flat polygon, a sphere, and a torus rendered with the brick shaders.)

Bricks Vertex Shader

Let's dive right in with the vertex shader, shown in Example 8.3. It has little to do with drawing brick, but does compute how the brick will be lit. If you wish, read through it, and if you've internalized the beginning of Chapter 7 as well as the first example given above, it should all start to make sense. The brick pattern will come from the fragment shader, and we'll explain that next.

Example 8.3   Vertex Shader for Drawing Bricks

```
#version 330 core

in vec4      MCvertex;
in vec3      MCnormal;

uniform mat4 MVMatrix;
uniform mat4 MVPMatrix;
uniform mat3 NormalMatrix;
uniform vec3 LightPosition;

const float SpecularContribution = 0.3;
const float DiffuseContribution  = 1.0 - SpecularContribution;

out float    LightIntensity;
out vec2     MCposition;

void main()
{
    vec3 ecPosition  = vec3(MVMatrix * MCvertex);
    vec3 tnorm       = normalize(NormalMatrix * MCnormal);
    vec3 lightVec    = normalize(LightPosition - ecPosition);
    vec3 reflectVec  = reflect(-lightVec, tnorm);
    vec3 viewVec     = normalize(-ecPosition);
    float diffuse    = max(dot(lightVec, tnorm), 0.0);
```

```
    float spec         = 0.0;

    if (diffuse > 0.0)
    {
        spec = max (dot (reflectVec, viewVec), 0.0);
        spec = pow (spec, 16.0);
    }

    LightIntensity     = DiffuseContribution * diffuse +
                         SpecularContribution * spec;

    MCposition         = MCvertex.xy;
    gl_Position        = MVPMatrix * MCvertex;
}
```

Bricks Fragment Shader

The fragment shader contains the core algorithm to make the brick
pattern. It is provided in Example 8.4, and we will point out the key
computations that make it work.

Example 8.4   Fragment Shader for Drawing Bricks

```
#version 330 core

uniform vec3 BrickColor, MortarColor;
uniform vec2 BrickSize;
uniform vec2 BrickPct;

in vec2   MCposition;
in float LightIntensity;

out vec4 FragColor;

void main()
{
    vec3 color;
    vec2 position, useBrick;

    position = MCposition / BrickSize;

    if (fract(position.y * 0.5) > 0.5)
        position.x += 0.5;

    position = fract(position);
    useBrick = step(position, BrickPct);

    color = mix(MortarColor, BrickColor, useBrick.x * useBrick.y);
    color *= LightIntensity;

    FragColor = vec4(color, 1.0);
}
```

The colors to make the brick and mortar are selected by the application and sent in as `BrickColor` and `MortarColor`. The size of the brick pattern uses two independent components for width and height and is also sent by the application, in `BrickSize`. Finally, the application selects what percentage of the pattern will be brick, in `BrickPct`, with the remaining being mortar.

The sizes are in the same units as the position coming from the vertex shader, `MCposition`, which in turn was passed into the vertex shader from the application. The input `MCposition` is effectively our texture coordinate.

The key to knowing *where* we are in the brick pattern is looking at the fractional part of dividing `MCposition` by the brick size: Each time the pattern completes, we are at a whole number of repetitions of the brick, hence the fractional part goes to 0. As we move through one iteration of the brick, the fractional part approaches 1.0. These computations are done with `vec2` math, so we get both dimensions answered at the same time. Because alternating rows of brick are offset, we conditionally add 0.5 to the *x* dimension for alternating counts of the repeat pattern in the *y* dimension. This is cryptically done as `fract(position.y * 0.5) > 0.5`, for which you might have other ways of expressing.

Once we know where we are in the brick pattern, we could use a bunch of `if` tests to select the right color, or we could use math. In this example, we chose math. The range of position is [0.0, 1.0), and we need `BrickPct` to be in the same range. The `step()` function says the first argument is an edge, the left of which should return 0.0 and the right of which should 1.0. So, for *a particular dimension*, `step(position, BrickPct)` will return 1.0 if we are in the brick and 0.0 if in the mortar. We want to draw mortar if *either dimension* says to draw mortar. Well, with these 0.0 and 1.0 results, multiplying them answers that question without using any `if` tests. Finally, the `mix()` function is used to pick one of the colors. No actual mixing occurs, because the ratio of mixing is either going to be 0.0 or 1.0; it simply selects the first or second argument. Additional reasons for using `step` and `mix` in this way will become clear when we antialias.

Toy Ball

Programmability is the key to procedurally defining all sorts of texture patterns. This next shader takes things a bit further by shading a sphere with a procedurally defined star pattern and a procedurally defined stripe. This shader was inspired by the ball in one of Pixar's early short animations, *Luxo Jr.* This shader is quite specialized. It shades any surface as long as it's a sphere. The reason is that the fragment shader exploits the following property of the sphere: The surface normal for any point on the surface points in the same direction as the vector from the center of the sphere to that point on the surface. This property is used to analytically compute the surface normal used in the shading calculations within the fragment shader. (This is actually a reasonable approximation for convex hulls that aren't too far from being spherical.)

The key to this shader is that the star pattern is defined by the coefficients for five half-spaces that define the star shape. These coefficients were chosen to make the star pattern an appropriate size for the ball. Points on the sphere are classified as "in" or "out", relative to each half space. Locations in the very center of the star pattern are "in" with respect to all five half-spaces. Locations in the points of the star are "in" with respect to four of the five half-spaces. All other locations are "in" with respect to three or fewer half-spaces. Fragments that are in the stripe pattern are simpler to compute. After we have classified each location on the surface as "star", "stripe", or "other", we can color each fragment appropriately. The color computations are applied in an order that ensures a reasonable result even if the ball is viewed from far away. A surface normal is calculated analytically (i.e., exactly) within the fragment shader. A lighting computation that includes a specular highlight calculation is also applied at every fragment.

Application Setup

The application needs only to provide vertex positions for this shader to work properly. Both colors and normals are computed algorithmically in the fragment shader. The only catch is that for this shader to work properly, the vertices must define a sphere. The sphere can be of arbitrary size because the fragment shader performs all the necessary computations, based on the known geometry of a sphere.

A number of parameters to this shader are specified with uniform variables. The values that produce the images shown in the remainder of this section are summarized in Example 8.5.

Example 8.5   Values for Uniform Variables Used by the Toy Ball Shader

```
HalfSpace[0]      1.0,              0.0,           0.0,  0.2
HalfSpace[1]      0.309016994,      0.951056516,   0.0,  0.2
HalfSpace[2]     -0.809016994,      0.587785252,   0.0,  0.2
HalfSpace[3]     -0.809016994,     -0.587785252,   0.0,  0.2
HalfSpace[4]      0.309016994,     -0.951056516,   0.0,  0.2
StripeWidth       0.3
```

```
InOrOutInit      -3.0
FWidth           0.005
StarColor        0.6, 0.0, 0.0, 1.0
StripeColor      0.0, 0.3, 0.6, 1.0
BaseColor        0.6, 0.5, 0.0, 1.0
BallCenter       0.0, 0.0, 0.0, 1.0
LightDir         0.57735, 0.57735, 0.57735, 0.0
HVector          0.32506, 0.32506, 0.88808, 0.0
SpecularColor    1.0, 1.0, 1.0, 1.0
SpecularExponent 200.0
Ka               0.3
Kd               0.7
Ks               0.4
```

Vertex Shader

The fragment shader is the workhorse for this shader duo, so the vertex shader needs only to compute the ball's center position in eye coordinates, the eye-coordinate position of the vertex, and the clip space position at each vertex. The application could provide the ball's center position in eye coordinates, but our vertex shader doesn't have much to do, and doing it this way means the application doesn't have to keep track of the model-view matrix. This value could easily be computed in the fragment shader, but the fragment shader will likely have a little better performance if we leave the computation in the vertex shader and pass the result as a `flat` interpolated `out` variable (see Example 8.6).

Example 8.6   Vertex Shader for Drawing a Toy Ball

```
#version 330 core

uniform vec4 MCBallCenter;
uniform mat4 MVMatrix;
uniform mat4 MVPMatrix;
uniform mat3 NormalMatrix;

in vec4 MCVertex;

     out vec3 OCPosition;
     out vec4 ECPosition;
flat out vec4 ECBallCenter;

void main (void)
{
   OCPosition = MCVertex.xyz;
   ECPosition = MVMatrix * MCVertex;
   ECBallCenter = MVMatrix * MCBallCenter;
   gl_Position = MVPMatrix * MCVertex;
}
```

Fragment Shader

The toy ball fragment shader is a little bit longer than some of the previous examples, so we build it up a few lines of code at a time and illustrate some intermediate results. The definitions for the local variables that are used in the toy ball fragment shader are as follows:

```
vec3   normal;      // Analytically computed normal
vec4   pShade;      // Point in shader space
vec4   surfColor;   // Computed color of the surface
float  intensity;   // Computed light intensity
vec4   distance;    // Computed distance values
float  inorout;     // Counter for classifying star pattern
```

The first thing we do is turn the surface location that we're shading into a point on a sphere with a radius of 1.0. We can do this with the normalize function:

```
pShade.xyz  = normalize(OCPosition.xyz);
pShade.w    = 1.0;
```

We don't want to include the *w* coordinate in the computation, so we use the component selector `.xyz` to select the first three components of `OCposition`. This normalized vector is stored in the first three components of `pShade`. With this computation, `pShade` represents a point on the sphere with radius 1, so all three components of `pShade` are in the range $[-1, 1]$. The *w* coordinate isn't really pertinent to our computations at this point, but to make subsequent calculations work properly, we initialize it to a value of 1.0.

We are always going to be shading spheres with this fragment shader, so we analytically calculate the surface normal of the sphere:

```
normal = normalize(ECPosition.xyz-ECBallCenter.xyz);
```

Next, we perform our half-space computations. We initialize a counter `inorout` to a value of −3.0. We increment the counter each time the surface location is "in" with respect to a half-space. Because five half-spaces are defined, the final counter value will be in the range $[-3, 2]$. Values of 1 or 2 signify that the fragment is within the star pattern. Values of 0 or less signify that the fragment is outside the star pattern.

```
inorout = InOrOutInit;    // initialize inorout to -3
```

We have defined the half-spaces as an array of five **vec4** values, done our "in" or "out" computations, and stored the results in an array of five float values. But we can take a little better advantage of the parallel nature of the underlying graphics hardware if we do things a bit differently. You'll see how in a minute. First, we compute the distance between pShade and the first four half-spaces by using the built-in dot-product function:

```
distance[0] = dot(p, HalfSpace[0]);
distance[1] = dot(p, HalfSpace[1]);
distance[2] = dot(p, HalfSpace[2]);
distance[3] = dot(p, HalfSpace[3]);
```

The results of these half-space distance calculations are visualized in (A)–(D) of Figure 8.4. Surface locations that are "in" with respect to the half-space are shaded in gray, and points that are "out" are shaded in black.

You may have been wondering why our counter was defined as a `float` instead of an `int` . We're going to use the counter value as the basis for a smoothly antialiased transition between the color of the star pattern and the color of the rest of the ball's surface. To this end, we use the **smoothstep()** function to set the distance to 0 if the computed distance is less than -FWidth, to 1 if the computed distance is greater than FWidth, and to a smoothly interpolated value between 0 and 1 if the computed distance is between those two values. By defining distance as a `vec4` , we can perform the smooth-step computation on four values in parallel. The built-in function **smoothstep()** implies a divide operation, and because FWidth is a float, only one divide operation is necessary. This makes it all very efficient.

```
distance = smoothstep(-FWidth, FWidth, distance);
```

Now we can quickly add the values in distance by performing a dot product between distance and a `vec4` containing 1.0 for all components:

```
inorout += dot(distance, vec4(1.0));
```

Because we initialized inorout to −3, we add the result of the dot product to the previous value of inorout. This variable now contains a value in the range [−3, 1] and we have one more half-space distance to compute. We compute the distance to the fifth half-space, and we do the computation to determine whether we're "in" or "out" of the stripe around the ball. We call the **smoothstep()** function to do the same operation on these two values as was performed on the previous four half-space distances. We update the inorout counter by adding the result from the distance computation with the final half-space. The distance computation with respect to the fifth half-space is illustrated in (E) of Figure 8.4.

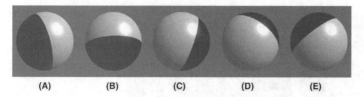

(A)   (B)   (C)   (D)   (E)

Figure 8.4   Visualizing the results of the half-space distance calculations (courtesy of AMD)

```
distance.x  = dot(pShade, HalfSpace[4]);
distance.y  = StripeWidth - abs(pShade.z);
distance.xy = smoothstep(-FWidth, FWidth, distance.xy);
inorout     += distance.x;
```

(In this case, we're performing a smooth-step operation only on the *x* and *y* components.)

The value for `inorout` is now in the range $[-3, 2]$. This intermediate result is illustrated in Figure 8.5 (A). By clamping the value of `inorout` to the range $[0, 1]$, we obtain the result shown in Figure 8.5 (B).

```
inorout     = clamp(inorout, 0.0, 1.0);
```

At this point, we can compute the surface color for the fragment. We use the computed value of `inorout` to perform a linear blend between yellow and red to define the star pattern. If we were to stop here, the result would look like ball (A) in Figure 8.6. If we take the results of this calculation and do a linear blend with the color of the stripe, we get the result shown for ball (B) Figure 8.6. Because we used **smoothstep()**, the values of `inorout` and `distance.y` provide a nicely antialiased edge at the border between colors.

```
surfColor   = mix(BaseColor, StarColor, inorout);
surfColor   = mix(surfColor, StripeColor, distance.y);
```

The result at this stage is flat and unrealistic. Performing a lighting calculation will fix this. The first step is to analytically compute the normal for this fragment, which we can do because we know the eye-coordinate position of the center of the ball (it's provided in the in variable `ECballCenter`) and we know the eye-coordinate position of the fragment (it's passed in the in variable `ECposition`).

```
// Calculate analytic normal of a sphere
normal      = normalize(ECPosition.xyz - ECBallCenter.xyz);
```

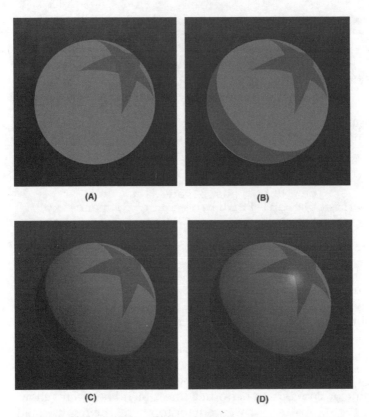

(A) (B)

(C) (D)

Figure 8.5   Intermediate results from the toy ball shader
(In (A), the procedurally defined star pattern is displayed. In (B), the stripe is added. In (C), diffuse lighting is applied. In (D), the analytically defined normal is used to apply a specular highlight. (Courtesy of ATI Research, Inc.))

The diffuse part of the lighting equation is computed with these three lines of code:

```
// Per-fragment diffuse lighting
intensity  = Ka; // ambient
intensity += Kd * clamp(dot(LightDir.xyz, normal), 0.0, 1.0);
surfColor *= intensity;
```

The result of diffuse-only lighting is shown as ball C in Figure 8.5. The final step is to add a specular contribution with these three lines of code:

```
// Per-fragment specular lighting
intensity  = clamp(dot(HVector.xyz, normal), 0.0, 1.0);
intensity  = Ks * pow(intensity, SpecularExponent);
surfColor.rgb += SpecularColor.rgb * intensity;
```

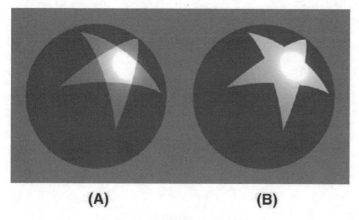

(A)   **(B)**

Figure 8.6   Intermediate results from "in" or "out" computation
(Surface points that are "in" with respect to all five half-planes are shown in
white, and points that are "in" with respect to four half-planes are shown
in gray (A). The value of inorout is clamped to the range [0, 1] to produce
the result shown in (B). (Courtesy of AMD.))

Notice in ball D in Figure 8.5 that the specular highlight is perfect! Because
the surface normal at each fragment is computed exactly, there is no
misshapen specular highlight caused by tessellation facets like we're used
to seeing. The resulting value is written to `FragColor` and sent on for final
processing before ultimately being written into the framebuffer.

```
FragColor = surfColor;
```

Voila! Your very own toy ball, created completely out of thin air! The
complete listing of the toy ball fragment shader is shown in Example 8.7.

Example 8.7   Fragment Shader for Drawing a Toy Ball

```
#version 330 core

uniform vec4   HalfSpace[5];  // half-spaces used to define star pattern
uniform float StripeWidth;
uniform float InOrOutInit;  // -3.0
uniform float FWidth;       // = 0.005

uniform vec4   StarColor;
uniform vec4   StripeColor;
uniform vec4   BaseColor;

uniform vec4   LightDir;    // light direction, should be normalized
uniform vec4   HVector;     // reflection vector for infinite light
```

```
uniform vec4  SpecularColor;
uniform float SpecularExponent;

uniform float Ka;
uniform float Kd;
uniform float Ks;

        in vec4  ECPosition;    // surface position in eye coordinates
        in vec3  OCPosition;    // surface position in object coordinates
flat in vec4  ECBallCenter; // ball center in eye coordinates

out vec4 FragColor;

void main()
{
    vec3  normal;            // Analytically computed normal
    vec4  pShade;            // Point in shader space
    vec4  surfColor;         // Computed color of the surface
    float intensity;         // Computed light intensity
    vec4  distance;          // Computed distance values
    float inorout;           // Counter for classifying star pattern

    pShade.xyz  = normalize(OCPosition.xyz);
    pShade.w    = 1.0;

    inorout     = InOrOutInit;     // initialize inorout to -3.0

    distance[0] = dot(pShade, HalfSpace[0]);
    distance[1] = dot(pShade, HalfSpace[1]);
    distance[2] = dot(pShade, HalfSpace[2]);
    distance[3] = dot(pShade, HalfSpace[3]);

    //float FWidth = fwidth(pShade);
    distance    = smoothstep(-FWidth, FWidth, distance);

    inorout     += dot(distance, vec4(1.0));

    distance.x  = dot(pShade, HalfSpace[4]);
    distance.y  = StripeWidth - abs(pShade.z);
    distance.xy = smoothstep(-FWidth, FWidth, distance.xy);
    inorout     += distance.x;

    inorout     = clamp(inorout, 0.0, 1.0);

    surfColor   = mix(BaseColor, StarColor, inorout);
    surfColor   = mix(surfColor, StripeColor, distance.y);

    // Calculate analytic normal of a sphere
    normal      = normalize(ECPosition.xyz-ECBallCenter.xyz);

    // Per-fragment diffuse lighting
    intensity = Ka; // ambient
    intensity += Kd * clamp(dot(LightDir.xyz, normal), 0.0, 1.0);
```

```
    surfColor *= intensity;

    // Per-fragment specular lighting
    intensity  = clamp(dot(HVector.xyz, normal), 0.0, 1.0);
    intensity  = Ks * pow(intensity, SpecularExponent);
    surfColor.rgb += SpecularColor.rgb * intensity;
    FragColor = surfColor;
}
```

Lattice

Here's a little bit of a gimmick. In this example, we show how not to draw the object procedurally.

In this example, we look at how the discard command can be used in a fragment shader to achieve some interesting effects. The discard command causes fragments to be discarded rather than used to update the framebuffer. We use this to draw geometry with "holes". The vertex shader is the exact same vertex shader used for stripes ("Regular Patterns"). The fragment shader is shown in Example 8.8.

Example 8.8   Fragment Shader for Procedurally Discarding Part of an Object

```
in vec3 DiffuseColor;
in vec3 SpecularColor;
in vec2 TexCoord

out vec3 FragColor;

uniform vec2   Scale;
uniform vec2   Threshold;
uniform vec3   SurfaceColor;

void main()
{
    float ss = fract(TexCoord.s * Scale.s);
    float tt = fract(TexCoord.t * Scale.t);

    if ((ss > Threshold.s) && (tt > Threshold.t))
        discard;

    vec3 finalColor = SurfaceColor * DiffuseColor + SpecularColor;
    FragColor = vec4(finalColor, 1.0);
}
```

The part of the object to be discarded is determined by the values of the s and t texture coordinates. A scale factor is applied to adjust the frequency of the lattice. The fractional part of this scaled texture-coordinate value is computed to provide a number in the range [0, 1]. These values are compared with the threshold values that have been provided. If both values exceed the threshold, the fragment is discarded. Otherwise, we do a simple lighting calculation and render the fragment.

In Figure 8.7, the threshold values were both set to 0.13. This means that more than three-quarters of the fragments were being discarded!

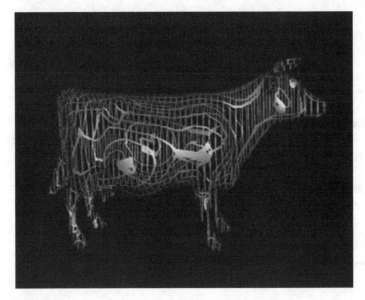

Figure 8.7　　The lattice shader applied to the cow model (3Dlabs, Inc.)

Procedural Shading Summary

A master magician can make it look like something is created out of thin air. With procedural textures, you, as a shader writer, can express algorithms that turn flat gray surfaces into colorful, patterned, bumpy, or reflective ones. The trick is to come up with an algorithm that expresses the texture you envision. By coding this algorithm into a shader, you too can create something out of thin air.

In this section, we only scratched the surface of what's possible. We created a stripe shader, but grids and checkerboards and polka dots are no more difficult. We created a toy ball with a star, but we could have created a beach ball with snowflakes. Shaders can be written to procedurally include or exclude geometry or to add bumps or grooves. Additional procedural texturing effects are illustrated in this rest of this chapter. In particular, "Noise" shows how an irregular function (`noise`) can achieve a wide range of procedural texturing effects.

Procedural textures are mathematically precise, are easy to parameterize, and don't require large amounts of texture memory, bandwidth, or filtering. The end goal of a fragment shader is to produce a color value (and possibly a depth value) that will be written into the framebuffer. Because the OpenGL Shading Language is a procedural programming language, the only limit to this computation is your imagination.

Bump Mapping

We have already seen procedural shader examples that modified color (brick and stripes) and opacity (lattice). Another class of interesting effects can be applied to a surface with a technique called *bump mapping*. Bump mapping involves modulating the surface normal before lighting is applied. We can perform the modulation algorithmically to apply a regular pattern, we can add noise to the components of a normal, or we can look up a perturbation value in a texture map. Bump mapping has proved to be an effective way of increasing the apparent realism of an object without increasing the geometric complexity. It can be used to simulate surface detail or surface irregularities.

The technique does not truly alter the shape of the surface being shaded; it merely "tricks" the lighting calculations. Therefore, the "bumping" does not show up on the silhouette edges of an object. Imagine modeling a planet as a sphere and shading it with a bump map so that it appears to have mountains that are quite large relative to the diameter of the planet. Because nothing has been done to change the underlying geometry, which is perfectly round, the silhouette of the sphere always appears perfectly round, even if the mountains (bumps) should stick out of the silhouette edge. In real life, you would expect the mountains on the silhouette edges to prevent the silhouette from looking perfectly round. Also, bump-to-bump interactions of lighting and occlusion aren't necessarily correct. For these reasons, it is a good idea to use bump mapping to apply only "small" effects to a surface (at least relative to the size of the surface) or to surfaces that won't be viewed near edge on. Wrinkles on an orange, embossed logos, and pitted bricks are all good examples of things that can be successfully bump mapped.

Bump mapping adds apparent geometric complexity during fragment processing, so once again the key to the process is our fragment shader. This implies that the lighting operation must be performed by our fragment shader instead of by the vertex shader where it is often handled. Again, this points out one of the advantages of the programmability that is available through the OpenGL Shading Language. We are free to perform whatever operations are necessary, in either the vertex shader or the fragment shader. We don't need to be bound to the fixed functionality ideas of where things like lighting are performed.

The key to bump mapping is that we need a valid surface normal at each fragment location, and we also need a light source vector and a viewing direction vector. If we have access to all these values in the fragment shader, we can procedurally perturb the normal prior to the light source calculation to produce the appearance of "bumps". In this case, we really are attempting to produce bumps or small spherical nodules on the surface being rendered.

The light source computation is typically performed with dot products. For the result to have meaning, all the components of the light source calculation must be defined in the same coordinate space. So if we used the vertex shader to perform lighting, we would typically define light source positions or directions in eye coordinates and would transform incoming normals and vertex values into this space to do the calculation.

However, the eye-coordinate system isn't necessarily the best choice for doing lighting in the fragment shader. We could normalize the direction to the light and the surface normal after transforming them to eye space and then pass them to the fragment shader as out variables. However, the light direction vector would need to be renormalized after interpolation to get accurate results. Moreover, whatever method we use to compute the perturbation normal, it would need to be transformed into eye space and added to the surface normal; that vector would also need to be normalized. Without renormalization, the lighting artifacts would be quite noticeable. Performing these operations at every fragment might be reasonably costly in terms of performance. There is a better way.

Let us look at another coordinate space called the *surface-local coordinate space*. This coordinate system adapts over a rendered object's surface, assuming that each point is at $(0, 0, 0)$ and that the unperturbed surface normal at each point is $(0, 0, 1)$. This is a highly convenient coordinate system in which to do our bump mapping calculations. But to do our lighting computation, we need to make sure that our light direction, viewing direction, and the computed perturbed normal are all defined in the same coordinate system. If our perturbed normal is defined in *surface-local coordinates*, that means we need to transform our light direction and viewing direction into surface-local space as well. How is that accomplished?

What we need is a transformation matrix that transforms each incoming vertex into surface-local coordinates (i.e., incoming vertex (x, y, z) is transformed to $(0, 0, 0)$). We need to construct this transformation matrix at each vertex. Then, at each vertex, we use the surface-local transformation matrix to transform both the light direction and the viewing direction. In this way, the surface local coordinates of the light direction and the viewing direction are computed at each vertex and interpolated across the primitive. At each fragment, we can use these values to perform our lighting calculation with the perturbed normal that we calculate.

But we still haven't answered the real question. How do we create the transformation matrix that transforms from object coordinates to surface-local coordinates? An infinite number of transforms will transform a particular vertex to $(0, 0, 0)$. To transform incoming vertex values, we need a way that gives consistent results as we interpolate between them.

The solution is to require the application to send down one more attribute value for each vertex, a surface tangent vector. Furthermore, we require the application to send us tangents that are consistently defined across the surface of the object. By definition, this tangent vector is in the plane of the surface being rendered and perpendicular to the incoming surface normal. If defined consistently across the object, it serves to orient consistently the coordinate system that we derive. If we perform a cross-product between the tangent vector and the surface normal, we get a third vector that is perpendicular to the other two. This third vector is called the *binormal*, and it's something that we can compute in our vertex shader. Together, these three vectors form an orthonormal basis of a new coordinate system, which is what we need to define the transformation from object coordinates into surface-local coordinates. Because this particular surface-local coordinate system is defined with a tangent vector as one of the basis vectors, this coordinate system is sometimes referred to as *tangent spaces*.

The transformation from object space to surface-local space is as follows:

$$\begin{bmatrix} S_x \\ S_y \\ S_z \end{bmatrix} = \begin{bmatrix} T_x & T_y & T_z \\ B_x & B_y & B_z \\ N_x & N_y & N_z \end{bmatrix} \begin{bmatrix} O_x \\ O_y \\ O_z \end{bmatrix}$$

We transform the object space vector (O_x, O_y, O_z) into surface-local space by multiplying it by a matrix that contains the tangent vector (T_x, T_y, T_z) in the first row, the binormal vector (B_x, B_y, B_z) in the second row, and the surface normal (N_x, N_y, N_z) in the third row. We can use this process to transform both the light direction vector and the viewing direction vector into surface-local coordinates. The transformed vectors are interpolated across the primitive, and the interpolated vectors are used in the fragment shader to compute the reflection with the procedurally perturbed normal.

Application Setup

For our procedural bump map shader to work properly, the application must send a vertex position, a surface normal, and a tangent vector in the plane of the surface being rendered. The application passes the tangent vector as a generic vertex attribute and binds the index of the generic attribute to be used to the vertex shader variable tangent by calling **glBindAttribLocation()**. The application is also responsible for providing values for the uniform variables LightPosition, SurfaceColor, BumpDensity, BumpSize, and SpecularFactor.

You must be careful to orient the tangent vectors consistently between vertices; otherwise, the transformation into surface-local coordinates will be inconsistent, and the lighting computation will yield unpredictable results. To be consistent, vertices near each other need to have tangent vectors that point in nearly the same direction. (Flat surfaces would have the same tangent direction everywhere.) Consistent tangents can be computed algorithmically for mathematically defined surfaces. Consistent tangents for polygonal objects can be computed with neighboring vertices and by application of a consistent orientation with respect to the object's texture coordinate system.

The problem with inconsistently defined normals is illustrated in Figure 8.8. This diagram shows two triangles, one with consistently defined tangents and one with inconsistently defined tangents. The gray arrowheads indicate the tangent and binormal vectors (the surface normal is pointing straight out of the page). The white arrowheads indicate the direction toward the light source (in this case, a directional light source is illustrated).

When we transform vertex 1 to surface-local coordinates, we get the same initial result in both cases. When we transform vertex 2, we get a large difference because the tangent vectors are very different between the two vertices. If tangents were defined consistently, this situation would not occur unless the surface had a high degree of curvature across this polygon. And if that were the case, we would really want to tessellate the geometry further to prevent this from happening.

The result is that in case 1, our light direction vector is smoothly interpolated from the first vertex to the second, and all the interpolated

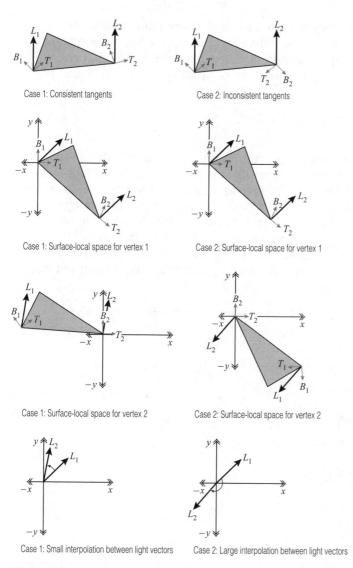

Case 1: Consistent tangents

Case 2: Inconsistent tangents

Case 1: Surface-local space for vertex 1

Case 2: Surface-local space for vertex 1

Case 1: Surface-local space for vertex 2

Case 2: Surface-local space for vertex 2

Case 1: Small interpolation between light vectors

Case 2: Large interpolation between light vectors

Figure 8.8 Inconsistently defined tangents leading to large lighting errors

vectors are roughly the same length. If we normalize this light vector at each vertex, the interpolated vectors are very close to unit length as well.

But in case 2, the interpolation causes vectors of wildly different lengths to be generated, some of them near zero. This causes severe artifacts in the lighting calculation.

Remember OpenGL does not need to send down a binormal vertex attribute, only a normal vector and a tangent vector. So, we don't compute the binormal in the application; rather we have the vertex shader compute it automatically. (Simple computation is typically faster than memory access or transfer.)

Vertex Shader

The vertex shader for our procedural bump-map shader is shown in Example 8.9. This shader is responsible for computing the surface-local direction to the light and the surface-local direction to the eye. To do this, it accepts the incoming vertex position, surface normal, and tangent vector; computes the binormal; and transforms the eye space light direction and viewing direction, using the created surface-local transformation matrix. The texture coordinates are also passed on to the fragment shader because they are used to determine the position of our procedural bumps.

Example 8.9   Vertex Shader for Doing Procedural Bump Mapping

```
#version 330 core

uniform vec3 LightPosition;

uniform mat4 MVMatrix;
uniform mat4 MVPMatrix;
uniform mat3 NormalMatrix;

in   vec4 MCVertex;
in   vec3 MCNormal;
in   vec3 MCTangent;
in   vec2 TexCoord0;

out vec3 LightDir;
out vec3 EyeDir;
out vec2 TexCoord;

void main()
{
    EyeDir = vec3(MVMatrix * MCVertex);
    TexCoord = TexCoord0.st;
    vec3 n = normalize(NormalMatrix * MCNormal);
    vec3 t = normalize(NormalMatrix * MCTangent);
    vec3 b = cross(n, t);
    vec3 v;
    v.x = dot(LightPosition, t);
    v.y = dot(LightPosition, b);
    v.z = dot(LightPosition, n);
    LightDir = normalize(v);
    v.x = dot(EyeDir, t);
```

```
    v.y = dot(EyeDir, b);
    v.z = dot(EyeDir, n);
    EyeDir = normalize(v);
    gl_Position = MVPMatrix * MCVertex;
}
```

Fragment Shader

The fragment shader for doing procedural bump mapping is shown in
Example 8.10. A couple of the characteristics of the bump pattern are
parameterized by being declared as uniform variables, namely,
BumpDensity (how many bumps per unit area) and BumpSize (how wide
each bump will be). Two of the general characteristics of the overall surface
are also defined as uniform variables: SurfaceColor (base color of the
surface) and SpecularFactor (specular reflectance property).

The bumps that we compute are round. Because the texture coordinate
is used to determine the positioning of the bumps, the first thing
we do is multiply the incoming texture coordinate by the density value.
This controls whether we see more or fewer bumps on the surface. Using
the resulting grid, we compute a bump located in the center of each grid
square. The components of the perturbation vector p are computed as the
distance from the center of the bump in the x direction and the distance
from the center of the bump in the y direction. (We only perturb the
normal in the x and y directions; the z value for our perturbation normal is
always 1.0.) We compute a "pseudodistance" d by squaring the components
of p and summing them. (The real distance could be computed at the cost
of doing another square root, but it's not really necessary if we consider
BumpSize to be a relative value rather than an absolute value.)

To perform a proper reflection calculation later on, we really need to
normalize the perturbation normal. This normal must be a unit vector so
that we can perform dot products and get accurate cosine values for use in
the lighting computation. We generally normalize a vector by multiplying
each component of the normal by:

$$\frac{1.0}{\sqrt{x^2 + y^2 + z^2}}$$

Because of our computation for d, we've already computed part of what we
need (i.e., $x^2 + y^2$). Furthermore, because we're not perturbing z at all, we
know that z^2 will always be 1.0. To minimize the computation, we just
finish computing our normalization factor at this point in the shader by
computing:

$$\frac{1.0}{\sqrt{d + 1.0}}$$

Next, we compare d to BumpSize to see if we're in a bump or not. If we're not, we set our perturbation vector to 0 and our normalization factor to 1.0. The lighting computation happens in the next few lines. We compute our normalized perturbation vector by multiplying through with the normalization factor f. The diffuse and specular reflection values are computed in the usual way, except that the interpolated surface-local coordinate light and view direction vectors are used. We get decent results without normalizing these two vectors as long as we don't have large differences in their interpolated values between vertices.

Example 8.10   Fragment Shader for Procedural Bump Mapping

```
#version 330 core

uniform vec4  SurfaceColor;      // = (0.7, 0.6, 0.18, 1.0)
uniform float BumpDensity;       // = 16.0
uniform float BumpSize;          // = 0.15
uniform float SpecularFactor;    // = 0.5

in  vec3 LightDir;
in  vec3 EyeDir;
in  vec2 TexCoord;

out vec4 FragColor;

void main()
{
    vec3 litColor;
    vec2 c = BumpDensity * TexCoord.st;
    vec2 p = fract(c) - vec2(0.5);

    float d, f;
    d = dot(p,p);
    f = inversesqrt(d + 1.0);

    if (d >= BumpSize) {
        p = vec2(0.0);
        f = 1.0;
    }

    vec3 normDelta = vec3(p.x, p.y, 1.0) * f;
    litColor = SurfaceColor.rgb * max(dot(normDelta, LightDir), 0.0);
    vec3 reflectDir = reflect(LightDir, normDelta);

    float spec = max(dot(EyeDir, reflectDir), 0.0);
    spec = pow(spec, 6.0);
    spec *= SpecularFactor;
    litColor = min(litColor + spec, vec3(1.0));

    FragColor = vec4(litColor, SurfaceColor.a);
}
```

The results from the procedural bump map shader are shown applied to two objects, a simple box and a torus, in Figure 8.9. The texture coordinates are used as the basis for positioning the bumps, and because the texture coordinates go from 0.0 to 1.0 four times around the diameter of the torus, the bumps look much closer together on that object.

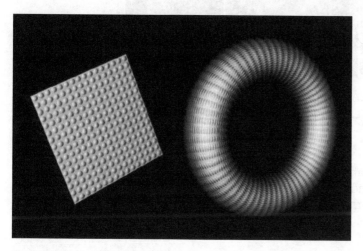

Figure 8.9   Simple box and torus with procedural bump mapping (3Dlabs, inc.)

Normal Maps

It is easy to modify our shader so that it obtains the normal perturbation values from a texture rather than generating them procedurally. A texture that contains normal perturbation values for the purpose of bump mapping is called a *bump map* or a *normal map*.

An example of a normal map and the results applied to our simple box object are shown in Figure 8.10. Individual components for the normals can be in the range $[-1, 1]$. To be encoded into an RGB texture with 8 bits per component, they must be mapped into the range $[0, 1]$. The normal map appears chalk blue because the default perturbation vector of $(0, 0, 1)$ is encoded in the normal map as $(0.5, 0.5, 1.0)$. The normal map could be stored in a floating-point texture. Today's graphics hardware supports textures both with 16-bit floating-point values per color component and 32-bit floating-point values per color component. If you use a floating-point texture format for storing normals, your image quality tends to increase (for instance, reducing banding effects in specular highlights). Of course, textures that are 16 bits per component require twice as much texture memory as 8-bit per component textures, and performance might be reduced.

Figure 8.10   Normal mapping
(A normal map (left) and the rendered result on a simple box and a sphere. (3Dlabs, Inc.))

The vertex program is identical to the one described in "Bump Mapping". The fragment shader is almost the same, except that instead of computing the perturbed normal procedurally, the fragment shader obtains it from a normal map stored in texture memory.

Antialiasing Procedural Textures

Jaggies, popping, sparkling, stair steps, strobing, and marching ants. They're all names used to describe the anathema of computer graphics— aliasing. Anyone who has used a computer has seen it. For still images, it's not always that noticeable or objectionable. But as soon as you put an object in motion, the movement of the jagged edges catches your eye and distracts you. From the early days of computer graphics, the fight to eliminate these nasty artifacts has been called antialiasing.

This section introduces the main reasons aliasing occurs, techniques to avoid it, and the facilities within the OpenGL Shading Language to help with antialiasing. Armed with this knowledge, you should be well on your way to fighting the jaggies in your own shaders.

Sources of Aliasing

Aliasing can be generally explained by sampling theory, while specific forms of aliasing can be explained more concretely by specific situations. We will tie together both approaches, and this will become clearer as the forms are discussed. Most generally, from a sampling theory perspective, a graphics image is made from point samples of the scene. If patterns in the scene vary at a high spatial frequency with respect to the samples, the samples can't accurately reproduce the scene; they are hit and miss on interesting features. A periodic pattern needs to be sampled at at least twice the frequency of the pattern itself; otherwise the image will break down when it has a pattern changing faster than every two samples, causing moiré patterns in a static image and sparkling in a moving image. The edge of an object is an interesting case, as it forms a step function as it is crossed. This is effectively a square wave, which includes super-high frequencies (it's an infinite sum of ever increasing frequencies). So, it is impossible to correctly sample an edge with point samples without undersampling. This is discussed further as we go and should become more clear.

The human eye is extremely good at noticing edges. This is how we comprehend shape and form and how we recognize letters and words. Our eye is naturally good at it, and we spend our whole lives practicing it, so naturally it is something we do very, very well.

A computer display is limited in its capability to present an image. The display is made up of a finite number of discrete elements (pixels). At a given time, each pixel can produce only one color. This makes it impossible for a computer display to accurately represent detail that is smaller than one pixel in screen space, such as an edge, especially when each pixel is only representing a point sample for the pixel's center.

When you combine these two things, the human eye's ability to discern edges and the computer graphics display's limitations in replicating them, you have a problem, and this problem is known as aliasing. In a nutshell, aliasing occurs when we try to reproduce a signal with an insufficient sampling frequency (less than two times the highest frequency present in the image). With a computer graphics display, we'll always have a fixed number of samples (pixels) with which to reconstruct our image, and this will always be insufficient to provide adequate sampling for edges, so we will always have aliasing, unless we use the pixels to represent something other than point samples. In the end, we can eliminate aliasing by reducing the spatial frequency in the image to half the spatial frequency of the pixels, exchanging aliasing for some other problem that is less objectionable, like loss of detail, blurriness, or noise, and sometimes also lowering the render-time performance.

The problem is illustrated in Figure 8.11. In this diagram, we show the results of trying to draw a gray object. The intended shape is shown in Figure 8.11 (A). The computer graphics display limits us to a discrete sampling grid. If we choose only one location within each grid square (usually the center) and determine the color to be used by sampling the desired image at that point, we see some apparent artifacts. This is called *point sampling* and is illustrated in Figure 8.11 (B). The result is ugly aliasing artifacts for edges that don't line up naturally with the sampling grid (see Figure 8.11 (C)). It actually depends on your display device technology whether pixels are more like overlapping circles (CRT), or collections of smaller red, green, and blue sub pixels (LCD), but the artifacts are obvious in all cases.

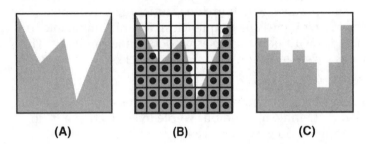

(A)   **(B)**   **(C)**

Figure 8.11   Aliasing artifacts caused by point sampling
(The gray region represents the shape of the object to be rendered (A). The computer graphics display presents us with a limited sampling grid (B). The result of choosing to draw or not draw gray at each pixel results in jaggies, or aliasing artifacts (C).)

Aliasing takes on other forms as well. If you are developing a sequence of images for an animation and you don't properly time-sample objects that are in motion, you might notice *temporal aliasings*. This is caused by objects that are moving too rapidly for the time sampling frequency being used. Objects may appear to stutter as they move or blink on and off. The classic example of temporal aliasing comes from the movies: A vehicle (car, truck, or covered wagon) in motion is going forward, but the spokes of its wheels appear to be rotating backwards. This effect is caused when the time sampling rate (movie frames per second) is too low relative to the motion of the wheel spokes. In reality, the wheel may be rotating two- and three-quarter revolutions per frame, but on film it looks like it's rotating one-quarter revolution *backward* each frame.

To render images that look truly realistic rather than computer generated, we need to develop techniques for overcoming the inherent limitations of the graphics display, both spatially and temporally.

Avoiding Aliasing

One way to achieve good results without aliasing is to avoid situations in which aliasing occurs.

For instance, if you know that a particular object will always be a certain size in the final rendered image, you can design a shader that looks good while rendering that object at that size. This is the assumption behind some of the shaders presented previously in this book. The **smoothstep()**, **mix()**, and **clamp()** functions are handy functions to use to avoid sharp transitions and to make a procedural texture look good at a particular scale.

Aliasing is often a problem when you are rendering an object at different sizes. Mipmap textures address this very issue, and you can do something similar with shaders. If you know that a particular object must appear at different sizes in the final rendering, you can design a shader for each different size. Each of these shaders would provide an appropriate level of detail and avoid aliasing for an object of that size. For this to work, the application must determine the approximate size of the final rendered object before it is drawn and then install the appropriate shader. In addition, if a continuous zoom (in or out) is applied to a single object, some "popping" will occur when the level of detail changes.

You can avoid aliasing in some situations by using a texture instead of computing something procedurally. This lets you take advantage of the filtering support that is built into the texture mapping. However, linear filtering between adjacent texels is only a solution to aliasing when the resolution of the texels is similar to the resolution of the pixels. Otherwise, you can still end up undersampling a texture and still get aliasing. Proper use of mipmaps will help keep you in antialiasing territory. Of course, there are other issues with using stored textures as opposed to doing things procedurally, as discussed earlier in this chapter.

Increasing Resolution

The effects of aliasing can be reduced through a brute force method called *supersampling* that performs sampling at several locations within a pixel and averages the result of those samples. This is exactly the approach supported in today's graphics hardware with the multisample buffer. This method of antialiasing replaces a single-point sampling operation with a several-point sampling operation, so it doesn't actually eliminate aliasing, but it can reduce aliasing to the point that it is no longer objectionable. You may be able to ignore the issue of aliasing if your shaders will always be used in conjunction with a multisample buffer.

But this approach does use up hardware resources (graphics board memory for storing the multisample buffer), and even with hardware acceleration, it still may be slower than performing the antialiasing as part of the procedural texture-generation algorithm. And because this approach doesn't eliminate aliasing, your result is still apt to exhibit signs of aliasing, albeit at a higher frequency (less visibly) than before.

Supersampling is illustrated in Figure 8.12. Each of the pixels is rendered by sampling at four locations rather than at one. The average of the four samples is used as the value for the pixel. This averaging provides a better result, but it is not sufficient to eliminate aliasing because high-frequency components can still be misrepresented.

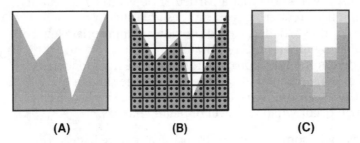

(A)   (B)   (C)

Figure 8.12   Supersampling
(Supersampling with four samples per pixel yields a better result, but aliasing artifacts are still present. The shape of the object to be rendered is shown in (A). Sampling occurs at four locations within each pixel as shown in (B). The results are averaged to produce the final pixel value as shown in (C). Some samples that are almost half covered were sampled with just one supersample point instead of two, and one pixel contains image data that was missed entirely, even with supersampling.)

Supersampling can also be implemented within a fragment shader. The code that is used to produce the fragment color can be constructed as a function, and this function can be called several times from within the main function of the fragment shader to sample the function at several discrete locations. The returned values can be averaged to create the final value for the fragment. Results are improved if the sample positions are varied stochastically rather than spaced on a regular grid. Supersampling within a fragment shader has the obvious downside of requiring N times as much processing per fragment, where N is the number of samples computed at each fragment.

There will be times when aliasing is unavoidable and supersampling is infeasible. If you want to perform procedural texturing and you want a single shader that is useful at a variety of scales, there's little choice but to take steps to counteract aliasing in your shaders.

Antialiasing High Frequencies

Aliasing does not occur until we attempt to represent a continuous image with discrete samples. This conversion occurs during rasterization. There are only two choices: either don't have high-frequency detail in the image to render, or somehow deal with undersampling of high-frequency detail. Since the former is almost never desirable due to viewing with a variety of scales, we focus on the latter. Therefore, our attempts to mitigate its effects will always occur in the fragment shader. They will still include both tools of removing high-frequencies or sampling at higher rates, but both are done after rasterization, where we can compare the frequencies of detail present in the image with the frequency of the pixels. The OpenGL Shading Language has several functions for this purpose that are available only to fragment shaders. To help explain the motivation for some of the language facilities for filter estimation, we develop a worst-case scenario—alternating black and white stripes drawn on a sphere. Developing a fragment shader that performs antialiasing enables us to further illustrate the aliasing problem and the methods for reducing aliasing artifacts. Bert Freudenberg developed the first version of the GLSL shaders discussed in this section.

Generating Stripes

The antialiasing fragment shader determines whether each fragment is to be drawn as white or black to create lines on the surface of an object. The first step is to determine the method to be used for drawing lines. We use a single parameter as the basis for our stripe pattern. For illustration, let's assume that the parameter is the s coordinate of the object's texture coordinate. We have the vertex shader pass this value to us as a floating-point out variable named V, eventually giving us a method for creating vertical stripes on a sphere. Figure 8.13 (A) shows the result of using the s texture coordinate directly as the intensity (grayscale) value on the surface of the sphere. The viewing position is slightly above the sphere, so we are looking down at the "north pole". The s texture coordinate starts off at 0 (black) and increases to 1 (white) as it goes around the sphere. The edge where black meets white can be seen at the pole, and it runs down the back side of the sphere. The front side of the sphere looks mostly gray but increases from left to right.

We create a sawtooth wave by multiplying the s texture coordinate by 16 and taking the fractional part (see Figure 8.13 (B)). This causes the intensity value to start at 0, rise quickly to 1, and then drop back down to 0. This sequence is repeated 16 times. The GLSL shader code to implement this is

```
float sawtooth = fract(V * 16.0);
```

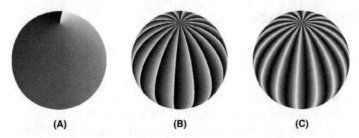

(A)   (B)   (C)

Figure 8.13   Using the *s* texture coordinate to create stripes on a sphere (In (A), the *s* texture coordinate is used directly as the intensity (gray) value. In (B), a modulus function creates a sawtooth function. In (C), the absolute value function turns the sawtooth function into a triangle function. (Courtesy of Bert Freudenberg, University of Magdeburg, 2002.))

This isn't quite the stripe pattern we're after. To get closer, we employ the absolute value function (see Figure 8.13 (C)). By multiplying the value of sawtooth by 2 and subtracting 1, we get a function that varies in the range $[-1, 1]$. Taking the absolute value of this function results in a function that goes from 1 down to 0 and then back to 1 (i.e., a *triangle* wave). The line of code to do this is

```
float triangle = abs(2.0 * sawtooth - 1.0);
```

A stripe pattern is starting to appear, but it's either too blurry or our glasses need adjustment. We make the stripes pure black and white by using the **step()** function. When we compare our triangle variable to 0.5, this function returns 0 whenever triangle is less than or equal to 0.5, and 1 whenever triangle is greater than 0.5. This could be written as

```
float square = step(0.5, triangle);
```

This effectively produces a square wave, and the result is illustrated in Figure 8.14 (A). We can modify the relative size of the alternating stripes by adjusting the threshold value provided in the step function.

Analytic Pre-filtering

In Figure 8.14 (A), we see that the stripes are now distinct, but aliasing has reared its ugly head. The step function returns values that are either 0 or 1, with nothing in between, so the jagged edges in the transitions between white and black are easy to spot. They will not go away if we increase the resolution of the image; they'll just be smaller. The problem is caused by the fact that the step function introduced an immediate transition from

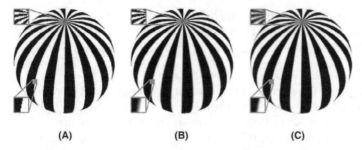

(A)   (B)   (C)

Figure 8.14   Antialiasing the stripe pattern
(We can see that the square wave produced by the step function produces aliasing artifacts (A). The **smoothstep()** function with a fixed-width filter produces too much blurring near the equator but not enough at the pole (B). An adaptive approach provides reasonable antialiasing in both regions (C). (Courtesy of Bert Freudenberg, University of Magdeburg, 2002.))

white to black or an edge, which includes frequencies marching up toward infinity. There is no way to sample this transition at a high enough frequency to eliminate the aliasing artifacts. To get good results, we need to take steps within our shader to remove such high frequencies.

A variety of antialiasing techniques rely on eliminating overly high frequencies before sampling. This is called *low-pass filtering* because low frequencies are passed through unmodified, whereas high frequencies are eliminated. The visual effect of low-pass filtering is that the resulting image is blurred.

To eliminate the high frequencies from the stripe pattern, we use the **smoothstep()** function. We know that this function produces a smooth transition between white and black. It requires that we specify two edges, and a smooth transition occurs between those two edges. Figure 8.14 (B) illustrates the result from the following line of code:

```
float square = smoothstep(0.4, 0.6, triangle);
```

Adaptive Analytic Pre-filtering

Analytic pre-filtering produces acceptable results in some regions of the sphere but not in others. The size of the smoothing filter (0.2) is defined in parameter space. But the parameter does not vary at a constant rate in screen space. In this case, the s texture coordinate varies quite rapidly in screen space near the poles and less rapidly at the equator. Our fixed-width filter produces blurring across several pixels at the equator and very little effect at the poles. What we need is a way to determine the size of the smoothing filter adaptively so that transition can be appropriate at all scales in screen space. This requires a measurement of how rapidly the function we're interested in is changing at a particular position in screen space.

Fortunately, GLSL provides a built-in function that can give us the rate of change (derivative) of any parameter in screen space. The function **dFdx()** gives the rate of change in screen coordinates in the x direction, and **dFdy()** gives the rate of change in the y direction. Because these functions deal with screen space, they are available only in a fragment shader. These two functions can provide the information needed to compute a *gradient vector* for the position of interest.

Given a function $f(x, y)$, the gradient of f at the position (x, y) is defined as the vector

$$G[f(x, y)] = \begin{bmatrix} \frac{\partial f}{\partial x} \\ \frac{\partial f}{\partial y} \end{bmatrix}$$

In English, the gradient vector comprises the partial derivative of function f with respect to x (i.e., the measure of how rapidly f is changing in the x direction) and the partial derivative of the function f with respect to y (i.e., the measure of how rapidly f is changing in the y direction). The important properties of the gradient vector are that it points in the direction of the maximum rate of increase of the function $f(x, y)$ (the gradient direction) and that the magnitude of this vector equals the maximum rate of increase of $f(x, y)$ in the gradient direction. (These properties are useful for image processing too, as we see later.) The built-in functions **dFdx()** and **dFdy()** give us exactly what we need to define the gradient vector for functions used in fragment shaders.

The magnitude of the gradient vector for the function $f(x, y)$ is commonly called the *gradient* of the function $f(x, y)$. It is defined as

$$\|G[f(x, y)]\| = +\sqrt{\frac{\partial f}{\partial x}^2 + \frac{\partial f}{\partial y}^2}$$

In practice, it is not always necessary to perform the (possibly costly) square root operation. The gradient can be approximated with absolute values:

$$\|G[f(x, y)]\| \cong \|f(x, y) - f(x + 1, y)\| + \|f(x, y) - f(x, y + 1)\|$$

This is exactly what is returned by the built-in function **fwidth()**. The sum of the absolute values is an upper bound on the width of the sampling filter needed to eliminate aliasing. If it is too large, the resulting image looks somewhat blurrier than it should, but this is usually acceptable.

The two methods of computing the gradient are compared in Figure 8.15. As you can see, there is little visible difference. Because the value of the gradient was quite small for the function being evaluated on this object, the values were scaled so that they would be visible.

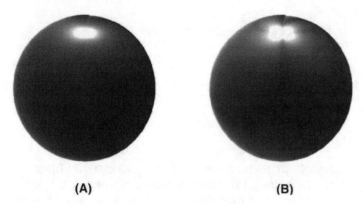

(A)   **(B)**

Figure 8.15   Visualizing the gradient
(In (A), the magnitude of the gradient vector is used as the intensity (gray) value. In (B), the gradient is approximated with absolute values. (Actual gradient values are scaled for visualization.) (Courtesy of Bert Freudenberg, University of Magdeburg, 2002.))

To compute the actual gradient for the `in` variable V within a fragment shader, we use

```
float width = length(vec2(dFdx(V), dFdy(V)));
```

To approximate it, we use the potentially higher-performance calculation.

```
float width = fwidth(V);
```

We then use the filter width within our call to **smoothstep()** as follows:

```
float edge = dp * Frequency * 2.0;
float square = smoothstep(0.5 - edge, 0.5 + edge, triangle);
```

If we put this all together in a fragment shader, we get Example 8.11.

Example 8.11   Fragment Shader for Adaptive Analytic Antialiasing

```
#version 330 core

uniform float Frequency;        // Stripe frequency = 6
uniform vec3  Color0;
uniform vec3  Color1;
```

```
in   float V;                          // generic varying
in   float LightIntensity;

out vec4 FragColor;

void main()
{
    float sawtooth = fract(V * Frequency);
    float triangle = abs(2.0 * sawtooth - 1.0);
    float dp = length(vec2(dFdx(V), dFdy(V)));
    float edge = dp * Frequency * 2.0;
    float square = smoothstep(0.5 - edge, 0.5 + edge, triangle);
    vec3 color = mix(Color0, Color1, square);
    FragColor = vec4(color, 1.0);
    FragColor.rgb *= LightIntensity;
}
```

If we scale the frequency of our texture, we must also increase the filter width accordingly. After the value of the function is computed, it is replicated across the red, green, and blue components of a `vec3` and used as the color of the fragment. The results of this adaptive antialiasing approach are shown in Figure 8.14 (C). The results are much more consistent across the surface of the sphere. A simple lighting computation is added, and the resulting shader is applied to the teapot in Figure 8.16.

Figure 8.16   Effect of adaptive analytical antialiasing on striped teapots (On the left, the teapot is drawn with no antialiasing. On the right, the adaptive antialiasing shader is used. A small portion of the striped surface is magnified 200 percent to make it easier to see the difference.)

This approach to antialiasing works well until the filter width gets larger than the frequency. This is the situation that occurs at the north pole of the sphere. The stripes very close to the pole are much thinner than one pixel, so no step function will produce the correct gray value here. In such regions, you need to switch to integration or frequency clamping, both of which are discussed in subsequent sections.

Analytic Integration

The weighted average of a function over a specified interval is called a *convolution*. The values that do the weighting are called the *convolution kernel* or the *convolution filter*. In some cases, we can reduce or eliminate aliasing by determining the convolution of a function ahead of time and then sampling the convolved function rather than the original function. The convolution can be performed over a fixed interval in a computation that is equivalent to convolving the input function with a box filter. A box filter is far from ideal, but it is simple and easy to compute and often good enough.

This method corresponds to the notion of antialiasing by *area sampling*. It is different from point sampling or super sampling in that we attempt to calculate the area of the object being rendered relative to the sampling region. Referring to Figure 8.12, if we used an area sampling technique, we would get more accurate values for each of the pixels, and we wouldn't miss that pixel that just had a sliver of coverage.

In *Advanced RenderMan: Creating CGI for Motion Pictures*, Apodaca and Gritz (1999) explain how to perform analytic antialiasing of a periodic step function, sometimes called a *pulse train*. Darwyn Peachey described how to apply this method to his procedural brick RenderMan shader in *Texturing and Modeling: A Procedural Approach*, and Dave Baldwin published a GLSL version of this shader in the original paper on the OpenGL Shading Language. We use this technique to analytically antialias the procedural brick shader we introduced at the beginning of this chapter in the subsection "Regular Patterns" on Page 414.

This example uses the step function to produce the periodic brick pattern. The function that creates the brick pattern in the horizontal direction is illustrated in Figure 8.17. From 0 to BrickPct.x (the brick-width fraction), the function is 1.0. At the value of BrickPct.x, there is an edge with infinite slope as the function drops to 0. At the value 1, the function jumps back up to 1.0, and the process is repeated for the next brick.

The key to antialiasing this function is to compute its integral, or accumulated, value. We have to consider the possibility that, in areas of high complexity, the filter width that is computed by **fwidth()** will cover several of these pulses. By sampling the integral rather than the function itself, we get a properly weighted average and avoid the high frequencies caused by point sampling that would produce aliasing artifacts.

So what is the integral of this function? It is illustrated in Figure 8.18. From 0 to BrickPct.x, the function value is 1, so the integral increases with a slope of 1. From BrickPct.x to 1.0, the function has a value of 0, so the integral stays constant in this region. At 1, the function jumps back to 1.0, so the integral increases until the function reaches BrickPct.x + 1. At this point, the integral changes to a slope of 0 again, and this pattern of ramps and plateaus continues.

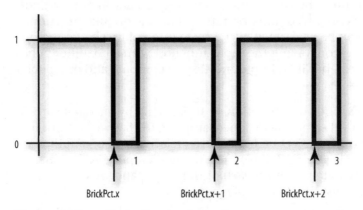

Figure 8.17   Periodic step function
(The periodic step function, or pulse train, that defines the horizontal component of the procedural brick texture.)

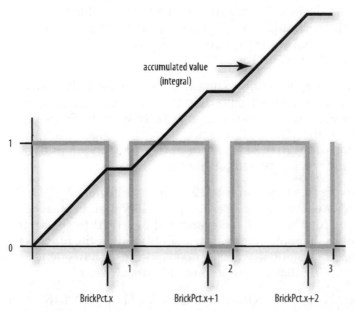

Figure 8.18   Periodic step function (pulse train) and its integral

We perform antialiasing by determining the value of the integral over the area of the filter, and we do that by evaluating the integral at the edges of the filter and subtracting the two values. The integral for this function consists of two parts: the sum of the area for all the pulses that have been fully completed before the edge we are considering and the area of the partially completed pulse for the edge we are considering.

For our procedural brick shader, we use the variable `position.x` as the basis for generating the pulse function in the horizontal direction. So, the number of fully completed pulses is just `floor(position.x)`. Because the height of each pulse is 1.0, the area of each fully completed pulse is just `BrickPct.x`. Multiplying `floor(position.x)` by `BrickPct.x` gives the area for all the fully completed pulses. The edge that we're considering may be in the part of the function that is equal to 0, or it may be in the part of the function that is equal to 1. We can find out by computing `fract(position.x) - (1.0 - BrickPct.x)`. If the result of this subtraction is less than 0, we were in the part of the function that returns 0, so nothing more needs to be done. But if the value is greater than 0, we are partway into a region of the function that is equal to 1. Because the height of the pulse is 1, the area of this partial pulse is `fract(position.x) - (1.0 - BrickPct.x)`. Therefore, the second part of our integral is the expression `max(fract(position.x) - (1.0 - BrickPct.x), 0.0)`.

We use this integral for both the horizontal and vertical components of our procedural brick pattern. Because the application knows the brick width and height fractions (`BrickPct.x` and `BrickPct.y`), it can easily compute `1.0 - BrickPct.x` and `1.0 - BrickPct.y` and provide them to our fragment shader as well. This keeps us from unnecessarily computing these values several times for every fragment that is rendered. We call these values the mortar percentage. Because we evaluate this expression twice with different arguments, we define it as a macro or a function for convenience.

```
#define Integral(x, p, notp) ((floor(x)*(p))+max(fract(x)-(notp), 0.0))
```

The parameter p indicates the value that is part of the pulse (i.e., when the function is 1.0), and `notp` indicates the value that is not part of the pulse (i.e., when the function is 0). Using this macro, we can write the code to compute the value of the integral over the width of the filter as follows:

```
vec2 fw, useBrick;

fw = fwidth(position);

useBrick = (Integral(position + fw, BrickPct, MortarPct) -
            Integral(position, BrickPct, MortarPct)) / fw;
```

The result is divided by the area of the filter (a box filter is assumed in this case) to obtain the average value for the function in the selected interval.

Antialiased Brick Fragment Shader

Now we can put all this to work to build better bricks. We replace the simple point sampling technique with analytic integration. The resulting shader is shown in Example 8.12. The difference between the aliased and antialiased brick shaders is shown in Figure 8.19.

Figure 8.19   Brick shader with and without antialiasing
(On the left, the results of the brick shader without antialiasing. On the right, results of antialiasing by analytic integration. (3Dlabs, Inc.))

Example 8.12   Source Code for an Antialiased Brick Fragment Shader

```
#version 330 core

uniform vec3   BrickColor, MortarColor;
uniform vec2   BrickSize;
uniform vec2   BrickPct;
uniform vec2   MortarPct;

in   vec2   MCPosition;
in   float LightIntensity;

out vec4    FragColor;

#define Integral(x, p, notp) ((floor(x)*(p)) + max(fract(x)-(notp), 0.0))

void main()
{
    vec2 position, fw, useBrick;
    vec3 color;
    // Determine position within the brick pattern
```

```
    position = MCPosition / BrickSize;
    // Adjust every other row by an offset of half a brick
    if (fract(position.y * 0.5) > 0.5)
        position.x += 0.5;
    // Calculate filter size
    fw = fwidth(position);
    // Perform filtering by integrating the 2D pulse made by the
    // brick pattern over the filter width and height
    useBrick = (Integral(position + fw, BrickPct, MortarPct) -
                Integral(position, BrickPct, MortarPct)) / fw;
    // Determine final color
    color = mix(MortarColor, BrickColor, useBrick.x * useBrick.y);
    color *= LightIntensity;
    FragColor = vec4(color, 1.0);
}
```

Frequency Clamping

Certain functions do not have an analytic solution, or they are just too difficult to solve. If this is the case, you might try a technique called *frequency clampings*. In this technique, the average value of the function replaces the actual value of the function when the filter width is too large. This is convenient for functions such as sine and noise, whose average is known.

Antialiased Checkerboard Fragment Shader

The checkerboard pattern is the standard measure of the quality of an antialiasing technique (see Figure 8.20). Larry Gritz wrote a checkerboard

RenderMan shader that performs antialiasing by frequency sampling, and Dave Baldwin translated this shader to GLSL. Example 8.13 shows a fragment shader that produces a procedurally generated, antialiased checkerboard pattern. The vertex shader transforms the vertex position and passes along the texture coordinate, nothing more. The application provides values for the two colors of the checkerboard pattern, the average of these two colors (the application can compute this and provide it through a uniform variable, rather than having the fragment shader compute it for every fragment), and the frequency of the checkerboard pattern.

The fragment shader computes the appropriate size of the filter and uses it to perform smooth interpolation between adjoining checkerboard squares. If the filter is too wide (i.e., the in variable is changing too quickly for proper filtering), the average color is substituted. Even though this fragment shader uses a conditional statement, care is taken to avoid aliasing. In the transition zone between the if clause and the else clause,

Figure 8.20   Checkerboard pattern
(Rendered with the antialiased checkerboard shader. On the left, the filter width is set to 0, so aliasing occurs. On the right, the filter width is computed using the **fwidth()** function.)

a smooth interpolation is performed between the computed color and the average color.

Example 8.13   Source Code for an Antialiased Checkerboard
Fragment Shader

```
#version 330 core

uniform vec3  Color0;
uniform vec3  Color1;
uniform vec3  AvgColor;
uniform float Frequency;

in vec2 TexCoord;

out vec4 FragColor;

void main()
{
    vec3 color;
```

```
// Determine the width of the projection of one pixel into
// s-t space
vec2 fw = fwidth(TexCoord);

// Determine the amount of fuzziness
vec2 fuzz = fw * Frequency * 2.0;

float fuzzMax = max(fuzz.s, fuzz.t);

// Determine the position in the checkerboard pattern
vec2 checkPos = fract(TexCoord * Frequency);

if (fuzzMax < 0.5)
{
    // If the filter width is small enough,
    // compute the pattern color
    vec2 p = smoothstep(vec2(0.5), fuzz + vec2(0.5), checkPos) +
            (1.0 - smoothstep(vec2(0.0), fuzz, checkPos));

    color = mix(Color0, Color1,
                p.x * p.y + (1.0 - p.x) * (1.0 - p.y));

    // Fade in the average color when we get close to the limit
    color=mix(color,AvgColor,smoothstep(0.125,0.5,fuzzMax));
}
else
{
    // Otherwise, use only the average color
    color = AvgColor;
}

FragColor = vec4(color, 1.0);
}
```

Procedural Antialiasing Summary

With increased freedom comes increased responsibility. The OpenGL
Shading Language permits the computation of procedural textures without
restriction. It is quite easy to write a shader that exhibits unsightly aliasing
artifacts (using a conditional or a step function is all it takes), and it can be
difficult to eliminate these artifacts. After describing the aliasing problem
in general terms, this chapter explored several options for antialiasing
procedural textures. Facilities in the language, such as the built-in
functions for smooth interpolation (**smoothstep()**), for determining
derivatives in screen space (**dFdx()**, **dFdy()**), and for estimating filter width
(**fwidth()**) can assist in the fight against jaggies, moiré patterns, and
sparkling points. These functions were fundamental components of
shaders that were presented to perform antialiasing by prefiltering,
adaptive prefiltering, integration, and frequency clamping.

Noise

In computer graphics, it's easy to make things look good. By definition, geometry is drawn and rendered precisely. However, when realism is a goal, perfection isn't always such a good thing. Real-world objects have dents and dings and scuffs. They show wear and tear. Computer graphics artists have to work hard to make a perfectly defined bowling pin look like it has been used and abused for 20 years in a bowling alley or to make a spaceship that seems a little worse for wear after many years of galactic travel.

This was the problem that Ken Perlin was trying to solve when he worked for a company called Magi in the early 1980s. Magi was working with Disney on the original feature film *Tron* that was the most ambitious film in its use of computer graphics until that time. Perlin recognized the "imperfection" of the perfectly rendered objects in that film, and he resolved to do something about it, with techniques still highly useful today.

In a seminal paper published in 1985, Perlin described a renderer that he had written that used a technique he called *noise*. His definition of noise was a little different from the common definition of noise. Normally, when we refer to noise, we're referring to something like a random changing pattern of pixels on an old television with no signal (also called *snow*) or a grainy image taken with a digital camera in low light, induced by thermal noise.

However, an always changing randomness like this isn't that useful for computer graphics. For computer graphics, we need a function that is repeatable so that an object can be drawn from different view angles. We also need the ability to draw the object the same way, frame after frame, in an animation. Normal random-number functions do not depend on any input location, so an object rendered with such a function would look different each time it was drawn.

The visual artifacts caused by this type of rendering would look horrible as the object was moved around the screen. What is needed is a function that produces the same output value for a given input location every time and yet gives the appearance of randomness. That is, for a typical surface, we want random variation across space, but not across time, unless that is also desired. This function also needs to be continuous at all levels of detail, fast to compute, and have some other important properties discussed shortly.

Perlin was the first to come up with a usable function, *Perlin noise*, for that purpose. Since then, a variety of similar noise functions have been defined and used in combinations to produce interesting rendering effects such as

- Rendering natural phenomena (clouds, fire, smoke, wind effects, etc.)

- Rendering natural materials (marble, granite, wood, mountains, etc.)

- Rendering man-made materials (stucco, asphalt, cement, etc.)

- Adding imperfections to perfect models (rust, dirt, smudges, dents, etc.)

- Adding imperfections to perfect patterns (wiggles, bumps, color variations, etc.)

- Adding imperfections to time periods (time between blinks, amount of change between successive frames, etc.)

- Adding imperfections to motion (wobbles, jitters, bumps, etc.)

Actually, the list is endless. Today, most rendering libraries include support for Perlin noise or something nearly equivalent. It is a staple of realistic rendering, and it's been heavily used in the generation of computer graphics images for the movie industry. For his groundbreaking work in this area, Perlin was presented with an Academy Award for technical achievement in 1997.

Because noise is such an important technique, it is included as a built-in function in the OpenGL Shading Language. However, not all GLSL platforms implement it, or implement it in exactly the same way. So if you need maximum portability, you'll want to use methods you have complete control over, giving complete portability. We'll focus on such a portable method in this section.

Once you have a source of noise, there are several ways to make use of it within a fragment shader. After laying the groundwork for a portable noise, we take a look at several shader examples that employ noise to achieve a variety of interesting effects.

Definition of Noise

The purpose of this section is to provide a definition and enough of an intuitive feel that you can grasp the noise-based OpenGL shaders presented in this section and then use GLSL to create additional noise-based effects.

As Ken Perlin describes it, you can think of noise as "seasoning" for graphics. It often helps to add a little noise. A perfect model looks a little less perfect and, therefore, a little more realistic if some subtle noise effects are applied.

The ideal noise function has the following important qualities that make it the valuable tool we need for creating a variety of interesting effects, needed for successful use in modeling, rendering, or animation:

- It does not show any obvious regular or repeated patterns.

- It is a continuous function, and its derivative is also continuous. That is, there are no sudden steps or sharp bends, only smooth variation, and zooming in to smaller and smaller scales still shows only smooth variation.

- It is a function that is repeatable across time (i.e., it generates the same value each time it is presented with the same input).

- It has a well-defined range of output values (usually the range is $[-1, 1]$ or $[0, 1]$).

- It is a function whose small-scale form is roughly independent of large-scale position (there is an underlying frequency to variation, or statistical character, that is the same everywhere).

- It is a function that is isotropic (its statistical character is the same in all directions).

- It can be defined for 1, 2, 3, 4, or even more dimensions.

- It is fast to compute for any given input.

In practice, all this adds up to a noise function that quickly and smoothly perturbs, or adds an apparent element of "randomness", to an initial regular periodic pattern, for example, taking a normal square grid and moving each intersection a bit in a some psuedo-random direction. A variety of functions can do this, but each makes various trade-offs in quality and performance, so they meet the preceding criteria with varying degrees of success.

We can construct a simple noise function (called *value noise* by Peachey) by first assigning a pseudorandom number in the range $[-1, 1]$ to each integer value along the x axis, as shown in Figure 8.21, and then smoothly

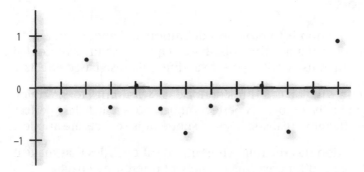

Figure 8.21   A discrete 1D noise function

interpolating between these points, as shown in Figure 8.22. The function is repeatable in that, for a given input value, it always returns the same output value.

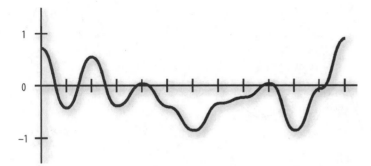

Figure 8.22   A continuous 1D noise function

A key choice to be made in this type of noise function is the method used to interpolate between successive points. Linear interpolation is not good enough because it is not continuous, making the resulting noise pattern show obvious artifacts. A cubic interpolation method is usually used to produce smooth-looking results.

By varying the frequency and the amplitude, you can get a variety of noise functions (see Figure 8.23).

As you can see, the "features" in these functions get smaller and closer together as the frequency increases and the amplitude decreases. When two frequencies are related by a ratio of 2:1, it's called an *octave*. Figure 8.23 illustrates five octaves of the 1D noise function. These images of noise don't look all that useful, but by themselves they can provide some interesting characteristics to shaders. If we add the functions at different frequencies (see Figure 8.24), we start to see something that looks even more interesting.

The result is a function that contains features of various sizes. The larger bumps from the lower-frequency functions provide the overall shape, whereas the smaller bumps from the higher-frequency functions provide detail and interest at a smaller scale. The function that results from summing the noise of consecutive octaves, each at half the amplitude of the previous octave, was called $1/f$ noise by Perlin, but the terms *fractional Brownian motion* or *fBm* are used more commonly today.

If you sum octaves of noise in a procedural shader, at some point you will begin to add frequencies that cause aliasing artifacts. When the frequency

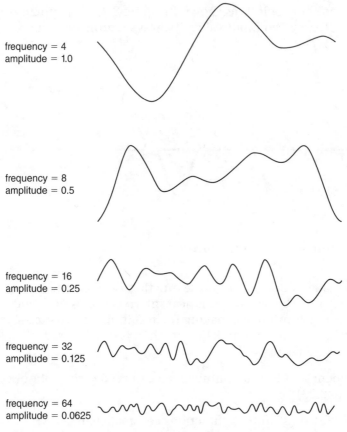

frequency = 4
amplitude = 1.0

frequency = 8
amplitude = 0.5

frequency = 16
amplitude = 0.25

frequency = 32
amplitude = 0.125

frequency = 64
amplitude = 0.0625

Figure 8.23   Varying the frequency and the amplitude of the noise
function

of noise is greater than twice the frequency of sampling (e.g., pixel
spacing), you really do start getting random sample values that will cause
the flickering forms of aliasing. Hence, algorithms for antialiasing noise
functions typically stop adding detail (higher-frequency noise) before this
occurs. This is another useful feature of the noise function—it can be faded
to the average sample value at the point at which aliasing artifacts would
begin to occur.

The noise function defined by Perlin (Perlin noise) is sometimes called
gradient noise. It is defined as a function whose value is 0 at each integer
input value, and its shape is created by defining a pseudorandom gradient
vector for the function at each of these points. The characteristics of this
noise function make it a somewhat better choice, in general, for the effects
we're after. It is used for the implementation of the noise function in

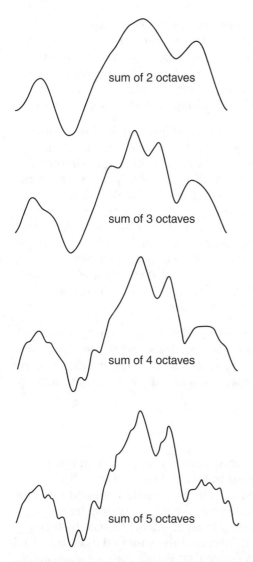

sum of 2 octaves

sum of 3 octaves

sum of 4 octaves

sum of 5 octaves

Figure 8.24   Summing noise functions
(Shows the result of summing noise functions of different amplitude and
frequency.)

RenderMan, and it is also intended to be used for implementations of the
noise function built into GLSL.

Lots of other noise functions have been defined, and there are many ways
to vary the basic ideas. The examples of Perlin noise shown previously
have a frequency multiplier of 2, but it can be useful to use a frequency

multiplier, such as 2.21, that is not an integer value. This frequency multiplier is called the *lacunarity* of the function. The word comes from the Latin word *lacuna*, which means *gap*. Using a value larger than 2 allows us to build up more "variety" more quickly (e.g., by summing fewer octaves to achieve the same apparent visual complexity). Similarly, it is not necessary to divide the amplitude of each successive octave by 2.

Summed noise functions are the basis for the terrain and features found in the planet-building software package MojoWorld from Pandromeda. In *Texturing and Modeling: A Procedural Approach*, Ken Musgrave defines a fractal as "a geometrically complex object, the complexity of which arises through the repetition of a given form over a range of scales". The relationship between the change in frequency and the change in amplitude determines the fractal dimension of the resulting function. If we use a noise function as the basis for generating a terrain model, we can take steps to make it behave differently at different locations. For instance, natural terrain has plains, rolling hills, foothills, and mountains. Varying the fractal dimension based on location can create a similar appearance—such a function is called a *multifractal*.

You can achieve interesting effects by using different noise functions for different situations or by combining noise functions of different types. It's not that easy to visualize in advance the results of calculations that depend on noise values, so varied experience will be a key ally as you try to achieve the effect you're after.

2D Noise

Armed with a basic idea of what the noise function looks like in one dimension, we can take a look at two-dimensional noise. Figure 8.25 contains images of 2D Perlin noise at various frequencies mapped into the range [0, 1] and displayed as a grayscale image. Each successive image is twice the frequency of the previous one. In each image, the contrast has been enhanced to make the peaks brighter and the valleys darker. In actual use, each subsequent image has an average that is half the previous one and an amplitude that is half the previous one. If we were to print images of the actual values, the images would be much grayer, and it would be harder to see what 2D noise really looks like.

As in the 1D case, adding the different frequency functions provides more interesting results (Figure 8.26).

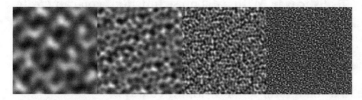

Figure 8.25 Basic 2D noise, at frequencies 4, 8, 16, and 32 (contrast enhanced)

Figure 8.26 Summed noise, at 1, 2, 3, and 4 octaves (contrast enhanced)

The first image in Figure 8.26 is exactly the same as the first image in Figure 8.25. The second image in Figure 8.26 is the sum of the first image in Figure 8.26 plus half of the second image in Figure 8.25 shifted so that its average intensity value is 0. This causes intensity to be increased in some areas and decreased in others. The third image in Figure 8.26 adds the third octave of noise to the first two, and the fourth image in Figure 8.26 adds the fourth octave. The fourth picture is starting to look a little bit like clouds in the sky.

Higher Dimensions of Noise

3D and 4D noise functions are obvious extensions of the 1D and 2D functions. It's a little hard to generate pictures of 3D noise, but the images in Figure 8.25 can be thought of as 2D slices out of a 3D noise function. Neighboring slices have continuity between them.

Often, a higher dimension of noise is used to control the time aspect of the next lower-dimension noise function. For instance, 1D noise can add some wiggle to otherwise straight lines in a drawing. If you have a 2D noise function, one dimension can control the wiggle, and the second dimension can animate the effect (i.e., make the wiggles move in successive frames). Similarly, a 2D noise function can create a 2D cloud pattern, whereas a 3D noise function can generate the 2D cloud pattern and animate it in a realistic way. With a 4D noise function, you can create a 3D object like a planet, and use the fourth dimension to watch it evolve in "fits and starts".

Using Noise in the OpenGL Shading Language

You include noise in a shader in the following three ways:

1. Use GLSL built-in noise functions.

2. Write your own noise function in GLSL.

3. Use a texture map to store a previously computed noise function.

With today's graphics systems, options 2 and 3 give the best portability, and option 3 typically gives the best performance. Here, we will focus on techniques based on option 3. Option 3 is not done to the exclusion of options 1 and 2, as the "previously computed noise function" comes from them. The difference is really whether the function is computed on the fly for arbitrary inputs (options 1 and 2), or precomputed and stored away for a predetermined set of inputs (option 3), typically as a texture map.

Noise Textures

The programmability offered by GLSL lets us use values stored in texture memory in new and unique ways. We can precompute a noise function and save it in a 1D, 2D, or 3D texture map. We can then access this texture map (or texture maps) from within a shader. Because textures can contain up to four components, we can use a single texture map to store four octaves of noise or four completely separate noise functions.

Example 8.14 shows a "C" function that generates a 3D noise texture. This function creates an RGBA texture with the first octave of noise stored in the red texture component, the second octave stored in the green texture component, the third octave stored in the blue component, and the fourth octave stored in the alpha component. Each octave has twice the frequency and half the amplitude as the previous one.

This function assumes the existence of a noise3 function that can generate 3D noise values in the range $[-1, 1]$. If you want, you can start with Perlin's C implementation. John Kessenich made some changes to that code (adding a setNoiseFrequency function) to produce noise values that wrap smoothly from one edge of the array to the other. This means we can use the texture with the wrapping mode set to GL_REPEAT, and we won't see any discontinuities in the function when it wraps. The revised version of the code is in the GLSLdemo program from 3Dlabs.

Example 8.14   C function to Generate a 3D Noise Texture

```c
int noise3DTexSize = 128;

GLuint noise3DTexName = 0;
GLubyte *noise3DTexPtr;

void make3DNoiseTexture(void)
{
    int f, i, j, k, inc;
    int startFrequency = 4;
    int numOctaves = 4;
    double ni[3];
    double inci, incj, inck;
    int frequency = startFrequency;
    GLubyte *ptr;
    double amp = 0.5;

    if ((noise3DTexPtr = (GLubyte *) malloc(noise3DTexSize *
                                            noise3DTexSize *
                                            noise3DTexSize * 4))
        == NULL)
    {
        fprintf(stderr,
                "ERROR: Could not allocate 3D noise texture\n");
        exit(1);
    }

    for (f = 0, inc = 0; f < numOctaves;
         ++f, frequency *= 2, ++inc, amp *= 0.5)
    {
        setNoiseFrequency(frequency);
        ptr = noise3DTexPtr;
        ni[0] = ni[1] = ni[2] = 0;

        inci = 1.0 / (noise3DTexSize / frequency);
        for (i = 0; i < noise3DTexSize; ++i, ni[0] += inci)
        {
            incj = 1.0 / (noise3DTexSize / frequency);
            for (j = 0; j < noise3DTexSize; ++j, ni[1] += incj)
            {
                inck = 1.0 / (noise3DTexSize / frequency);
                for (k = 0; k < noise3DTexSize;
                     ++k, ni[2] += inck, ptr += 4)
                {
                    *(ptr+inc) = (GLubyte)(((noise3(ni)+1.0) * amp)
                                            * 128.0);
                }
            }
        }
    }
}
```

This function computes noise values for four octaves of noise and stores them in a 3D RGBA texture of size 128 × 128 × 128. This code also assumes that each component of the texture is stored as an 8-bit integer value. The first octave has a frequency of 4 and an amplitude of 0.5. In the innermost part of the loop, we call the noise3 function to generate a noise value based on the current value of ni. The noise3 function returns a value in the range $[-1, 1]$, so by adding 1, we end up with a noise value in the range $[0, 2]$. Multiplying by our amplitude value of 0.5 gives a value in the range $[0, 1]$. Finally, we multiply by 128 to give us an integer value in the range $[0, 128]$ that can be stored in the red component of a texture. (When accessed from within a shader, the value is a floating-point value in the range $[0, 0.5]$.)

The amplitude value is cut in half and the frequency is doubled in each pass through the loop. The result is that integer values in the range $[0, 64]$ are stored in the green component of the noise texture, integer values in the range $[0, 32]$ are stored in the blue component of the noise texture, and integer values in the range $[0, 16]$ are stored in the alpha component of the texture. We generated the images in Figure 8.25 by looking at each of these channels independently after scaling the values by a constant value that allowed them to span the maximum intensity range (i.e., integer values in the range $[0, 255]$ or floating-point values in the range $[0, 1]$).

After the values for the noise texture are computed, the texture can be provided to the graphics hardware with the code in Example 8.15. First, we pick a texture unit and bind to it the 3D texture we've created. We set up its wrapping parameters so that the texture wraps in all three dimensions. This way, we always get a valid result for our noise function no matter what input values are used. We still have to be somewhat careful to avoid using the texture in a way that makes obvious repeating patterns. The next two lines set the texture-filtering modes to linear because the default is mipmap linear and we're not using mipmap textures here. We are controlling the scaling factors from within our noise shaders, so a single texture is sufficient.

Though we won't go into it more deeply here, using a mipmapped texture will improve quality when using a broad range of level of detail. When zoomed in, to avoid seeing blockiness in the noise, you'll need a base texel frequency two times greater than the highest-frequency noise. When zoomed out, you'll need a properly filtered mipmap to avoid seeing aliasing when the pixel frequency approaches or surpasses the noise frequency.

When all the parameters are set up, we can download the noise texture to the hardware by using the glTexImage3D function.

Example 8.15   A Function for Activating the 3D Noise Texture

```
void init3DNoiseTexture()
{
    glGenTextures(1, & noise3DTexName);

    glActiveTexture(GL_TEXTURE6);
    glBindTexture(GL_TEXTURE_3D, noise3DTexName);
    glTexParameterf(GL_TEXTURE_3D, GL_TEXTURE_WRAP_S, GL_REPEAT);
    glTexParameterf(GL_TEXTURE_3D, GL_TEXTURE_WRAP_T, GL_REPEAT);
    glTexParameterf(GL_TEXTURE_3D, GL_TEXTURE_WRAP_R, GL_REPEAT);
    glTexParameterf(GL_TEXTURE_3D, GL_TEXTURE_MAG_FILTER, GL_LINEAR);
    glTexParameterf(GL_TEXTURE_3D, GL_TEXTURE_MIN_FILTER, GL_LINEAR);

    glTexImage3D(GL_TEXTURE_3D, 0, GL_RGBA, noise3DTexSize,
                 noise3DTexSize, noise3DTexSize, 0, GL_RGBA,
                 GL_UNSIGNED_BYTE, noise3DTexPtr);
}
```

This is an excellent approach if the period of repeatability can be avoided in the final rendering. One way to avoid it is to make sure that no texture value is accessed more than once when the target object is rendered. For instance, if a $128 \times 128 \times 128$ texture is being used and the position on the object is used as the input to the noise function, the repeatability won't be visible if the entire object fits within the texture.

Trade-offs

As previously mentioned, three methods can be used to generate noise values in a shader. How do you know which is the best choice for your application? A lot depends on the underlying implementation, but generally speaking, if we assume a hardware computation of noise that does not use texturing, the points favoring usage of GLSL built-in noise function are the following:

- It doesn't consume any texture memory (a $128 \times 128 \times 128$ texture map stored as RGBA with 8 bits per component uses 8MB of texture memory).

- It doesn't use a texture unit.

- It is a continuous function rather than a discrete one, so it does not look "pixelated" no matter what the scaling is.

- The repeatability of the function should be undetectable, especially for 2D and 3D noise (but it depends on the hardware implementation).

- Shaders written with the built-in noise function don't depend on the application to set up appropriate textures.

The advantages of using a texture map to implement the noise function are as follows:

- Because the noise function is computed by the application, the application has total control of this function and can ensure matching behavior on every hardware platform.

- You can store four noise values (i.e., one each for the R, G, B, and A values of the texture) at each texture location. This lets you precompute four octaves of noise, for instance, and retrieve all four values with a single texture access.

- Accessing a texture map may be faster than calling the built-in noise function.

User-defined functions can implement noise functions that provide a different appearance from that of the built-in noise functions. A user-defined function can also provide matching behavior on every platform, whereas the built-in noise functions cannot (at least not until all graphics hardware developers support the noise function in exactly the same way). But hardware developers will optimize the built-in noise function, perhaps accelerating it with special hardware, so it is apt to be faster than user-defined noise functions.

In the long run, using the built-in noise function or user-defined noise functions will be the way to go for most applications. This will result in noise that doesn't show a repetitive pattern, has greater numerical precision, and doesn't use up any texture resources. Applications that want full control over the noise function and can live within the constraints of a fixed-size noise function can be successful using textures for their noise. With current generation hardware, noise textures may also provide better performance and require fewer instructions in the shader.

A Simple Noise Shader

Now we put all these ideas into some shaders that do some interesting rendering for us. The first shader we look at uses noise in a simple way to produce a cloud effect.

Application Setup

Very little needs to be passed to the noise shaders discussed in this section, or in "Turbulence" and "Granite". The vertex position must be passed in as always, and the surface normal is needed for performing lighting computations. Colors and scale factors are parameterized as uniform variables for the various shaders.

Vertex Shader

The code shown in Example 8.16 is the vertex shader that we use for the four noise fragment shaders that follow. It is fairly simple because it really only needs to accomplish three things.

- As in all vertex shaders, our vertex shader transforms the incoming vertex value and stores it in the built-in special variable `gl_Position`.

- Using the incoming normal and the uniform variable `LightPos`, the vertex shader computes the light intensity from a single white light source and applies a scale factor of 1.5 to increase the amount of illumination.

- The vertex shader scales the incoming vertex value and stores it in the out variable `MCposition`. This value is available to us in our fragment shader as the modeling coordinate position of the object at every fragment. It is an ideal value to use as the input for our 3D texture lookup.

No matter how the object is drawn, fragments always produce the same position values (or very close to them); therefore, the noise value obtained for each point on the surface is also the same (or very close to it). The application can set a uniform variable called `Scale` to optimally scale the object in relationship to the size of the noise texture.

Example 8.16   Cloud Vertex Shader

```
#version 330 core

uniform mat4 MVMatrix;
uniform mat4 MVPMatrix;
uniform mat3 NormalMatrix;

uniform vec3 LightPos;
uniform float Scale;

in   vec4   MCvertex;
in   vec3   MCnormal;

out float LightIntensity;
out vec3   MCposition;

void main()
{
    vec3 ECposition = vec3(MVMatrix * MCVertex);
    MCposition       = vec3(MCVertex) * Scale;
    vec3 tnorm      = normalize(vec3(NormalMatrix * MCNormal));
    LightIntensity  = dot(normalize(LightPos - ECposition), tnorm);
    LightIntensity *= 1.5;
    gl_Position     = MVPMatrix * MCVertex;
}
```

Fragment Shader

After we've computed a noise texture and used OpenGL calls to download it to the graphics card, we can use a fairly simple fragment shader together with the vertex shader described in the previous section to make an interesting "cloudy sky" effect (see Example 8.17). This shader results in something that looks like the sky on a mostly cloudy day. You can experiment with the color values to get a result that is visually pleasing.

This fragment shader receives as input the two in variables— LightIntensity and MCposition—that were computed by the vertex shader shown in the previous section. These values were computed at each vertex by the vertex shader and then interpolated across the primitive by the rasterization hardware. Here, in our fragment shader, we have access to the interpolated value of each of these variables at every fragment.

The first line of code in the shader performs a 3D texture lookup on our 3D noise texture to produce a four-component result. We compute the value of intensity by summing the four components of our noise texture. This value is then scaled by 1.5 and used to perform a linear blend between two colors: white and sky blue. The four channels in our noise texture have mean values of 0.25, 0.125, 0.0625, and 0.03125. An additional 0.03125 term is added to account for the average values of all the octaves at higher frequencies. You can think of this as fading to the average values of all the higher frequency octaves that aren't being included in the calculation, as described earlier in "Definition of Noise". Scaling the sum by 1.5 stretches the resulting value to use up more of the range from $[0, 1]$.

The computed color is then scaled by LightIntensity value to simulate a diffuse surface lit by a single light source. The result is assigned to the out variable FragColor with an alpha value of 1.0 to produce the color value that is used by the remainder of the OpenGL pipeline. An object rendered with this shader is shown in Figure 8.27. Notice that the texture on the teapot looks a lot like the final image in Figure 8.26.

Example 8.17   Fragment Shader for Cloudy Sky Effect

```
#version 330 core

uniform sampler3D Noise;
uniform vec3 SkyColor;        // (0.0, 0.0, 0.8)
uniform vec3 CloudColor;      // (0.8, 0.8, 0.8)

in   float LightIntensity;
in   vec3  MCposition;

out vec4  FragColor;
```

```
void main()
{
    vec4 noisevec = texture(Noise, MCposition);

    float intensity = (noisevec[0] + noisevec[1] +
                       noisevec[2] + noisevec[3] + 0.03125) * 1.5;

    vec3 color = mix(SkyColor, CloudColor, intensity) *
                 LightIntensity;
    FragColor = vec4(color, 1.0);
}
```

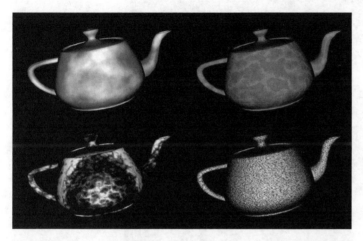

Figure 8.27   Teapots rendered with noise shaders
(Clockwise from upper left: a cloud shader that sums four octaves of noise and uses a blue-to-white color gradient to code the result; a sun surface shader that uses the absolute value function to introduce discontinuities (turbulence); a granite shader that uses a single high-frequency noise value to modulate between white and black; a marble shader that uses noise to modulate a sine function to produce alternating "veins" of color. (3Dlabs, Inc.))

Turbulence

We can obtain some additional interesting effects by taking the absolute value of the noise function. This technique introduces a discontinuity of the derivative because the function folds on itself when it reaches 0. When this folding is done to noise functions at several frequencies and the results are summed, the result is cusps or creases in the texture at various scales. Perlin started referring to this type of noise as *turbulence* because it is reminiscent of turbulent flow. It shows up in a variety of places in nature, so this type of noise can be used to simulate various things like flames or lava. The two-dimensional appearance of this type of noise is shown in Figure 8.28.

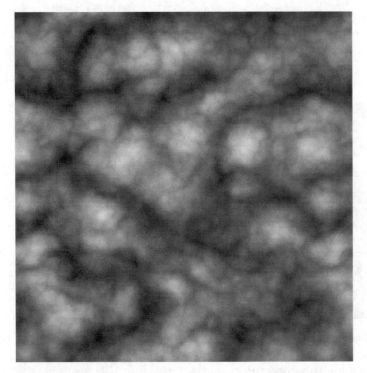

Figure 8.28   Absolute value noise or "turbulence"

Sun Surface Shader

We can achieve an effect that looks like a pit of hot molten lava or the surface of the sun by using the same vertex shader as the cloud shader and a slightly different fragment shader. The main difference is that we scale each noise value and shift it over so that it is centered at 0; then we take its absolute value. After summing the values, we scale the result again to occupy nearly the full range of [0, 1]. We clamp this value and use it to mix between yellow and red to get the result shown in Figure 8.27 (see Example 8.18). This technique can be extended to change the results over time, using another dimension of noise for time, resulting in animation of the effect.

Example 8.18   Sun Surface Fragment Shader

```
#version 330 core

in float LightIntensity;
in vec3 MCposition;

uniform sampler3D Noise;
uniform vec3  Color1;        // (0.8, 0.7, 0.0)
uniform vec3  Color2;        // (0.6, 0.1, 0.0)
uniform float NoiseScale;    // 1.2

out vec4 FragColor;

void main()
{
    vec4 noisevec = texture(Noise, MCposition * NoiseScale);

    float intensity = abs(noisevec[0] - 0.25) +
                      abs(noisevec[1] - 0.125) +
                      abs(noisevec[2] - 0.0625) +
                      abs(noisevec[3] - 0.03125);

    intensity = clamp(intensity * 6.0, 0.0, 1.0);
    vec3 color = mix(Color1, Color2, intensity) * LightIntensity;
    FragColor = vec4(color, 1.0);
}
```

Marble

Yet another variation on the noise function is to use it as part of a periodic function such as sine. By adding noise to the input value for the sine function, we get a "noisy" oscillating function. We use this to create a look similar to the alternating color veins of some types of marble. Example 8.19 shows the fragment shader to do it. Again, we use the same vertex shader. Results of this shader are also shown in Figure 8.27.

Example 8.19   Fragment Shader for Marble

```
#version 330 core

uniform sampler3D Noise;
uniform vec3 MarbleColor;
uniform vec3 VeinColor;

in float LightIntensity;
in vec3  MCposition;

out vec4 FragColor;
```

```
void main()
{
    vec4 noisevec = texture(Noise, MCposition);
    float intensity = abs(noisevec[0] - 0.25) +
                      abs(noisevec[1] - 0.125) +
                      abs(noisevec[2] - 0.0625) +
                      abs(noisevec[3] - 0.03125);
    float sineval = sin(MCposition.y * 6.0 + intensity * 12.0)
                    * 0.5 + 0.5;
    vec3 color    = mix(VeinColor, MarbleColor, sineval)
                    * LightIntensity;
    FragColor     = vec4(color, 1.0);
}
```

Granite

With noise, it's also easy just to try to make stuff up. In this example, we want to simulate a grayish rocky material with small black specks. To generate a relatively high-frequency noise texture, we use only the fourth component (the highest frequency one). We scale it by an arbitrary amount to provide an appropriate intensity level and then use this value for each of the red, green, and blue components. The shader in Example 8.20 generates an appearance similar to granite, as shown in Figure 8.27.

Example 8.20   Granite Fragment Shader

```
#version 330 core

uniform sampler3D Noise;
uniform float NoiseScale;

in float LightIntensity;
in vec3  MCposition;

out vec4 FragColor;

void main()
{
    vec4 noisevec   = texture(Noise, NoiseScale * MCposition);
    float intensity = min(1.0, noisevec[3] * 18.0);
    vec3 color      = vec3(intensity * LightIntensity);
    FragColor       = vec4(color, 1.0);
}
```

Wood

We can do a fair approximation of wood with this approach as well. In *Advanced Renderman*, Anthony A. Apodaca and Larry Gritz describe a model for simulating the appearance of wood. We can adapt their approach to create wood shaders in GLSL. Following are the basic ideas behind the wood fragment shader shown in Example 8.21:

- Wood is composed of light and dark areas alternating in concentric cylinders surrounding a central axis.

- Noise is added to warp the cylinders to create a more natural-looking pattern.

- The center of the "tree" is taken to be the y axis.

- Throughout the wood, a high-frequency grain pattern gives the appearance of wood that has been sawed, exposing the open grain nature of the wood.

The wood shader uses the same vertex shader as the other noise-based shaders discussed in this section.

Application Setup

The wood shaders don't require too much from the application. The application is expected to pass in a vertex position and a normal, per vertex, using the usual OpenGL entry points. In addition, the vertex shader takes a light position and a scale factor that are passed in as uniform variables. The fragment shader takes a number of uniform variables that parameterize the appearance of the wood.

The uniform variables needed for the wood shaders are initialized as follows:

```
LightPos          0.0, 0.0, 4.0
Scale             2.0
LightWood         0.6, 0.3, 0.1
DarkWood          0.4, 0.2, 0.07
RingFreq          4.0
LightGrains       1.0
DarkGrains        0.0
GrainThreshold    0.5
NoiseScale        0.5, 0.1, 0.1
Noisiness         3.0
GrainScale        27.0
```

Fragment Shader

Example 8.21 shows the fragment shader for procedurally generated wood.

Example 8.21   Fragment Shader for Wood

```
#version 330 core

uniform sampler3D Noise;
uniform vec3 LightWood;
uniform vec3 DarkWood;
uniform float RingFreq;
uniform float LightGrains;
uniform float DarkGrains;
uniform float GrainThreshold;
uniform vec3 NoiseScale;
uniform float Noisiness;
uniform float GrainScale;

in   float LightIntensity;
in   vec3  MCposition;

out vec4  FragColor;

void main()
{
    vec3 noisevec = vec3(texture(Noise, MCposition * NoiseScale) *
                                            Noisiness);
    vec3 location = MCposition + noisevec;
    float dist = sqrt(location.x * location.x + location.z * location.z);
    dist *= RingFreq;
    float r = fract(dist + noisevec[0] + noisevec[1] + noisevec[2])
              * 2.0;
    if (r > 1.0)
        r = 2.0 - r;
    vec3 color = mix(LightWood, DarkWood, r);
    r = fract((MCposition.x + MCposition.z) * GrainScale + 0.5);
    noisevec[2] *= r;
    if (r < GrainThreshold)
        color += LightWood * LightGrains * noisevec[2];
    else
        color -= LightWood * DarkGrains * noisevec[2];
    color *= LightIntensity;
    FragColor = vec4(color, 1.0);
}
```

As you can see, we've parameterized quite a bit of this shader through the use of uniform variables to make it easy to manipulate through the application's user interface. As in many procedural shaders, the object position is the basis for computing the procedural texture. In this case, the object position is multiplied by `NoiseScale` (a `vec3` that allows us to scale the noise independently in the *x*, *y*, and *z* directions), and the computed value is used as the index into our 3D noise texture. The noise values obtained from the texture are scaled by the value `Noisiness`, which allows us to increase or decrease the contribution of the noise.

Our tree is assumed to be a series of concentric rings of alternating light wood and dark wood. To give some interest to our grain pattern, we add the noise vector to our object position. This has the effect of adding our low-frequency (first octave) noise to the x coordinate of the position and the third-octave noise to the z coordinate (the y coordinate won't be used). The result is rings that are still relatively circular but have some variation in width and distance from the center of the tree.

To compute where we are in relation to the center of the tree, we square the x and z components and take the square root of the result. This gives us the distance from the center of the tree. The distance is multiplied by RingFreq, a scale factor that gives the wood pattern more rings or fewer rings.

Following this, we attempt to create a function that goes from 0 up to 1.0 and then back down to 0. We add three octaves of noise to the distance value to give more interest to the wood grain pattern. We could compute different noise values here, but the ones we've already obtained will do just fine. Taking the fractional part of the resulting value gives us a function in the range $[0.0, 1.0)$. Multiplying this value by 2.0 gives us a function in the range $[0.0, 2.0)$. And finally, by subtracting 1.0 from values that are greater than 1.0, we get our desired function that varies from 0 to 1.0 and back to 0.

We use this "triangle" function to compute the basic color for the fragment, using the built-in **mix()** function. The **mix()** function linearly blends LightWood and DarkWood according to our computed value r.

At this point, we would have a pretty nice result for our wood function, but we attempt to make it a little better by adding a subtle effect to simulate the look of open-grain wood that has been sawed. (You may not be able to see this effect on the object shown in Figure 8.29.)

Our desire is to produce streaks that are roughly parallel to the y axis. So we add the x and z coordinates, multiply by the GrainScale factor (another uniform variable that we can adjust to change the frequency of this effect), add 0.5, and take the fractional part of the result. Again, this gives us a function that varies from $[0.0, 1.0)$, but for the default values for GrainScale (27.0) and RingFreq (4.0), this function for r goes from 0 to 1.0 much more often than our previous function for r.

We could just make our "grains" go linearly from light to dark, but we try something a little more subtle. We multiply the value of r by our third octave noise value to produce a value that increases nonlinearly. Finally, we compare our value of r to the GrainThreshold value (the default is 0.5). If the value of r is less than GrainThreshold, we modify our current

Figure 8.29   A bust of Beethoven rendered with the wood shader
(3Dlabs, Inc.)

color by adding to it a value we computed by multiplying the `LightWood`
color, the `LightGrains` color, and our modified noise value. Conversely, if
the value of `r` is greater than `GrainThreshold`, we modify our current
color by subtracting from it a value we computed by multiplying the
`DarkWood` color, the `DarkGrains` color, and our modified noise value. (By
default, the value of `LightGrains` is 1.0 and the value of `DarkGrains` is 0,
so we don't actually see any change if `r` is greater than `GrainThreshold`.)

You can play around with this effect and see if it really does help the
appearance. It seemed to me that it added to the effect of the wood texture
for the default settings I've chosen, but there probably is a way to achieve a
better effect more simply.

With our final color computed, all that remains is to multiply the color by
the interpolated diffuse lighting factor and add an alpha value of 1.0 to
produce our final fragment value. The results of our shader are applied to a
bust of Beethoven in Figure 8.29.

Noise Summary

This section introduced noise, an incredibly useful function for adding irregularity to procedural shaders. After a brief description of the mathematical definition of this function, we used it as the basis for shaders that simulated clouds, turbulent flow, marble, granite, and wood. There is a noise function available as a built-in function in some implementations of GLSL. Portable noise functions can be created with user-defined shader functions or textures. However it is implemented, noise can increase the apparent realism of an image or an animation by adding imperfections, complexity, and an element of apparent randomness.

Further Information

The book *Texturing and Modeling: A Procedural Approach, Third Edition*, by David S. Ebert et al. (2002) is entirely devoted to creating images procedurally. This book contains a wealth of information and inspires a ton of ideas for the creation and use of procedural models and textures. It contains several significant discussions of noise, including a description by Perlin of his original noise function. Darwyn Peachey also provides a taxonomy of noise functions called *Making Noises*. The application of different noise functions and combinations of noise functions are discussed by Ken Musgrave in his section on building procedural planets.

The shaders written in the RenderMan Shading Language are often procedural in nature, and *The RenderMan Companion* by Steve Upstill (1990) and *Advanced RenderMan: Creating CGI for Motion Pictures* by Anthony A. Apodaca and Larry Gritz (1999) contain some notable examples.

Bump mapping was invented by Jim Blinn and described in his 1978 SIGGRAPH paper, *Simulation of Wrinkled Surfaces*. A very good overview of bump mapping techniques can be found in a paper titled *A Practical and Robust Bump-mapping Technique for Today's GPUs* by Mark Kilgard (2000).

A Photoshop plug-in for creating a normal map from an image is available at NVIDIA's developer Web site http://developer.nvidia.com/.

Most signal-processing and image-processing books contain a discussion of the concepts of sampling, reconstruction, and aliasing. Books by Glassner, Wolberg, and Gonzalez and Woods can be consulted for additional information on these topics. Technical memos by Alvy Ray Smith address the issues of aliasing in computer graphics directly.

The book *Advanced RenderMan: Creating CGI for Motion Pictures* by Anthony A. Apodaca and Larry Gritz (1999) contains a chapter that describes shader antialiasing in terms of the RenderMan shading language, and much of the discussion is germane to the OpenGL Shading Language as well. Darwyn Peachey has a similar discussion in *Texturing & Modeling: A Procedural Approach, Third Edition*, by David Ebert et al. (2002).

Bert Freudenberg developed a GLSL shader to do adaptive antialiasing and presented this work at the SIGGRAPH 2002 in San Antonio, Texas. This subject is also covered in his Ph.D. thesis, "Real-Time Stroke-based Halftoning".

Ken Perlin has a tutorial and history of the noise function as well as a reference implementation in the Java programming language at his Web site. A lot of other interesting things are available on Ken's home page at NYU (http://mrl.nyu.edu/~perlin). His paper, *An Image Synthesizer*, appeared in the 1985 SIGGRAPH proceedings, and his improvements to the original algorithm were published in the paper "Improving Noise" as part of SIGGRAPH 2002. He also described a clever method for combining two small 3D textures to get a large 3D Perlin-like noise function in the article *Implementing Improved Perlin Noise* in the book *GPU Gems*.

Chapter 9

Tessellation Shaders

Chapter Objectives

After reading this chapter, you'll be able to do the following:

- Understand the differences between tessellation shaders and vertex shaders.

- Identify the phases of processing that occur when using tessellation shaders.

- Recognize the various *tessellation domains* and know which one best matches the type of geometry you need to generate.

- Initialize data and draw using the patch geometric primitive.

This chapter introduces OpenGL's tessellation shader stages. It has the following major sections:

- "Tessellation Shaders" provides an overview of how tessellation shaders work in OpenGL.

- "Tessellation Patches" introduces tessellation's rendering primitive, the patch.

- "Tessellation Control Shaders" explains the operation and purpose of the first tessellation shading.

- "Tessellation Evaluation Shaders" describes the second tessellation stage and how it operates.

- "A Tessellation Example: The Teapot" shows an example of rendering a teapot using tessellation shaders and Bézier patches.

- "Additional Tessellation Techniques" discusses some additional techniques that are enabled by tessellation shading.

Tessellation Shaders

Up to this point, only vertex shaders have been available for us to manipulate geometric primitives. While there are numerous graphics techniques you can do using vertex shaders, they do have their limitations. One limitation is that they can't create additional geometry during their execution. They really only update the data associated with the current vertex they are processing, and they can't even access the data of other vertices in the primitives.

To address those issues, the OpenGL pipeline contains several other shader stages that address those limitations. In this chapter, we introduce *tessellation shaders* which, for example, can generate a mesh of triangles, using a new geometric primitive type called a patch.

Tessellation shading adds two shading stages to the OpenGL pipeline to generate a mesh of geometric primitives. As compared to having to specify all of the lines or triangles to form your model as you do with vertex shading—with tessellation, you begin by specifying a patch, which is just an ordered list of vertices. When a patch is rendered, the *tessellation control shaders* executes first, operating on your patch vertices, and specifying how much geometry should be generated from your patch. Tessellation control shaders are optional, and we'll see what's required if you don't use one. After the tessellation control shader completes, the second shader, the *tessellation evaluation shaders*, positions the vertices of the generated mesh using *tessellation coordinates* and sends them to the rasterizer, or for more processing by a geometry shader (which we describe in Chapter 10, "Geometry Shaders").

As we describe OpenGL's process of tessellation, we'll start at the beginning with describing patches in "Tessellation Patches" on Page 487, then move to describe the tessellation control shader's operation detail in "Tessellation Control Shaders" on Page 488. OpenGL passes the output of the tessellation control shader to the *primitive generator*, which generates the mesh of geometric primitives and tessellation coordinates that the tessellation evaluation shader stage uses. Finally, the tessellation evaluation shader positions each of the vertices in the final mesh, a process described in "Tessellation Evaluation Shaders" on Page 496.

We conclude the chapter with a few examples, including a demonstration of *displacement mapping*, which combines texture-mapping for vertices (which is discussed in Chapter 6, "Textures") with tessellation shaders.

Tessellation Patches

The tessellation process doesn't operate on OpenGL's classic geometric primitives: points, lines, and triangles, but uses a new primitive (added in OpenGL Version 4.0) called a patch. Patches are processed by all of active shading stages in the pipeline. By comparison, other primitive types are only processed by vertex, fragment, and geometry shaders, and bypass the tessellation stage. In fact, if any tessellation shaders are active, passing any other type of geometry will generate a GL_INVALID_OPERATION error. Conversely, you'll get a GL_INVALID_OPERATION error if you try to render a patch without any tessellation shaders (specifically, a tessellation evaluation shader; we'll see that tessellation control shaders are optional) bound.

Patches are nothing more than a list of vertices that you pass into OpenGL, which preserves their order during processing. When rendering with tessellation and patches, you use OpenGL rendering commands, like **glDrawArrays()**, and specify the total number of vertices to be read from the bound vertex-buffer objects and processed for that draw call. When you're rendering with the other OpenGL primitives, OpenGL implicitly knows how many vertices to use based on the primitive type you specified in your draw call, like using three vertices to make a triangle. However, when you use a patch, OpenGL needs to be told how many vertices from your vertex array to use to make one patch, which you specify using **glPatchParameteri()**. Patches processed by the same draw call will all be the same size.

---

void **glPatchParameteri**(GLenum *pname*, GLint *value*);

Specifies the number of vertices in a patch using *value*. *pname* must be set to GL_PATCH_VERTICES.

A GL_INVALID_ENUM error is generated if *value* is less than zero, or greater than GL_MAX_PATCH_VERTICES.

The default number of vertices for a patch is three. If the number of vertices for a patch is less that *value*, the patch is ignored, and no geometry will be generated.

To specify a patch, use the input type GL_PATCHES into any OpenGL drawing command. Example 9.1 demonstrates issuing two patches, each with four vertices

Example 9.1　　Specifying Tessellation Patches

```
GLfloat vertices [] [2] = {
   {-0.75, -0.25}, {-0.25, -0.25}, {-0.25, 0.25}, {-0.75, 0.25},
   { 0.25, -0.25}, { 0.75, -0.25}, { 0.75, 0.25}, { 0.25, 0.25}
};

glBindVertexArray(VAO);
glBindBuffer(GL_ARRAY_BUFFER, VBO);
glBufferData(GL_ARRAY_BUFFER, sizeof(vertices), vertices,
             GL_STATIC_DRAW);

glVertexAttribPointer(vPos, 2, GL_FLOAT, GL_FALSE, 0, BUFFER_OFFSET(0));
glPatchParameteri(GL_PATCH_VERTICES, 4);
glDrawArrays(GL_PATCHES, 0, 8);
```

The vertices of each patch are first processed by the currently bound vertex shader, and then used to initialize the array gl_in, which is implicitly declared in the tessellation control shader. The number of elements in gl_in is the same as the patch size specified by **glPatchParameteri()**. Inside of a tessellation control shader, the variable gl_PatchVerticesIn provides the number of elements in gl_in (as does querying gl_in.length()).

Tessellation Control Shaders

Once your application issues a patch, the tessellation control shader will be called (if one is bound) and is responsible for completing the following actions:

- Generate the *tessellation output patch vertices* that are passed to the tessellation evaluation shader, as well as update any per-vertex, or per-patch attribute values as necessary.

- Specify the *tessellation level factors* that control the operation of the primitive generator. These are special tessellation control shader variables called `gl_TessLevelInner` and `gl_TessLevelOuter`, and are implicitly declared in your tessellation control shader.

We'll discuss each of these actions in turn.

Generating Output-Patch Vertices

Tessellation control shaders use the vertices specified by the application, which we'll call *input-patch vertexs*, to generate a new set of vertices, the output-patch vertices, which are stored in the `gl_out` array of the tessellation control shader. At this point, you might be asking what's going on; why not just pass in the original set of vertices from the application, and skip all this work? Tessellation control shaders can modify the values passed from the application, but can also create or remove vertices from the input-patch vertices when producing the output-patch vertices. You might use this functionality when working with sprites, or when minimizing the amount of data sent from the application to OpenGL, which may increase performance.

You already know how to set the number of input-patch vertices using **glPatchParameteri()**. You specify the number of output-patch vertices using a `layout` construct in your tessellation control shader, as demonstrated below, which sets the number of output-patch vertices to 16.

```
layout (vertices = 16) out;
```

The value set by the `vertices` parameter in the `layout` directive does two things: it sets the size of the output-patch vertices, `gl_out`; and specifies how many times the tessellation control shader will execute: once for each output-patch vertex.

In order to determine which output vertex is being processed, the tessellation control shader can use the `gl_InvocationID` variable. Its value is most often used as an index into the `gl_out` array. While a tessellation control shader is executing, it has access to all patch vertex data—both input and output. This can lead to issues where a shader invocation might need data values from a shader invocation that hasn't happened yet. tessellation control shaders can use the GLSL **barrier()** function, which causes all of the control shaders for an input patch to execute and wait until all of them have reached that point, thus guaranteeing that all of the data values you might set will be computed.

A common idiom of tessellation control shaders is just passing the input-patch vertices out of the shader. Example 9.2 demonstrates this for an output patch with four vertices.

Example 9.2 Passing Through Tessellation Control Shader Patch Vertices

```
#version 420 core

layout (vertices = 4) out;

void
main()
{
    gl_out[gl_InvocationID].gl_Position
                    = gl_in[gl_InvocationID].gl_Position;

    // and then set tessellation levels
}
```

Tessellation Control Shader Variables

The gl_in array is actually an array of structures, with each element defined as:

```
in gl_PerVertex {
    vec4 gl_Position;
    float gl_PointSize;
    float gl_ClipDistance[]
} gl_in[gl_PatchVerticesIn];
```

and for each value that you need downstream (e.g., in the tessellation evaluation shader), you'll need to assign values similar to what we did with the gl_Position field.

The gl_out array has the same fields, but is a different size specified by gl_PatchVerticesOut, which as we saw, was set in the tessellation control shader's out layout qualifier. Additionally, the following scalar values, described in Table 9.1 are provided for determining which primitive and output vertex invocation is being shaded:

Table 9.1 Tessellation Control Shader Input Variables

Variable Declaration	Description
gl_InvocationID	Invocation index for the output vertex of the current tessellation control shader
gl_PrimitiveID	Primitive index for current input patch
gl_PatchVerticesIn	Number of vertices in the input patch, which is the dimension of gl_in
gl_PatchVerticesOut	Number of vertices in the output patch, which is the dimension of gl_out

If you have additional per-vertex attribute values, either for input or output, these need to be declared as either in or out arrays in your tessellation control shader. The size of an input array needs to be sized to the input-patch size, or can be declared unsized, and OpenGL will appropriately allocate space for all its values. Similarly, per-vertex output attributes, which you will be able to access in the tessellation evaluation shader need to be sized to the number of vertices in the output patch, or can be declared unsized as well.

Controlling Tessellation

The other function of a tessellation control shader is to specify how much to tessellate the output patch. While we haven't discussed tessellation evaluation shaders in detail yet, they control the type of output patch for rendering, and consequently, the domain where tessellation occurs. OpenGL supports three tessellation domains: a quadrilateral, a triangle, and a collection of isolines.

The amount of tessellation is controlled by specifying two sets of values: the inner- and outer-tessellation levels. The outer-tessellation levels control how the perimeter of the domain is subdivided, and is stored in an implicitly declared four-element array named gl_TessLevelOuter. Similarly, the inner-tessellation levels specify how the interior of the domain is subdivided and stored in a two-element array named gl_TessLevelInner. All tessellation level factors are floating-point values, and we'll see the effect that fractional values have on tessellations in a bit. One final point is that while the dimensions of the implicitly declared tessellation level factors arrays are fixed, the number of values used from those arrays depends on the type of tessellation domain.

Understanding how the inner- and outer-tessellation levels operate is key to getting tessellation to do what you want. Each of the tessellation level factors specifies how many "segments" to subdivide a region, as well as how many tessellation coordinates and geometric primitives to generate. How that subdivision is done varies by domain type. We'll discuss each type of domain in turn, as they operate differently.

Quad Tessellation

Using the quadrilaterial domain may be the most intuitive, so we'll begin with it. It's useful when your input patches are rectangular in shape, as you might have when using two-dimensional spline surfaces, like Bézier surfaces. The quad domain subdivides the *unit square* using all of the inner- and outer-tessellation levels. For instance, if we were to set the tessellation level factors to the following values, OpenGL would tessellate the quad domain as illustrated in Figure 9.1.

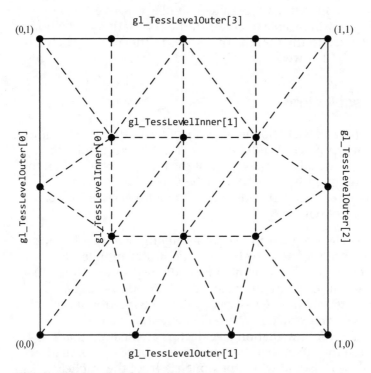

Figure 9.1 Quad tessellation
(A tessellation of a quad domain using the tessellation levels from Example 9.3.)

Example 9.3 Tessellation Levels for Quad Domain Tessellation Illustrated in Figure 9.1

```
gl_TessLevelOuter[0] = 2.0;
gl_TessLevelOuter[1] = 3.0;
gl_TessLevelOuter[2] = 2.0;
gl_TessLevelOuter[3] = 5.0;

gl_TessLevelInner[0] = 3.0;
gl_TessLevelInner[1] = 4.0;
```

Notice that the outer-tessellation levels values correspond to the number of segments for each edge around the perimeter, while the inner-tessellation levels specify how many "regions" are in the horizontal and vertical directions in the interior of the domain. Also shown in Figure 9.1 is a possible triangularization of the domain,[1] shown using the dashed lines. Likewise, the solid circles represent the tessellation coordinates, each of which will be provided as input into the tessellation evaluation shader. In the case of the quad domain, the Tessellation coordinates will have two coordinates, (u, v), which will both be in the range $[0, 1]$, and each Tessellation coordinate will be passed into an invocation of an tessellation evaluation shader.

Isoline Tessellation

Similar to the quad domain, the isoline domain also generates (u, v) pairs as tessellation coordinates for the tessellation evaluation shader. Isolines, however, use only two of the outer-tessellation levels to determine the amount of subdivsion (and none of the inner-tessellation levels). This is illustrated in Figure 9.2 for the tessellation level factors shown in Example 9.4.

Example 9.4   Tesslation Levels for an Isoline Domain Tessellation
Shown in Figure 9.2

```
gl_TessLevelOuter[0]  = 6;
gl_TessLevelOuter[1]  = 8;
```

You'll notice that there's a dashed line along the $v = 1$ edge. That's because isolines don't include a tessellated isoline along that edge, and if you place two isoline patches together (i.e., two patches share an edge), there isn't overlap of the edges.

Triangle Tessellation

Finally, let's discuss tessellation using a triangle domain. As compared to either the quad or isolines domains, coordinates related to the three vertices of a triangle aren't very conveniently represented by a (u, v) pair. Instead, triangular domains use *barycentric coordinates* to specify their Tessellation coordinates. Barycentric coordinates are represented by a triplet of numbers (a, b, c), each of which lies in the range $[0, 1]$, and which

---

1. Triangularization of the domain is implementation-dependent.

have the property that $a + b + c = 1$. Think of a, b, or c as weights for each individual triangle vertex.

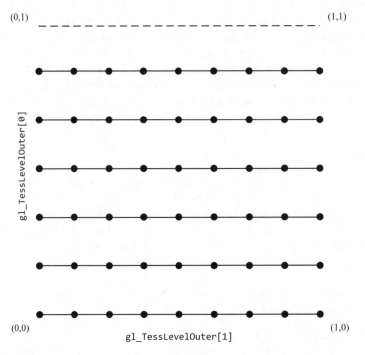

Figure 9.2   Isoline tessellation
(A tessellation of an isolines domain using the tessellations levels from Example 9.4.)

As with any of the other domains, the generated tessellation coordinates are a function of the tessellation level factors, and in particular, the first three outer-tessellation levels, and only inner-tessellation level zero. The tessellation of a triangular domain with tessellation level factors set as in Example 9.5 is shown in Figure 9.3.

Example 9.5   Tesslation Levels for a Triangular Domain Tessellation Shown in Figure 9.3

```
gl_TessLevelOuter[0]  = 6;
gl_TessLevelOuter[1]  = 5;
gl_TessLevelOuter[2]  = 8;

gl_TessLevelInner[0]  = 5;
```

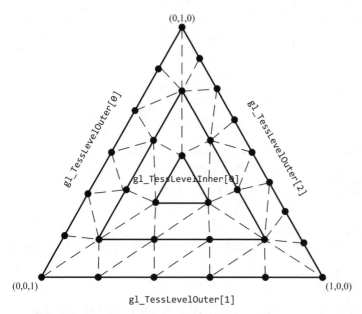

Figure 9.3   Triangle tessellation
(A tessellation of a triangular domain using the tessellation levels from
Example 9.5.)

As with the other domains, the outer-tessellation levels control the
subdivision of the perimeter of the triangle and the inner-tessellation level
controls how the interior is partitioned. As compared to the rectangular
domains, where the interior is partitioned in a set of rectangles forming a
grid, the interior of the triangular domain is partitioned into a set of
concentric triangles that form the regions. Specifically, let t represent the
inner-tessellation level. If t is an even value, then the center of the
triangular domain (barycentric coordinate $(\frac{1}{2}, \frac{1}{2}, \frac{1}{2})$ is located, and then
$(t/2) - 1$ concentric triangles are generated between the center point and
the perimeter. Conversely, if t is an odd value, then $(t/2) - 1$ concentric
triangles are out to the perimeter, however, the center point (in barycentric
coordinates) will not be a tessellation coordinate. These two scenarios are
shown in Figure 9.4.

Bypassing the Tessellation Control Shader

As we mentioned, often your tessellation control shader will just be a
pass-through shader, copying data from input to output. In such a case,
you can actually bypass using a tessellation control shader and set the

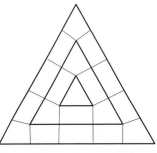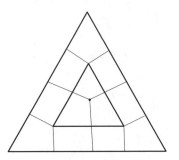

Odd inner tessellation levels
create a small triangle in the
center of the triangular
tessellation domain

Even inner tessellation levels
create a single tessellation
coordinate in the center of the
triangular tessellation domain

Figure 9.4   Even and odd tessellation
(Examples of how even and odd inner tessellation levels affect triangular
tessellation.)

tessellation level factors using the OpenGL API, as compared to using a
shader. The **glPatchParameterfv()** function can be used to set the inner-
and outer-tessellation levels.

---

void **glPatchParameterfv**(GLenum *pname*, const GLfloat **values*);

Sets the inner- and outer-tessellation levels for when no tessellation
control shader is bound. *pname* must be either
GL_PATCH_DEFAULT_OUTER_LEVEL, or
GL_PATCH_DEFAULT_INNER_LEVEL.

When *pname* is GL_PATCH_DEFAULT_OUTER_LEVEL, values must be an
array of four floating-point values that specify the four outer-tessellation
levels.

Similarly, when *pname* is GL_PATCH_DEFAULT_INNER_LEVEL, values
must be an array of two floating-point values that specify the two
inner-tessellation levels.

Tessellation Evaluation Shaders

The final phase in OpenGL's tessellation pipeline is the tessellation
evaluation shader execution. The bound tessellation evaluation shader is
executed one for each tessellation coordinate that the primitive generator

emits, and is responsible for determining the position of the vertex derived from the tessellation coordinate. As we'll see, tessellation evaluation shaders look similar to vertex shaders in transforming vertices into screen positions (unless the tessellation evaluation shader's data is going to be further processed by a geometry shader).

The first step in configuring a tessellation evaluation shader is to configure the primitive generator, which is done using a `layout` directive, similar to what we did in the tessellation control shader. Its parameters specify the tessellation domain and subsequently, the type of primitives generated; face orientation for solid primitives (used for face culling); and how the tessellation levels should be applied during primitive generation.

Specifying the Primitive Generation Domain

We'll now describe the parameters that you will use to set up the tessellation evaluation shader's `out layout` directive. First, we'll talk about specifying the tessellation domain. As you've seen, There are three types of domains used for generating tessellation coordinates, which are described in Table 9.2.

Table 9.2   Evaluation Shader Primitive Types

Primitive Type	Description	Domain Coordinates
quads	A rectangular domain over the unit square	a (u, v) pair with u, v values ranging from 0 to 1.
triangles	A triangular shaped domain using barycentric coordinates	(a, b, c) with a, b, and c values ranging from 0 to 1 and where $a + b + c = 1$
isolines	A collection of lines across the unit square	a (u, v) pair with u values ranging from 0 to 1 and v values ranging from 0 to almost 1

Specifying the Face Winding for Generated Primitives

As with any filled primitive in OpenGL, the order the vertices are issued determines the facedness of the primitive. Since we don't issue the vertices directly in this case, but rather have the primitive generator do it on our behalf, we need to tell it the face winding of our primitives. In the `layout` directive, specify cw for clockwise *vertex winding* or ccw for counterclock-wise vertex winding.

Specifying the Spacing of Tessellation Coordinates

Additionally, we can control how fractional values for the outer-tessellation levels are used in determining the tessellation coordinate generation for the perimeter edges. (Inner-tessellation levels are affected by these options.) Table 9.3 describes the three spacing options available, where *max* represents an OpenGL implementation's maximum accepted value for a tessellation level.

Table 9.3   Options for Controlling Tessellation Level Effects

Option	Description
equal_spacing	Tessellation level is clamped to [1, *max*], and is then rounded up to the next largest integer value
fractional_even_spacing	The value is clamped to [2, *max*], and then rounded up to the next largest even integer value *n*. The edge is then divided into *n* − 2 equal length parts, and two other parts, one at either end, which may be shorter than the other lengths.
fractional_odd_spacing	The value is clamped to [1, *max* − 1], and then rounded up to the next largest odd integer value *n*. The edge is then divided into *n* − 2 equal length parts, and two other parts, one at either end, which may be shorter than the other lengths.

Additional Tessellation Evaluation Shader `layout` Options

Finally, should you want to output points, as compared to isolines or filled regions, you can supply the `point_mode` option, which will render a single point for each vertex processed by the tessellation evaluation shader.

The order of options within the `layout` directive is not important. As an example, the following `layout` directive will request primitives generated on a triangular domain using equal spacing, counterclockwise-oriented triangles, but only rendering points, as compared to connected primitives.

```
layout (triangles, equal_spacing, ccw, points) out;
```

Specifying a Vertex's Position

The vertices output from the tessellation control shader (i.e., the `gl_Position` values in `gl_out` array) are made available in the evaluation shader in the `gl_in` variable, which when combined with tessellation coordinates, can be used to generate the output vertex's position.

Tessellation coordinates are provided to the shader in the variable `gl_TessCoord`. In Example 9.6, we use a combination of equal-spaced quads to render a simple patch. In this case, the tessellation coordinates are used to color the surface, and illustrates how to compute the vertex's position.

Example 9.6   A Sample Tessellation Evaluation Shader

```
#version 420 core

layout (quads, equal_spacing, ccw) in;

out vec4 color;

void main()
{
    float u = gl_TessCoord.x;
    float omu = 1 - u; // one minus "u"
    float v = gl_TessCoord.y;
    float omv = 1 - v; // one minus "v"

    color = gl_TessCoord;

    gl_Position =
        omu * omv * gl_in[0].gl_Position +
        u * omv * gl_in[1].gl_Position +
        u * v * gl_in[2].gl_Position +
        omu * v * gl_in[3].gl_Position;
}
```

Tessellation Evaluation Shader Variables

Similar to tessellation control shaders, tessellation evaluation shaders have a `gl_in` array that is actually an array of structures, with each element defined as shown in Example 9.7.

Example 9.7   `gl_in` Parameters for Tessellation Evaluation Shaders

```
in gl_PerVertex {
    vec4 gl_Position;
    float gl_PointSize;
    float gl_ClipDistance[]
} gl_in[gl_PatchVerticesIn];
```

Additionally, the following scalar values, described in Table 9.4, are provided for determining which primitive and for computing the position of the output vertex.

Table 9.4 Tessellation Control Shader Input Variables

Variable Declaration	Description
`gl_PrimitiveID`	Primitive index for current input patch
`gl_PatchVerticesIn`	Number of vertices in the input patch, which is the dimension of `gl_in`
`gl_TessLevelOuter[4]`	Outer-tessellation level values
`gl_TessLevelInner[2]`	Inner-tessellation level values
`gl_TessCoord`	Coordinates in patch domain space of the vertex being shaded in the evaluation shader

The output vertex's data is stored in an interface block defined as follows:

```
out gl_PerVertex {
    vec4 gl_Position;
    float gl_PointSize;
    float gl_ClipDistance[]
};
```

A Tessellation Example: The Teapot

All of that theory could use a concrete demonstration. In this section, we'll render the famous *Utah teapot* using Bézier patches. A Bézier patch, named after French engineer Pierre Bézier, defines a parametric surface evaluated over the unit square using control points arranged in a grid. For our example, we'll use 16 control points arranged in a 4 × 4 grid. As such, we make the following observations to help us set up our tessellation:

- Bézier patches are defined over the unit square, which indicates we should use the `quads` domain type that we'll specify in our `layout` directive in the tessellation evaluation shader.

- Each patch has 16 control points, so our GL_PATCH_VERTICES should be set to 16 using **glPatchParameteri()**.

- The 16 control points also define the number of input-patch vertices, which tells us our maximum index into the `gl_in` array in our tessellation control shader.

- Finally, since the tessellation control shader doesn't add or remove any vertices to the patch, the number of output-patch vertices will also be 16, which specifies the value we'll use in our `layout` directive in the tessellation control shader.

Processing Patch Input Vertices

Given the information from our patches, we can easily construct the tessellation control shader for our application, which is shown in Example 9.8.

Example 9.8   Tessellation Control Shader for Teapot Example

```
#version 420 core

layout (vertices = 16) out;

void main()
{
    gl_TessLevelInner[0] = 4;
    gl_TessLevelInner[1] = 4;

    gl_TessLevelOuter[0] = 4;
    gl_TessLevelOuter[1] = 4;
    gl_TessLevelOuter[2] = 4;
    gl_TessLevelOuter[3] = 4;

    gl_out[gl_InvocationID].gl_Position
                 = gl_in[gl_InvocationID].gl_Position;
}
```

Using the tessellation level factors from Example 9.8, Figure 9.5 shows the patches of the teapot (shrunk slightly to expose each individual patch).

This is a very simple example of a tessellation control shader. In fact, it's a great example of a pass-through shader, where mostly the inputs are copied to the output. The shader also sets the inner- and outer-tessellation levels to constant values, which could also be done in the application using a call to **glPatchParameterfv()**. However, we include the example here for completeness.

Evaluating Tessellation Coordinates for the Teapot

Bézier patches use a bit of mathematics to determine the final vertex position from the input control points. The equation mapping a tessellation coordinate to a vertex position for our 4 × 4 patch is:

$$\vec{p}(u, v) = \sum_{i=0}^{3} \sum_{j=0}^{3} B(i, u)B(j, v)\vec{v}_{ij}$$

Figure 9.5   The tessellated patches of the teapot

with $\vec{p}$ being the final vertex position, $\vec{v}_{ij}$ the input control point at index (i, j) in our input patch (both of which are `vec4`s in GLSL), and B which are two scaling functions.

While it might not seem like it, we can map easily the formula to a tessellation evaluation shader, as show in Example 9.9. In the following shader, the B function will be a GLSL function we'll define in a moment.

We also specify our `quads` domain, spacing options, and polygon face orientation in the `layout` directive.

Example 9.9   The `Main` Routine of the Teapot Tessellation
           Evaluation Shader

```
#version 420 core

layout (quads, equal_spacing, ccw) out;

uniform mat4 MV; // Model-view matrix
uniform mat4 P; // Projection matrix

void main()
```

```
{
    vec4 p = vec4(0.0);

    float u = gl_TessCoord.x;
    float v = gl_TessCoord.y;

    for (int j = 0; j < 4; ++j) {
        for (int i = 0; i < 4; ++i) {
            p += B(i, u) * B(j, v) * gl_in[4*j+i].gl_Position;
        }
    }

    gl_Position = P * MV * p;
}
```

Our B function is one of the *Bernstein polynomials*, which is an entire family of mathematical functions. Each one returns a scalar value. We're using a small, select set of functions, which we index using the first parameter, and evaluate the function's value at one component of our tessellation coordinate. Here's the mathematical definition of our functions

$$B(i, u) = \binom{3}{i} u^i (1 - u)^{3-i}$$

where the $\binom{3}{i}$ is a particular instance of a mathematical construct called a *binomial coefficient*.[2] We'll spare you the gory details and just say we're lucky that it evaluates to either 1 or 3 in our cases, and which we'll hard code into a lookup table, *bc* in the function's definition, and that we'll index using *i*. As such, we can rewrite $B(i, u)$ as

$$B(i, u) = bc_i\, u^i (1 - u)^{3-i}$$

This also translates easily into GLSL, shown in Example 9.10.

Example 9.10   Definition of $B(i, u)$ for the Teapot Tessellation Evaluation Shader

```
float
B(int i, float u)
{
    // Binomial coefficient lookup table
    const vec4 bc = vec4(1, 3, 3, 1);

    return bc[i] * pow(u, i) * pow(1.0 - u, 3 - i);
}
```

---

2. Binomial coefficients in generally defined using the formula $\binom{n}{k} = \frac{n!}{k!(n-k)!}$, where $n!$ is the *factorial* of n, which is just the product of the values n to 1: $n! = (n)(n-1)(n-2)\ldots(2)(1)$.

While that conversation involved more mathematics than most of the other techniques we've described in the book, it is representative of what you will encounter when working with tessellated surfaces. While discussion of the mathematics of surfaces is outside of this text, copious resources are available that describe the required techniques.

Additional Tessellation Techniques

In this final section, we briefly describe a few additional techniques you can employ while using tessellation shaders.

View-Dependent Tessellation

Most of the examples in this chapter have set the tessellation level factors to constant values (either in the shader or through uniform variables). One key feature of tessellation is being able to compute tessellation levels dynamically in the tessellation control shader, and in particular, basing the amount of tessellation on view-dependent parameters.

For example, you might implement a level-of-detail scheme based on the distance of the patch from the eye's location in the scene. In Example 9.11, we use the average of all the input-patch vertices to specify a single representative point for the patch, and derive all the tessellation level factors from the distance of that point to the eye point.

Example 9.11   Computing Tessellation Levels Based on View-Dependent Parameters

```
uniform vec3 EyePosition;

void main()
{
    vec4 center = vec4(0.0);

    for (int i = 0; i < gl_in.length(); ++i) {
        center += gl_in[i].gl_Position;
    }

    center /= gl_in.length();

    float d = distance(center, vec4(EyePosition, 1.0));

    const float lodScale = 2.5; // distance scaling variable

    float tessLOD = mix(0.0, gl_MaxTessGenLevel, d * lodScale
```

```
for (int i = 0; i < 4; ++i) {
    gl_TessLevelOuter[i] = tessLOD;
}

tessLOD = clamp(0.5 * tessLOD, 0.0, gl_MaxTessGenLevel);
gl_TessLevelInner[0] = tessLOD;
gl_TessLevelInner[1] = tessLOD;

gl_out[gl_InvocationID].gl_Position
                       = gl_in[gl_InvocationID].gl_Position;
}
```

Example 9.11 is a very rudimentary method for computing a patch's level of detail. In particular, each perimeter edge is tessellated the same amount, regardless of its distance from the eye. This doesn't take full advantage of tessellation possibilities based on view information, which is usually employed as a geometry optimization technique (i.e., reducing the object's geometric complexity the farther from the eye that object is, assuming a perspective projection is used). Another failing of this approach is that if you have multiple patches that share edges, it's likely that the shared edges may be assigned different levels of tessellation depending on the objects' orientation with respect to the eye's position, and that might lead to *cracking* along the shared edges. Cracking is an important issue with tessellation, and we address another concern in "Shared Tessellated Edges and Cracking" on Page 506.

To address guaranteeing that shared edges are tessellated the same, we need to find a method that returns the same tessellation factor for those edges. However, as compared to Example 9.11, which doesn't need to know anything about the logical ordering of input-patch vertices, any algorithm that needs to know which vertices are incident on a perimeter edge is data-dependent. This is because a patch is a logical ordering—only the application knows how it ordered the input-patch vertices. For Example 9.12, we introduce the following array of structures that contain our edge information for our tessellation control shader.

```
struct EdgeCenters {
    vec4 edgeCenter[4];
};
```

The application would need to populate this array using the world-space positions of the centers of each edge. In that example, we'll assume we're working with the quads domain, which is why there are four points in each EdgeCenters structure; the number of points would need to be modified for the other domains. The number of EdgeCenters structures in the array is the number of patches that will be issued in the draw call process. We would modify the tessellation control shader to implement the following:

Example 9.12   Specifying Tessellation Level Factors Using Perimeter Edge Centers

```
struct EdgeCenters { vec4 edgeCenter[4]; };

uniform vec3 EyePosition;

uniform EdgeCenters patch[];

void main()
{
    for (int i = 0; i < 4; ++i) {
        float d = distance(patch[gl_PrimitiveID].edgeCenter[i],
                           vec4(EyePosition, 1.0));
        const float lodScale = 2.5; // distance scaling variable

        float tessLOD = mix(0.0, gl_MaxTessGenLevel, d * lodScale);

        gl_TessLevelOuter[i] = tessLOD;
    }
    tessLOD = clamp(0.5 * tessLOD, 0.0, gl_MaxTessGenLevel);
    gl_TessLevelInner[0] = tessLOD;
    gl_TessLevelInner[1] = tessLOD;

    gl_out[gl_InvocationID].gl_Position
                      = gl_in[gl_InvocationID].gl_Position;
}
```

Shared Tessellated Edges and Cracking

Often a geometric model that uses tessellation will have patches with shared edges. Tessellation in OpenGL guarantees that the geometry generated for the primitives within a patch won't have any cracks between them, but it can't make the same claim for patches that share edges. That's something the application needs to address, and clearly the starting point is that shared edges need to be tessellated the same amounts. However, there's a secondary issue that can creep in—precision in mathematical computations done by a computer.

For all but trivial tessellation applications, the points along a perimeter edge will be positioned using multiple tessellation control shader output-patch vertices, which are combined with the tessellation coordinates in the tessellation evaluation shader. In order to truly prevent cracking along edges between similarly tessellated adjacent patches, the order of accumulation of mathematical operations in the tessellation evaluation shader must also match. Depending upon how the tessellation evaluation shader generates the mesh's vertices final positions, you may need to reorder the processing of vertices in the tessellation evaluation shader. A common approach to this problem is to recognize the output-patch vertices that contribute to a vertex incident to a perimeter edge, and sort those vertices in a predictable manner, say, in terms of increasing magnitude along the edge.

Another technique to avoid cracking is applying the `precise` qualifier to shader computations where points might be in reversed order between two shader invocations. This is illustrated in Figure 9.6.

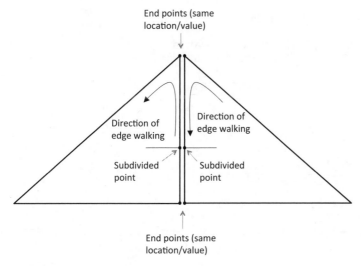

Figure 9.6   Tessellation cracking
(When walking the interior edge in opposite directions, the computed sub-division points need to result in the same value, or the edge may crack.)

As explained in "The `precise` Qualifier" on Page 55 in Chapter 2, this computation can result in different values if the expression is the same and the input values are the same but some of them are swapped due to the opposite direction of edge walking. Qualifying the results of such computations as `precise` will prevent this.

Displacement Mapping

A final technique we'll discuss in terms of tessellation is displacement mapping, which is merely a form of vertex texture mapping, like we described in Chapter 6, "Textures". In fact, there's really not much to say, other than you would likely use the tessellation coordinate provided to the tessellation evaluation shader in some manner to sample a texture map containing displacement information.

Adding displacement mapping to the teapot from Example 9.9, would requite adding two lines into the tessellation evaluation shader, as shown in Example 9.13.

Example 9.13   Displacement Mapping in `main` Routine of the Teapot
               Tessellation Evaluation Shader

```
#version 420 core

layout (quads, equal_spacing, ccw) out;

uniform mat4  MV; // Model-view matrix
uniform mat4  P;  // Projection matrix

uniform sampler2D DisplacementMap;

void main()
{
    vec4  p = vec4(0.0);

    float  u = gl_TessCoord.x;
    float  v = gl_TessCoord.y;

    for (int j = 0; j < 4; ++j) {
        for (int i = 0; i < 4; ++i) {
            p += B(i, u) * B(j, v) * gl_in[4*j+i].gl_Position
        }
    }

    p += texture(DisplacementMap, gl_TessCoord.xy);

    gl_Position = P * MV * p;
}
```

Chapter 10

Geometry Shaders

Chapter Objectives

After reading this chapter, you'll be able to do the following:

- Create and use geometry shaders to further process geometry within the OpenGL pipeline.

- Create additional geometric primitives using a geometry shader.

- Use geometry shaders in combination with transform feedback to generate multiple streams of geometric data.

- Render to multiple viewports in a single rendering pass.

In this chapter, we introduce an entirely new shader stage—the geometry shader. The geometry shader sits logically right before primitive assembly and fragment shading. It receives as its input complete primitives as a collection of vertices, and these inputs are represented as arrays. Typically, the inputs are provided by the vertex shader. However, when tessellation is active, the input to the geometry shader is provided by the tessellation evaluation shader. Because each invocation of the geometry shader processes an entire primitive, it is possible to implement techniques that require access to all of the vertices of that primitive.

In addition to this enhanced, multivertex access, the geometry shader can output a variable amount of data. Outputting nothing amounts to culling geometry and outputting more vertices than were in the original primitive results in geometry amplification. The geometry shader is also capable of producing a different primitive type at its output than it accepts on its input, allowing it to change the type of geometry as it passes through the pipeline. There are four special primitive types provided for use as inputs to geometry shaders. Finally, geometry shaders can be used with transform feedback to split an input stream of vertex data into several substreams. These are very powerful features that enable a large array of techniques and algorithms to be implemented on the GPU.

It has the following major sections:

- "Creating a Geometry Shader" describes the fundamental mechanics of using geometry shaders.

- "Geometry Shader Inputs and Outputs" defines the input and output data structures used with geometry shaders.

- "Producing Primitives" illustrates how primitives can be generated within a geometry shader.

- "Advanced Transform Feedback" extends the transform feedback mechanism (described in "Transform Feedback" on Page 239) to support more advanced techniques.

- "Geometry Shader Instancing" describes optimization techniques available when using geometry shaders for geometric instancing.

- "Multiple Viewports and Layered Rendering" explains rendering to multiple viewports in a single rendering pass.

Creating a Geometry Shader

Geometry shaders are created in exactly the same manner as any other type of shader—by using the **glCreateShader()** function. To create a geometry shader, pass GL_GEOMETRY_SHADER as the shader *type* parameter to **glCreateShader()**. The shader source is passed as normal using the **glShaderSource()** function and then the shader is compiled using **glCompileShader()**. Multiple geometry shaders may be attached to a single program object and when that program is linked, the attached geometry shaders will be linked into an executable that can run on the GPU. When a program object containing a geometry shader is active the geometry shader will run on each primitive produced by OpenGL. These primitives may be points, lines, triangles or one of the special adjacency primitives, which will be discussed shortly.

The geometry shader is an optional stage in OpenGL—your program object does not need to contain one. It sits right before rasterization and fragment shading. The output of the geometry shader can be captured using transform feedback, and it is often used in this mode to process vertices for use in subsequent rendering, or even nongraphics tasks. If no fragment shader is present, rasterization can even be turned off by calling **glEnable()** with the parameter GL_RASTERIZER_DISCARD. This makes transform feedback the end of the pipeline and it can be used in this mode when only the captured vertex data is of interest and the rendering of primitives is not required.

One of the unique aspects of the geometry shader is that it is capable of changing the type and number of primitives that are passing through the OpenGL pipeline. The methods and applications of doing these things will be explained shortly. However, before a geometry shader may be linked, the input primitive type, output primitive type, and the maximum number of vertices that it might produce must be specified. These parameters are given in the form of *layout qualifiers* in the geometry shader source code.

Example 10.1 shows a very basic example of a geometry shader that simply passes primitives through unmodified (a pass-through geometry shader).

Example 10.1   A Simple Pass-Through Geometry Shader

```
// This is a very simple pass-through geometry shader
#version 330 core

// Specify the input and output primitive types, along
// with the maximum number of vertices that this shader
// might produce. Here, the input type is triangles and
// the output type is triangle strips.
layout (triangles) in;
layout (triangle_strip, max_vertices = 3) out;

// Geometry shaders have a main function just
// like any other type of shader
```

```
void main()
{
    int n;

    // Loop over the input vertices
    for (n = 0; n < gl_in.length(); n++)
    {
        // Copy the input position to the output
        gl_Position = gl_in[0].gl_Position;
        // Emit the vertex
        EmitVertex();
    }
    // End the primitive. This is not strictly necessary
    // and is only here for illustrative purposes.
    EndPrimitive();
}
```

This shader simply copies its input into its output. You don't need to worry about how this works right now, but you might notice several features of this example that are unique to geometry shaders. First, at the top of the shader is a pair of layout qualifiers containing the declaration of the input and output primitive types and the maximum number of vertices that may be produced. These are shown in Example 10.2.

Example 10.2   Geometry Shader Layout Qualifiers

```
layout (triangles) in;
layout (triangle_strip, max_vertices = 3) out;
```

The first line specifies that the input primitive type is triangles. This means that the geometry shader will be run once for each triangle rendered. Drawing commands used by the program must use a primitive mode that is compatible with the primitive type expected by the geometry shader (if present). If a drawing command specifies strips or fans (GL_TRIANGLE_STRIP or GL_TRIANGLE_FAN, in the case of triangles), the geometry shader will run once for each triangle in the strip or fan. The second line of the declaration specifies that the output of the geometry shader is triangle strips and that the maximum number of vertices that will be produced is three. The accepted primitive types accepted as inputs to the geometry shader and the corresponding primitive types that are allowed to be used in drawing commands are listed in Table 10.1.

Notice that even though we are only producing a single triangle in this example, we still specify that the output primitive type is triangle strips. Geometry shaders are designed to produce only points, line strips, or triangle strips, but not individual lines or triangles, nor loops or fans. This is because strips are a superset of individual primitive types—think of an independent triangle or line as a strip of only one primitive. By

Table 10.1   Geometry Shader Primitive Types and Accepted Drawing
Modes

Geometry Shader Primitive Type	Accepted Drawing Command Modes
points	GL_POINTS, GL_PATCHES[1]
lines	GL_LINES, GL_LINE_STRIP, GL_LINE_LOOP, GL_PATCHES[1]
triangles	GL_TRIANGLES, GL_TRIANGLE_STRIP GL_TRIANGLE_FAN, GL_PATCHES[1]
lines_adjacency[2]	GL_LINES_ADJACENCY, GL_LINE_STRIP_ADJACENCY
triangles_adjacency[2]	GL_TRIANGLES_ADJACENCY, GL_TRIANGLE_STRIP_ADJACENCY

terminating the strip after only a single triangle, independent triangles
may be drawn.

The special GLSL function EmitVertex() produces a new vertex at the
output of the geometry shader. Each time it is called, a vertex is appended
to the end of the current strip if the output primitive type is line_strip
or triangle_strip. If the output primitive type is points, then each call
to EmitVertex() produces a new, independent point. A second special
geometry shader function, EndPrimitive(), breaks the current strip
and signals OpenGL that a new strip should be started the next time
EmitVertex() is called. As discussed, single primitives such as lines or
triangles are not directly supported, although they may be generated by
calling EndPrimitive() after every two or three vertices in the case of
lines or triangles, respectively. By calling EndPrimitive() after every two
vertices are emitted when producing line strips or after every three vertices
are emitted when producing triangle strips, it is possible to generate
independent lines or triangles. As there is no such thing as a point
strip, each point is treated as an individual primitive and so calling
EndPrimitive() when the output primitive mode is points has no
effect (although it is still legal).

When the geometry shader exits, the current primitive is ended implicitly
and so it is not strictly necessary to call EndPrimitive() explicitly at the
end of the geometry shader. When EndPrimitive() is called (or at the

---

1. GL_PATCHES are accepted by drawing commands when a geometry shader is present so
long as the selected tessellation mode will cause the patches to be converted to something
compatible with the geometry shader input.

2. The adjacency primitive types lines_adjacency and triangles_adjacency are special
types introduced for geometry shaders and will be discussed shortly.

end of the shader), any incomplete primitives will simply be discarded. That is, if the shader produces a triangle strip with only two vertices or if it produces a line strip with only one vertex, the extra vertices making up the partial strip will be thrown away.

Geometry Shader Inputs and Outputs

The inputs and outputs of the geometry shader are specified using layout qualifiers and the `in` and `out` keywords in GLSL. In addition to user-defined inputs and outputs, there are several built-in inputs and outputs that are specific to geometry shaders. These are described in some detail in the following subsections. The `in` and `out` keywords are also used in conjunction with layout qualifiers to specify how the geometry shader fits into the pipeline, how it behaves, and how it interacts with adjacent shader stages.

Geometry Shader Inputs

The input to the geometry shader is fed by the output of the vertex shader, or if tessellation is active, the output of the tessellation evaluation shader.[3] As the geometry shader runs once per input primitive, outputs from the previous stage (vertex shader or tessellation evaluation shader) become arrays in the geometry shader. This includes all user-defined inputs and the special built-in input variable, `gl_in`, which is array containing the built-in outputs that are available in the previous stage. The `gl_in` input is implicitly declared as an interface block. The definition of `gl_in` is shown in Example 10.3.

Example 10.3   Implicit Declaration of `gl_in[]`

```
in gl_PerVertex {
    vec4        gl_Position;
    float       gl_PointSize;
    float       gl_ClipDistance[];
} gl_in[];
```

As noted, `gl_in` is implicitly declared as an array. The length of the array is determined by the input primitive type. Whatever is written to `gl_Position`, `gl_PointSize`, or `gl_ClipDistance` in the vertex shader (or tessellation evaluation shader) becomes visible to the geometry shader in the appropriate member of each member of the `gl_in` array. Like any

---

3. Tessellation shaders are covered in detail in Chapter 9.

array, the number of elements in the `gl_in` array can be found using the `.length()` method. Returning to our example geometry shader, we see a loop:

```
// Loop over the input vertices
for (n = 0; n < gl_in.length(); n++)
{
    . . .
}
```

The loop runs over the elements of the `gl_in` array, whose length is dependent on the input primitive type declared at the top of the shader. In this particular shader, the input primitive type is `triangles`, meaning that each invocation of the geometry shader processes a single triangle, and so the `gl_in.length()` function will return three. This is very convenient as it allows us to change the input primitive type of the geometry shader without changing any source code except the input primitive type layout qualifier. For example, if we change the input primitive type to `lines`, the geometry shader will now run once per line, and `gl_in.length()` will return two. The rest of the code in the shader need not change.

The size of the input arrays is determined by the type of primitives that the geometry shader accepts. The accepted primitive types are `points`, `lines`, `triangles`, `lines_adjacency`, and `triangles_adjacency`. The number of vertices in each primitive of these types is shown in Table 10.2 below.

Table 10.2   Geometry Shader Primitives and the Vertex Count for Each

Primitive Type	Input Array Size
points	1
lines	2
triangles	3
lines_adjacency	4
triangles_adjacency	6

The first three represent points, lines, and triangles, respectively. Points are represented by single vertices, and so although the inputs to the geometry shader are still arrays, the length of those arrays is one. Lines and triangles are generated both by independent triangles (GL_TRIANGLES and GL_LINES primitive types) and from the individual members of strips and fans (GL_TRIANGLE_STRIP, for example). Even if the drawing command specified GL_TRIANGLE_STRIP, GL_TRIANGLE_FAN, GL_LINE_STRIP, or GL_LINE_LOOP, the geometry shader still receives individual primitives as appropriate.

The last two input primitive types represent *adjacency* primitives, which are special primitives that are accepted by the geometry shader. They have special meaning and interpretation when no geometry shader is present (which will be described shortly), but for most cases where a geometry shader is present can be considered to be simple collections of four or six vertices and it is up to the geometry shader to convert them into some other primitive type. You cannot specify an adjacency primitive type as the output mode of the geometry shader.

Just as the built-in variable gl_in is an array with a length determined by the input primitive type, so are user-defined inputs. Consider the following vertex shader output declarations:

```
out vec4 position;
out vec3 normal;
out vec4 color;
out vec2 tex_coord;
```

In the geometry shader, these must be declared as arrays as follows:

```
in vec4 position[];
in vec3 normal[];
in vec4 color[];
in vec2 tex_coord[];
```

Note that the size of the arrays does not have to be given explicitly. If the array declarations are left unsized, then the size is implied by the input primitive type declared earlier in the shader. If the size is given explicitly then it is cross-checked at compile time against the input primitive type, giving an additional layer of error checking. If an input array is declared with an explicit size and that size does not match what is expected given the input primitive type, the GLSL compiler will generate an error.

GLSL versions earlier than 4.3 did not contain support for two-dimensional arrays. So, what happened to vertex shader outputs that are declared as arrays? To pass an array from a vertex shader to a geometry shader, we took advantage of an *interface block*. Using an interface block helps group all the data for a single vertex, rather than managing collections of arrays, so you may want to use interface blocks regardless of arrays or version numbers. The interface block can contain arrays, but it is the interface block itself that becomes an array when passed into a geometry shader. This technique is already used in the definition of the gl_in[] built-in variable—the gl_ClipDistance[] array is a member of the block.

Consider the example above. Let's assume that we wish to pass more than one texture coordinate from the vertex shader to the fragment shader. We will do that by making tex_coord an array. We can re-declare the variables listed in the example in an interface block and see how that affects their declaration in the geometry shader.

First, in the vertex shader:

```
out VS_GS_INTERFACE
{
    out vec4 position;
    out vec3 normal;
    out vec4 color;
    out vec2 tex_coord[4];
} vs_out;
```

Now, in the geometry shader:

```
in VS_GS_INTERFACE
{
    out vec4 position;
    out vec3 normal;
    out vec4 color;
    out vec2 tex_coord[4];
} gs_in[];
```

Now we have declared the output of the vertex shader as `vs_out` using an interface block, which is matched to `gs_in[]` in the geometry shader. Remember that interface block matching is performed by *block name* (`VS_GS_INTERFACE` in this example) rather than instance name. This allows the variables representing the block instance to have a different name in each shader stage. `gs_in[]` is an array, and the four texture coordinates are available in the geometry shader as `gs_in[n].tex_coord[m]`. Anything that can be passed from a vertex shader to a fragment shader can be passed in this manner, including arrays, structures, matrices, and other compound types.

In addition to the built-in members of `gl_in[]` and to user-defined inputs, there are a few other special inputs to the geometry shader. These are `gl_PrimitiveIDIn` and `gl_InvocationID`. The first, `gl_PrimitiveIDIn`, is the equivalent of `gl_PrimitiveID` that is available to the fragment shader. The *In* suffix distinguishes it from `gl_PrimitiveID`, which is actually an output in the geometry shader and must be assigned by the geometry shader if it is to be made available in the subsequent fragment shader. The second input, `gl_InvocationID`, is used during geometry shader instancing, which will be explained shortly. Both `gl_PrimitiveIDIn` and `gl_InvocationID` are intrinsically declared as integers.

Special Geometry Shader Primitives

Special attention should be paid to the adjacency primitive types available to geometry shaders (`lines_adjacency` and `triangles_adjacency`).

These primitives have four and six vertices, respectively, and allow adjacency information—information about adjacent primitives or edges—to be passed into the geometry shader. Lines with adjacency information are generated by using the GL_LINES_ADJACENCY or GL_LINE_STRIP_ADJACENCY primitive *mode* in a draw command such as **glDrawArrays()**. Likewise, triangles with adjacency information are produced by using the GL_TRIANGLES_ADJACENCY or GL_TRIANGLE_STRIP_ADJACENCY primitive types. These primitive types can be used without a geometry shader present and will be interpreted as lines or triangles with additional vertices being discarded.

Lines with Adjacency

At the input of the geometry shader, each *lines_adjacency* primitive is represented as a four-vertex primitive (i.e., the geometry shader inputs such as `gl_in` and user-defined inputs are four element arrays). In the OpenGL API, there are two adjacency primitives representing lines—GL_LINES_ADJACENCY or GL_LINE_STRIP_ADJACENCY. The first represents individual line primitives and each primitive sent to the geometry shader is formed from an independent collection of four vertices. Four vertices are consumed from the input arrays each time a primitive is assembled. The vertex layout is shown in Figure 10.1, where the first primitive passed to the geometry shader is made up from vertices A, B, C, and D. The second primitive is made up of vertices E, F, G, and H. This sequence continues, four vertices at a time for the length of the draw.

Figure 10.1   Lines adjacency sequence
(Vertex sequence for GL_LINES_ADJACENCY primitives.)

The second of these line primitive types (GL_LINE_STRIP_ADJACENCY) represents a line strip in much the same way as the regular GL_LINE_STRIP primitive does. Each primitive to the geometry shader is still made up of four vertices. The first primitive in a draw is constructed from the first four vertices in the enabled arrays,[4] and then a new four-vertex primitive is constructed from each successive vertex together with the preceding three

---

4. When using vertex indices with a draw command like **glDrawElements()**, primitives are not actually constructed from the first vertices in the arrays, rather they are constructed from the vertices referred to by the first few indices in the element array. For simplicity of explanation though, we will refer to these as the *first few vertices*, even though there may be an indirection involved.

vertices. Figure 10.2 below demonstrates this. In Figure 10.2, the first primitive passed to the geometry shader is made up from vertices A, B, C, and D, the second from B, C, D, and E, the third from C, D, E, and F and so on.

Figure 10.2   Line-strip adjacency sequence
(Vertex sequence for GL_LINE_STRIP_ADJACENCY primitives.)

The *lines_adjacency* primitive type is a good way to pass an arbitrary four-vertex primitive to the geometry shader (which does not actually have to represent a line). This is particularly true when the GL_LINES_ADJACENCY primitive mode is used as it does not infer any connectivity semantics. Note that the geometry shader cannot *emit* a *lines_adjacency* primitive. It must convert the primitive to another type. For example, if the vertices really do represent lines, then the geometry output primitive type can be set to *lines* and the shader can simply emit lines. However, it is possible to represent any arbitrary quadrilateral with four vertices, and in such a case the geometry shader can be used to convert it into a pair of triangles.

You may be wondering why we call them *line* primitives if any arbitrary four-vertex primitive can be passed to the geometry shader using the lines with adjacency primitive types. After all, the geometry shader can't actually produce lines with adjacency primitive and must convert them to another primitive type to be rendered. The answer is in how the primitives are interpreted by OpenGL when there is no geometry shader present. For each four-vertex primitive (whether it originated from the GL_LINES_ADJACENCY or GL_LINE_STRIP_ADJACENCY primitive mode), the additional vertices representing adjacency information are considered to be the first and last vertices in the primitive and those representing the line itself are the second and third vertices (the middle two vertices). When no geometry shader is present, the adjacency vertices are discarded and a line is formed from the two central vertices in the four-vertex primitive. In this manner, the vertex information is still interpreted as lines, although much of it may ultimately be discarded.

In Figures 10.1 and 10.2, the solid arrows represent the lines that will be generated by OpenGL when no geometry shader is present, and the dotted arrows represent the virtual lines that will be discarded.

Triangles with Adjacency

Like the lines with adjacency primitive types, the *triangles_adjacency* input primitive type is designed to allow triangles with adjacency information to be passed into a geometry shader. Each *triangles_adjacency* primitive is constructed from six vertices and so gl_in and the other geometry shader inputs become six-element arrays. There are also two primitive modes that may be used with OpenGL drawing commands, GL_TRIANGLES_ADJACENCY and GL_TRIANGLE_STRIP_ADJACENCY. Like GL_LINES_ADJACENCY, each GL_TRIANGLES_ADJACENCY primitive is formed from six independent vertices. Again, the geometry shader cannot emit a *triangles_adjacency* primitive and so must generate another type of primitive from the six incoming vertices.

Figure 10.3 illustrates the layout of vertices in a triangles_adjacency primitive and how they are passed to the geometry shader. When the primitive mode is GL_TRIANGLES_ADJACENCY, the first primitive will be formed from vertices A through F, the second from G through L, and so on. When no geometry shader is present, a triangle is formed from *every other* vertex. As in Figure 10.1, solid arrows represent triangles that will be rendered, and dotted arrows represent the virtual triangles that will be discarded. In this case, a triangle is formed from vertices A, C, and E, and another is formed from vertices G, I, and K. Vertices B, D, F, H, and J are discarded in the absence of a geometry shader.

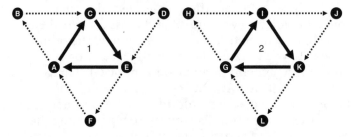

Figure 10.3   Triangles adjacency sequence
(Vertex sequence for GL_TRIANGLES_ADJACENCY primitives.)

Finally, we come to the GL_TRIANGLE_STRIP_ADJACENCY primitive mode. This primitive can be hard to understand and is possibly best illustrated using a diagram. Figure 10.4 shows how vertices are assembled into triangles, where the extra vertices come from, and as in previous figures shows which vertices are used to form triangles when no geometry shader is present. When the primitive mode is GL_TRIANGLE_STRIP_ADJACENCY, six vertices are still used to construct each primitive passed to the geometry shader. The first primitive is made from the first six vertices in the enabled arrays and then a new primitive is constructed for each vertex, reusing the previous five.

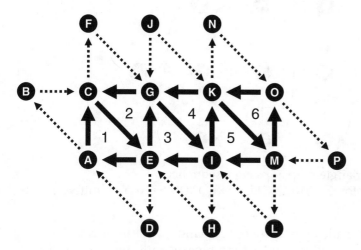

Figure 10.4   Triangle-strip adjacency layout
(Vertex layout for GL_TRIANGLE_STRIP_ADJACENCY primitives.)

If the pattern of triangles is removed and instead arrows representing the order of vertices are overlaid onto Figure 10.4, a pattern emerges that can be helpful in understanding the ordering of vertices in the arrays. This is shown in Figure 10.5.

Notice how, in Figures 10.4 and 10.5, it appears that adjacency information about every triangle is not conveyed. Instead, additional vertices *outside* the strip are passed to the geometry shader. However, which vertices are used to fill the inputs to the geometry shader vary based on whether the triangle is the only one in the strip, the first in a strip, an odd- or even-numbered triangle within the strip or the last triangle in a strip containing an even or odd number of triangles. This is described in some detail in the OpenGL specification.[5]

Given the geometry shown in Figure 10.4, triangle 1 will have its inputs made from vertices A, C, and E with vertices B, D, and G forming the additional adjacency vertices. Triangle 2 will have its inputs filled from vertices E, C, and G, with A, F, and I forming the adjacency vertices.

---

5. See Table 10.1 of the OpenGL Specification, Version 4.3.

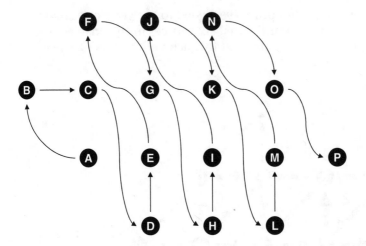

Figure 10.5   Triangle-strip adjacency sequence
(Vertex sequence for GL_TRIANGLE_STRIP_ADJACENCY primitives.)

Triangle 3 will be made up of vertices E, G, and I, and the adjacency vertices will be C, K, and H. This pattern repeats until the end of the strip, where triangle 6 is made from vertices M, K, and O, and the adjacency vertices are I, N, and P. Remember that in the geometry shader, the first, third, and fifth elements of gl_in represent the triangle while the second, fourth, and sixth elements represent the adjacency vertices. Putting all this together tells us that gl_in for triangle 1 will be constructed from vertices A, B, C, D, E, and G (in that order), for triangle 2 it is constructed from vertices E, A, C, F, G, and I, and in triangle 3 it is E, C, G, K, I, and H. Finally, for triangle 6 it is constructed from vertices M, I, K, N, O, and P.

Generating Data for Adjacency Primitives

Seeing the strange patterns of vertices in Figures 10.1 through 10.4 might make you think that you need to have specialized software or jump though some mental contortions to generate geometry data to feed to OpenGL when these primitive types are used. While it is possible to hijack the adjacency primitive types (especially GL_LINES_ADJACENCY and GL_TRIANGLES_ADJACECNCY) to pass arbitrary groups of four or six vertices into the pipeline, these primitive types are often used with vertex indices stored in a buffer bound to the GL_ELEMENT_ARRAY_BUFFER binding and a drawing command such as **glDrawElements()**.

The additional vertices in the adjacency primitives are intended to allow the geometry shader to obtain knowledge of the primitives *adjacent* to the one that it's processing in the mesh. For triangles, the extra vertex is often the third vertex of a triangle sharing an edge (and therefore two vertices) with the current primitive. This vertex likely *already exists* in the mesh. If indexed vertices are used, then no additional vertex data is required to represent this—only additional indices in the element buffer. In many cases, these extra indices can be generated by a preprocessing tool. Of course it is also possible to store information about an edge in the adjacency vertex, and it's also possible that the adjacency vertex is used only for that purpose and is not referenced as a real vertex at all.

Geometry Shader Outputs

The output of the geometry shader is fed into the primitive setup engine, rasterizer, and eventually into the fragment shader. In general, the output of the geometry shader is equivalent to the output of the vertex shader if no geometry shader is present. As many of the same outputs exist in the geometry shader as exist in the vertex shader. The same `gl_PerVertex` interface block specification is used for per-vertex outputs in the geometry shader. The definition of this block is given in Example 10.4.

Example 10.4   Implicit Declaration of Geometry Shader Outputs

```
out gl_PerVertex
{
    vec4     gl_Position;
    float    gl_PointSize;
    float    gl_ClipDistance[];
};
```

Note that although the same `gl_PerVertex` interface block is used to declare the geometry shader outputs, in this instance it has no name, and so the outputs are essentially in global scope. Of course, user-defined outputs may be declared as well, and these will be passed to the fragment shader along with the built-in interface block members. Because each geometry shader invocation can produce multiple output vertices, each vertex must be explicitly produced by calling the `EmitVertex()` function. When `EmitVertex()` is called, the current values of all outputs of the geometry shader are recorded and used to form a new vertex. After `EmitVertex()` is called, the values of all geometry shader outputs become *undefined* and thus it is necessary to write all outputs in the geometry shader before producing a vertex, even if the values of some of those outputs are the same from vertex to vertex. The only exception to this general rule for outputs that are marked with the `flat` keyword. In this case, only the value generated for the *provoking vertex* is used in subsequent stages and so, although the value of the outputs is still undefined for the other vertices, that doesn't really matter as those undefined values will never be used.

To specify which vertex is to be used as the provoking vertex, you can call **glProvokingVertex**() with the desired mode. The default is GL_LAST_VERTEX_CONVENTION, which means that flat shaded interpolants will be taken from the last vertex in each primivite. However, you can specify that they can take their values from the first vertex by passing GL_FIRST_VERTEX_CONVENTION to **glProvokingVertex**(). The prototype for **glProvokingVertex**() is as follows:

void **glProvokingVertex**(GLenum *provokeMode*);

Sets the provoking vertex mode to *provokeMode*, which may be one of GL_LAST_VERTEX_CONVENTION, or GL_FIRST_VERTEX_CONVENTION to specify that flat interpolants be taken from the last vertex or the first vertex, respectively.

Which vertex is considered the provoking vertex depends not only on the provoking vertex convention set with **glProvokingVertex**(), but also on the primitive type. Table 10.3 shows which vertices are considered the provoking vertex for each primitive mode.

Table 10.3   Provoking Vertex Selection by Primitive Mode

Primitive Mode	First Vertex Index	Last Vertex Index
GL_POINTS	i	i
GL_LINES	$2i - 1$	$2i$
GL_LINE_LOOP	i	$i + 1$ if $i < n$ and 1 if $i = n$
GL_LINE_STRIP	i	$i + 1$
GL_TRIANGLES	$3i - 2$	$3i$
GL_TRIANGLE_STRIP	i	$i + 2$
GL_TRIANGLE_FAN	$i + 1$	$i + 2$
GL_LINES_ADJACENCY	$4i - 2$	$4i - 1$
GL_LINE_STRIP_ADJACENCY	$i + 1$	$i + 2$
GL_TRIANGLES_ADJACENCY	$6i - 5$	$6i - 1$
GL_TRIANGLE_STRIP_ADJACENCY	$2i - 1$	$2i + 3$

In addition to the built-in and user-defined per-vertex outputs from the geometry shader, there are three further special built-in variables that are passed to the subsequent stage. These are gl_PrimitiveID, gl_Layer, and gl_ViewportIndex. The first of these should be familiar to you already—it is available in the fragment shader to identify the primitive to which the fragment belongs. Because the geometry shader may produce a variable amount of output primitives (or none at all), it is not possible for the system to generate `gl_PrimitiveID` automatically. Instead, the value that would have been generated if no geometry shader were present is passed as an input to the geometry shader in the built-in input `gl_PrimitiveIDIn` and it is the responsibility of the geometry shader to produce a value for the fragment shader to use if required. In a simple geometry shader that produces at most one output primitive per input primitive, the value in `gl_PrimitiveIDIn` can be written directly to `gl_PrimitiveID` and the expected behavior will occur. In a more complex geometry shader that might produce more than one primitive per invocation (this is known as *amplification*), a more in-depth scheme might be devised. For example, the shader could multiply the incoming `gl_PrimitiveIDIn` by the maximum number of primitives expected to be produced by the shader invocation and then apply an offset to that value for each generated primitive.

The other two variables, `gl_Layer` and `gl_ViewportIndex`, are used in *layered rendering* and with *viewport arrays*, respectively. Both of these topics will be covered shortly.

Producing Primitives

Primitives are produced in the geometry shader with the two special built-in functions, `EmitVertex()` and `EndPrimitive()`. As already discussed, a single geometry shader invocation must call `EmitVertex()` and possibly `EndPrimitive()` to produce output primitives. If the geometry shader does not call these functions, no output geometry is produced, and the inputs to the shader are essentially discarded. This is *culling*. On the other hand, if the geometry shader calls `EmitVertex()` many times, it can produce more output than it receives at its input, *amplifying* the geometry.

Another unique feature of geometry shaders is that they can have a different primitive type for their output than they do for their input. This can be used for techniques like wireframe rendering, *billboards* and even interesting instancing effects.

Culling Geometry

The simplest possible geometry shader is a culling geometry shader. The shader does absolutely nothing. We already gave an example of a simple geometry shader earlier in this chapter. The pass-through geometry shader is possibly the simplest geometry that actually does anything. However, Example 10.5 contains a perfectly legal geometry shader.

Example 10.5   A Geometry Shader that Drops Everything

```
#version 330 core

layout (triangles) in;
layout (triangle_strip, max_vertices = 3) out;

void main()
{
    /* Do nothing */
}
```

However, this isn't particularly useful—it doesn't produce any output primitives and using it in a program will result in absolutely nothing being rendered. Now, consider that the geometry shader can *conditionally* discard geometry. It's possible to discard primitives in the geometry shader based on some predefined condition in order to implement selective culling. Take a look at the shader in Example 10.6 below.

Example 10.6   Geometry Shader Passing Only Odd-Numbered
                    Primitives

```
#version 330 core

layout (triangles) in;
layout (triangle_strip, max_vertices = 3) out;

void main()
{
    int n;

    // Check the LSB of the primitive ID.
    // If it's set, emit a primitive.
    if (gl_PrimitiveIDIn & 1)
    {
        for (n = 0; n < gl_in.length(); ++n)
        {
            gl_Position = gl_in[n].gl_Position;
            EmitVertex();
        }
        EndPrimitive();
    }
}
```

The shader in Example 10.6 is similar to the pass-through shader shown earlier, except that it only runs when gl_PrimitiveIDIn is odd, allowing odd-numbered input primitives to pass and discarding, or culling the even-numbered ones.

Geometry Amplification

As you have read, it is possible for a geometry shader to output a different amount of primitives in than it accepts as input. So far we have looked at a simple pass-through geometry shader and at a shader that selectively culls geometry. Now we will look at a shader that produces more primitives on its output than it accepts on its input. This is known as *amplification*. Amplification can be used to implement fur shells or moderate tessellation, for example (although tessellation is best left to fixed-function tessellation hardware). Also, in combination with layered rendering or viewport indices, the geometry shader can produce several versions of the same geometry as slices of an array texture or different regions of the framebuffer.

Amplification in a geometry shader cannot be unlimited. Most OpenGL implementations have a moderate upper bound on the number of vertices that a single geometry shader invocation can produce. The maximum number of output vertices supported by the implementation is given in the built-in shader variable `gl_MaxGeometryOutputVertices`. It can also be found by the application by calling **glGetIntegerv()** to read the value of the GL_MAX_GEOMETRY_OUTPUT_VERTICES constant. The minimum required value of this constant is 256, so you can be sure that all implementations support at least this many output vertices in the geometry shader stage. However, the geometry shader is not really intended for large amplification, and performance may drop off dramatically when a very large number of primitives are generated in a single geometry shader invocation. So, even though your implementation might support a larger number of output vertices, measurements should be taken to ensure that producing a large amount of geometry isn't going to be detrimental to performance.

Fur Rendering Using a Geometry Shader

The following is a worked example of using amplification in a geometry shader to produce a fur-rendering effect. This is an implementation of the fur shell method—there are several methods for rendering fur and hair, but this method neatly demonstrates how moderate amplification in a geometry shader can be used to implement the effect. The basic principle is that hair or fur on a surface is modeled as a volume that is rendered using slices, and the geometry shader is used to generate those slices. The more slices that are rendered, the more detailed and continuous the hair effect will be. This number can be varied to hit a particular performance or quality target. The input to the geometry shader is the triangles forming the underlying mesh and the effect parameters are the number of layers

(shells) and the depth of the fur. The geometry shader produces the fur
shells by displacing the incoming vertices along their normals and
essentially producing multiple copies of the incoming geometry. As the
shells are rendered, the fragment shader uses a fur texture to selectively
blend and ultimately discard pixels that are not part of a hair. The
geometry shader is shown in Example 10.7.

Example 10.7   Fur Rendering Geometry Shader

```
// Fur rendering geometry shader
#version 330 core

// Triangles in, triangles out, large max_vertices as we're amplifying
layout (triangles) in;
layout (triangle_strip, max_vertices = 120) out;

uniform mat4 model_matrix;
uniform mat4 projection_matrix;

// The number of layers in the fur volume and the depth of the volume
uniform int fur_layers = 30;
uniform float fur_depth = 5.0;

// Input from the vertex shader
in VS_GS_VERTEX
{
    vec3 normal;
    vec2 tex_coord;
} vertex_in[];

// Output to the fragment shader
out GS_FS_VERTEX
{
    vec3 normal;
    vec2 tex_coord;
    flat float fur_strength;
} vertex_out;

void main()
{
    int i, layer;
    // The displacement between each layer
    float disp_delta = 1.0 / float(fur_layers);
    float d = 0.0;

    // For each layer...
    for (layer = 0; layer < fur_layers; layer++)
    {
        // For each incoming vertex (should be three of them)
        for (i = 0; i < gl_in.length(); i++) {
            // Get the vertex normal
```

```
        vec3 n = vertex_in[i].normal;
        // Copy it to the output for use in the fragment shader
        vertex_out.normal = n;
        // Copy the texture coordinate too - we'll need that to
        // fetch from the fur texture
        vertex_out.tex_coord = vertex_in[i].tex_coord;
        // Fur "strength" reduces linearly along the length of
        // the hairs
        vertex_out.fur_strength = 1.0 - d;
        // This is the core - displace each vertex along its normal
        // to generate shells
        position = gl_in[i].gl_Position +
                   vec4(n * d * fur_depth, 0.0);
        // Transform into place and emit a vertex
        gl_Position = projection_matrix * (model_matrix * position);
        EmitVertex();
    }
    // Move outwards by our calculated delta
    d += disp_delta;
    // End the "strip" ready for the next layer
    EndPrimitive();
  }
}
```

The geometry shader in Example 10.7 begins by specifying that it takes triangles as input and will produce a triangle strip as output with a maximum of 120 vertices. This is quite a large number, but we will not use them all unless the number of fur layers is increased significantly. A maximum of 120 vertices output from the geometry shader will allow for 40 fur layers. The shader will displace vertices along their normal vectors (which are assumed to point outwards) and amplify the incoming geometry to produce the shells that will be used to render the fur. The displacement for each shell is calculated into `disp_delta`. Then for each layer (the number of layers is in the `fur_layers` uniform) the vertex position is displaced by scaling the normal and adding it to the original position. A displaced version of the triangle is thus generated by performing the operation on each vertex. A call to `EndPrimitive()` causes the geometry shader to create unconnected triangles as its output.

Next, we pass into the fragment shader, which is given in Example 10.8 below.

Example 10.8   Fur Rendering Fragment Shader

```
// Fur rendering fragment shader
#version 330 core

// One output
layout (location = 0) out vec4 color;
```

```
// The fur texture
uniform sampler2D fur_texture;
// Color of the fur. Silvery gray by default...
uniform vec4 fur_color = vec4(0.8, 0.8, 0.9, 1.0);

// Input from the geometry shader
in GS_FS_VERTEX
{
    vec3 normal;
    vec2 tex_coord;
    flat float fur_strength;
} fragment_in;

void main()
{
    // Fetch from the fur texture. We'll only use the alpha channel
    // here, but we could easily have a color fur texture.
    vec4 rgba = texture(fur_texture, fragment_in.tex_coord);
    float t = rgba.a;
    // Multiply by fur strength calculated in the GS for the
    // current shell t *= fragment_in.fur_strength;
    // Scale fur color alpha by fur strength.
    color = fur_color * vec4(1.0, 1.0, 1.0, t);
}
```

Figure 10.6   Texture used to represent hairs in the fur rendering
example

The fur fragment shader uses a texture to represent the layout of hairs in
the fur. The texture used in the fur example is shown in Figure 10.6. The
brightness of each texel maps to the length of the hair at that point. Zero
essentially means no hair, and white represents hairs whose length is equal
to the full depth of the fur volume.

The texture in Figure 10.6 is generated using a simple random placement
of hairs. A more sophisticated algorithm could be developed to allow hair

density and distribution to be controlled programmatically. The current depth of the shell being rendered is passed from the geometry shader into the fragment shader. The fragment shader uses this, along with the contents of the fur texture to determine how far along the hair the fragment being rendered is. This information is used to calculate the fragment's color and opacity, which are used to generate the fragment shader output.

A first pass of the underlying geometry is rendered without the fur shaders active. This represents the *skin* of the object and prevents holes or gaps appearing when the hair is sparse. Next, the fur rendering shader is activated and another pass of the original geometry is rendered. Depth testing is used to quickly reject fur fragments that are behind the solid geometry. However, while the fur is being rendered, depth writes are turned off. This causes the very fine tips of the hairs to not occlude thicker hairs that may be behind them. Figure 10.7 shows the result of the algorithm.

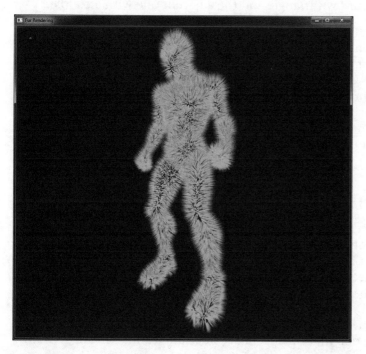

Figure 10.7   The output of the fur rendering example

As you can see from Figure 10.7, the fur rendered with this method is reasonably convincing. There are ways to improve on the algorithm though. For example, when polygons are seen edge-on, it is possible to see the individual slices that make up the shells. This means that we need a lot of shells (and thus a lot of amplification in the geometry shader) to produce a visually compelling result and hide this artifact. This can be detrimental to performance. When fur shells are used, we will generally also generate *fur fins*.

Fins are additional primitives emitted perpendicular to the edges of the mesh that are determined to be silhouettes (edges that make the outline of the shape). The fins are generated in the geometry shader, possibly at the same time as generating the shells. We only generate fins for edges that are silhouettes, and to make that decision we need to examine the two triangles that share the edge. If the triangle on one side of the edge faces towards the viewer and the triangle on the other side of the edge faces away from the viewer then the edge is considered to be a silhouette. To obtain information about the face normal of the adjacent face, we use the adjacency primitive type. With access to the additional vertex forming a triangle sharing an edge with our own, we can calculate the face normal of both our own triangle and the adjacent one with a couple of cross-products.

Another way to improve appearance is to use a true volume texture to represent the hair. In this example, we used a simple two-dimensional texture containing the length of a hair at each texel to represent fur. This is a fairly crude approximation, and better results can be obtained by using a real three-dimensional texture to store the density of the hair at all points within the volume of the fur. This obviously requires a lot more storage space but can improve visual quality and increase the level of control over the effect.

Advanced Transform Feedback

We have already covered the concept of transform feedback and seen how it works when only a vertex shader is present. In summary, the output of the vertex shader is captured and recorded into one or more buffer objects. Those buffer objects can subsequently be used for rendering (e.g., as vertex buffers) or read back by the CPU using functions like **glMapBuffer()** or **glGetBufferSubData()**. We have also seen how to disable rasterization such that only the vertex shader is active. However, the vertex shader is a relatively simple one-in, one-out shader stage and cannot create or destroy vertices. Also, it only has a single set of outputs.

You have just read about the ability of a geometry shader to produce a variable amount of output vertices. When a geometry shader is present, transform feedback captures the output of the geometry shader. In addition to the stream of vertices that is usually sent to primitive assembly and rasterization, the geometry shader is capable of producing other, ancillary streams of vertex information that can be captured using transform feedback. By combining the geometry shader's ability to produce a variable amount of vertices at its output and its ability to send those input vertices to any one of several output streams, some sophisticated sorting, bucketing, and processing algorithms can be implemented using the geometry shader and transform feedback.

In this subsection, we will introduce the concept of multiple vertex streams as outputs from the geometry shader. We also introduce methods to determine how many vertices were produced by the geometry shader, both when using a single output stream and when using multiple output streams. Finally, we discuss methods to use data generated by a geometry shader and stored into a transform feedback buffer in subsequent draw commands without requiring a round-trip to the CPU.

Multiple Output Streams

Multiple streams of vertices can be declared as outputs in the geometry shader. Output streams are declared using the `stream` layout qualifier. This layout qualifier may be applied globally, to an interface block, or to a single output declaration. Each stream is numbered, starting from zero and an implementation defined maximum number of streams can be declared. That maximum can be found by calling **glGetIntegerv()** with the parameter GL_MAX_VERTEX_STREAMS, and all OpenGL implementations are required to support at least four geometry shader output streams. When the stream number is given at global scope, all subsequently declared geometry shader outputs become members of that stream until another output stream layout qualifier is specified. The default output stream for all outputs is zero. That is, unless otherwise specified, all outputs belong to stream zero. The global stream layout qualifiers shown in Example 10.9 demonstrate how to assign geometry shader outputs to different streams.

Example 10.9   Global Layout Qualifiers Used to Specify a Stream Map

```
// Redundant as the default stream is 0
layout (stream=0) out;
// foo and bar become members of stream 0
out vec4 foo;
out vec4 bar;

// Switch the output stream to stream 1
layout (stream=1) out;
// proton and electron are members of stream 1
out vec4 proton;
```

```
flat out float electron;

// Output stream declarations have no effect on input
// declarations elephant is just a regular input
in vec2 elephant;

// It's possible to go back to a previously
// defined stream
layout (stream=0) out;
// baz joins it's cousins foo and bar in stream 0
out vec4 baz;

// And then jump right to stream 3, skipping stream 2
// altogether
layout (stream=3) out;
// iron and copper are members of stream 3
flat out int iron;
out vec2 copper;
```

The declarations in Example 10.9 set up three output streams from a geometry shader, numbered zero, one, and three. Stream zero contains foo, bar, and baz, stream one contains proton and electron and stream three contains iron and copper. Note that stream two is not used at all and there are no outputs in it. An equivalent stream mapping can be constructed using output interface blocks and is shown in Example 10.10.

Example 10.10   Example 10.9 Rewritten to Use Interface Blocks

```
// Again, redundant as the default output stream is 0
layout (stream=0) out stream0
{
    vec4 foo;
    vec4 bar;
    vec4 baz;
};

// All of stream 1 output
layout (stream=1) out stream1
{
    vec4 proton;
    flat float electron;
};

// Skip stream 2, go directly to stream 3
layout (stream=3) out stream3
{
    flat int iron;
    vec2 copper;
};
```

As can be seen in Example 10.10, grouping members of a single stream in an interface block can make the declarations appear more organized and so easier to read. Now that we have defined which outputs belong to which streams, we need to direct output vertices to one or more of those streams. As with a regular, single-stream geometry shader, vertices are emitted and primitives are ended programmatically using special built-in GLSL functions. When multiple output streams are active, the function to emit vertices on a specific stream is `EmitStreamVertex(int stream)` and the function to end a primitive on a specific stream is `EndStreamPrimitive(int stream)`. Calling `EmitVertex` is equivalent to calling `EmitStreamVertex` with `stream` set to zero. Likewise, calling `EndPrimitive` is equivalent to calling `EndStreamPrimitive` with `stream` set to zero.

When `EmitStreamVertex` is called, the current values for any variables associated with the specified stream are recorded and used to form a new vertex on that stream. Just as when `EmitVertex` is called, the values of all output variables become undefined, so too do they become undefined when `EmitStreamVertex` is called. In fact, the current values of *all* output variables on *all* streams become undefined. This is an important consideration as code that assumes that the values of output variables remain consistent across a call to `EmitStreamVertex` (or `EmitVertex`) may work on some OpenGL implementations and not others, and most shader compilers will not warn about this—especially on implementations where it will work!

To illustrate, consider the example shown in Example 10.11.

Example 10.11   Incorrect Emission of Vertices into Multiple Streams

```
// Set up outputs for stream 0
foo = vec4(1.0, 2.0, 3.0, 4.0);
bar = vec4(5.0);
baz = vec4(4.0, 3.0, 2.0, 1.0);

// Set up outputs for stream 1
proton = atom;
electron = 2.0;

// Set up outputs for stream 3
iron = 4;
copper = shiny;

// Now emit all the vertices
EmitStreamVertex(0);
EmitStreamVertex(1);
EmitStreamVertex(3);
```

This example will produce *undefined results* because it assumes that the values of the output variables associated with streams 1 and 3 remain valid across the calls to `EmitStreamVerex`. This is incorrect, and on some OpenGL implementations, the values of `proton`, `electron`, `iron` and `copper` will become undefined after the first call to `EmitStreamVerex`. Such a shader should be written as shown in Example 10.12.

Example 10.12   Corrected Emission of Vertices into Multiple Streams

```
// Set up and emit outputs for stream 0
foo = vec4(1.0, 2.0, 3.0, 4.0);
bar = vec4(5.0);
baz = vec4(4.0, 3.0, 2.0, 1.0);
EmitStreamVertex(0);

// Set up and emit outputs for stream 1
proton = atom;
electron = 2.0;
EmitStreamVertex(1);

// Note, there's nothing in stream 2

// Set up and emit outputs for stream 3
iron = 4;
copper = shiny;
EmitStreamVertex(3);
```

Now that we have a shader that outputs vertices on multiple output streams, we need to inform OpenGL how those streams are mapped into transform feedback buffers. This mapping is specified with the **glTransformFeedbackVaryings()** function just as when only a single output stream is present. Under normal circumstances, all output variables are to be captured by transform feedback recorded into a single buffer (by specifying GL_INTERLEAVED_ATTRIBS as the *bufferMode* parameter to **glTransformFeedbackVaryings()**) or into a separate buffer for each variable (by specifying GL_SEPARATE_ATTRIBS). When multiple streams are active, it is required that variables associated with a single stream are not written into the same buffer binding point as those associated with any other stream.[6] It may be desirable, however, to have some or all of the varyings associated with a single stream written, interleaved, into a single buffer. To provide this functionality, the reserved variable name `gl_NextBuffer` is used to signal that the following output variables are to be recorded into the buffer object bound to the next transform feedback binding point. Recall from Chapter 3 that `gl_NextBuffer` is not a real variable—it cannot be used in the shader; it is provided solely as a marker to delimit groups of variables that will be written into the same buffer. For

---

6. Although it is not possible to direct output variables from different streams into the same transform feedback buffer binding point, it is possible to bind the same buffer object (or better, different sections of the same buffer) to different transform feedback buffer binding points. This allows variables from different streams to be written into the same buffer.

Examples 10.9 and 10.10, we will record the variables for the first stream (foo, bar, and baz) into the buffer object bound to the first transform feedback buffer binding point, the variables for the second stream (proton and electron) into the buffer bound to the second binding point, and finally the variables associated with stream 3 (iron and copper) into the buffer bound to the third buffer binding point. Example 10.13 shows how to express this layout.

Example 10.13   Assigning Transform Feedback Outputs to Buffers

```
static const char * const vars[] =
{
    "foo", "bar", "baz",      // Variables from stream 0
    "gl_NextBuffer",          // Move to binding point 1
    "proton", "electron",     // Variables from stream 1
    "gl_NextBuffer",          // Move to binding point 2
                              // Note, there are no variables
                              // in stream 2
    "iron", "copper"          // Variables from stream 3
};

glTransformFeedbackVaryings(prog,
                            sizeof(vars) / sizeof(vars[0]),
                            varyings,
                            GL_INTERLEAVED_ATTRIBS);
glLinkProgram(prog);
```

Notice the call to **glLinkProgram()** after the call to **glTransformFeedbackVaryings()** in Example 10.13. As previously mentioned, the mapping specified by **glTransformFeedbackVaryings()** does not take effect until the next time the program object is linked. Therefore, it is necessary to call **glLinkProgram()** after **glTransformFeedbackVaryings()** before the program object is used.

If rasterization is enabled and there is a fragment shader present, the output variables belonging to stream 0 (foo, bar, and baz) will be used to form primitives for rasterization and will be passed into the fragment shader. Output variables belonging to other streams (proton, electron, iron, and copper) will not be visible in the fragment shader and if transform feedback is not active, they will be discarded. Also note that when multiple output streams are used in a geometry shader, they must all have points as the primitive type. This means that if rasterization is used in conjunction with multiple geometry shader output streams, an application is limited to rendering points with that shader.

Primitive Queries

Transform feedback was introduced in "Transform Feedback" on Page 239 as a method to record the output of a vertex shader into a buffer that could be used in subsequent rendering. Because the vertex shader is a simple, one-in, one-out pipeline stage, it is known up front how many vertices the vertex shader will generate. Assuming that the transform feedback buffer is large enough to hold all of the output data, the number of vertices stored in the transform feedback buffer is simply the number of vertices processed by the vertex shader. Such a simple relationship is not present for the geometry shader. Because the geometry shader can emit a variable number of vertices per invocation, the number of vertices recorded into transform feedback buffers when a geometry shader is present may not be easy to infer. In addition to this, should the space available in the transform feedback buffers be exhausted, the geometry shader will produce more vertices than are actually recorded. Those vertices will still be used to generate primitives for rasterization (if they are emitted on stream 0), but they will not be written into the transform feedback buffers.

To provide this information to the application, two types of queries are available to count both the number of primitives the geometry shader generates, and the number of primitives actually written into the transform feedback buffers. These are the GL_PRIMITIVES_GENERATED and GL_TRANSFORM_FEEDBACK_PRIMITIVES_WRITTEN queries. The GL_PRIMITIVES_GENERATED query counts the number of vertices output by the geometry shader, even if space in the transform feedback buffers was exhausted and the vertices were not recorded. The GL_TRANSFORM_FEEDBACK_PRIMITIVES_WRITTEN query counts the number of vertices actually written into a transform feedback buffer. Note that the GL_PRIMITIVES_GENERATED query is valid at any time, even when transform feedback is not active (hence the lack of TRANSFORM_FEEDBACK in the name of the query), whereas GL_TRANSFORM_FEEDBACK_PRIMITIVES_WRITTEN only counts when transform feedback is active.[7]

Because a geometry shader can output to multiple transform feedback streams, primitive queries are *indexed*. That is, there are multiple binding points for each type of query—one for each supported output stream. To begin and end a primitive query for a particular primitive stream, call:

---

void **glBeginQueryIndexed**(GLenum *target*, GLuint *index*,
                             GLuint *id*);

Begins a query using the query object *id* on the indexed query target point specified by *target* and *index*.

---

7. This makes sense. In a way, a GL_TRANSFORM_FEEDBACK_PRIMITIVES_WRITTEN query does continue to count when transform feedback is not active, but as no primitives are written, it will not increment, and so the result is the same.

and

> void **glEndQueryIndexed**(GLenum *target*, GLuint *index*);
>
> Ends the active query on the indexed query target point specified by *target* and *index*.

Here, *target* is set to either GL_PRIMITIVES_GENERATED or GL_TRANSFORM_FEEDBACK_PRIMITIVES_WRITTEN, *index* is the index of the primitive query binding point on which to execute the query, and *id* is the name of a query object that was previously created using the **glGenQueries**() function. Once the primitive query has been ended, the availability of the result can be checked by calling **glGetQueryObjectuiv**() with the *pname* parameter set to GL_QUERY_RESULT_AVAILABLE and the actual value of the query can be retrieved by calling **glGetQueryObjectuiv**() with *pname* set to GL_QUERY_RESULT. Don't forget that if the result of the query object is retrieved by calling **glGetQueryObjectuiv**() with *name* set to GL_QUERY_RESULT and the result was not available yet, the GPU will likely stall, significantly reducing performance.

It is possible to run both a GL_PRIMITIVES_GENERATED and a GL_TRANSFORM_FEEDBACK_PRIMITIVES_WRITTEN query simultaneously on the same stream. If the result of the GL_PRIMITIVES_GENERATED query is greater than the result of the GL_TRANSFORM_FEEDBACK_PRIMITIVES_WRITTEN query, it may indicate that the transform feedback buffer was not large enough to record all of the results.

Using Transform Feedback Results

Now that the number of vertices recorded into a transform feedback buffer is known, it is possible to pass that vertex count into a function like **glDrawArrays**() to use it as the source of vertex data in subsequent rendering. However, to retrieve this count requires the CPU to read information generated by the GPU, which is generally detrimental to performance. In this case, the CPU will wait for the GPU to finish rendering anything that might contribute to the primitive count, and then the GPU will wait for the CPU to send a new rendering command using that count. Ideally, the count would never make the round trip from the GPU to the CPU and back again. To achieve this, the OpenGL commands

glDrawTransformFeedback() and **glDrawTransformFeedbackStream()** are supplied. The prototypes of these functions are as follows:

---

void **glDrawTransformFeedback**(GLenum *mode*, GLuint *id*);
void **glDrawTransformFeedbackStream**(GLenum *mode*,
                                                            GLuint *id*,
                                                            GLuint *stream*);

Draw primitives as if **glDrawArrays()** had been called with *mode* set as specified, *first* set to zero and *count* set to the number of primitives captured by transform feedback stream *stream* on the transform feedback object *id*. Calling **glDrawTransformFeedback()** is equivalent to calling **glDrawTransformFeedbackStream()** with *stream* set to zero.

When **glDrawTransformFeedbackStream()** is called, it is equivalent to calling **glDrawArrays()** with the same *mode* parameter, with *first* set to zero, and with the *count* parameter taken from a virtual GL_TRANSFORM_FEEDBACK_PRIMITIVES_WRITTEN query running on stream *stream* of the transform feedback object *id*. Note that there is no need to execute a real GL_TRANSFORM_FEEDBACK_PRIMITIVES_WRITTEN query and the primitive count is never actually transferred from the GPU to the CPU. Also, there is no requirement that the buffers used to record the results of the transform feedback operation need to be bound for use in the new draw. The vertex count used in such a draw is whatever was recorded the last time **glEndTransformFeedback()** was called while the transform feedback object *id* was bound. It is possible for transform feedback to still be active for *id*—the previously recorded vertex count will be used.

By using the **glDrawTransformFeedbackStream()** function, it is possible to circulate the result of rendering through the pipeline. By repeatedly calling **glDrawTransformFeedbackStream()**, vertices will be transformed by the OpenGL vertex and geometry shaders. Combined with double buffering of vertex data,[8] it is possible to implement recursive algorithms that change the number of vertices in flight on each iteration of the loop.

Drawing transform feedback may be combined with instancing to allow you to draw many instances of the data produced by transform feedback. To support this, the functions **glDrawTransformFeedbackInstanced()** and

---

8. Double buffering is required because undefined results will be produced if the same buffer objects are bound both for transform feedback and as the source of data.

glDrawTransformFeedbackStreamInstanced() are provided. Their prototypes are as follows:

```
void glDrawTransformFeedbackInstanced(GLenum mode,
                                       GLuint id,
                                       GLsizei instancecount);
void glDrawTransformFeedbackStreamInstanced(GLenum mode,
                                             GLuint id,
                                             GLuint stream,
                                             GLsizei instancecount);
```

Draw primitives as if **glDrawArraysInstanced()** had been called with *first* set to zero, *count* set to the number of primitives captured by transform feedback stream *stream* on the transform feedback object *id* and with *mode* and *instancecount* passed as specified. Calling **glDrawTransformFeedbackInstanced()** is equivalent to calling **glDrawTransformFeedbackStreamInstanced()** with *stream* set to zero.

Combining Multiple Streams and DrawTransformFeedback

As a worked example of the techniques just described, we'll go over an application that demonstrates how to use a geometry shader to sort incoming geometry, and then render subsets of it in subsequent passes. In this example, we'll use the geometry shader to sort "left-facing" and "right-facing" polygons—that is, polygons whose face normal points to the left or right. The left-facing polygons will be sent to stream zero, while the right-facing polygons will be sent to stream one. Both streams will be recorded into transform feedback buffers. The contents of those buffers will then be drawn using **glDrawTransformFeedbackStream()** while a different program object is active. This causes left-facing primitives to be rendered with a completely different state from right-facing primitives, even though they are physically part of the same mesh.

First, we will use a vertex shader to transform incoming vertices into view space. This shader is shown in Example 10.14 below.

Example 10.14   Simple Vertex Shader for Geometry Sorting

```
#version 330 core

uniform mat4 model_matrix;

layout (location = 0) in vec4 position;
layout (location = 1) in vec3 normal;

out vec3 vs_normal;
```

```
void main()
{
    vs_normal = (model_matrix * vec4(normal, 0.0)).xyz;
    gl_Position = model_matrix * position;
}
```

Vertices enter the geometry shader shown in Example 10.15 in view space.
This shader takes the incoming stream of primitives, calculates a per-face
normal, and then uses the sign of the X component of the normal to
determine whether the triangle is left-facing or right-facing. The face
normal for the triangle is calculated by taking the cross product of two of
its edges. Left-facing triangles are emitted to stream zero and right-facing
triangles are emitted to stream one, where outputs belonging to each
stream will be recorded into separate transform feedback buffers.

Example 10.15   Geometry Shader for Geometry Sorting

```
#version 330 core

// Triangles input, points output (although we'll write
// three points for each incoming triangle.
layout (triangles) in;
layout (points, max_vertices = 3) out;

uniform mat4 projection_matrix;

in vec3 vs_normal[];

// Stream 0 - left-facing polygons
layout (stream = 0) out vec4 lf_position;
layout (stream = 0) out vec3 lf_normal;

// Stream 1 - right-facing polygons
layout (stream = 1) out vec4 rf_position;
layout (stream = 1) out vec3 rf_normal;

void main()
{
    // Take the three vertices and find the (unnormalized face normal)
    vec4 A = gl_in[0].gl_Position;
    vec4 B = gl_in[1].gl_Position;
    vec4 C = gl_in[2].gl_Position;
    vec3 AB = (B - A).xyz;
    vec3 AC = (C - A).xyz;
    vec3 face_normal = cross(AB, AC);
    int i;

    // If the normal's X coordinate is negative, it faces to the left of
    // the viewer and is "left-facing", so stuff it in stream 0
    if (face_normal.x < 0.0)
    {
        // For each input vertex ...
```

```
        for (i = 0; i < gl_in.length(); i++)
        {
            // Transform to clip space
            lf_position = projection_matrix *
                          (gl_in[i].gl_Position -
                          vec4(30.0, 0.0, 0.0, 0.0));
            // Copy the incoming normal to the output stream
            lf_normal = vs_normal[i];
            // Emit the vertex
            EmitStreamVertex(0);
        }
        // Calling EndStreamPrimitive is not strictly necessary as
        // these are points
        EndStreamPrimitive(0);
    }
    // Otherwise, it's "right-facing" and we should write it to stream 1.
    else
    {
        // Exactly as above but writing to rf_position and rf_normal
        // for stream 1.
        for (i = 0; i < gl_in.length(); i++)
        {
            rf_position = projection_matrix *
                          (gl_in[i].gl_Position -
                          vec4(30.0, 0.0, 0.0, 0.0));
            rf_normal = vs_normal[i];
            EmitStreamVertex(1);
        }
        EndStreamPrimitive(1);
    }
}
```

When rendering the sorting pass, we will not be rasterizing any polygons, and so our first pass program has no fragment shader. To disable rasterization we will call glEnable(GL_RASTERIZER_DISCARD). If an attempt is made to render with a program object that does not contain a fragment shader and rasterization is not disabled, an error will be generated. Before linking the sorting program, we need to specify where the transform feedback varyings will be written to. To do this, we use the code shown in Example 10.16 below.

Example 10.16   Configuring Transform Feedback for Geometry Sorting

```
static const char * varyings[] =
{
    // These two varyings belong to stream 0
    "rf_position", "rf_normal",
    // Move to the next binding point (can't write
    // varyings from different streams to the same buffer
    // binding point.)
    "gl_NextBuffer",
    // These two varyings belong to stream 1
```

```
        "lf_position", "lf_normal"
};

glTransformFeedbackVaryings(sort_prog,
                            5,
                            varyings,
                            GL_INTERLEAVED_ATTRIBS);
```

Notice that the output of the geometry shader for stream zero and stream
one are identical. The same data is written to the selected stream regardless
of whether the polygon is left- or right-facing. In the first pass, all of the
vertex data recorded into the transform feedback buffers have already been
transformed into clip space and so we can reuse that work on the second
and third passes that will be used to render it. All we need to supply is a
pass-through vertex shader (shown in Example 10.17 below) to read the
pre-transformed vertices and feed the fragment shader. There is no
geometry shader in the second pass.

Example 10.17   Pass-Through Vertex Shader used for Geometry Shader
                     Sorting

```
#version 330 core

layout (location = 0) in vec4 position;
layout (location = 1) in vec3 normal;

out vec3 vs_normal;

void main()
{
    vs_normal = normal;
    gl_Position = position;
}
```

We'll use the same fragment shader in the second and third passes, but in a
more complex application of this technique, a different shader could be
used for each pass.

Now, to drive this system we need several objects to manage data and logic
at the OpenGL API level. First, we need two program objects for the
programs that will be used in the three passes (one containing the vertex
and geometry shaders for sorting the left-facing and right-facing
primitives, and one containing the pass-through vertex and fragment
shaders for the two rendering passes). We need buffer objects for storing
the input geometry shader and the intermediate data produced by the
geometry shader. We need a pair of vertex array objects (VAOs) to represent
the vertex inputs to the two rendering passes. Finally, we need a transform

feedback object to manage transform feedback data and primitive counts. The code to set all this up is given in Example 10.18 below.

Example 10.18   OpenGL Setup Code for Geometry Shader Sorting

```
// Create a pair of vertex array objects and buffer objects
// to store the intermediate data.
glGenVertexArrays(2, vao);
glGenBuffers(2, vbo);

// Create a transform feedback object upon which transform
// feedback operations (including the following buffer
// bindings) will operate, and then bind it.
glGenTransformFeedbacks(1, &xfb);
glBindTransformFeedback(GL_TRANSFORM_FEEDBACK, xfb);

// For each of the two streams ...
for (i = 0; i < 2; i++)
{
    // Bind the buffer object to create it.
    glBindBuffer(GL_TRANSFORM_FEEDBACK_BUFFER, vbo[i]);
    // Call glBufferData to allocate space. 220 floats
    // should be enough for this example. Note GL_DYNAMIC_COPY.
    // This means that the data will change often (DYNAMIC)
    // and will be both written by and used by the GPU (COPY).
    glBufferData(GL_TRANSFORM_FEEDBACK_BUFFER,
                 1024 * 1024 * sizeof(GLfloat),
                 NULL, GL_DYNAMIC_COPY);
    // Now bind it to the transform feedback buffer binding
    // point corresponding to the stream.
    glBindBufferBase(GL_TRANSFORM_FEEDBACK_BUFFER, i, vbo[i]);

    // Now set up the VAOs. First, bind to create.
    glBindVertexArray(vao[i]);
    // Now bind the VBO to the ARRAY_BUFFER binding.
    glBindBuffer(GL_ARRAY_BUFFER, vbo[i]);
    // Set up the vertex attributes for position and normal ...
    glVertexAttribPointer(0, 4, GL_FLOAT, GL_FALSE,
                          sizeof(vec4) + sizeof(vec3),
                          NULL);
    glVertexAttribPointer(1, 3, GL_FLOAT, GL_FALSE,
                          sizeof(vec4) + sizeof(vec3),
                          (GLvoid *)(sizeof(vec4)));
    // ... and remember to enable them!
    glEnableVertexAttribArray(0);
    glEnableVertexAttribArray(1);
}
```

Once we have created and set up all of our data management objects, we need to write our rendering loop. The general flow is shown in Figure 10.8 below. The first pass is responsible for sorting the geometry into front- and back-facing polygons and performs no rasterization. The second and third passes are essentially identical in this example, although a completely different shading algorithm could be used in each. These passes actually render the sorted geometry as if it were supplied by the application.

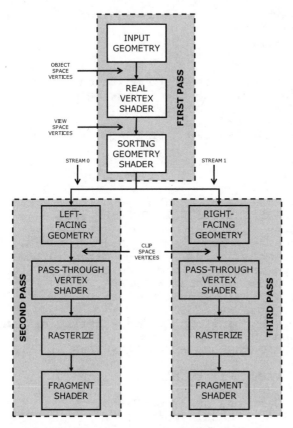

Figure 10.8   Schematic of geometry shader sorting example

For the first pass, we bind the VAO representing the original input geometry and the program object containing the sorting geometry shader. We bind the transform feedback object and the intermediate buffer to the transform feedback buffer binding, start transform feedback, and draw the original geometry. The geometry shader sorts the incoming triangles into left- and right-facing groups and sends them to the appropriate stream. After the first pass, we turn off transform feedback. For the second pass, bind the VAO representing the intermediate data written to stream zero, bind the second pass program object, and use **glDrawTransformFeedbackStream()** to draw the intermediate left-facing geometry using the primitives-written count from stream zero on the first pass. Likewise, in the third pass we draw the right-facing geometry by using **glDrawTransformFeedbackStream()** with stream one.

Example 10.19   Rendering Loop for Geometry Shader Sorting

```
// First pass - start with the "sorting" program object.
glUseProgram(sort_prog);

// Set up projection and model-view matrices
mat4 p(frustum(-1.0f, 1.0f, aspect, -aspect, 1.0f, 5000.0f));
mat4 m;

m = mat4(translation(0.0f,
                     0.0f,
                     100.0f * sinf(6.28318531f * t) - 230.0f) *
                     rotation(360.0f * t, X) *
                     rotation(360.0f * t * 2.0f, Y) *
                     rotation(360.0f * t * 5.0f, Z) *
                     translation(0.0f, -80.0f, 0.0f));

glUniformMatrix4fv(model_matrix_pos, 1, GL_FALSE, m[0]);
glUniformMatrix4fv(projection_matrix_pos, 1, GL_FALSE, p);

// Turn off rasterization
glEnable(GL_RASTERIZER_DISCARD);

// Bind the transform feedback object and start
// recording (note GL_POINTS used here...)
glBindTransformFeedback(GL_TRANSFORM_FEEDBACK, xfb);
glBeginTransformFeedback(GL_POINTS);

// Render the object
object.Render();

// Stop recording and unbind the transform feedback object
glEndTransformFeedback();
glBindTransformFeedback(GL_TRANSFORM_FEEDBACK, 0);

// Turn rasterization back on
glDisable(GL_RASTERIZER_DISCARD);

static const vec4 colors[2] =
{
    vec4(0.8f, 0.8f, 0.9f, 0.5f),
    vec4(0.3f, 1.0f, 0.3f, 0.8f)
};

// Use the rendering program
glUseProgram(render_prog);

// Second pass - left facing polygons. Regular rendering
glUniform4fv(0, 1, colors[0]);
```

```
glBindVertexArray(vao[0]);
glDrawTransformFeedbackStream(GL_TRIANGLES, xfb, 0);

// Now draw stream 1, which contains right facing polygons.
glUniform4fv(0, 1, colors[1]);
glBindVertexArray(vao[1]);
glDrawTransformFeedbackStream(GL_TRIANGLES, xfb, 1);
```

The output of the program shown in Example 10.19 is shown in
Figure 10.9. While this is not the most exciting program ever written,
it does demonstrate the techniques involved in configuring and
using transform feedback with multiple streams and the
glDrawTransformFeedback() function.

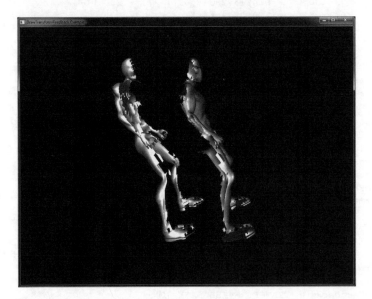

Figure 10.9   Final output of geometry shader sorting example

An interesting note is that although we are drawing triangles when
rendering the original model, the transform feedback mode is GL_POINTS.
This is because the sorting geometry shader converts the incoming
triangles into points. OpenGL requires that when multiple output streams
are in use in a geometry shader, the output primitive type is points
(although the input can be anything). If this restriction were not present,
this application would run in two passes rather than three. Even though
we recorded points into the transform feedback buffers, we can still draw
the second and third passes using GL_TRIANGLES. Once the vertices have
been recorded into the transform feedback buffers, they are simply
interpreted as raw data and can be used for any purpose.

Geometry Shader Instancing

One type of instancing has already been covered in Chapter 3. In this first type of instancing, functions like **glDrawArraysInstanced()** or **glDrawElementsInstanced()** are used to simply run the whole OpenGL pipeline on a set of input data multiple times. This results in the vertex shader running several times on all of the input vertices, with the same vertex data being fetched from memory for each instance of the draw. Also, if tessellation is active, primitives will be tessellated multiple times, resulting in a potentially huge processing load for the GPU. To differentiate between members of each instance in the shader, the built-in GLSL variable gl_InstanceID is provided. Another type of instancing, known as *geometry shader instancing*, is available that only runs the geometry shader and subsequent stages (rasterization and fragment shading) multiple times, rather than the whole pipeline. Geometry shader instancing requires that a geometry shader is present, and so cannot be used without a geometry shader in the currently active program. Both methods of instancing may be used simultaneously. That is, **glDrawArraysInstanced()** may be called while a geometry shader is present that uses geometry shader instancing.

Geometry shader instancing is enabled in the shader by specifying the invocations layout qualifier as part of the input definition as follows:

```
layout (triangles, invocations = 4) in;
```

This example specifies that the geometry shader will be invoked four times for each input primitive (in this case, triangles). The special built-in GLSL input variable gl_InvocationID will contain the invocation number while the geometry shader is running (starting at zero). In effect, all geometry shaders are instanced, although the default invocation count is one. gl_InvocationID is always available as a geometry shader input, but when instancing is not active, its value will be zero. When using instancing in the geometry shader, it is advisable to move as much work as possible from the geometry shader to the vertex shader. By doing so, any such work is performed only once and then shared across all geometry shader invocations. If that work were to be performed in the geometry shader, it would run once per instance.

The maximum invocation count for geometry shader supported by the OpenGL implementation can be found by calling **glGetIntegerv()** with *pname* set to GL_MAX_GEOMETRY_SHADER_INVOCATIONS. All OpenGL implementations must support at least 32 invocations for instanced geometry shaders, but the count may be higher. Each invocation of the geometry shader may still output the maximum number of vertices allowed by the OpenGL implementation. In this way, an instanced geometry shader may reach a much higher amplification level as with a noninstanced geometry shader, any amplification performed must be limited to the maximum number of output vertices supported by the implementation. By combining API level instancing with geometry shader instancing and amplification in the geometry shader, it is possible to essentially nest three levels of geometry in a single draw. Pseudo-code for this is shown in Example 10.20 below.

Example 10.20   Geometry Amplification Using Nested Instancing

```
for each API instance // glDrawArraysInstanced
{
    for each geometry shader invocation // layout (invocations=N)
    {
        for each primitive produced by the geometry shader
        {
            render primitive
        }
    }
}
```

Multiple Viewports and Layered Rendering

This section of the chapter covers two output variables available in the geometry shader that can redirect rendering into different regions of the framebuffer, or to layers of array textures. These variables are gl_ViewportIndex and gl_Layer, respectively. Their values are also available as inputs to fragment shaders.[9]

Viewport Index

The first of these two variables, gl_ViewportIndex is used to specify which set of viewport parameters will be used to perform the viewport transformation by OpenGL. These parameters are passed to OpenGL by calling **glViewportIndexedf()** or **glViewportIndexedfv()** to specify how window x and y coordinates are generated from clip coordinates. Additionally, **glDepthRangeIndexed()** can be used to specify how the window z coordinate is generated. The prototypes of these functions are as follows:

---

9. As of GLSL version 4.3, gl_Layer and gl_Viewport are available as inputs to the fragment shader. In earlier versions of OpenGL (and GLSL), if you need the values of these variables in the fragment shader, you would need to pass them explicitly as a user-defined variable.

void **glViewportIndexedf**(GLuint *index*, GLfloat *x*, GLfloat *y*,
                 GLfloat *w*, GLfloat *h*);
void **glViewportIndexedfv**(GLuint *index*, const GLfloat * *v*);
void **glDepthRangeIndexed**(GLuint *index*, GLclampd *n*,
                 GLclampd *f*);

Sets the bounds of a specific viewport. **glViewportIndexedf()** sets the
bounds of the viewport determined by *index* to the rectangle whose
upper left is at (*x*, *y*) and whose width and height ar *w* and *h*, respectively.
glViewportIndexedfv() performs the same action, but with *x*, *y*, *w*, and *h*
taken from the first through fourth elements of the array *v*.
glDepthRangeIndexed() sets the depth extent of the viewport indexed
by *index*. *n* and *f* represent the near and far planes, respectively.

The viewport origins, widths, and heights are stored in an array by
OpenGL and when a geometry shader is active that writes to
`gl_ViewportIndex`, that value is used to index into the array of viewport
parameters. If the geometry shader does not write to `gl_ViewportIndex`,
or if no geometry shader is present, the first viewport is used.

If you need to set the extent of a number of viewports (and their depth
ranges), you can also use the **glViewportArrayv()** and
glDepthRangeArrayv() functions. These functions take a count of the
number of viewports whose bounds to update, the index of the first
viewport to update, and an array of parameters that will be used to
update the viewports' bounds. Their prototypes are as follows:

void **glViewportArrayv**(GLuint *first*, GLsizei *count*,
                const GLfloat * *v*);
void **glDepthRangeArrayv**(GLuint *first*, GLsizei *count*,
                  const GLdouble * *v*);

Set the bounds of number of viewports with a single command. For
both functions, *first* contains the index of the first viewport to
update and *count* contains the number of viewports to update. For
glViewportArrayv(), *v* contains the address of an array if 4 × *count*
floating point values—one set of four for each viewport, which represent
the *x*, *y*, *w*, and *h* parameters to a call to **glViewportIndexedf()**, in that
order. For **glDepthRangeArrayv()**, *v* contains the address of an array of
2 × *count* double-precision floating point values—one set of two for each
viewport, which represent the *n* and *f* parameters to a call to
glDepthRangeIndexed().

An example use case is to specify multiple viewports within a single framebuffer (e.g., a top, side, and front view in a 3D modeling application) and use the geometry shader to render the same input vertex data into each of the viewports. This can be performed using any of the techniques discussed previously. For example, the geometry shader could perform a simple loop and amplify the geometry—outputting more primitives than it receives as input. Alternatively, the geometry shader could be made to perform instancing with an invocation count of three, and redirect the geometry to the appropriate viewport during each invocation. In either case, it's advisable to perform per-vertex operations in the vertex shader and simply direct rendering to the appropriate viewport in the geometry shader. The geometry shader will also need to perform any operations that are unique for each viewport. In this example, a different projection matrix will be needed for each viewport.

Example 10.21 below contains a simple but a complete example of a geometry shader that uses instancing and multiple invocations to direct rendering to an array of four viewports.

Example 10.21   Directing Geometry to Different Viewports with a Geometry Shader

```
#version 330 core

// Triangles in, four invocations (instances)
layout (triangles, invocations = 4) in;
// Triangles (strips) out, 3 vertices each
layout (triangle_strip, max_vertices = 3) out;

// Four model matrices and a common projection matrix
uniform mat4 model_matrix[4];
uniform mat4 projection_matrix;

// Normal input from the vertex shader
in vec3 vs_normal[];

// Color and normal output to the fragment shader
out vec4 gs_color;
out vec3 gs_normal;

// Colors that will be used for the four instances
const vec4 colors[4] = vec4[4]
(
    vec4(1.0, 0.7, 0.3, 1.0),
    vec4(1.0, 0.2, 0.3, 1.0),
    vec4(0.1, 0.6, 1.0, 1.0),
    vec4(0.3, 0.7, 0.5, 1.0)
);

void main()
```

```
{
    for (int i = 0; i < gl_in.length(); i++)
    {
        // Set the viewport index for every vertex.
        gl_ViewportIndex = gl_InvocationID;
        // Color comes from the "colors" array, also
        // indexed by gl_InvocationID.
        gs_color = colors[gl_InvocationID];
        // Normal is transformed using the model matrix.
        // Note that this assumes that there is no
        // shearing in the model matrix.
        gs_normal = (model_matrix[gl_InvocationID] *
                     vec4(vs_normal[i], 0.0)).xyz;
        // Finally, transform the vertex into position
        // and emit it.
        gl_Position = projection_matrix *
                      (model_matrix[gl_InvocationID] *
                       gl_in[i].gl_Position);
        EmitVertex();
    }
}
```

In this shader, the viewport index is simply initialized using the invocation number (gl_InvocationID). Note that this is set for every vertex in the output primitive, even though it is the same for each. An array of four model matrices is used to apply a different transformation to each of several copies of the incoming geometry. The geometry shader invocation number is also used to index into the array of transformation matrices. Finally, an array of colors is used to color each instance of the geometry differently and this is also indexed using the invocation number.

Before drawing each frame, the array of model matrices is updated using the code shown in Example 10.22 below. A different translation and rotation is used for each of the four matrices.

Example 10.22 Creation of Matrices for Viewport Array Example

```
static const vec3 X(1.0f, 0.0f, 0.0f);
static const vec3 Y(0.0f, 1.0f, 0.0f);
static const vec3 Z(0.0f, 0.0f, 1.0f);
mat4 m[4];

for (int i = 0; i < 4; i++)
{
    m[i] = mat4(
            translation(
                0.0f,
                0.0f,
                100.0f * sin(6.28318531f * t + i) - 230.0f) *
```

```
                    rotation(360.0f * t * float(i + 1), X) *
                    rotation(360.0f * t * float(i + 2), Y) *
                    rotation(360.0f * t * float(5 - i), Z) *
                    translation(0.0f, -80.0f, 0.0f));
    }

    glUniformMatrix4fv(model_matrix_pos, 4, GL_FALSE, m[0]);
```

Notice in Example 10.22 how **glUniformMatrix4fv()** is used to set the
complete array of four matrix uniforms with a single function call. In the
window resize handler for the program, the four viewports are set using
the code shown in Example 10.23.

Example 10.23   Specifying Four Viewports

```
void ViewportArrayApplication::Reshape(int width, int height)
{
    const float wot = float(width) * 0.5f;
    const float hot = float(height) * 0.5f;

    glViewportIndexedf(0, 0.0f, 0.0f, wot, hot);
    glViewportIndexedf(1, wot, 0.0f, wot, hot);
    glViewportIndexedf(2, 0.0f, hot, wot, hot);
    glViewportIndexedf(3, wot, hot, wot, hot);
}
```

In Example 10.23, wot and hot represent the width and height on two,
respectively. This code divides the window into four quadrants with a
viewport for each. The **glViewportIndexedf()** function is used to set the
viewports individually. Figure 10.10 shows the output of the program.

In addition to the multiple viewports supported by OpenGL, multiple
scissor rectangles are also supported. Individual scissor rectangles may be
specified using the **glScissorIndexed()** and **glScissorIndexedv()** functions,
whose prototypes are as follows:

---

void **glScissorIndexed**(GLuint *index*, GLint *left*, GLint *bottom*,
                    GLsizei *width*, GLsizei *height*);
void **glScissorIndexedv**(GLuint *index*, const GLint * *v*);

Set the bounds of a specific scissor rectangle. **glScissorIndexed()** sets the
bounds of the scissor rectangle determined by *index* to the rectangle
whose lower left is at (*left*, *bottom*) and whose width and height are *width*
and *height*, respectively. **glScissorIndexedv()** performs the same action,
but with *left*, *bottom*, *width*, and *height* taken from the first through
fourth elements of the array *v*.

Figure 10.10　　Output of the viewport-array example

As with **glDepthRangeArrayv()** and **glViewportArrayv()**, there is an array
form of **glScissorIndexed()**, which sets multiple scissor rectangles
simultaneously. Its prototype is as follows:

void **glScissorArrayv**(GLuint *first*, GLsizei *count*, const GLint * *v*);

Sets the bounds of multiple scissor rectangles with a single command.
first contains the index of the first scissor rectangle to update, *count*
contains the number of scissor rectangles to update, and *v* contains the
address of an array of 4 × *count* integers—four integers for each scissor
rectangle, which are equivalent to the *left*, *bottom*, *width*, and *height*
parameters to **glScissorIndexed()**, in that order.

The same index written to gl_ViewportIndex is used to specify which
scissor rectangle should be used for the pixel ownership test. Both
viewport and scissor rectangles are specified in screen coordinates. Thus,
you may wish to offset each scissor rectangle by the origin of the viewport
whose index it shares. Although the same index is used to determine both
the scissor rectangle and the viewport to use, they may be effectively
decoupled by specifying the same viewport for multiple indices, but a
different scissor rectangle for each, or vice-versa. The maximum number of
viewports (and scissor rectangles) that an implementation supports can be
found by calling **glGetIntegerv()** with *pname* set to GL_MAX_VIEWPORTS.
The minimum requirement for this value is 16, and so you can be sure that
your implementation supports at least that many. Having large arrays of

viewports and scissor rectangles allows for some combinatorial use. For example, you could specify four viewports and four scissor rectangles, producing 16 possible combinations of viewport and scissor rectangles, which can be indexed in the geometry shader independently.

Layered Rendering

When rendering into a framebuffer object, it is possible to use a 2D array texture as a color attachment and render into the slices of the array using a geometry shader. To create a 2D array texture and attach it to a framebuffer object, use code such as that shown in Example 10.24.

Example 10.24   Example Code to Create an FBO with an Array
                       Texture Attachment

```
// Declare variables
GLuint tex;        // This will be the 2D array texture
GLuint fbo;        // The framebuffer object

// Create and allocate a 1024x1024x32 2D array texture
glGenTextures(1, &tex);
glBindTexture(GL_TEXTURE_2D_ARRAY, tex);
glTexImage3D(GL_TEXTURE_2D_ARRAY,
             0,
             GL_RGBA,
             1024,
             1024,
             32,
             0,
             GL_RGBA,
             GL_UNSIGNED_BYTE,
             NULL);

// Now create a framebuffer object and attach the
// 2D array texture to one of its color attachments
glGenFramebuffers(1 &fbo);
glBindFramebuffer(GL_FRAMEBUFFER, fbo);
glFramebufferTexture(GL_FRAMEBUFFER,
                     GL_COLOR_ATTACHMENT0,
                     tex,
                     0);

// Now, make the framebuffer's color attachment(s) the
// current draw buffer.
static const GLenum draw_buffers[] =
{
    GL_COLOR_ATTACHMENT0
};
glDrawBuffers(1, draw_buffers);
```

A different array texture can be attached to each of the framebuffer's color attachments (GL_COLOR_ATTACHMENT*i*, where *i* is the index of the color attachment). It is also possible to create a 2D array texture with a format of GL_DEPTH_COMPONENT, GL_DEPTH_STENCIL, or GL_STENCIL_INDEX and attach it to GL_DEPTH_ATTACHMENT, GL_STENCIL_ATTACHMENT, or GL_DEPTH_STENCIL_ATTACHMENT. This will allow the array texture to be used as a layered depth or stencil buffer. Note that this type of 2D array texture must be used for this purpose because there is no such thing as an array renderbuffer in OpenGL.

Now we have a layered framebuffer that we can render into. A restriction exists that when using layered attachments to a framebuffer, *all* the attachments of that framebuffer must be layered. Also, all attachments of a layered framebuffer must be of the same type (one- or two-dimensional array textures, cube maps, etc.). Thus, it is not possible, for example, to bind a six-slice 2D array texture and the six faces of a cube-map texture to the same framebuffer object at the same time. Attempting to render into such a framebuffer object will result in **glCheckFramebufferStatus()** returning GL_FRAMEBUFFER_INCOMPLETE_LAYER_TARGETS.

It is also possible to render into the slices of a 3D texture by attaching each of the slices individually as layers of the framebuffer using the **glFramebufferTextureLayer()** function.

Now that an array texture is attached to the color attachment point of the current framebuffer object, the geometry shader can be used to direct rendering into the slices of the array. To do this, the geometry shader can write into the GLSL built-in variable `gl_Layer`. `gl_Layer` is used to specify the zero-based index of the layer into which rendering will be directed. An example of such a geometry shader is shown in Example 10.25.

Note: Be careful when writing to `gl_Layer` that the value written is a valid index into the current layered framebuffer object. Writing outside this range will produce *undefined results*, which may include discarding the geometry, rendering it into the first or last slice, corrupting other slices, or even corrupting other areas of memory.

Example 10.25   Geometry Shader for Rendering into an Array Texture

```
#version 330 core

layout (triangles) in;
layout (triangle_strip, max_vertices=128) out;

in VS_GS_VERTEX
{
    vec4 color;
```

```
    vec3 normal;
} vertex_in[];

out GS_FS_VERTEX
{
    vec4 color;
    vec3 normal;
} vertex_out;

uniform mat4 projection_matrix;
uniform int output_slices;

void main()
{
    int i, j;
    mat4 slice_matrix;
    float alpha = 0.0;
    float delta = float(output_slices - 1) * 0.5 / 3.1415927;

    for (j = 0; j < output_slices; ++j)
    {
        float s = sin(alpha);
        float c = cos(alpha);
        slice_matrix = mat4(vec4(c, 0.0, -s, 0.0),
                            vec4(0.0, 1.0, 0.0, 0.0),
                            vec4(s, 0.0, c, 0.0),
                            vec4(0.0, 0.0, 0.0, 1.0));
        slice_matrix = slice_matrix * projection_matrix;
        for (i = 0; i < gl_in.length(); ++i)
        {
            gl_Layer = j;
            gl_Position = slice_matrix * gl_in[i].gl_Position;
            vertex_out.color = vertex_in[i].color;
            vertex_out.normal = vertex_in[i].normal;
            EmitVertex();
        }
    EndPrimitive();
    }
}
```

Example 10.25 amplifies the incoming geometry and renders a complete copy of it into each layer of the layered color attachment of the current framebuffer. Each copy is a rotated version of the incoming geometry such that after a single pass of rendering, the output array texture contains a view of the geometry as seen from several different angles. This can be used, for example to update *impostors*.[10]

---

10. *Impostors* are views of real geometry rendered into textures and then used in place of that geometry when many instances are needed, rather than rendering the entire mesh. An example use is a forest of trees. Trees are rendered as seen from an array of angles into a texture and the appropriate view of the tree selected when the forest is rendered.

In this particular example, a simple loop is used to amplify the incoming geometry. This is sufficient when the number of layers in the framebuffer attachment is relatively small—less than one third of the maximum number of output vertices allowed by the implementation in a geometry shader. When a larger number of array slices must be rendered, instanced rendering or even geometry shader instancing can be employed and gl_InstanceID (or gl_InvocationID) used to derive the output layer. In the second case, attention should be paid to the maximum geometry shader invocations allowed, as 32 is the minimum requirement. The maximum number of layers in an array texture can be determined by calling **glGetIntegerv()** with a *pname* of GL_MAX_ARRAY_TEXTURE_LAYERS, and the minimum required value of this parameter is 2048.

Another application of layered rendering using a geometry shader is to update the faces of a cube-map texture that might be used as an environment map in another pass. When a cube-map texture is attached as a color attachment to a framebuffer object, it appears as a six-layer array texture. The faces of the cube map appear as the slices of the array in the order shown in Table 10.4 below.

Table 10.4   Ordering of Cube-Map Face Indices

Layer Number	Cube-Map Face
0	GL_TEXTURE_CUBE_MAP_POSITIVE_X
1	GL_TEXTURE_CUBE_MAP_NEGATIVE_X
2	GL_TEXTURE_CUBE_MAP_POSITIVE_Y
3	GL_TEXTURE_CUBE_MAP_NEGATIVE_Y
4	GL_TEXTURE_CUBE_MAP_POSITIVE_Z
5	GL_TEXTURE_CUBE_MAP_NEGATIVE_Z

To render an environment map into a cube map using a geometry shader, set up six projection matrices representing the view frustums for each of the faces. Next, use an instanced geometry shader with an invocation count of six to emit the same incoming geometry into each of the faces. Use gl_InvocationID to the output gl_Layer and to index into the array of projection matrices. In a single pass, the cube-map environment map will be updated.

Chapter Summary

In this chapter, we have covered geometry shaders—a shader stage that runs per-primitive, has access to all vertices in the primitive, and can create and destroy geometry as it passes through the OpenGL pipeline. It can even change the types of primitives. The geometry shader can be used for user-controlled culling, geometric transformations, and even sorting algorithms. It provides access to features such as multiple viewports and rendering into texture arrays, three-dimensional textures, and cube maps. The geometry shader can be *instanced*, which when combined with its other features is an extremely powerful tool. The geometry shader is perhaps the most versatile and flexible shader stage. Geometry shaders even have their own special primitive modes—GL_LINES_ADJACENCY, GL_LINE_STRIP_ADJACENCY, GL_TRIANGLES_ADJACENCY, and GL_TRIANGLE_STRIP_ADJACENCY.

Effective use of geometry shaders, in conjunction with features such as layered framebuffers, transform feedback, primitive queries, and instancing allows some very advanced and interesting algorithms to be implemented.

Geometry Shader Redux

To use a geometry shader in your program:

- Create a geometry shader with
  `glCreateShader(GL_GEOMETRY_SHADER)`.

- Set the shader source with `glShaderSource` and compile it with
  `glCompileShader`.

- Attach it to a program object with `glAttachShader`, and link the
  program with `glLinkProgram`.

Inside your geometry shader do the following:

- Specify input and output primitive types with the
  `layout (<primitive_type>) in;` or
  `layout (<primitive_type>) out;` layout qualifiers.

- Specify the maximum number of vertices the shader might produce
  with the `layout (max_vertices = <vertex_count>) in;` layout
  qualifier.

- Declare all inputs to the geometry shader as arrays (using the `in`
  keyword). You can use the `.length()` method on the input arrays
  (including `gl_in[]`) to retrieve the size of the primitive being
  processed.

- If using multiple output streams with transform feedback, declare
  outputs using the `layout(stream = <stream>) out;` layout
  qualifier. Use interface blocks to group outputs for a single stream
  together, keeping your code neat and tidy.

To produce geometry do the following:

- Use `EmitVertex()` or `EmitStreamVertex(<stream>)` to produce vertices and `EndPrimitive()` or `EndStreamPrimitive(<stream>)` to break apart long output strips (remember, geometry shaders can only produce points, line strips or triangle strips).

The special inputs and outputs available to geometry shaders are as follows:

- `gl_in[]`—an input array containing all the per-vertex built-in data (`gl_Position`, `gl_PointSize` and `gl_ClipDistance[]`.
- `gl_InvocationID`—an input containing invocation index for an instanced geometry shader. For noninstanced geometry shaders, this is still available; it will just be zero, always.
- `gl_PrimitiveIDIn`—an input containing the index of the incoming primitive. So named because in a geometry shader, `gl_PrimitiveID` is an output.
- `gl_PrimitiveID`—an output that is to be written with the primitive index as seen by the subsequent fragment shader.
- `gl_Layer`—an output that contains the index of the layer within a layered framebuffer to render the primitive to. This is also an input to the fragment shader.
- `gl_ViewportIndex`—an output that contains the index of the viewport to use for the viewport transformation before rasterization. This is also an input to the fragment shader.

Geometry Shader Best Practices

The following are some tips for using geometry shaders wisely. This will help you obtain the best possible performance from a program using geometry shaders. These aren't hard-and-fast rules, but if followed should allow you to use geometry shaders effectively in your programs.

Do Work in the Right Place

If you have work that is to be done per-vertex, do it in the vertex shader (or tessellation evaluation shader, if present). When rendering triangle strips or fans, each triangle is presented individually to the geometry shader. Performing per-vertex work in the geometry shader will result in it being done multiple times per vertex. Likewise, if you have work that is to be done per-face (such as calculating the values for attributes with flat interpolation qualifiers), perform it in the geometry shader rather than in the vertex shader. If independent triangles are rendered, calculating the values of flat interpolated attributes in the vertex shader will result in that computation being performed for vertices that are not the *provoking vertex* for the primitive. Moving that work to the geometry shader allows it to be performed only once and then the value (which should be stored in local variables) propagated to all of the output variables.

Only Use a Geometry Shader When You Need One

Geometry shaders are not free. Even a pass-through geometry shader will have some impact on the performance of your program. Consider whether you really need a geometry shader. Do you need per-primitive calculations that can't be performed in the vertex shader? Do you need access to all the vertices of the primitive, or to adjacency information? If your algorithm can be implemented with reasonable efficiency using only the vertex shader (or tessellation shaders, if you're using tessellation), then that may be worth considering.

Allocate Carefully

When specifying the `max_vertices` input layout qualifier, only make it as large as is needed by the algorithm you intend to implement. The `max_vertices` qualifier essentially acts as an allocation. Depending on the OpenGL implementation you're using, performance may be degraded if you allocate too many output vertices—even if you don't use them all. It's very easy to simply specify the maximum allowed, but care should be taken to only allocate as many as is necessary.

Don't Amplify Too Aggressively

For the same reasons that you shouldn't allocate too many output vertices with the `max_vertices` layout qualifier, care should be taken with producing a very large amount of vertices in the geometry shader. While it is possible to implement algorithms like tessellation in the geometry shader, some OpenGL implementations may run at a reduced performance level if this is attempted. This is why OpenGL includes tessellation! The geometry shader is best suited to algorithms that need access to whole-primitive information, and perform culling or small amounts of primitive amplification.

Chapter 11

Memory

Chapter Objectives

After reading this chapter, you'll be able to do the following:

- Read from and write to memory from shaders.

- Perform simple mathematical operations directly on memory from shaders.

- Synchronize and communicate between different shader invocations.

Everything in the OpenGL pipeline thus far has essentially been free from side effects. That is, the pipeline is constructed from a sequence of stages, either programmable (such as the vertex and fragment shaders) or fixed function (such as the tessellation engine) with well-defined inputs and outputs (such as vertex attributes or color outputs to a framebuffer). Although it has been possible to read from arbitrary memory locations using textures or texture buffer objects (TBOs), in general, writing has been allowed only to fixed and predictable locations. For example, vertices captured during transform feedback operations are written in well-defined sequences to transform feedback buffers, and pixels produced in the fragment shader are written into the framebuffer in a regular pattern defined by rasterization.

In this chapter we introduce mechanisms by which shaders may both read from *and* write to user-specified locations. This allows shaders to construct data structures in memory and, by carefully updating the same memory locations, effect a level of communication between each other. To this end, we also introduce special functions both in the shading language and in the OpenGL API that provide control over the order of access and of the operations performed during those memory accesses.

This chapter has the following major sections:

- "Using Textures for Generic Data Storage" shows how to read and write memory held in a texture object, through GLSL built-in functions.

- "Shader Storage Buffer Objects" shows how to read and write a generic memory buffer, directly through user-declared variables.

- "Atomic Operations and Synchronization" explains multiple-writer synchronization problems with images, and how to solve them.

- "Example" discusses an interesting use of many of the features outlined in the chapter in order to demonstrate the power and flexibility that generalized memory access provides to the experienced OpenGL programmer.

Using Textures for Generic Data Storage

It is possible to use the memory representing a buffer object or a single level of a texture object for general purpose read and write access in shaders. To support this, the OpenGL Shading Language provides several *image* types to represent raw image data.

Images are declared in shaders as uniforms in a similar manner to samplers. Just like samplers, they are assigned locations by the shader compiler that can be passed to **glUniform1i()** to specify the *image unit* which they represent. The OpenGL Shading Language image types are shown in Table 11.1.

Table 11.1   Generic Image Types in GLSL

Image Type	Meaning
image1D	Floating-Point 1D
image2D	Floating-Point 2D
image3D	Floating-Point 3D
imageCube	Floating-Point Cube Map
image2DRect	Floating-Point Rectangle
image1DArray	Floating-Point 1D Array
image2DArray	Floating-Point 2D Array
imageBuffer	Floating-Point Buffer
image2DMS	Multisample 2D Floating Point
image2DMSArray	Floating-Point 2D Multisample Array
imageCubeArray	Floating-Point Cube-Map Array
iimage1D	Signed Integer 1D
iimage2D	Signed Integer 2D
iimage3D	Signed Integer 3D
iimageCube	Signed Integer Cube Map
iimage2DRect	Signed Integer Rectangle
iimage1DArray	Signed Integer 1D Array
iimage2DArray	Signed Integer 2D Array
iimageBuffer	Signed Integer Buffer
iimage2DMS	Multisample 2D Signed Integer
iimage2DMSArray	Signed Integer 2D Multisample Array
iimageCubeArray	Signed Integer Cube-Map Array
uimage1D	Unsigned Integer 1D
uimage2D	Unsigned Integer 2D
uimage3D	Unsigned Integer 3D
uimageCube	Unsigned Integer Cube Map
uimage2DRect	Unsigned Integer Rectangle
uimage1DArray	Unsigned Integer 1D Array

Table 11.1 (continued) Generic Image Types in GLSL

Image Type	Meaning
uimage2DArray	Unsigned Integer 2D Array
uimageBuffer	Unsigned Integer Buffer
uimage2DMS	Multisample 2D Unsigned Integer
uimage2DMSArray	Unsigned Integer 2D Multisample Array
uimageCubeArray	Unsigned Integer Cube-Map Array

Notice that most of GLSL sampler types have an analog as an image type. The primary differences between a sampler type (such as `sampler2D`) and an image type (such as `image2D`) are first, that the image type represents a single layer of the texture, not a complete mipmap chain and second, that image types do not support sampler operations such as filtering. Note that these unsupported sampling operations include depth comparison, which is why the shadow sampler types such as `sampler2DShadow` do not have an equivalent image type.

The three basic classes of image types, `image*`, `iimage*`, and `uimage*` are used to declare images containing floating point, signed integer, or unsigned integer data, respectively.

In addition to the general data type (floating point, signed, or unsigned integer) associated with the image variable, a *format* layout qualifier may also be given to further specify the underlying image format of the data in memory. Any image from which data will be read must be declared with a format layout qualifier, but in general it is a good idea to explicitly state the format of the data in the image at declaration time. The format layout qualifiers and their corresponding OpenGL internal format types are shown in Table 11.2.

Table 11.2 Image Format Qualifiers

Image Type	OpenGL Internal Format
rgba32f	GL_RGBA32F
rgba16f	GL_RGBA16F
rg32f	GL_RG32F
rg16f	GL_RG16F
r11f_g11f_b10f	GL_R11F_G11F_B10F
r32f	GL_R32F
r16f	GL_R16F

Table 11.2 **(continued)** Image Format Qualifiers

Image Type	OpenGL Internal Format
rgba16	GL_RGBA16UI
rgb10_a2	GL_RGB10_A2UI
rgba8	GL_RGBA8UI
rg16	GL_RG16UI
rg8	GL_RG8UI
r16	GL_R16UI
r8	GL_R8UI
rgba16_snorm	GL_RGBA16_SNORM
rgba8_snorm	GL_RGBA8_SNORM
rg16_snorm	GL_RG16_SNORM
rg8_snorm	GL_RG8_SNORM
r16_snorm	GL_R16_SNORM
r8_snorm	GL_R8_SNORM
rgba32i	GL_RGBA32I
rgba16i	GL_RGBA16I
rgba8i	GL_RGBA8I
rg32i	GL_RG32I
rg16i	GL_RG16I
rg8i	GL_RG8I
r32i	GL_R32I
r16i	GL_R16I
r8i	GL_R8I
rgba32ui	GL_RGBA32UI
rgba16ui	GL_RGBA16UI
rgba8ui	GL_RGBA8UI
rg32ui	GL_RG32UI
rg16ui	GL_RG16UI
rg8ui	GL_RG8UI
r32ui	GL_R32UI
r16ui	GL_R16UI
r8ui	GL_R8UI

The image format qualifier is provided as part of the image variable declaration and must be used when declaring an image variable that will be used to read from an image. It is optional if the image will only ever be written to (see the explanation of `writeonly` below for more details). The image format qualifier used in the declaration of such variables (if present) must batch the basic data type of the image. That is, floating-point format specifiers such as `r32f` or `rgba16_unorm` must be used with floating-point image variables such as `image2D`, while nonfloating-point qualifiers (such as `rg8ui`) may not. Likewise, signed integer format qualifiers such as `rgba32i` must be used to declare signed integer image variables (`iimage2D`) and unsigned format qualifiers (`rgba32ui`) must be used to declare unsigned integer image variables (`uimage2D`).

Examples of using the format layout qualifiers to declare image uniforms are shown in Example 11.1.

Example 11.1   Examples of Image Format Layout Qualifiers

```
// 2D image whose data format is 4-component floating point
layout (rgba32f) uniform image2D image1;

// 2D image whose data format is 2-component integer
layout (rg32i) uniform iimage2D image2;

// 1D image whose data format is single-component unsigned integer
layout (r32ui) uniform uimage1D image3;

// 3D image whose data format is single-component integer, and is
// initialized to refer to image unit 4
layout (binding=4, r32) uniform iimage3D image4;
```

The format type used in the declaration of the image variable does not need to exactly match the underlying format of the data in the image (as given by the texture's internal format), but should be *compatible* as defined by the OpenGL specification. In general, if the amount of data storage required *per texel* is the same between two formats, then they are considered to be compatible. For example, a texture whose internal format is GL_RGBA32F has four, 32-bit (floating point) components, for a total of 128 bits per texel. Levels of this texture may be accessed in a shader through image variables whose format is `rgba32f`, `rgba32ui`, or `rgba32i` as all of these formats represent a single texel using 128 bits. Furthermore, a texture whose internal format is GL_RG16F is represented as 32 bits per texel. This type of texture may be accessed using image variables declared as `r32f`, `rgba8ui`, `rgb10_a2ui`, or any other format that represents a texel using 32 bits. When texture and image variable formats do not match exactly but are otherwise compatible, the raw data in the image is reinterpreted as the type specified in the shader. For example, reading from a texture with the GL_R32F internal format using an image variable declared as `r32ui` will return an unsigned integer whose bit-pattern represents the floating-point data stored in the texture.

The maximum number of image uniforms that may be used in a single shader stage may be determined by querying the value of GL_MAX_VERTEX_IMAGE_UNIFORMS for vertex shaders, GL_MAX_TESS_CONTROL_IMAGE_UNIFORMS, and GL_MAX_TESS_EVALUATION_IMAGE_UNIFORMS for tessellation control and evaluation shaders, respectively, GL_MAX_GEOMETRY_IMAGE_UNIFORMS for geometry shaders and finally, GL_MAX_FRAGMENT_IMAGE_UNIFORMS for fragment shaders. Additionally, the maximum number of image uniforms that may be used across all active shaders is given by GL_MAX_COMBINED_IMAGE_UNIFORMS. In addition to these limits, some implementations may have restrictions upon the number of image uniforms available to a fragment shader when that shader also writes to the framebuffer using traditional output variables. To determine whether this is the case, retrieve the value of GL_MAX_COMBINED_IMAGE_UNITS_AND_FRAGMENT_OUTPUTS. A final note is that although the OpenGL API supports image uniforms in every shader stage, it only mandates that implementations provide support in the fragment shader and that only GL_MAX_FRAGMENT_IMAGE_UNIFORMS be nonzero.

Binding Textures to Image Units

Just as sampler variables represent texture units in the OpenGL API, so do image variables represent a binding to an *image unit* in the OpenGL API. Image uniforms declared in a shader have a location that may be retrieved by calling **glGetUniformLocation()**. This is passed in a call to **glUniform1i()** to set the index of the image unit to which the image uniform refers. This binding may also be specified directly[1] in the shader using a `binding` layout qualifier as shown in the declaration of `image4` in Example 11.1. By default, an image uniform has the binding 0, and so if only one image is used in a shader, there is no need to explicitly set its

---

1. The option of specifying the image unit in the shader using the `binding` layout qualifier is generally preferred. This is because some OpenGL implementations may provide a multi-threaded shader compiler. If properties of a linked program, such as the locations of uniforms, are queried too soon after the program is linked, the implementation may need to stall to allow compilation and linking to complete before it can return. By specifying the bindings explicitly, the uniform location query and the potential stall may be avoided.

binding to 0. The number of image units supported by the OpenGL implementation may be determined by retrieving the value of GL_MAX_IMAGE_UNITS. A single layer of a texture object must be bound to an image unit before it can be accessed in a shader. To do this, call **glBindImageTexture()** whose prototype is as follows:

---

void **glBindImageTexture**(GLuint *unit*, Gluint *texture*, GLint *level*,
                            GLboolean *layered*, GLint *layer*,
                            GLenum *access*, GLenum *format*);

Binds level *level* of texture *texture* to image unit *unit*. *unit* is the zero-based unit index of the image unit to which to bind the texture level. If *texture* is zero, any texture currently bound to the specified image unit is unbound. If *texture* refers to an array texture type, such as a 1D- or 2D-array texture type, it is possible to either bind the entire array or only a single layer of the array to the image unit. If *layered* is GL_TRUE then the entire array is bound and *layer* is ignored whereas if *layered* is GL_FALSE then only layer *layer* of the texture is bound. When a single layer of an array texture is bound, it is treated as if it were a single-layer, nonarray texture.

access may be GL_READ_ONLY, GL_WRITE_ONLY, or GL_READ_WRITE and describes how the image will be accessed by the shader. *format* specifies the format that the elements of the image will be treated as when performing formatted stores and should be one of the OpenGL enumerants listed in Table 11.2.

Texture objects that will be used for generic memory access are created and allocated as usual by calling **glGenTextures()** and one of the texture allocation functions such as **glTexImage2D()** or **glTexStorage3D()**. Once created and allocated, they are bound to an image unit using **glBindImageTexture()** for either read, write, or both read and write access, as specified by the *access* parameter to **glBindImageTexture()**. Violating this declaration (for example by writing to an image bound using GL_READ_ONLY for *access*) will cause undesired behavior, possibly crashing the application.

An example of creating, allocating, and binding a texture for read and write access in shaders is given in Example 11.2.

Example 11.2   Creating, Allocating, and Binding a Texture to an Image
Unit

```
GLuint tex;

// Generate a new name for our texture
glGenTextures(1, &tex);
// Bind it to the regular 2D texture target to create it
glBindTexture(GL_TEXTURE_2D, tex);
// Allocate immutable storage for the texture
glTexStorage2D(GL_TEXTURE_2D, 1, GL_RGBA32F, 512, 512);
// Unbind it from the 2D texture target
glBindTexture(GL_TEXTURE_2D, 0);
// Now bind it for read-write to one of the image units
glBindImageTexture(0, tex, 0, GL_FALSE, 0, GL_READ_WRITE, GL_RGBA32F);
```

glBindImageTexture() works similarly to **glBindTexture()**. There are,
however, a few subtle differences. Firstly, the index of the image unit to
which to bind the texture is specified directly in the *unit* parameter rather
than being inferred through the current active texture unit. This makes
calls to **glActiveTexture()** unnecessary when binding texture levels to
image units. Secondly, the format in which formatted stores (writes from
the shader) will be performed is specified during the API call. This format
should match the format of the image uniform in the shaders that will
access the texture. However, it need not match the format of the actual
texture. For textures allocated by calling one of the **glTexImage()** or
glTexStorage() functions, any format that matches in *size* may be specified
for *format*. For example, formats GL_R32F, GL_RGBA8, and
GL_R11F_G11F_B10F are all considered to consist of 32 bits per texel and
therefore to match in size. A complete table of all of the sizes of the texture
formats is given in the OpenGL specification.

To use a buffer object as the backing store for an `imageBuffer` image in a
shader, it must still be represented as a texture by creating a buffer texture,
attaching the buffer object to the texture object and then binding the
buffer texture to the image unit as shown in Example 11.3. The format of
the data in the buffer object is specified when it is attached to the texture
object. The same buffer may be attached to multiple texture objects
simultaneously with different formats, allowing some level of format
aliasing to be implemented.

Example 11.3   Creating and Binding a Buffer Texture to an Image Unit

```
GLuint tex, buf;

// Generate a name for the buffer object, bind it to the
// GL_TEXTURE_BINDING, and allocate 4K for the buffer
glGenBuffers(1, &buf);
glBindBuffer(GL_TEXTURE_BUFFER, buf);
glBufferData(GL_TEXTURE_BUFFER, 4096, NULL, GL_DYNAMIC_COPY);

// Generate a new name for our texture
glGenTextures(1, &tex);
// Bind it to the buffer texture target to create it
glBindTexture(GL_TEXTURE_BUFFER, tex);
// Attach the buffer object to the texture and specify format as
// single channel floating point
glTexBuffer(GL_TEXTURE_BUFFER, GL_R32F, buf);

// Now bind it for read-write to one of the image units
glBindImageTexture(0, tex, 0, GL_FALSE, 0, GL_READ_WRITE, GL_RGBA32F);
```

Reading from and Writing to Images

Once an image has been declared in the shader and a level and layer of a texture have been bound to the corresponding image unit, the shader may access the data in the texture directly for both *read* and *write*. Reading and writing are done only through built-in functions that load or store their arguments to or from an image. To load texels from an image, call **imageLoad()**. There are many overloaded variants of **imageLoad()**. They are as follows:

gvec4 **imageLoad**(readonly gimage1D *image*, int *P*);
gvec4 **imageLoad**(readonly gimage2D *image*, ivec2 *P*);
gvec4 **imageLoad**(readonly gimage3D *image*, ivec3 *P*);
gvec4 **imageLoad**(readonly gimage2DRect *image*, ivec2 *P*);
gvec4 **imageLoad**(readonly gimageCube *image*, ivec3 *P*);
gvec4 **imageLoad**(readonly gimageBuffer *image*, int *P*);
gvec4 **imageLoad**(readonly gimage1DArray *image*, ivec2 *P*);
gvec4 **imageLoad**(readonly gimage2DArray *image*, ivec3 *P*);
gvec4 **imageLoad**(readonly gimageCubeArray *image*, ivec3 *P*);
gvec4 **imageLoad**(readonly gimage2DMS *image*, ivec2 *P*,
                    int *sample*);
gvec4 **imageLoad**(readonly gimage2DMSArray *image*, ivec3 *P*,
                    int *sample*);

Load the texel at coordinate *P* from the image unit *image*. For loads from multisample images, the sample number is given in *sample*.

The **imageLoad()** functions operate similarly to **texelFetch()**, which is used to directly read texels from textures without any filtering applied. In order to store into images, the **imageStore()** function may be used. **imageStore()** is defined as follows:

```
gvec4 imageStore(writeonly gimage1D image, int P, gvec4 data);
gvec4 imageStore(writeonly gimage2D image, ivec2 P, gvec4
                 data);
gvec4 imageStore(writeonly gimage3D image, ivec3 P, gvec4
                 data);
gvec4 imageStore(writeonly gimage2DRect image, ivec2 P, gvec4
                 data);
gvec4 imageStore(writeonly gimageCube image, ivec3 P, gvec4
                 data);
gvec4 imageStore(writeonly gimageBuffer image, int P, gvec4
                 data);
gvec4 imageStore(writeonly gimage1DArray image, ivec2 P, gvec4
                 data);
gvec4 imageStore(writeonly gimage2DArray image, ivec3 P, gvec4
                 data);
gvec4 imageStore(writeonly gimageCubeArray image, ivec3 P,
                 gvec4 data);
gvec4 imageStore(writeonly gimage2DMS image, ivec2 P,
                 int sample, gvec4 data);
gvec4 imageStore(writeonly gimage2DMSArray image, ivec3 P,
                 int sample, gvec4 data);
```

Store *data* into the texel at coordinate *P* in the image specified by *image*. For multisample stores, the sample number is given by *sample*.

If you need to know the size of an image in the shader, you can query with the **imageSize()** functions listed below.

```
int imageSize(gimage1D image);
int imageSize(gimageBuffer image);
ivec2 imageSize(gimage2D image);
ivec2 imageSize(gimageCube image);
ivec2 imageSize(gimageRect image);
ivec2 imageSize(gimage1DArray image);
ivec2 imageSize(gimage2DMS image);
ivec3 imageSize(gimageCubeArray image);
```

```
ivec3 imageSize(gimage3D image);
ivec3 imageSize(gimage2DArray image);
ivec3 imageSize(gimage2DMSArray image);
```

Return the dimensions of the image. For arrayed images, the last
component of the return value will hold the size of the array. Cube
images return only the dimensions of one face and the number of cubes
in the cube-map array, if arrayed.

Example 11.4 shows a simple but complete example of a fragment shader
that performs both image loads and stores from and to multiple images. It
also performs multiple stores per invocation.

Example 11.4   Simple Shader Demonstrating Loading and Storing into
                    Images

```
#version 420 core

// Buffer containing a palette of colors to mark primitives by ID
layout (binding = 0, rgba32f) uniform imageBuffer colors;

// The buffer that we will write to
layout (binding = 1, rgba32f) uniform image2D output_buffer;

out vec4 color;

void main(void)
{
    // Load a color from the palette based on primitive ID % 256
    vec4 col = imageLoad(colors, gl_PrimitiveID & 255);

    // Store the resulting fragment at two locations. First at the
    // fragments window space coordinate shifted left...
    imageStore(output_buffer,
            ivec2(gl_FragCoord.xy) - ivec2(200, 0), col);

    // ... then at the location shifted right
    imageStore(output_buffer,
            ivec2(gl_FragCoord.xy) +ivec2(200, 0), col);
}
```

The shader in Example 11.4 loads a color from a buffer texture indexed by
a function of `gl_PrimitiveID` and then writes it *twice* into a single image
indexed by functions of the current two-dimensional fragment coordinate.
Notice that the shader has no other per-fragment outputs. The result of
running this shader on some simple geometry is shown in Figure 11.1

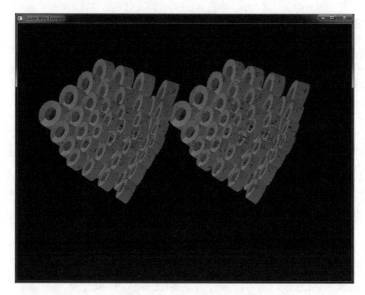

Figure 11.1   Output of the simple load-store shader

As can be seen in Figure 11.1, two copies of the output geometry have been rendered—one in the left half of the image and the other in the right half of the image. The data in the resulting texture was explicitly placed with the shader of Example 11.4. While this may seem like a minor accomplishment, it actually illustrates the power of image store operations. It demonstrates that a fragment shader is able to write to arbitrary locations in a surface. In traditional rasterization into a framebuffer, the location at which the fragment is written is determined by fixed function processing before the shader executes. However, with image stores, this location is determined by the shader. Another thing to consider is that the number of stores to images is not limited, whereas the number of attachments allowed on a single framebuffer object is, and only one fragment is written to each attachment. This means that a much larger amount of data may be written by a fragment shader using image stores than would be possible using a framebuffer and its attachments. In fact, an arbitrary amount of data may be written to memory by a single shader invocation using image stores.

Figure 11.1 also demonstrates another facet of stores from shaders. That is, they are unordered and can be subject to race conditions. The program that generated the image disabled both depth testing and back-face culling, meaning that each pixel has at least two primitives rendering into it. The speckled corruption that can be seen in the image is the result of the nondeterministic order with which the primitives are rendered by OpenGL. We will cover race conditions and how to avoid them later in this chapter.

Shader Storage Buffer Objects

Reading data from and writing data to memory using image variables works well for simple cases where large arrays of homogeneous data are needed, or where the data is naturally image-based (such as the output of OpenGL rendering or where the shader is writing into an OpenGL texture). However, in some cases, large blocks of structured data may be required. For these use cases, we can use a `buffer` variable to store the data. Buffer variables are declared in shaders by placing them in an interface block which in turn is declared using the `buffer` keyword. A simple example is given in Example 11.5.

Example 11.5   Simple Declaration of a Buffer Block

```
#version 430 core

// create a readable-writeable buffer
layout (std430, binding = 0) buffer BufferObject {
    int mode;              // preamble members
    vec4 points[];     // last member can be unsized array
};
```

In addition to declaring the interface block `BufferObject` as a buffer block, Example 11.5 also includes two further layout qualifiers attached to the block. The first, `std430`, indicates that the memory layout of the block should follow the `std430` standard, which is important if you want to read the data produced by the shader in your application, or possibly generate data in the application and then consume it from the shader. The `std430` layout is documented in Appendix I, "Buffer Object Layouts" and is similar to the `std140` layout used for uniform blocks, but a bit more economical with its use of memory.

The second qualifier, `binding = 0`, specifies that the block should be associated with the GL_SHADER_STORAGE_BUFFER binding at index zero. Declaring an interface block using the `buffer` keyword indicates that the block should be stored in memory and backed by a buffer object. This is similar to how a uniform block is backed by buffer object bound to one of the GL_UNIFORM_BUFFER indexed binding points. The big difference between a uniform buffer and a shader storage buffer is that the shader storage buffer can both be read *and* written from the shader. Any writes to the storage buffer via a buffer block will eventually be seen by other shader invocations and can be read back by the application.

An example of how to initialize a buffer object and bind it to one of the indexed GL_SHADER_STORAGE_BUFFER bindings is shown in Example 11.6.

Example 11.6   Creating a Buffer and Using it for Shader Storage

```
GLuint buf;

// Generate the buffer, bind it to create it and declare storage
glGenBuffers(1, &buf);
glBindBuffer(GL_SHADER_STORAGE_BUFFER, buf);
glBufferData(GL_SHADER_STORAGE_BUFFER, 8192, NULL, GL_DYNAMIC_COPY);

// Now bind the buffer to the zeroth GL_SHADER_STORAGE_BUFFER
// binding point
glBindBufferBase(GL_SHADER_STORAGE_BUFFER, 0, buf);
```

Writing Structured Data

In the beginning of the section, we mentioned reading and writing structured data. If all you had was an array of `vec4`, you probably could get by with using image buffers. However, if you really have a collection of structured objects, where each is a heterogeneous collection of types, image buffers would become quite cumbersome. With shader storage buffers, however, you get full use of GLSL structure definitions and arrays to define the layout of your buffer. See the example in Example 11.7 to get the idea.

Example 11.7   Declaration of Structured Data

```
#version 430 core

// structure of a single data item
struct ItemType {
    int count;
    vec4 data[3];
    // ... other fields
};

// declare a buffer block using ItemType
layout (std430, binding = 0) buffer BufferObject {
    // ... other data here
    ItemType items[];    // render-time sized array of
                         // items typed above
};
```

As you see existing examples of using images to play the role of accessing memory, it will be easy to imagine smoother sailing through the more direct representation enabled by using buffer blocks (shader storage buffer objects).

Atomic Operations and Synchronization

Now that you have seen how shaders may read and write arbitrary locations in textures (through built-in functions) and buffers (through direct memory access), it is important to understand how these accesses can be controlled such that simultaneous operations to the same memory location do not destroy each other's effects. In this section, you will be introduced to a number of *atomic* operations that may be performed safely by many shader invocations simultaneously on the same memory location. Also, we will cover functionality that allows your application to provide ordering information to OpenGL. This to ensure that reads observe the results of any previous writes and that writes occur in desired order, leaving the correct value in memory.

Atomic Operations on Images

The number of applications for simply being able to store randomly into images and buffers is limited. However, GLSL provides many more built-in functions for manipulating images. These include atomic functions that perform simple mathematical operations directly on the image in an atomic fashion. Atomic operations (or *atomics*) are important in these applications because multiple shader instances could attempt to write to the same memory location. OpenGL does not guarantee the order of operations for shader invocations produced by the same draw command or even between invocations produced by separate drawing commands. It is this undefined ordering that allows OpenGL to be implemented on massively parallel architectures and provide extremely high performance. However, this also means that the fragment shader might be run on multiple fragments generated from a single primitive or even fragments making up multiple primitives simultaneously. In some cases, different fragment shader invocations could literally access the same memory location at the same instant in time, could run out of order with respect to one another, or could even pass each other in execution order. As an example, consider the naïve shader shown in Example 11.8.

Example 11.8   Naïvely Counting Overdraw in a Scene

```
#version 420 core

// This is an image that will be used to count overdraw in the scene.
layout (r32ui) uniform uimage2D overdraw_count;

void main(void)
{
    // Read the current overdraw counter
```

```
uint count = imageLoad(overdraw_count, ivec2(gl_FragCoord.xy));
// Add one
count = count + 1;
// Write it back to the image
imageStore(output_buffer, ivec2(gl_FragCoord.xy), count);
}
```

The shader in Example 11.8 attempts to count overdraw in a scene. It does so by storing the current overdraw count for each pixel in an image. Whenever a fragment is shaded, the current overdraw count is loaded into a variable, incremented, and then written back into the image. This works well when there is no overlap in the processing of fragments that make up the final pixel. However, when image complexity grows and multiple fragments are rendered into the final pixel, strange results will be produced. This is because the read-modify-write cycle performed explicitly by the shader can be interrupted by *another instance* of the same shader. Take a look at the timeline shown in Figure 11.2.

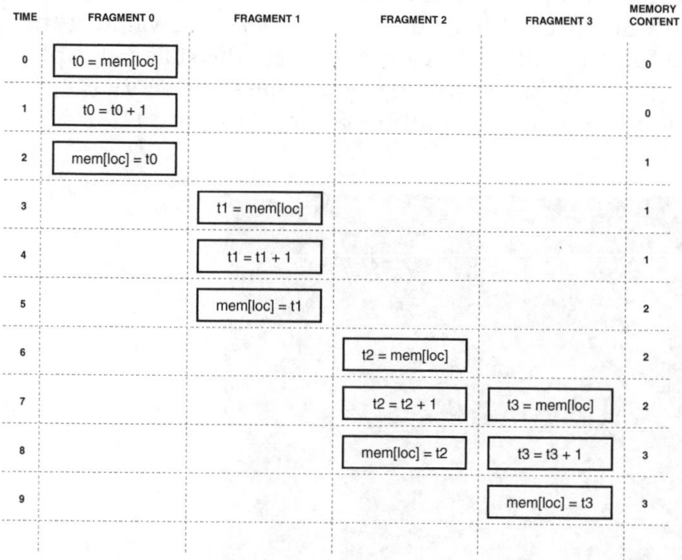

TIME	FRAGMENT 0	FRAGMENT 1	FRAGMENT 2	FRAGMENT 3	MEMORY CONTENT
0	t0 = mem[loc]				0
1	t0 = t0 + 1				0
2	mem[loc] = t0				1
3		t1 = mem[loc]			1
4		t1 = t1 + 1			1
5		mem[loc] = t1			2
6			t2 = mem[loc]		2
7			t2 = t2 + 1	t3 = mem[loc]	2
8			mem[loc] = t2	t3 = t3 + 1	3
9				mem[loc] = t3	3

Figure 11.2   Timeline exhibited by the naïve overdraw counter shader

Figure 11.2 shows a simplified timeline of four fragment shader invocations running in parallel. Each shader is running the code in Example 11.8 and reads a value from memory, increments it, and then writes it back to memory over three consecutive time steps. Now, consider what happens if all four invocations of the shader end up accessing the same location in memory. At time 0, the first invocation reads the memory location, at time 1, it increments it, and at time 2, it writes the value back to memory. The value in memory (shown in the right-most column) is now 1 as expected. Starting at time 3, the second invocation of the shader (fragment 1) executes the same sequence of operations—load, increment, and write, over three time steps. The value in memory at the end of time Step 5 is now 2, again as expected.

Now consider what happens during the third and fourth invocations of the shader. In time Step 6, the third invocation reads the value from memory (which is currently 2) into a local variable and at time Step 7, it increments the variable ready to write it back to memory. However, also during time Step 7, the fourth invocation of the shader reads the same location in memory (which still contains the value 2) into its own local variable. It increments that value in time Step 8 while the third invocation writes its local variable back to memory. Memory now contains the value 3. Finally, the fourth invocation of the shader writes its own copy of the value into memory in time Step 9. However, because it read the original value in time Step 7—after the third invocation had read from memory but before it had written the updated value back—the data written is *stale*. The value of the local variable in the fourth shader invocation is three (the stale value plus one), not four as might be expected. The desired value in memory is 4, not 3, and the result is the blocky corruption as seen in Figure 11.3.

Figure 11.3   Output of the naïve overdraw counter shader

The reason for the corruption seen in this example is that the increment operations performed by the shader are not *atomic* with respect to each other. That is, they do not operate as a single, indivisible operation but rather as a sequence of independent operations that may be interrupted or may overlap with the processing performed by other shader invocations accessing the same resources. Although the simple explanation above only describes the hypothetical behavior of four invocations, when considering that modern GPUs typically have hundreds or even thousands of concurrently executing invocations, it becomes easy to see how this type of issue can be more likely to encounter than one would imagine.

To avoid this, OpenGL provides a set of atomic functions that operate directly on memory. They have two properties that make them suitable for accessing and modifying shared memory locations. Firstly, they apparently operate in a single time step[2] without interruption by other shader invocations and secondly, the graphics hardware provides mechanisms to ensure that even if multiple concurrent invocations perform an atomic operation on the same memory location at the same instant, they will appear to be *serialized* such that they take turns executing and produce the expected result. Note that there is still no guarantee of order—just a guarantee that all invocations execute their operation without stepping on each other's results.

The shader in Example 11.8 may be rewritten using an atomic function as shown in Example 11.9. In Example 11.9, the imageAtomicAdd function is used to directly add one to the value stored in memory. This is executed by OpenGL as a single, indivisible operation and therefore isn't susceptible to the issues illustrated in Figure 11.2.

Example 11.9 Counting Overdraw with Atomic Operations

```
#version 420 core

// This is an image that will be used to count overdraw in
// the scene.
layout (r32ui) uniform uimage2D overdraw_count;

void main(void)
{
    // Atomically add one to the contents of memory
    imageAtomicAdd(overdraw_count, ivec2(gl_FragCoord.xy), 1);
}
```

---

2. This may not actually be true—they could take several tens of clock cycles, but the graphics hardware will make them appear as if they are single, indivisible operations.

The result of executing the shader shown in Example 11.9 is shown in Figure 11.4. As you can see, the output is much cleaner.

Figure 11.4   Output of the atomic overdraw counter shader

imageAtomicAdd is one of many atomic built-in functions in GLSL. These functions include addition and subtraction, logical operations, and comparison and exchange operations. The complete list of GLSL atomics is shown below.

```
uint imageAtomicAdd(IMAGE_PARAMS mem, uint data);
int  imageAtomicAdd(IMAGE_PARAMS mem, int data);
uint imageAtomicMin(IMAGE_PARAMS mem, uint data);
int  imageAtomicMin(IMAGE_PARAMS mem, int data);
uint imageAtomicMax(IMAGE_PARAMS mem, uint data);
int  imageAtomicMax(IMAGE_PARAMS mem, int data);
uint imageAtomicAnd(IMAGE_PARAMS mem, uint data);
int  imageAtomicAnd(IMAGE_PARAMS mem, int data);
uint imageAtomicOr(IMAGE_PARAMS mem, uint data);
int  imageAtomicOr(IMAGE_PARAMS mem, int data);
uint imageAtomicXor(IMAGE_PARAMS mem, uint data);
int  imageAtomicXor(IMAGE_PARAMS mem, int data);
uint imageAtomicExchange(IMAGE_PARAMS mem, uint data);
```

```
int  imageAtomicExchange(IMAGE_PARAMS mem, int data);
uint imageAtomicCompSwap(IMAGE_PARAMS mem,
                        uint compare uint data);
int  imageAtomicCompSwap(IMAGE_PARAMS mem, int compare,
                        int data);
```

`imageAtomicAdd`, `imageAtomicMin`, and `imageAtomicMax` perform an atomic addition, minimum, and maximum operation between *data* and the contents of the specified image at the specified coordinates, respectively. `imageAtomicAnd`, `imageAtomicOr`, and `imageAtomicXor` perform an atomic logical AND, OR, and XOR operation between *data* and the contents of the specified image at the specified coordinates, respectively. Each function returns the value originally in memory before the operation was performed.

`imageAtomicExchange` writes the value of *data* into the specified image at the specified coordinates and returns the value originally in memory before the write was performed.

`imageAtomicCompSwap` compares the value of *compare* with the value in the specified image at the specified coordinates and if they are equal, it writes the value of *data* into that memory location. The compare and write operations are performed atomically. The value originally in memory before the write occurred is returned.

In the declarations of the atomic image functions, IMAGE_PARAMS may be replaced with any of the definitions given in Example 11.10. The effect of this is that there are several overloaded versions of each of the atomic functions.

Example 11.10   Possible Definitions for IMAGE_PARAMS

```
#define IMAGE_PARAMS gimage1D image, int P              // or
#define IMAGE_PARAMS gimage2D image, ivec2 P            // or
#define IMAGE_PARAMS gimage3D image, ivec3 P            // or
#define IMAGE_PARAMS gimage2DRect image, ivec2 P        // or
#define IMAGE_PARAMS gimageCube image, ivec3 P          // or
#define IMAGE_PARAMS gimageBuffer image, int P          // or
#define IMAGE_PARAMS gimage1DArray image, ivec2 P       // or
#define IMAGE_PARAMS gimage2DArray image, ivec3 P       // or
#define IMAGE_PARAMS gimageCubeArray image, ivec3 P     // or
#define IMAGE_PARAMS gimage2DMS image, ivec2 P, int sample   // or
#define IMAGE_PARAMS gimage2DMSArray image, ivec3 P, int sample
```

Atomic functions can operate only on single signed or unsigned integers—that is, neither floating-point images nor images of vectors of any type are supported in atomic operations. Each atomic function returns the value that was *previously* in memory at the specified location. If this value is not required by the shader, it may be safely ignored. Shader compilers may then perform data-flow analysis and eliminate unnecessary memory reads if it is advantageous to do so. As an example, the equivalent code for `imageAtomicAdd` is given in Example 11.11. Although Example 11.11 shows `imageAtomicAdd` implemented as several lines of code, it is important to remember that this is for illustration only and that the built-in `imageAtomicAdd` function operates as a single, indivisible operation.

Example 11.11   Equivalent Code for `imageAtomicAdd`

```
// THIS FUNCTION OPERATES ATOMICALLY
uint imageAtomicAdd(uimage2D image, ivec2 P, uint data)
{
    // Read the value that's currently in memory
    uint val = imageLoad(image, P).x;
    // Write the new value to memory
    imageStore(image, P, uvec4(val + data));
    // Return the *old* value.
    return val;
}
```

As has been shown in Example 11.9, this atomic behavior may be used to effectively serialize access to a memory location. Similar functionality for other operations such as logical operations is achieved through the use of `imageAtomicAnd`, `imageAtomicXor`, and so on. For example, two shader invocations may simultaneously set different bits in a single memory location using the `imageAtomicOr` function. The two atomic functions that do not perform arithmetic or logical operations on memory are `imageAtomicExchange` and `imageAtomicCompSwap`. `imageAtomicExchange` is similar to a regular store, except that it returns the value that was previously in memory. In effect, it exchanges the value in memory with the value passed to the function, returning the old value to the shader. `imageAtomicCompSwap` is a generic compare-and-swap operation that conditionally stores the specified data in memory. The equivalent code for these functions is shown in Example 11.12.

Example 11.12 Equivalent Code for `imageAtomicExchange` and `imageAtomicComp`

```
// THIS FUNCTION OPERATES ATOMICALLY
uint imageAtomicExchange(uimage2D image, ivec2 P, uint data)
{
    uint val = imageLoad(image, P);
    imageStore(image, P, data);
    return val;
}

// THIS FUNCTION OPERATES ATOMICALLY
uint imageAtomicCompSwap(uimage2D image, ivec2 P,
                         uint compare, uint data)
{
    uint val = imageLoad(image, P);
    if (compare == val)
    {
        imageStore(image, P, data);
    }
    return val;
}
```

Again, it is important to remember that the code given in Example 11.12 is for illustrative purposes only and that the `imageAtomicExchange` and `imageAtomicCompSwap` functions are truly implemented using hardware support as opposed to a sequence of lower-level operations. One of the primary use cases for `imageAtomicExchange` is in the implementation of linked lists or other complex data structures. In a linked list, the head and tail pointers may be swapped with references to new items inserted into the list atomically to effectively achieve parallel list insertion. Likewise, `imageAtomicCompSwap` may be used to implement *locks* (also known as *mutexes*) to prevent simultaneous access to a shared resource (such as another image). An example of taking a lock using an atomic compare-and-swap operation (as implemented by `imageAtomicCompSwap`) is shown in Example 11.13.

Example 11.13 Simple Per-Pixel Mutex Using `imageAtomicCompSwap`

```
#version 420 core

layout (r32ui) uniform uimage2D lock_image;
layout (rgba8f) uniform image2D protected_image;
```

```
void takeLock(ivec2 pos)
{
    int lock_available;

    do {
        // Take the lock - the value in lock_image is 0 if the lock
        // is not already taken. If so, then it is overwritten with
        // 1 otherwise it is left alone. The function returns the value
        // that was originally in memory - 0 if the lock was not taken,
        // 1 if it was. We terminate the loop when we see that the lock
        // was not already taken and thus we now hold it because we've
        // written a one to memory.
        lock_available = imageAtomicCompSwap(lock_image, pos, 0, 1);
    } while (lock_available == 0);
}

void releaseLock(ivec2 pos)
{
    imageStore(lock_image, pos, 0);
}

void operateOnFragment()
{
    // Perform a sequence of operations on the current fragment
    // that need to be indivisible. Here, we simply perform
    // multiplication by a constant as there is no atomic version
    // of this (imageAtomicMult, for example). More complex functions
    // could easily be implemented.

    vec4 old_fragment;

    old_fragment = imageLoad(protected_image,
    ivec2(gl_FragCoord.xy));

    imageStore(protected_image,
               ivec2(gl_FragCoord.xy),
               old_fragment * 13.37);
}

void main(void)
{
    // Take a per-pixel lock
    takeLock(ivec2(gl_FragCoord.xy));

    // Now we own the lock and can safely operate on a shared resource
    operateOnPixel();

    // Be sure to release the lock...
    releaseLock(ivec2(gl_FragCoord.xy));
}
```

The code shown in Example 11.13 implements a simple per-pixel mutex using the imageAtomicCompSwap function. To do this, it compares the value already in memory to zero (the third parameter to imageAtomicCompSwap). If they are equal (i.e., if the current value in memory is zero), it writes the new value (one, here) into memory. imageAtomicCompSwap then returns the value that was originally in memory. That is, if the lock was not previously taken, the value in memory will be zero (which is what is returned), but this will be replaced with one, reserving the lock. If the lock was previously taken by another shader invocation, the value in memory will already be one, and this is what will be returned. Therefore, we know that we received the lock when imageAtomicCompSwap returns zero. This loop therefore executes until imageAtomicCompSwap returns zero, indicating that the lock was available. When it does, this shader invocation will have the lock. The first invocation (after serialization by the hardware) that receives a zero from imageAtomicComSwap will hold the lock until it places a zero back into memory (which is what releaseLock does). All other invocations will spin in the loop in takeLock. They will be released from this loop one at a time until all invocations have taken the lock, performed their operations, and then released it again.

The functionality implemented in operateOnFragment can be anything. It does not have to use atomics because the whole function is running while the lock is taken by the current shader invocation. For example, programmable blending[3] operations could be implemented here by using imageLoad and imageStore to read and write a texture. Also, operations for which there is no built-in atomic function can be implemented—for example, multiplication, arithmetic shift, or transcendental functions can be performed on images.

Atomic Operations on Buffers

In addition to the atomic operations that may be performed on images, atomic operations may also be performed on buffer variables. Buffer variables are variables inside interface blocks that have been declared with the buffer keyword. As with images, several built-in functions to perform atomic operations are defined. The atomic operations that may be performed on buffer variables are the same set that may be performed on image variables.

---

3. Note that there is still no ordering guarantee, so only blending operations that are order-independent can be implemented here. A more complete example that includes order-independent blending is given at the end of this chapter.

```
uint atomicAdd(inout uint mem, uint data);
int  atomicAdd(inout int mem, int data);
uint atomicMin(inout uint mem, uint data);
int  atomicMin(inout int mem, int data);
uint atomicMax(inout uint mem, uint data);
int  atomicMax(inout int mem, int data);
uint atomicAnd(inout uint mem, uint data);
int  atomicAnd(inout int mem, int data);
uint atomicOr(inout uint mem, uint data);
int  atomicOr(inout int mem, int data);
uint atomicXor(inout uint mem, uint data);
int  atomicXor(inout int mem, int data);
uint atomicExchange(inout uint mem, uint data);
int  atomicExchange(inout int mem, int data);
uint atomicCompSwap(inout uint mem, uint compare uint data);
int  atomicCompSwap(inout int mem, int compare, int data);
```

`atomicAdd`, `atomicMin`, and `atomicMax` perform an atomic addition, minimum, and maximum operation between *data* and *mem*, respectively. `atomicAnd`, `atomicOr`, and `atomicXor` perform an atomic logical AND, OR, and XOR operation between *data* and *mem*, respectively. Each function returns the value originally in memory before the operation was performed.

`atomicExchange` writes the value of *data* into the memory location referenced by *mem* and returns the value originally in memory before the write was performed.

`atomicCompSwap` compares the value of *compare* with the value in the memory location referenced by *mem* and if they are equal, it writes the value of *data* into that memory location. The compare and write operations are performed atomically. The value originally in memory before the write occurred is returned.

Each of the atomic functions listed above takes an `inout` parameter that serves as a reference to a memory location. The value passed to any of these atomic functions in the *mem* parameter must[4] be a member of a block declared with the `buffer` keyword. Like the image atomic functions, each of these functions returns the value originally in memory before it was updated. This effectively allows you to swap the content of memory for a new value, possibly conditionally as in the case of `atomicCompSwap`.

---

4. Actually, these atomic functions may also be used on variables declared as `shared`. This will be discussed further in "Compute Shaders".

Sync Objects

OpenGL operates in a client-server model, where a server operates *asynchronously* to the client. Originally, this allowed the user's terminal to render high-performance graphics and for the application to run on a server in a remote location. This was an extension of the X protocol, which was always designed with remote rendering and network operations in mind. In modern graphics workstations, we have a similar arrangement, with a slightly different interpretation. Here, the *client* is the CPU and the application runs on it, sending commands to the *server*, which is a high-performance GPU. However, the bandwidth between the two is still relatively low compared to the throughput and performance of either one. Therefore, for maximum performance, the GPU runs asynchronously to the CPU and can often be several OpenGL commands behind the application.

In some circumstances, it is necessary, however, to ensure that the client and the server—the CPU and the GPU execute in a synchronized manner. To achieve this, we can use a *sync object*, which can also be known as a *fence*. A fence is essentially a marker in the stream of commands that can be sent along with drawing and state change commands to the GPU. The fence starts life in an *unsignaled* state and becomes *signaled* when the GPU has executed it. At any given time, the application can look at the state of the fence to see if the GPU has reached it yet, and it can wait for the GPU to have executed the fence before moving on. To inject a fence into the OpenGL command stream, call **glFenceSync()**:

GLsync **glFenceSync**(GLenum *condition*, GLbitfield *flags*);

Creates a new fence sync object by inserting a fence into the OpenGL command stream and returning a handle to the newly created fence. The fence begins in an unsignaled state and becomes signaled when the conditions specified by *condition* becomes true. The only legal value for *condition* is GL_SYNC_GPU_COMMANDS_COMPLETE. *flags* is currently unused and must be set to zero.

When you call **glFenceSync()**, a new fence sync object is created, and the corresponding fence is inserted into the OpenGL command stream. The sync starts of unsignaled and will eventually become signaled when the GPU processes it. Because (although asynchronous) OpenGL has a well-defined order of execution, when a fence becomes signaled, you know that any commands that precede it in the command stream have finished executing, although nothing is known about commands that follow. To check if a fence has been executed by the GPU yet, you can call **glGetSynciv()**:

> void **glGetSynciv**(GLsync *sync*, GLenum *pname*, GLsizei *bufSize*,
> GLsizei **length*, GLint **values*);
>
> Retrieves the properties of a sync object. *sync* specifies a handle to the
> sync object from which to read the property specified by *pname*. *bufSize* is
> the size in bytes of the buffer whose address is given in *values*. *length* is
> the address of an integer variable that will receive the number of bytes
> written into *values*.

To check to see if a fence object has become signaled yet, call
glGetSynciv() with *pname* set to GL_SYNC_STATUS. Assuming no error is
generated, and the buffer is big enough, either GL_SIGNALED or
GL_UNSIGNALED will be written into the buffer pointed to by *values*
depending on whether the fence had been reached by the GPU or not. You
can use this to poll a sync object to wait for it to become signaled, but this
can be quite inefficient, with control passing backwards between your
application and the OpenGL implementation, and with all the error
checking and other validation that the OpenGL drivers might do on your
system occurring for each transition. If you wish to wait for a sync object
to become signaled, you should call **glClientWaitSync()**:

> GLenum **glClientWaitSync**(GLsync *sync*, GLbitfields *flags*,
> GLuint64 *timeout*);
>
> Causes the client to wait for the sync object *sync* to become signaled.
> **glClientWaitSync()** will wait at most *timeout* nanoseconds for the object
> to become signaled before generating a timeout. The *flags* parameter may
> be used to control flushing behavior of the command. Specifying
> GL_SYNC_FLUSH_COMMANDS_BIT is equivalent to calling **glFlush()**
> before executing the wait.

The **glClientWaitSync()** function is used to wait in the client for a fence to
be reached by the server. It will wait for up to *timeout* nanoseconds for the
sync object given by *sync* to become signaled before giving up. If *flags*
contains GL_SYNC_FLUSH_COMMANDS_BIT then **glClientWaitSync()**
will implicitly send any pending commands to the server before beginning
to wait. It's generally a good idea to always set this bit as without it, the
OpenGL driver might buffer up commands and never send them to the
server, ensuring that your call to **glClientWaitSync()** will generate a
timeout. **glClientWaitSync()** will generate one of four return values:

- GL_ALREADY_SIGNALED is returned if *sync* was already signaled when the call to **glClientWaitSync()** was made.

- GL_TIMEOUT_EXPIRED is returned if *sync* did not enter the signaled state before *nanoseconds* nanoseconds passed.

- GL_CONDITION_SATISFIED is returned if *sync* was not signaled when the call to **glClientWaitSync()** was made, but became signaled before *nanoseconds* nanoseconds elapsed.

- GL_WAIT_FAILED is returned if the call to **glClientWaitSync()** failed for some reason, such as *sync* not being the name of a sync object. In this case, a regular OpenGL error is also generated and should be checked with **glGetError()**. Furthermore, if you are using a debug context, then there is a good chance that its log will tell you exactly what went wrong.

Sync objects can only go from the unsignaled state (which is the state that they are created in) into the signaled state. Thus, they are basically a single-use object. Once you have finished waiting for a sync object, or if you decide you don't need it any more, you should delete the sync object. To delete a sync object, call **glDeleteSync()**:

---

void **glDeleteSync**(GLsync *sync*);

Deletes the sync object specified by *sync*. If *sync* is already signaled at this time, it is deleted immediately, otherwise it is marked for deletion and will be deleted when the implementation determines that it is safe to do so.

A very common use-case for sync objects is to ensure that the GPU is done using data in a mapped buffer before overwriting the data. This can occur if the buffer (or a range of it) was mapped using the **glMapBufferRange()** function with the GL_MAP_UNSYNCHRONIZED_BIT set. This causes OpenGL to not wait for any pending commands that may be about to read from the buffer to complete before handing your application a pointer to write into. Under some circumstances, this pointer may actually address memory that the GPU is about to use. To make sure that you don't stomp all over data that hasn't been used yet, you can insert a fence right after the last command that might read from a buffer, and then issue a call to **glClientWaitSync()** right before you write into the buffer. Ideally, you'd execute something that takes some time between the call to **glFenceSync()** and the call to **glClientWaitSync()**. A simple example is shown in Example 11.14.

Example 11.14   Example Use of a Sync Object

```
// This will be our sync object.
GLsync s;

// Bind a vertex array and draw a bunch of geometry
glBindVertexArray(vao);

glDrawArrays(GL_TRIANGLES, 0, 30000);

// Now create a fence that will become signaled when the
// above drawing command has completed
s = glFenceSync();

// Map the uniform buffer that's in use by the above draw
void * data = glMapBufferRange(GL_UNIFORM_BUFFER,
                               0, 256,
                               GL_WRITE_BIT |
                               GL_MAP_UNSYNCHRONIZED_BIT);

// Now go do something that will last a while...
// ... say, calculate the new values of the uniforms
do_something_time_consuming();

// Wait for the sync object to become signaled.
// 1,000,000 ns = 1 ms.
switch (glClientWaitSync(s, 0, 1000000);

// Now delete the sync object, write over the uniform
// buffer and unmap it
glDeleteSync(s);

memcpy(data, source_data, source_data_size);

glUnmapBuffer(GL_UNIFORM_BUFFER);
```

As with many other object types in OpenGL, it is possible to simply ask whether the object you have is what you think it is. To find out if an object is a valid sync object, you can call **glIsSync()**:

GLboolean **glIsSync**(GLsync *sync*);

Returns GL_TRUE if *sync* is the name of an existing sync object that has not been deleted and GL_FALSE otherwise.

Advanced

If you are sharing objects between two or more contexts, it is possible to wait in one context for a sync object to become signaled as the result of commands issued in another. To do this, call **glFenceSync()** in the source context (the one which you want to wait on) and then call **glWaitSync()** in the destination context (the one that will do the waiting). The prototype for **glWaitSync()** is as follows:

---

void **glWaitSync**(GLsync *sync*, GLbitfield *flags*, GLuint64 *timeout*);

Causes the server to wait for the sync object indicated by *sync* to become signaled. *flags* is not used and must be set to zero. *timeout* is also unused, but must be set to the special value, GL_TIMEOUT_IGNORED. The server will wait an implementation-dependent amount of time before considering the sync object to have timed out and will then continue execution of subsequent commands.

---

glWaitSync() presents a rather limited form of what may be achieved with **glClientWaitSync()**. The major differences are the GL_SYNC_FLUSH_COMMANDS_BIT flag is not accepted in the *flags* parameter (nor is any other flag), and the timeout is implementation-defined. You still have to ask for this implementation-defined timeout value by passing GL_TIMEOUT_IGNORED in *timeout*. However, you can find out what that implementation-dependent timeout value is by calling **glGetIntegerv()** with the parameter GL_MAX_SERVER_WAIT_TIMEOUT.

An example use for **glWaitSync()** synchronizing two contexts is when you are writing data into a buffer using transform feedback and want to consume that data in another context. In this case, you would issue the drawing commands that would ultimately update the transform feedback buffer and then issue the fence with a call to **glFenceSync()**. Next, switch to the consuming thread (either with a true context switch or by handing control to another application thread) and then wait on the fence to become signaled by calling **glWaitSync()** before issuing any drawing commands that might consume the data.

Image Qualifiers and Barriers

The techniques outlined above work well when compilers don't perform overly aggressive optimizations on your shaders. However, under certain circumstances, the compiler might change the order or frequency of image loads or stores, and may eliminate them altogether if it believes they are redundant. For example, consider the simple example loop in Example 11.15.

Example 11.15   Basic Spin-Loop Waiting on Memory

```
#version 420 core

// Image that we'll read from in the loop
layout (r32ui} uniform uimageBuffer my_image;

void waitForImageToBeNonZero()
{
    uint val;

    do
    {
        // (Re-)read from the image at a fixed location.
        val = imageLoad(my_image, 0).x;
        // Loop until the value is nonzero
    } while (val == 0);
}
```

In Example 11.15, the function waitForImageToBeNonZero contains a tight loop that repeatedly reads from the same location in the image and only breaks out of the loop when the data returned is nonzero. The compiler might assume that the data in the image does not change and therefore, the imageLoad function will always return the same value. In such a case, it may move the imageLoad out of the loop. This is a very common optimization known as *hoisting* and effectively replaces waitForImageToBeNonZero with the version shown in Example 11.16.

Example 11.16   Result of Loop-Hoisting on Spin-Loop

```
#version 420 core

// Image that we'll read from in the loop
layout (r32ui} uniform uimageBuffer my_image;

void waitForImageToBeNonZero()
{
    uint val;

    // The shader complier has assumed that the image
    // data does not change and has moved the load
    // outside the loop.
    val = imageLoad(my_image, 0).x;

    do
    {
        // Nothing remains in the loop. It will either
        // exit after one iteration, or execute forever!
    } while (val == 0);
}
```

As may be obvious, each call to the optimized version of `waitForImageToBeNonZero` in Example 11.16 will either read a nonzero value from the image and return immediately or enter an infinite loop—quite possibly crashing or hanging the graphics hardware. In order to avoid this situation, the `volatile` keyword must be used when declaring the image uniform to instruct the compiler to not perform such an optimization on any loads or stores to the image. To declare an image uniform (or parameter to a function) as volatile, simply include the `volatile` keyword in its declaration. This is similar to the `volatile` keyword supported by the "C" and C++ languages, and examples of this type of declaration are shown in Example 11.17.

Example 11.17   Examples of Using the `volatile` Keyword

```
#version 420 core

// Declaration of image uniform that is volatile. The
// compiler will not make any assumptions about the
// content of the image and will not perform any
// unsafe optimizations on code accessing the image.
layout (r32ui} uniform volatile uimageBuffer my_image;

// Declaration of function that does declares its
// parameter as volatile...
void functionTakingVolatileImage(volatile uimageBuffer i)
{
    // Read and write i here.
}
```

The `volatile` keyword may be applied to global declarations and uniforms, function parameters, or local variables. In particular, image variables that have not been declared as volatile may be passed to functions as parameters that *do* have the `volatile` keyword. In such cases, the operations performed by the called function will be treated as volatile, whereas operations on the image elsewhere will not be volatile. In effect, the `volatile` qualifier may be *added* to a variable based on scope. However, the `volatile` keyword (or any other keyword discussed in this section) may not be *removed* from a variable. That is, it is illegal to pass an image variable declared as `volatile` as a parameter to a function that does not also declare that parameter as `volatile`.

Another qualifier originating in the "C" languages that is available in GLSL is the `restrict` keyword, which instructs the compiler that data referenced by one image does not alias[5] the data referenced by any other.

---

5. That is, no two images reference the same piece of memory, so stores to one cannot possibly affect the result of loads from the other.

In such cases, writes to one image do not affect the contents of any other image. The compiler can therefore be more aggressive about making optimizations that might otherwise be unsafe. Note that by default, the compiler assumes that aliasing of external buffers is possible and is less likely to perform optimizations that may break otherwise well-formed code. (Note GLSL assumes no aliasing of variables and parameters residing within the shader, and fully optimizes based on that.) The `restrict` keyword is used in a similar manner to the `volatile` keyword as described above—that is, it may be added to global or local declarations to effectively add the restrict qualifier to existing image variables in certain scope. In essence, references to memory buffers through `restrict` qualified image variables behave similarly to references to memory through restricted pointers in "C" and C++.

There are three further qualifiers available in GLSL that do not have an equivalent in C. These are `coherent`, `readonly`, and `writeonly`. First, `coherent` is used to control *cache behavior* for images. This type of functionality is generally not exposed by high-level languages. However, as GLSL is designed for writing code that will execute on highly parallel and specialized hardware, `coherent` is included to allow some level of management of where data is placed.

Consider a typical graphics processing unit (GPU). It is made up of hundreds or potentially thousands of separate processors grouped into blocks. Different models of otherwise similar GPUs may contain different numbers of these blocks depending on their power and performance targets. Now, such GPUs will normally include large, multilevel caches that may or may not be fully coherent.[6] If the data store for an image is placed in a noncoherent cache, then changes made by one client of that cache may not be noticed by another client until that cache is explicitly flushed back to a lower level in a memory hierarchy. A schematic of this is shown in Figure 11.5, which depicts the memory hierarchy of a fictitious GPU with a multilevel cache hierarchy.

---

6. A coherent cache is a cache that allows local changes to be immediately observed by other clients of the same memory subsystem. Caches in CPUs tend to be coherent (a write performed by one CPU core is seen immediately by other CPU cores), whereas caches in GPUs may or may not be coherent.

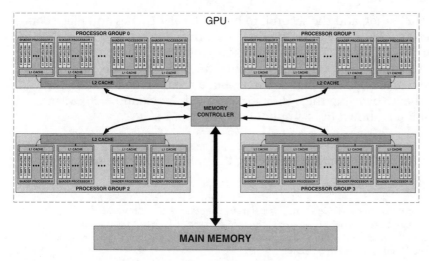

Figure 11.5   Cache hierarchy of a fictitious GPU

In Figure 11.5, each shader processor is made up of a 16-wide vector processor that concurrently processes 16 data items (these may be fragments, vertices, patches, or primitives depending on what type of shader is executing). Each vector processor has its own, small, level-1 cache, which is coherent among all of the shader invocations running in that processor. That is, a write performed by one invocation on that processor will be observed by and its data made available to any other invocation executing on the same processor. Furthermore, there are four shader processor groups, each with 16, 16-element-wide vector processors and a single, shared, level-2 cache, that is, there is a level-2 cache per shader processor group that is shared by 16, 16-wide vector processors (256 data items). There are therefore four independent level-2 caches, each serving 16 processors with 16-wide vectors for a total of 1024 concurrently processing data items. Each of the level-2 caches is a client of the memory controller.

For highest performance, the GPU will attempt to keep data in the highest-level cache, that is, in caches labeled with the smallest number, closest to the processor accessing the data. If data is only to be read from memory, but not written, then data can be stored in noncoherent caches. In such cases, our fictitious GPU will place data in the level-1 caches within the vector processors. However, if memory writes made by one processor must be seen by another processor, (this includes atomics that implicitly read, modify, and write data), the data must be placed in a coherent memory location. Here, we have two choices: the first, to bypass cache altogether, and the second, to bypass level-1 caches and place data in level-2 caches while ensuring that any work that needs to share data is run only in that cache's shader processor group. Other GPUs may have ways of keeping the level-2 caches coherent. This type of decision is generally made by the OpenGL driver, but a requirement to do so is given in the shader by using the `coherent` keyword. An example `coherent` declaration is shown in Example 11.18.

Example 11.18   Examples of Using the `coherent` Keyword

```
#version 420 core

// Declaration of image uniform that is coherent. The OpenGL
// implementation will ensure that the data for the image is
// placed in caches that are coherent, or perhaps used an uncached
// location for data storage.
layout (r32ui} uniform coherent uimageBuffer my_image;

// Declaration of function that does declares its parameter
// as coherent...
uint functionTakingCoherentImage(coherent uimageBuffer i, int n)
{
    // Write i here...
    imageStore(my_image, n, uint(n));

    // Any changes will be visible to all other shader invocations.
    // Likewise, changes made by invocations are visible here.
    uint m = imageStore(my_image, n - 1).x;

    return m;
}
```

The final two image qualifier keywords, `readonly` and `writeonly`, control access to image data. `readonly` behaves somewhat like `const`, being a contract between the programmer and the OpenGL implementation that the programmer will not access a `readonly` image for writing. The difference between `const` and `readonly` applied to an image variable is that `const` applies to the variable itself. That is, an image variable declared as `const` may not be written, however, the shader may write to the image bound to the image unit referenced by that variable. On the other hand, `readonly` applies to the underlying image data. A shader may assign new values to an image variable declared as `readonly`, but it may not write to an image through that variable. An image variable may be declared both `const` and `readonly` at the same time.

The `writeonly` keyword also applies to the image data attached to the image unit to which an image variable refers. Attempting to read from an image variable declared as `writeonly` will generate an error. Note that atomic operations implicitly perform a read operation as part of their read-modify-write cycle and so are not allowed on `readonly` or `writeonly` image variables.

Memory Barriers

Now that we understand how to control compiler optimizations using the `volatile` and `restrict` keywords and control caching behavior using the `coherent` keyword, we can accurately describe how image data is to be used. However, the compiler may still reorder memory operations, or allow different shader invocations to run out of order with respect to each other. This is particularly true in the case of shaders from different stages of the OpenGL pipeline. Some level of asynchrony is required in order to achieve best performance. Because of this, GLSL includes the `memoryBarrier()` function that may be used to ensure that any writes made to a particular location in memory are observed by other shader invocations in the order that they were made in. It causes a singe shader invocation to wait until any outstanding memory transactions have completed.[7] As an example, see Example 11.19.

Example 11.19   Example of Using the `memoryBarrier()` Function

```
#version 420 core

layout (rgba32f} uniform coherent image2D my_image;

// Declaration of function
void functionUsingBarriers(coherent uimageBuffer i)
{
    uint val;

    // This loop essentially waits until at least one fragment from
    // an earlier primitive (that is, one with gl_PrimitiveID - 1)
    // has reached the end of this function point. Note that this is
    // not a robust loop as not every primitive will generate
    // fragments.
    do
```

7. Writes to memory may be *posted*. This means that a request is made to the memory subsystem (caches and controller) to write data at a specific address. The memory system inserts this request in a queue and services one or more requests at a time until the data is written to memory. At this time, it signals the original requester that the write has completed. Because there may be multiple caches and memory controllers in a system and each may service multiple requests at a time, the requests may complete out of order. The `memoryBarrier` function forces a shader invocation to wait until the completion signal comes back from the memory subsystem for all pending writes before continuing execution.

```
{
    val = imageLoad(i, 0).x;
} while (val != gl_PrimitiveID);

// At this point, we can load data from another global image
vec4 frag = imageLoad(my_image, gl_FragCoord.xy);

// Operate on it...
frag *= 0.1234;
frag = pow(frag, 2.2);

// Write it back to memory
imageStore(my_image, gl_FragCoord.xy, frag);

// Now, we're about to signal that we're done with processing
// the pixel. We need to ensure that all stores thus far have
// been posted to memory. So, we insert a memory barrier.
memoryBarrier();

// Now we write back into the original "primitive count" memory
// to signal that we have reached this point. The stores
// resulting from processing "my_image" will have reached memory
// before this store is committed due to the barrier.
imageStore(i, 0, gl_PrimitiveID + 1);

// Now issue another barrier to ensure that the results of the
// image store are committed to memory before this shader
// invocation ends.
memoryBarrier();
}
```

Example 11.19 shows a very simple use case for memory barriers. It allows some level of ordering between fragments to be ensured. At the top of functionUsingBarriers, a simple loop is used to wait for the contents of a memory location to reach our current primitive ID. Because we know that no two fragments from the same primitive can land on the same pixel,[8] we know that when we're executing the code in the body of the function, at least one fragment from the previous primitive has been processed. We then go about modifying the contents of memory at our fragment's location using nonatomic operations. We signal to other shader invocations that we are done by writing to the shared memory location originally polled at the top of the function.

---

8. This is true except for patches or other complex geometry generated by the geometry shader. In such cases, the primitive ID seen by the fragment shader is generated explicitly by the upstream shader (tessellation evaluation or geometry shader) and it is up to the user to ensure that no two overlapping fragments see the same primitive ID if this is required by the algorithm.

To ensure that our modified image contents are written back to memory before other shader invocations start into the body of the function, we use a call to `memoryBarrier` between updates of the color image and the primitive counter to enforce ordering. We then insert another barrier after the primitive counter update to ensure that other shader invocations see our update. This doesn't guarantee full per-pixel ordering (especially if fragments from multiple primitives are packed into a single vector), but it may be close enough for many purposes. Also, it should be noted that if primitives are discarded (because they are clipped, back-facing, or have no area), they will generate no fragments and will not update the primitive ID counter. In such a case, this loop will deadlock waiting for primitives that never come.

Not only can barriers be used inside shader code to ensure that memory operations are ordered with respect to one another, some level of control over memory transactions and caching behavior is provided by the OpenGL API through the **glMemoryBarrier()** function. Its prototype is as follows:

---

void **glMemoryBarrier**(GLbitfield *barriers*);

Defines a barrier ordering memory transactions issued before the command relative to those issued after the command. Memory transactions performed by shaders are considered to be issued by the rendering command that invoked the execution of the shader. The *bitfield* parameter contains a set of bits indicating that operations are to be synchronized with stores performed by shaders.

The **glMemoryBarrier()** function may be used to ensure ordering of memory operations performed by shaders relative to those performed by other parts of the OpenGL pipeline. Which operations are to be synchronized is specified using the *barriers* parameter to **glMemoryBarrier()** and is a logical combination of any of the following values.

- GL_VERTEX_ATTRIB_ARRAY_BARRIER_BIT specifies that data read from vertex buffers after the barrier should reflect data written to those buffers by commands issued before the barrier.

- GL_ELEMENT_ARRAY_BARRIER_BIT specifies that indices read from the bound element array buffer should reflect data written to that buffer by commands issued before the barrier.

- GL_UNIFORM_BARRIER_BIT specifies that uniforms sourced from uniform buffer objects whose backing store was written before the barrier was issued should reflect those values.

- GL_TEXTURE_FETCH_BARRIER_BIT specifies that any fetch from a texture issued after the barrier should reflect data written to the texture by commands issued before the barrier.

- GL_SHADER_IMAGE_ACCESS_BARRIER_BIT specifies that data read from an image variable in shaders executed by commands after the barrier should reflect data written into those images by commands issued before the barrier.

- GL_COMMAND_BARRIER_BIT specifies that command parameters source from buffer objects using the `glDraw*Indirect` commands should reflect data written into those buffer objects by commands issued before the barrier.

- GL_PIXEL_BUFFER_BARRIER_BIT specifies that accesses to buffers bound to the GL_PIXEL_UNPACK_BUFFER or GL_PIXEL_PACK_BUFFER should be ordered with respect to accesses to those buffers by commands issued before the barrier.

- GL_TEXTURE_UPDATE_BARRIER_BIT specifies that writes to textures via calls like **glTexImage*D()**, **glTexSubImage*D()**, or other texture commands, and reads from textures via **glGetTexImage()** issued after the barrier will reflect data written to the texture by commands issued before the barrier.

- GL_BUFFER_UPDATE_BARRIER_BIT specifies that reads from buffer objects either through **glCopyBufferSubData()** or **glGetBufferSubData()**, or via mapping, will reflect data written by shaders before the barrier. Likewise, writes to buffers through mapping or **glBufferData()** and **glBufferSubData()** before the barrier, will be reflected in the data read from buffers in shaders executed after the barrier.

- GL_FRAMEBUFFER_BARRIER_BIT specifies that reads or writes through framebuffer attachments issued after the barrier will reflect data written to those attachments by shaders executed before the barrier. Further, writes to framebuffers issued after the barrier will be ordered with respect to writes performed by shaders before the barrier.

- GL_TRANSFORM_FEEDBACK_BARRIER_BIT specifies that writes performed through transform feedback before the barrier will be visible to shaders issued after the barrier. Likewise, writes performed by transform feedback after the barrier will be ordered with respect to writes performed by shaders before the barrier.

- GL_ATOMIC_COUNTER_BARRIER_BIT specifies that any accesses to atomic counters after the barrier will reflect writes prior to the barrier.

In addition to the flags listed above, the special value GL_ALL_BARRIER_BITS may be used to specify that all caches be flushed or invalidated and all pending operations be finished before proceeding. This value is included to allow additional bits to be added to the accepted set by future versions of OpenGL or by extensions in a forward compatible manner. The extension documentation will provide instruction on how to use any such added flags, but they will be implicitly included in the set specified by GL_ALL_BARRIER_BITS.

Note that calling **glMemoryBarrier()** may have no effect, or may be crucial to the correct functioning of your application. This depends on the OpenGL implementation that its running on. Some implementations may have specialized caches for each major functional block (vertex fetching, framebuffers and so on) and these caches will need to be flushed or invalidated[9] before data written by one block may be read by another. Meanwhile, other implementations may have fully unified and coherent cache systems (or no caches at all) and therefore any data written by one block will be immediately visible to other blocks.

In addition to controlling cache behavior, **glMemoryBarrier()** controls ordering. Given the lengthy OpenGL pipeline and highly parallel nature of the operations it performs (such as fragment shading), commands issued by your application can be executing at the same time and possibly even out of order. For example, OpenGL may be reading vertices from vertex buffers for one draw while the fragments from the previous draw are still being shaded. If the fragment shader for the first draw writes to a buffer that may be the source of vertex data for the second, the first draw must complete before the second may begin—even if the memory subsystem is coherent. Of course, the amount of overlap between draws will also depend on the OpenGL implementation and will vary depending on architecture and performance.

For these reasons, it's generally a good idea to use **glMemoryBarrier()** to delineate dependent operations on buffer and texture objects through image operations in shaders and by other fixed functionality in OpenGL. Implementations that are implicitly ordered and coherent can effectively ignore barrier operations while implementations that require explicit

---

9. In the context of caches, *flushing* the cache involves writing any modified data still held in the cache back into memory, whereas *invalidating* the cache means to mark the data currently held in cache as stale. Subsequent reads from an invalidated cache will cause new data to be fetched from the next level of the memory hierarchy. However, no data transfer is performed during invalidation. Flushing is generally performed on writable caches while invalidation is performed on read-only caches.

synchronization will depend on the barriers in order to perform cache control and ordering functions.

Controlling Early Fragment Test Optimizations

The OpenGL pipeline is defined to perform fragment shading followed by depth and stencil tests before writing to the framebuffer. This is almost always the desired behavior—certainly when a fragment shader writes to `gl_FragDepth`. However, modern graphics hardware employs optimizations like discarding fragments before shading when it can guarantee those fragments would have failed the depth test, and therefore saving the processing power required to execute the fragment shader. It can also do the same with the stencil test—perform the test early in the pipeline and discard the fragment *before* the shader runs. If a shader writes to `gl_FragDepth`, however, the optimization becomes invalid and is therefore not used. This is because the value written into `gl_FragDepth` is the one that should be used to perform the per-fragment depth test.

In the context of a traditional OpenGL pipeline, this is the correct behavior. Now consider a case where a fragment shader writes data into an image and the desired result is that data is only written if the fragment passes the depth and stencil tests. In this case, running these tests after the fragment shader has run will cause all rasterized fragments to have an effect on the output image, regardless of whether they will eventually pass or fail the depth or stencil tests. This is likely not the desired behavior and the shader author intends that the tests be run before the fragment shader such that the shader only has effects for fragments that pass the tests.

In order to specify that per-fragment tests should be evaluated before the fragment shader executes, GLSL provides the `early_fragment_tests` layout qualifier. This can be used with an input declaration in at least one fragment shader to turn on early depth test and early stencil test as shown in Example 11.20. *Not* including the `early_fragment_tests` layout qualifier in any fragment shader implies that depth and stencil test should run after the shader as normal.

Example 11.20   Using the `early_fragment_tests` Layout Qualifier

```
#version 420 core

layout (early_fragment_tests) in;
```

High Performance Atomic Counters

The OpenGL Shading Language also supports a dedicated, high-performance set of atomic counters. However, to motivate their use, we will start with the ones already introduced; that is, the large suite of functions that perform atomic operations on the content of images, as described in "Atomic Operations on Images" on Page 578. These functions are extremely powerful and provide a great deal of flexibility when it comes to dealing with image data. Let's imagine that we want to count fragments in a shader. This can often be accomplished using an occlusion query. However, an occlusion query blindly counts *all* fragments that pass the depth and stencil tests and runs after the shader has executed. Look at the example in Example 11.21.

Example 11.21   Counting Red and Green Fragments Using General
Atomics

```
#version 420 core

uniform (r32ui) uimageBuffer counter_buffer;
uniform sampler2D my_texture;

in vec2 tex_coord;

layout (location=0) out vec4 fragment_color;

void main(void)
{
    vec4 texel_color = texture(my_texture, tex_coord);

    if (texel_color.r > texel_color.g)
    {
        imageAtomicAdd(counter_buffer, 0, 1);
    }
    else
    {
        imageAtomicAdd(counter_buffer, 1, 1);
    }

    fragment_color = texel_color;
}
```

The shader shown in Example 11.21 samples a texture and compares the resulting red channel to the green channel. If the red channel is greater than the green channel (i.e., the fragment will be generally red in color), it atomically increments the memory in the first location of the counter_buffer image, otherwise it increments the second location. After rendering a scene with this shader, the result is that there are two counts in the buffer—the first being the count of all fragments whose red channel is greater than its green channel and the second being the count of all other fragments. Obviously, the sum is the total number of fragments that executed this shader and is what would have been generated by an occlusion query.

This type of operation is fairly common—counting events by incrementing a counter. In the example shown in Example 11.21, a very large amount of memory traffic is generated by the atomic operations used to count fragments. Every transaction accesses one of two adjacent memory operations. Depending on the implementation of atomics provided by OpenGL, this can have a serious impact on performance. Because simply incrementing or decrementing counters is such a common operation used in a large number of algorithms, GLSL includes special functionality specifically for this purpose. *Atomic counters* are special objects that represent elements used for counting. The only operations supported by them are to increment them, decrement them, or to obtain their current value. Example 11.22 shows the algorithm of Example 11.21 modified to use atomic counters rather than regular image operations.

Example 11.22   Counting Red and Green Fragments Using Atomic Counters

```
#version 420 core

layout (binding = 0, offset = 0) uniform atomic_uint red_texels;
layout (binding = 0, offset = 4) uniform atomic_unit green_texels;

uniform sampler2D my_texture;

in vec2 tex_coord;

layout (location=0) out vec4 fragment_color;

void main(void)
{
    vec4 texel_color = texture(my_texture, tex_coord);

    if (texel_color.r > texel_color.g)
    {
        atomicCounterIncrement(red_texels);
    }
    else
    {
        atomicCounterInrement(green_texels);
    }

    fragment_color = texel_color;
}
```

Notice the two new uniforms declared at the top of Example 11.22, `red_texels` and `green_texels`. They are declared with the type `atomic_uint` and are atomic counter uniforms. The values of atomic counters may be reset to particular values and their contents read by the application. To provide this functionality, atomic counters are backed by buffer objects bound to the GL_ATOMIC_COUNTER_BUFFER bindings that are indexed buffer bindings. The atomic counter buffer binding point to which the buffer object will be bound and the offset within that buffer are specified by the layout qualifiers used in Example 11.22.

The `binding` layout qualifier, when applied to `atomic_uint` uniforms is used to specify the index of the atomic counter buffer binding point that the counter refers to. Likewise, the `offset` layout qualifier is used to specify the offset within that buffer (in bytes, or basic machine units) at which the counter resides. This way, many counters may be placed into a single buffer, or several buffers can be used, each containing one or more counters.

The maximum number of counters that may be used in each shader stage is given by the OpenGL constants GL_MAX_VERTEX_ATOMIC_COUNTERS, GL_MAX_TESS_CONTROL_ATOMIC_COUNTERS, GL_MAX_TESS_EVALUATION_ATOMIC_COUNTERS, GL_MAX_GEOMETRY_ATOMIC_COUNTERS, and GL_MAX_FRAGMENT_ATOMIC_COUNTERS for vertex, tessellation control, tessellation evaluation, geometry, and fragment shaders, respectively. This includes cases where many counters are packed into a single buffer object, or when they are distributed across multiple buffer objects. Further, the maximum combined total number of atomic counters that may be used in all programs attached to a single program pipeline object can be determined by reading the value of the GL_MAX_COMBINED_ATOMIC_COUNTERS limit.

Likewise, the number of atomic counter buffer binding points supported by each of the shading stages may be determined by retrieving the values of GL_MAX_VERTEX_ATOMIC_COUNTER_BUFFERS, GL_MAX_TESS_CONTROL_ATOMIC_COUNTER_BUFFERS, GL_MAX_TESS_EVALUATION_ATOMIC_COUNTER_BUFFERS, GL_MAX_GEOMETRY_ATOMIC_COUNTER_BUFFERS, and GL_MAX_FRAGMENT_ATOMIC_COUNTER_BUFFERS for the vertex, tessellation control, tessellation evaluation, geometry, and fragment stages, respectively. Again, the GL_MAX_COMBINED_ATOMIC_COUNTER_BUFFERS limit is provided to indicate the maximum number of atomic counter buffers that may be referred to from all shader stages combined. For example, if each of the vertex, geometry, and fragment shader stages referred to one atomic counter buffer but the value reported for GL_MAX_COMBINED_ATOMIC_COUNTER_BUFFERS is 2, the program will fail to link.

Note: Note that while these limits are queryable, it is only required that an OpenGL implementation support atomic counters in the fragment shader—at least one atomic counter buffer binding and 8 atomic counters are supported in the fragment shader, and all other stages may report zero counters and zero buffers supported.

In the application, the code in Example 11.23 is used to create and bind buffers to the atomic counter buffer binding points. A small buffer large enough to contain GLuint variables is created and initialized and then it is bound to the indexed GL_ATOMIC_COUNTER_BUFFER binding at index 0. This provides backing store for the counters. Note that even though a buffer object is used to provide storage for atomic counters, hardware implementations may not operate directly on memory. Some implementations may provide dedicated hardware to extremely quickly increment and decrement counters without accessing memory at all.

Example 11.23   Initializing an Atomic Counter Buffer

```
// Local variables
GLuint buffer;
GLuint *counters;

// Generate a name for the buffer and create it by bind
// the name to the generic GL_ATOMIC_COUNTER_BUFFER
// binding point
glGenBuffers(1, &buffer);
glBindBuffer(GL_ATOMIC_COUNTER_BUFFER, buffer);

// Allocate enough space for two GLuints in the buffer
glBufferData(GL_ATOMIC_COUNTER_BUFFER, 2 * sizeof(GLuint),
             NULL, GL_DYNAMIC_COPY);

// Now map the buffer and initialize it
counters = (GLuint*)glMapBuffer(GL_ATOMIC_COUNTER_BUFFER,
                                GL_MAP_WRITE_ONLY);
counters[0] = 0;
counters[1] = 0;
glUnmapBuffer(GL_ATOMIC_COUNTER_BUFFER);

// Finally, bind the now initialized buffer to the 0th indexed
// GL_ATOMIC_COUNTER_BUFFER binding point
glBindBufferBase(GL_ATOMIC_COUNTER_BUFFER, 0, buffer);
```

Example

The following section includes an example of the types of effect and techniques that can implemented using the functionality described in this chapter.

Order-Independent Transparency

Order-independent transparency is a technique where blending operations are carried out in a manner such that rasterization order is not important. The fixed function blending provided by OpenGL through functions such as **glBlendEquation()** and **glBlendFunc()** are fairly restrictive. They provide a small, fixed set of operations that may be performed, most of which are not commutative. That is, the order of their operations matters—blend(a, blend(b, c)) does not produce the same result as blend(blend(a, b), c). This means that geometry must be sorted into a fixed, known order before being rendered. This can be very time-consuming, especially for complex geometry and in some cases, such as where geometry may self-intersect, may be impossible. The implementation in this example is based on a technique devised by demo engineers at AMD that uses sorted fragment lists to reorder fragments after rasterization and then perform blending in the fragment shader. This provides two benefits. First, the order in which the geometry is submitted to the GPU is not important and it can be rasterized in any order. Second, arbitrary blending functions can be implemented as all operations are performed in the shader and so *programmable blending* is achievable.

Principles of Operation

The order-independent transparency technique described here uses OpenGL to rasterize transparent polygons. However, rather than rendering directly to the framebuffer, the fragment shader builds a set of *linked lists* into a large, one-dimensional buffer image. Each element in the list is a record of a fragment that contributes to the final pixel color and includes the fragment's color, alpha, and perhaps most importantly, its depth. Also included in each record is the classic *next* pointer[10] seen in almost any linked-list implementation. An *atomic counter* is used to keep track of the *total number of fragments* appended to the list so far. Each pixel on the screen generates a separate linked list of all of the transparent fragments that contribute to it. Although the fragments for all pixels are contained in

---

10. Note that when the term *pointer* is used here, it is not used to refer to a physical (or virtual) address but to an offset into the fragment buffer.

Example **609**

the same buffer image, the resulting linked lists are *interleaved* and each pixel has its own *head* pointer, stored in a 2D image that is the size of the framebuffer. The head pointer is updated using atomic operations—items are always appended at the head of the image and use of an atomic exchange operation ensures that multiple shader invocations attempting to append to the same list will not corrupt each other's results.

A simplified diagram of the data structures used by this algorithm is shown in Figure 11.6. Each element in the linked list is represented by a `uvec4` vector and the fields used for different purposes. As `uvec4` is a native type in GLSL and the OpenGL API, no special handling is required to interpret it as a structure.

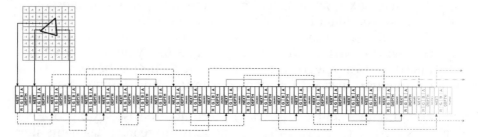

Figure 11.6   Data structures used for order-independent transparency

In Figure 11.6, the first field (`.x`) of each record is used to store the *next* pointer (the index of the next item in the linked list). The second field (`.y`) is used to store the color of the fragment. It is stored in a single `uint` component by packing the red, green, blue, and alpha channels together in the shader as will be shown shortly. The third component (`.z`) is used to store the depth of the fragment that will later be used to sort the list. As depth is a floating-point vlaue, but we're using integer components here, we'll cast the floating-point value to an unsigned integer and store its bit-wise representation in the vector directly. This is a completely reversible operation and will provide the exact depth value during the sorting stage. The final component (`.w`) is not used currently, but will be used during an enhancement to the algorithm shown later.

Once the linked list data structures have been built, a second pass is performed over the entire framebuffer. In this pass, the fragment shader traverses the linked list corresponding to its pixel and sorts all of the fragments in the list in order of depth. Once the fragments are in depth order, they can be blended together from back to front using any desired function.

To summarize, what is required for this algorithm to function are

- A buffer large enough to hold all of the fragments that might be rasterized.

- An atomic counter to serve as an *allocator* for records within the linked list.

- A 2D image the size of the framebuffer that will be used to store the head pointer for each pixel's linked list of fragments.

Initialization

Before any rendering can occur, we need to create the resources that our algorithm will use and initialize them to known values. In particular, we need to create our atomic counter that will be used to allocate items from our buffer object to store our linked list, create a 2D image the size of the framebuffer, and create a one-dimensional buffer object that is large enough to store all of the transparent fragments. Note that this doesn't have to be large enough to store the number of pixels on the screen times the maximum expected overdraw as most pixels will have no visible transparent fragments or perhaps very few transparent fragments. The code shown in Example 11.24 creates the required resources but does not initialize them because they need to be initialized before each frame anyway.

Example 11.24   Initializing for Order-Independent Transparency

```
// This is the maximum supported framebuffer width and height. We
// could support higher resolutions, but this is reasonable for
// this application
#define MAX_FRAMEBUFFER_WIDTH     2048
#define MAX_FRAMEBUFFER_HEIGHT    2048

// Local variables
GLuint * data;
size_t total_pixels = MAX_FRAMEBUFFER_WIDTH *
                      MAX_FRAMEBUFFER_HEIGHT;

// Create the 2D image that will be used to store the head pointers
// for the per-pixel linked lists.
GLuint head_pointer_texture;
glGenTextures(1, &head_pointer_texture);
glBindTexture(GL_TEXTURE_2D, head_pointer_texture);
glTexImage2D(GL_TEXTURE_2D, 0,          // 2D texture, level 0
            GL_R32UI,                    // 32-bit GLuint per texel
            MAX_FRAMEBUFFER_WIDTH,       // Width
            MAX_FRAMEBUFFER_HEIGHT,      // Height
```

Example   **611**

```
                0,                              // No border
                GL_RED_INTEGER,                 // Single channel
                GL_UNSIGNED_INT,                // Unsigned int
                NULL);                          // No data... yet

    // We will need to re-initialize the head pointer each frame. The
    // easiest way to do this is probably to copy from a PBO. We'll
    // create that here...
    GLuint head_pointer_initializer;
    glGenBuffers(1, &head_pointer_initializer);
    glBindBuffer(GL_PIXEL_UNPACK_BUFFER, head_pointer_initializer);
    glBufferData(GL_PIXEL_UNPACK_BUFFER,
                total_pixels *
                sizeof(GLuint),                 // 1 uint per pixel
                NULL,                           // No data - we'll map it
                GL_STATIC_DRAW);                // Never going to change
    data = (GLuint)glMapBuffer(GL_PIXEL_UNPACK_BUFFER, GL_WRITE_ONLY);
    // 0xFF will be our "end of list" marker.
    memset(data, 0xFF, total_pixels * sizeof(GLuint));
    glUnmapBuffer(GL_PIXEL_UNPACK_BUFFER);

    // Next, create our atomic counter buffer to back our atomic
    // counter.  We only need one counter, so a small buffer will
    // suffice.
    GLuint atomic_counter_buffer;
    glGenBuffers(1, &atomic_counter_buffer);
    glBindBuffer(GL_ATOMIC_COUNTER_BUFFER, atomic_counter_buffer);
    glBufferData(GL_ATOMIC_COUNTER_BUFFER,  // Allocate buffer...
                sizeof(GLuint), NULL,       // with space for 1 GLuint
                GL_DYNAMIC_COPY);           // written to by GPU

    // Finally, our large, one-dimensional buffer for fragment storage.
    // We're going to allocate enough storage for 2 fragments for every
    // pixel on the screen. Note again that this is average overdraw and
    // should be sufficient and allow a few pixels to include tens of
    // fragments so long as the average remains low.
    GLuint fragment_storage_buffer;
    glGenBuffers(1, &fragment_storage_buffer);
    glBindBuffer(GL_TEXTURE_BUFFER, fragment_storage_buffer);
    glBufferData(GL_TEXTURE_BUFFER,
                2 * total_pixels *    // Twice the maximum number of pixels
                sizeof(vec4),         // Times vec4
                NULL,                 // No data
                GL_DYNAMIC_COPY);     // Updated often by GPU
```

Rendering

For each frame, we will render the transparent objects in the scene using a
fragment shader that determines the color and opacity for each fragment
and then appends that information, along with the fragment's depth into
the linked list data structures. Before each frame's transparent objects are

drawn, the head pointer and atomic counter buffers must be initialized to known values; otherwise, our shader will continue to append to the structures created in the previous frame. The code for this is given in Example 11.25.

Example 11.25   Per-Frame Reset for Order-Independent Transparency

```
// First, clear the head-pointer 2D image with known values. Bind it
// to the GL_TEXTURE_2D target and then initialize it from a PBO that
// has been pre-loaded with the value 0x00
glBindBuffer(GL_PIXEL_UNPACK_BUFFER, head_pointer_initializer);
glBindTexture(GL_TEXTURE_2D, head_pointer_texture);
glTexImage2D(GL_TEXTURE_2D, 0,          // 2D texture, first level
            GL_R32UI,                   // 32-bit GLuint per texel
            MAX_FRAMEBUFFER_WIDTH,      // Width
            MAX_FRAMEBUFFER_HEIGHT,     // Height
            0,                          // No border
            GL_UNSIGNED_INT,            // Unsigned int
            NULL);                      // Consume data from PBO
// Now bind it to the image unit that will be used for
// read-write access
glBindImageTexture(0,                   // Image unit 0
                head_pointer_texture,
                GL_FALSE, 0,            // Not layered
                GL_READ_WRITE,         // Read and write access
                GL_R32UI);             // 32-bit GLuint per pixel

// Now bind the atomic counter buffer ready for use and reset the
// counter to zero
glBindBufferBase(GL_ATOMIC_COUNTER_BUFFER,   // Atomic counter...
                0,                           // Binding point 0
                atomic_counter_buffer);
// Note that this also binds the buffer to the generic buffer
// binding  point, so we can use that to initialize the buffer.
const GLuint zero = 0;
glBufferSubData(GL_ATOMIC_COUNTER_BUFFER, 0, sizeof(zero), &zero);
```

Once the code in Example 11.25 has executed, the head pointer image contains the value 0x00 in all texels and the buffer that stores our atomic counter contains zero, which resets the atomic counter to zero. Note that it is not necessary to clear the one-dimensional buffer that is used to store the linked lists as these lists will be completely rebuilt during each frame.

Now we are ready to render the frame. First, we render all nontransparent objects as there is no reason to append their fragments into the per-pixel fragment lists. Next, we render all of the transparent objects in an arbitrary order (this is the point of the algorithm, after all). The transparent objects are rendered using the fragment shader shown in Example 11.26.

Example   **613**

Example 11.26   Appending Fragments to Linked List for Later Sorting

```
#version 420 core

// Turn on early fragment testing
layout (early_fragment_tests) in;

// This is the atomic counter used to allocate items in the
// linked list
layout (binding = 0, offset = 0) uniform atomic_uint index_counter;

// Linked list 1D buffer
layout (binding = 0, rgba32ui) uniform imageBuffer list_buffer;

// Head pointer 2D buffer
layout (binding = 1, r32ui) uniform imageRect head_pointer_image;

void main(void)
{
    // First, shade the fragment - how is not important right now.
    vec4 frag_color = shadeFragment();

    // Allocate an index in the linked list buffer. Remember,
    // atomicCounterIncrement increments the atomic counter and
    // returns the _old_ value of the counter. Thus, the first
    // fragment to execute this code will receive the value 0, the
    // next will receive 1, and so on.
    uint new = atomicCounterIncrement(index_counter);

    // Now, insert the fragment into the list. To do this, we
    // atomically exchange our newly allocated index with the
    // current content of the head pointer image. Remember
    // imageAtomicExchange, writes our new value to memory and
    // returns the _old_ value.
    uint old_head = imageAtomicExchange(head_pointer_image,
                                        ivec2(gl_FragCoord.xy),
                                        index);

    // Before this code executed, we had:
    // head_pointer_image(x,y) -> old_item

    // Now we have:
    // head_pointer_image(x,y) -> new_item
    // _and_
    // old_head -> old_item

    // Now assemble the fragment into the buffer.
    // This will be the item...
    uvec4 item;
    // item.x = next pointer
    item.x = old_head;
    // Now we have
    // head_pointer_image(x,y) -> new_item (.x) -> old_item.
```

```
// item.y = color
item.y = packUnorm4x8(frag_color);
// item.z = depth (gl_FragCoord.z)
item.z = floatBitsToUint(gl_FragCoord.z);
// item.w = unused (so far...)
item.w = 0;

// Write the data into the buffer at the right location
imageStore(list_buffer, index, item);
}
```

The shader shown in Example 11.26 appends fragments into the per-pixel linked list using atomics counters, general purpose atomic operations, bit packing, and bit casting. First, the global atomic counter is incremented in order to allocate a record in the one-dimensional linked-list buffer. This can be used as an allocator because the atomic increment operation doesn't necessarily return $(n + 1)$, but rather a new, unique value that is greater than (n). This is shown in Figure 11.7 (a). In Figure 11.7 (a), the head pointer contains the index of the first item in the linked list and the index of the newly allocated item is stored in the new variable.

Next, this value is inserted into the head pointer texture and the previous value of head retrieved. This is performed in a single step by using an atomic exchange operation. This is shown in Figure 11.7 (b), where the head of the list is now pointing at the newly allocated item, and old_head contains the previous value of the head pointer—the index of the first item in the list. At this stage, the list is actually *broken* as the head pointer indexes an item without a valid next pointer. However, this doesn't matter because the list is never traversed as it is built.

Finally, the old value of the head pointer is used as the new next value for the inserted item. This means that the head pointer now refers to the item we allocated using the atomic counter, and the next pointer for that item points to what was previously the first item in the list. This is achieved by simply writing the old value of the head pointer into the next field of the new item as shown in Figure 11.7 (c). In all parts of Figure 11.7, the new item is marked with a gray crosshatch pattern.

Example **615**

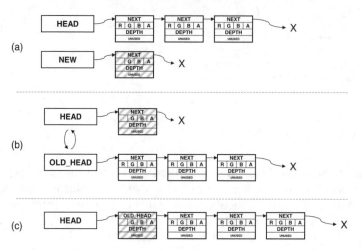

Figure 11.7   Inserting an item into the per-pixel linked lists

The end result is set of unsorted lists of fragment records, each containing a color, depth, and link to the next item in the list, with one list per pixel. Notice that all of the data that might be shared between shader invocations—the atomic counter and the head pointer—is only ever modified by using atomic operations. We never actually traversed the linked list during building as we only prepended items to the head. We are now ready to consume this data by sorting the fragments in order of depth and blending them together to form the final fragment color.

Finally, notice that the shader in Example 11.26 turns on early fragment testing using the `early_fragment_tests` layout qualifier. This is because we wish to ensure that fragments that are obscured by previously rendered opaque geometry are not added to the linked lists. As the transparent geometry is rendered with depth testing on but the shader has side effects (writing into the linked list), OpenGL would normally perform the depth test *after* it has executed by default. Using the `early_fragment_tests` input layout qualifier instructs OpenGL to perform depth testing *before* the shader runs and to not execute it if the fragment fails the test. This ensures that the shader will not be executed for obscured fragments and those fragments will not be added to the lists.

Sorting and Blending

Once the data structures have been built, the per-pixel linked lists are essentially a compressed representation of the scene. The next step is to walk the per-pixel lists and blend all of the fragments together in order to build the final output colors. To do this, we render a full-screen quad using a fragment shader that will read from the list corresponding to its output pixel, sort all of the fragments into order, and then perform the blending operations of our choice. Because the number of fragments per-pixel is expected to be low, a simple sorting algorithm can be used.

In this pass, we again take our head pointer image and our linked-list buffer and access them from the shader. However, as we are only going to be reading from them, we can bind them as a regular 2D texture and as a texture buffer object (TBO), respectively. This gives additional hints to the implementation that it can access the image in a read-only manner without worrying about coherency or caching issues. The atomic counter used to allocate list items is not required in the blending pass as we are not going to allocate more items on the list. The main body of the sorting and blending shader is shown in Example 11.27.

Example 11.27   Main Body of Final Order-Independent Sorting Fragment Shader

```
#version 420 core

// Head pointer 2D buffer
uniform sampler2D head_pointer_image;

// Linked list 1D buffer
uniform samplerBuffer list_buffer;

#define MAX_FRAGMENTS 15

// Small buffer to hold all of the fragments corresponding
// to this pixel
uvec4 fragments[MAX_FRAGMENTS];

layout (location = 0) out vec4 output_color;

void main(void)
{
    int frag_count;

    // Traverse the list and build an array of fragments
    frag_count = build_local_fragment_list();

    // Sort the array in depth order
    sort_fragment_list(frag_count);

    // Blend the sorted fragments together  to compute the final
```

Example   **617**

```
    // output color
    output_color = calculate_final_color(frag_count);
}
```

Example 11.27 makes use of three functions. First,
build_local_fragment_list traverses the linked list of fragments
corresponding to the current pixel and places all of the fragments into the
fragments[] array. The code for this function is shown in Example 11.28.
Notice that the size of the per-pixel fragment array is defined as 15 here,
even though the buffer allocated in Example 11.24 is only twice the
number of pixels in the framebuffer. This is possible because the fragment
lists only needs to be large enough to store the *average* number of
fragments per-pixel, but the *maximum* overdraw supported can be much
larger.

Example 11.28   Traversing Linked-Lists in a Fragment Shader

```
// Traverse the linked list, place all of the fragments into the
// fragments[] array and return the number of fragments retrieved
// from the list.
int build_local_fragment_list(void)
{
    uint current;
    int frag_count = 0;

    // Get the initial head pointer from the header-pointer image
    current = texelFetch(head_pointer_image,
                        ivec2(gl_FragCoord.xy), 0);

    // While we haven't reached the end of the list or exhausted
    // the storage available in fragments[]...
    while (current != 0xFFFFFFFF && frag_count < MAX_FRAGMENTS)
    {
        // Read an item from the linked list
        item = texelFetch(list_buffer, current);
        // item.x contains the "next" pointer - update current
        current = item.x;
        // Store the fragment in the array
        uvec4 fragments[frag_count] = item;
        // Update the fragment count
        frag_count++;
    }

    // Done - return the fragment count
    return frag_count;
}
```

After the local array of fragments has been built, it is sorted in order of depth using the `sort_fragment_list` function shown in Example 11.29. This function implements a simple bubble-sort algorithm. While this is a very simple algorithm and is not well suited for sorting large amounts of data, because the number of items is very low, the cost of the function is still small, and the algorithm suffices.

Example 11.29   Sorting Fragments into Depth Order for OIT

```
// Simple bubble-sort for sorting the fragments[] array
void sort_fragment_list(int frag_count)
{
    int i;
    int j;

    for (i = 0; i < frag_count; i++)
    {
        for (j = i + 1; j < frag_count; j++)
        {
            // The depth of each fragment is bit-encoded into the
            // .z channel of the fragment array. Unpack it here.
            float depth_i = uintBitsToFloat(fragments[i].z);
            float depth_j = uintBitsToFloat(fragments[j].z);

            // Compare depth and if the comparison fails...
            if (depth_i > depth_j)
            {
                // Swap the fragments in the array
                uvec4 temp = fragments[i];
                fragments[i] = fragments[j];
                fragments[j] = temp;
            }
        }
    }
}
```

Once the fragments in the `fragments[]` array have been sorted into depth order, we can traverse the array and blend the fragments together using a blending operation of our choice. This is implemented in the `calculate_final_color` function that is shown in Example 11.30.

Example 11.30   Blending Sorted Fragments for OIT

```
// Simple alpha blending function -- we could replace
// this with anything...
vec4 blend(vec4 current_color, vec4 new_color)
{
    return mix(current_color, new_color, new_color.a);
}
```

Example   **619**

```
// Function for calculating the final output color. Walks the
// fragments[] array and blends each pixel on top of each other
vec4 calculate_final_color(int frag_count)
{
    // Initialize the final color output
    vec4 final_color = vec4(0.0);

    // For each fragment in the array...
    for (i = 0; i < frag_count; i++)
    {
        // The color is stored packed into the .y channel of the
        // fragment vector. Unpack it here.
        vec4 frag_color = unpackUnorm4x8(fragments[i].y);
        // Now call the blending function.
        final_color = blend(final_color, frag_color);
    }

    // Done -- return the final color.
    return final_color;

}
```

The blend function shown in Example 11.30 simply uses the mix function to implement basic alpha blending. This is equivalent to using fixed-function OpenGL blending with the blend equation set to GL_FUNC_ADD and the blend functions set to GL_SRC_ALPHA and GL_ONE_MINUS_SRC_ALPHA for source and destination factors, respectively.

Results

The results of rendering with this algorithm are shown in Figure 11.8. The image on the left is produced using fixed-function OpenGL blending. As can be seen, the image does not look correct in all areas. This is because geometry is rendered in order of submission rather than in order of depth. Because the blending equations used are not commutative and are therefore sensitive to order, they produce different results depending on the submission order of the geometry. Contrast this to the result shown on the right of Figure 11.8. This is rendered with the order-independent algorithm described in this example. The result is correct in all areas.

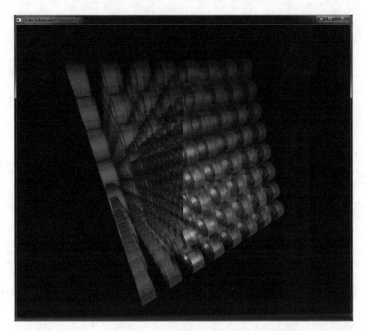

Figure 11.8   Result of order-independent transparency incorrect order on left; correct order on right.

Example   **621**

Chapter 12

Compute Shaders

Chapter Objectives

After reading this chapter, you'll be able to do the following:

- Create, compile, and link compute shaders.

- Launch compute shaders, which operate on buffers, images, and counters.

- Allow compute shader invocations to communicate with each other and to synchronize their execution.

Compute shaders run in a completely separate stage of the GPU than the rest of the graphics pipeline. They allow an application to make use of the power of the GPU for general purpose work that may or may not be related to graphics. Compute shaders have access to many of the same resources as graphics shaders, but have more control over their application flow and how they execute. This chapter introduces the compute shader and describes its use.

This chapter has the following major sections:

- "Overview" gives a brief introduction to compute shaders and outlines their general operation.

- The organization and detailed working of compute shaders with regards to the graphics processor is given in "Workgroups and Dispatch".

- Next, methods for communicating between the individual invocations of a compute shader are presented in "Communication and Synchronization", along with the synchronization mechanisms that can be used to control the flow of data between those invocations.

- A few examples of compute shaders are shown, including both graphics and nongraphics work are given in "Examples".

Overview

The graphics processor is an immensely powerful device capable of performing *trillions* of calculations each second. Over the years, it has been developed to crunch the huge amount of math operations required to render real-time graphics. However, it is possible to use the computational power of the processor for tasks that are not considered graphics, or that don't fit neatly into the relatively fixed graphical pipeline. To enable this type of use, OpenGL includes a special shader stage called the *compute shader*. The compute shader can be considered a special, single-stage pipeline that has no fixed input or output. Instead, all automatic input is through a handful of built-in variables. If additional input is needed, those fixed-function inputs may be used to control access to textures and buffers. All visible side effects are through image stores, atomics, and access to atomic counters. While at first this seems like it would be quite limiting, it includes general read and write of memory, and this level of flexibility and lack of graphical idioms open up a wide range of applications for compute shaders.

Compute shaders in OpenGL are very similar to any other shader stage. They are created using the **glCreateShader()** function, compiled using **glCompileShader()**, and attached to program objects using

glAttachShader(). These programs are linked as normal by using
glLinkProgram(). Compute shaders are written in GLSL and in general,
any functionality accessible to normal graphics shaders (for example,
vertex, geometry or fragment shaders) is available. Obviously, this excludes
graphics pipeline functionality such as the geometry shaders'
`EmitVertex()` or `EndPrimitive()`, or to the similarly pipeline-specific
built-in variables. On the other hand, several built-in functions and
variables are available to a compute shader that are available nowhere else
in the OpenGL pipeline.

Workgroups and Dispatch

Just as the graphics shaders fit into the pipeline at specific points and
operate on graphics-specific elements, compute shaders effectively fit into
the (single-stage) compute pipeline and operate on compute-specific
elements. In this analogy, vertex shaders execute per vertex, geometry
shaders execute per primitive and fragment shaders execute per fragment.
Performance of graphics hardware is obtained through parallelism, which
in turn is achieved through the very large number of vertices, primitives, or
fragments, respectively, passing through each stage of the pipeline. In the
context of compute shaders, this parallelism is more explicit, with work
being launched in groups known as *workgroups*. Workgroups have a local
neighborhood known as a *local workgroup*, and these are again grouped to
form a *global workgroup* as the result of one of the dispatch commands.

The compute shader is then executed once for each element of each local
workgroup within the global workgroup. Each element of the workgroup is
known as a *work item* and is processed by an *invocation*. The invocations of
the compute shader can communicate with each other via variables and
memory, and can perform synchronization operations to keep their work
coherent. Figure 12.1 shows a schematic of this work layout. In this
simplified example, the global workgroup consists of 16 local workgroups,
and each local workgroup consists of 16 invocations, arranged in a 4×4
grid. Each invocation has a local index that is a two-dimensional vector.

While Figure 12.1 visualizes the global and local workgroups as two-
dimensional entities, they are in fact in three dimensions. To issue work
that is logically one- or two-dimensional, we simply make a
three-dimensional work size where the extent in one or two of the
dimensions is of size one. The invocations of a compute shader are
essentially independent and may run in parallel on some implementations
of OpenGL. In practice, most OpenGL implementations will group subsets
of the work together and run it in lockstep, grouping yet more of these
subsets together to form the local workgroups. The size of a local

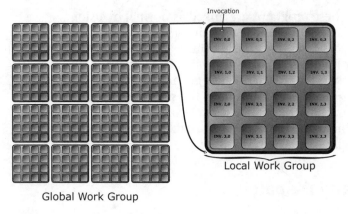

Invocation

INV. 0,0   INV. 0,1   INV. 0,2   INV. 0,3

INV. 1,0   INV. 1,1   INV. 1,2   INV. 1,3

INV. 2,0   INV. 2,1   INV. 2,2   INV. 2,3

INV. 3,0   INV. 3,1   INV. 3,2   INV. 3,3

Local Work Group

Global Work Group

Figure 12.1   Schematic of a compute workload

workgroup is defined in the compute shader source code using an input layout qualifier. The global workgroup size is measured as an integer multiple of the local workgroup size. As the compute shader executes, it is provided with its location within the local workgroup, the size of the workgroup, and the location of its local workgroup within the global workgroup through built-in variables. There are further variables available that are derived from these providing the location of the invocation within the global workgroup, among other things. The shader may use these variables to determine which elements of the computation it should work on and also can know its neighbors within the workgroup, which facilitates some amount of data sharing.

The input layout qualifiers that are used in the compute shader to declare the local workgroup size are `local_size_x`, `local_size_y`, and `local_size_z`. The defaults for these are all one, and so omitting `local_size_z`, for example, would create an $N \times M$ two-dimensional workgroup size. An example of declaring a shader with a local workgroup size of 16×16 is shown in Example 12.1.

Example 12.1   Simple Local Workgroup Declaration

```
#version 430 core

// Input layout qualifier declaring a 16 x 16 (x 1) local
// workgroup size
layout (local_size_x = 16, local_size_y = 16) in;

void main(void)
{
    // Do nothing.
}
```

Although the simple shader of Example 12.1 does nothing, it is a valid compute shader and will compile, link, and execute on an OpenGL implementation. To create a compute shader, simply call **glCreateShader()** with *type* set to GL_COMPUTE_SHADER, set the shader's source code with **glShaderSource()** and compile it as normal. Then, attach the shader to a program and call **glLinkProgram()**. This creates the executable for the compute shader stage that will operate on the work items. A complete example of creating and linking a compute program[1] is shown in Example 12.2.

Example 12.2   Creating, Compiling, and Linking a Compute Shader

```
GLuint shader, program;

static const GLchar* source[] =
{
    "#version 430 core\n"
    "\n"
    "// Input layout qualifier declaring a 16 x 16 (x 1) local\n"
    "// workgroup size\n"
    "layout (local_size_x = 16, local_size_y = 16) in;\n"
    "\n"
    "void main(void)\n"
    "{\n"
    "    // Do nothing.\n"
    "}\n"
};

shader = glCreateShader(GL_COMPUTE_SHADER);
glShaderSource(shader, 1, source, NULL);
glCompileShader(shader);

program = glCreateProgram();
glAttachShader(program, shader);
glLinkProgram(program);
```

Once we have created and linked a compute shader as shown in Example 12.2, we can make the program current using **glUseProgram()** and then dispatch workgroups into the compute pipeline using the function **glDispatchCompute()**, whose prototype is as follows:

---

1. We use the term *compute program* to refer to a linked program object containing a compute shader.

> void **glDispatchCompute**(GLuint *num_groups_x*,
> GLuint *num_groups_y*,
> GLuint *num_groups_z*);
>
> Dispatch compute workgroups in three dimensions. *num_groups_x*, *num_groups_y*, and *num_groups_z* specify the number of workgroups to launch in the X, Y, and Z dimensions, respectively. Each parameter must be greater than zero and less than or equal to the corresponding element of the implementation-dependent constant vector GL_MAX_COMPUTE_WORK_GROUP_SIZE.

When you call **glDispatchCompute()**, OpenGL will create a three-dimensional array of local workgroups whose size is *num_groups_x* by *num_groups_y* by *num_groups_z* groups. Remember, the size of the workgroup in one or more of these dimensions may be one, as may be any of the parameters to **glDispatchCompute()**. Thus the total number of invocations of the compute shader will be the size of this array times the size of the local workgroup declared in the shader code. As you can see, this can produce an extremely large amount of work for the graphics processor and it is relatively easy to achieve parallelism using compute shaders.

As **glDrawArraysIndirect()** is to **glDrawArrays()**, so **glDispatchComputeIndirect()** is to **glDispatchCompute()**. **glDispatchComputeIndirect()** launches compute work using parameters stored in a buffer object. The buffer object is bound to the GL_DISPATCH_INDIRECT_BUFFER binding point and the parameters stored in the buffer consist of three unsigned integers, tightly packed together. Those three unsigned integers are equivalent to the parameters to **glDispatchCompute()**. The prototype for **glDispatchComputeIndirect()** is as follows:

> void **glDispatchComputeIndirect**(GLintptr *indirect*);
>
> Dispatch compute workgroups in three dimensions using parameters stored in a buffer object. *indirect* is the offset, in basic machine units, into the buffer's data store at which the parameters are located. The parameters in the buffer at this offset are three, tightly packed unsigned integers representing the number of local workgroups to be dispatch. These unsigned integers are equivalent to the *num_groups_x*, *num_groups_y*, and *num_groups_z* parameters to **glDispatchCompute()**. Each parameter must be greater than zero and less than or equal to the corresponding element of the implementation-dependent constant vector GL_MAX_COMPUTE_WORK_GROUP_SIZE.

The data in the buffer bound to GL_DISPATCH_INDIRECT_BUFFER binding could come from anywhere—including another compute shader. As such, the graphics processor can be made to feed work to itself by writing the parameters for a dispatch (or draws) into a buffer object. Example 12.3 shows an example of dispatching compute workloads using **glDispatchComputeIndirect()**.

Example 12.3   Dispatching Compute Workloads

```
// program is a successfully linked program object containing
// a compute shader executable
GLuint program =  ...;

// Activate the program object
glUseProgram(program);

// Create a buffer, bind it to the DISPATCH_INDIRECT_BUFFER
// binding point and fill it with some data.
glGenBuffers(1, &dispatch_buffer);
glBindBuffer(GL_DISPATCH_INDIRECT_BUFFER, dispatch_buffer);

static const struct
{
    GLuint num_groups_x;
    GLuint num_groups_y;
    GLuint num_groups_z;
} dispatch_params = { 16, 16, 1 };

glBufferData(GL_DISPATCH_INDIRECT_BUFFER,
             sizeof(dispatch_params),
             &dispatch_params,
             GL_STATIC_DRAW);

// Dispatch the compute shader using the parameters stored
// in the buffer object
glDispatchComputeIndirect(0);
```

Notice how in Example 12.3 we simply use **glUseProgram()** to set the current program object to the compute program. Aside from having no access to the fixed-function graphics pipeline (such as the rasterizer or framebuffer), compute shaders and the programs that they are linked into are completely normal, first-class shader and program objects. This means that you can use **glGetProgramiv()** to query their properties (such as active uniform or storage blocks) and can access uniforms as normal. Of course, compute shaders also have access to almost all of the resources that other types shaders have, including images, samplers, buffers, atomic counters, and uniform blocks.

Compute shaders and their linked programs also have several compute-specific properties. For example, to retrieve the local workgroup size of a compute shader (which would have been set using a layout qualifier in the source of the compute shader), call **glGetProgramiv()** with *pname* set to GL_MAX_COMPUTE_WORK_GROUP_SIZE and *param* set to the address of an array of three unsigned integers. The three elements of the array will be filled with the size of the local workgroup size in the X, Y, and Z dimensions, in that order.

Knowing Where You Are

Once your compute shader is executing, it likely has the responsibility to set the value of one or more elements of some output array (such as an image or an array of atomic counters), or to read data from a specific location in an input array. To do this, you will need to know where in the local workgroup you are and where that workgroup is within the larger global workgroup. For these purposes, OpenGL provides several built-in variables to compute shaders. These built-in variables are implicitly declared as shown in Example 12.4.

Example 12.4   Declaration of Compute Shader Built-in Variables

```
const uvec3 gl_WorkGroupSize;
in    uvec3 gl_NumWorkGroups;

in    uvec3 gl_LocalInvocationID;
in    uvec3 gl_WorkGroupID;

in    uvec3 gl_GlobalInvocationID;
in    uint  gl_LocalInvocationIndex;
```

The compute shader built-in variables have the following definitions:

- gl_WorkGroupSize is a constant that stores the size of the local workgroup as declared by the local_size_x, local_size_y and local_size_z layout qualifiers in the shader. Replicating this information here serves two purposes; first, it allows the workgroup size to be referred to multiple times in the shader without relying on the preprocessor and second, it allows multidimensional workgroup size to be treated as a vector without having to construct it explicitly.

- gl_NumWorkGroups is a vector that contains the parameters that were passed to **glDispatchCompute()** (*num_groups_x*, *num_groups_y*, and *num_groups_z*). This allows the shader to know the extent of the global workgroup that it is part of. Besides being more convenient than needing to set the values of uniforms by hand, some OpenGL implementations may have a very efficient path for setting these constants.

- `gl_LocalInvocationID` is the location of the current invocation of a compute shader within the local workgroup. It will range from `uvec3(0)` to `gl_WorkGroupSize - uvec3(1)`.

- `gl_WorkGroupID` is the location of the current local workgroup within the larger global workgroup. This variable will range from `uvec3(0)` to `gl_NumWorkGroups - uvec3(1)`.

- `gl_GlobalInvocationID` is derived from `gl_LocalInvocationID`, `gl_WorkGroupSize`, and `gl_WorkGroupID`. Its exact value is equal to `gl_WorkGroupID * gl_WorkGroupSize + gl_LocalInvocationID` and as such, it is effectively the three-dimensional index of the current invocation within the global workgroup.

- `gl_LocalInvocationIndex` is a flattened form of `gl_LocalInvocationID`. It is equal to `gl_LocalInvocationID.z * gl_WorkGroupSize.x * gl_WorkGroupSize.y + gl_LocalInvocationID.y * gl_WorkGroupSize.x + gl_LocalInvocationID.x`. It can be used to index into one-dimensional arrays that represent two- or three-dimensional data.

Given that we now know where we are within both the local workgroup and the global workgroup, we can use this information to operate on data. Taking the example of Example 12.5 and adding an image variable allows us to write into the image at a location derived from the coordinate of the invocation within the global workgroup and update it from our compute shader. This modified shader is shown in Example 12.5.

Example 12.5   Operating on Data

```
#version 430 core

layout (local_size_x = 32, local_size_y = 16) in;

// An image to store data into.
layout (rg32f) uniform image2D data;

void main(void)
{
    // Store the local invocation ID into the image.
    imageStore(data,
               ivec2(gl_GlobalInvocationID.xy),
               vec4(vec2(gl_LocalInvocationID.xy) /
                    vec2(gl_WorkGroupSize.xy),
                    0.0, 0.0));
}
```

The shader shown in Example 12.5 simply takes the local invocation index, normalizes it to the local workgroup size, and stores the result into the data image at the location given by the global invocation ID. The resulting image shows the relationship between the global and local invocation IDs and clearly shows the rectangular local workgroup size specified in the compute shader (in this case, 32 × 16 work items). The resulting image is shown in Figure 12.2.

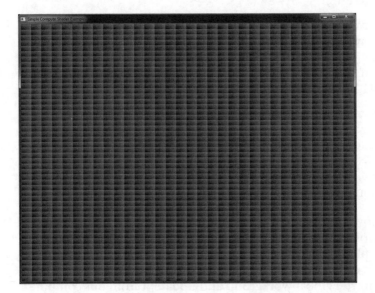

Figure 12.2   Relationship of global and local invocation ID

To generate the image of Figure 12.2, after being written by the compute shader, the texture is simply rendered to a full screen triangle fan.

Communication and Synchronization

When you call **glDispatchCompute()** (or **glDispatchComputeIndirect()**), a potentially huge amount of work is sent to the graphics processor. The graphics processor will run that work in parallel if it can, and the invocations that execute the compute shader can be considered to be a team trying to accomplish a task. Teamwork is facilitated greatly by communication and so, while the order of execution and level of parallelism is not defined by OpenGL, some level of cooperation between the invocations is enabled by allowing them to communicate via *shared* variables. Furthermore, it is possible to sync up all the invocations in the local workgroup so that they reach the same part of your shader at the same time.

Communication

The `shared` keyword is used to declare variables in shaders in a similar manner to other keywords such as `uniform`, `in`, or `out`. Some example declarations using the `shared` keyword are shown in Example 12.6.

Example 12.6   Example of Shared Variable Declarations

```
// A single shared unsigned integer;
shared uint foo;

// A shared array of vectors
shared vec4 bar[128];

// A shared block of data
shared struct baz_struct
{
    vec4 a_vector;
    int an_integer;
    ivec2 an_array_of_integers[27];
} baz[42];
```

When a variable is declared as `shared`, that means it will be kept in storage that is visible to all of the compute shader invocations in the same local workgroup. When one invocation of the compute shader writes to a `shared` variable, then the data it wrote will eventually become visible to other invocations of that shader within the same local workgroup. We say *eventually* because the relative order of execution of compute shader invocations is not defined—even within the same local workgroup. Therefore, one shader invocation may write to a `shared` variable long before another invocation reads from that variable, or even long after the other invocation has read from that variable. To ensure that you get the results you expect, you need to include some synchronization primitives in your code. These are covered in detail in the next section.

The performance of accesses to `shared` variables is often significantly better than accesses to images or to shader storage buffers (i.e., main memory). As shared memory is local to a shader processor and may be duplicated throughout the device, access to shared variables can be even faster than hitting the cache. For this reason, it is recommended that if your shader performs more than a few accesses to a region of memory, and especially if multiple shader invocations will access the same memory locations, that you first copy that memory into some shared variables in the shader, operate on them there, and then write the results back into main memory if required.

Because it is expected that variables declared as `shared` will be stored inside the graphics processor in dedicated high-performance resources, and because those resources may be limited, it is possible to query the combined maximum size of all shared variables that can be accessed by a single compute program. To retrieve this limit, call **glGetIntegerv()** with *pname* set to GL_MAX_COMPUTE_SHARED_MEMORY_SIZE.

Synchronization

If the order of execution of the invocations of a local workgroup and all of the local workgroups that make up the global workgroup are not defined, the operations that an invocation performs can occur out of order with respect to other invocations. If no communication between the invocations is required and they can all run completely independently of each other, then this likely isn't going to be an issue. However, if the invocations need to communicate with each other either through images and buffers or through shared variables, then it may be necessary to synchronize their operations with each other.

There are two types of synchronization commands. The first is an execution barrier, which is invoked using the **barrier()** function. This is similar to the **barrier()** function you can use in a tessellation control shader to synchronize the invocations that are processing the control points. When an invocation of a compute shader reaches a call to **barrier()**, it will stop executing and wait for all other invocations within the same local workgroup to catch up. Once the invocation resumes executing, having returned from the call to **barrier()**, it is safe to assume that all other invocations have also reached their corresponding call to **barrier()**, and have completed any operations that they performed before this call. The usage of **barrier()** in a compute shader is somewhat more flexible than what is allowed in a tessellation control shader. In particular, there is no requirement that **barrier()** be called only from the shader's `main()` function. Calls to **barrier()** must, however, only be executed inside uniform flow control. That is, if one invocation within a local workgroup executes a **barrier()** function, then all invocations within that workgroup must also execute the same call. This seems logical as one invocation of the shader has no knowledge of the control flow of any other and must assume that the other invocations will eventually reach the barrier—if they do not, then deadlock can occur.

When communicating between invocations within a local workgroup, you can write to shared variables from one invocation and then read from them in another. However, you need to make sure that by the time you read from a shared variable in the destination invocation that the source invocation has completed the corresponding write to that variable. To ensure this, you can write to the variable in the source invocation, and then in both invocations execute the **barrier()** function. When the destination invocation returns from the **barrier()** call, it can be sure that the source invocation has also executed the function (and therefore completed the write to the shared variable), and so it is safe to read from the variable.

The second type of synchronization primitive is the memory barrier. The heaviest, most brute-force version of the memory barrier is **memoryBarrier()**. When **memoryBarrier()** is called, it ensures that any writes to memory that have been performed by the shader invocation have been committed to memory rather than lingering in caches or being scheduled after the call to **memoryBarrier()**, for example. Any operations that occur after the call to **memoryBarrier()** will see the results of those memory writes if the same memory locations are read again—even in different invocations of the same compute shader. Furthermore, **memoryBarrier()** can serve as instruction to the shader compiler to not reorder memory operations if it means that they will cross the barrier. If **memoryBarrier()** seems somewhat heavy handed, that would be an astute observation. In fact, there are several other memory barrier functions that serve as subsets of the **memoryBarrier()** mega function. In fact, **memoryBarrier()** is simply defined as calling each of these subfunctions back to back in some undefined (but not really relevant) order.

The **memoryBarrierAtomicCounter()** function wait for any updates to atomic counters to complete before continuing. The **memoryBarrierBuffer()** and **memoryBarrierImage()** functions wait for any write accesses to buffer and image variables to complete, respectively. The **memoryBarrierShared()** function waits for any updates to variables declared with the `shared` qualifier. These functions allow much finer-grained control over what types of memory accesses are waited for. For example, if you are using an atomic counter to arbitrate accesses to a buffer variable, you might want to ensure that updates to atomic counters are seen by other invocations of the shader without necessarily waiting for any prior writes to the buffer to complete, as the latter may take much longer than the former. Also, calling **memoryBarrierAtomicCounter()** will allow the shader compiler to reorder accesses to buffer variables without violating the logic implied by atomic counter operations.

Note that even after a call to **memoryBarrier()** or one of its subfunctions, there is still no guarantee that all other invocations have reached this point in the shader. To ensure this, you will need to call the execution barrier function, **barrier()**, before reading from memory that would have been written prior to the call to **memoryBarrier()**.

Use of memory barriers is not necessary to ensure the observed order of memory transactions within a single shader invocation. Reading the value of a variable in a particular invocation of a shader will always return the value most recently written to that variable, even if the compiler reordered them behind the scenes.

One final function, **groupMemoryBarrier()** is effectively equivalent to **memoryBarrier()**, except that it applies only to other invocations within the same local workgroup. All of the other memory barrier functions apply globally. That is, they ensure that memory writes performed by any invocation in the global workgroup is committed before continuing.

Examples

This section includes a number of example use cases for compute shaders. As compute shaders are designed to execute arbitrary work with very little fixed-function plumbing to tie them to specific functionality, they are very flexible and very powerful. As such, the best way to see them in action is to work through a few examples in order to see their application in real-world scenarios.

Physical Simulation

The first example is a simple particle simulator. In this example, we use a compute shader to update the positions of close to a million particles in real time. Although the physical simulation is very simple, it produces visually interesting results and demonstrates the relative ease with which this type of algorithm can be implemented in a compute shader.

The algorithm implemented in this example is as follows. Two large buffers are allocated, one which stores the current velocity of each particle and a second which stores the current position. At each time step, a compute shader executes and each invocation processes a single particle. The current velocity and position are read from their respective buffers. A new velocity is calculated for the particle and then this velocity is used to update the particle's position. The new velocity and position are then written back into the buffers. To make the buffers accessible to the shader, they are attached to buffer textures that are then used with image load and store operations. An alternative to buffer textures is to use shader storage buffers, declared with as a `buffer` interface block.

In this toy example, we don't consider the interaction of the particles with each other, which would be an $O(n^2)$ problem. Instead, we use a small number of attractors, each with a position and a mass. The mass of each particle is also considered to be the same. Each particle is considered to be gravitationally attracted to the attractors. The force exerted on the particle by each of the attractors is used to update the velocity of the particle by integrating over time. The positions and masses of the attractors are stored in a uniform block.

In addition to a position and velocity, the particles have a life expectancy. The life expectancy of the particle is stored in the *w* component of its position vector and each time the particle's position is updated, its life expectancy is reduced slightly. Once its life expectancy is below a small threshold, it is reset to one, and rather than update the particle's position, we reset it to be close to the origin. We also reduce the particle's velocity by two orders of magnitude. This causes aged particles (including those that may have been flung to the corners of the universe) to reappear at the center, creating a stream of fresh young particles to keep our simulation going.

The source code for the particle simulation shader is given in Example 12.7.

Example 12.7   Particle Simulation Compute Shader

```
#version 430 core

// Uniform block containing positions and masses of the attractors
layout (std140, binding = 0) uniform attractor_block
{
    vec4 attractor[64]; // xyz = position, w = mass
};

// Process particles in blocks of 128
layout (local_size_x = 128) in;

// Buffers containing the positions and velocities of the particles
layout (rgba32f, binding = 0) uniform imageBuffer velocity_buffer;
layout (rgba32f, binding = 1) uniform imageBuffer position_buffer;

// Delta time
uniform float dt;

void main(void)
{
    // Read the current position and velocity from the buffers
    vec4 vel = imageLoad(velocity_buffer, int(gl_GlobalInvocationID.x));
    vec4 pos = imageLoad(position_buffer, int(gl_GlobalInvocationID.x));

    int i;

    // Update position using current velocity * time
    pos.xyz += vel.xyz * dt;
    // Update "life" of particle in w component
```

```
            pos.w -= 0.0001 * dt;

        // For each attractor...
        for (i = 0; i < 4; i++)
        {
            // Calculate force and update velocity accordingly
            vec3 dist = (attractor[i].xyz - pos.xyz);
            vel.xyz += dt * dt *
                        attractor[i].w *
                        normalize(dist) / (dot(dist, dist) + 10.0);
        }

        // If the particle expires, reset it
        if (pos.w <= 0.0)
        {
            pos.xyz = -pos.xyz * 0.01;
            vel.xyz *= 0.01;
            pos.w += 1.0f;
        }

        // Store the new position and velocity back into the buffers
        imageStore(position_buffer, int(gl_GlobalInvocationID.x), pos);
        imageStore(velocity_buffer, int(gl_GlobalInvocationID.x), vel);
    }
```

To kick off the simulation, we first create the two buffer objects that will store the positions and velocities of all of the particles. The position of each particle is set to a random location in the vicinity of the origin and its life expectancy is set to random value between zero and one. This means that each particle will reach the end of its first iteration and be brought back to the origin after a random amount of time. The velocity of each particle is also initialized to a random vector with a small magnitude. The code to do this is shown in Example 12.8.

Example 12.8 Initializing Buffers for Particle Simulation

```
// Generate two buffers, bind them and initialize their data stores
glGenBuffers(2, buffers);
glBindBuffer(GL_ARRAY_BUFFER, position_buffer);
glBufferData(GL_ARRAY_BUFFER,
            PARTICLE_COUNT * sizeof(vmath::vec4),
            NULL,
            GL_DYNAMIC_COPY);

// Map the position buffer and fill it with random vectors
vmath::vec4 * positions = (vmath::vec4 *)
    glMapBufferRange(GL_ARRAY_BUFFER,
                    0,
                    PARTICLE_COUNT * sizeof(vmath::vec4),
                    GL_MAP_WRITE_BIT |
                    GL_MAP_INVALIDATE_BUFFER_BIT);
```

```
for (i = 0; i < PARTICLE_COUNT; i++)
{
    positions[i] = vmath::vec4(random_vector(-10.0f, 10.0f),
                               random_float());
}

glUnmapBuffer(GL_ARRAY_BUFFER);

// Initialization of the velocity buffer - also filled with random vectors
glBindBuffer(GL_ARRAY_BUFFER, velocity_buffer);
glBufferData(GL_ARRAY_BUFFER,
             PARTICLE_COUNT * sizeof(vmath::vec4),
             NULL,
             GL_DYNAMIC_COPY);

vmath::vec4 * velocities = (vmath::vec4 *)
    glMapBufferRange(GL_ARRAY_BUFFER,
                     0,
                     PARTICLE_COUNT * sizeof(vmath::vec4),
                     GL_MAP_WRITE_BIT |
                     GL_MAP_INVALIDATE_BUFFER_BIT);

for (i = 0; i < PARTICLE_COUNT; i++)
{
    velocities[i] = vmath::vec4(random_vector(-0.1f, 0.1f), 0.0f);
}

glUnmapBuffer(GL_ARRAY_BUFFER);
```

The masses of the attractors are also set to random numbers between 0.5 and 1.0. Their positions are initialized to zero, but these will be moved during the rendering loop. Their masses are stored in a variable in the application because, as they are fixed, they need to be restored after each update of the uniform buffer containing the updated positions of the attractors. Finally, the position buffer is attached to a vertex array object so that the particles can be rendered as points.

The rendering loop is quite simple. First, we execute the compute shader with sufficient invocations to update all of the particles. Then, we render all of the particles as points with a single call to **glDrawArrays()**. The shader vertex shader simply transforms the incoming vertex position by a perspective transformation matrix and the fragment shader outputs solid white. The result of rendering the particle system as simple, white points is shown in Figure 12.3.

The initial output of the program is not terribly exciting. While it does demonstrate that the particle simulation is working, the visual complexity of the scene isn't high. To add some interest to the output (this is a graphics API after all), we add some simple shading to the points.

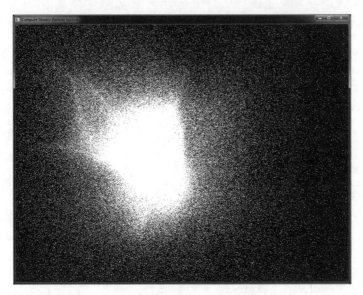

Figure 12.3   Output of the physical simulation program as simple points

In the fragment shader for rendering the points, we first use the age of the point (which is stored in its *w* component) to fade the point from red hot to cool blue as it gets older. Also, we turn on additive blending by enabling GL_BLEND and setting both the source and destination factors to GL_ONE. This causes the points to accumulate in the framebuffer and for more densely populated areas to "glow" due to the number of particles in the region. The fragment shader used to do this is shown in Listing 12.9.

Example 12.9   Particle Simulation Fragment Shader

```
#version 430 core

layout (location = 0) out vec4 color;

// This is derived from the age of the particle read
// by the vertex shader
in float intensity;

void main(void)
{
    // Blend between red-hot and cool-blue based on the
    // age of the particle.
    color = mix(vec4(0.0f, 0.2f, 1.0f, 1.0f),
                vec4(0.2f, 0.05f, 0.0f, 1.0f),
                intensity);
}
```

In our rendering loop, the positions and masses of the attractors are updated before we dispatch the compute shader over the buffers containing the positions and velocities. We then render the particles as points having issued a memory barrier to ensure that the writes performed by the compute shader have been completed. This loop is shown in Example 12.10.

Example 12.10   Particle Simulation Rendering Loop

```
// Update the buffer containing the attractor positions and masses
vmath::vec4 * attractors =
    (vmath::vec4 *)glMapBufferRange(GL_UNIFORM_BUFFER,
                                    0,
                                    32 * sizeof(vmath::vec4),
                                    GL_MAP_WRITE_BIT |
                                    GL_MAP_INVALIDATE_BUFFER_BIT);

int i;

for (i = 0; i < 32; i++)
{
    attractors[i] =
        vmath::vec4(sinf(time * (float)(i + 4) * 7.5f * 20.0f) * 50.0f,
                    cosf(time * (float)(i + 7) * 3.9f * 20.0f) * 50.0f,
                    sinf(time * (float)(i + 3) * 5.3f * 20.0f) *
                        cosf(time * (float)(i + 5) * 9.1f) * 100.0f,
                    attractor_masses[i]);
}

glUnmapBuffer(GL_UNIFORM_BUFFER);

// Activate the compute program and bind the position
// and velocity buffers
glUseProgram(compute_prog);
glBindImageTexture(0, velocity_tbo, 0,
                   GL_FALSE, 0,
                   GL_READ_WRITE, GL_RGBA32F);
glBindImageTexture(1, position_tbo, 0,
                   GL_FALSE, 0,
                   GL_READ_WRITE, GL_RGBA32F);

// Set delta time
glUniform1f(dt_location, delta_time);

// Dispatch the compute shader
glDispatchCompute(PARTICLE_GROUP_COUNT, 1, 1);

// Ensure that writes by the compute shader have completed
glMemoryBarrier(GL_SHADER_IMAGE_ACCESS_BARRIER_BIT);

// Set up our mvp matrix for viewing
vmath::mat4 mvp = vmath::perspective(45.0f, aspect_ratio,
                                     0.1f, 1000.0f) *
```

```
              vmath::translate(0.0f, 0.0f, -60.0f) *
              vmath::rotate(time * 1000.0f,
                    vmath::vec3(0.0f, 1.0f, 0.0f));

// Clear, select the rendering program and draw a full screen quad
glClear(GL_COLOR_BUFFER_BIT | GL_DEPTH_BUFFER_BIT);
glUseProgram(render_prog);
glUniformMatrix4fv(0, 1, GL_FALSE, mvp);
glBindVertexArray(render_vao);
glEnable(GL_BLEND);
glBlendFunc(GL_ONE, GL_ONE);
glDrawArrays(GL_POINTS, 0, PARTICLE_COUNT);
```

Finally, the result of rendering the particle system with the fragment shader
of Example 12.9 and with blending turned on is shown in Figure 12.4.

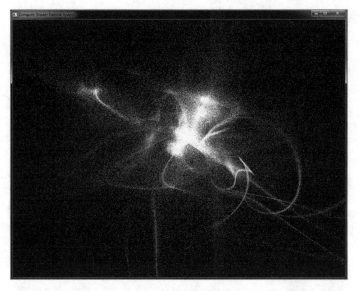

Figure 12.4   Output of the physical simulation program

Image Processing

This example of compute shaders uses them as a means to implement
image processing algorithms. In this case, we implement a simple
edge-detection algorithm by convolving an input image with an
edge-detection filter. The filter chosen is an example of a separable filter. A
separable filter is one that can be applied one dimension at a time in a
multidimensional space to produce a final result. Here, it is is applied to a

two-dimensional image by applying it first in the horizontal dimension and then again in the vertical dimension. The actual kernel is a central difference kernel $\begin{bmatrix} -1 & 0 & 1 \end{bmatrix}$.

To implement this kernel, each invocation of the compute shader produces a single pixel in the output image. It must read from the input image and subtract the samples to either side of the target pixel. Of course, this means that each invocation of the shader must read from the input image twice and that two invocations of the shader will read from the same location. To reduce memory accesses, this implementation uses *shared* variables to store a row of the input image.

Rather than reading the needed input samples directly from the input image, each invocation reads the value of its target pixel from the input image and stores it in an element of a shared array. After all invocations of the shader have read from the input image, the shared array contains a complete copy of the current scanline of the input image—each pixel of that image having been read only once. However, now that the pixels are stored in the shared array, all other invocations in the local workgroup can read from that array to retrieve the pixel values they need at very high speed.

The edge-detection compute shader is shown in Example 12.11.

Example 12.11   Central Difference Edge Detection Compute Shader

```
#version 430 core

// One scanline of the image... 1024 is the minimum maximum
// guaranteed by OpenGL
layout (local_size_x = 1024) in;

// Input and output images
layout (rgba32f, binding = 0) uniform image2D input_image;
layout (rgba32f, binding = 1) uniform image2D output_image;

// Shared memory for the scanline data -- must be the same size
// as (or larger than) as the local workgroup
shared vec4 scanline[1024];

void main(void)
{
    // Get the current position in the image.
    ivec2 pos = ivec2(gl_GlobalInvocationID.xy);

    // Read an input pixel and store it in the shared array
    scanline[pos.x] = imageLoad(input_image, pos);

    // Ensure that all other invocations have reached this point
    // and written their shared data by calling barrier()
```

```
        barrier();

        // Compute our result and write it back to the image
        vec4 result = scanline[min(pos.x + 1, 1023)] -
                      scanline[max(pos.x - 1, 0)];
        imageStore(output_image, pos.yx, result);
}
```

The image processing shader of Example 12.11 uses a one-dimensional local workgroup size of 1024 pixels (which is the largest workgroup size that is guaranteed to be supported by an OpenGL implementation). This places an upper bound on the width or height of the image of 1024 pixels. While this is sufficient for this rather simple example, a more complex approach would be required to implement larger filters or operate on larger images.

The global invocation ID is converted to a signed integer vector and is used to read from the input image. The result is written into the scanline shared variable. Then the shader calls **barrier()**. This is to ensure that all of the invocations in the local workgroup have reached this point in the shader. Next, the shader takes the difference between the pixels to the left and the right of the target pixel. These values have been placed into the shared array by the invocations logically to the left and right of the current invocation. The resulting difference is placed into the output image.

Another thing to note about this shader is that when it stores the resulting pixel, it transposes the coordinates of the output pixel, effectively writing in a vertical line down the image. This has the effect of transposing the image. An alternative is to read from the input image in vertical strips and write horizontally. The idea behind this is that the same shader can be used for both passes of the separable filter—the second pass re-transposing the already transposed intermediate image, restoring it to its original orientation.

The code to invoke the compute shader is shown in Example 12.12.

Example 12.12   Dispatching the Image Processing Compute Shader

```
// Activate the compute program...
glUseProgram(compute_prog);

// Bind the source image as input and the intermediate
// image as output
glBindImageTexture(0, input_image, 0,
                   GL_FALSE, 0,
                   GL_READ_ONLY, GL_RGBA32F);
glBindImageTexture(1, intermediate_image, 0,
                   GL_FALSE, 0, GL_WRITE_ONLY,
                   GL_RGBA32F);

// Dispatch the horizontal pass
```

```
glDispatchCompute(1, 1024, 1);

// Issue a memory barrier between the passes
glMemoryBarrier(GL_SHADER_IMAGE_ACCESS_BARRIER_BIT);

// Now bind the intermediate image as input and the final
// image for output
glBindImageTexture(0, intermediate_image, 0,
                   GL_FALSE, 0,
                   GL_READ_ONLY, GL_RGBA32F);
glBindImageTexture(1, output_image, 0,
                   GL_FALSE, 0,
                   GL_WRITE_ONLY, GL_RGBA32F);

// Dispatch the vertical pass
glDispatchCompute(1, 1024, 1);
```

Figure 12.5 shows the original input image[2] at the top and the resulting output image at the bottom. The edges are clearly visible in the output image.

The image-processing example shader includes a call to `barrier` after all of the input image data has been read into the shared variable `scanline`. This ensures that all of the invocations in the local workgroup (including the current invocation's neighbors) have completed the read from the input image and have written the result into the shared variable. Without the barrier, it is possible to suffer from a *race condition* where some invocations of the shader will read from the shared variable before the adjacent invocations have completed their writes into it. The result can be sparkling corruption in the output image.

Figure 12.6 shows the result of applying this shader with the call to `barrier` removed. A horizontal and vertical grid-like pattern of seemingly random pixels is visible. This is due to some invocations of the shader receiving stale or uninitialized data because they move ahead of their neighbors within the local workgroup. The reason that the corruption appears as a grid-like pattern is that the graphics processor used to generate this example processes a number of invocations in lockstep and therefore those invocations cannot get out of sync with each other. However, the local workgroup is broken up into a number of these subgroups, and they *can* get ahead of each other. Therefore, we see corrupted pixels produced by the invocations that happen to be executed by the first and last members of the subgroups. If the number of invocations working in lockstep were different then the spacing of the grid pattern would change accordingly.

---

2. This image is a picture of the Martian surface as seen from the Curiosity rover and was obtained from NASA's Web site in August of 2012. NASA does not endorse this simple image processing example—they have much better ones.

Figure 12.5   Image processing
(Input image (top) and resulting output image (bottom), generated by the image-processing compute-shader example.)

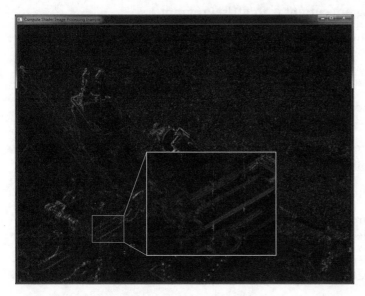

Figure 12.6   Image processing artifacts
(Output of the image processing example, without barriers, showing artifacts.)

Chapter Summary

In this chapter, you have read an introduction to compute shaders. As they
are not tied to a specific part of the traditional graphics pipeline and have
no fixed intended use, the amount that could be written about compute
shaders is enormous. Instead, we have covered the basics and provided a
couple of examples that should demonstrate how compute shaders may be
used to perform the nongraphics parts of your graphics applications.

Compute Shader Redux

To use a compute shader in your program:

- Create a compute shader with **glCreateShader()** using the type
  GL_COMPUTE_SHADER.

- Set the shader source with **glShaderSource()** and compile it with
  glCompileShader().

- Attach it to a program object with **glAttachShader()** and link it with
  glLinkProgram().

- Make the program current with **glUseProgram()**.

- Launch compute workloads with **glDispatchCompute()** or **glDispatchComputeIndirect()**.

In your compute shader:

- Specify the local workgroup size using the `local_size_x`, `local_size_y` and `local_size_z` input layout qualifiers.

- Read and write memory using buffer or image variables, or by updating the values of atomic counters.

The special built-in variables available to a compute shader are as follows:

- `gl_WorkGroupSize` is a constant containing the three-dimensional local size as declared by the input layout qualifiers.

- `gl_NumWorkGroups` is a copy of the global workgroup count as passed to the **glDispatchCompute()** or **glDispatchCompute()** function.

- `gl_LocalInvocationID` is the coordinate of the current shader invocation within the local workgroup.

- `gl_WorkGroupID` is the coordinate of the local workgroup within the global workgroup.

- `gl_GlobalInvocationID` is the coordinate of the current shader invocation within the global workgroup.

- `gl_LocalInvocationIndex` is a flattened version of `gl_LocalInvocationID`.

Compute Shader Best Practices

The following are a handful of tips for making effective use of compute shaders. By following this advice, your compute shaders are more likely to perform well and work correctly on a wide range of hardware.

Choose the Right Workgroup Size

Choose a local workgroup size that is appropriate for the workload you need to process. Choosing a size that is too large may not allow you to fit everything you need into `shared` variables. On the other hand, choosing a size that is too small may reduce efficiency, depending on the architecture of the graphics processor.

Use Barriers

Remember to insert control flow and memory barriers before attempting to communicate between compute shader invocations. If you leave out memory barriers, you open your application up to the effects of race conditions. It may appear to work on one machine but could produce corrupted data on others.

Use Shared Variables

Make effective use of `shared` variables. Try to structure your workload into blocks—especially if it is memory intensive and multiple invocations will read the same memory locations. Read blocks of data into `shared` variables, issue a barrier, and then operate on the data in the `shared` variable. Write the results back to memory at the end of the shader. Ideally, each memory location accessed by an invocation will be read exactly once and written exactly once.

Do Other Things While Your Compute Shader Runs

If you can, insert graphics work (or even more compute work) between producing data with a compute shader and consuming that data in a graphics shader. Not doing this will force the compute shader to complete execution before the graphics shader can begin execution. By placing unrelated work between the compute shader producer and the graphics shader consumer, that work may be overlapped, improving overall performance.

Basics of GLUT: The OpenGL Utility Toolkit

In this text, we used the OpenGL Utility Toolkit (GLUT) as a simple, cross-platform application framework to simplify our examples.

The two versions of GLUT in circulation are as follows:

- Freeglut, written by Pawel W. Olszta with contributions from Andreas Umbach and Steve Baker, is the most up-to-date version and the one that we've used in this book.

- The original version was written by Mark Kilgard many years ago. This version hasn't been kept up to date with respect to recent changes. However, its Version 3.7 (which is the most recent) is the foundation of Apple Computer's Mac OS X 10.8 (aka "Mountain Lion") GLUT framework.

This appendix describes a subset of functions available in the Freeglut version.

GLUT makes the process of creating an OpenGL application simple, since in its most basic form, only four steps are required to get the application going.

1. Initialize the GLUT library

2. Create a GLUT window

3. Register the **display()** callback

4. Enter GLUT's main loop

In this appendix, we explain those steps and expand on other options that the GLUT library makes available. For complete details on Freeglut (which is the version we recommend), please visit their Web site http://freeglut.sourceforge.net/.

This appendix contains the following major sections:

- "Initializing and Creating a Window"

- "Accessing Functions"

- "Handling Window and Input Events"

- "Managing a Background Process"

- "Running the Program"

Initializing and Creating a Window

To use GLUT, you first need to initialize the GLUT library by calling **glutInit()**. The function also parses any relevant command-line options you pass for specifying GLUT options.

---

void **glutInit**(int *argc*, char ****argv*);

glutInit() should be called before any other GLUT routine because it initializes the GLUT library. **glutInit()** will also process command-line options, but the specific options are window system dependent. For many windowing systems, command-line options like `-iconic`, `-geometry`, and `-display` are examples of options you might set that are processed by **glutInit()**.

Following that, you'll usually call **glutInitDisplayMode()** to configure the characteristics of the window, like having a depth or stencil buffer, its pixel type, or controlling multisampling. Likewise, you'll use **glutInitContextVersion()**, **glutInitContextProfile()**, and **glutInitContextFlags()** to configure the type of OpenGL implementation your application requires. Additionally, you might call **glutInitWindowSize()** or **glutInitWindowPosition()** to set the geometry of the window. To finally open your configured window, call **glutCreateWindow()** to open the window.

void **glutInitDisplayMode**(unsigned int *mode*);

Specifies a display mode for windows created when **glutCreateWindow**() is called. You can specify that the window have an associated depth, stencil, or be an RGB or RGBA window. The *mode* argument is a bitwise OR combination of GLUT_RGB, GLUT_RGBA, GLUT_DOUBLE, GLUT_ALPHA, GLUT_DEPTH, GLUT_STENCIL, GLUT_MULTISAMPLE, or GLUT_STEREO. Additionally, if you're using the compatibility profile, you can include the following options: GLUT_INDEX (for color-index mode), GLUT_SINGLE (for single-buffered rendering), GLUT_ACCUM (to use the accumulation buffer), and GLUT_LUMINANCE (for luminance [greyscale] only rendering).

The default mode is the bitwise OR of GLUT_INDEX, GLUT_SINGLE, and GLUT_DEPTH (which relies on a compatibility mode context).

void **glutInitContextVersion**(int *majorVersion*, int *minorVersion*);

Specifies the major and minor versions of the OpenGL implementation that you want a context created for. To use OpenGL Version 3.0 or greater, you need to call this routine before calling **glutCreateWindow**(), due to the different context creation semantics introduced by OpenGL Version 3.0.

If you don't specify a context version, a compatibility profile version of the most recent OpenGL version will be created for you.

void **glutInitContextProfile**(int *profile*);

Specifies the context profile you want created: core or compatibility. To specify a core profile (as we did in this manual), use GLUT_CORE_PROFILE; for a compatibility profile, use GLUT_COMPATIBILITY_PROFILE.

void **glutInitContextFlags**(int *flags*);

Specifies any attribute flags to be used in the creation of the OpenGL context. The *flags* argument is a bitwise OR of the following values: GLUT_DEBUG to specify a context with debug facilities enabled or

GLUT_FORWARD_COMPATIBLE to specify a testing context for forward application compatibility.

void **glutInitWindowSize**(int *width*, int *height*);
void **glutInitWindowPosition**(int *x*, int *y*);

Request windows created by **glutCreateWindow()** to have an initial size and position. The arguments (x, y) indicate the location of a corner of the window, relative to the entire display. The parameters *width* and *height* indicate the window's size (in pixels). The initial window size and position are hints and may be overridden by other requests.

int **glutCreateWindow**(char **name*);

Opens a window with previously set characteristics (display mode, width, height, etc.). The string *name* may appear in the title bar if your window system does that sort of thing. The window is not initially displayed until **glutMainLoop()** is entered, so do not render into the window until then.

The value returned is a unique integer identifier for the window. This identifier can be used for controlling and rendering to multiple windows (each with an OpenGL rendering context) from the same application.

Accessing Functions

Depending on the operating system you're using, there may be differences in the compilation (or specifically, the program-linking phase) libraries, and the libraries used by the application when it runs. For example, in Microsoft Windows, your application will link with `opengl32.lib` but execute using `opengl32.dll` (along with other libraries). In this particular case (and also in other operating systems), the set of functions available in the link-time library differs from those available in the run-time library. To solve this problem, each window system that supports OpenGL has a mechanism for obtaining function pointers at run time. GLUT abstracts away the window–system-specific functions, and presents **glutGetProcAddress()**, which will call the window-specific function to return a function address for your use.

> void (*GLUTproc)() **glutGetProcAddress**(const char *procName);
>
> Retrieves the function address associated with *procName* or returns NULL
> if *procName* names a function that's not supported in the OpenGL
> implementation.

Note: In our examples, you may notice we don't use
glutGetProcAddress() explicitly. Instead, we use GLEW, the
OpenGL Extension Wrangler library, which further abstracts away
all of this function pointer inconvenience and allows you to just
write OpenGL routines.

Handling Window and Input Events

After the window is created, but before you enter the main loop, you
should register callback functions using the following routines. Callback
functions are routines you write that you present to GLUT as a function
pointer, and that GLUT will call when the right circumstances occur. You
will specify certain callback functions once, and never change them
throughout the execution of your program. Others, however, you may
specify when a certain event occurs (like when a mouse button is pressed),
and disable that callback function by specifying NULL (or zero) as the new
callback function.

The most important routine is **glutDisplayFunc()**, which is where you will
do all of your rendering in your application. It's required for every GLUT
program.

> void **glutDisplayFunc**(void (*func)(void));
>
> Specifies the function to be called whenever the contents of the window
> need to be redrawn. The contents of the window will need to be drawn
> when the window is initially opened, and likely when the window is
> raised above other windows and previously obscured areas are exposed,
> or when **glutPostRedisplay()** is explicitly called.

Likewise, when your window changes geometry or position, you'll
probably need to update things like the window's viewport and projection

transformation. The **glutReshapeFunc()** callback is the right place to make those updates.

---

void **glutReshapeFunc**(void (*func*)(int *width*, int *height*));

Specifies the function that's called whenever the window is resized or moved. The argument *func* is a pointer to a function that expects two arguments, the new width and height of the window. Typically, *func* calls **glViewport()**, so that the display is clipped to the new size and it redefines the projection matrix so that the aspect ratio of the projected image matches the viewport, avoiding aspect-ratio distortion. If **glutReshapeFunc()** isn't called or is deregistered by passing NULL, a default reshape function is called, which calls **glViewport**(0, 0, width, height).

Responding to user input is crucial in interactive graphics applications. The most common forms of input are keyboard and mouse events. GLUT makes it easy to process those events as well, using the same callback mechanism. **glutKeyboardFunc()**, as the name suggests, is called when a user presses a keyboard key.

---

void **glutKeyboardFunc**(void (*func*)(unsigned char *key*, int *x*, int *y*));

Specifies the function, *func*, that's called when a key that generates an ASCII character is pressed. The *key* callback parameter is the generated ASCII value. The *x* and *y* callback parameters indicate the location of the mouse (in window-relative coordinates) when the key was pressed.

If, however, you're interested when a key is released, use **glutKeyboardUpFunc()**.

---

void **glutKeyboardUpFunc**(void (*func*)(unsigned char *key*, int *x*, int *y*));

Specifies the function, *func*, that's called when a key that generates an ASCII character is released. The *key* callback parameter is the generated ASCII value. The *x* and *y* callback parameters indicate the location of the mouse (in window-relative coordinates) when the key was pressed.

Processing mouse input events is more varied. For instance, does your application require that a mouse button be pressed to have the application respond to events? Or are you only interested in knowing if the mouse if moving, regardless of the button state. There are different mouse-event processing routines for these situations.

---

void **glutMouseFunc**(void (*func)(int *button,* int *state,* int *x,* int *y*));

Specifies the function, *func,* that's called when a mouse button is pressed or released. The *button* callback parameter is GLUT_LEFT_BUTTON, GLUT_MIDDLE_BUTTON, or GLUT_RIGHT_BUTTON. The *state* callback parameter is either GLUT_UP or GLUT_DOWN, depending on whether the mouse has been released or pressed. The *x* and *y* callback parameters indicate the location (in window-relative coordinates) of the mouse when the event occurred.

---

void **glutMotionFunc**(void (*func)(int *x,* int *y*));

Specifies the function, *func,* that's called when the mouse pointer moves within the window while one or more mouse buttons are pressed. The *x* and *y* callback parameters indicate the location (in window-relative coordinates) of the mouse when the event occurred.

Similar is **glutPassiveMotionEvent()**, which reports the mouse's position regardless of the state of the mouse's buttons.

---

void **glutPassiveMotionFunc**(void (*func)(int *x,* int *y*));

Specifies the function, *func,* that's called when the mouse pointer moves within the window. The *x* and *y* callback parameters indicate the location (in window-relative coordinates) of the mouse when the event occurred.

In order to keep interactive programs responding rapidly to lots of input events, it's best to process all input events and then update your image by rendering. Generally speaking, it takes much less time to process an input event than it does to render your scene. As such, the GLUT event loop will continue to retrieve events and call your application's callback functions while there are events to process. How, though, do you know when you're completed processing input events and it's time to render? That's what **glutPostRedisplay()** is for. Place a call to it as the last operation any input-processing callback. When GLUT detects that there are no more input events, it will call the display callback (the one set with **glutDisplayFunc()**).

---

void **glutPostRedisplay**(void);

Marks the current window as needing to be redrawn. At the next opportunity, the callback function registered by **glutDisplayFunc()** will be called.

Managing a Background Process

You can specify a function to be executed if no other events are pending—for example, when the event loop would otherwise be idle—with **glutIdleFunc()**. This is particularly useful for continuous animation or other background processing.

---

void **glutIdleFunc**(void (*_func_)(void));

Specifies the function, _func_, to be executed if no other events are pending. If NULL (zero) is passed in, execution of _func_ is disabled.

Running the Program

After all the setup is completed, GLUT programs enter an event-processing loop, **glutMainLoop()**.

---

void **glutMainLoop**(void);

Enters the GLUT-processing loop, never to return. Registered callback functions will be called when the corresponding events instigate them.

Note: For those of you familiar with previous versions of GLUT (regardless of whether it's the Freeglut version or the original), various features—like menus and shapes, for example—will not work when you ask for a core profile, as they use deprecated features. If you need those features, the simplest approach is to ask for a compatibility profile.

OpenGL ES and WebGL

While the OpenGL API is great for many computer graphics applications, under certain circumstances, it may not be the best solution, which is why the OpenGL API has spawned two other APIs. The first is OpenGL ES, where the "ES" stands for "Embedded Subsystem", and was crafted from the "desktop" version of OpenGL for use in embedded devices like mobile phones, Internet tablets, televisions, and other devices with color screens, but limited system resources. The other API is WebGL, which enables OpenGL-style rendering within most Web browsers using the JavaScript Web programming language.

This appendix provides an overview of the OpenGL ES and WebGL, highlighting the differences between OpenGL as described throughout the rest of this book, and these derivative versions. It contains the following major sections:

- "OpenGL ES"
- "WebGL"

OpenGL ES

OpenGL ES is developed to meet the need of early embedded devices like mobile phones and set-top boxes. The original version, OpenGL ES Version 1.0 was derived from OpenGL Version 1.3, and was quickly expanded to OpenGL ES Version 1.1, which is based on OpenGL Version 1.5, and released in April of 2007. This version reached much popularity in original mobile phones with fixed-function graphics hardware.

As mobile graphics hardware became more capable, principally by programmable shaders, a new version of OpenGL ES was required, and OpenGL ES Version 2.0—based on OpenGL Version 2.0—was originally specified in January of 2008. Keeping with its minimalist mantra of supporting only a single method for processing graphics, the API switched to an entirely shader-based rendering pipeline using both vertex and fragment shaders (which also broke source-code compatibility with OpenGL ES Version 1.1). OpenGL ES Version 2.0 has become very influential in dictating hardware requirements for many different types of devices. With the release of OpenGL Version 4.1, all functionality for OpenGL ES Version 2.0 was added to OpenGL, making OpenGL ES a proper subset of OpenGL's functionality.

At SIGGRAPH 2012, OpenGL ES Version 3.0 was announced, expanding on the rendering capabilities of OpenGL ES (however, not adding any additional programmable shader stages like geometry or tessellation shading). This version did retain backwards compatibility with OpenGL ES Version 2.0, with most of the new features focusing on increased shader programmabilty (leveraging sampler objects, for example), instanced rendering and transform feedback, and extended pixel and framebuffer formats.

As OpenGL ES is a subset of OpenGL in terms of both features and functions, everything you've read in this text applies in terms of techniques it supports. In fact, perhaps the largest noticeable difference between an OpenGL ES program and that of OpenGL core profile may be in creating a window for rendering. In most systems (but notably not Apple's iOS), OpenGL ES is connected to the system's windowing system by a binding layer named EGL. EGL was patterned after the X Window System's binding layer, GLX (as described in Appendix F).

We now provide a brief example of creating an OpenGL ES Version 2.0 context (since, at the time of this writing, there are no OpenGL ES Version 3.0 capable devices available). Example B.1 demonstrates creating an RGB-capable rendering context with a depth buffer for use in a window.

Example B.1   An Example of Creating an OpenGL ES Version 2.0
Rendering Context

```
EGLBoolean initializeWindow(EGLNativeWindow nativeWindow)
{
    const EGLint  configAttribs[] = {
        EGL_RENDER_TYPE, EGL_WINDOW_BIT,
        EGL_RED_SIZE, 8,
        EGL_GREEN_SIZE, 8,
        EGL_BLUE_SIZE, 8,
        EGL_DEPTH_SIZE, 24,
        EGL_NONE
    };

    const EGLint  contextAttribs[] = {
        EGL_CONTEXT_CLIENT_VERSION, 2,
        EGL_NONE
    };

    EGLDisplay dpy;

    dpy = eglGetNativeDispay(EGL_DEFAULT_DISPLAY);

    if (dpy == EGL_NO_DISPLAY) { return EGL_FALSE; }

    EGLint major, minor;
    if (!eglInitialize(dpy, &major, &minor)) { return EGL_FALSE;

    EGLConfig  config;
    EGLint  numConfigs;
    if (!eglChooseConfig(dpy, configAttribs, &config, 1, &numConfigs)) {
        return EGL_FALSE;
    }

    EGLSurface window;
    window = eglCreateWindowSurface(dpy, config, nativeWindow, NULL);

    if (window == EGL_NO_SURFACE) { return EGL_FALSE; }

    EGLContext context;
    context = eglCreateContext(dpy, config, EGL_NO_CONTEXT,
        contextAttribs);

    if (context == EGL_NO_CONTEXT) { return EGL_FALSE; }
    if (!eglMakeCurrent(dpy, window, window, context)) {
        return EGL_FALSE;
    }

    return EGL_TRUE;
}
```

WebGL

WebGL takes OpenGL (or specifically, OpenGL ES Version 2.0) to the Internet by adding high-performance, 3D rendering within HTML5's Canvas element. Virtually all functions from OpenGL ES Version 2.0 are available in their exact form, except for small changes necessitated because of its JavaScript interface.

This section provides a brief introduction to WebGL through a simple example, which works natively in all modern Web browsers (except Microsoft's Internet Explorer, which requires a plug-in for support). Our example focuses exclusively on rendering; event processing and user interaction aren't discussed.

Setting up WebGL within an HTML5 page

To provide a "window" for WebGL to use for rendering, you first create an HTML5 Canvas element within your Web page. Example B.2 demonstrates creating a 512 × 512-sized Canvas with a blue background. In the case that the browser doesn't support WebGL, a simple page stating the browser doesn't support Canvas elements is shown. In the example, we name the Canvas *gl-canvas* by setting its *id* attribute. We'll use its *id* later when we initialize WebGL.

Example B.2   Creating an HTML5 Canvas Element

```
<html>
<style type="text/css">
  canvas { background: blue; }
</style>
<body>
<canvas id="gl-canvas" width="512" height="512">
  Oops ... your browser doesn't support HTML5's Canvas elements!
</canvas>
</body>
</html>
```

Note: Example B.2 uses a cascading style sheet for specifying the Canvas element's background color.

Assuming this worked in your browser, we can now continue to the next step: creating a WebGL context. There are multiple ways to do this; however, we'll use a utility function defined in a JavaScript file hosted by the Khronos Group from their Web site, https://www.khronos.org/registry/webgl/sdk/demos/common/webgl-utils.js. You will likely find it convenient to include this JavaScript file in your WebGL applications.[1] It includes the package WebGLUtils and its method **setupWebGL()**, which makes it easy to enable WebGL on an HTML5 Canvas. Example B.3 expands on the previous example and handles setting up a WebGL context that works in all supported Web browsers. The return value from **setupWebGL()** is a JavaScript object containing methods for all OpenGL functions supported in WebGL.

Example B.3   Creating an HTML5 Canvas Element that Supports WebGL

```
<html>
<style type="text/css">
  canvas { background: blue; }
</style>

<script type="text/javascript"
src="https://www.khronos.org/registry/webgl/sdk/demos/common/webgl-utils.js">
</script>

<script type="text/javascript">
var canvas;
var gl;

window.onload = init;

function init() {
    canvas = document.getElementById("gl-canvas");

    gl = WebGLUtils.setupWebGL(canvas);
    if (!gl) { alert("WebGL isn't available"); }

    gl.viewport(0, 0, canvas.width, canvas.height);
    gl.clearColor(1.0, 0.0, 0.0, 1.0);
    gl.clear(gl.COLOR_BUFFER_BIT);
}
</script>

<body>
<canvas id="gl-canvas" width="512" height="512">
  Oops ... your browser doesn't support HTML5's Canvas elements!
</canvas>
</body>
</html>
```

Example B.3 specifies an **init()** function that is executed when the page loads (specified by the line `window.onload = init`). Our **init()** function retrieves our *gl-canvas* Canvas id, passes it to **setupWebGL()**, which will return a WebGL object that we can use if initialization was successful; or

---

1. This file can also be hosted from the Web server serving the pages composing the WebGL application.

false otherwise, which we use to emit an error message. Assuming WebGL is available, we set up some WebGL state, and clear the window—to red now. Once WebGL takes over the Canvas, all of its contents are controlled by WebGL.

Now that we know WebGL is supported, we'll expand our example by initializing the required shaders, setting up vertex buffers, and finally rendering.

Initializing Shaders in WebGL

OpenGL ES Version 2.0—and therefore WebGL—is a shader-based API, like OpenGL, requiring every application to use vertex and fragment shaders for its rendering. As such, you encounter the same requirement of loading shaders as you saw in OpenGL.

To include vertex and fragment shaders in a WebGL application, it's simplest to include the shader as a script in the HTML page.[2] A shader within an HTML page needs to be identified correctly. There are two mime-types associated with WebGL shaders, as shown in Table B.1.

Table B.1   Type Strings for WebGL Shaders

`<script>` Tag Type	Shader Type
x-shader/x-vertex	Vertex
x-shader/x-fragment	Fragment

For our WebGL application, Example B.4 shows our main HTML page including the shader sources. You'll also notice that we include two more JavaScript files, which are as follows:

- demo.js, which includes the JavaScript implementation of our application (including the final version of our **init()** routine).

- InitShaders.js, which is a helper function for loading shaders similar to our **LoadShaders()** routine.

Example B.4   Our WebGL Applications Main HTML Page

```
<html>
<style type="text/css">
    canvas { background: blue; }
</style>
```

2. It is possible to store the shader in a separate file from the original HTML page, but the mechanism is very cumbersome with current Web technology. We've opted for the simple approach here.

```
<script id="vertex-shader" type="x-shader/x-vertex">
attribute vec4   vPos;
attribute vec2   vTexCoord;
uniform float uFrame;   // Frame number
varying vec2   texCoord;

void
main()
{
    float angle = radians(uFrame);
    float c = cos(angle);
    float s = sin(angle);

    mat4   m = mat4(1.0);

    m[0][0] = c;
    m[0][1] = s;
    m[1][1] = c;
    m[1][0] = -s;

    texCoord = vTexCoord;
    gl_Position = m * vPos;
}
</script>

<script id="fragment-shader" type="x-shader/x-fragment">
#ifdef GL_ES
precision highp float;
#endif

uniform sampler2D uTexture;
varying vec2      texCoord;

void
main()
{
    gl_FragColor = texture2D(uTexture, texCoord);
}
</script>

<script type="text/javascript"
<src="http://www.khronos.org/registry/webgl/sdk/demos/common/webgl-utils.js">
</script>
<script type="text/javascript" src="InitShaders.js"></script>
<script type="text/javascript" src="demo.js"></script>

<body>
<canvas id="gl-canvas" width="512" height="512"
Oops ... your browser doesn't support the HTML5 canvas element
</canvas>
</body>
</html>
```

To simplify compiling and linking our shaders in WebGL, we created a
routine similar to **LoadShaders()** that we've used in the book. Here, we call

it **InitShaders()**, since there are no files to load; shaders are defined in the
HTML source for the page. In order to organize our code better, we created
a JavaScript file named InitShaders.js to store the code.

Example B.5   Our WebGL Shader Loader: InitShaders.js

```
//
//  InitShaders.js
//

function InitShaders(gl, vertexShaderId, fragmentShaderId)
{
    var vertShdr;
    var fragShdr;

    var vertElem = document.getElementById(vertexShaderId);
    if (!vertElem) {
        alert("Unable to load vertex shader " + vertexShaderId);
        return -1;
    }
    else {
        vertShdr = gl.createShader(gl.VERTEX_SHADER);
        gl.shaderSource(vertShdr, vertElem.text);
        gl.compileShader(vertShdr);
        if (!gl.getShaderParameter(vertShdr, gl.COMPILE_STATUS)) {
            var msg = "Vertex shader failed to compile."
                + "The error log is:"
          + "<pre>" + gl.getShaderInfoLog(vertShdr) + "</pre>";
            alert(msg);
            return -1;
        }
    }

    var fragElem = document.getElementById(fragmentShaderId);
    if (!fragElem) {
        alert("Unable to load vertex shader " + fragmentShaderId);
        return -1;
    }
    else {
        fragShdr = gl.createShader(gl.FRAGMENT_SHADER);
        gl.shaderSource(fragShdr, fragElem.text);
        gl.compileShader(fragShdr);
        if (!gl.getShaderParameter(fragShdr, gl.COMPILE_STATUS)) {
            var msg = "Fragment shader failed to compile. "
                + "The error log is:"
          + "<pre>" + gl.getShaderInfoLog(fragShdr) + "</pre>";

            alert(msg);
            return -1;
        }
    }

    var program = gl.createProgram();
    gl.attachShader(program, vertShdr);
```

```
    gl.attachShader(program, fragShdr);
    gl.linkProgram(program);

    if (!gl.getProgramParameter(program, gl.LINK_STATUS)) {
        var msg = "Shader program failed to link."
            + "The error log is:"
            + "<pre>" + gl.getProgramInfoLog(program) + "</pre>";
        alert(msg);
        return -1;
    }

    return program;
}
```

While **InitShaders()** is JavaScript, most of it should look recognizable. The major difference here is that compared to **LoadShaders()**, which took file names for our vertex and fragment shaders, **InitShaders()** takes HTML element ids (*vertex-shader* and *fragment-shader* in our example). The routine returns a program name that can be passed into the JavaScript equivalent of **glUseProgram()**.

Example B.6   Loading WebGL Shaders Using **InitShaders()**

```
var program = InitShaders(gl, "vertex-shader", "fragment-shader");
gl.useProgram(program);
```

Armed with a method for compiling and linking our shaders, we can move on to initializing our graphics data, loading textures, and completing the setup of the rest of our WebGL application.

Initializing Vertex Data in WebGL

One major addition to JavaScript that came from WebGL were *typed arrays*, which extend the concept of a JavaScript array but match the type support required for OpenGL-style rendering. Several types of typed arrays are listed in Table B.2.

Table B.2   WebGL Typed Arrays

Array Type	C Type
Int8Array	signed char
Uint8Array	unsigned char
Uint8ClampedArray	unsigned char
Int16Array	signed short
Uint16Array	unsigned short
Int32Array	signed int
Uint32Array	unsigned int
Float32Array	float
Float64Array	double

You first allocate and populate (both of which you can do in a single operation) a typed array to store your vertex data. After that, setting up your VBOs is identical to what you've done in OpenGL. We show our initialization in Example B.7.

Example B.7   Initializing Vertex Buffers in WebGL

```
var vertices = {};
vertices.data = new Float32Array(
[
  -0.5,  -0.5,
   0.5,  -0.5,
   0.5,   0.5,
  -0.5,   0.5
]);

vertices.bufferId = gl.createBuffer();
gl.bindBuffer(gl.ARRAY_BUFFER, vertices.bufferId);
gl.bufferData(gl.ARRAY_BUFFER, vertices.data, gl.STATIC_DRAW);
var vPos = gl.getAttribLocation(program, "vPos");
gl.vertexAttribPointer(vPos, 2, gl.FLOAT, false, 0, 0);
gl.enableVertexAttribArray(vPos);
```

Using Texture Maps in WebGL

Using textures in WebGL is also the same as in OpenGL, but handling the loading and setup is much simpler, since HTML lends a helping hand. In fact, loading a texture from a file is a one-line operation. In our demo, we use a single texture named OpenGL-logo.png.

```
var image = new Image();
image.src = "OpenGL-logo.png";
```

Yes; that's all there is to loading the pixels from the image into a variable. However, HTML pages load asynchronously, so knowing when the image file has been received and loaded needs to be handled in a callback. Fortunately, JavaScript has a ready-made method in the Image class for handling that situation: **onload()**. We can specify the **onload()** method as follows:

```
image.onload = function () {
    configureTexture(image);
    render();
}
```

The **onload()** method defined above will be called once our image has been completely loaded and ready for use by WebGL. We group all of our texture-initialization code in a local function: `configureTexture`.

```
function configureTexture(image) {
    texture = gl.createTexture();
```

```
        gl.activeTexture(gl.TEXTURE0);
        gl.bindTexture(gl.TEXTURE_2D, texture);
        gl.pixelStorei(gl.UNPACK_FLIP_Y_WEBGL, true);
        gl.texImage2D(gl.TEXTURE_2D, 0, gl.RGB, gl.RGB, gl.UNSIGNED_BYTE,
                      image);
        gl.generateMipmap(gl.TEXTURE_2D);
        gl.texParameteri(gl.TEXTURE_2D, gl.TEXTURE_MIN_FILTER,
                         gl.NEAREST_MIPMAP_LINEAR);
        gl.texParameteri(gl.TEXTURE_2D, gl.TEXTURE_MAG_FILTER, gl.NEAREST);
    }
```

The code sequence in `configureTexture` should look very similar to
what was presented in Chapter 6, "Textures". The one notable addition is
the WebGL extension to **glPixelStore*()** for flipping image data. The
WebGL token UNPACK_FLIP_Y_WEBGL will orient the image data to
match what WebGL is expecting.

Note: As with OpenGL ES Version 2.0, WebGL only supports
power-of-two textures.

Having covered the important parts of our demo.js, we now show the file
in its entirety, and the resulting image.

Example B.8   Our demo.js WebGL Application

```
var canvas;
var gl;
var texture;
var uFrame;   // vertex shader angle uniform variable

window.onload = init;

function CheckError(msg)   {
    var error = gl.getError();
    if (error != 0) {
        var errMsg = "OpenGL error: " + error.toString(16);

        if (msg) { errMsg = msg + "\n" + errMsg; }
        alert(errMsg);
    }
}

function configureTexture(image) {
    texture = gl.createTexture();
    gl.activeTexture(gl.TEXTURE0);
    gl.bindTexture(gl.TEXTURE_2D, texture);
    gl.pixelStorei(gl.UNPACK_FLIP_Y_WEBGL, true);
    gl.texImage2D(gl.TEXTURE_2D, 0, gl.RGB, gl.RGB, gl.UNSIGNED_BYTE,
                  image);
    gl.generateMipmap(gl.TEXTURE_2D);
    gl.texParameteri(gl.TEXTURE_2D, gl.TEXTURE_MIN_FILTER,
                     gl.NEAREST_MIPMAP_LINEAR);
    gl.texParameteri(gl.TEXTURE_2D, gl.TEXTURE_MAG_FILTER, gl.NEAREST);
```

```
    }

    function init() {
        canvas = document.getElementById("gl-canvas");

        gl = WebGLUtils.setupWebGL(canvas);
        if (!gl) { alert("WebGL isn't available"); }

        gl.viewport(0, 0, canvas.width, canvas.height);
        gl.clearColor(1.0, 0.0, 0.0, 1.0);

        //
        //  Load shaders and initialize attribute buffers
        //
        var program = InitShaders(gl, "vertex-shader", "fragment-shader");
        gl.useProgram(program);

        var vertices = {};
        vertices.data = new Float32Array(
            [
                -0.5, -0.5,
                 0.5, -0.5,
                 0.5,  0.5,
                -0.5,  0.5
            ]);

        vertices.bufferId = gl.createBuffer();
        gl.bindBuffer(gl.ARRAY_BUFFER, vertices.bufferId);
        gl.bufferData(gl.ARRAY_BUFFER, vertices.data, gl.STATIC_DRAW);
        var vPos = gl.getAttribLocation(program, "vPos");
        gl.vertexAttribPointer(vPos, 2, gl.FLOAT, false, 0, 0);
        gl.enableVertexAttribArray(vPos);

        var texCoords = {};
        texCoords.data = new Float32Array(
            [
                0.0, 0.0,
                1.0, 0.0,
                1.0, 1.0,
                0.0, 1.0
            ]);

        texCoords.bufferId = gl.createBuffer();
        gl.bindBuffer(gl.ARRAY_BUFFER, texCoords.bufferId);
        gl.bufferData(gl.ARRAY_BUFFER, texCoords.data, gl.STATIC_DRAW);
        var vTexCoord = gl.getAttribLocation(program, "vTexCoord");
        gl.vertexAttribPointer(vTexCoord, 2, gl.FLOAT, false, 0, 0);
        gl.enableVertexAttribArray(vTexCoord);

        //
        // Initialize a texture
        //
        var image = new Image();
        image.onload = function() {
            configureTexture(image);
```

```
        render();
    }
    image.src = "OpenGL-logo.png";

    gl.activeTexture(gl.TEXTURE0);
    var uTexture = gl.getUniformLocation(program, "uTexture");
    gl.uniform1i(uTexture, 0);

    uFrame = gl.getUniformLocation(program, "uFrame");
}

var frameNumber = 0;

function render() {
    gl.uniform1f(uFrame, frameNumber++);

    gl.clear(gl.COLOR_BUFFER_BIT | gl.DEPTH_BUFFER_BIT);
    gl.drawArrays(gl.TRIANGLE_FAN, 0, 4);

    window.requestAnimFrame(render, canvas);
}
```

Figure B.1   Our WebGL demo

Built-in GLSL Variables and Functions

The OpenGL Shading Language has a small number of built-in variables, a set of constants, and a large collection of built-in functions. This appendix describes each of these, in the following major sections:

- "Built-in Variables" lists the variables, first showing the declarations for all stages, followed by the description of each.

- "Built-in Constants" lists all the built-in constants.

- "Built-in Functions" describes all GLSL built-in functions. You'll need to refer to the table at the beginning of the section to decode the types.

Built-in Variables

Each programmable stage has a different set of built-in variables, though there is some overlap. We'll first show all the built-in variable declarations in "Built-in Variable Declarations" and then describe each one in "Built-in Variable Descriptions".

Built-in Variable Declarations

Vertex Shader Built-in Variables

```
in   int   gl_VertexID;
in   int   gl_InstanceID;

out gl_PerVertex {
    vec4  gl_Position;
    float gl_PointSize;
    float gl_ClipDistance[];
};
```

Tessellation Control Shader Built-in Variables

```
in gl_PerVertex {
    vec4 gl_Position;
    float gl_PointSize;
    float gl_ClipDistance[];
} gl_in[gl_MaxPatchVertices];

in int gl_PatchVerticesIn;
in int gl_PrimitiveID;
in int gl_InvocationID;

out gl_PerVertex {
    vec4 gl_Position;
    float gl_PointSize;
    float gl_ClipDistance[];
} gl_out[];

patch out float gl_TessLevelOuter[4];
patch out float gl_TessLevelInner[2];
```

Tessellation Evaluation Shader Built-in Variables

```
in gl_PerVertex {
    vec4 gl_Position;
    float gl_PointSize;
    float gl_ClipDistance[];
} gl_in[gl_MaxPatchVertices];

in int gl_PatchVerticesIn;
in int gl_PrimitiveID;
```

```
in vec3 gl_TessCoord;

patch in float gl_TessLevelOuter[4];
patch in float gl_TessLevelInner[2];

out gl_PerVertex {
    vec4 gl_Position;
    float gl_PointSize;
    float gl_ClipDistance[];
};
```

Geometry Shader Built-in Variables

```
in gl_PerVertex {
    vec4  gl_Position;
    float gl_PointSize;
    float gl_ClipDistance[];
} gl_in[];

in int gl_PrimitiveIDIn;
in int gl_InvocationID;

out gl_PerVertex {
    vec4  gl_Position;
    float gl_PointSize;
    float gl_ClipDistance[];
};

out int gl_PrimitiveID;
out int gl_Layer;
out int gl_ViewportIndex;
```

Fragment Shader Built-in Variables

```
in   vec4   gl_FragCoord;
in   bool   gl_FrontFacing;
in   float  gl_ClipDistance[];
in   vec2   gl_PointCoord;
in   int    gl_PrimitiveID;
in   int    gl_SampleID;
in   vec2   gl_SamplePosition;
in   int    gl_SampleMaskIn[];
in   int    gl_Layer;
in   int    gl_ViewportIndex;

out float gl_FragDepth;
out int   gl_SampleMask[];
```

Compute Shader Built-in Variables

```
// work group dimensions
in    uvec3 gl_NumWorkGroups;
const uvec3 gl_WorkGroupSize;
```

```
// work group and invocation IDs
in     uvec3 gl_WorkGroupID;
in     uvec3 gl_LocalInvocationID;

// derived variables
in     uvec3 gl_GlobalInvocationID;
in     uint  gl_LocalInvocationIndex;
```

All Shaders' Built-in State Variables

```
struct gl_DepthRangeParameters {
    float near;
    float far;
    float diff;
};
uniform gl_DepthRangeParameters gl_DepthRange;

uniform int gl_NumSamples;
```

Built-in Variable Descriptions

The descriptions of each of the declared variables above are given below in alphabetical order.

gl_ClipDistance[]

This provides the mechanism for controlling user clipping. The element gl_ClipDistance[i] specifies a clip distance for each plane [i]. A distance of 0 means the vertex is on the plane, a positive distance means the vertex is inside the clip plane, and a negative distance means the point is outside the clip plane. The output clip distances will be linearly interpolated across the primitive, and the portion of the primitive with interpolated distances less than 0 will be clipped.

The gl_ClipDistance[] array is predeclared as unsized and must be sized by the shader either redeclaring it with a size or indexing it only with integral constant expressions. This needs to size the array to include all the clip planes that are enabled via the OpenGL API; if the size does not include all enabled planes, results are undefined. The size can be at most gl_MaxClipDistances. The number of varying components (gl_MaxVaryingComponents) consumed by gl_ClipDistance[] will match the size of the array, no matter how many planes are enabled. The shader must also set all values in gl_ClipDistance[] that have been enabled via the OpenGL API, or results are undefined. Values written into gl_ClipDistance[] for planes that are not enabled have no effect.

As an output variable, gl_ClipDistance[] provides the place for the shader to write these distances. As an input in all shaders except fragment shaders, it reads the values written in the previous shader stage. In a fragment shader, gl_ClipDistance[] array contains linearly interpolated values for the vertex values written by a shader to the gl_ClipDistance[] vertex output variable. Only elements in this array that have clipping enabled will have defined values.

gl_DepthRange

The structure gl_DepthRange contains the locations of the near clip plane and far clip plane for viewport 0. Values are given in window coordinates. The field diff contains the difference far − near.

gl_FragCoord

The fixed functionality computed depth for a fragment may be obtained by reading gl_FragCoord.z.

The gl_FragCoord fragment shader input variable holds the window relative coordinates $(x, y, z, \frac{1}{w})$ values for the current fragment.

If multisampling, this value can be for any location within the pixel. It is the result of the fixed functionality that interpolates primitives after vertex processing to generate fragments. The z component is the depth value that would be used for the fragment's depth if no shader contained any writes to gl_FragDepth. This is useful for invariance if a shader conditionally computes gl_FragDepth but otherwise wants the fixed functionality fragment depth.

gl_FragDepth

Writing to gl_FragDepth in a fragment shader will establish the depth value for the fragment being processed. If depth buffering is enabled, and no shader writes gl_FragDepth, then the fixed function value for depth will be used as the fragment's depth value. If a shader in the fragment stage contains any assignment anywhere to gl_FragDepth, and there is an execution path through the shader that does not set gl_FragDepth, the value of the fragment's depth might not be undefined when the nonassigning path is taken. So, if you write it anywhere, make sure all paths write it.

gl_FrontFacing

Fragment shaders can read the input built-in variable gl_FrontFacing, whose value is true if the fragment belongs to a front-facing primitive.

One use of this is to emulate two-sided lighting by selecting one of two colors calculated by a vertex or geometry shader.

gl_GlobalInvocationID

The compute shader input gl_GlobalInvocationID contains the global index of the current work item. This value uniquely identifies this invocation from all other invocations across all local and global work groups initiated by the current glDispatchCompute call. This is computed as follows:

```
gl_GlobalInvocationID =
    gl_WorkGroupID * gl_WorkGroupSize + gl_LocalInvocationID;
```

gl_InstanceID

The vertex shader input gl_InstanceID holds the instance number of the current primitive in an instanced draw call. If the current primitive does not come from an instanced draw call, the value of gl_InstanceID is zero.

gl_InvocationID

Tessellation control and geometry shaders can read gl_InvocationID. In the tessellation control shader, it identifies the number of the output patch vertex assigned to the tessellation control shader invocation. In the geometry shader, it identifies the invocation number assigned to the geometry shader invocation. In both cases, gl_InvocationID is assigned integer values in the range $[0, N - 1]$, where N is the number of output patch vertices or geometry shader invocations per primitive.

gl_Layer

The gl_Layer variable is both an output from geometry shaders and an input to fragment shaders. In a geometry shader, it is used to select a specific layer (or face and layer of a cube map) of a multilayer framebuffer attachment. The actual layer used will come from one of the vertices in the primitive being shaded. Which vertex the layer comes from is undefined, so it is best to write the same layer value for all vertices of a primitive. If any geometry shader in a program contains an assignment to gl_Layer, layered rendering mode is enabled. Once enabled, if there is an execution path through the shader that does not set gl_Layer, it will be undefined. So, ensure you always set it for all paths through the shader.

The output variable gl_Layer takes on a special value when used with an array of cube-map textures. Instead of only referring to the layer, it is used to select a cube-map face and a layer. Setting gl_Layer to the value $layer \times 6 + face$ will render to face *face* of the cube defined in layer *layer*. The face values are listed in Table C.1.

Table C.1   Cube-Map Face Targets

Face Value	Face Target
0	TEXTURE_CUBE_MAP_POSITIVE_X
1	TEXTURE_CUBE_MAP_NEGATIVE_X
2	TEXTURE_CUBE_MAP_POSITIVE_Y
3	TEXTURE_CUBE_MAP_NEGATIVE_Y
4	TEXTURE_CUBE_MAP_POSITIVE_Z
5	TEXTURE_CUBE_MAP_NEGATIVE_Z

For example, to render to the positive *y* cube-map face located in the 5th layer of the cube-map array, gl_Layer should be set to $5 \times 6 + 2$.

The gl_Layer input to a fragment shader will have the same value that was written to the gl_Layer output from the geometry shader. If no shader in the geometry stage dynamically assigns a value to gl_Layer, the value of gl_Layer in the fragment shaders will be undefined. If the geometry stage contains no assignment at all to gl_Layer, the input gl_Value in the fragment stage will be zero. Otherwise, the fragment stage will read the same value written by the geometry stage, even if that value is out of range. If a fragment shader contains any access to gl_Layer, it will count against the implementation-defined limit for the maximum number of inputs to the fragment stage.

gl_LocalInvocationID

The compute shader input gl_LocalInvocationID contains the *t*-dimensional index of the local work group within the global work group that the current invocation is executing in. The possible values for this variable range across the local work group size are as follows:

```
(0,0,0)
    to
(gl_WorkGroupSize.x - 1, gl_WorkGroupSize.y - 1, gl_WorkGroupSize.z - 1)
```

gl_LocalInvocationIndex

The compute shader input gl_LocalInvocationIndex contains the one-dimensional representation of the gl_LocalInvocationID. This is useful for uniquely identifying a unique region of shared memory within the local work group for this invocation to use. It is computed as follows:

```
gl_LocalInvocationIndex =
    gl_LocalInvocationID.z * gl_WorkGroupSize.x * gl_WorkGroupSize.y +
    gl_LocalInvocationID.y * gl_WorkGroupSize.x +
    gl_LocalInvocationID.x;
```

gl_NumSamples

The uniform input gl_NumSamples to all stages contains the total number of samples in the framebuffer, when using a multisample framebuffer. When using nonmultisample framebuffer, gl_NumSamples just contains 1.

gl_NumWorkGroups

The compute shader input gl_NumWorkGroups contains the total number of global work items in each dimension of the work group that will execute the compute shader. Its content is equal to the values specified in the num_groups_x, num_groups_y, and num_groups_z parameters passed to the glDispatchCompute API entry point.

gl_PatchVerticesIn

Tessellation shaders can read gl_PatchVerticesIn. It is an integer specifying the number of vertices in the input patch being processed by the shader. A single tessellation control or evaluation shader can read patches of differing sizes, so the value of gl_PatchVerticesIn may differ between patches.

gl_PointCoord

The values in gl_PointCoord are two-dimensional coordinates indicating where within a point primitive the current fragment is located when point sprites are enabled. They range from 0.0 to 1.0 across the point. If the current primitive is not a point, or if point sprites are not enabled, then the values read from gl_PointCoord are undefined.

gl_PointSize

As an output variable, gl_PointSize is intended for a shader to write the size of the point to be rasterized. It is measured in pixels. If gl_PointSize is not written to, its value is undefined in subsequent stages. As an input variable, gl_PointSize reads the value written to gl_PointSize in the previous shader stage.

gl_Position

As an output variable, gl_Position is intended for writing the homogeneous vertex position. This value will be used by primitive assembly, clipping, culling, and other fixed functionality operations, if present, that operate on primitives after vertex processing has occurred. Its value is undefined after the vertex processing stage if the vertex shader executable does not write gl_Position, and it is undefined after geometry processing if the geometry executable calls EmitVertex without having written gl_Position since the last EmitVertex (or hasn't written it at all). As an input variable, gl_Position reads the output written in the previous shader stage to gl_Position.

gl_PrimitiveID

Geometry shaders output gl_PrimitiveID to provide a single integer that serves as a primitive identifier. This is then available to fragment shaders as the fragment input gl_PrimitiveID, which will select the written primitive ID from the provoking vertex in the primitive being shaded. If a fragment shader using gl_PrimitiveID is active and a geometry shader is also active, the geometry shader must write to gl_PrimitiveID or the fragment shader input gl_PrimitiveID is undefined.

For tessellation control and evaluation shaders the input variable gl_PrimitiveID is filled with the number of primitives processed by the shader since the current set of rendering primitives was started. For the fragment shader, it is filled with the value written to the gl_PrimitiveID geometry shader output if a geometry shader is present. Otherwise, it is assigned in the same manner as with tessellation control and evaluation shaders.

gl_PrimitiveIDIn

The geometry shader input variable gl_PrimitiveIDIn behaves identically to the tessellation control and evaluation shader input variable gl_PrimitiveID, described just above.

gl_SampleID

The fragment shader input variable gl_SampleID is filled with the sample number of the sample currently being processed. This variable is in the range 0 to gl_NumSamples−1, where gl_NumSamples is the total number of samples in the framebuffer, or 1 if rendering to a nonmultisample framebuffer. Any use of this variable in a fragment shader causes the entire shader to be evaluated per-sample.

gl_SampleMask

The fragment output array gl_SampleMask[] sets the sample mask for the fragment being processed. Coverage for the current fragment will become the logical AND of the coverage mask and the output gl_SampleMask. This array must be sized in the fragment shader either implicitly or explicitly to be the same size described above.

If any fragment shader contains any assignment to gl_SampleMask, the sample mask will be undefined for any array elements of any fragment shader invocations that fail to assign a value. If no shader has any assignment to gl_SampleMask, the sample mask has no effect on the processing of a fragment.

Bit B of mask gl_SampleMask[M] corresponds to sample $32 \times M + B$. There are $ceil(s/32)$ array elements, where s is the maximum number of color samples supported by the implementation.

gl_SampleMaskIn

The fragment shader input gl_SampleMaskIn indicates the set of samples covered by the primitive generating the fragment during multisample rasterization. It has a sample bit set if and only if the sample is considered covered for this fragment shader invocation.

Bit B of mask gl_SampleMaskIn[M] corresponds to sample $32 \times M + B$. There are $ceil(s/32)$ array elements, where s is the maximum number of color samples supported by the implementation.

gl_SamplePosition

The fragment shader input gl_SamplePosition contains the position of the current sample within the multisample draw buffer. The x and y components of gl_SamplePosition contain the sub-pixel coordinate of the current sample and will have values in the range 0.0 to 1.0. Any use of this variable in any fragment shader causes the entire fragment stage to be evaluated per sample.

gl_TessCoord

The variable gl_TessCoord is available only in tessellation evaluation shaders. It specifies a three-component (u, v, w) vector identifying the position of the vertex being processed by the shader relative to the primitive being tessellated. Its values will obey the properties

```
gl_TessCoord.x == 1.0 - (1.0 - gl_TessCoord.x)
gl_TessCoord.y == 1.0 - (1.0 - gl_TessCoord.y)
gl_TessCoord.z == 1.0 - (1.0 - gl_TessCoord.z)
```

to aid in replicating subdivision computations.

gl_TessLevelOuter and gl_TessLevelOuter

The input variables gl_TessLevelOuter[] and gl_TessLevelInner[] are available only in tessellation evaluation shaders. If a tessellation control shader is active, these variables are filled with corresponding outputs written by the tessellation control shader. Otherwise, they are assigned with default tessellation levels.

The output variables gl_TessLevelOuter[] and gl_TessLevelInner[] are available only in tessellation control shaders. The values written to these variables are assigned to the corresponding outer and inner tessellation levels of the output patch. They are used by the tessellation primitive generator to control primitive tessellation and may be read by tessellation evaluation shaders.

gl_ViewportID

The vertex shader input gl_VertexID holds an integer index for the vertex. While the variable gl_VertexID is always present, its value is not always defined.

gl_ViewportIndex

The variable gl_ViewportIndex is available as an output variable from geometry shaders and an input variable to fragment shaders. In geometry shaders, it provides the index of the viewport to which the next primitive emitted from the geometry shader should be drawn. Primitives generated by the geometry shader will undergo viewport transformation and scissor testing using the viewport transformation and scissor rectangle selected by the value of gl_ViewportIndex. The viewport index used will come from one of the vertices in the primitive being shaded. However, which vertex the viewport index comes from is implementation-dependent, so it is best to use the same viewport index for all vertices of the primitive. If a geometry shader does not assign a value to gl_ViewportIndex, viewport transform and scissor rectangle zero will be used. If any geometry shader assigns a value to gl_ViewportIndex, and there is a path through the geometry stage that does not assign a value to gl_ViewportIndex, the value of gl_ViewportIndex is undefined for executions of the shader that take that path.

As a fragment shader input, gl_ViewportIndex will have the same value that was written to the output variable gl_ViewportIndex in the geometry stage. If the geometry stage does not dynamically assign to gl_ViewportIndex, the value of gl_ViewportIndex in the fragment shader will be undefined. If the geometry stage contains no assignment to gl_ViewportIndex, the fragment stage will read zero. Otherwise, the fragment stage will read the same value written by the geometry stage, even if that value is out of range. If a fragment shader contains any access to gl_ViewportIndex, it will count against the implementation defined limit for the maximum number of inputs to the fragment stage.

gl_WorkGroupSize

The built-in constant gl_WorkGroupSize is a compute shader constant containing the local workgroup size of the shader. The size of the work group in the x, y, and z dimensions is stored in the x, y, and z components. The values stored in gl_WorkGroupSize match those specified in the required local_size_x, local_size_y, and local_size_z layout qualifiers for the current shader. This value is a constant so that it can be used to size arrays of memory that can be shared within the local work group.

gl_WorkGroupID

The compute shader input gl_WorkGroupID contains the three-dimensional index of the global work group that the current invocation is executing in. The possible values range across the parameters passed into glDispatchCompute, i.e., from:

```
(0, 0, 0)
   to
(gl_NumWorkGroups.x - 1, gl_NumWorkGroups.y - 1, gl_NumWorkGroups.z - 1)
```

Built-in Constants

The constants are relatively self-explanatory and referred to as needed by other sections. The numbers below are the not necessarily the numbers you will see on your rendering platform. Rather, the numbers you will see on any particular platform will be at least as big as these.

```
const ivec3 gl_MaxComputeWorkGroupCount = { 65535, 65535,
                                             65535 };
const ivec3 gl_MaxComputeWorkGroupSize = { 1024, 1024,
                                           64 };
const int gl_MaxComputeUniformComponents = 1024;
const int gl_MaxComputeTextureImageUnits = 16;
```

```
const int gl_MaxComputeImageUniforms = 8;
const int gl_MaxComputeAtomicCounters = 8;
const int gl_MaxComputeAtomicCounterBuffers = 1;

const int  gl_MaxVertexAttribs = 16;
const int  gl_MaxVertexUniformComponents = 1024;

const int  gl_MaxVaryingComponents = 60;
const int  gl_MaxVertexOutputComponents = 64;
const int  gl_MaxGeometryInputComponents = 64;
const int  gl_MaxGeometryOutputComponents = 128;
const int  gl_MaxFragmentInputComponents = 128;
const int  gl_MaxVertexTextureImageUnits = 16;
const int  gl_MaxCombinedTextureImageUnits = 80;
const int  gl_MaxTextureImageUnits = 16;
const int  gl_MaxImageUnits = 8;
const int  gl_MaxCombinedImageUnitsAndFragmentOutputs = 8;
const int  gl_MaxImageSamples = 0;
const int  gl_MaxVertexImageUniforms = 0;
const int  gl_MaxTessControlImageUniforms = 0;
const int  gl_MaxTessEvaluationImageUniforms = 0;
const int  gl_MaxGeometryImageUniforms = 0;
const int  gl_MaxFragmentImageUniforms = 8;
const int  gl_MaxCombinedImageUniforms = 8;
const int  gl_MaxFragmentUniformComponents = 1024;
const int  gl_MaxDrawBuffers = 8;
const int  gl_MaxClipDistances = 8;
const int  gl_MaxGeometryTextureImageUnits = 16;
const int  gl_MaxGeometryOutputVertices = 256;
const int  gl_MaxGeometryTotalOutputComponents = 1024;
const int  gl_MaxGeometryUniformComponents = 1024;
const int  gl_MaxGeometryVaryingComponents = 64;

const int gl_MaxTessControlInputComponents = 128;
const int gl_MaxTessControlOutputComponents = 128;
const int gl_MaxTessControlTextureImageUnits = 16;
const int gl_MaxTessControlUniformComponents = 1024;
const int gl_MaxTessControlTotalOutputComponents = 4096;

const int gl_MaxTessEvaluationInputComponents = 128;
const int gl_MaxTessEvaluationOutputComponents = 128;
const int gl_MaxTessEvaluationTextureImageUnits = 16;
const int gl_MaxTessEvaluationUniformComponents = 1024;

const int gl_MaxTessPatchComponents = 120;
const int gl_MaxPatchVertices = 32;
const int gl_MaxTessGenLevel = 64;

const int gl_MaxViewports = 16;

const int gl_MaxVertexUniformVectors = 256;
const int gl_MaxFragmentUniformVectors = 256;
const int gl_MaxVaryingVectors = 15;
```

```
const int gl_MaxVertexAtomicCounters = 0;
const int gl_MaxTessControlAtomicCounters = 0;
const int gl_MaxTessEvaluationAtomicCounters = 0;
const int gl_MaxGeometryAtomicCounters = 0;
const int gl_MaxFragmentAtomicCounters = 8;
const int gl_MaxCombinedAtomicCounters = 8;
const int gl_MaxAtomicCounterBindings = 1;
const int gl_MaxVertexAtomicCounterBuffers = 0;
const int gl_MaxTessControlAtomicCounterBuffers = 0;
const int gl_MaxTessEvaluationAtomicCounterBuffers = 0;
const int gl_MaxGeometryAtomicCounterBuffers = 0;
const int gl_MaxFragmentAtomicCounterBuffers = 1;
const int gl_MaxCombinedAtomicCounterBuffers = 1;
const int gl_MaxAtomicCounterBufferSize = 16384;

const int gl_MinProgramTexelOffset = -8;
const int gl_MaxProgramTexelOffset = 7;
```

Built-in Functions

The OpenGL Shading Language defines an assortment of built-in convenience functions for scalar and vector operations. These are grouped as shown below, and use the subsequently defined notation for types.

- "Angle and Trigonometry Functions"

- "Exponential Functions"

- "Common Functions"

- "Floating-Point Pack and Unpack Functions"

- "Geometric Functions"

- "Matrix Functions"

- "Vector Relational Functions"

- "Integer Functions"

- "Texture Functions"

- "Atomic-Counter Functions"

- "Atomic Memory Functions"

- "Image Functions"

- "Fragment Processing Functions"

- "Noise Functions"

- "Geometry Shader Functions"

- "Shader Invocation Control Functions"

- "Shader Memory Control Functions"

Listing all the prototypes for all the GLSL built-in functions would fill this entire book. Instead, we use some generic notations that represent multiple types. These are listed in Table C.2, and allow a single prototype listing below to represent multiple actual prototypes.

Table C.2   Notation for Argument or Return Type

Generic Notation	Specific Types
genType	float vec2 vec3 vec4
genDType	double dvec2 dvec3 dvec4
genIType	int ivec2 ivec3 ivec4
genUType	uint uvec2 uvec3 uvec4
genBType	bool bvec2 bvec3 bvec4
vec	vec2 vec3 vec4
ivec	ivec2 ivec3 ivec4
uvec	uvec2 uvec3 uvec4
bvec	bvec2 bvec3 bvec4
gvec4	vec4 ivec4 uvec4
gsampler[...]	sampler[...] isampler[...] usampler[...]
gimage[...]	image[...] iimage[...] uimage[...]
mat	any single-precision matrix type; mat4, mat2x3, ...
dmat	any double-precision matrix type; dmat4, dmat2x3, ...

For any specific use of a function, the actual types substituted for genType, genIType, and so on, have to have the same number of components for all arguments as well as the return type. When gsampler... is used, the underlying type (floating point, signed integer, and unsigned integer) must match the underlying type in the gvec4.

One final note: most built-in functions operate component-wise and are described as if operating on a single component. That is, if the actual type is, say, a `vec3`, the x component will be operated on as described, independently of the y and z components. Similarly, each of y and z will be operated on independently of the other two components. Unless otherwise noted, the functions operate component-wise. Dot product is a great counterexample, where each component of the result is affected by all the components of the input.

Angle and Trigonometry Functions

Function parameters specified as *angle* are assumed to be in units of radians.

---

genType **radians**(genType *degrees*);

Converts *degrees* to radians:

$$\frac{\pi}{180}degrees$$

---

genType **degrees**(genType *radians*);

Converts *radians* to degrees:

$$\frac{180}{\pi}radians$$

---

genType **sin**(genType *angle*);

The standard trigonometric sine function.

---

genType **cos**(genType *angle*);

The standard trigonometric cosine function.

---

genType **tan**(genType *angle*);

The standard trigonometric tangent.

genType **asin**(genType x);

Arc sine. Returns an angle whose sine is x. The range of values returned by this function is $-\frac{\pi}{2}$ to $\frac{\pi}{2}$, inclusive.

Results are undefined if $x > 1$ or $x < -1$.

genType **acos**(genType x);

Arc cosine. Returns an angle whose cosine is x. The range of values returned by this function is 0 to π, inclusive.

Results are undefined if $x > 1$ or $x < -1$.

genType **atan**(genType y, genType x);

Arc tangent. Returns an angle whose tangent is $\frac{y}{x}$. The signs of x and y are used to determine what quadrant the angle is in. The range of values returned by this function is $-\pi$ to π, inclusive.

Results are undefined if x and y are both 0.

genType **atan**(genType y_over_x);

Arc tangent. Returns an angle whose tangent is y_over_x. The range of values returned by this function is $-\frac{\pi}{2}$ to $\frac{\pi}{2}$, inclusive.

genType **sinh**(genType x);

Returns the hyperbolic sine function $\frac{e^x - e^{-x}}{2}$.

genType **cosh**(genType x);

Returns the hyperbolic cosine function $\frac{e^x + e^{-x}}{2}$.

genType **tanh**(genType *x*);

Returns the hyperbolic tangent function $\frac{sinh(x)}{cosh(x)}$.

genType **asinh**(genType *x*);

Arc hyperbolic sine; returns the inverse of **sinh**.

genType **acosh**(genType *x*);

Arc hyperbolic cosine; returns the nonnegative inverse of **cosh**.

Results are undefined if $x < 1$.

genType **atanh**(genType *x*);

Arc hyperbolic tangent; returns the inverse of **tanh**.

Results are undefined if $x \geq 1$ or if $x \leq -1$.

Exponential Functions

genType **pow**(genType *x*, genType *y*);

Returns *x* raised to the *y* power, i.e., x^y.

Results are undefined if $x < 0$.

Results are undefined if $x = 0$ and $y \leq 0$.

genType **exp**(genType *x*);

Returns the natural exponentiation of *x*; e^x.

genType **log**(genType x);

Returns the natural logarithm of x, i.e., returns the value y that satisfies the equation $x = e^y$.

Results are undefined if $x \leq 0$.

genType **exp2**(genType x);

Returns 2 raised to the x power; 2^x.

genType **log2**(genType x);

Returns the base 2 logarithm of x, i.e., returns the value y that satisfies the equation $x = 2^y$.

Results are undefined if $x \leq 0$.

genType **sqrt**(genType x);
genDType **sqrt**(genDType x);

Returns $\sqrt{x}$.

Results are undefined if $x < 0$.

genType **inversesqrt**(genType x);
genDType **inversesqrt**(genDType x);

Returns $\frac{1}{\sqrt{x}}$.

Results are undefined if $x \leq 0$.

Common Functions

genType **abs**(genType x);
genIType **abs**(genIType x);
genDType **abs**(genDType x);

Return x if $x \geq 0$; otherwise it returns $-x$.

genType **sign**(genType x);
genIType **sign**(genIType x);
genDType **sign**(genDType x);

Return 1.0 if $x > 0$, 0.0 if $x = 0$, or -1.0 if $x < 0$.

genType **floor**(genType x);
genDType **floor**(genDType x);

Return a value equal to the nearest integer that is less than or equal to x.

genType **trunc**(genType x);
genDType **trunc**(genDType x);

Return a value equal to the nearest integer to x whose absolute value is not larger than the absolute value of x.

genType **round**(genType x);
genDType **round**(genDType x);

Return a value equal to the nearest integer to x. The fraction 0.5 will round in a direction chosen by the implementation, presumably the direction that is fastest. This includes the possibility that **round(x)** returns the same value as **roundEven(x)** for all values of x.

genType **roundEven**(genType *x*);
genDType **roundEven**(genDType *x*);

Return a value equal to the nearest integer to *x*. A fractional part of 0.5 will round toward the nearest even integer. (Both 3.5 and 4.5 for *x* will return 4.0.)

genType **ceil**(genType *x*);
genDType **ceil**(genDType *x*);

Return a value equal to the nearest integer that is greater than or equal to *x*.

genType **fract**(genType *x*);
genDType **fract**(genDType *x*);

Return $x - floor(x)$.

genType **mod**(genType *x*, float *y*);
genType **mod**(genType *x*, genType *y*);
genDType **mod**(genDType *x*, double *y*);
genDType **mod**(genDType *x*, genDType *y*);

Modulus. Return $x - y \times floor(x/y)$.

genType **modf**(genType *x*, out genType *i*);
genDType **modf**(genDType *x*, out genDType *i*);

Return the fractional part of *x* and sets *i* to the integer part (as a whole number floating-point value). Both the return value and the output argument will have the same sign as *x*.

genType **min**(genType *x*, genType *y*);
genType **min**(genType *x*, float *y*);

genDType **min**(genDType *x*, genDType *y*);
genDType **min**(genDType *x*, double *y*);
genIType **min**(genIType *x*, genIType *y*);
genIType **min**(genIType *x*, int *y*);
genUType **min**(genUType *x*, genUType *y*);
genUType **min**(genUType *x*, uint *y*);

Return *y* if *y* < *x*; otherwise it returns *x*.

genType **max**(genType *x*, genType *y*);
genType **max**(genType *x*, float *y*);
genDType **max**(genDType *x*, genDType *y*);
genDType **max**(genDType *x*, double *y*);
genIType **max**(genIType *x*, genIType *y*);
genIType **max**(genIType *x*, int *y*);
genUType **max**(genUType *x*, genUType *y*);
genUType **max**(genUType *x*, uint *y*);

Return *y* if *x* < *y*; otherwise it returns *x*.

genType **clamp**(genType *x*, genType *minVal*, genType *maxVal*);
genType **clamp**(genType *x*, float *minVal*, float *maxVal*);
genDType **clamp**(genDType *x*, genDType *minVal*,
                genDType *maxVal*);
genDType **clamp**(genDType *x*, double *minVal*, double *maxVal*);
genIType **clamp**(genIType *x*, genIType *minVal*, genIType *maxVal*);
genIType **clamp**(genIType *x*, int *minVal*, int *maxVal*);
genUType **clamp**(genUType *x*, genUType *minVal*,
                genUType *maxVal*);
genUType **clamp**(genUType *x*, uint *minVal*, uint *maxVal*);

Return min(max(x, minVal), maxVal).

Results are undefined if *minVal* > *maxVal*.

```
genType mix(genType x, genType y, genType a);
genType mix(genType x, genType y, float a);
genDType mix(genDType x, genDType y, genDType a);
genDType mix(genDType x, genDType y, double a);
```

Return the linear blend of x and y, i.e., $x(1 - a) + ya$.

```
genType mix(genType x, genType y, genBType a);
genDType mix(genDType x, genDType y, genBType a);
```

Select which vector each returned component comes from. For a component of a that is `false` the corresponding component of x is returned. For a component of a that is `true`, the corresponding component of y is returned. Components of x and y that are not selected are allowed to be invalid floating-point values and will have no effect on the results. Thus, this provides different functionality than, for example,

```
genType mix(genType x, genType y, genType(a))
```

where a is a Boolean vector.

```
genType step(genType edge, genType x);
genType step(float edge, genType x);
genDType step(genDType edge, genDType x);
genDType step(double edge, genDType x);
```

Return 0.0 if $x < edge$; otherwise it returns 1.0.

```
genType smoothstep(genType edge0, genType edge1, genType x);
genType smoothstep(float edge0, float edge1, genType x);
genDType smoothstep(genDType edge0, genDType edge1,
                    genDType x);
genDType smoothstep(double edge0, double edge1, genDType x);
```

Return 0.0 if $x \leq edge0$ and 1.0 if $x \geq edge1$, and performs smooth Hermite interpolation between 0 and 1 when $edge0 < x < edge1$. This is useful in cases where you would want a threshold function with a smooth transition. This is equivalent to:

```
genType t;
t = clamp ((x - edge0) / (edge1 - edge0), 0, 1);
return t * t * (3 - 2 * t);
```

(And similarly for doubles.) Results are undefined if $edge0 \geq edge1$.

---

genBType **isnan**(genType *x*);
genBType **isnan**(genDType *x*);

Return `true` if *x* holds a NaN. Returns `false` otherwise. Always return `false` if NaNs are not implemented.

---

genBType **isinf**(genType *x*);
genBType **isinf**(genDType *x*);

Return `true` if *x* holds a positive infinity or negative infinity. Return `false` otherwise.

---

genIType **floatBitsToInt**(genType *value*);
genUType **floatBitsToUint**(genType *value*);

Return a signed or unsigned integer value representing the encoding of a float. The float value's bit-level representation is preserved.

---

genType **intBitsToFloat**(genIType *value*);
genType **uintBitsToFloat**(genUType *value*);

Return a float value corresponding to a signed or unsigned integer encoding of a float. If a NaN is passed in, it will not signal, and the resulting value is unspecified. If an Inf is passed in, the resulting value is the corresponding Inf.

genType **fma**(genType *a*, genType *b*, genType *c*);
genDType **fma**(genDType *a*, genDType *b*, genDType *c*);

Compute and return $a \times b + c$.

In uses where the return value is eventually consumed by a variable declared as precise:

- **fma** is considered a single operation, whereas the expression $a \times b + c$ consumed by a variable declared precise is considered two operations.

- The precision of **fma** can differ from the precision of the expression $a \times b + c$.

- **fma** will be computed with the same precision as any other **fma** consumed by a precise variable, giving invariant results for the same input values of *a*, *b*, and *c*.

Otherwise, in the absence of precise consumption, there are no special constraints on the number of operations or difference in precision between **fma** and the expression $a \times b + c$.

---

genType **frexp**(genType *x*, out genIType *exp*);
genDType **frexp**(genDType *x*, out genIType *exp*);

Split *x* into a floating-point significand in the range $[0.5, 1.0)$ and an integral exponent of two, such that:

$$x = significand \times 2^{exponent}$$

The significand is returned by the function and the exponent is returned in the argument *exp*. For a floating-point value of zero, the significand and exponent are both zero. For a floating-point value that is an infinity or is not a number, the results are undefined.

---

genType **ldexp**(genType *x*, in genIType *exp*);
genDType **ldexp**(genDType *x*, in genIType *exp*);

Build a floating-point number from *x* and the corresponding integral exponent of two in *exp*, returning:

$$significand \times 2^{exponent}$$

If this product is too large to be represented in the floating-point type, the result is undefined.

Floating-Point Pack and Unpack Functions

These functions do not operate component-wise, rather, as described in each case.

---

uint **packUnorm2x16**(vec2 *v*);
uint **packSnorm2x16**(vec2 *v*);
uint **packUnorm4x8**(vec4 *v*);
uint **packSnorm4x8**(vec4 *v*);

First, converts each component of the normalized floating-point value *v* into 8- or 16-bit integer values. Then, the results are packed into the returned 32-bit unsigned integer. The conversion for component *c* of *v* to fixed point is done as follows:

```
packUnorm2x16:   round(clamp(c,   0,  +1) * 65535.0)
packSnorm2x16:   round(clamp(c,  -1,  +1) * 32767.0)
packUnorm4x8:    round(clamp(c,   0,  +1) * 255.0)
packSnorm4x8:    round(clamp(c,  -1,  +1) * 127.0)
```

The first component of the vector will be written to the least significant bits of the output; the last component will be written to the most significant bits.

---

vec2 **unpackUnorm2x16**(uint *p*);
vec2 **unpackSnorm2x16**(uint *p*);
veç4 **unpackUnorm4x8**(uint *p*);
vec4 **unpackSnorm4x8**(uint *p*);

First, unpacks a single 32-bit unsigned integer *p* into a pair of 16-bit unsigned integers, four 8-bit unsigned integers, or four 8-bit signed integers. Then, each component is converted to a normalized floating-point value to generate the returned two- or four-component vector.

The conversion for unpacked fixed-point value *f* to floating point is done as follows:

```
unpackUnorm2x16:   f / 65535.0
unpackSnorm2x16:   clamp(f / 32767.0, -1, +1)
unpackUnorm4x8:    f / 255.0
unpackSnorm4x8:    clamp(f / 127.0, -1, +1)
```

The first component of the returned vector will be extracted from the least significant bits of the input; the last component will be extracted from the most significant bits.

double **packDouble2x32**(uvec2 *v*);

Returns a double-precision value obtained by packing the components of *v* into a 64-bit value. If an IEEE 754 Inf or NaN is created, it will not signal, and the resulting floating-point value is unspecified. Otherwise, the bit-level representation of *v* is preserved. The first vector component specifies the 32 least significant bits; the second component specifies the 32 most significant bits.

uvec2 **unpackDouble2x32**(double *v*);

Returns a two-component unsigned integer vector representation of *v*. The bit-level representation of *v* is preserved. The first component of the vector contains the 32 least significant bits of the double; the second component consists of the 32 most significant bits.

uint **packHalf2x16**(vec2 *v*);

Returns an unsigned integer obtained by converting the components of a two-component floating-point vector to a 16-bit floating-point representation, and then packing these two 16-bit integers into a 32-bit unsigned integer.

The first vector component specifies the 16 least-significant bits of the result; the second component specifies the 16 most-significant bits.

vec2 **unpackHalf2x16**(uint *v*);

Returns a two-component floating-point vector with components obtained by unpacking a 32-bit unsigned integer into a pair of 16-bit values, interpreting those values as 16-bit floating-point numbers, and converting them to 32-bit floating-point values.

The first component of the vector is obtained from the 16 least-significant bits of *v*; the second component is obtained from the 16 most-significant bits of *v*.

Geometric Functions

These operate on vectors as vectors, not component-wise.

---

float **length**(genType *x*);
double **length**(genDType *x*);

Return the length of vector *x*, i.e.,

$$\sqrt{x[0]^2 + x[1]^2 + \cdots}$$

---

float **distance**(genType *p0*, genType *p1*);
double **distance**(genDType *p0*, genDType *p1*);

Return the distance between *p0* and *p1*: length (p0 − p1).

---

float **dot**(genType *x*, genType *y*);
double **dot**(genDType *x*, genDType *y*);

Return the dot product of *x* and *y*, i.e.,

$$x[0] \times y[0] + x[1] \times y[1] + \cdots$$

---

vec3 **cross**(vec3 *x*, vec3 *y*);
dvec3 **cross**(dvec3 *x*, dvec3 *y*);

Return the cross product of *x* and *y*, i.e.,

$$\begin{bmatrix} x[1] \times y[2] - y[1] \times x[2] \\ x[2] \times y[0] - y[2] \times x[0] \\ x[0] \times y[1] - y[0] \times x[1] \end{bmatrix}$$

genType **normalize**(genType *x*);
genDType **normalize**(genDType *x*);

Return a vector in the same direction as *x* but with a length of 1.

genType **faceforward**(genType *N*, genType *I*, genType *Nref*);
genDType **faceforward**(genDType *N*, genDType *I*,
                    genDType *Nref*);

```
if (dot(Nref, I) < 0.0)
    return N;
else
    return -N;
```

genType **reflect**(genType *I*, genType *N*);
genDType **reflect**(genDType *I*, genDType *N*);

For the incident vector *I* and surface orientation *N*, returns the reflection direction:

```
I - 2 * dot(N, I) * N
```

N must already be normalized in order to achieve the desired result.

genType **refract**(genType *I*, genType *N*, float *eta*);
genDType **refract**(genDType *I*, genDType *N*, float *eta*);

For the incident vector *I* and surface normal *N*, and the ratio of indices of refraction *eta*, return the refraction vector. The result is computed by

```
k = 1.0 - eta * eta * (1.0 - dot(N, I) * dot(N, I));
if (k < 0.0)
    return genType(0.0);    // or genDType(0.0)
else
    return eta * I - (eta * dot(N, I) + sqrt(k)) * N;
```

The input arguments for the incident vector *I* and the surface normal *N* must already be normalized to get the desired results.

Matrix Functions

For each of the following built-in matrix functions, there is both a single-precision floating-point version, where all arguments and return values are single precision, and a double-precision floating-point version, where all arguments and return values are double precision. Only the single-precision floating-point version is shown.

---

mat **matrixCompMult**(mat *x*, mat *y*);

Multiply matrix *x* by matrix *y* component-wise, i.e.,

$$result[i][j] = x[i][j] \times y[i][j]$$

for all *i* and *j*.

Note: to get linear algebraic matrix multiplication, use the multiply operator (*).

---

mat2 **outerProduct**(vec2 *c*, vec2 *r*);
mat3 **outerProduct**(vec3 *c*, vec3 *r*);
mat4 **outerProduct**(vec4 *c*, vec4 *r*);
mat2x3 **outerProduct**(vec3 *c*, vec2 *r*);
mat3x2 **outerProduct**(vec2 *c*, vec3 *r*);
mat2x4 **outerProduct**(vec4 *c*, vec2 *r*);
mat4x2 **outerProduct**(vec2 *c*, vec4 *r*);
mat3x4 **outerProduct**(vec4 *c*, vec3 *r*);
mat4x3 **outerProduct**(vec3 *c*, vec4 *r*);

Treat the first argument *c* as a column vector (matrix with one column), the second argument *r* as a row vector (matrix with one row), and do a linear algebraic matrix multiply *c* × *r*, yielding a matrix whose number of rows is the number of components in *c* and whose number of columns is the number of components in *r*.

---

mat2 **transpose**(mat2 *m*);
mat3 **transpose**(mat3 *m*);
mat4 **transpose**(mat4 *m*);

```
mat2x3 transpose(mat3x2 m);
mat3x2 transpose(mat2x3 m);
mat2x4 transpose(mat4x2 m);
mat4x2 transpose(mat2x4 m);
mat3x4 transpose(mat4x3 m);
mat4x3 transpose(mat3x4 m);
```

Return a matrix that is the transpose of *m*. The input matrix *m* is not modified.

```
float determinant(mat2 m);
float determinant(mat3 m);
float determinant(mat4 m);
```

Return the determinant of *m*.

```
mat2 inverse(mat2 m);
mat3 inverse(mat3 m);
mat4 inverse(mat4 m);
```

Return a matrix that is the inverse of *m*. The input matrix *m* is not modified. The values in the returned matrix are undefined if *m* is singular or poorly-conditioned (nearly singular).

Vector Relational Functions

The following are for comparing vectors. (Scalars are compared with operators.)

In all cases, the sizes of all the input and return vectors for any particular call must match.

bvec **lessThan**(vec x, vec y);
bvec **lessThan**(ivec x, ivec y);
bvec **lessThan**(uvec x, uvec y);

Return the component-wise compare of $x < y$.

bvec **lessThanEqual**(vec x, vec y);
bvec **lessThanEqual**(ivec x, ivec y);
bvec **lessThanEqual**(uvec x, uvec y);

Return the component-wise compare of $x \leq y$.

bvec **greaterThan**(vec x, vec y);
bvec **greaterThan**(ivec x, ivec y);
bvec **greaterThan**(uvec x, uvec y);

Return the component-wise compare of $x > y$.

bvec **greaterThanEqual**(vec x, vec y);
bvec **greaterThanEqual**(ivec x, ivec y);
bvec **greaterThanEqual**(uvec x, uvec y);

Return the component-wise compare of $x \geq y$.

bvec **equal**(vec x, vec y);
bvec **equal**(ivec x, ivec y);
bvec **equal**(uvec x, uvec y);
bvec **equal**(bvec x, bvec y);

Return the component-wise compare of $x = y$.

bvec **notEqual**(vec *x*, vec *y*);
bvec **notEqual**(ivec *x*, ivec *y*);
bvec **notEqual**(uvec *x*, uvec *y*);
bvec **notEqual**(bvec *x*, bvec *y*);

Return the component-wise compare of $x \neq y$.

bool **any**(bvec *x*);

Returns `true` if any component of *x* is `true`.

bool **all**(bvec *x*);

Returns `true` only if all components of *x* are `true`.

bvec **not**(bvec *x*);

Returns the component-wise logical complement of *x*.

Integer Functions

For these functions, the notation [*a*, *b*] means the set of bits from bit-number *a* through bit-number *b*, inclusive. The lowest-order bit is bit 0. "Bit number" will always refer to counting up from the lowest-order bit as bit 0.

genUType **uaddCarry**(genUType *x*, genUType *y*,
　　　　　　　　out genUType *carry*);

Adds 32-bit unsigned integer *x* and *y*, returning the sum modulo 2^{32}. The value *carry* is set to 0 if the sum was less than 2^{32}, or to 1 otherwise.

genUType **usubBorrow**(genUType *x*, genUType *y*,
       out genUType *borrow*);

Subtracts the 32-bit unsigned integer *y* from *x*, returning the difference if nonnegative, or 2^{32} plus the difference otherwise. The value *borrow* is set to 0 if $x \geq y$, or to 1 otherwise.

---

void **umulExtended**(genUType *x*, genUType *y*,
      out genUType *msb*, out genUType *lsb*);
void **imulExtended**(genIType *x*, genIType *y*, out genIType *msb*,
      out genIType *lsb*);

Multiply 32-bit integers *x* and *y*, producing a 64-bit result. The 32 least-significant bits are returned in *lsb*. The 32 most-significant bits are returned in *msb*.

---

genIType **bitfieldExtract**(genIType *value*, int *offset*, int *bits*);
genUType **bitfieldExtract**(genUType *value*, int *offset*, int *bits*);

Extract bits [*offset*, *offset* + *bits* − 1] from *value*, returning them in the least significant bits of the result.

For unsigned data types, the most significant bits of the result will be set to zero. For signed data types, the most significant bits will be set to the value of bit *offset* + *bits* − 1.

If *bits* is zero, the result will be zero. The result will be undefined if *offset* or *bits* is negative or if the sum of *offset* and *bits* is greater than the number of bits used to store the operand.

---

genIType **bitfieldInsert**(genIType *base*, genIType *insert*, int *offset*,
      int *bits*);
genUType **bitfieldInsert**(genUType *base*, genUType *insert*,
      int *offset*, int *bits*);

Return the insertion of the *bits* least-significant bits of *insert* into *base*.

The result will have bits [*offset*, *offset* + *bits* − 1] taken from bits [0, *bits* − 1] of *insert*, and all other bits taken directly from the corresponding bits of *base*. If *bits* is zero, the result will simply be *base*. The result will be undefined if *offset* or *bits* is negative or if the sum of *offset* and *bits* is greater than the number of bits used to store the operand.

genIType **bitfieldReverse**(genIType *value*);
genUType **bitfieldReverse**(genUType *value*);

Return the reversal of the bits of *value*. The bit numbered *n* of the result will be taken from bit (*bits* − 1) − *n* of *value*, where *bits* is the total number of bits used to represent *value*.

genIType **bitCount**(genIType *value*);
genIType **bitCount**(genUType *value*);

Return the number of bits set to 1 in the binary representation of *value*.

genIType **findLSB**(genIType *value*);
genIType **findLSB**(genUType *value*);

Return the bit number of the least significant bit set to 1 in the binary representation of *value*. If *value* is zero, −1 will be returned.

genIType **findMSB**(genIType *value*);
genIType **findMSB**(genUType *value*);

Return the bit number of the most significant bit in the binary representation of *value*.

For positive integers, the result will be the bit number of the most significant bit set to 1. For negative integers, the result will be the bit number of the most significant bit set to 0. For a *value* of zero or negative one, −1 will be returned.

Texture Functions

Texture lookup functions are available in all shading stages. However, level of detail is implicitly computed only for fragment shaders, so that OpenGL can automatically perform mipmap filtering. Other shading stages use a base level of detail of zero or use the texture directly if it is not mipmapped. When texture functions require implicit derivatives, they must be called outside of nonuniform flow control. That is, if they are called within flow control that varies from fragment to fragment, there is not enough information to properly compute the level of detail, giving undefined implicit derivatives and hence undefined results from the texture lookup.

Texture data can be stored by the GL as single-precision floating point, unsigned normalized integer, unsigned integer, or signed integer data. This is determined by the type of the internal format of the texture. Texture lookups on unsigned normalized integer and floating-point data return floating-point values in the range $[0.0, 1.0]$.

Texture lookup functions that can return their result as floating point, unsigned integer, or signed integer are provided, depending on the sampler type passed to the lookup function. Care must be taken to use the right sampler type for texture access. If an integer sampler type is used, the result of a texture lookup is an ivec4. If an unsigned integer sampler type is used, the result of a texture lookup is a uvec4. If a floating-point sampler type is used, the result of a texture lookup is a vec4, where each component is in the range $[0, 1]$.

For shadow forms (the *sampler* parameter is a shadow-type), a depth comparison lookup on the depth texture bound to *sampler* is done. See the table below for which component specifies D_{ref}. The texture bound to *sampler* must be a depth texture, or results are undefined. If a nonshadow texture call is made to a sampler that represents a depth texture with depth comparisons turned on, then results are undefined. If a shadow texture call is made to a sampler that represents a depth texture with depth comparisons turned off, then results are undefined. If a shadow texture call is made to a sampler that does not represent a depth texture, then results are undefined.

In all functions below, the *bias* argument is optional for fragment-stage shaders. The *bias* argument is not accepted in any other stages. For a fragment shader, if *bias* is present, it is added to the implicit level of detail prior to performing the texture access operation. No *bias* or *lod* arguments for rectangle textures, multisample textures, or texture buffers are supported because mipmaps are not allowed for these types of textures.

For **Cube** forms, the direction of P is used to select which face to do a two-dimensional texture lookup in.

For **Array** forms, the array layer used will be

$$max(0, min(d - 1, floor(layer + 0.5)))$$

where d is the depth of the texture array and *layer* comes from the component indicated in the tables below.

For depth-stencil textures, the sampler type should match the component being accessed as set through the OpenGL API. When the depth-stencil texture mode is set to DEPTH_COMPONENT, a floating-point sampler type should be used. When the depth-stencil texture mode is set to STENCIL_INDEX, an unsigned integer sampler type should be used. Doing a texture lookup with an unsupported combination will return undefined values.

Texture Query Functions

The **textureSize** functions query the dimensions of a specific texture level for a sampler.

The **textureQueryLod** functions are available only in a fragment shader. They take the components of P and compute the level of detail information that the texture pipe would use to access that texture through a normal texture lookup. The level of detail is obtained after any LOD bias, but prior to clamping to [TEXTURE_MIN_LOD, TEXTURE_MAX_LOD]. The mipmap array(s) that would be accessed are also computed. If a single level of detail would be accessed, the level-of-detail number relative to the base level is returned. If multiple levels of detail would be accessed, a floating-point number between the two levels is returned, with the fractional part equal to the fractional part of the computed and clamped level of detail.

```
int textureSize(gsampler1D sampler, int lod);
ivec2 textureSize(gsampler2D sampler, int lod);
ivec3 textureSize(gsampler3D sampler, int lod);
ivec2 textureSize(gsamplerCube sampler, int lod);
int textureSize(sampler1DShadow sampler, int lod);
ivec2 textureSize(sampler2DShadow sampler, int lod);
ivec2 textureSize(samplerCubeShadow sampler, int lod);
ivec3 textureSize(gsamplerCubeArray sampler, int lod);
ivec3 textureSize(samplerCubeArrayShadow sampler, int lod);
```

ivec2 **textureSize**(gsampler2DRect *sampler*);
ivec2 **textureSize**(sampler2DRectShadow *sampler*);
ivec2 **textureSize**(gsampler1DArray *sampler*, int *lod*);
ivec3 **textureSize**(gsampler2DArray *sampler*, int *lod*);
ivec2 **textureSize**(sampler1DArrayShadow *sampler*, int *lod*);
ivec3 **textureSize**(sampler2DArrayShadow *sampler*, int *lod*);
int **textureSize**(gsamplerBuffer *sampler*);
ivec2 **textureSize**(gsampler2DMS *sampler*);
ivec3 **textureSize**(gsampler2DMSArray *sampler*);

Return the dimensions of level *lod* (if present) for the texture bound to *sampler*. The components in the return value are filled in, in order, with the width, height, and depth of the texture. For the array forms, the last component of the return value is the number of layers in the texture array, or the number of cubes in the texture cube-map array.

---

vec2 **textureQueryLod**(gsampler1D *sampler*, float *P*);
vec2 **textureQueryLod**(gsampler2D *sampler*, vec2 *P*);
vec2 **textureQueryLod**(gsampler3D *sampler*, vec3 *P*);
vec2 **textureQueryLod**(gsamplerCube *sampler*, vec3 *P*);
vec2 **textureQueryLod**(gsampler1DArray *sampler*, float *P*);
vec2 **textureQueryLod**(gsampler2DArray *sampler*, vec2 *P*);
vec2 **textureQueryLod**(gsamplerCubeArray *sampler*, vec3 *P*);
vec2 **textureQueryLod**(sampler1DShadow *sampler*, float *P*);
vec2 **textureQueryLod**(sampler2DShadow *sampler*, vec2 *P*);
vec2 **textureQueryLod**(samplerCubeShadow *sampler*, vec3 *P*);
vec2 **textureQueryLod**(sampler1DArrayShadow *sampler*, float *P*);
vec2 **textureQueryLod**(sampler2DArrayShadow *sampler*, vec2 *P*);
vec2 **textureQueryLod**(samplerCubeArrayShadow *sampler*,
                              vec3 *P*);

Return the mipmap array(s) that would be accessed in the *x* component of the return value.

Return the computed level of detail relative to the base level in the *y* component of the return value.

If called on an incomplete texture, the results are undefined.

```
int textureQueryLevels(gsampler1D sampler);
int textureQueryLevels(gsampler2D sampler);
int textureQueryLevels(gsampler3D sampler);
int textureQueryLevels(gsamplerCube sampler);
int textureQueryLevels(gsampler1DArray sampler);
int textureQueryLevels(gsampler2DArray sampler);
int textureQueryLevels(gsamplerCubeArray sampler);
int textureQueryLevels(gsampler1DShadow sampler);
int textureQueryLevels(gsampler2DShadow sampler);
int textureQueryLevels(gsamplerCubeShadow sampler);
int textureQueryLevels(gsampler1DArrayShadow sampler);
int textureQueryLevels(gsampler2DArrayShadow sampler);
int textureQueryLevels(gsamplerCubeArrayShadow sampler);
```

Return the number of mipmap levels accessible in the texture associated with *sampler*.

The value zero will be returned if no texture or an incomplete texture is associated with *sampler*.

Available in all shader stages.

Texel Lookup Functions

```
gvec4 texture(gsampler1D sampler, float P [, float bias]);
gvec4 texture(gsampler2D sampler, vec2 P [, float bias]);
gvec4 texture(gsampler3D sampler, vec3 P [, float bias]);
gvec4 texture(gsamplerCube sampler, vec3 P [, float bias]);
float texture(sampler1DShadow sampler, vec3 P [, float bias]);
float texture(sampler2DShadow sampler, vec3 P [, float bias]);
float texture(samplerCubeShadow sampler, vec4 P [, float bias]);
gvec4 texture(gsampler1DArray sampler, vec2 P [, float bias]);
gvec4 texture(gsampler2DArray sampler, vec3 P [, float bias]);
gvec4 texture(gsamplerCubeArray sampler, vec4 P [, float bias]);
float texture(sampler1DArrayShadow sampler, vec3 P [,
              float bias]);
float texture(sampler2DArrayShadow sampler, vec4 P);
gvec4 texture(gsampler2DRect sampler, vec2 P);
float texture(sampler2DRectShadow sampler, vec3 P);
float texture(gsamplerCubeArrayShadow sampler, vec4 P,
              float compare);
```

Use the texture coordinate *P* to do a texture lookup in the texture currently bound to *sampler*. For shadow forms: When *compare* is present, it is used as D_{ref} and the array layer comes from *P.w*. When *compare* is not present, the last component of *P* is used as D_{ref} and the array layer comes from the second to last component of *P*. (The second component of *P* is unused for 1D shadow lookups.)

For nonshadow forms the array layer comes from the last component of *P*.

---

gvec4 **textureProj**(gsampler1D *sampler*, vec2 *P* [, float *bias*]);
gvec4 **textureProj**(gsampler1D *sampler*, vec4 *P* [, float *bias*]);
gvec4 **textureProj**(gsampler2D *sampler*, vec3 *P* [, float *bias*]);
gvec4 **textureProj**(gsampler2D *sampler*, vec4 *P* [, float *bias*]);
gvec4 **textureProj**(gsampler3D *sampler*, vec4 *P* [, float *bias*]);
float **textureProj**(sampler1DShadow *sampler*, vec4 *P* [, float *bias*]);
float **textureProj**(sampler2DShadow *sampler*, vec4 *P* [, float *bias*]);
gvec4 **textureProj**(gsampler2DRect *sampler*, vec3 *P*);
gvec4 **textureProj**(gsampler2DRect *sampler*, vec4 *P*);
float **textureProj**(sampler2DRectShadow *sampler*, vec4 *P*);

Do a texture lookup with projection. The texture coordinates consumed from *P*, not including the last component of *P*, are divided by the last component of *P*. The resulting 3rd component of *P* in the shadow forms is used as D_{ref}. After these values are computed, texture lookup proceeds as in **texture**.

---

gvec4 **textureLod**(gsampler1D *sampler*, float *P*, float *lod*);
gvec4 **textureLod**(gsampler2D *sampler*, vec2 *P*, float *lod*);
gvec4 **textureLod**(gsampler3D *sampler*, vec3 *P*, float *lod*);
gvec4 **textureLod**(gsamplerCube *sampler*, vec3 *P*, float *lod*);
float **textureLod**(sampler1DShadow *sampler*, vec3 *P*, float *lod*);
float **textureLod**(sampler2DShadow *sampler*, vec3 *P*, float *lod*);
gvec4 **textureLod**(gsampler1DArray *sampler*, vec2 *P*, float *lod*);
gvec4 **textureLod**(gsampler2DArray *sampler*, vec3 *P*, float *lod*);
float **textureLod**(sampler1DArrayShadow *sampler*, vec3 *P*,
                  float *lod*);
gvec4 **textureLod**(gsamplerCubeArray *sampler*, vec4 *P*, float *lod*);

Do a texture lookup as in **texture** but with explicit level of detail; *lod* specifies λ_{base} and sets the partial derivatives as follows:

$$\frac{\partial u}{\partial x} = 0 \quad \frac{\partial v}{\partial x} = 0 \quad \frac{\partial w}{\partial x} = 0$$

$$\frac{\partial u}{\partial y} = 0 \quad \frac{\partial v}{\partial y} = 0 \quad \frac{\partial w}{\partial y} = 0$$

---

gvec4 **textureOffset**(gsampler1D *sampler*, float *P*, int *offset* [, float *bias*]);

gvec4 **textureOffset**(gsampler2D *sampler*, vec2 *P*, ivec2 *offset* [, float *bias*]);

gvec4 **textureOffset**(gsampler3D *sampler*, vec3 *P*, ivec3 *offset* [, float *bias*]);

gvec4 **textureOffset**(gsampler2DRect *sampler*, vec2 *P*, ivec2 *offset*);

float **textureOffset**(sampler2DRectShadow *sampler*, vec3 *P*, ivec2 *offset*);

float **textureOffset**(sampler1DShadow *sampler*, vec3 *P*, int *offset* [, float *bias*]);

float **textureOffset**(sampler2DShadow *sampler*, vec3 *P*, ivec2 *offset* [, float *bias*]);

gvec4 **textureOffset**(gsampler1DArray *sampler*, vec2 *P*, int *offset* [, float *bias*]);

gvec4 **textureOffset**(gsampler2DArray *sampler*, vec3 *P*, ivec2 *offset* [, float *bias*]);

float **textureOffset**(sampler1DArrayShadow *sampler*, vec3 *P*, int *offset* [, float *bias*]);

float **textureOffset**(sampler2DArrayShadow *sampler*, vec4 *P*, vec2 *offset* [, float *bias*]);

Do a texture lookup as in **texture** but with *offset* added to the (u, v, w) texel coordinates before looking up each texel. The offset value must be a constant expression. A limited range of offset values are supported; the minimum and maximum offset values are implementation-dependent and given by gl_MinProgramTexelOffset and gl_MaxProgramTexelOffset, respectively.

Note that *offset* does not apply to the layer coordinate for texture arrays.

Note that texel offsets are also not supported for cube maps.

---

gvec4 **texelFetch**(gsampler1D *sampler*, int *P*, int *lod*);
gvec4 **texelFetch**(gsampler2D *sampler*, ivec2 *P*, int *lod*);
gvec4 **texelFetch**(gsampler3D *sampler*, ivec3 *P*, int *lod*);
gvec4 **texelFetch**(gsampler2DRect *sampler*, ivec2 *P*);
gvec4 **texelFetch**(gsampler1DArray *sampler*, ivec2 *P*, int *lod*);
gvec4 **texelFetch**(gsampler2DArray *sampler*, ivec3 *P*, int *lod*);
gvec4 **texelFetch**(gsamplerBuffer *sampler*, int *P*);
gvec4 **texelFetch**(gsampler2DMS *sampler*, ivec2 *P*, int *sample*);
gvec4 **texelFetch**(gsampler2DMSArray *sampler*, ivec3 *P*,
                   int *sample*);

Use integer texture coordinate *P* to look up a single texel from *sampler*. The array layer comes from the last component of *P* for the array forms.

---

gvec4 **texelFetchOffset**(gsampler1D *sampler*, int *P*, int *lod*,
                   int *offset*);
gvec4 **texelFetchOffset**(gsampler2D *sampler*, ivec2 *P*, int *lod*,
                   ivec2 *offset*);
gvec4 **texelFetchOffset**(gsampler3D *sampler*, ivec3 *P*, int *lod*,
                   ivec3 *offset*);
gvec4 **texelFetchOffset**(gsampler2DRect *sampler*, ivec2 *P*,
                   ivec2 *offset*);
gvec4 **texelFetchOffset**(gsampler1DArray *sampler*, ivec2 *P*, int *lod*,
                   int *offset*);
gvec4 **texelFetchOffset**(gsampler2DArray *sampler*, ivec3 *P*, int *lod*,
                   ivec2 *offset*);

Fetch a single texel as in **texelFetch** offset by *offset* as described in **textureOffset**.

gvec4 **textureProjOffset**(gsampler1D *sampler*, vec2 P, int *offset* [,
float *bias*]);
gvec4 **textureProjOffset**(gsampler1D *sampler*, vec4 P, int *offset* [,
float *bias*]);
gvec4 **textureProjOffset**(gsampler2D *sampler*, vec3 P, ivec2 *offset*
[, float *bias*]);
gvec4 **textureProjOffset**(gsampler2D *sampler*, vec4 P, ivec2 *offset*
[, float *bias*]);
gvec4 **textureProjOffset**(gsampler3D *sampler*, vec4 P, ivec3 *offset*
[, float *bias*]);
gvec4 **textureProjOffset**(gsampler2DRect *sampler*, vec3 P,
ivec2 *offset*);
gvec4 **textureProjOffset**(gsampler2DRect *sampler*, vec4 P,
ivec2 *offset*);
float **textureProjOffset**(sampler2DRectShadow *sampler*, vec4 P,
ivec2 *offset*);
float **textureProjOffset**(sampler1DShadow *sampler*, vec4 P,
int *offset* [, float *bias*]);
float **textureProjOffset**(sampler2DShadow *sampler*, vec4 P,
ivec2 *offset* [, float *bias*]);

Do a projective texture lookup as described in **textureProj** offset by *offset*
as described in **textureOffset**.

---

gvec4 **textureLodOffset**(gsampler1D *sampler*, float P, float *lod*,
int *offset*);
gvec4 **textureLodOffset**(gsampler2D *sampler*, vec2 P, float *lod*,
ivec2 *offset*);
gvec4 **textureLodOffset**(gsampler3D *sampler*, vec3 P, float *lod*,
ivec3 *offset*);
float **textureLodOffset**(sampler1DShadow *sampler*, vec3 P,
float *lod*, int *offset*);
float **textureLodOffset**(sampler2DShadow *sampler*, vec3 P,
float *lod*, ivec2 *offset*);
gvec4 **textureLodOffset**(gsampler1DArray *sampler*, vec2 P,
float *lod*, int *offset*);
gvec4 **textureLodOffset**(gsampler2DArray *sampler*, vec3 P,
float *lod*, ivec2 *offset*);
float **textureLodOffset**(sampler1DArrayShadow *sampler*, vec3 P,
float *lod*, int *offset*);

Do an offset texture lookup with explicit level of detail.

See **textureLod** and **textureOffset**.

---

gvec4 **textureProjLod**(gsampler1D *sampler*, vec2 *P*, float *lod*);
gvec4 **textureProjLod**(gsampler1D *sampler*, vec4 *P*, float *lod*);
gvec4 **textureProjLod**(gsampler2D *sampler*, vec3 *P*, float *lod*);
gvec4 **textureProjLod**(gsampler2D *sampler*, vec4 *P*, float *lod*);
gvec4 **textureProjLod**(gsampler3D *sampler*, vec4 *P*, float *lod*);
float **textureProjLod**(sampler1DShadow *sampler*, vec4 *P*,
        float *lod*);
float **textureProjLod**(sampler2DShadow *sampler*, vec4 *P*,
        float *lod*);

Do a projective texture lookup with explicit level of detail.

See **textureProj** and **textureLod**.

---

gvec4 **textureProjLodOffset**(gsampler1D *sampler*, vec2 *P*,
        float *lod*, int *offset*);
gvec4 **textureProjLodOffset**(gsampler1D *sampler*, vec4 *P*,
        float *lod*, int *offset*);
gvec4 **textureProjLodOffset**(gsampler2D *sampler*, vec3 *P*,
        float *lod*, ivec2 *offset*);
gvec4 **textureProjLodOffset**(gsampler2D *sampler*, vec4 *P*,
        float *lod*, ivec2 *offset*);
gvec4 **textureProjLodOffset**(gsampler3D *sampler*, vec4 *P*,
        float *lod*, ivec3 *offset*);
float **textureProjLodOffset**(sampler1DShadow *sampler*, vec4 *P*,
        float *lod*, int *offset*);
float **textureProjLodOffset**(sampler2DShadow *sampler*, vec4 *P*,
        float *lod*, ivec2 *offset*);

Do an offset projective texture lookup with explicit level of detail.

See **textureProj**, **textureLod**, and **textureOffset**.

gvec4 **textureGrad**(gsampler1D *sampler*, float *P*, float *dPdx*,
                float *dPdy*);

gvec4 **textureGrad**(gsampler2D *sampler*, vec2 *P*, vec2 *dPdx*,
                vec2 *dPdy*);

gvec4 **textureGrad**(gsampler3D *sampler*, vec3 *P*, vec3 *dPdx*,
                vec3 *dPdy*);

gvec4 **textureGrad**(gsamplerCube *sampler*, vec3 *P*, vec3 *dPdx*,
                vec3 *dPdy*);

gvec4 **textureGrad**(gsampler2DRect *sampler*, vec2 *P*, vec2 *dPdx*,
                vec2 *dPdy*);

float **textureGrad**(sampler2DRectShadow *sampler*, vec3 *P*,
                vec2 *dPdx*, vec2 *dPdy*);

float **textureGrad**(sampler1DShadow *sampler*, vec3 *P*, float *dPdx*,
                float *dPdy*);

float **textureGrad**(sampler2DShadow *sampler*, vec3 *P*, vec2 *dPdx*,
                vec2 *dPdy*);

float **textureGrad**(samplerCubeShadow *sampler*, vec4 *P*,
                vec3 *dPdx*, vec3 *dPdy*);

gvec4 **textureGrad**(gsampler1DArray *sampler*, vec2 *P*, float *dPdx*,
                float *dPdy*);

gvec4 **textureGrad**(gsampler2DArray *sampler*, vec3 *P*, vec2 *dPdx*,
                vec2 *dPdy*);

float **textureGrad**(sampler1DArrayShadow *sampler*, vec3 *P*,
                float *dPdx*, float *dPdy*);

float **textureGrad**(sampler2DArrayShadow *sampler*, vec4 *P*,
                vec2 *dPdx*, vec2 *dPdy*);

gvec4 **textureGrad**(gsamplerCubeArray *sampler*, vec4 *P*,
                vec3 *dPdx*, vec3 *dPdy*);

Do a texture lookup as in **texture** but with explicit gradients. The partial derivatives of *P* are with respect to window *x* and window *y*.

For a 1D texture, set

$$\frac{\partial s}{\partial x} = \frac{\partial P}{\partial x} \qquad \frac{\partial t}{\partial x} = 0 \qquad \frac{\partial r}{\partial x} = 0$$

$$\frac{\partial s}{\partial y} = \frac{\partial P}{\partial y} \qquad \frac{\partial t}{\partial y} = 0 \qquad \frac{\partial r}{\partial y} = 0$$

For a multidimensional texture, set

$$\frac{\partial s}{\partial x} = \frac{\partial P.s}{\partial x} \qquad \frac{\partial t}{\partial x} = \frac{\partial P.t}{\partial x} \qquad \frac{\partial r}{\partial x} = \frac{\partial P.p}{\partial x}$$

$$\frac{\partial t}{\partial y} = \frac{\partial P.t}{\partial y} \qquad \frac{\partial s}{\partial y} = \frac{\partial P.s}{\partial y} \qquad \frac{\partial r}{\partial y} = \frac{\partial P.p}{\partial y}$$

For the cube version, the partial derivatives of P are assumed to be in the coordinate system used before texture coordinates are projected onto the appropriate cube face.

---

gvec4 **textureGradOffset**(gsampler1D *sampler*, float *P*, float *dPdx*, float *dPdy*, int *offset*);

gvec4 **textureGradOffset**(gsampler2D *sampler*, vec2 *P*, vec2 *dPdx*, vec2 *dPdy*, ivec2 *offset*);

gvec4 **textureGradOffset**(gsampler3D *sampler*, vec3 *P*, vec3 *dPdx*, vec3 *dPdy*, ivec3 *offset*);

gvec4 **textureGradOffset**(gsampler2DRect *sampler*, vec2 *P*, vec2 *dPdx*, vec2 *dPdy*, ivec2 *offset*);

float **textureGradOffset**(sampler2DRectShadow *sampler*, vec3 *P*, vec2 *dPdx*, vec2 *dPdy*, ivec2 *offset*);

float **textureGradOffset**(sampler1DShadow *sampler*, vec3 *P*, float *dPdx*, float *dPdy*, int *offset*);

float **textureGradOffset**(sampler2DShadow *sampler*, vec3 *P*, vec2 *dPdx*, vec2 *dPdy*, ivec2 *offset*);

gvec4 **textureGradOffset**(gsampler1DArray *sampler*, vec2 *P*, float *dPdx*, float *dPdy*, int *offset*);

gvec4 **textureGradOffset**(gsampler2DArray *sampler*, vec3 *P*, vec2 *dPdx*, vec2 *dPdy*, ivec2 *offset*);

float **textureGradOffset**(sampler1DArrayShadow *sampler*, vec3 *P*, float *dPdx*, float *dPdy*, int *offset*);

float **textureGradOffset**(sampler2DArrayShadow *sampler*, vec4 *P*, vec2 *dPdx*, vec2 *dPdy*, ivec2 *offset*);

Do a texture lookup with both explicit gradient and offset, as described in **textureGrad** and **textureOffset**.

gvec4 **textureProjGrad**(gsampler1D *sampler*, vec2 *P*, float *dPdx*,
float *dPdy*);
gvec4 **textureProjGrad**(gsampler1D *sampler*, vec4 *P*, float *dPdx*,
float *dPdy*);
gvec4 **textureProjGrad**(gsampler2D *sampler*, vec3 *P*, vec2 *dPdx*,
vec2 *dPdy*);
gvec4 **textureProjGrad**(gsampler2D *sampler*, vec4 *P*, vec2 *dPdx*,
vec2 *dPdy*);
gvec4 **textureProjGrad**(gsampler3D *sampler*, vec4 *P*, vec3 *dPdx*,
vec3 *dPdy*);
gvec4 **textureProjGrad**(gsampler2DRect *sampler*, vec3 *P*,
vec2 *dPdx*, vec2 *dPdy*);
gvec4 **textureProjGrad**(gsampler2DRect *sampler*, vec4 *P*,
vec2 *dPdx*, vec2 *dPdy*);
float **textureProjGrad**(sampler2DRectShadow *sampler*, vec4 *P*,
vec2 *dPdx*, vec2 *dPdy*);
float **textureProjGrad**(sampler1DShadow *sampler*, vec4 *P*,
float *dPdx*, float *dPdy*);
float **textureProjGrad**(sampler2DShadow *sampler*, vec4 *P*,
vec2 *dPdx*, vec2 *dPdy*);

Do a texture lookup both projectively, as described in **textureProj**, and
with explicit gradient as described in **textureGrad**.

The partial derivatives *dPdx* and *dPdy* are assumed to be already
projected.

---

gvec4 **textureProjGradOffset**(gsampler1D *sampler*, vec2 *P*,
float *dPdx*, float *dPdy*, int *offset*);
gvec4 **textureProjGradOffset**(gsampler1D *sampler*, vec4 *P*,
float *dPdx*, float *dPdy*, int *offset*);
gvec4 **textureProjGradOffset**(gsampler2D *sampler*, vec3 *P*,
vec2 *dPdx*, vec2 *dPdy*, ivec2 *offset*);
gvec4 **textureProjGradOffset**(gsampler2D *sampler*, vec4 *P*,
vec2 *dPdx*, vec2 *dPdy*, ivec2 *offset*);
gvec4 **textureProjGradOffset**(gsampler2DRect *sampler*, vec3 *P*,
vec2 *dPdx*, vec2 *dPdy*, ivec2 *offset*);
gvec4 **textureProjGradOffset**(gsampler2DRect *sampler*, vec4 *P*,
vec2 *dPdx*, vec2 *dPdy*, ivec2 *offset*);

float **textureProjGradOffset**(sampler2DRectShadow *sampler*,
                    vec4 *P*, vec2 *dPdx*, vec2 *dPdy*,
                    ivec2 *offset*);
gvec4 **textureProjGradOffset**(gsampler3D *sampler*, vec4 *P*,
                    vec3 *dPdx*, vec3 *dPdy*, ivec3 *offset*);
float **textureProjGradOffset**(sampler1DShadow *sampler*, vec4 *P*,
                    float *dPdx*, float *dPdy*, int *offset*);
float **textureProjGradOffset**(sampler2DShadow *sampler*, vec4 *P*,
                    vec2 *dPdx*, vec2 *dPdy*, ivec2 *offset*);

Do a texture lookup projectively and with explicit gradient as described in **textureProjGrad**, as well as with offset, as described in **textureOffset**.

Texture Gather Functions

The texture gather functions take components of a single floating-point vector operand as a texture coordinate, determine a set of four texels to sample from the base level of detail of the specified texture image, and return one component from each texel in a four-component result vector.

When performing a texture gather operation, the minification and magnification filters are ignored, and the rules for LINEAR filtering are applied to the base level of the texture image to identify the four texels i_0j_1, i_1j_1, i_1j_0, and i_0j_0. The texels are then converted to texture base colors (R_s, G_s, B_s, A_s), followed by application of the texture swizzle. A four-component vector is assembled by taking the selected component from each of the post-swizzled texture source colors in the order $(i_0j_1, i_1j_1, i_1j_0, i_0j_0)$.

For texture gather functions using a shadow sampler type, each of the four texel lookups performs a depth comparison against the depth reference value passed in *refZ*, and returns the result of that comparison in the appropriate component of the result vector.

As with other texture lookup functions, the results of a texture gather are undefined for shadow samplers if the texture referenced is not a depth texture or has depth comparisons disabled; or for nonshadow samplers if the texture referenced is a depth texture with depth comparisons enabled.

gvec4 **textureGather**(gsampler2D *sampler*, vec2 P [, int *comp*]);
gvec4 **textureGather**(gsampler2DArray *sampler*, vec3 P [, int *comp*]);
gvec4 **textureGather**(gsamplerCube *sampler*, vec3 P [, int *comp*]);
gvec4 **textureGather**(gsamplerCubeArray *sampler*, vec4 P [, int *comp*]);
gvec4 **textureGather**(gsampler2DRect *sampler*, vec2 P [, int *comp*]);
vec4 **textureGather**(sampler2DShadow *sampler*, vec2 P, float *refZ*);
vec4 **textureGather**(sampler2DArrayShadow *sampler*, vec3 P, float *refZ*);
vec4 **textureGather**(samplerCubeShadow *sampler*, vec3 P, float *refZ*);
vec4 **textureGather**(samplerCubeArrayShadow *sampler*, vec4 P, float *refZ*);
vec4 **textureGather**(sampler2DRectShadow *sampler*, vec2 P, float *refZ*);

Return a vec4 value from the following four components:

Sample $i_0 j_1 (P, base).comp$

Sample $i_1 j_1 (P, base).comp$

Sample $i_1 j_0 (P, base).comp$

Sample $i_0 j_0 (P, base).comp$

If specified, the value of *comp* must be a constant integer expression with a value of 0, 1, 2, or 3, identifying the *x*, *y*, *z*, or *w* post-swizzled component of the four-component vector lookup result for each texel, respectively. If *comp* is not specified, it is treated as 0, selecting the *x* component of each texel to generate the result.

gvec4 **textureGatherOffset**(gsampler2D *sampler*, vec2 P, ivec2 *offset* [, int *comp*]);
gvec4 **textureGatherOffset**(gsampler2DArray *sampler*, vec3 P, ivec2 *offset* [, int *comp*]);
gvec4 **textureGatherOffset**(gsampler2DRect *sampler*, vec2 P, ivec2 *offset* [, int *comp*]);

vec4 **textureGatherOffset**(sampler2DShadow *sampler*, vec2 *P*,
float *refZ*, ivec2 *offset*);
vec4 **textureGatherOffset**(sampler2DArrayShadow *sampler*,
vec3 *P*, float *refZ*, ivec2 *offset*);
vec4 **textureGatherOffset**(sampler2DRectShadow *sampler*, vec2 *P*,
float *refZ*, ivec2 *offset*);

Perform a texture gather operation as in **textureGather** by *offset* as
described in **textureOffset** except that *offset* can be variable (non
constant) and the implementation-dependent minimum and maximum
offset values are given by MIN_PROGRAM_TEXTURE_GATHER_OFFSET
and MAX_PROGRAM_TEXTURE_GATHER_OFFSET, respectively.

gvec4 **textureGatherOffsets**(gsampler2D *sampler*, vec2 *P*,
ivec2 *offsets[4]* [, int *comp*]);
gvec4 **textureGatherOffsets**(gsampler2DArray *sampler*, vec3 *P*,
ivec2 *offsets[4]* [, int *comp*]);
gvec4 **textureGatherOffsets**(gsampler2DRect *sampler*, vec3 *P*,
ivec2 *offsets[4]* [, int *comp*]);
vec4 **textureGatherOffsets**(sampler2DShadow *sampler*, vec2 *P*,
float *refZ*, ivec2 *offsets[4]*);
vec4 **textureGatherOffsets**(sampler2DArrayShadow *sampler*,
vec3 *P*, float *refZ*, ivec2 *offsets[4]*);
vec4 **textureGatherOffsets**(sampler2DRectShadow *sampler*,
vec2 *P*, float *refZ*, ivec2 *offsets[4]*);

Operate identically to **textureGatherOffset** except that *offsets* is used to
determine the location of the four texels to sample. Each of the four
texels is obtained by applying the corresponding offset in *offsets* as a (u, v)
coordinate offset to *P*, identifying the four-texel LINEAR footprint, and
then selecting the texel i_0j_0 of that footprint. The specified values in
offsets must be set with constant integral expressions.

Atomic-Counter Functions

The atomic-counter operations in this section operate atomically with
respect to each other. They are atomic for any single counter, meaning any
of these operations on a specific counter in one shader instantiation will be
indivisible by any of these operations on the same counter from another
shader instantiation. There is no guarantee that these operations are atomic

with respect to other forms of access to the counter or that they are serialized when applied to separate counters. Such cases would require additional use of fences, barriers, or other forms of synchronization, if atomicity or serialization is desired. The value returned by an atomic-counter function is the value of an atomic counter, which may be returned and incremented in an atomic operation, or decremented and returned in an atomic operation, or simply returned. The underlying counter is a 32-bit unsigned integer. Increments and decrements at the limit of the range will wrap to $[0, 2^{32} - 1]$.

uint **atomicCounterIncrement**(atomic_uint *c*);

Atomically

1. increments the counter for *c*, and

2. returns its value prior to the increment operation.

These two steps are done atomically with respect to the atomic-counter functions in this table.

uint **atomicCounterDecrement**(atomic_uint *c*);

Atomically

1. decrements the counter for *c*, and

2. returns the value resulting from the decrement operation.

These two steps are done atomically with respect to the atomic-counter functions in this table.

uint **atomicCounter**(atomic_uint *c*);

Returns the counter value for *c*.

Atomic Memory Functions

Atomic memory functions perform atomic operations on an individual signed or unsigned integer stored in buffer-object or shared-variable storage. All of the atomic memory operations read a value from memory, compute a new value using one of the operations described below, write the new value to memory, and return the original value read. The contents of the memory being updated by the atomic operation are guaranteed not to be modified by any other assignment or atomic memory function in any shader invocation between the time the original value is read and the time the new value is written. Atomic memory functions are supported only for a limited set of variables. A shader will fail to compile if the value passed to the *mem* argument of an atomic memory function does not correspond to a buffer or shared variable. It is acceptable to pass an element of an array or a single component of a vector to the *mem* argument of an atomic memory function, as long as the underlying array or vector is a buffer or shared variable.

uint **atomicAdd**(inout uint *mem*, uint *data*);
int **atomicAdd**(inout int *mem*, int *data*);

Compute a new value by adding the value of *data* to the contents *mem*.

uint **atomicMin**(inout uint *mem*, uint *data*);
int **atomicMin**(inout int *mem*, int *data*);

Compute a new value by taking the minimum of the value of *data* and the contents of *mem*.

uint **atomicMax**(inout uint *mem*, uint *data*);
int **atomicMax**(inout int *mem*, int *data*);

Compute a new value by taking the maximum of the value of *data* and the contents of *mem*.

uint **atomicAnd**(inout uint *mem*, uint *data*);
int **atomicAnd**(inout int *mem*, int *data*);

Compute a new value by performing a bit-wise *and* of the value of *data* and the contents of *mem*.

uint **atomicOr**(inout uint *mem*, uint *data*);
int **atomicOr**(inout int *mem*, int *data*);

Compute a new value by performing a bit-wise *or* of the value of *data* and the contents of *mem*.

uint **atomicXor**(inout uint *mem*, uint *data*);
int **atomicXor**(inout int *mem*, int *data*);

Compute a new value by performing a bit-wise *exclusive or* of the value of *data* and the contents of *mem*.

uint **atomicExchange**(inout uint *mem*, uint *data*);
int **atomicExchange**(inout int *mem*, int *data*);

Compute a new value by simply copying the value of *data*.

uint **atomicCompSwap**(inout uint *mem*, uint *compare*, uint *data*);
int **atomicCompSwap**(inout int *mem*, int *compare*, int *data*);

Compare the value of *compare* and the contents of *mem*. If the values are equal, the new value is given by *data*; otherwise, it is taken from the original contents of *mem*.

Image Functions

Variables using one of the image basic types may be used by the built-in shader image memory functions defined in this section to read and write individual texels of a texture. Each image variable references an image unit, which has a texture image attached.

When the image functions access memory, an individual texel in the image is identified using an (i), (i, j), or (i, j, k) coordinate corresponding to the values of P. For image2DMS and image2DMSArray variables (and the corresponding signed- and unsigned-int types) corresponding to multisample textures, each texel may have multiple samples and an individual sample is identified using the integer *sample* argument.

Loads and stores support float, integer, and unsigned integer types. The *IMAGE_PARAMS* in the prototypes below is a placeholder representing 33 separate functions, each for a different type of image variable. The *IMAGE_PARAMS* placeholder is replaced by one of the following parameter lists:

- gimage1D *image*, int *P*
- gimage2D *image*, ivec2 *P*
- gimage3D *image*, ivec3 *P*
- gimage2DRect *image*, ivec2 *P*
- gimageCube *image*, ivec3 *P*
- gimageBuffer *image*, int *P*
- gimage1DArray *image*, ivec2 *P*
- gimage2DArray *image*, ivec3 *P*
- gimageCubeArray *image*, ivec3 *P*
- gimage2DMS *image*, ivec2 *P*, int *sample*
- gimage2DMSArray *image*, ivec3 *P*, int *sample*

where each of the lines represents one of three different image variable types, and *image*, *P*, and *sample* specify the individual texel to operate on.

The atomic functions perform atomic operations on individual texels or samples of an image variable. Atomic memory operations read a value from the selected texel, compute a new value using one of the operations described below, write the new value to the selected texel, and return the original value read. The contents of the texel being updated by the atomic operation are guaranteed not to be modified by any other image store or atomic function between the time the original value is read and the time the new value is written.

Atomic memory operations are supported on only a subset of all image variable types; image must be either

- a signed integer image variable (type starts "iimage") and a format qualifier of *r32i*, used with a *data* argument of type int, or
- an unsigned image variable (type starts "uimage") and a format qualifier of *r32ui*, used with a *data* argument of type uint.

```
int imageSize(gimage1D image);
ivec2 imageSize(gimage2D image);
ivec3 imageSize(gimage3D image);
ivec2 imageSize(gimageCube image);
ivec3 imageSize(gimageCubeArray image);
ivec2 imageSize(gimageRect image);
ivec2 imageSize(gimage1DArray image);
ivec3 imageSize(gimage2DArray image);
int imageSize(gimageBuffer image);
ivec2 imageSize(gimage2DMS image);
ivec3 imageSize(gimage2DMSArray image);
```

Return the dimensions of the image or images bound to *image*. For arrayed images, the last component of the return value will hold the size of the array. Cube images return only the dimensions of one face, and the number of cubes in the cube-map array, if arrayed.

```
gvec4 imageLoad(readonly IMAGE_PARAMS);
```

Loads the texel at the coordinate *P* from the image unit *image* (in *IMAGE_PARAMS*). For multisample loads, the sample number is given by *sample*. When *image*, *P*, and *sample* identify a valid texel, the bits used to represent the selected texel in memory are converted to a vec4, ivec4, or uvec4.

```
void imageStore(writeonly IMAGE_PARAMS, gvec4 data);
```

Stores *data* into the texel at the coordinate *P* from the image specified by *image*. For multisample stores, the sample number is given by *sample*. When *image*, *P*, and *sample* identify a valid texel, the bits used to represent *data* are converted to the format of the image unit.

```
uint imageAtomicAdd(IMAGE_PARAMS, uint data);
int imageAtomicAdd(IMAGE_PARAMS, int data);
```

Compute a new value by adding the value of *data* to the contents of the selected texel.

uint **imageAtomicMin**(*IMAGE_PARAMS*, uint *data*);
int **imageAtomicMin**(*IMAGE_PARAMS*, int *data*);

Compute a new value by taking the minimum of the value of *data* and the contents of the selected texel.

uint **imageAtomicMax**(*IMAGE_PARAMS*, uint *data*);
int **imageAtomicMax**(*IMAGE_PARAMS*, int *data*);

Compute a new value by taking the maximum of the value *data* and the contents of the selected texel.

uint **imageAtomicAnd**(*IMAGE_PARAMS*, uint *data*);
int **imageAtomicAnd**(*IMAGE_PARAMS*, int *data*);

Compute a new value by performing a bit-wise *and* of the value of *data* and the contents of the selected texel.

uint **imageAtomicOr**(*IMAGE_PARAMS*, uint *data*);
int **imageAtomicOr**(*IMAGE_PARAMS*, int *data*);

Compute a new value by performing a bit-wise *or* of the value of *data* and the contents of the selected texel.

uint **imageAtomicXor**(*IMAGE_PARAMS*, uint *data*);
int **imageAtomicXor**(*IMAGE_PARAMS*, int *data*);

Compute a new value by performing a bit-wise *exclusive or* of the value of *data* and the contents of the selected texel.

uint **imageAtomicExchange**(*IMAGE_PARAMS*, uint *data*);
int **imageAtomicExchange**(*IMAGE_PARAMS*, int *data*);

Compute a new value by simply copying the value of *data*.

uint **imageAtomicCompSwap**(*IMAGE_PARAMS*, uint *compare*,
uint *data*);
int **imageAtomicCompSwap**(*IMAGE_PARAMS*, int *compare*,
int *data*);

Compare the value of *compare* and the contents of the selected texel. If
the values are equal, the new value is given by *data*; otherwise, it is taken
from the original value loaded from the texel.

Fragment Processing Functions

Fragment processing functions are available only in fragment shaders.

Derivative Functions

OpenGL implementations typically approximate derivatives by comparing
a computed expression's value at neighboring fragments. Hence, when this
is requested within nonuniform control flow (lines of the shader that are
conditionally executed, where the condition varies from pixel to pixel),
the derivative is undefined.

genType **dFdx**(genType *p*);

Returns the derivative in the *x* direction, based on the value of *p* at
neighboring fragments.

genType **dFdy**(genType *p*);

Returns the derivative in the *y* direction, based on the value of *p* at
neighboring fragments.

genType **fwidth**(genType *p*);

Returns the sum of the absolute derivative in *x* and *y* for the input
argument *p*.

```
abs (dFdx (p))   + abs (dFdy (p));
```

Interpolation Functions

Built-in interpolation functions are available to compute an interpolated value of a fragment shader input variable at a shader-specified (x, y) location. A separate (x, y) location may be used for each invocation of the built-in function, and those locations may differ from the default (x, y) location used to produce the default value of the input. For all of the interpolation functions, *interpolant* must be an input variable or an element of an input variable declared as an array. Component selection operators (e.g., *.xy*) may not be used when specifying *interpolant*. If *interpolant* is declared with a `flat` or `centroid` qualifier, the qualifier will have no effect on the interpolated value. If *interpolant* is declared with the `noperspective` qualifier, the interpolated value will be computed without *perspective correction*.

---

float **interpolateAtCentroid**(float *interpolant*);
vec2 **interpolateAtCentroid**(vec2 *interpolant*);
vec3 **interpolateAtCentroid**(vec3 *interpolant*);
vec4 **interpolateAtCentroid**(vec4 *interpolant*);

Return the value of the input *interpolant* sampled at a location inside both the pixel and the primitive being processed. The value obtained would be the same value assigned to the input variable if declared with the `centroid` qualifier.

---

float **interpolateAtSample**(float *interpolant*, int *sample*);
vec2 **interpolateAtSample**(vec2 *interpolant*, int *sample*);
vec3 **interpolateAtSample**(vec3 *interpolant*, int *sample*);
vec4 **interpolateAtSample**(vec4 *interpolant*, int *sample*);

Return the value of the input *interpolant* variable at the location of sample number *sample*. If multisample buffers are not available, the input variable will be evaluated at the center of the pixel. If sample *sample* does not exist, the position used to interpolate the input variable is undefined.

---

float **interpolateAtOffset**(float *interpolant*, vec2 *offset*);
vec2 **interpolateAtOffset**(vec2 *interpolant*, vec2 *offset*);

vec3 **interpolateAtOffset**(vec3 *interpolant*, vec2 *offset*);
vec4 **interpolateAtOffset**(vec4 *interpolant*, vec2 *offset*);

Return the value of the input *interpolant* variable sampled at an offset from the center of the pixel specified by *offset*. The two floating-point components of *offset* give the offset in pixels in the x and y directions, respectively. An offset of $(0, 0)$ identifies the center of the pixel.

The range and granularity of offsets supported by this function are implementation-dependent.

Noise Functions

Portability Note: Built-in noise functions are not reproducible from platform to platform. Verify their support and appearance on all platforms you care about.

Noise functions can be used to increase visual complexity. Values returned by the following noise functions give the appearance of randomness but are not random. Rather, they give the same result for the same input, allowing reproduction of the same variance from frame to frame.

The noise functions below are defined to have the following characteristics:

- The return value(s) are always in the range [–1.0, 1.0], and cover at least the range [–0.6, 0.6], with a Gaussian-like distribution.

- The return value(s) have an overall average of 0.0.

- They are repeatable, in that a particular input value will always produce the same return value.

- They have a statistical invariance under translation (i.e., no matter how the domain is translated, it has the same statistical character).

- They give different results under translation.

- The spatial frequency is narrowly concentrated, centered somewhere between 0.5 and 1.0.

- They are C1 continuous everywhere (i.e., the first derivative is continuous).

float **noise1**(genType *x*);

Returns a 1D noise value based on the input value *x*.

vec2 **noise2**(genType *x*);

Returns a 2D noise value based on the input value *x*.

vec3 **noise3**(genType *x*);

Returns a 3D noise value based on the input value *x*.

vec4 **noise4**(genType *x*);

Returns a 4D noise value based on the input value *x*.

Geometry Shader Functions

These functions are available only in geometry shaders to manage the output data streams created by this stage.

The function **EmitStreamVertex** specifies that a vertex is completed. A vertex is added to the current output primitive in vertex stream *stream* using the current values of all output variables associated with *stream*. These include gl_PointSize, gl_ClipDistance[], gl_Layer, gl_Position, gl_PrimitiveID, and gl_ViewportIndex. The values of all output variables for all output streams are undefined after a call to **EmitStreamVertex**. If a geometry shader invocation has emitted more vertices than permitted by the output layout qualifier max_vertices, the results of calling **EmitStreamVertex** are undefined.

The function **EndStreamPrimitive** specifies that the current output primitive for vertex stream *stream* is completed and a new output primitive (of the same type) will be started by any subsequent **EmitStreamVertex**. This function does not emit a vertex. If the output layout is declared to be "points", calling **EndStreamPrimitive** is optional.

A geometry shader starts with an output primitive containing no vertices for each stream. When a geometry shader terminates, the current output primitive for each stream is automatically completed. It is not necessary to call **EndStreamPrimitive** if the geometry shader writes only a single primitive.

Multiple output streams are supported only if the output primitive type is declared to be points. A program will fail to link if it contains a geometry shader calling **EmitStreamVertex** or **EndStreamPrimitive** if its output primitive type is not points.

---

void **EmitStreamVertex**(int *stream*);

Emits the current values of output variables to the current output primitive on stream *stream*. The argument to *stream* must be a constant integral expression. On return from this call, the values of all output variables are undefined.

Can be used only if multiple output streams are supported.

---

void **EndStreamPrimitive**(int *stream*);

Completes the current output primitive on stream *stream* and starts a new one. The argument to *stream* must be a constant integral expression. No vertex is emitted.

Can be used only if multiple output streams are supported.

---

void **EmitVertex**();

Emits the current values of output variables to the current output primitive. On return from this call, the values of output variables are undefined. When multiple output streams are supported, this is equivalent to calling **EmitStreamVertex(0)**.

---

void **EndPrimitive**();

Completes the current output primitive and starts a new one. No vertex is emitted.

When multiple output streams are supported, this is equivalent to calling **EndStreamPrimitive(0)**.

Shader Invocation Control Functions

The shader invocation control function is available only in tessellation control shaders and compute shaders. It is used to control the relative execution order of multiple shader invocations used to process a patch (in the case of tessellation control shaders) or a local work group (in the case of compute shaders), which are otherwise executed with an undefined relative order.

void **barrier**();

For any given static instance of **barrier**, all tessellation control shader invocations for a single input patch must enter it before any will be allowed to continue beyond it, or all invocations for a single work group must enter it before any will continue beyond it.

The function **barrier** provides a partially defined order of execution between shader invocations. This ensures that values written by one invocation prior to a given static instance of **barrier** can be safely read by other invocations after their call to the same static instance **barrier**. Because invocations may execute in undefined order between these barrier calls, the values of a per-vertex or per-patch output variable or shared variables for compute shaders will be undefined in some cases. The **barrier** function may only be placed inside the function **main** of the tessellation control shader and may not be called within any control flow. Barriers are also disallowed after a return statement in the function **main**. Any such misplaced barriers result in a compile-time error.

Shader Memory Control Functions

Shaders of all types may read and write the contents of textures and buffer objects using image variables. While the order of reads and writes within a single shader invocation is well defined, the relative order of reads and writes to a single shared memory address from multiple separate shader invocations is largely undefined. The order of memory accesses performed by one shader invocation, as observed by other shader invocations, is also largely undefined but can be controlled through memory control functions.

void **memoryBarrier**();

Controls the ordering of memory transactions issued by a single shader invocation.

void **memoryBarrierAtomicCounter**();

Controls the ordering of accesses to atomic-counter variables issued by a single shader invocation.

void **memoryBarrierBuffer**();

Controls the ordering of memory transactions to buffer variables issued within a single shader invocation.

void **memoryBarrierShared**();

Controls the ordering of memory transactions to shared variables issued within a single shader invocation. Only available in compute shaders.

void **memoryBarrierImage**();

Controls the ordering of memory transactions to images issued within a single shader invocation.

void **groupMemoryBarrier**();

Controls the ordering of all memory transactions issued within a single shader invocation, as viewed by other invocations in the same work group. Only available in compute shaders.

The memory barrier built-in functions can be used to order reads and writes to variables stored in memory accessible to other shader invocations. When called, these functions will wait for the completion of all reads and writes previously performed by the caller that accessed selected variable types, and then return with no other effect. The built-in functions **memoryBarrierAtomicCounter**, **memoryBarrierBuffer**, **memoryBarrierImage**, and **memoryBarrierShared** wait for the completion of accesses to atomic counter, buffer, image, and shared variables, respectively. The built-in functions **memoryBarrier** and **groupMemoryBarrier** wait for the completion of accesses to all of the above variable types. The functions **memoryBarrierShared** and **groupMemoryBarrier** are available only in compute shaders; the other functions are available in all shader types.

When these functions return, the results of any memory stores performed using coherent variables performed prior to the call will be visible to any future coherent access to the same memory performed by any other shader invocation. In particular, the values written this way in one shader stage are guaranteed to be visible to coherent memory accesses performed by shader invocations in subsequent stages when those invocations were triggered by the execution of the original shader invocation (e.g., fragment shader invocations for a primitive resulting from a particular geometry shader invocation).

Additionally, memory barrier functions order stores performed by the calling invocation, as observed by other shader invocations. Without memory barriers, if one shader invocation performs two stores to coherent variables, a second shader invocation might see the values written by the second store prior to seeing those written by the first. However, if the first shader invocation calls a memory barrier function between the two stores, selected other shader invocations will never see the results of the second store before seeing those of the first. When using the function **groupMemoryBarrier**, this ordering guarantee applies only to other shader invocations in the same compute shader work group; all other memory barrier functions provide the guarantee to all other shader invocations. No memory barrier is required to guarantee the order of memory stores as observed by the invocation performing the stores; an invocation reading from a variable that it previously wrote will always see the most recently written value unless another shader invocation also wrote to the same memory.

State Variables

This appendix lists the queryable OpenGL state variables, their default values, and the commands for obtaining the values of these variables, and contains the following major sections:

- "The Query Commands"
- "OpenGL State Variables"

The Query Commands

In addition to the basic commands, such as **glGetIntegerv()** and **glIsEnabled()**, to obtain the values of simple state variables, there are other specialized commands to return more complex state variables. The prototypes for these specialized commands are listed here. Some of these routines, such as **glGetError()** and **glGetString()**, were discussed in more detail in Chapter 1.

To find out when you need to use these commands and their corresponding symbolic constants, use the tables in the next section, "OpenGL State Variables" on Page 745.

```
void glGetActiveAtomicCounterBufferiv(GLuint program,
                                      GLuint bufferIndex,
                                      GLenum pname,
                                      GLint *params);

void glGetActiveAttrib(GLuint program, GLuint index,
                       GLsizei bufSize, GLsizei *length,
                       GLint *size, GLenum *type,
                       GLchar *name);

void glGetActiveSubroutineName(GLuint program,
                               GLenum shadertype,
                               GLuint index, GLsizei bufsize,
                               GLsizei *length,
                               GLchar *name);

void glGetActiveSubroutineUniformiv(GLuint program,
                                    GLenum shadertype,
                                    GLuint index,
                                    GLenum pname,
                                    GLint *values);

void glGetActiveSubroutineUniformName(GLuint program,
                                      GLenum shadertype,
                                      GLuint index,
                                      GLsizei bufsize,
                                      GLsizei *length,
                                      GLchar *name);

void glGetActiveUniform(GLuint program, GLuint index,
                        GLsizei bufSize, GLsizei *length,
                        GLint *size, GLenum *type,
                        GLchar *name);
```

void **glGetActiveUniformBlockiv**(GLuint *program,*
                                   GLuint *uniformBlockIndex,*
                                   GLenum *pname,*
                                   GLint **params*);

void **glGetActiveUniformBlockName**(GLuint *program,*
                                     GLuint *uniformBlockIndex,*
                                     GLsizei *bufSize,*
                                     GLsizei **length,*
                                     GLchar **uniformBlockName*);

void **glGetActiveUniformName**(GLuint *program,*
                                GLuint *uniformIndex,*
                                GLsizei *bufSize,* GLsizei **length,*
                                GLchar **uniformName*);

void **glGetActiveUniformsiv**(GLuint *program,*
                               GLsizei *uniformCount,*
                               const GLuint **uniformIndices,*
                               GLenum *pname,* GLint **params*);

void **glGetAttachedShaders**(GLuint *program,* GLsizei *maxCount,*
                              GLsizei **count,* GLuint **obj*);

GLint **glGetAttribLocation**(GLuint *program,*
                              const GLchar **name*);

void **glGetBooleanv**(GLenum *pname,* GLboolean **params*);

void **glGetBooleani_v**(GLenum *target,* GLuint *index,*
                         GLboolean **data*);

void **glGetBufferParameteriv**(GLenum *target,* GLenum *pname,*
                                GLint **params*);

void **glGetBufferParameteri64v**(GLenum *target,* GLenum *pname,*
                                  GLint64 **params*);

void **glGetBufferPointerv**(GLenum *target,* GLenum *pname,*
                             GLvoid* **params*);

void **glGetBufferSubData**(GLenum *target,* GLintptr *offset,*
                            GLsizeiptr *size,* GLvoid **data*);

void **glGetCompressedTexImage**(GLenum *target,* GLint *level,*
                                 GLvoid **img*);

GLuint **glGetDebugMessageLog**(GLuint *count*, GLsizei *bufsize*,
                    GLenum **sources*,
                    GLenum **types*, GLuint **ids*,
                    GLenum **severities*,
                    GLsizei **lengths*,
                    GLchar **messageLog*);

void **glGetDoublev**(GLenum *pname*, GLdouble **params*);

void **glGetDoublei_v**(GLenum *target*, GLuint *index*,
                    GLdouble **data*);

GLenum **glGetError**(void);

void **glGetFloatv**(GLenum *pname*, GLfloat **params*);

void **glGetFloati_v**(GLenum *target*, GLuint *index*, GLfloat **data*);

GLint **glGetFragDataIndex**(GLuint *program*,
                    const GLchar **name*);

GLint **glGetFragDataLocation**(GLuint *program*,
                    const GLchar **name*);

void **glGetFramebufferAttachmentParameteriv**(GLenum *target*,
                    GLenum *attachment*,
                    GLenum *pname*,
                    GLint **params*);

void **glGetFramebufferParameteriv**(GLenum *target*,
                    GLenum *pname*,
                    GLint **params*);

void **glGetIntegerv**(GLenum *pname*, GLint **params*);

void **glGetInteger64v**(GLenum *pname*, GLint64 **params*);

void **glGetIntegeri_v**(GLenum *target*, GLuint *index*, GLint **data*);

void **glGetInteger64i_v**(GLenum *target*, GLuint *index*,
                    GLint64 **data*);

void **glGetInternalformativ**(GLenum *target*,
                    GLenum *internalformat*,
                    GLenum *pname*, GLsizei *bufSize*,
                    GLint **params*);

void **glGetInternalformati64v**(GLenum *target*,
                                 GLenum *internalformat*,
                                 GLenum *pname*, GLsizei *bufSize*,
                                 GLint64 **params*);

void **glGetMultisamplefv**(GLenum *pname*, GLuint *index*,
                            GLfloat **val*);

void **glGetObjectLabel**(GLenum *identifier*, GLuint *name*,
                          GLsizei *bufSize*, GLsizei **length*,
                          GLchar **label*);

void **glGetObjectPtrLabel**(const void **ptr*, GLsizei *bufSize*,
                             GLsizei **length*, GLchar **label*);

void **glGetPointerv**(GLenum *pname*, GLvoid* **params*);

void **glGetProgramBinary**(GLuint *program*, GLsizei *bufSize*,
                            GLsizei **length*,
                            GLenum **binaryFormat*,
                            GLvoid **binary*);

void **glGetProgramInfoLog**(GLuint *program*, GLsizei *bufSize*,
                             GLsizei **length*, GLchar **infoLog*);

void **glGetProgramiv**(GLuint *program*, GLenum *pname*,
                        GLint **params*);

void **glGetProgramPipelineInfoLog**(GLuint *pipeline*,
                                     GLsizei *bufSize*,
                                     GLsizei **length*,
                                     GLchar **infoLog*);

void **glGetProgramPipelineiv**(GLuint *pipeline*, GLenum *pname*,
                                GLint **params*);

void **glGetProgramInterfaceiv**(GLuint *program*,
                                 GLenum *programInterface*,
                                 GLenum *pname*, GLint **params*);

GLuint **glGetProgramResourceIndex**(GLuint *program*,
                                     GLenum *programInterface*,
                                     const GLchar **name*);

GLint **glGetProgramResourceLocation**(GLuint *program*,
                                       GLenum *programInterface*,
                                       const GLchar **name*);

GLint **glGetProgramResourceLocationIndex**(GLuint *program,*
GLenum *programInterface,*
const GLchar **name*);

void **glGetProgramResourceName**(GLuint *program,*
GLenum *programInterface,*
GLuint *index,* GLsizei *bufSize,*
GLsizei **length,*
GLchar **name*);

void **glGetProgramResourceiv**(GLuint *program,*
GLenum *programInterface,*
GLuint *index,* GLsizei *propCount,*
const GLenum **props,*
GLsizei *bufSize,* GLsizei **length,*
GLint **params*);

void **glGetProgramStageiv**(GLuint *program,* GLenum *shadertype,*
GLenum *pname,* GLint **values*);

void **glGetQueryIndexediv**(GLenum *target,* GLuint *index,*
GLenum *pname,* GLint **params*);

void **glGetQueryiv**(GLenum *target,* GLenum *pname,*
GLint **params*);

void **glGetQueryObjectiv**(GLuint *id,* GLenum *pname,*
GLint **params*);

void **glGetQueryObjecti64v**(GLuint *id,* GLenum *pname,*
GLint64 **params*);

void **glGetQueryObjectuiv**(GLuint *id,* GLenum *pname,*
GLuint **params*);

void **glGetQueryObjectui64v**(GLuint *id,* GLenum *pname,*
GLuint64 **params*);

void **glGetRenderbufferParameteriv**(GLenum *target,*
GLenum *pname,*
GLint **params*);

void **glGetSamplerParameterfv**(GLuint *sampler,* GLenum *pname,*
GLfloat **params*);

void **glGetSamplerParameteriv**(GLuint *sampler,* GLenum *pname,*
GLint **params*);

void **glGetSamplerParameterIiv**(GLuint *sampler*,
                                  GLenum *pname*,
                                  GLint **params*);

void **glGetSamplerParameterIuiv**(GLuint *sampler*,
                                    GLenum *pname*,
                                    GLuint **params*);

void **glGetShaderInfoLog**(GLuint *shader*, GLsizei *bufSize*,
                            GLsizei **length*, GLchar **infoLog*);

void **glGetShaderiv**(GLuint *shader*, GLenum *pname*,
                       GLint **params*);

void **glGetShaderPrecisionFormat**(GLenum *shadertype*,
                                     GLenum *precisiontype*,
                                     GLint **range*,
                                     GLint **precision*);

void **glGetShaderSource**(GLuint *shader*, GLsizei *bufSize*,
                           GLsizei **length*, GLchar **source*);

const GLubyte * **glGetString**(GLenum *name*);

const GLubyte * **glGetStringi**(GLenum *name*, GLuint *index*);

GLuint **glGetSubroutineIndex**(GLuint *program*,
                                GLenum *shadertype*,
                                const GLchar **name*);

GLint **glGetSubroutineUniformLocation**(GLuint *program*,
                                          GLenum *shadertype*,
                                          const GLchar **name*);

void **glGetSynciv**(GLsync *sync*, GLenum *pname*, GLsizei *bufSize*,
                     GLsizei **length*, GLint **values*);

void **glGetTexImage**(GLenum *target*, GLint *level*, GLenum *format*,
                       GLenum *type*, GLvoid **pixels*);

void **glGetTexLevelParameterfv**(GLenum *target*, GLint *level*,
                                   GLenum *pname*,
                                   GLfloat **params*);

void **glGetTexLevelParameteriv**(GLenum *target*, GLint *level*,
                                   GLenum *pname*, GLint **params*);

void **glGetTexParameterfv**(GLenum *target*, GLenum *pname*,
GLfloat **params*);

void **glGetTexParameteriv**(GLenum *target*, GLenum *pname*,
GLint **params*);

void **glGetTexParameterIiv**(GLenum *target*, GLenum *pname*,
GLint **params*);

void **glGetTexParameterIuiv**(GLenum *target*, GLenum *pname*,
GLuint **params*);

void **glGetTransformFeedbackVarying**(GLuint *program*,
GLuint *index*,
GLsizei *bufSize*,
GLsizei **length*,
GLsizei **size*,
GLenum **type*,
GLchar **name*);

GLuint **glGetUniformBlockIndex**(GLuint *program*,
const GLchar **uniformBlockName*);

void **glGetUniformdv**(GLuint *program*, GLint *location*,
GLdouble **params*);

void **glGetUniformfv**(GLuint *program*, GLint *location*,
GLfloat **params*);

void **glGetUniformiv**(GLuint *program*, GLint *location*,
GLint **params*);

void **glGetUniformuiv**(GLuint *program*, GLint *location*,
GLuint **params*);

void **glGetUniformIndices**(GLuint *program*,
GLsizei *uniformCount*,
const GLchar* **uniformNames*,
GLuint **uniformIndices*);

GLint **glGetUniformLocation**(GLuint *program*,
const GLchar **name*);

void **glGetUniformSubroutineuiv**(GLenum *shadertype*,
GLint *location*,
GLuint **params*);

void **glGetVertexAttribdv**(GLuint *index*, GLenum *pname*,
GLdouble **params*);

void **glGetVertexAttribfv**(GLuint *index*, GLenum *pname*,
GLfloat **params*);

void **glGetVertexAttribiv**(GLuint *index*, GLenum *pname*,
GLint **params*);

void **glGetVertexAttribIiv**(GLuint *index*, GLenum *pname*,
GLint **params*);

void **glGetVertexAttribIuiv**(GLuint *index*, GLenum *pname*,
GLuint **params*);

void **glGetVertexAttribLdv**(GLuint *index*, GLenum *pname*,
GLdouble **params*);

void **glGetVertexAttribPointerv**(GLuint *index*, GLenum *pname*,
GLvoid* **pointer*);

OpenGL State Variables

The following pages contain tables that list the names of queryable state
variables that OpenGL maintains. Variables are grouped by their related
functionality. For each variable in a table, the token you pass to query its
value, along with a description, its initial values, and a recommended
glGet*() function are provided. Most state variables can be obtained using
glGetBooleanv(), **glGetIntegerv**(), **glGetFloatv**(), or **glGetDoublev**(). The
tables list the most appropriate one given the type of data to be returned.
However, state variables for which **glIsEnabled**() is listed as the query
command can also be obtained using any of **glGetBooleanv**(),
glGetIntegerv(), **glGetFloatv**(), or **glGetDoublev**(). State variables for
which any other command is listed can be obtained only by using that
command.

More detail on all the query functions and values is available online at
http://www.opengl.org/sdk/docs/.

Current Values and Associated Data

Table D.1 Current Values and Associated Data

State Variable	Description	Initial Value	Get Command
GL_PATCH_VERTICES	Number of vertices in an input patch	3	glGetIntegerv()
GL_PATCH_DEFAULT_OUTER_LEVEL	Default outer tessellation level when not using a tessellation control shader	(1.0, 1.0, 1.0, 1.0)	glGetFloatv()
GL_PATCH_DEFAULT_INNER_LEVEL	Default inner tessellation level when not using a tessellation control shader	(1.0, 1.0)	glGetFloatv()

Vertex Array Object State

Table D.2   State Variables for Vertex Array Objects

State Variable	Description	Initial Value	Get Command
GL_VERTEX_ATTRIB_ARRAY_ENABLED	Vertex attribute array enable	GL_FALSE	glGetVertexAttribiv()
GL_VERTEX_ATTRIB_ARRAY_SIZE	Vertex attribute array size	4	glGetVertexAttribiv()
GL_VERTEX_ATTRIB_ARRAY_STRIDE	Vertex attribute array stride	0	glGetVertexAttribiv()
GL_VERTEX_ATTRIB_ARRAY_TYPE	Vertex attribute array type	GL_FLOAT	glGetVertexAttribiv()
GL_VERTEX_ATTRIB_ARRAY_NORMALIZED	Vertex attribute array normalized	GL_FALSE	glGetVertexAttribiv()
GL_VERTEX_ATTRIB_ARRAY_INTEGER	Vertex attribute array has unconverted integers	GL_FALSE	glGetVertexAttribiv()
GL_VERTEX_ATTRIB_ARRAY_LONG	Vertex attribute array has unconverted integers	GL_FALSE	glGetVertexAttribiv()
GL_VERTEX_ATTRIB_ARRAY_DIVISOR	Vertex attribute array instance divisor	0	glGetVertexAttribiv()

Table D.2 (continued)   State Variables for Vertex Array Objects

State Variable	Description	Initial Value	Get Command
GL_VERTEX_ATTRIB_ARRAY_POINTER	Vertex attribute array pointer	NULL	glGetVertexAttrib Pointerv()
GL_LABEL	Debug label	empty string	glGetObjectLabel()
GL_ELEMENT_ARRAY_BUFFER_BINDING	Element array buffer binding	0	glGetIntegerv()
GL_VERTEX_ATTRIB_ARRAY_BUFFER_BINDING	Attribute array buffer binding	0	glGetVertexAttribiv()
GL_VERTEX_ATTRIB_BINDING	Vertex buffer binding used by vertex attribute i	i	glGetVertexAttribiv()
GL_VERTEX_ATTRIB_RELATIVE_OFFSET	Byte offset added to vertex binding offset for this attribute	0	glGetVertexAttribiv()
GL_VERTEX_BINDING_OFFSET	Byte offset of the first element in the bound buffer	i	glGetInteger64i_v()
GL_VERTEX_BINDING_STRIDE	Vertex buffer binding stride	16	glGetIntegeri_v()

Vertex Array Data

Table D.3 State Variables for Vertex Array Data (Not Stored in a Vertex Array Object)

State Variable	Description	Initial Value	Get Command
GL_ARRAY_BUFFER_BINDING	Current buffer binding	0	glGetIntegerv()
GL_DRAW_INDIRECT_BUFFER_BINDING	Indirect command buffer binding	0	glGetIntegerv()
GL_VERTEX_ARRAY_BINDING	Current vertex array object binding	0	glGetIntegerv()
GL_PRIMITIVE_RESTART	Primitive restart enable	GL_FALSE	glIsEnabled()
GL_PRIMITIVE_RESTART_INDEX	Primitive restart index	0	glGetIntegerv()

Buffer Object State

Table D.4   State Variables for Buffer Objects

State Variable	Description	Initial Value	Get Command
GL_BUFFER_SIZE	Buffer data size	0	glGetBuffer Parameteri64v()
GL_BUFFER_USAGE	Buffer usage pattern	GL_STATIC_DRAW	glGetBuffer Parameteriv()
GL_BUFFER_ACCESS	Buffer access flag	GL_READ_WRITE	glGetBuffer Parameteriv()
GL_BUFFER_ACCESS_FLAGS	Extended buffer access flag	0	glGetBuffer Parameteriv()
GL_BUFFER_MAPPED	Buffer map flag	GL_FALSE	glGetBuffer Parameteriv()
GL_BUFFER_MAP_POINTER	Mapped buffer pointer	NULL	glGetBufferPointerv()
GL_BUFFER_MAP_OFFSET	Start of mapped buffer range	0	glGetBuffer Parameteri64v()
GL_BUFFER_MAP_LENGTH	Size of mapped buffer range	0	glGetBuffer Parameteri64v()
GL_LABEL	Debug label	empty string	glGetObjectLabel()

Transformation State

Table D.5   Transformation State Variables

State Variable	Description	Initial Value	Get Command
GL_VIEWPORT	Viewport origin and extent	(0, 0, *width, height*) where *width* and *height* represent the dimensions of the window that OpenGL will render into	glGetFloati_v()
GL_DEPTH_RANGE	Depth range near and far	0,1	glGetDoublei_v()
GL_CLIP_DISTANCE*i*	ith user clipping plane enabled	GL_FALSE	glIsEnabled()
GL_DEPTH_CLAMP	Depth clamping enabled	GL_FALSE	glIsEnabled()
GL_TRANSFORM_FEEDBACK_BINDING	Object bound for transform feedback operations	0	glGetIntegerv()

Coloring State

Table D.6 State Variables for Controlling Coloring

State Variable	Description	Initial Value	Get Command
GL_CLAMP_READ_COLOR	Read color clamping	GL_FIXED_ONLY	glGetIntegerv()
GL_PROVOKING_VERTEX	Provoking vertex convention	GL_LAST_VERTEX_CONVENTION	glGetIntegerv()

Rasterization State

Table D.7   State Variables for Controlling Rasterization

State Variable	Description	Initial Value	Get Command
GL_RASTERIZER_DISCARD	Discard primitives before rasterization	GL_FALSE	glIsEnabled()
GL_POINT_SIZE	Point size	1.0	glGetFloatv()
GL_POINT_FADE_THRESHOLD_SIZE	Threshold for alpha attenuation	1.0	glGetFloatv()
GL_POINT_SPRITE_COORD_ORIGIN	Origin orientation for point sprites	GL_UPPER_LEFT	glGetIntegerv()
GL_LINE_WIDTH	Line width	1.0	glGetFloatv()
GL_LINE_SMOOTH	Line antialiasing on	GL_FALSE	glIsEnabled()
GL_CULL_FACE	Polygon culling enabled	GL_FALSE	glIsEnabled()
GL_CULL_FACE_MODE	Cull front-/back-facing polygons	GL_BACK	glGetIntegerv()
GL_FRONT_FACE	Polygon frontface CW/CCW indicator	GL_CCW	glGetIntegerv()
GL_POLYGON_SMOOTH	Polygon antialiasing on	GL_FALSE	glIsEnabled()

State Variable	Description	Initial Value	Get Command
GL_POLYGON_MODE	Polygon rasterization mode (front and back)	GL_FILL	glGetIntegerv()
GL_POLYGON_OFFSET_FACTOR	Polygon offset factor	0	glGetFloatv()
GL_POLYGON_OFFSET_UNITS	Polygon offset units	0	glGetFloatv()
GL_POLYGON_OFFSET_POINT	Polygon offset enable for GL_POINT mode rasterization	GL_FALSE	glIsEnabled()
GL_POLYGON_OFFSET_LINE	Polygon offset enable for GL_LINE mode rasterization	GL_FALSE	glIsEnabled()
GL_POLYGON_OFFSET_FILL	Polygon offset enable for GL_FILL mode rasterization	GL_FALSE	glIsEnabled()

Multisampling

Table D.8   State Variables for Multisampling

State Variable	Description	Initial Value	Get Command
GL_MULTISAMPLE	Multisample rasterization	GL_TRUE	glIsEnabled()
GL_SAMPLE_ALPHA_TO_COVERAGE	Modify coverage from alpha	GL_FALSE	glIsEnabled()
GL_SAMPLE_ALPHA_TO_ONE	Set alpha to maximum	GL_FALSE	glIsEnabled()
GL_SAMPLE_COVERAGE	Mask to modify coverage	GL_FALSE	glIsEnabled()
GL_SAMPLE_COVERAGE_VALUE	Coverage mask value	1	glGetFloatv()
GL_SAMPLE_COVERAGE_INVERT	Invert coverage mask value	GL_FALSE	glGetBooleanv()
GL_SAMPLE_SHADING	Sample shading enable	GL_FALSE	glIsEnabled()
GL_MIN_SAMPLE_SHADING_VALUE	Fraction of multisamples to use for sample shading	0	glGetFloatv()
GL_SAMPLE_MASK	Sample mask enable	GL_FALSE	glIsEnabled()
GL_SAMPLE_MASK_VALUE	Sample mask words	all bits of all words set	glGetIntegeri_v()

Textures

Table D.9   State Variables for Texture Units

State Variable	Description	Initial Value	Get Command
GL_TEXTURE_xD	True if xD texturing is enabled; x is 1, 2, or 3	GL_FALSE	glIsEnabled()
GL_TEXTURE_CUBE_MAP	True if cube-map texturing is enabled	GL_FALSE	glIsEnabled()
GL_TEXTURE_BINDING_xD	Texture object bound to GL_TEXTURE_xD	0	glGetIntegerv()
GL_TEXTURE_BINDING_1D_ARRAY	Texture object bound to GL_TEXTURE_1D_ARRAY	0	glGetIntegerv()
GL_TEXTURE_BINDING_2D_ARRAY	Texture object bound to GL_TEXTURE_2D_ARRAY	0	glGetIntegerv()
GL_TEXTURE_BINDING_CUBE_MAP_ARRAY	Texture object bound to GL_TEXTURE_CUBE_MAP_ARRAY	0	glGetIntegerv()
GL_TEXTURE_BINDING_RECTANGLE	Texture object bound to GL_TEXTURE_RECTANGLE	0	glGetIntegerv()
GL_TEXTURE_BINDING_BUFFER	Texture object bound to GL_TEXTURE_BUFFER	0	glGetIntegerv()
GL_TEXTURE_BINDING_CUBE_MAP	Texture object bound to GL_TEXTURE_CUBE_MAP	0	glGetIntegerv()

Table D.9 (continued) State Variables for Texture Units

State Variable	Description	Initial Value	Get Command
GL_TEXTURE_BINDING_2D_MULTISAMPLE	Texture object bound to GL_TEXTURE_2D_MULTISAMPLE	0	glGetIntegerv()
GL_TEXTURE_BINDING_2D_MULTISAMPLE_ARRAY	Texture object bound to GL_TEXTURE_2D_MULTISAMPLE_ARRAY	0	glGetIntegerv()
GL_SAMPLER_BINDING	Sampler object bound to active texture unit	0	glGetIntegerv()
GL_TEXTURE_xD	xD texture image at level-of-detail i	—	glGetTexImage()
GL_TEXTURE_1D_ARRAY	1D texture array image at row i	—	glGetTexImage()
GL_TEXTURE_2D_ARRAY	2D texture array image at slice i	—	glGetTexImage()
GL_TEXTURE_CUBE_MAP_ARRAY	Cube-map array texture image at level-of-detail i	—	glGetTexImage()
GL_TEXTURE_RECTANGLE	Rectangular texture image at level-of-detail zero	—	glGetTexImage()
GL_TEXTURE_CUBE_MAP_POSITIVE_X	+x face cube-map texture image at level-of-detail i	—	glGetTexImage()

Table D.9 (continued) State Variables for Texture Units

State Variable	Description	Initial Value	Get Command
GL_TEXTURE_CUBE_MAP_NEGATIVE_X	$-x$ face cube-map texture image at level-of-detail i	—	glGetTexImage()
GL_TEXTURE_CUBE_MAP_POSITIVE_Y	$+y$ face cube-map texture image at level-of-detail i	—	glGetTexImage()
GL_TEXTURE_CUBE_MAP_NEGATIVE_Y	$-y$ face cube-map texture image at level-of-detail i	—	glGetTexImage()
GL_TEXTURE_CUBE_MAP_POSITIVE_Z	$+z$ face cube-map texture image at level-of-detail i	—	glGetTexImage()
GL_TEXTURE_CUBE_MAP_NEGATIVE_Z	$-z$ face cube-map texture image at level-of-detail i	—	glGetTexImage()

Textures

Table D.10 State Variables for Texture Objects

State Variable	Description	Initial Value	Get Command
GL_TEXTURE_SWIZZLE_R	Red component swizzle	GL_RED	glGetTexParameter*()
GL_TEXTURE_SWIZZLE_G	Green component swizzle	GL_GREEN	glGetTexParameter*()
GL_TEXTURE_SWIZZLE_B	Blue component swizzle	GL_BLUE	glGetTexParameter*()
GL_TEXTURE_SWIZZLE_A	Alpha component swizzle	GL_ALPHA	glGetTexParameter*()
GL_TEXTURE_BORDER_COLOR	Border color	(0.0, 0.0, 0.0, 0.0)	glGetTexParameter*()
GL_TEXTURE_MIN_FILTER	Minification function	GL_NEAREST_MIPMAP_LINEAR, or GL_LINEAR for rectangle textures	glGetTexParameter*()
GL_TEXTURE_MAG_FILTER	Magnification function	GL_LINEAR	glGetTexParameter*()
GL_TEXTURE_WRAP_S	Texcoord *s* wrap mode	GL_REPEAT, or GL_CLAMP_TO_EDGE for rectangle textures	glGetTexParameter*()
GL_TEXTURE_WRAP_T	Texcoord *t* wrap mode (2D, 3D, cube-map textures only)	GL_REPEAT, or GL_CLAMP_TO_EDGE for rectangle textures	glGetTexParameter*()

Table D.10 (continued) State Variables for Texture Objects

State Variable	Description	Initial Value	Get Command
GL_TEXTURE_WRAP_R	Texcoord r wrap mode (3D textures only)	GL_REPEAT	glGetTexParameter*()
GL_TEXTURE_MIN_LOD	Minimum level of detail	−1000	glGetTexParameterfv()
GL_TEXTURE_MAX_LOD	Maximum level of detail	1000	glGetTexParameterfv()
GL_TEXTURE_BASE_LEVEL	Base texture array	0	glGetTexParameterfv()
GL_TEXTURE_MAX_LEVEL	Maximum texture array level	1000	glGetTexParameterfv()
GL_TEXTURE_LOD_BIAS	Texture level of detail bias	0.0	glGetTexParameterfv()
GL_DEPTH_STENCIL_TEXTURE_MODE	Depth stencil texture mode	GL_DEPTH_COMPONENT	glGetTexParameteriv()
GL_TEXTURE_COMPARE_MODE	Comparison mode	GL_NONE	glGetTexParameteriv()
GL_TEXTURE_COMPARE_FUNC	Comparison function	GL_LEQUAL	glGetTexParameteriv()
GL_TEXTURE_IMMUTABLE_FORMAT	Size and format immutable	GL_FALSE	glGetTexParameter*()

Table D.10 (continued)   State Variables for Texture Objects

State Variable	Description	Initial Value	Get Command
GL_IMAGE_FORMAT_COMPATIBILITY_TYPE	Compatibility rules for texture use with image units	Implementation-dependent selection from either GL_IMAGE_FORMAT_COMPATIBILITY_BY_SIZE or GL_IMAGE_FORMAT_COMPATIBILITY_BY_CLASS	**glGetTexParameteriv()**
GL_TEXTURE_IMMUTABLE_LEVELS	Number of texture storage levels	0	**glGetTexParameter*()**
GL_TEXTURE_VIEW_MIN_LEVEL	View base texture level	0	**glGetTexParameter*()**
GL_TEXTURE_VIEW_NUM_LEVEL	Number of view texture levels	0	**glGetTexParameter*()**
GL_TEXTURE_VIEW_MIN_LAYER	View minimum array level	0	**glGetTexParameter*()**
GL_TEXTURE_VIEW_NUM_LEVEL	Number of view array layers	0	**glGetTexParameter*()**
GL_LABEL	Debug label	empty string	**glGetObjectLabel()**

Textures

Table D.11 State Variables for Texture Images

State Variable	Description	Initial Value	Get Command
GL_TEXTURE_WIDTH	Specified width	0	glGetTexLevel Parameter*()
GL_TEXTURE_HEIGHT	Specified height (2D/3D)	0	glGetTexLevel Parameter*()
GL_TEXTURE_DEPTH	Specified depth (3D)	0	glGetTexLevel Parameter*()
GL_TEXTURE_SAMPLES	Number of samples per texel	0	glGetTexLevel Parameter*()
GL_TEXTURE_FIXED_SAMPLE_LOCATIONS	Whether the image uses a fixed sample pattern	GL_TRUE	glGetTexLevel Parameter*()
GL_TEXTURE_INTERNAL_FORMAT	Internal format	GL_RGBA or GL_R8	glGetTexLevel Parameter*()
GL_TEXTURE_x_SIZE	Component resolution (x is GL_RED, GL_GREEN, GL_BLUE, GL_ALPHA, GL_DEPTH, or GL_STENCIL)	0	glGetTexLevel Parameter*()
GL_TEXTURE_SHARED_SIZE	Shared exponent field resolution	0	glGetTexLevel Parameter*()

Table D.11 (continued)   State Variables for Texture Images

State Variable	Description	Initial Value	Get Command
GL_TEXTURE_x_TYPE	Component type (x is GL_RED, GL_GREEN, GL_BLUE, GL_ALPHA, or GL_DEPTH)	GL_NONE	glGetTexLevel Parameter*()
GL_TEXTURE_COMPRESSED	True if image has a compressed internal format	GL_FALSE	glGetTexLevel Parameter*()
GL_TEXTURE_COMPRESSED_IMAGE_SIZE	Size (in GLubytes) of compressed image	0	glGetTexLevel Parameter*()
GL_TEXTURE_BUFFER_DATA_STORE_BINDING	Buffer object bound as the data store for the active image unit's buffer texture	0	glGetTexLevel Parameter*()
GL_TEXTURE_BUFFER_OFFSET	Offset into buffer's data used for the active image unit's buffer texture	0	glGetTexLevel Parameter*()
GL_TEXTURE_BUFFER_SIZE	Sizes into buffer's data used for the active image unit's buffer texture	0	glGetTexLevel Parameter*()

Textures

Table D.12   State Variables Per Texture Sampler Object

State Variable	Description	Initial Value	Get Command
GL_TEXTURE_BORDER_COLOR	Border color	(0.0, 0.0, 0.0, 0.0)	glGetSampler Parameter*()
GL_TEXTURE_COMPARE_FUNC	Comparison function	GL_LEQUAL	glGetSampler Parameteriv()
GL_TEXTURE_COMPARE_MODE	Comparison mode	GL_NONE	glGetSampler Parameteriv()
GL_TEXTURE_LOD_BIAS	Texture level of detail bias	0.0	glGetSampler Parameterfv()
GL_TEXTURE_MAX_LOD	Maximum level of detail	1000	glGetSampler Parameterfv()
GL_TEXTURE_MAG_FILTER	Magnification function	GL_LINEAR	glGetSampler Parameter*()
GL_TEXTURE_MIN_FILTER	Minification function	GL_NEAREST_ MIPMAP_LINEAR, or GL_LINEAR for rectangle textures	glGetSampler Parameter*()
GL_TEXTURE_MIN_LOD	Minimum level of detail	–1000	glGetSampler Parameterfv()

Table D.12 (continued) State Variables Per Texture Sampler Object

State Variable	Description	Initial Value	Get Command
GL_TEXTURE_WRAP_S	Texcoord *s* wrap mode	GL_REPEAT, or GL_CLAMP_TO_EDGE for rectangle textures	**glGetSampler Parameter*()**
GL_TEXTURE_WRAP_T	Texcoord *t* wrap mode (2D, 3D, cube-map textures only)	GL_REPEAT, or GL_CLAMP_TO_EDGE for rectangle textures	**glGetSampler Parameter*()**
GL_TEXTURE_WRAP_R	Texcoord *r* wrap mode (3D textures only)	GL_REPEAT	**glGetSampler Parameter*()**
GL_LABEL	Debug label	empty string	**glGetObjectLabel()**

Texture Environment

Table D.13 State Variables for Texture Environment and Generation

State Variable	Description	Initial Value	Get Command
GL_ACTIVE_TEXTURE	Active texture unit	GL_TEXTURE0	glGetIntegerv()

Pixel Operations

Table D.14   State Variables for Pixel Operations

State Variable	Description	Initial Value	Get Command
GL_SCISSOR_TEST	Scissoring enabled	GL_FALSE	glIsEnabledi()
GL_SCISSOR_BOX	Scissor box	(0, 0, width, height) where width and height represent the dimensions of the window that OpenGL will render into	glGetIntegeri_v()
GL_STENCIL_TEST	Stenciling enabled	GL_FALSE	glIsEnabled()
GL_STENCIL_FUNC	Front stencil function	GL_ALWAYS	glGetIntegerv()
GL_STENCIL_VALUE_MASK	Front stencil mask	$2^s - 1$ where s is at least the number of bits in the deepest stencil buffer supported by the OpenGL implementation	glGetIntegerv()
GL_STENCIL_REF	Front stencil reference value	0	glGetIntegerv()
GL_STENCIL_FAIL	Front stencil fail action	GL_KEEP	glGetIntegerv()

Table D.14 **(continued)**   State Variables for Pixel Operations

State Variable	Description	Initial Value	Get Command
GL_STENCIL_PASS_DEPTH_FAIL	Front stencil depth buffer fail action	GL_KEEP	**glGetIntegerv()**
GL_STENCIL_PASS_DEPTH_PASS	Front stencil depth buffer pass action	GL_KEEP	**glGetIntegerv()**
GL_STENCIL_BACK_FUNC	Back stencil function	GL_ALWAYS	**glGetIntegerv()**
GL_STENCIL_BACK_VALUE_MASK	Back stencil mask	$2^s - 1$ where s is at least the number of bits in the deepest stencil buffer supported by the OpenGL implementation	**glGetIntegerv()**
GL_STENCIL_BACK_REF	Back stencil reference value	0	**glGetIntegerv()**
GL_STENCIL_BACK_FAIL	Back stencil fail action	GL_KEEP	**glGetIntegerv()**
GL_STENCIL_BACK_PASS_DEPTH_FAIL	Back stencil depth buffer fail action	GL_KEEP	**glGetIntegerv()**
GL_STENCIL_BACK_PASS_DEPTH_PASS	Back stencil depth buffer pass action	GL_KEEP	**glGetIntegerv()**
GL_DEPTH_TEST	Depth buffer enabled	GL_FALSE	**glIsEnabled()**
GL_DEPTH_FUNC	Depth buffer test function	GL_LESS	**glGetIntegerv()**

Table D.14 (continued)   State Variables for Pixel Operations

State Variable	Description	Initial Value	Get Command
GL_BLEND	Blending enabled for draw buffer i	GL_FALSE	glIsEnabledi()
GL_BLEND_SRC_RGB	Blending source RGB function for draw buffer i	GL_ONE	glGetIntegeri_v()
GL_BLEND_SRC_ALPHA	Blending source A function for draw buffer i	GL_ONE	glGetIntegeri_v()
GL_BLEND_DST_RGB	RGB destination blending function for draw buffer i	GL_ZERO	glGetIntegeri_v()
GL_BLEND_DST_ALPHA	Alpha destination blending function for draw buffer i	GL_ZERO	glGetIntegeri_v()
GL_BLEND_EQUATION_RGB	RGB blending equation for draw buffer i	GL_FUNC_ADD	glGetIntegeri_v()
GL_BLEND_EQUATION_ALPHA	Alpha blending equation for draw buffer i	GL_FUNC_ADD	glGetIntegeri_v()
GL_BLEND_COLOR	Constant blend color	(0.0, 0.0, 0.0, 0.0)	glGetFloatv()
GL_FRAMEBUFFER_SRGB	sRGB update and blending enable	GL_FALSE	glIsEnabled()
GL_DITHER	Dithering enabled	GL_TRUE	glIsEnabled()
GL_COLOR_LOGIC_OP	Color logic op enabled	GL_FALSE	glIsEnabled()
GL_LOGIC_OP_MODE	Logic op function	GL_COPY	glGetIntegerv()

Framebuffer Controls

Table D.15 State Variables Controlling Framebuffer Access and Values

State Variable	Description	Initial Value	Get Command
GL_COLOR_WRITEMASK	Color write enables (R,G,B,A) for draw buffer *i*	(GL_TRUE,GL_TRUE, GL_TRUE,GL_TRUE)	glGetBooleani_v()
GL_DEPTH_WRITEMASK	Depth buffer enabled for writing	GL_TRUE	glGetBooleanv()
GL_STENCIL_WRITEMASK	Front stencil buffer writemask	1s	glGetIntegerv()
GL_STENCIL_BACK_WRITEMASK	Back stencil buffer writemask	1s	glGetIntegerv()
GL_COLOR_CLEAR_VALUE	Color buffer clear value	(0.0, 0.0, 0.0, 0.0)	glGetFloatv()
GL_DEPTH_CLEAR_VALUE	Depth buffer clear value	1	glGetFloatv()
GL_STENCIL_CLEAR_VALUE	Stencil clear value	0	glGetIntegerv()

Framebuffer State

Table D.16 State Variables for Framebuffers per Target

State Variable	Description	Initial Value	Get Command
GL_DRAW_FRAMEBUFFER_BINDING	Framebuffer object bound to GL_DRAW_FRAMEBUFFER	0	glGetIntegerv()
GL_READ_FRAMEBUFFER_BINDING	Framebuffer object bound to GL_READ_FRAMEBUFFER	0	glGetIntegerv()

Framebuffer State

Table D.17   State Variables for Framebuffer Objects

State Variable	Description	Initial Value	Get Command
GL_DRAW_BUFFER*i*	Draw buffer selected for color output *i*	GL_BACK if there is a back buffer, otherwise GL_FRONT, unless there is no default framebuffer, then GL_NONE. GL_COLOR_ATTACHMENT0 for framebuffer object fragment color zero, otherwise GL_NONE	glGetIntegerv()
GL_READ_BUFFER	Read source buffer	GL_BACK if there is a back buffer, otherwise GL_FRONT, unless there is no default framebuffer, then GL_NONE	glGetIntegerv()
GL_LABEL	Debug label	empty string	glGetObjectLabel()

Framebuffer State

Table D.18 State Variables for Framebuffer Attachments

State Variable	Description	Initial Value	Get Command
GL_FRAMEBUFFER_ATTACHMENT_OBJECT_TYPE	Type of image attached to framebuffer attachment point	GL_NONE	glGetFramebuffer Attachment Parameteriv()
GL_FRAMEBUFFER_ATTACHMENT_OBJECT_NAME	Name of object attached to framebuffer attachment point	0	glGetFramebuffer Attachment Parameteriv()
GL_FRAMEBUFFER_ATTACHMENT_TEXTURE_LEVEL	Mipmap level of texture image attached, if object attached is texture	0	glGetFramebuffer Attachment Parameteriv()
GL_FRAMEBUFFER_ATTACHMENT_TEXTURE_CUBE_MAP_FACE	Cube-map face of texture image attached, if object attached is cube-map texture	GL_NONE	glGetFramebuffer Attachment Parameteriv()
GL_FRAMEBUFFER_ATTACHMENT_TEXTURE_LAYER	Layer of texture image attached, if object attached is 3D texture	0	glGetFramebuffer Attachment Parameteriv()

Table D.18 (continued)   State Variables for Framebuffer Attachments

State Variable	Description	Initial Value	Get Command
GL_FRAMEBUFFER_ATTACHMENT_LAYERED	Framebuffer attachment is layered	GL_FALSE	glGetFramebuffer Attachment Parameteriv()
GL_FRAMEBUFFER_ATTACHMENT_COLOR_ENCODING	Encoding of components in the attached image	—	glGetFramebuffer Attachment Parameteriv()
GL_FRAMEBUFFER_ATTACHMENT_COMPONENT_TYPE	Data type of components in the attached image	—	glGetFramebuffer Attachment Parameteriv()
GL_FRAMEBUFFER_ATTACHMENT_x_SIZE	Size in bits of attached image's x component; x is GL_RED, GL_GREEN, GL_BLUE, GL_ALPHA, GL_DEPTH, or GL_STENCIL	—	glGetFramebuffer Attachment Parameteriv()

Renderbuffer State

Table D.19   Renderbuffer State

State Variable	Description	Initial Value	Get Command
GL_RENDERBUFFER_BINDING	Renderbuffer object bound to GL_RENDERBUFFER	0	glGetIntegerv()

Renderbuffer State

Table D.20 State Variables per Renderbuffer Object

State Variable	Description	Initial Value	Get Command
GL_RENDERBUFFER_WIDTH	Width of renderbuffer	0	glGetRenderbuffer Parameteriv()
GL_RENDERBUFFER_HEIGHT	Height of renderbuffer	0	glGetRenderbuffer Parameteriv()
GL_RENDERBUFFER_INTERNAL_FORMAT	Internal format of renderbuffer	GL_RGBA	glGetRenderbuffer Parameteriv()
GL_RENDERBUFFER_RED_SIZE	Size in bits of renderbuffer image's red component	0	glGetRenderbuffer Parameteriv()
GL_RENDERBUFFER_GREEN_SIZE	Size in bits of renderbuffer image's green component	0	glGetRenderbuffer Parameteriv()
GL_RENDERBUFFER_BLUE_SIZE	Size in bits of renderbuffer image's blue component	0	glGetRenderbuffer Parameteriv()
GL_RENDERBUFFER_ALPHA_SIZE	Size in bits of renderbuffer image's alpha component	0	glGetRenderbuffer Parameteriv()

Table D.20 **(continued)** State Variables Per Renderbuffer Object

State Variable	Description	Initial Value	Get Command
GL_RENDERBUFFER_DEPTH_SIZE	Size in bits of renderbuffer image's depth component	0	**glGetRenderbuffer Parameteriv**()
GL_RENDERBUFFER_STENCIL_SIZE	Size in bits of renderbuffer image's stencil component	0	**glGetRenderbuffer Parameteriv**()
GL_RENDERBUFFER_SAMPLES	Number of samples	0	**glGetRenderbuffer Parameteriv**()
GL_LABEL	Debug label	empty string	**glGetObjectLabel**()

Pixel State

Table D.21   State Variables Controlling Pixel Transfers

State Variable	Description	Initial Value	Get Command
GL_UNPACK_SWAP_BYTES	Value of GL_UNPACK_SWAP_BYTES	GL_FALSE	glGetBooleanv()
GL_UNPACK_LSB_FIRST	Value of GL_UNPACK_LSB_FIRST	GL_FALSE	glGetBooleanv()
GL_UNPACK_IMAGE_HEIGHT	Value of GL_UNPACK_IMAGE_HEIGHT	0	glGetIntegerv()
GL_UNPACK_SKIP_IMAGES	Value of GL_UNPACK_SKIP_IMAGES	0	glGetIntegerv()
GL_UNPACK_ROW_LENGTH	Value of GL_UNPACK_ROW_LENGTH	0	glGetIntegerv()
GL_UNPACK_SKIP_ROWS	Value of GL_UNPACK_SKIP_ROWS	0	glGetIntegerv()
GL_UNPACK_SKIP_PIXELS	Value of GL_UNPACK_SKIP_PIXELS	0	glGetIntegerv()
GL_UNPACK_ALIGNMENT	Value of GL_UNPACK_ALIGNMENT	4	glGetIntegerv()
GL_UNPACK_COMPRESSED_BLOCK_WIDTH	Value of GL_UNPACK_COMPRESSED_BLOCK_WIDTH	0	glGetIntegerv()

Table D.21 (continued)   State Variables Controlling Pixel Transfers

State Variable	Description	Initial Value	Get Command
GL_UNPACK_COMPRESSED_BLOCK_HEIGHT	Value of GL_UNPACK_COMPRESSED_BLOCK_HEIGHT	0	glGetIntegerv()
GL_UNPACK_COMPRESSED_BLOCK_DEPTH	Value of GL_UNPACK_COMPRESSED_BLOCK_DEPTH	0	glGetIntegerv()
GL_UNPACK_COMPRESSED_BLOCK_SIZE	Value of GL_UNPACK_COMPRESSED_BLOCK_SIZE	0	glGetIntegerv()
GL_PIXEL_UNPACK_BUFFER_BINDING	Pixel unpack buffer binding	0	glGetIntegerv()
GL_PACK_SWAP_BYTES	Value of GL_PACK_SWAP_BYTES	GL_FALSE	glGetBooleanv()
GL_PACK_LSB_FIRST	Value of GL_PACK_LSB_FIRST	GL_FALSE	glGetBooleanv()
GL_PACK_IMAGE_HEIGHT	Value of GL_PACK_IMAGE_HEIGHT	0	glGetIntegerv()
GL_PACK_SKIP_IMAGES	Value of GL_PACK_SKIP_IMAGES	0	glGetIntegerv()
GL_PACK_ROW_LENGTH	Value of GL_PACK_ROW_LENGTH	0	glGetIntegerv()

Table D.21 (continued) State Variables Controlling Pixel Transfers

State Variable	Description	Initial Value	Get Command
GL_PACK_SKIP_ROWS	Value of GL_PACK_SKIP_ROWS	0	glGetIntegerv()
GL_PACK_SKIP_PIXELS	Value of GL_PACK_SKIP_PIXELS	0	glGetIntegerv()
GL_PACK_ALIGNMENT	Value of GL_PACK_ALIGNMENT	4	glGetIntegerv()
GL_PACK_COMPRESSED_BLOCK_WIDTH	Value of GL_PACK_COMPRESSED_BLOCK_WIDTH	0	glGetIntegerv()
GL_PACK_COMPRESSED_BLOCK_HEIGHT	Value of GL_PACK_COMPRESSED_BLOCK_HEIGHT	0	glGetIntegerv()
GL_PACK_COMPRESSED_BLOCK_DEPTH	Value of GL_PACK_COMPRESSED_BLOCK_DEPTH	0	glGetIntegerv()
GL_PACK_COMPRESSED_BLOCK_SIZE	Value of GL_PACK_COMPRESSED_BLOCK_SIZE	0	glGetIntegerv()
GL_PIXEL_PACK_BUFFER_BINDING	Pixel pack buffer binding	0	glGetIntegerv()

Shader Object State

Table D.22   State Variables for Shader Objects

State Variable	Description	Initial Value	Get Command
GL_SHADER_TYPE	Type of shader (vertex, geometry, or fragment)	—	glGetShaderiv()
GL_DELETE_STATUS	Shader flagged for deletion	GL_FALSE	glGetShaderiv()
GL_COMPILE_STATUS	Last compile succeeded	GL_FALSE	glGetShaderiv()
GL_INFO_LOG_LENGTH	Info log for shader objects	empty string	glGetShaderInfoLog()
GL_SHADER_SOURCE_LENGTH	Length of info log	0	glGetShaderiv()
GL_LABEL	Source code for a shader	empty string	glGetShaderSource()
	Length of source code	0	glGetShaderiv()
	Debug label	empty string	glGetObjectLabel()

Shader Program Pipeline Object State

Table D.23 State Variables for Program Pipeline Object State

State Variable	Description	Initial Value	Get Command
GL_ACTIVE_PROGRAM	Program object updated by **Uniform*** when PPO bound	0	glGetProgram Pipelineiv()
GL_VERTEX_SHADER	Name of current vertex shader program object	0	glGetProgram Pipelineiv()
GL_GEOMETRY_SHADER	Name of current geometry shader program object	0	glGetProgram Pipelineiv()
GL_FRAGMENT_SHADER	Name of current fragment shader program object	0	glGetProgram Pipelineiv()
GL_TESS_CONTROL_SHADER	Name of current tessellation-control shader program object	0	glGetProgram Pipelineiv()
GL_TESS_EVALUATION_SHADER	Name of current tessellation-evaluation shader program object	0	glGetProgram Pipelineiv()
GL_VALIDATE_STATUS	Validate status of program pipeline object	GL_FALSE	glGetProgram Pipelineiv()
	Info log for program pipeline object	empty	glGetProgramPipeline InfoLog()
GL_INFO_LOG_LENGTH	Length of info log	0	glGetProgram Pipelineiv()
GL_LABEL	Debug label	empty string	glGetObjectLabel()

Shader Program Object State

Table D.24   State Variables for Shader Program Objects

State Variable	Description	Initial Value	Get Command
GL_CURRENT_PROGRAM	Name of current program object	0	glGetIntegerv()
GL_PROGRAM_PIPELINE_BINDING	Current program pipeline object binding	0	glGetIntegerv()
GL_PROGRAM_SEPARABLE	Program object capable of being bound for separate pipeline stages	GL_FALSE	glGetProgramiv()
GL_DELETE_STATUS	Program object deleted	GL_FALSE	glGetProgramiv()
GL_LINK_STATUS	Last link attempt succeeded	GL_FALSE	glGetProgramiv()
GL_VALIDATE_STATUS	Last validate attempt succeeded	GL_FALSE	glGetProgramiv()
GL_ATTACHED_SHADERS	Number of attached shader objects	0	glGetProgramiv()
	Shader objects attached	empty	glGetAttachedShaders()
	Info log for program object	empty	glGetProgramInfoLog()
GL_INFO_LOG_LENGTH	Length of info log	0	glGetProgramiv()
GL_PROGRAM_BINARY_LENGTH	Length of program binary	0	glGetProgramiv()

Table D.24 (continued) State Variables for Shader Program Objects

State Variable	Description	Initial Value	Get Command
GL_PROGRAM_BINARY_RETRIEVABLE_HINT	Retrievable binary hint enabled	GL_FALSE	glGetProgramiv()
	Binary representation of program	—	glGetProgramBinary()
GL_COMPUTE_WORK_GROUP_SIZE	Local work group size of a linked compute program	glGetProgramiv()	0, …
GL_LABEL	Debug label	empty string	glGetObjectLabel()
GL_ACTIVE_UNIFORMS	Number of active uniforms	0	glGetProgramiv()
	Location of active uniforms	—	glGetUniformLocation()
	Size of active uniform	—	glGetActiveUniform()
	Type of active uniform	—	glGetActiveUniform()
	Name of active uniform	empty string	glGetActiveUniform()
GL_ACTIVE_UNIFORM_MAX_LENGTH	Maximum active uniform name length	0	glGetProgramiv()
	Uniform value	0	glGetUniform*()
GL_ACTIVE_ATTRIBUTES	Number of active attributes	0	glGetProgramiv()
	Location of active generic attribute	—	glGetAttribLocation()
	Size of active attribute	—	glGetActiveAttrib()

Table D.24 (continued)   State Variables for Shader Program Objects

State Variable	Description	Initial Value	Get Command
	Type of active attribute	—	glGetActiveAttrib()
	Name of active attribute	empty string	glGetActiveAttrib()
GL_ACTIVE_ATTRIBUTE_MAX_LENGTH	Maximum active attribute name length	0	glGetProgramiv()
GL_GEOMETRY_VERTICES_OUT	Maximum number of output vertices	0	glGetProgramiv()
GL_GEOMETRY_INPUT_TYPE	Primitive input type	GL_TRIANGLES	glGetProgramiv()
GL_GEOMETRY_OUTPUT_TYPE	Primitive output type	GL_TRIANGLE_STRIP	glGetProgramiv()
GL_GEOMETRY_SHADER_INVOCATIONS	Number of times a geometry shader should be executed for each input primitive	1	glGetProgramiv()
GL_TRANSFORM_FEEDBACK_BUFFER_MODE	Transform feedback mode for the program	GL_INTERLEAVED_ATTRIBS	glGetProgramiv()
GL_TRANSFORM_FEEDBACK_VARYINGS	Number of outputs to stream to buffer object(s)	0	glGetProgramiv()
GL_TRANSFORM_FEEDBACK_VARYING_MAX_LENGTH	Maximum transform feedback output variable name length	0	glGetProgramiv()
	Size of each transform feedback output variable	—	glGetTransformFeedbackVarying()

Table D.24 (continued) State Variables for Shader Program Objects

State Variable	Description	Initial Value	Get Command
	Type of each transform feedback output variable	—	glGetTransform FeedbackVarying()
	Name of each transform feedback output variable	—	glGetTransform FeedbackVarying()
GL_UNIFORM_BUFFER_BINDING	Uniform buffer object bound to the context for buffer object manipulation	0	glGetIntegerv()
GL_UNIFORM_BUFFER_BINDING	Uniform buffer object bound to the specified context binding point	0	glGetIntegeri_v()
GL_UNIFORM_BUFFER_START	Start of bound uniform buffer region	0	glGetInteger64i_v()
GL_UNIFORM_BUFFER_SIZE	Size of bound uniform buffer region	0	glGetInteger64i_v()
GL_ACTIVE_UNIFORM_BLOCKS	Number of active uniform blocks in a program	0	glGetProgramiv()
GL_ACTIVE_UNIFORM_BLOCK_ MAX_NAME_LENGTH	Length of longest active uniform block name	0	glGetProgramiv()
GL_UNIFORM_TYPE	Type of active uniform	—	glGetActiveUniformsiv()
GL_UNIFORM_SIZE	Size of active uniform	—	glGetActiveUniformsiv()

Table D.24 (continued) State Variables for Shader Program Objects

State Variable	Description	Initial Value	Get Command
GL_UNIFORM_NAME_LENGTH	Uniform name length	—	glGetActiveUniformsiv()
GL_UNIFORM_BLOCK_INDEX	Uniform block index	—	glGetActiveUniformsiv()
GL_UNIFORM_OFFSET	Uniform buffer offset	—	glGetActiveUniformsiv()
GL_UNIFORM_ARRAY_STRIDE	Uniform buffer array stride	—	glGetActiveUniformsiv()
GL_UNIFORM_MATRIX_STRIDE	Uniform buffer intra-matrix stride	—	glGetActiveUniformsiv()
GL_UNIFORM_IS_ROW_MAJOR	Whether uniform is a row-major matrix	—	glGetActiveUniformsiv()
GL_UNIFORM_BLOCK_BINDING	Uniform buffer binding points associated with the specified uniform block	0	glGetActiveUniform Blockiv()
GL_UNIFORM_BLOCK_DATA_SIZE	Size of the storage needed to hold this uniform block's data	—	glGetActiveUniform Blockiv()
GL_UNIFORM_BLOCK_ACTIVE_UNIFORMS	Count of active uniforms in the specified uniform block	—	glGetActiveUniform Blockiv()
GL_UNIFORM_BLOCK_ACTIVE_UNIFORM_INDICES	Array of active uniform indices of the specified uniform block	—	glGetActiveUniform Blockiv()

Table D.24 (continued)   State Variables for Shader Program Objects

State Variable	Description	Initial Value	Get Command
GL_UNIFORM_BLOCK_ REFERENCED_BY_VERTEX_ SHADER	True if uniform block is actively referenced by the vertex stage	GL_FALSE	**glGetActiveUniform Blockiv()**
GL_UNIFORM_BLOCK_ REFERENCED_BY_TESS_ CONTROL_SHADER	True if uniform block is actively referenced by tessellation control stage	GL_FALSE	**glGetActiveUniform Blockiv()**
GL_UNIFORM_BLOCK_ REFERENCED_BY_TESS_ EVALUTION_SHADER	True if uniform block is actively referenced by tessellation evaluation stage	GL_FALSE	**glGetActiveUniform Blockiv()**
GL_UNIFORM_BLOCK_ REFERENCED_BY_GEOMETRY_ SHADER	True if uniform block is actively referenced by the geometry stage	GL_FALSE	**glGetActiveUniform Blockiv()**
GL_UNIFORM_BLOCK_ REFERENCED_BY_FRAGMENT_ SHADER	True if uniform block is actively referenced by the fragment stage	GL_FALSE	**glGetActiveUniform Blockiv()**
GL_UNIFORM_BLOCK_ REFERENCED_BY_COMPUTE_ SHADER	True if uniform block is actively referenced by the compute stage	GL_FALSE	**glGetActiveUniform Blockiv()**
GL_TESS_CONTROL_OUTPUT_ VERTICES	Output patch size for tessellationcontrol shader	0	**glGetProgramiv()**

Table D.24 (continued) State Variables for Shader Program Objects

State Variable	Description	Initial Value	Get Command
GL_TESS_GEN_MODE	Base primitive type for tessellation primitive generator	GL_QUADS	glGetProgramiv()
GL_TESS_GEN_SPACING	Spacing of tessellation primitive generator edge subdivision	GL_EQUAL	glGetProgramiv()
GL_TESS_GEN_VERTEX_ORDER	Order of vertices in primitives generated by tessellation prim generator	GL_CCW	glGetProgramiv()
GL_TESS_GEN_POINT_MODE	Tessellation primitive generator emits primitives or points	GL_FALSE	glGetProgramiv()
GL_ACTIVE_SUBROUTINE_UNIFORM_LOCATIONS	Number of subroutine uniform locations in the shader	0	glGetProgramStageiv()
GL_ACTIVE_SUBROUTINE_UNIFORMS	Number of subroutine uniform variables in the shader	0	glGetProgramStageiv()
GL_ACTIVE_SUBROUTINES	Number of subroutine functions in the shader	0	glGetProgramStageiv()
GL_ACTIVE_SUBROUTINE_UNIFORM_MAX_LENGTH	Maximum subroutine uniform name length	0	glGetProgramStageiv()

Table D.24 (continued) State Variables for Shader Program Objects

State Variable	Description	Initial Value	Get Command
GL_ACTIVE_SUBROUTINE_MAX_LENGTH	Maximum subroutine name length	0	**glGetProgramStageiv()**
GL_NUM_COMPATIBLE_SUBROUTINES	Number of subroutines compatible with a subroutine uniform	–	**glGetActiveSub routineUniformiv()**
GL_COMPATIBLE_SUBROUTINES	List of subroutines compatible with a subroutine uniform	–	**glGetActiveSub routineUniformiv()**
GL_UNIFORM_SIZE	Number of elements in subroutine uniform array	–	**glGetActiveSub routineUniformiv()**
GL_UNIFORM_NAME_LENGTH	Length of subroutine uniform name	–	**glGetActiveSub routineUniformiv()**
	Subroutine uniform name string	–	**glGetActiveSubroutine UniformName()**
	Length of subroutine name	–	**glGetActiveSubroutine Name()**
	Subroutine name string	–	**glGetActiveSubroutine Name()**
GL_ACTIVE_ATOMIC_COUNTER_BUFFERS	Number of active atomic-counter buffers used by a program	0	**glGetProgramiv()**

Table D.24 (continued)   State Variables for Shader Program Objects

State Variable	Description	Initial Value	Get Command
GL_ATOMIC_COUNTER_BUFFER_ BINDING	Binding point associated with an active atomic-counter buffer	—	**glGetActiveAtomic CounterBufferiv()**
GL_ATOMIC_COUNTER_BUFFER_ DATA_SIZE	Minimum size required by an active atomic-counter buffer	—	**glGetActiveAtomic CounterBufferiv()**
GL_ATOMIC_COUNTER_BUFFER_ ACTIVE_ATOMIC_COUNTERS	Number of active atomic counters in an active atomic-counter buffer	—	**glGetActiveAtomic CounterBufferiv()**
GL_ATOMIC_COUNTER_BUFFER_ ACTIVE_ATOMIC_COUNTER_- INDICES	List of active atomic counters in an active atomic-counter buffer	—	**glGetActiveAtomic CounterBufferiv()**
GL_ATOMIC_COUNTER_BUFFER_ REFERENCED_BY_VERTEX_ SHADER	Active atomic-counter buffer has a counter used by vertex shaders	GL_FALSE	**glGetActiveAtomic CounterBufferiv()**
GL_ATOMIC_COUNTER_BUFFER_ REFERENCED_BY_TESS_ CONTROL_SHADER	Active atomic-counter buffer has a counter used by tessellation control shaders	GL_FALSE	**glGetActiveAtomic CounterBufferiv()**

Table D.24   (continued)   State Variables for Shader Program Objects

State Variable	Description	Initial Value	Get Command
GL_ATOMIC_COUNTER_BUFFER_ REFERENCED_BY_TESS_ EVALUTION_SHADER	Active atomic-counter buffer has a counter used by tessellation evaluation shaders	GL_FALSE	**glGetActiveAtomic CounterBufferiv**()
GL_ATOMIC_COUNTER_BUFFER_ REFERENCED_BY_GEOMETRY_ SHADER	Active atomic-counter buffer has a counter used by geometry shaders	GL_FALSE	**glGetActiveAtomic CounterBufferiv**()
GL_ATOMIC_COUNTER_BUFFER_ REFERENCED_BY_FRAGMENT_ SHADER	Active atomic-counter buffer has a counter used by fragment shaders	GL_FALSE	**glGetActiveAtomic CounterBufferiv**()
GL_ATOMIC_COUNTER_BUFFER_ REFERENCED_BY_COMPUTE_ SHADER	Active atomic-counter buffer has a counter used by compute shaders	GL_FALSE	**glGetActiveAtomic CounterBufferiv**()
GL_UNIFORM_ATOMIC_ COUNTER_BUFFER_INDEX	Active atomic-counter buffer associated with an active uniform	—	**glGetActiveUniformsiv**()

Program Interface State

Table D.25   State Variables for Program Interfaces

State Variable	Description	Initial Value	Get Command
GL_ACTIVE_RESOURCES	Number of active resources on a program interface	0	glGetProgram Interfaceiv()
GL_MAX_NAME_LENGTH	Maximum name length for active resources	0	glGetProgram Interfaceiv()
GL_MAX_NUM_ACTIVE_VARIABLES	Maximum number of active variables for active resources	0	glGetProgram Interfaceiv()
GL_MAX_NUM_COMPATIBLE_SUBROUTINES	Maximum number of compatible subroutines for subroutine uniforms	0	glGetProgram Interfaceiv()

Program Object Resource State

Table D.26   State Variables for Program Object Resources

State Variable	Description	Initial Value	Get Command
GL_NAME_LENGTH	Length of active resource name	—	glGetProgramResourceiv()
GL_TYPE	Active resource type	—	glGetProgramResourceiv()
GL_ARRAY_SIZE	Active resource array size	—	glGetProgramResourceiv()
GL_OFFSET	Active resource offset in memory	—	glGetProgramResourceiv()
GL_BLOCK_INDEX	Index of interface block owning resource	—	glGetProgramResourceiv()
GL_ARRAY_STRIDE	Active resource array stride in memory	—	glGetProgramResourceiv()
GL_MATRIX_STRIDE	Active resource matrix stride in memory	—	glGetProgramResourceiv()
GL_IS_ROW_MAJOR	Active resource stored as a row major matrix	—	glGetProgramResourceiv()

Table D.26 (continued)   State Variables for Program Object Resources

State Variable	Description	Initial Value	Get Command
GL_ATOMIC_COUNTER_BUFFER_ INDEX	Index of atomic-counter buffer owning resource	—	**glGetProgram Resourceiv()**
GL_BUFFER_BINDING	Buffer binding assigned to active resource	—	**glGetProgram Resourceiv()**
GL_BUFFER_DATA_SIZE	Minimum buffer data size required for resource	—	**glGetProgram Resourceiv()**
GL_NUM_ACTIVE_VARIABLES	Number of active variables owned by active resource	—	**glGetProgram Resourceiv()**
GL_ACTIVE_VARIABLES	List of active variables owned by active resource	—	**glGetProgram Resourceiv()**
GL_REFERENCED_BY_VERTEX_ SHADER	Active resource used by vertex shader	—	**glGetProgram Resourceiv()**
GL_REFERENCED_BY_TESS_ CONTROL_SHADER	Active resource used by tessellation control shader	—	**glGetProgram Resourceiv()**
GL_REFERENCED_BY_TESS_ EVALUATION_SHADER	Active resource used by tessellation evaluation shader	—	**glGetProgram Resourceiv()**

State Variable	Description	Initial Value	Get Command
GL_REFERENCED_BY_GEOMETRY_SHADER	Active resource used by geometry shader	—	glGetProgram Resourceiv()
GL_REFERENCED_BY_FRAGMENT_SHADER	Active resource used by fragment shader	—	glGetProgram Resourceiv()
GL_REFERENCED_BY_COMPUTE_SHADER	Active resource used by compute shader	—	glGetProgram Resourceiv()
GL_TOP_LEVEL_ARRAY_SIZE	Array size of top level shared storage block member	—	glGetProgram Resourceiv()
GL_TOP_LEVEL_ARRAY_STRIDE	Array stride of top level shared storage block member	—	glGetProgram Resourceiv()
GL_LOCATION	Location assigned to active resource	—	glGetProgram Resourceiv()
GL_LOCATION_INDEX	Location index assigned to active resource	—	glGetProgram Resourceiv()
GL_IS_PER_PATCH	As active input or output a per-patch attribute	—	glGetProgram Resourceiv()
GL_NUM_COMPATIBLE_SUBROUTINES	Number of compatible subroutines for active subroutine uniform	—	glGetProgram Resourceiv()
GL_COMPATIBLE_SUBROUTINES	List of compatible subroutines for active subroutine uniform	—	glGetProgram Resourceiv()

Vertex and Geometry Shader State

Table D.27   State Variables for Vertex and Geometry Shader State

State Variable	Description	Initial Value	Get Command
GL_CURRENT_VERTEX_ATTRIB	Current generic vertex attribute values	0.0,0.0,0.0,1.0	glGetVertexAttribfv()
GL_PROGRAM_POINT_SIZE	Point size mode	GL_FALSE	glIsEnabled()

Query Object State

Table D.28   State Variables for Query Objects

State Variable	Description	Initial Value	Get Command
GL_QUERY_RESULT	Query object result	0 or GL_FALSE	glGetQueryObjectuiv()
GL_QUERY_RESULT_AVAILABLE	Is the query object result available?	GL_FALSE	glGetQueryObjectiv()
GL_LABEL	Debug label	empty string	glGetObjectLabel()

Image State

Table D.29   State Variables per Image Unit

State Variable	Description	Initial Value	Get Command
GL_IMAGE_BINDING_NAME	Name of bound texture object	0	glGetIntegeri_v()
GL_IMAGE_BINDING_LEVEL	Level of bound texture object	0	glGetIntegeri_v()
GL_IMAGE_BINDING_LAYERED	Texture object bound with multiple layers	GL_FALSE	glGetBooleani_v()
GL_IMAGE_BINDING_LAYER	Layer of bound texture, if not layered	0	glGetIntegeri_v()
GL_IMAGE_BINDING_ACCESS	Read and/or write access for bound texture	GL_READ_ONLY	glGetIntegeri_v()
GL_IMAGE_BINDING_FORMAT	Format used for accesses to bound texture	GL_R8	glGetIntegeri_v()

Transform Feedback State

Table D.30   State Variables for Transform Feedback

State Variable	Description	Initial Value	Get Command
GL_TRANSFORM_FEEDBACK_BUFFER_BINDING	Buffer object bound to generic bind point for transform feedback	0	glGetIntegerv()
GL_TRANSFORM_FEEDBACK_BUFFER_BINDING	Buffer object bound to each transform feedback attribute stream	0	glGetIntegeri_v()
GL_TRANSFORM_FEEDBACK_BUFFER_START	Start offset of binding range for each transform feedback attribute stream	0	glGetInteger64i_v()
GL_TRANSFORM_FEEDBACK_BUFFER_SIZE	Size of binding range for each transform feedback attribute stream	0	glGetInteger64i_v()
GL_TRANSFORM_FEEDBACK_PAUSED	Is transform feedback paused on this object?	GL_FALSE	glGetBooleanv()
GL_TRANSFORM_FEEDBACK_ACTIVE	Is transform feedback active on this object?	GL_FALSE	glGetBooleanv()
GL_LABEL	Debug label	empty string	glGetObjectLabel()

Atomic Counter State

Table D.31   State Variables for Atomic Counters

State Variable	Description	Initial Value	Get Command
GL_ATOMIC_COUNTER_BUFFER_BINDING	Current value of generic atomic-counter buffer binding	0	glGetIntegerv()
GL_ATOMIC_COUNTER_BUFFER_BINDING	Buffer object bound to each atomic counter buffer binding point	0	glGetIntegeri_v()
GL_ATOMIC_COUNTER_BUFFER_START	Start offset of binding range for each atomic counter buffer	0	glGetInteger64i_v()
GL_ATOMIC_COUNTER_BUFFER_SIZE	Size of binding range for each atomic counter buffer	0	glGetInteger64i_v()

Shader Storage Buffer State

Table D.32 State Variables for Shader Storage Buffers

State Variable	Description	Initial Value	Get Command
GL_SHADER_STORAGE_BUFFER_BINDING	Current value of generic shader storage buffer binding	0	glGetIntegerv()
GL_SHADER_STORAGE_BUFFER_BINDING	Buffer object bound to each shader storage buffer binding point	0	glGetIntegeri_v()
GL_SHADER_STORAGE_BUFFER_START	Start offset of binding range for each shader storage buffer	0	glGetInteger64i_v()
GL_SHADER_STORAGE_BUFFER_SIZE	Size of binding range for each shader storage buffer	0	glGetInteger64i_v()

Sync Object State

Table D.33   State Variables for Sync Objects

State Variable	Description	Initial Value	Get Command
GL_OBJECT_TYPE	Type of sync object	GL_SYNC_FENCE	glGetSynciv()
GL_SYNC_STATUS	Sync object status	GL_UNSIGNALED	glGetSynciv()
GL_SYNC_CONDITION	Sync object condition	GL_SYNC_GPU_COMMANDS_COMPLETE	glGetSynciv()
GL_SYNC_FLAGS	Sync object flags	0	glGetSynciv()
GL_LABEL	Debug label	empty string	glGetObjectLabel()

Hints

Table D.34   Hints

State Variable	Description	Initial Value	Get Command
GL_LINE_SMOOTH_HINT	Line smooth hint	GL_DONT_CARE	glGetIntegerv()
GL_POLYGON_SMOOTH_HINT	Polygon smooth hint	GL_DONT_CARE	glGetIntegerv()
GL_TEXTURE_COMPRESSION_HINT	Texture compression quality hint	GL_DONT_CARE	glGetIntegerv()
GL_FRAGMENT_SHADER_DERIVATIVE_HINT	Fragment shader derivative accuracy hint	GL_DONT_CARE	glGetIntegerv()

Compute Dispatch State

Table D.35   State Variables for Compute Shader Dispatch

State Variable	Description	Initial Value	Get Command
GL_DISPATCH_INDIRECT_BUFFER_BINDING	Indirect dispatch buffer binding	0	glGetIntegerv()

Implementation-Dependent Values

Table D.36   State Variables Based on Implementation-Dependent Values

State Variable	Description	Initial Value	Get Command
GL_MAX_CLIP_DISTANCES	Maximum number of user clipping planes	8	glGetIntegerv()
GL_SUBPIXEL_BITS	Number of bits of subpixel precision in screen x_w and y_w	4	glGetIntegerv()
GL_IMPLEMENTATION_COLOR_READ_TYPE	Implementation preferred pixel *type*	GL_UNSIGNED_BYTE	glGetIntegerv()
GL_IMPLEMENTATION_COLOR_READ_FORMAT	Implementation preferred pixel *format*	GL_RGBA	glGetIntegerv()
GL_MAX_3D_TEXTURE_SIZE	Maximum 3D texture image dimension	2048	glGetIntegerv()
GL_MAX_TEXTURE_SIZE	Maximum 2D/1D texture image dimension	16384	glGetIntegerv()
GL_MAX_ARRAY_TEXTURE_LAYERS	Maximum number of layers for texture arrays	2048	glGetIntegerv()
GL_MAX_TEXTURE_LOD_BIAS	Maximum absolute texture level of detail bias	2.0	glGetFloatv()
GL_MAX_CUBE_MAP_TEXTURE_SIZE	Maximum cube-map texture image dimension	16384	glGetIntegerv()

Table D.36 (continued)   State Variables Based on Implementation-Dependent Values

State Variable	Description	Initial Value	Get Command
GL_MAX_RENDERBUFFER_SIZE	Maximum width and height of renderbuffers	16384	**glGetIntegerv()**
GL_MAX_VIEWPORT_DIMS	Maximum viewport dimensions	Implementation-dependent maximum values	**glGetFloatv()**
GL_MAX_VIEWPORTS	Maximum number of active viewports	16	**glGetIntegerv()**
GL_VIEWPORT_SUBPIXEL_BITS	Number of bits of subpixel precision for viewport bounds	0	**glGetIntegerv()**
GL_VIEWPORT_BOUNDS_RANGE	Viewport bounds range [*min*, *max*] (at least [−32768, 32767])	Implementation dependent	**glGetFloatv()**
GL_LAYER_PROVOKING_VERTEX	Vertex convention followed by gl_Layer	Implementation dependent	**glGetIntegerv()**
GL_VIEWPORT_INDEX_ PROVOKING_VERTEX	Vertex convention followed by gl_ViewportIndex	Implementation dependent	**glGetIntegerv()**
GL_POINT_SIZE_RANGE	Range (low to high) of point sprite sizes	1,1	**glGetFloatv()**
GL_POINT_SIZE_GRANULARITY	Point sprite size granularity	—	**glGetFloatv()**

State Variable	Description	Initial Value	Get Command
GL_ALIASED_LINE_WIDTH_RANGE	Range (low to high) of aliased line widths	1,1	glGetFloatv()
GL_SMOOTH_LINE_WIDTH_RANGE	Range (low to high) of antialiased line widths	1,1	glGetFloatv()
GL_SMOOTH_LINE_WIDTH_GRANULARITY	Antialiased line width granularity	—	glGetFloatv()
GL_MAX_ELEMENTS_INDICES	Recommended maximum number of glDrawRangeElements() indices	—	glGetIntegerv()
GL_MAX_ELEMENTS_VERTICES	Recommended maximum number of glDrawRangeElements() vertices	—	glGetIntegerv()
GL_COMPRESSED_TEXTURE_FORMATS	Enumerated compressed texture formats	—	glGetIntegerv()
GL_MAX_VERTEX_ATTRIB_RELATIVE_OFFSET	Maximum offset added to vertex buffer binding offset	2047	glGetIntegerv()
GL_MAX_VERTEX_ATTRIB_BINDINGS	Maximum number of vertex buffers	16	glGetIntegerv()
GL_NUM_COMPRESSED_TEXTURE_FORMATS	Number of compressed texture formats	0	glGetIntegerv()

Table D.36 (continued)   State Variables Based on Implementation-Dependent Values

State Variable	Description	Initial Value	Get Command
GL_MAX_TEXTURE_BUFFER_SIZE	Number of addressable texels for buffer textures	65536	glGetIntegerv()
GL_MAX_RECTANGLE_TEXTURE_SIZE	Maximum width and height of rectangular textures	16384	glGetIntegerv()
GL_PROGRAM_BINARY_FORMATS	Enumerated program binary formats	N/A	glGetIntegerv()
GL_NUM_PROGRAM_BINARY_FORMATS	Number of program binary formats	0	glGetIntegerv()
GL_SHADER_BINARY_FORMATS	Enumerated shader binary formats	–	glGetIntegerv()
GL_NUM_SHADER_BINARY_FORMATS	Number of shader binary formats	0	glGetIntegerv()
GL_SHADER_COMPILER	Shader compiler supported	–	glGetBooleanv()
GL_MIN_MAP_BUFFER_ALIGNMENT	Minimum byte alignment of pointers returned by **glMapBuffer()**	64	glGetIntegerv()
GL_TEXTURE_BUFFER_OFFSET_ALIGNMENT	Minimum required alignment for texture buffer offsets	1	glGetIntegerv()
GL_MAJOR_VERSION	Major version number supported	–	glGetIntegerv()

Table D.36 (continued)   State Variables Based on Implementation-Dependent Values

State Variable	Description	Initial Value	Get Command
GL_MINOR_VERSION	Minor version number supported	—	glGetIntegerv()
GL_CONTEXT_FLAGS	Context full/forward-compatible flag	—	glGetIntegerv()
GL_EXTENSIONS	Supported individual extension names	—	glGetStringi()
GL_NUM_EXTENSIONS	Number of individual extension names	—	glGetIntegerv()
GL_SHADING_LANGUAGE_VERSION	Latest shading language version supported	—	glGetString()
GL_SHADING_LANGUAGE_VERSION	Supported shading language versions	—	glGetStringi()
GL_NUM_SHADING_LANGUAGE_VERSIONS	Number of shading languages supported	3	glGetIntegerv()
GL_VENDOR	Vendor string	—	glGetString()
GL_VERSION	OpenGL version supported	—	glGetString()
GL_MAX_VERTEX_ATTRIBS	Number of active vertex attributes	16	glGetIntegerv()
GL_MAX_VERTEX_UNIFORM_COMPONENTS	Number of components for vertex shader uniform variables	1024	glGetIntegerv()

Table D.36 **(continued)**   State Variables Based on Implementation-Dependent Values

State Variable	Description	Initial Value	Get Command
GL_MAX_VERTEX_UNIFORM_VECTORS	Number of vectors for vertex shader uniform variables	256	glGetIntegerv()
GL_MAX_VERTEX_UNIFORM_BLOCKS	Maximum number of vertex uniform buffers per program	14	glGetIntegerv()
GL_MAX_VERTEX_OUTPUT_COMPONENTS	Maximum number of components of outputs written by a vertex shader	64	glGetIntegerv()
GL_MAX_VERTEX_TEXTURE_IMAGE_UNITS	Number of texture image units accessible by a vertex shader	16	glGetIntegerv()
GL_MAX_VERTEX_ATOMIC_COUNTER_BUFFERS	Number of atomic-counter buffers accessed by a vertex shader	0	glGetIntegerv()
GL_MAX_VERTEX_ATOMIC_COUNTERS	Number of atomic counters accessed by a vertex shader	0	glGetIntegerv()
GL_MAX_VERTEX_SHADER_STORAGE_BLOCKS	Number of shader storage blocks accessed by a vertex shader	0	glGetIntegerv()

Tessellation Shader Implementation-Dependent Limits

Table D.37   State Variables for Implementation-Dependent Tessellation Shader Values

State Variable	Description	Initial Value	Get Command
GL_MAX_TESS_GEN_LEVEL	Maximum level supported by tessellation primitive generator	64	glGetIntegerv()
GL_MAX_PATCH_VERTICES	Maximum patch size	32	glGetIntegerv()
GL_MAX_TESS_CONTROL_UNIFORM_COMPONENTS	Number of words for tessellation control shader (tessellation-control shader) uniforms	1024	glGetIntegerv()
GL_MAX_TESS_CONTROL_TEXTURE_IMAGE_UNITS	Number of texture image units for tessellation-control shader	16	glGetIntegerv()
GL_MAX_TESS_CONTROL_OUTPUT_COMPONENTS	Number components for tessellation-control shader per-vertex outputs	128	glGetIntegerv()
GL_MAX_TESS_PATCH_COMPONENTS	Number components for tessellation-control shader per-patch outputs	120	glGetIntegerv()
GL_MAX_TESS_CONTROL_TOTAL_OUTPUT_COMPONENTS	Number components for tessellation-control shader per-patch outputs	4096	glGetIntegerv()

Table D.37 (continued)   State Variables for Implementation-Dependent Tessellation Shader Values

State Variable	Description	Initial Value	Get Command
GL_MAX_TESS_CONTROL_INPUT_COMPONENTS	Number components for tessellation-control shader per-vertex inputs	128	**glGetIntegerv()**
GL_MAX_TESS_CONTROL_UNIFORM_BLOCKS	Number of supported uniform blocks for tessellation-control shader	14	**glGetIntegerv()**
GL_MAX_TESS_CONTROL_ATOMIC_COUNTER_BUFFERS	Number of atomic-counter buffers accessed by a tessellation-control shader	0	**glGetIntegerv()**
GL_MAX_TESS_CONTROL_ATOMIC_COUNTERS	Number of atomic-counters accessed by a tessellation-control shader	0	**glGetIntegerv()**
GL_MAX_TESS_CONTROL_SHADER_STORAGE_BLOCKS	Number of supported shader storage blocks for tessellation-control shader	0	**glGetIntegerv()**
GL_MAX_TESS_EVALUATION_UNIFORM_COMPONENTS	Number of words for tessellation evaluation shader (tessellation-evaluation shader) uniforms	1024	**glGetIntegerv()**
GL_MAX_TESS_EVALUATION_TEXTURE_IMAGE_UNITS	Number of texture image units for tessellation-evaluation shader	16	**glGetIntegerv()**

Table D.37 (continued) State Variables for Implementation-Dependent Tessellation Shader Values

State Variable	Description	Initial Value	Get Command
GL_MAX_TESS_EVALUATION_OUTPUT_COMPONENTS	Number components for tessellation-evaluation shaderper-vertex outputs	128	glGetIntegerv()
GL_MAX_TESS_EVALUATION_INPUT_COMPONENTS	Number components for tessellation-evaluation shaderper-vertex inputs	128	glGetIntegerv()
GL_MAX_TESS_EVALUATION_UNIFORM_BLOCKS	Number of supported uniform blocks for tessellation-evaluation shader	12	glGetIntegerv()
GL_MAX_TESS_EVALUATION_ATOMIC_COUNTER_BUFFERS	Number of atomic-counter buffers accessed by a tessellation-evaluation shader	0	glGetIntegerv()
GL_MAX_TESS_EVALUATION_ATOMIC_COUNTERS	Number of atomic counters accessed by a tessellation-evaluation shader	0	glGetIntegerv()
GL_MAX_TESS_EVALUATION_SHADER_STOAGE_BLOCKS	Number of shader storage blocks accessed by a tessellation-evaluation shader	0	glGetIntegerv()

Geometry Shader Implementation-Dependent Limits

Table D.38 State Variables for Implementation-Dependent Geometry Shader Values

State Variable	Description	Initial Value	Get Command
GL_MAX_GEOMETRY_UNIFORM_COMPONENTS	Number of components for geometry shader uniform variables	512	glGetIntegerv()
GL_MAX_GEOMETRY_UNIFORM_BLOCKS	Maximum number of geometry uniform buffers per program	14	glGetIntegerv()
GL_MAX_GEOMETRY_INPUT_COMPONENTS	Maximum number of components of inputs read by a geometry shader	64	glGetIntegerv()
GL_MAX_GEOMETRY_OUTPUT_COMPONENTS	Maximum number of components of outputs written by a geometry shader	128	glGetIntegerv()
GL_MAX_GEOMETRY_OUTPUT_VERTICES	Maximum number of vertices that any geometry shader can can emit	256	glGetIntegerv()

Table D.38 (continued) State Variables for Implementation-Dependent Geometry Shader Values

State Variable	Description	Initial Value	Get Command
GL_MAX_GEOMETRY_TOTAL_OUTPUT_ COMPONENTS	Maximum number of total components (all vertices) of active outputs that a geometry shader can emit	1024	glGetIntegerv()
GL_MAX_GEOMETRY_TEXTURE_IMAGE_UNITS	Number of texture image units accessible by a geometry shader	16	glGetIntegerv()
GL_MAX_GEOMETRY_SHADER_INVOCATIONS	Maximum supported geometry shader invocation count	32	glGetIntegerv()
GL_MAX_VERTEX_STREAMS	Total number of vertex streams	4	glGetIntegerv()
GL_MAX_GEOMETRY_ATOMIC_COUNTER_ BUFFERS	Number of atomic-counter buffers accessed by a geometry shader	0	glGetIntegerv()
GL_MAX_GEOMETRY_ATOMIC_COUNTERS	Number of atomic counters accessed by a geometry shader	0	glGetIntegerv()
GL_MAX_GEOMETRY_SHADER_STOAGE_BLOCKS	Number of shader storage blocks accessed by a geometry shader	0	glGetIntegerv()

Fragment Shader Implementation-Dependent Limits

Table D.39   State Variables for Implementation-Dependent Fragment Shader Values

State Variable	Description	Initial Value	Get Command
GL_MAX_FRAGMENT_UNIFORM_COMPONENTS	Number of components for fragment shader uniform variables	1024	glGetIntegerv()
GL_MAX_FRAGMENT_UNIFORM_VECTORS	Number of vectors for fragment shader uniform variables	256	glGetIntegerv()
GL_MAX_FRAGMENT_UNIFORM_BLOCKS	Maximum number of fragment uniform buffers per program	14	glGetIntegerv()
GL_MAX_FRAGMENT_INPUT_COMPONENTS	Maximum number of components of inputs read by a fragment shader	128	glGetIntegerv()
GL_MAX_TEXTURE_IMAGE_UNITS	Number of texture image units accessible by a fragment shader	16	glGetIntegerv()
GL_MIN_PROGRAM_TEXTURE_GATHER_OFFSET	Minimum texel offset for textureGather	−8	glGetIntegerv()
GL_MAX_PROGRAM_TEXTURE_GATHER_OFFSET	Maximum texel offset for textureGather	7	glGetIntegerv()
GL_MAX_FRAGMENT_ATOMIC_COUNTER_BUFFERS	Number of atomic-counter buffers accessed by a fragment shader	1	glGetIntegerv()
GL_MAX_FRAGMENT_ATOMIC_COUNTERS	Number of atomic counters accessed by a fragment shader	8	glGetIntegerv()
GL_MAX_FRAGMENT_SHADER_STOAGE_BLOCKS	Number of shader storage blocks accessed by a fragment shader	8	glGetIntegerv()

Implementation-Dependent Compute Shader Limits

Table D.40   State Variables for Implementation-Dependent Compute Shader Limits

State Variable	Description	Initial Value	Get Command
GL_MAX_COMPUTE_WORK_GROUP_COUNT	Maximum number of work groups that may be dispatched by a single dispatch command (per dimension)	65535	glGetIntegeri_v()
GL_MAX_COMPUTE_WORK_GROUP_SIZE	Maximum local size of a compute work group (per dimension)	1024 (x, y), 64 (z)	glGetIntegeri_v()
GL_MAX_COMPUTE_WORK_GROUP_INVOCATIONS	Maximum total compute shader invocations in a single local work group	1024	glGetIntegerv()
GL_MAX_COMPUTE_UNIFORM_BLOCKS	Maximum number of uniform blocks per compute program	14	glGetIntegerv()
GL_MAX_COMPUTE_TEXTURE_IMAGE_UNITS	Maximum number of texture image units accessible by a compute shader	16	glGetIntegerv()
GL_MAX_COMPUTE_ATOMIC_COUNTER_BUFFERS	Number of atomic-counter buffers accessed by a compute shader	8	glGetIntegerv()

Table D.40 (continued) State Variables for Implementation-Dependent Compute Shader Limits

State Variable	Description	Initial Value	Get Command
GL_MAX_COMPUTE_ATOMIC_COUNTERS	Number of atomic counters accessed by a compute shader	8	glGetIntegerv()
GL_MAX_COMPUTE_SHARED_MEMORY_SIZE	Maximum total storage size of all variables declared as *shared* in all compute shaders linked into a single program object	32768	glGetIntegerv()
GL_MAX_COMPUTE_UNIFORM_COMPONENTS	Number of components for compute shader uniform variables	512	glGetIntegerv()
GL_MAX_COMPUTE_IMAGE_UNIFORMS	Number of image variables in compute shaders	8	glGetIntegerv()
GL_MAX_COMBINED_COMPUTE_UNIFORM_COMPONENTS	Number of words for compute shader uniform variables in all uniform blocks, including the default	—	glGetIntegerv()
GL_MAX_COMPUTE_SHADER_STORAGE_BLOCKS	Number of shader storage blocks accessed by a compute shader	8	glGetIntegerv()

Implementation-Dependent Shader Limits

Table D.41   State Variables for Implementation-Dependent Shader Limits

State Variable	Description	Initial Value	Get Command
GL_MIN_PROGRAM_TEXEL_OFFSET	Minimum texel offset allowed in lookup	−8	glGetIntegerv()
GL_MAX_PROGRAM_TEXEL_OFFSET	Maximum texel offset allowed in lookup	7	glGetIntegerv()
GL_MAX_UNIFORM_BUFFER_BINDINGS	Maximum number of uniform buffer binding points on the context	72	glGetIntegerv()
GL_MAX_UNIFORM_BLOCK_SIZE	Maximum size in basic machine units of a uniform block	16384	glGetIntegerv()
GL_UNIFORM_BUFFER_OFFSET_ALIGNMENT	Minimum required alignment for uniform buffer sizes and offsets	1	glGetIntegerv()
GL_MAX_COMBINED_UNIFORM_BLOCKS	Maximum number of uniform buffers per program	70	glGetIntegerv()
GL_MAX_VARYING_COMPONENTS	Number of components for output variables	60	glGetIntegerv()
GL_MAX_VARYING_VECTORS	Number of vectors for output variables	15	glGetIntegerv()

Table D.41 (continued) State Variables for Implementation-Dependent Shader Limits

State Variable	Description	Initial Value	Get Command
GL_MAX_COMBINED_TEXTURE_IMAGE_UNITS	Total number of texture units accessible by the GL	96	glGetIntegerv()
GL_MAX_SUBROUTINES	Maximum number of subroutines per shader stage	256	glGetIntegerv()
GL_MAX_SUBROUTINE_UNIFORM_LOCATIONS	Maximum number of subroutine uniform locations per stage	1024	glGetIntegerv()
GL_MAX_UNIFORM_LOCATIONS	Maximum number of user-assignable uniform locations	1024	glGetIntegerv()
GL_MAX_ATOMIC_COUNTER_BUFFER_BINDINGS	Maximum number of atomic-counter buffer bindings	1	glGetIntegerv()
GL_MAX_ATOMIC_COUNTER_BUFFER_SIZE	Maximum size in basic machine units of an atomic-counter buffer	32	glGetIntegerv()
GL_MAX_COMBINED_ATOMIC_COUNTER_BUFFERS	Maximum number of atomic-counter buffers per program	1	glGetIntegerv()
GL_MAX_COMBINED_ATOMIC_COUNTERS	Maximum number of atomic-counter uniforms per program	8	glGetIntegerv()

Table D.41   (continued)   State Variables for Implementation-Dependent Shader Limits

State Variable	Description	Initial Value	Get Command
GL_MAX_SHADER_STORAGE_BUFFER_BINDINGS	Maximum number of shader storage buffer binding	8	glGetIntegerv()
GL_MAX_SHADER_STORAGE_BLOCK_SIZE	Maximum size of shader storage buffer binding	2^{24}	glGetInteger64v()
GL_MAX_COMBINED_SHADER_STORAGE_BLOCKS	Maximum number of shader storage buffer accessed by a program	8	glGetIntegerv()
GL_SHADER_STORAGE_BUFFER_OFFSET_ALIGNMENT	Minimum required alignment for shader storage buffer binding offsets	256	glGetIntegerv()
GL_MAX_IMAGE_UNITS	Number of units for image load/store/atom	8	glGetIntegerv()
GL_MAX_COMBINED_IMAGE_UNITS_AND_FRAGMENT_OUTPUTS	Limit on active image units + fragment outputs	8	glGetIntegerv()
GL_MAX_IMAGE_SAMPLES	Maximum allowed samples for a texture level bound to an image unit	0	glGetIntegerv()
GL_MAX_VERTEX_IMAGE_UNIFORMS	Number of image variables in vertex shaders	0	glGetIntegerv()

Table D.41 (continued)   State Variables for Implementation-Dependent Shader Limits

State Variable	Description	Initial Value	Get Command
GL_MAX_TESS_CONTROL_IMAGE_UNIFORMS	Number of image variables in tessellation control shaders	0	glGetIntegerv()
GL_MAX_TESS_EVALUATION_IMAGE_UNIFORMS	Number of image variables in tessellation evaluation shaders	0	glGetIntegerv()
GL_MAX_GEOMETRY_IMAGE_UNIFORMS	Number of image variables in geometry shaders	0	glGetIntegerv()
GL_MAX_FRAGMENT_IMAGE_UNIFORMS	Number of image variables in fragment shaders	8	glGetIntegerv()
GL_MAX_COMBINED_IMAGE_UNIFORMS	Number of image variables in all shaders	8	glGetIntegerv()
GL_MAX_COMBINED_VERTEX_UNIFORM_COMPONENTS	Number of words for vertex shader uniform variables in all uniform blocks (including default)	Implementation dependent	glGetIntegerv()
GL_MAX_COMBINED_GEOMETRY_UNIFORM_COMPONENTS	Number of words for geometry shader uniform variables in all uniform blocks (including default)	Implementation dependent	glGetIntegerv()

State Variable	Description	Initial Value	Get Command
GL_MAX_COMBINED_TESS_ CONTROL_UNIFORM_ COMPONENTS	Number of words for tessellation-control shader uniform variables in all uniform blocks (including default)	Implementation dependent	glGetIntegerv()
GL_MAX_COMBINED_TESS_ EVALUATION_UNIFORM_ COMPONENTS	Number of words for tessellation-evaluation shaderuniform variables in all uniform blocks (including default)	Implementation dependent	glGetIntegerv()
GL_MAX_COMBINED_ FRAGMENT_UNIFORM_ COMPONENTS	Number of words for fragment shader uniform variables in all uniform blocks (including default)	Implementation dependent	glGetIntegerv()

Implementation-Dependent Debug Output State

Table D.42 State Variables for Debug Output State

State Variable	Description	Initial Value	Get Command
GL_MAX_DEBUG_MESSAGE_LENGTH	The maximum length of a debug message string, including its null terminator	1	glGetIntegerv()
GL_MAX_DEBUG_LOGGED_MESSAGES	The maximum number of messages stored in the debug message log	1	glGetIntegerv()
GL_MAX_DEBUG_GROUP_STACK_DEPTH	Maximum debug group stack depth	64	glGetIntegerv()
GL_MAX_LABEL_LENGTH	Maximum length of a label string	256	glGetIntegerv()

Implementation-Dependent Values

Table D.43 Implementation-Dependent Values

State Variable	Description	Initial Value	Get Command
GL_MAX_SAMPLE_MASK_WORDS	Maximum number of sample mask words	1	glGetIntegerv()
GL_MAX_SAMPLES	Maximum number of samples supported for all noninteger formats	4	glGetIntegerv()
GL_MAX_COLOR_TEXTURE_SAMPLES	Maximum number of samples supported for all color formats in a multisample texture	1	glGetIntegerv()
GL_MAX_DEPTH_TEXTURE_SAMPLES	Maximum number of samples supported for all depth/stencil formats in a multisample texture	1	glGetIntegerv()
GL_MAX_INTEGER_SAMPLES	Maximum number of samples supported for all integer format multisample buffers	1	glGetIntegerv()

Table D.43   (continued)   Implementation-Dependent Values

State Variable	Description	Initial Value	Get Command
GL_QUERY_COUNTER_BITS	Asynchronous query counter bits	Implementation dependent	glGetQueryiv()
GL_MAX_SERVER_WAIT_ TIMEOUT	Maximum **glWaitSync()** timeout interval	0	glGetInteger64v()
GL_MIN_FRAGMENT_ INTERPOLATION_OFFSET	Furthest negative offset for interpolate AtOffset	−0.5	glGetFloatv()
GL_MAX_FRAGMENT_ INTERPOLATION_OFFSET	Furthest positive offset for interpolate AtOffset	+0.5	glGetFloatv()
GL_FRAGMENT_ INTERPOLATION_OFFSET_BITS	Subpixel bits for interpolate AtOffset	4	glGetIntegerv()
GL_MAX_DRAW_BUFFERS	Maximum number of active draw buffers	8	glGetIntegerv()
GL_MAX_DUAL_SOURCE_ DRAW_BUFFERS	Maximum number of active draw buffers when using dual-source blending	1	glGetIntegerv()
GL_MAX_COLOR_ATTACHMENTS	Maximum number of FBO attachment points for color buffers	8	glGetIntegerv()

Internal Format-Dependent Values

Table D.44   Internal Format-Dependent Values

State Variable	Description	Initial Value	Get Command
GL_SAMPLES	Supported sample counts	Implementation dependent	glGetInternalformativ()
GL_NUM_SAMPLE_COUNTS	Number of supported sample counts	1	glGetInternalformativ()

Implementation-Dependent Transform Feedback Limits

Table D.45   Implementation-Dependent Transform Feedback Limits

State Variable	Description	Initial Value	Get Command
GL_MAX_TRANSFORM_FEEDBACK_INTERLEAVED_COMPONENTS	Maximum number of components to write to a single buffer in interleaved mode	64	glGetIntegerv()
GL_MAX_TRANSFORM_FEEDBACK_SEPARATE_ATTRIBS	Maximum number of separate attributes or outputs that can be captured in transform feedback	4	glGetIntegerv()
GL_MAX_TRANSFORM_FEEDBACK_SEPARATE_COMPONENTS	Maximum number of components per attribute or output in separate mode	4	glGetIntegerv()
GL_MAX_TRANSFORM_FEEDBACK_BUFFERS	Maximum number of buffer objects to write with transform feedback	4	glGetIntegerv()

Framebuffer-Dependent Values

Table D.46 Framebuffer-Dependent Values

State Variable	Description	Initial Value	Get Command
GL_DOUBLEBUFFER	True if front and back buffers exist	—	glGetBooleanv()
GL_STEREO	True if left and right buffers exist	—	glGetBooleanv()
GL_SAMPLE_BUFFERS	Number of multisample buffers	0	glGetIntegerv()
GL_SAMPLES	Coverage mask size	0	glGetIntegerv()
GL_SAMPLE_POSITION	Explicit sample positions	—	glGetMultisamplefv()

Miscellaneous

Table D.47 Miscellaneous State Values

State Variable	Description	Initial Value	Get Command
GL_—	Current error code	GL_NO_ERROR	glGetError()
GL_CURRENT_QUERY	Active query object names	0	glGetQueryiv()
GL_COPY_READ_BUFFER_BINDING	Buffer object bound to copy buffer's "read" bind point	0	glGetIntegerv()
GL_COPY_WRITE_BUFFER_BINDING	Buffer object bound to copy buffer's "write" bind point	0	glGetIntegerv()
GL_TEXTURE_CUBE_MAP_SEAMLESS	Seamless cube-map filtering enable	GL_FALSE	glIsEnabled()

Homogeneous Coordinates and Transformation Matrices

This appendix presents a brief discussion of homogeneous coordinates, stated in a different way than Chapter 5, "Viewing Transformations, Clipping, and Feedback". It also summarizes the forms of the transformation matrices used for rotation, scaling, translation, perspective, and orthographic projection discussed in detail in Chapter 5. For a more detailed discussion on projection, see *The Real Projective Plane*, by H. S. M. Coxeter, 3rd ed. (Springer, 1992). To see how to use the library accompanying this book, see Chapter 5.

In the discussion that follows, the term homogeneous coordinates always means three-dimensional homogeneous coordinates, although projective geometries exist for all dimensions.

This appendix has the following major sections:

- "Homogeneous Coordinates"
- "Transformation Matrices"

Homogeneous Coordinates

OpenGL commands usually deal with two- and three-dimensional vertices, but in fact all are treated internally as three-dimensional homogeneous vertices comprising four coordinates. Every column vector

$$\begin{pmatrix} x \\ y \\ z \\ w \end{pmatrix}$$

(which we write as $(x, y, z, w)^\mathsf{T}$) represents a homogeneous vertex if at least one of its elements is nonzero. If the real number a is nonzero, then $(x, y, z, w)^\mathsf{T}$ and $(ax, ay, az, aw)^\mathsf{T}$ represent the same homogeneous vertex. (This is just like fractions: $x/y = (ax)/(ay)$.) A three-dimensional Euclidean space point $(x, y, z)^\mathsf{T}$ becomes the homogeneous vertex with coordinates $(x, y, z, 1.0)^\mathsf{T}$, and the two-dimensional Euclidean point $(x, y)^\mathsf{T}$ becomes $(x, y, 0.0, 1.0)^\mathsf{T}$.

As long as w is nonzero, the homogeneous vertex $(x, y, z, w)^\mathsf{T}$ corresponds to the three-dimensional point $(x/w, y/w, z/w)^\mathsf{T}$. If $w = 0.0$, it corresponds to no Euclidean point, but rather to some idealized "point at infinity." To understand this point at infinity, consider the point $(1, 2, 0, 0)$ and note that the sequence of points $(1, 2, 0, 1)$, $(1, 2, 0, 0.01)$, and $(1, 2.0, 0.0, 0.0001)$ corresponds to the Euclidean points $(1, 2)$, $(100, 200)$, and $(10, 000, 20, 000)$. This sequence represents points rapidly moving toward infinity along the line $2x = y$. Thus, you can think of $(1, 2, 0, 0)$ as the point at infinity in the direction of that line.

OpenGL might not handle homogeneous clip coordinates with $w < 0$ correctly. To be sure that your code is portable to all OpenGL systems, use only nonnegative w-values.

Transforming Vertices

Vertex transformations (such as rotations, translations, scaling, and shearing) and projections (such as perspective and orthographic) can all be represented by applying an appropriate 4×4 matrix to the coordinates representing the vertex. If v represents a homogeneous vertex and M is a 4×4 transformation matrix, then Mv is the image of v under the transformation by M. (In computer-graphics applications, the transformations used are usually nonsingular—in other words, the matrix M can be inverted. This isn't required, but some problems arise with singular matrices.)

After transformation, all transformed vertices are clipped so that x, y, and z are in the range $[-w, w]$ (assuming $w > 0$). Note that this range corresponds in Euclidean space to $[-1.0,\ 1.0]$.

Transforming Normals

Normal vectors aren't transformed in the same way as vertices or position vectors are. Mathematically, it's better to think of normal vectors not as vectors, but as planes perpendicular to those vectors. Then, the transformation rules for normal vectors are described by the transformation rules for perpendicular planes.

A homogeneous plane is denoted by the row vector (a, b, c, d), where at least one of a, b, c, and d is nonzero. If q is a nonzero real number, then (a, b, c, d) and (qa, qb, qc, qd) represent the same plane. A point $(x, y, z, w)^\mathsf{T}$ is on the plane (a, b, c, d) if $ax + by + cz + dw = 0$. (If $w = 1$, this is the standard description of a Euclidean plane.) In order for (a, b, c, d) to represent a Euclidean plane, at least one of a, b, or c must be nonzero. If they're all zero, then $(0, 0, 0, d)$ represents the "plane at infinity," which contains all the "points at infinity."

If p is a homogeneous plane and v is a homogeneous vertex, then the statement "v lies on plane p" is written mathematically as $pv = 0$, where pv is normal matrix multiplication. If M is a nonsingular vertex transformation (i.e., a 4×4 matrix that has an inverse M^{-1}), then $pv = 0$ is equivalent to $pM^{-1}Mv = 0$, so Mv lies in the plane pM^{-1}. Thus, pM^{-1} is the image of the plane under the vertex transformation M.

If you like to think of normal vectors as vectors instead of as the planes perpendicular to them, let v and n be vectors such that v is perpendicular to n. Then, $n^\mathsf{T} v = 0$. Thus, for an arbitrary nonsingular transformation M, $n^\mathsf{T} M - 1 M v = 0$, which means that $n^\mathsf{T} M^{-1}$ is the transpose of the transformed normal vector. Thus, the transformed normal vector is $M^{-1\mathsf{T}} n$. In other words, normal vectors are transformed by the inverse transpose of the transformation that transforms points. Whew!

Transformation Matrices

Although any nonsingular matrix M represents a valid projective transformation, a few special matrices are particularly useful. These matrices are listed in the following subsections.

Translation

$$T = \begin{bmatrix} 1 & 0 & 0 & x \\ 0 & 1 & 0 & y \\ 0 & 0 & 1 & z \\ 0 & 0 & 0 & 1 \end{bmatrix} \text{ and, } T^{-1} = \begin{bmatrix} 1 & 0 & 0 & -x \\ 0 & 1 & 0 & -y \\ 0 & 0 & 1 & -z \\ 0 & 0 & 0 & 1 \end{bmatrix}$$

Scaling

$$S = \begin{bmatrix} x & 0 & 0 & 1 \\ 0 & y & 0 & 1 \\ 0 & 0 & z & 1 \\ 0 & 0 & 0 & 1 \end{bmatrix} \text{ and, } S^{-1} = \begin{bmatrix} \frac{1}{x} & 0 & 0 & 1 \\ 0 & \frac{1}{y} & 0 & 1 \\ 0 & 0 & \frac{1}{z} & 1 \\ 0 & 0 & 0 & 1 \end{bmatrix}$$

Notice that S^{-1} is defined only if x, y, and z are all nonzero.

Rotation

Let $v = (x, y, z)^\mathsf{T}$, and $u = v/||v|| = (x', y', z')^\mathsf{T}$. Also let

$$S = \begin{bmatrix} 0 & -z' & y' \\ z' & 0 & -x' \\ -y' & x' & 0 \end{bmatrix}$$

and,

$$M = u u^\mathsf{T} + \cos \theta (I - u u^\mathsf{T}) + \sin \theta \, S$$

where

$$u u^\mathsf{T} = \begin{bmatrix} x^2 & xy & xz \\ xy & y^2 & yz \\ xz & yz & z^2 \end{bmatrix}$$

Then

$$R = \begin{bmatrix} m & m & m & 0 \\ m & m & m & 0 \\ m & m & m & 0 \\ 0 & 0 & 0 & 1 \end{bmatrix}$$

where m represents the elements from M, which is the 3×3 matrix defined on the preceding page. The R matrix is always defined. If $x = y = z = 0$, then R is the identity matrix. You can obtain the inverse of R, R^{-1}, by substituting $-\theta$ for θ, or by transposition.

Often, you're rotating about one of the coordinate axes; the corresponding matrices are as follows:

$$\text{Rotate}(\theta, 1, 0, 0) = \begin{bmatrix} 1 & 0 & 0 & 0 \\ 0 & \cos\theta & -\sin\theta & 0 \\ 0 & \sin\theta & \cos\theta & 0 \\ 0 & 0 & 0 & 1 \end{bmatrix}$$

$$\text{Rotate}(\theta, 0, 1, 0) = \begin{bmatrix} \cos\theta & 0 & \sin\theta & 0 \\ 0 & 1 & 0 & 0 \\ -\sin\theta & 0 & \cos\theta & 0 \\ 0 & 0 & 0 & 1 \end{bmatrix}$$

$$\text{Rotate}(\theta, 0, 0, 1) = \begin{bmatrix} \cos\theta & -\sin\theta & 0 & 0 \\ \sin\theta & \cos\theta & 0 & 0 \\ 0 & 0 & 1 & 0 \\ 0 & 0 & 0 & 1 \end{bmatrix}$$

As before, the inverses are obtained by transposition.

Perspective Projection

$$P = \begin{bmatrix} \dfrac{2n}{r-l} & 0 & \dfrac{r+l}{r-l} & 0 \\[2ex] 0 & \dfrac{2n}{t-b} & \dfrac{t+b}{t-b} & 0 \\[2ex] 0 & 0 & -\dfrac{f+n}{f-n} & -\dfrac{2fn}{f-n} \\[2ex] 0 & 0 & -1 & 0 \end{bmatrix}$$

P is defined as long as $l \neq r$, $t \neq b$, and $n \neq f$.

Orthographic Projection

$$P = \begin{bmatrix} \dfrac{2}{r-l} & 0 & 0 & -\dfrac{r+l}{r-l} \\[2ex] 0 & \dfrac{2}{t-b} & 0 & -\dfrac{t+b}{t-b} \\[2ex] 0 & 0 & -\dfrac{2}{f-n} & -\dfrac{f+n}{f-n} \\[2ex] 0 & 0 & 0 & 1 \end{bmatrix}$$

P is defined as long as $l \neq r$, $t \neq b$, and $n \neq f$.

Appendix F

OpenGL and Window Systems

OpenGL is available on many different platforms and works with many different window systems. It is designed to complement window systems, not duplicate their functionality. Therefore, OpenGL performs geometric and image rendering in two and three dimensions, but it does not manage windows or handle input events.

However, the basic definitions of most window systems don't support a library as sophisticated as OpenGL, with its complex and diverse pixel formats, including depth, and stencil buffers, as well as double-buffering. For most window systems, some routines are added to extend the window system to support OpenGL.

This appendix introduces the extensions defined for several window and operating systems: the X Window System that is supported on most Unix systems, Microsoft Windows, and Apple Computer's Mac OS X. You need to have some knowledge of the window systems to fully understand this appendix.

This appendix has the following major sections:

- "Accessing New OpenGL Functions"
- "GLX: OpenGL Extension for the X Window System"
- "WGL: OpenGL Extensions for Microsoft Windows"
- "OpenGL in Mac OS X: The Core OpenGL (CGL) API and the NSOpenGL Classes"

Accessing New OpenGL Functions

OpenGL changes all the time. The manufacturers of OpenGL graphics hardware add new extensions and the OpenGL Architecture Review Board approves those extensions and merges them into the core of OpenGL. Since each manufacturer needs to be able to update its version of OpenGL, the header files (like glcorearb.h[1]), and the library you use to compile (like opengl32.lib, on Microsoft Windows, for example) may be out of sync with the latest version. This would likely cause errors when compiling (or more specifically, linking) your application.

To help you work around this problem, a mechanism for accessing the new functions was added for many of the window system libraries. This method varies among the different window systems, but the idea is the same in all cases. You will need to retrieve function pointers for the functions that you want to use. You need to do this only if the function is not available explicitly from your library (you'll know when it isn't; you'll get a linker error).

Each window system that uses this mechanism has its own function for getting an OpenGL function pointer; check the respective section in this appendix for specifics.

Here is an example for Microsoft Windows:

```
#include <windows.h>   /* for wglGetProcAddress() */
#include "glext.h"     /* declares function pointer typedefs */

PFNGLBINDPROGRAMARBPROC   glBindProgramARB;

void
init(void)
{
  glBindProgramARB = (PFNGLBINDPROGRAMARB)
  wglGetProcAddress("glBindProgramARB");
  ...
}
```

The function pointer type—in this case, PFNGLBINDPROGRAMARBPROC—is defined in glext.h, as are all of the enumerants that you pass into OpenGL functions. If the returned value is zero (effectively a NULL pointer), the function is not available in the OpenGL implementation that your program is using.

GLUT includes a similar routine, **glutGetProcAddress()**, which simply wraps the window–system-dependent routine.

---

1. Newly named for Version 4.3. Preceeding version were named gl3.h, and before that, just gl.h. For those in the know, glext.h is still the compendium of all OpenGL extensions.

It's not sufficient in all cases to merely retrieve a function pointer to determine if functionality is present. To verify that the extension the functionality is defined from is available, check the extension string (see "The Query Commands" on Page 738 in Appendix D, "State Variables" for details).

GLEW: The OpenGL Extension Wrangler

To simplify both verifying extension support and dealing with the associated function pointers, we recommend using the open-source GLEW library (http://glew.sourceforge.net/) developed by Milan Ikits and Marcelo Magallon, which manages this process simply and elegantly.

To incorporate GLEW into your applications, follow these three simple steps:

1. Replace the OpenGL and glext.h header files with those of GLEW: glew.h.

2. Initialize GLEW by calling **glewInit()** after you've created your window (or more specifically, your OpenGL context). This causes GLEW to query and retrieve all available function pointers from your implementation as well as to provide a convenient set of variables for determining whether a particular version or extension is supported.

3. Verify that the OpenGL version or extension containing the functionality you want to use is available. GLEW provides a set of Boolean variables you can check at runtime. For example, the variable GL_version_4_3 will be available to verify if the OpenGL version is 4.3. Likewise, for each extension, a variable like GL_ARB_map_buffer_range (which is the OpenGL token for the map buffer range extension) is also defined. If the variable's value is true, you can use the extension's functions.

In the case of OpenGL versions and GLEW variables, all version variables will have a true value up to and including the current version.

Here's a short example using our **init()** routine, which is executed after calling **glutCreateWindow()**:

```
#include <GLEW.h>

void
init()
{
    GLuint vao;
```

```
glewInit(); // Initialize the GLEW library

if (GL_version_3_0) {
    // We know that OpenGL version 3.0 is supported, which is the
    // minimum version of OpenGL supporting vertex array objects
    glGenVertexArrays(1, &vao);
    glBindVertexArray(vao);
}

// Initialize and bind all other vertex arrays
...
}
```

GLX: OpenGL Extension for the X Window System

In the X Window System, OpenGL rendering is made available as an extension to X in the formal X sense. GLX is an extension to the X protocol (and its associated API) for communicating OpenGL commands to an extended X server. Connection and authentication are accomplished with the normal X mechanisms.

As with other X extensions, there is a defined network protocol for OpenGL's rendering commands encapsulated within the X byte stream, so client-server OpenGL rendering is supported. Since performance is critical in three-dimensional rendering, the OpenGL extension to X allows OpenGL to bypass the X server's involvement in data encoding, copying, and interpretation, and instead render directly to the graphics pipeline.

GLX Version 1.3 introduces several sweeping changes, starting with the new GLXFBConfig data structure, which describes the GLX framebuffer configuration (including the depth of the color buffer components, and the types, quantities, and sizes of the depth, stencil, accumulation, and auxiliary buffers). The GLXFBConfig structure describes these framebuffer attributes for a GLXDrawable rendering surface. (In X, a rendering surface is called a Drawable.)

GLX 1.3 also provides for three types of GLXDrawable surfaces: GLXWindow, GLXPixmap, and GLXPbuffer. A GLXWindow is on-screen; a GLXPixmap or GLXPbuffer is off-screen. Because a GLXPixmap has an associated X pixmap, both X and GLX may render into a GLXPixmap. GLX may be the only way to render into a GLXPbuffer. The GLXPbuffer is intended to store pixel data in nonvisible framebuffer memory. (Off-screen rendering isn't guaranteed to be supported for direct renderers.)

GLX version 1.4 (the current version at the time of this writing), increased support for framebuffer configuration by adding drawable configuration options for number of buffers and samples for multisampled drawables.

The X Visual is an important data structure for maintaining pixel format information about an OpenGL window. A variable of data type XVisualInfo keeps track of pixel format information, including pixel type (RGBA or color-index), single- or double-buffering, resolution of colors, and presence of depth, stencil, and accumulation buffers. The standard X Visuals (for example, PseudoColor and TrueColor) do not describe the pixel format details, so each implementation must extend the number of X Visuals supported.

In GLX 1.3, a GLXWindow has an X Visual, associated with its GLXFBConfig. For a GLXPixmap or a GLXPbuffer, there may or may not be a similar associated X Visual. Prior to GLX 1.3, all surfaces (windows or pixmaps) were associated with an X Visual. (Prior to 1.3, Pbuffers were not part of GLX.)

The GLX routines are discussed in more detail in the OpenGL Reference Manual. Integrating OpenGL applications with the X Window System and the Motif widget set is discussed in great detail in OpenGL Programming for the X Window System by Mark Kilgard (Addison-Wesley, 1996), which includes full source code examples. If you absolutely want to learn about the internals of GLX, you may want to read the GLX specification, which can be found at

http://www.opengl.org/registry/doc/glx1.4.pdf

Initialization

Use **glXQueryExtension()** and **glXQueryVersion()** to determine whether the GLX extension is defined for an X server and, if so, which version is present. **glXQueryExtensionsString()** returns extension information about the client-server connection. **glXGetClientString()** returns information about the client library, including extensions and version number. **glXQueryServerString()** returns similar information about the server.

glXChooseFBConfig() returns a pointer to an array of GLXFBConfig structures describing all GLX framebuffer configurations that meet the client's specified attributes. You may use **glXGetFBConfigAttrib()** to query a framebuffer configuration about its support of a particular GLX attribute. You may also call **glXGetVisualFromFBConfig()** to retrieve the X Visual associated with a GLXFBConfig.

Creation of rendering areas varies slightly, depending on the type of drawable. For a GLXWindow, first create an X Window with an X Visual that corresponds to the GLXFBConfig. Then use that X Window when calling **glXCreateWindow()**, which returns a GLXWindow. Similarly for a GLXPixmap, first create an X Pixmap with a pixel depth that matches the vGLXFBConfig. Then use that Pixmap when calling **glXCreatePixmap()** to create a GLXPixmap. A GLXPbuffer does not require an X Window or an X Pixmap; just call **glXCreatePbuffer()** with the appropriate GLXFBConfig.

Note: If you are using GLX 1.2 or earlier, you do not have a GLXFBConfig structure. Instead, use **glXChooseVisual()**, which returns a pointer to an XVisualInfo structure describing the X Visual that meets the client's specified attributes. You can query a visual about its support of a particular OpenGL attribute with **glXGetConfig()**. To render to an off-screen pixmap, you must use the earlier **glXCreateGLXPixmap()** routine.

Accessing OpenGL Functions

To access function pointers for extensions and new features in the X Window System, use the **glXGetProcAddress()** function. This function is defined in the glxext.h header file, which can be downloaded from the OpenGL Web site.

Controlling Rendering

Several GLX routines are provided for creating and managing an OpenGL rendering context. Routines are also provided for such tasks as handling GLX events, synchronizing execution between the X and OpenGL streams, swapping front and back buffers, and using an X font.

Managing an OpenGL Rendering Context

An OpenGL rendering context is created with either **glXCreateNewContext()** or **glXCreateContextAttribsARB()**, whose use is required in OpenGL Version 3.0 and greater. One of the arguments to these routines allows you to request a direct rendering context that bypasses the X server as described previously. (To perform direct rendering, the X server connection must be local, and the OpenGL implementation needs to support direct rendering.) Another argument also allows display-list and texture-object indices and definitions to be shared by multiple rendering contexts. You can determine whether a GLX context is direct with **glXIsDirect()**.

glXMakeContextCurrent() binds a rendering context to the current rendering thread and also establishes two current drawable surfaces. You can draw into one of the current drawable surfaces and read pixel data from the other drawable. In many situations, the draw and read drawables refer to the same GLXDrawable surface. **glXGetCurrentContext()** returns the current context. You can also obtain the current draw drawable with **glXGetCurrentDrawable()**, the current read drawable with **glXGetCurrentReadDrawable()**, and the current X Display with **glXGetCurrentDisplay()**. You can use **glXQueryContext()** to determine the current values for context attributes.

Only one context can be current for any thread at any one time. If you have multiple contexts, you can copy selected groups of OpenGL state variables from one context to another with **glXCopyContext()**. When you're finished with a particular context, destroy it with **glXDestroyContext()**.

Note: If you are using GLX 1.2 or earlier, use **glXCreateContext()** to create a rendering context and **glXMakeCurrent()** to make it current. You cannot declare a drawable as a separate read drawable, so you do not have **glXGetCurrentReadDrawable()**.

Handling GLX Events

GLX 1.3 introduces GLX events, which are returned in the event stream of standard X11 events. GLX event handling has been added specifically to deal with the uncertainty of the contents of a GLXPbuffer, which may be clobbered at any time. In GLX 1.3, you may use **glXSelectEvent()** to select only one event with GLX_PBUFFER_CLOBBER_MASK. With standard X event-handling routines, you can now determine if a portion of a GLXPbuffer (or GLXWindow) has been damaged and then take steps, if desired, to recover. (Also, you can call **glXGetSelectedEvent()** to find out if you are already monitoring this GLX event.)

Synchronizing Execution

To prevent X requests from executing until any outstanding OpenGL rendering is completed, call **glXWaitGL()**. Then, any previously issued OpenGL commands are guaranteed to be executed before any X rendering calls made after **glXWaitGL()**. Although the same result can be achieved with **glFinish()**, **glXWaitGL()** doesn't require a round-trip to the server and thus is more efficient in cases where the client and server are on separate machines.

To prevent an OpenGL command sequence from executing until any outstanding X requests are completed, use **glXWaitX()**. This routine guarantees that previously issued X rendering calls are executed before any OpenGL calls made after **glXWaitX()**.

Swapping Buffers

For drawables that are double-buffered, the front and back buffers can be exchanged by calling **glXSwapBuffers()**. An implicit **glFlush()** is done as part of this routine.

Using an X Font

A shortcut for using X *fonts* in OpenGL is provided with the command **glXUseXFont()**. This routine builds display lists for each requested character from the specified font and font size.

Note: **glXUseXFont()** uses functionality that was removed from the core profile of OpenGL in Version 3.1. You can still use **glXUseXFont()** if you use the compatibility profile.

Cleaning Up Drawables

Once rendering is completed, you can destroy the drawable surface with the appropriate call to **glXDestroyWindow()**, **glXDestroyPixmap()**, or **glXDestroyPbuffer()**. (These routines are not available prior to GLX 1.3, although there is **glXDestroyGLXPixmap()**, which is similar to **glXDestroyPixmap()**.)

GLX Prototypes

Initialization

Determine whether the GLX extension is defined on the X server:

Bool **glXQueryExtension**(Display *dpy*, int *errorBase*,
                        int *eventBase*);

Query version and extension information for client and server:

Bool **glXQueryVersion**(Display *dpy*, int *major*, int *minor*);

const char* **glXGetClientString**(Display *dpy*, int *name*);

const char* **glXQueryServerString**(Display *dpy*, int *screen*,
                                  int *name*);

const char* **glXQueryExtensionsString**(Display *dpy*, int *screen*);

Obtain available GLX framebuffer configurations:

GLXFBConfig * **glXGetFBConfigs**(Display *dpy*, int *screen*,
                                  int *nelements*);

GLXFBConfig * **glXChooseFBConfig**(Display *dpy*, int *screen*,
                                    const int *attribList*,
                                    int *nelements*);

Query a GLX framebuffer configuration for attribute or X Visual information:

int **glXGetFBConfigAttrib**(Display *dpy*, GLXFBConfig *config*,
                             int *attribute*, int *value*);

XVisualInfo * **glXGetVisualFromFBConfig**(Display *dpy*,
                                           GLXFBConfig *config*);

Create surfaces that support rendering (both on-screen and off-screen):

GLXWindow **glXCreateWindow**(Display *dpy*,
                             GLXFBConfig *config*,
                             Window *win*,
                             const int *attribList*);

GLXPixmap **glXCreatePixmap**(Display *dpy*,
                             GLXFBConfig *config*,
                             Pixmap *pixmap*,
                             const int *attribList*);

GLXPbuffer **glXCreatePbuffer**(Display *dpy*, GLXFBConfig *config*,
                                const int *attribList*);

Obtain a pointer to an OpenGL function:

__GLXextFuncPtr **glXGetProcAddress**(const char *funcName*);

Controlling Rendering

Manage and query an OpenGL rendering context:

GLXContext **glXCreateNewContext**(Display *dpy*,
                                   GLXFBConfig *config*,
                                   int *renderType*,
                                   GLXContext *shareList*,
                                   Bool *direct*);

GLXContext **glXCreateContextAttribsARB**((Display *dpy*,
                                                GLXFBConfig *config*,
                                                GLXContext *shareList*,
                                                Bool *direct*,
                                                const int **attribs*);

Bool **glXMakeContextCurrent**(Display **dpy*,
                                    GLXDrawable *drawable*,
                                    GLXDrawable *read*,
                                    GLXContext *context*);

void **glXCopyContext**(Display **dpy*, GLXContext *source*,
                              GLXContext *dest*, unsigned long *mask*);

Bool **glXIsDirect**(Display **dpy*, GLXContext *context*);

GLXContext **glXGetCurrentContext**(void);

Display* **glXGetCurrentDisplay**(void);

GLXDrawable **glXGetCurrentDrawable**(void);

GLXDrawable **glXGetCurrentReadDrawable**(void);

int **glXQueryContext**(Display **dpy*, GLXContext *context*,
                         int *attribute*, int **value*);

void **glXDestroyContext**(Display **dpy*, GLXContext *context*);

Ask to receive and query GLX events:

int **glXSelectEvent**(Display **dpy*, GLXDrawable *drawable*,
                       unsigned long *eventMask*);

int **glXGetSelectedEvent**(Display **dpy*, GLXDrawable *drawable*,
                       unsigned long **eventMask*);

Synchronize execution:

void **glXWaitGL**(void);

void **glXWaitX**(void);

Exchange front and back buffers:

void **glXSwapBuffers**(Display **dpy*, GLXDrawable *drawable*);

Use an X font:

void **glXUseXFont**(Font *font*, int *first*, int *count*, int *listBase*);

Clean up drawables:

void **glXDestroyWindow**(Display *dpy*, GLXWindow *win*);

void **glXDestroyPixmap**(Display *dpy*, GLXPixmap *pixmap*);

void **glXDestroyPbuffer**(Display *dpy*, GLXPbuffer *pbuffer*);

Deprecated GLX Prototypes

The following routines have been deprecated in GLX 1.3. If you are using GLX 1.2 or a predecessor, you may need to use several of these routines.

Obtain the desired visual:

XVisualInfo* **glXChooseVisual**(Display *dpy*, int *screen*,
                                int *attribList*);

int **glXGetConfig**(Display *dpy*, XVisualInfo *visual*, int *attrib*,
                    int *value*);

Manage an OpenGL rendering context:

GLXContext **glXCreateContext**(Display *dpy*,
                                XVisualInfo *visual*,
                                GLXContext *shareList*,
                                Bool *direct*);

Bool **glXMakeCurrent**(Display *dpy*, GLXDrawable *drawable*,
                        GLXContext *context*);

Perform off-screen rendering:

GLXPixmap **glXCreateGLXPixmap**(Display *dpy*,
                                XVisualInfo *visual*,
                                Pixmap *pixmap*);

void **glXDestroyGLXPixmap**(Display *dpy*, GLXPixmap *pix*);

WGL: OpenGL Extensions for Microsoft Windows

OpenGL rendering is supported on systems that run any modern version of Microsoft Windows (from Windows 95 and later). The functions and routines of the Win32 library are necessary to initialize the pixel format and control rendering, and for access to extensions for OpenGL. Some routines, which are prefixed by **wgl**, extend Win32 so that OpenGL can be fully supported.

For Win32/WGL, the PIXELFORMATDESCRIPTOR is the key data structure for maintaining pixel format information about the OpenGL window.

A variable of data type PIXELFORMATDESCRIPTOR keeps track of pixel information, including pixel type (RGBA or color-index); single- or double-buffering; resolution of colors; and presence of depth, stencil, and accumulation buffers.

To get more information about WGL, you may want to start with technical articles available through the Microsoft Developer Network Web site (http://msdn.microsoft.com/).

Initialization

Use **GetVersion()** or the newer **GetVersionEx()** to determine version information. **ChoosePixelFormat()** tries to find a PIXELFORMATDESCRIPTOR with specified attributes. If a good match for the requested pixel format is found, then **SetPixelFormat()** should be called for actual use of the pixel format. You should select a pixel format in the device context before creating a rendering context.

If you want to find out details about a given pixel format, use **DescribePixelFormat()** or, for overlays or underlays, **wglDescribeLayerPlane()**.

Accessing OpenGL Functions

To access function pointers for extensions and new features in Microsoft Windows, use the **wglGetProcAddress()** function. This function is defined in the wingdi.h header file, which is automatically included when you include windows.h in your application.

Controlling Rendering

Several WGL routines are provided for creating and managing an OpenGL rendering context, rendering to a bitmap, swapping front and back buffers, finding a color palette, and using either bitmap or outline fonts.

Managing an OpenGL Rendering Context

wglCreateContext() and **wglCreateContextAttribsARB()** (the latter for use with OpenGL Version 3.0 and greater) create an OpenGL rendering context for drawing on the device in the selected pixel format of the device context. (To create an OpenGL rendering context for overlay or underlay windows, use **wglCreateLayerContext()** instead.) To make a rendering context current, use **wglMakeCurrent()**; **wglGetCurrentContext()** returns the current context. You can also obtain the current device context with **wglGetCurrentDC()**. You can copy some OpenGL state variables from one context to another with **wglCopyContext()** or make two contexts share the same display lists and texture objects with **wglShareLists()**. When you're finished with a particular context, destroy it with **wglDestroyContext()**.

Accessing OpenGL Extensions

Use **wglGetProcAddress()** to access implementation-specific OpenGL extension procedure calls. To determine which extensions are supported by your implementation, first call **glGetIntegerv()** passing GL_NUM_EXTENSIONS to determine the number of extensions available, and then call **glGetStringi()** to retrieve each extension name. **wglGetProcAddress()**, when passed the exact name of the extension returned from **glGetStringi()**, returns a function pointer for the extension procedure call, or returns NULL if the extension is not supported.

OpenGL Rendering to a Bitmap

Win32 has a few routines for allocating (and deallocating) bitmaps, to which you can render OpenGL directly. **CreateDIBitmap()** creates a device-dependent bitmap (DDB) from a device-independent bitmap (DIB). **CreateDIBSection()** creates a DIB that applications can write to directly. When finished with your bitmap, you can use **DeleteObject()** to free it up.

Synchronizing Execution

If you want to combine GDI and OpenGL rendering, be aware that there are no equivalents to functions such as **glXWaitGL()**, or **glXWaitX()** in Win32. Although **glXWaitGL()** has no equivalent in Win32, you can achieve the same effect by calling **glFinish()**, which waits until all pending OpenGL commands are executed, or by calling **GdiFlush()**, which waits until all GDI drawing has been completed.

Swapping Buffers

For windows that are double-buffered, the front and back buffers can be exchanged by calling **SwapBuffers()** or **wglSwapLayerBuffers()**; the latter is used for overlays and underlays.

Finding a Color Palette

To access the color palette for the standard (nonlayer) bitplanes, use the standard GDI functions to set the palette entries. For overlay or underlay layers, use **wglRealizeLayerPalette()**, which maps palette entries from a given color-index layer plane into the physical palette or initializes the palette of an RGBA layer plane. **wglGetLayerPaletteEntries()** and **wglSetLayerPaletteEntries()** are used to query and set the entries in palettes of layer planes.

Using a Bitmap or Outline Font

WGL has two routines, **wglUseFontBitmaps()** and **wglUseFontOutlines()**, for converting system fonts for use with OpenGL. Both routines build a display list for each requested character from the specified font and font size.

Note: Display lists, a feature used by **wglUseFontBitmaps()** and **wglUseFontOutlines()**, were removed from the core profile of OpenGL since Version 3.1. As such, these routines will not work properly if you're using a core profile. However, they are supported if you use the compatiblity profile.

WGL Prototypes

Initialization

Determine version information:

BOOL **GetVersion**(LPOSVERSIONINFO *lpVersionInformation*);

BOOL **GetVersionEx**(LPOSVERSIONINFO *lpVersionInformation*);

Pixel format availability, selection, and capability:

int **ChoosePixelFormat**(HDC *hdc*,
                    CONST PIXELFORMATDESCRIPTOR **ppfd*);

BOOL **SetPixelFormat**(HDC *hdc*, int *iPixelFormat*,
                    CONST PIXELFORMATDESCRIPTOR **ppfd*);

int **DescribePixelFormat**(HDC *hdc*, int *iPixelFormat*, UINT *nBytes*,
                    LPPIXELFORMATDESCRIPTOR *ppfd*);

BOOL **wglDescribeLayerPlane**(HDC *hdc*, int *iPixelFormat*,
                    int *iLayerPlane*,
                    UINT *nBytes*,
                    LPLAYERPLANEDESCRIPTOR *plpd*);

Obtain a pointer to an OpenGL function:

PROC **wglGetProcAddress**(LPCSTR *funcNam*);

Controlling Rendering

Manage or query an OpenGL rendering context:

HGLRC **wglCreateContext**(HDC *hdc*);

HGLRC **wglCreateContextAttribsARB**(HDC *hdc*,
                             HGLRC *hShareContext*,
                             const int *attribList*);

HGLRC **wglCreateLayerContext**(HDC *hdc*, int *iLayerPlane*);

BOOL **wglShareLists**(HGLRC *hglrc1*, HGLRC *hglrc2*);

BOOL **wglDeleteContext**(HGLRC *hglrc*);

BOOL **wglCopyContext**(HGLRC *hglrcSource*, HGLRC *hlglrcDest*,
                     UINT *mask*);

BOOL **wglMakeCurrent**(HDC *hdc*, HGLRC *hglrc*);

HGLRC **wglGetCurrentContext**(void);

HDC **wglGetCurrentDC**(void);

Access implementation-dependent extension procedure calls:

PROC **wglGetProcAddress**(LPCSTR *lpszProc*);

Access and release the bitmap of the front buffer:

HBITMAP **CreateDIBitmap**(HDC *hdc*,
                CONST BITMAPINFOHEADER **lpbmih*,
                DWORD *fdwInit*,
                CONST VOID **lpbInit*,
                CONST BITMAPINFO **lpbmi*,
                UINT *fuUsage*);

HBITMAP **CreateDIBSection**(HDC *hdc*,
                CONST BITMAPINFO **pbmi*,
                UINT *iUsage*,
                VOID **ppvBits*,

                HANDLE *hSection*,
                DWORD *dwOffset*);

BOOL **DeleteObject**(HGDIOBJ *hObject*);

Exchange front and back buffers:

BOOL **SwapBuffers**(HDC *hdc*);

BOOL **wglSwapLayerBuffers**(HDC *hdc*, UINT *fuPlanes*);

Find a color palette for overlay or underlay layers:

int **wglGetLayerPaletteEntries**(HDC *hdc*, int *iLayerPlane*,
                int *iStart*, int *cEntries*,
                CONST COLORREF **pcr*);

int **wglSetLayerPaletteEntries**(HDC *hdc*, int *iLayerPlane*,
                int *iStart*,
                int *cEntries*,
                CONST COLORREF **pcr*);

BOOL **wglRealizeLayerPalette**(HDC *hdc*, int *iLayerPlane*,
                BOOL *bRealize*);

Use a bitmap or an outline font:

BOOL **wglUseFontBitmaps**(HDC *hdc*, DWORD *first*,
                DWORD *count*, DWORD *listBase*);

BOOL **wglUsexFontOutlines**(HDC *hdc*, DWORD *first*,
                DWORD *count*,
                DWORD *listBase*, FLOAT *deviation*,
                FLOAT *extrusion*, int *format*,
                LPGLYPHMETRICSFLOAT *lpgmf*);

OpenGL in Mac OS X: The Core OpenGL (CGL) API and the NSOpenGL Classes

In Apple Computer's Mac OS X, OpenGL is an integral part of the windowing system. In fact, the window manager Quartz uses OpenGL to display windows on the screen and perform all of the window transitions, (like minimizing, etc.). On Mac OS X, there are two methods for setting up an application to use OpenGL. They are as follows:

- Using CGL, the "Core OpenGL Library", which is a low-lever access API similar to those of the X Window System and Microsoft Windows.

- Using the NSOpenGL Objective-C classes for direct support in Apple's Cocoa framework.

Mac OS X also supports GLUT as an application framework, but its use for complex application development is discouraged, generally speaking.

Mac OS X also makes an implementation of the X Window System available as a client application, which supports GLX as described previously.

We'll begin by describing the CGL, and then discuss the NSOpenGL classes, as they use CGL for suppporting OpenGL.

Note: There current window-system framework of Mac OS X is called "Cocoa", and supports the topics described in the following sections. The previous window-system framework called "Carbon" also supported the CGL API (including some functions which were deprecated), and a deprecated API named AGL, which we do not describe.

Mac OS X's Core OpenGL Library

On Mac OS X, an OpenGL implementation is described using a concept called a *renderer*. Usually, Mac OS X manages renderers for you, but you can control the selection if you need. Once the renderer is chosen, you then select the buffer attributes your application requires, create a context, and your application is ready to render using OpenGL.

For complete details of Mac OS X's OpenGL implementations, go to the Apple developer Web site (http://developer.apple.com), which contains user guides and reference documents.

Initialization

Usually, renderers are selected and managed automatically for your by Mac OS X; however, if you need or want to explicitly control the renderer for your application, do the following: first, determine the available renderers by calling **CGLQueryRendererInfo**(), which returns an opaque data structure—CGLRendererInfoObj—that you need to use to query the characteristics of each renderer. Properties of a renderer can be determined by calling **CGLDescribeRenderer**(). Once you've completed all of your system queries, you need to release the returned CGLRendererInfoObj by calling **CGLDestroyRendererInfo**().

Once you've selected the appropriate renderer, you next specify the buffer attributes required for your application. Specify the attributes you need, and then verify that the configuration you need is supported by calling **CGLChoosePixelFormat**(), which returns a CGLPixelFormatObj object. As with other objects, you need to release its resource, and in this case, you'll call **CGLDestroyPixelFormat**().

Controlling Rendering

Like the other binding APIs, CGL has routines for controlling OpenGL's interaction with the windowing system, including managing OpenGL contexts.

Managing an OpenGL Rendering Context

After selecting a pixel format, create an OpenGL context by calling **CGLCreateContext()** using the returned CGLPixelFormatObj object. Once the context is created, you need to call **CGLSetCurrentContext()** to make the context current and available for OpenGL rendering.

Accessing OpenGL Extensions

Synchronizing Execution

Swapping Buffers

CGL Prototypes

Initialization

Managing Pixel Format Objects:

CGLError **CGLChoosePixelFormat**(const CGLPixelFormatAttribute *attribs,
                                   CGLPixelFormatObj *pix,
                                   GLint *npix);

CGLError **CGLDescribePixelFormat**(CGLPixelFormatObj pix,
                                     GLint pix num,
                                     CGLPixelFormatAttribute attrib,
                                     GLintp *value);

CGLPixelFormatObj **CGLGetPixelFormat**(CGLContextObj ctx);

CGLPixelFormatObj **CGLRetainPixelFormat**(CGLPixelFormatObj pix);

void **CGLReleasePixelFormat**(CGLPixelFormatObj pix);

GLuint **CGLGetPixelFormatRetainCount**(CGLPixelFormatObj pix);

CGLError **CGLDestroyPixelFormat**(CGLPixelFormatObj pix);

Controlling Rendering

Managing rendering contexts:

CGLError **CGLCreateContext**(CGLPixelFormatObj *pix*,
                              CGLContextObj *share*,
                              CGLContextObj **ctx*);

CGLContextObj **CGLRetainContext**(CGLContextObj *ctx*);

void **CGLReleaseContext**(CGLContextObj *ctx*);

GLuint **CGLGetContextRetainCount**(CGLContextObj *ctx*);

CGLError **CGLDestroyContext**(CGLContextObj *ctx*);

CGLContextObj **CGLGetCurrentContext**(void);

CGLError **CGLSetCurrentContext**(CGLContextObj *ctx*);

Getting and Setting Context Options:

CGLError **CGLEnable**(CGLContextObj *ctx*,
                       CGLContextEnable *pname*);

CGLError **CGLDisable**(CGLContextObj *ctx*,
                        CGLContextEnable *pname*);

CGLError **CGLIsEnabled**(CGLContextObj *ctx*,
                          CGLContextEnable *pname*,
                          GLint **enable*);

CGLError **CGLSetParameter**(CGLContextObj *ctx*,
                             CGLContextParameter *pname*,
                             const GLint **params*);

CGLError **CGLGetParameter**(CGLContextObj *ctx*,
                             CGLContextParameter *pname*,
                             GLint **params*);

Locking and unlocking contexts:

CGLError **CGLLockContext**(CGLContextObj *ctx*);

CGLError **CGLUnlockContext**(CGLContextObj *ctx*);

Managing drawable objects:

CGLError **CGLClearDrawable**(CGLContextObj *ctx*);

CGLError **CGLFlushDrawable**(CGLContextObj *ctx*);

Getting error information:

const char* **CGLErrorString**(CGLError *error*);

Managing global information:

CGLError **CGLSetGlobalOption**(CGLGlobalOption *pname,*
                               const GLint *params*);

CGLError **CGLGetGlobalOption**(CGLGlobalOption *pname,*
                               GLint *params*);

void **CGLGetVersion**(GLint *majorvers,* GLint *minorvers*);

Retrieve rendering information:

CGLError **CGLDescribeRenderer**(CGLRendererInfoObj *rend,*
                                GLint *rend_num,*
                                CGLRendererProperty *prop,*
                                GLint *value*);

CGLError **CGLDestroyRendererInfo**(CGLRendererInfoObj *rend*);

CGLError **CGLQueryRendererInfo**(GLuint *display_mask,*
                                 CGLRendererInfoObj *rend,*
                                 GLint *nrend*);

Managing virtual screens:

CGLError **CGLSetVirtualScreen**(CGLContextObj *ctx,*
                                GLint *screen*);

CGLError **CGLGetVirtualScreen**(CGLContextObj *ctx,*
                                GLint *screen*);

CGLError **CGLUpdateContext**(CGLContextObj *ctx*);

The NSOpenGL Classes

Initialization

Begin by adding an OpenGL view (through an instance of **NSOpenGLView**()) to your application window. Using an **NSOpenGLView**() takes care of managing the OpenGL context and the associated pixel formats; otherwise, you will need to specify the pixel format for the application's OpenGL window by allocating an **NSOpenGLPixelFormat**() class and using the returned class instance when creating an OpenGL context with **NSOpenGLContext**().

It is also possible to add an **NSOpenGLView**() to your application using the Interface Builder, but you will need to manually create the associated pixel format and context objects programmatically.

Once your view is created, you can proceed with OpenGL rendering.

Accessing OpenGL Functions

As compared to the GLX and WGL OpenGL implementations, Mac OS X provides full-linkage capabilities with its OpenGL framework. That is, there's no need (or supported functions) for retrieving function pointers to OpenGL extensions. All supported entry poins are exported.

Floating-Point Formats for Textures, Framebuffers, and Renderbuffers

This appendix describes the floating-point formats used for pixel storage in framebuffers and renderbuffers, and texel storage in textures. It has the following major sections:

- "Reduced-Precision Floating-Point Values"

- "16-bit Floating-Point Values"

- "10- and 11-bit Unsigned Floating-Point Values"

Reduced-Precision Floating-Point Values

In addition to the normal 32-bit single-precision floating-point values you usually use when you declare a GLfloat in your application, OpenGL supports reduced-precision floating-point representations for storing data more compactly than its 32-bit representation. In many instances, your floating-point data may not require the entire dynamic range of a 32-bit float, and storing or processing data in a reduced-precision format may save memory and increase data transfer rates.

OpenGL supports three reduced-precision floating-point formats: 16-bit (signed) floating-point values, and 10- and 11-bit unsigned floating-point values. Table G-1 describes the bit layout of each representation, and the associated pixel formats.

Table G.1   Reduced-Precision Floating-Point Formats

Floating-Point Type	Associated Pixel Formats	Sign Bit	Number of Exponents Bits	Number of Mantissa Bits
16-bit	GL_RGB16F, GL_RGBA16F	1	5	10
11-bit	GL_R11F_G11F_B10F (red and green components)	0	5	6
10-bit	GL_R11F_G11F_B10F (blue component)	0	5	5

16-bit Floating-Point Values

For signed 16-bit floating-point values, the minimum and maximum values that can be represented are (about) 6.103×10^{-5}, and 65504.0, respectively.

The following routine, **F32toF16()**, will convert a single, full-precision 32-bit floating-point value to a 16-bit reduced-precision form (stored as an unsigned short integer).

```
#define F16_EXPONENT_BITS    0x1F
#define F16_EXPONENT_SHIFT   10
#define F16_EXPONENT_BIAS    15
#define F16_MANTISSA_BITS    0x3ff
#define F16_MANTISSA_SHIFT   (23 - F16_EXPONENT_SHIFT)
#define F16_MAX_EXPONENT \
   (F16_EXPONENT_BITS << F16_EXPONENT_SHIFT)
```

```
GLushort
F32toF16(GLfloat val)
{
  GLuint   f32 = (*(GLuint *) &val);
  GLushort f16 = 0;

  /* Decode IEEE 754 little-endian 32-bit floating-point value */
  int sign     = (f32 >> 16) & 0x8000;
  /* Map exponent to the range [-127,128] */
  int exponent = ((f32 >> 23) & 0xff) - 127;
  int mantissa =   f32 & 0x007fffff;

  if (exponent == 128) { /* Infinity or NaN */
    f16 = sign | F16_MAX_EXPONENT;
    if (mantissa) f16 |= (mantissa & F16_MANTISSA_BITS);
  }
  else if (exponent > 15) { /* Overflow - flush to Infinity */
    f16 = sign | F16_MAX_EXPONENT;
  }
  else if (exponent > -15) { /* Representable value */
    exponent += F16_EXPONENT_BIAS;
    mantissa >>= F16_MANTISSA_SHIFT;
    f16 = sign | exponent << F16_EXPONENT_SHIFT | mantissa;
  }
  else {
    f16 = sign;
  }

  return f16;
}
```

Likewise, **F16toF32()** converts from the reduced-precision floating-point form into a normal 32-bit floating-point value.

```
#define F32_INFINITY 0x7f800000

GLfloat
F16toF32(GLushort val)
{
  union {
    GLfloat f;
    GLuint ui;
  } f32;

  int sign     = (val & 0x8000) << 15;
  int exponent = (val & 0x7c00) >> 10;
  int mantissa = (val & 0x03ff);

  f32.f = 0.0;

  if (exponent == 0) {
```

```
      if (mantissa != 0) {
        const GLfloat scale = 1.0 / (1 << 24);
        f32.f = scale * mantissa;
      }
    }
    else if (exponent == 31) {
      f32.ui = sign | F32_INFINITY | mantissa;
    }
    else {
      GLfloat scale, decimal;
      exponent -= 15;
      if (exponent < 0) {
        scale = 1.0 / (1 << -exponent);
      }
      else {
        scale = 1 << exponent;
      }
      decimal = 1.0 + (float) mantissa / (1 << 10);
      f32.f = scale * decimal;
    }

    if (sign) f32.f = -f32.f;

    return f32.f;
}
```

10- and 11-bit Unsigned Floating-Point Values

For normalized color values in the range [0, 1], unsigned 10- and 11-bit floating-point formats may provide a more compact format with better dynamic range than either floating-point values, or OpenGL's unsigned integer pixel formats. The maximum representable values are 65204 and 64512, respectively.

Routines for converting floating-point values into 10-bit unsigned floating-point values, and vice versa, are shown below.

```
#define UF11_EXPONENT_BIAS    15
#define UF11_EXPONENT_BITS    0x1F
#define UF11_EXPONENT_SHIFT   6
#define UF11_MANTISSA_BITS    0x3F
#define UF11_MANTISSA_SHIFT   (23 - UF11_EXPONENT_SHIFT)
#define UF11_MAX_EXPONENT     \
   (UF11_EXPONENT_BITS << UF11_EXPONENT_SHIFT)

GLushort
F32toUF11(GLfloat val)
{
```

```
  GLuint   f32  = (*(GLuint *) &val);
  GLushort uf11 = 0;

  /* Decode little-endian 32-bit floating-point value */
  int sign     = (f32 >> 16) & 0x8000;
  /* Map exponent to the range [-127,128] */
  int exponent = ((f32 >> 23) & 0xff) - 127;
  int mantissa = f32 & 0x007fffff;

  if (sign) return 0;

  if (exponent == 128) { /* Infinity or NaN */
    uf11 = UF11_MAX_EXPONENT;
    if (mantissa) uf11 |= (mantissa & UF11_MANTISSA_BITS);
  }
  else if (exponent > 15) { /* Overflow - flush to Infinity */
    uf11 = UF11_MAX_EXPONENT;
  }
  else if (exponent > -15) { /* Representable value */
    exponent += UF11_EXPONENT_BIAS;
    mantissa >>= UF11_MANTISSA_SHIFT;
    uf11 = exponent << UF11_EXPONENT_SHIFT | mantissa;
  }

  return uf11;
}

#define F32_INFINITY  0x7f800000

GLfloat
UF11toF32(GLushort val)
{
  union {
    GLfloat f;
    GLuint ui;
  } f32;

  int exponent = (val & 0x07c0) >> UF11_EXPONENT_SHIFT;
  int mantissa = (val & 0x003f);

  f32.f = 0.0;

  if (exponent == 0) {
    if (mantissa != 0) {
      const GLfloat scale = 1.0 / (1 << 20);
      f32.f = scale * mantissa;
    }
  }
  else if (exponent == 31) {
    f32.ui = F32_INFINITY | mantissa;
  }
  else {
    GLfloat scale, decimal;
```

```
  exponent -= 15;
  if (exponent < 0) {
    scale = 1.0 / (1 << -exponent);
  }
  else {
    scale = 1 << exponent;
  }
  decimal = 1.0 + (float) mantissa / 64;
  f32.f = scale * decimal;
}

return f32.f;
}
```

For completeness, we present similar routines for converting 10-bit unsigned floating-point values.

```
#define UF10_EXPONENT_BIAS   15
#define UF10_EXPONENT_BITS   0x1F
#define UF10_EXPONENT_SHIFT 5
#define UF10_MANTISSA_BITS   0x3F
#define UF10_MANTISSA_SHIFT (23 - UF10_EXPONENT_SHIFT)
#define UF10_MAX_EXPONENT \
(UF10_EXPONENT_BITS << UF10_EXPONENT_SHIFT)

GLushort
F32toUF10(GLfloat val)
{
  GLuint    f32  = (*(GLuint *) &val);
  GLushort uf10 = 0;

  /* Decode little-endian 32-bit floating-point value */
  int sign      = (f32 >> 16) & 0x8000;
  /* Map exponent to the range [-127,128] */
  int exponent = ((f32 >> 23) & 0xff) - 127;
  int mantissa = f32 & 0x007fffff;

  if (sign) return 0;

  if (exponent == 128) { /* Infinity or NaN */
    uf10 = UF10_MAX_EXPONENT;
    if (mantissa) uf10 |= (mantissa & UF10_MANTISSA_BITS);
  }
  else if (exponent > 15) { /* Overflow - flush to Infinity */
    uf10 = UF10_MAX_EXPONENT;
  }
  else if (exponent > -15) { /* Representable value */
    exponent += UF10_EXPONENT_BIAS;
    mantissa >>= UF10_MANTISSA_SHIFT;
    uf10 = exponent << UF10_EXPONENT_SHIFT | mantissa;
  }
```

```
    return uf10;
}

#define F32_INFINITY 0x7f800000

GLfloat
UF10toF32(GLushort val)
{
  union {
    GLfloat f;
    GLuint ui;
  } f32;

  int exponent = (val & 0x07c0) >> UF10_EXPONENT_SHIFT;
  int mantissa = (val & 0x003f);

  f32.f = 0.0;

  if (exponent == 0) {
    if (mantissa != 0) {
      const GLfloat scale = 1.0 / (1 << 20);
      f32.f = scale * mantissa;
    }
  }
  else if (exponent == 31) {
    f32.ui = F32_INFINITY | mantissa;
  }
  else {
    GLfloat scale, decimal;
    exponent -= 15;
    if (exponent < 0) {
      scale = 1.0 / (1 << -exponent);
    }
    else {
      scale = 1 << exponent;
    }
    decimal = 1.0 + (float) mantissa / 64;
    f32.f = scale * decimal;
  }

  return f32.f;
}
```

Debugging and Profiling OpenGL

This appendix describes the facilities provided by *debug contexts*, which can greatly assist you in finding errors in your programs and with getting the best possible performance from OpenGL. This appendix contains the following major sections:

- "Creating a Debug Context" explains how to create OpenGL contexts in debug mode, enabling debugging features.

- "Debug Output" describes how OpenGL communicates debugging information back to your application.

- "Debug Groups" delves deeper into debug output, showing how your application, any utility libraries, and tools you use can cooperate to group parts of your scenes for debug purposes.

- "Profiling" concludes the appendix with information about profiling and optimizing your application for performance.

Creating a Debug Context

To get the most from OpenGL's debugging facilities, it is necessary to create a *debug context*, which implies that you need control over the flags and parameters used to create the context. Context creation is a platform-specific task that is often handled by a wrapper layer such as GLUT. Modern implementations of GLUT (such as FreeGLUT, which we use in many of this book's samples) include the function **glutInitContextFlags()**. This function takes a number of flags that can be used to control how contexts subsequently created behave. One of these flags is GLUT_DEBUG, which will enable a debug context. Many other platform abstraction layers have similar mechanisms. If you are not using an abstraction layer, then you will need to interface to your platform's context-creation mechanisms directly.

In WGL (the window system layer for Microsoft Windows), you need to use the WGL_ARB_create_context extension and access the **wglCreateContextAttribsARB()** function. This function takes as one of its parameters an attribute list. By specifying the WGL_CONTEXT_DEBUG_BIT_ARB as one of the context flags, a debug context will be created. The code to create this context is given in Example H.1.

Example H.1   Creating a Debug Context Using WGL

```
HGLRC CreateDebugContext(HDC hDC, HGLRC hShareContext,
                         int major, int minor)
{
    const int attriblist[] =
    {
        // Major version of context
        WGL_CONTEXT_MAJOR_VERSION_ARB,
            major,
        // Minor version of context
        WGL_CONTEXT_MINOR_VERSION_ARB,
            minor,
        // Always select a core profile
        WGL_CONTEXT_PROFILE_MASK_ARB,
            WGL_CONTEXT_CORE_PROFILE_BIT_ARB,
        // Turn on the debug context
        WGL_CONTEXT_FLAGS_ARB,
            WGL_CONTEXT_DEBUG_BIT_ARB,
        0
    };

    return wglCreateContextAttribsARB(hDC, hShareContext,
                                      attribs);
}
```

Note that due to some nastiness in the design of WGL, it is not possible to use any WGL extensions without first creating a context. This is because **wglGetProcAddress()** will return NULL if no context is current at the time it is called. This means that you will need to create a context with **wglCreateContext()** first, make it current, get the address of the **wglCreateContextAttribsARB()** function and then create a *second* context using that function. If you wish, you may delete the first context. Ultimately, though, you will always end up creating at least two contexts in any new application that uses a core profile context or needs debugging features.

GLX has a similar mechanism, using the similarly named **glXCreateContextAttribsARB()** function. Unlike WGL, there is no requirement to create and activate a context before determining the address of **glXCreateContextAttribsARB()** and so you should use this function to create the first (and possibly only) context in your application. Code for GLX equivalent to Example H.1 is given in Example H.2.

Example H.2   Creating a Debug Context Using GLX

```
GLXContext CreateDebugContext(Display* dpy,
                              GLXFBConfig config,
                              GLXContext share_context,
                              int major, int minor)
{
    const int attriblist[] =
    {
        // Major version of context
        GLX_CONTEXT_MAJOR_VERSION_ARB,
            major,
        // Minor version of context
        GLX_CONTEXT_MINOR_VERSION_ARB,
            minor,
        // Always select a core profile
        GLX_CONTEXT_PROFILE_MASK_ARB,
            GLX_CONTEXT_CORE_PROFILE_BIT_ARB,
        // Turn on the debug context
        GLX_CONTEXT_FLAGS_ARB,
            GLX_CONTEXT_DEBUG_BIT_ARB,
        0
    };

    return glXCreateContextAttribsARB(dpy, config,
                                      share_context,
                                      True, attriblist);
}
```

Creating a debug context doesn't really do anything special—it just tells OpenGL that you're intending to use its debugging facilities and that it should turn them on. Once development of your application is completed and you're no longer debugging, you should turn the debug context off as some of the debugging features supported by OpenGL may come at a performance cost. Once your application is debugged and working correctly, you don't really need to use a debug context and it's best to avoid this potential performance loss in a shipping application.

Debug Output

The primary feature of a debug context is the ability to perform additional error checking and analysis. There are two ways that a debug context can get this information back to you. The first, which is really intended to support remote rendering is via a log that is part of the context and must be queried. The second, and far more efficient mechanism is through the use of a *callback function*. The reason that a log exists for remote rendering is that a remote server cannot call a callback function in the client application. However, whenever direct rendering is in use, it is strongly recommended to use the callback function.

A callback function is essentially a function pointer that you pass a third-party component (such as OpenGL). That component holds on to the pointer and calls it when it needs the attention of the host application. The callback function has an agreed-upon prototype and calling convention such that both sides of the call know how that call should be handled. The prototype for the callback function is shown in Example H.3. You hand the pointer to a function with this prototype using the **glDebugMessageCallback()** function, whose prototype and a simple implementation of which is shown below.

Example H.3   Prototype for the Debug Message Callback Function

```
typedef void (APIENTRY *DEBUGPROC) (GLenum source,
                                    GLenum type,
                                    GLuint id,
                                    GLenum severity,
                                    GLsizei length,
                                    const GLchar* message,
                                    void* userParam);

void APIENTRY DebugCallbackFunction (GLenum source,
                                     GLenum type,
                                     GLuint id,
                                     GLenum severity,
                                     GLsizei length,
                                     const GLchar* message,
                                     void* userParam)
{
```

```
    printf("Debug Message: SOURCE(0x%04X),"
           "TYPE(0x%04X),"
           "ID(0x%08X),"
           "SEVERITY(0x%04X), \"%s\"\n",
           source, type, id, severity, message);
}
```

void **glDebugMessageCallback**(DEBUGPROC *callback*,
                              void* *userParam*);

Sets the current debug message callback function pointer to the value
specified in *callback*. This function will be called when the
implementation needs to notify the client of the generation of a new
debug message. When the callback function is invoked, the *userParam*
argument to **glDebugMessageCallback()** will be passed in the *userParam*
argument of the callback. Otherwise, *userParam* has no meaning to
OpenGL and may be used for any purpose.

Debug Messages

Each message generated by OpenGL is comprised of a text string and a
number of attributes. These are passed back to the application in the
parameters to the callback function. The prototype of the callback function
is shown in Example H.3 and a declaration of the function is shown below.

void **callback**(GLenum *source*, GLenum *type*, GLuint *id*,
              GLenum *severity*, GLsizei *length*,
              const GLchar* *message*, void* *userParam*);

This is a callback function that will be called by OpenGL when it needs to
send the application a debug message. *source*, *type*, *id*, and *severity* indicate
the source, type, id, and severity of the message, respectively. *length*
contains the length of the string whose address is given by *message*.
userParam contains the value passed to **glDebugMessageCallback()** in
the *userParam* argument and otherwise holds no meaning to OpenGL.

Each debug message has several attributes associated with it—the source,
type, and severity of the message, and a unique identifier for that message.
These attributes are passed to the callback function you've specified and
can also be used as the basis for message filtering, which will be covered
shortly. The source may be one of the following:

* GL_DEBUG_SOURCE_API indicates that the message originates from
  direct usage of OpenGL.

- GL_DEBUG_SOURCE_WINDOW_SYSTEM indicates that the message originates from the window system (e.g., WGL, GLX, or EGL).

- GL_DEBUG_SOURCE_SHADER_COMPILER indicates that the message is generated by the shader compiler.

- GL_DEBUG_SOURCE_THIRD_PARTY indicates that the message is generated by a third-party source such as a utility library, middleware, or tool.

- GL_DEBUG_SOURCE_APPLICATION indicates that the message was generated explicitly by the application.

- GL_DEBUG_SOURCE_OTHER indicates that the message does not fit into any of the above categories.

Messages with the source GL_DEBUG_SOURCE_THIRD_PARTY or GL_DEBUG_SOURCE_APPLICATION should never be generated by the OpenGL implementation, but are instead injected into the debug message stream explicitly either by a tool or library, or by the application directly. The mechanisms to insert messages into the debug stream will be covered shortly.

Each debug message also has a type. This allows your application to determine what to do with the message. The available types of message are as follows:

- GL_DEBUG_TYPE_ERROR is generated when an error is generated.

- GL_DEBUG_TYPE_DEPRECATED_BEHAVIOR is produced by the use of deprecated functionality in OpenGL.

- GL_DEBUG_TYPE_UNDEFINED_BEHAVIOR is generated if the application has attempted to use functionality in a way that might produce undefined results.

- GL_DEBUG_TYPE_PERFORMANCE indicates that the application is using OpenGL in a way that is not optimal for performance.

- GL_DEBUG_TYPE_PORTABILITY is generated if the behavior of the application is relying on the functionality of the OpenGL implementation that may not be portable to other implementations or platforms.

- GL_DEBUG_TYPE_MARKER is used for annotation of the debug stream.

- GL_DEBUG_TYPE_PUSH_GROUP is generated when the application calls **glPushDebugGroup()**.

- GL_DEBUG_TYPE_POP_GROUP is generated when the application calls **glPopDebugGroup()**.

- GL_DEBUG_TYPE_OTHER is used when the type of the debug message does not fall into any of the above categories.

In addition to a source and a type, each debug message has a severity associated with it. Again, these may be used for filtering or otherwise directing output. For example, an application may choose to log all message, but cause a break into a debugger in the case that a high severity message is encountered. The available severities are as follows:

- GL_DEBUG_SEVERITY_HIGH is used to mark the most important messages and would generally be used for OpenGL errors, shader compiler failures, and so on.

- GL_DEBUG_SEVERITY_MEDIUM is used to mark messages that the application really should know about, but that may not be fatal. These might include portability issues or performance warnings.

- GL_DEBUG_SEVERITY_LOW is used when the OpenGL implementation needs the developer about issues that they should address, but that aren't going to be detrimental to the functioning of the application. These might include minor performance issues, redundant state changes, and so on.

- GL_DEBUG_SEVERITY_NOTIFICATION is used to mark messages that may not have a negative consequence such as a tool attaching to an application or initialization of the context.

Finally, the unique identifier assigned to each message is implementation dependent and may be used for any purpose.

Enabling Debug Output

It is possible to enable or disable debug output globally without affecting filter state. In a debug context, debug output is on by default, and you should receive fairly verbose messages from the context if your application does anything it shouldn't. However, in a nondebug context, while the default is to not produce any debug output, it is possible to enable debug messages anyway. You should be aware that a nondebug context may not generate very useful output—in fact, it may generate nothing at all. To enable or disable debug output, **glEnable()** or **glDisable()** with the GL_DEBUG_OUTPUT.

In many cases, OpenGL may operate somewhat asynchronously to the application. In some implementations, OpenGL might batch up several function calls and execute them later. In some cases this can help the implementation work around redundancy in the command stream, or to batch related state changes together and validate a lot of parameters in one go. In other implementations, the OpenGL driver might run in multiple threads that could be behind the application in processing order. The debug output is often generated when parameters are validated, or even cross-validated against each other, and this can happen some time after the actual error has occurred from the application's perspective. The net result is that the debug callback might not be called immediately when the application generates an error, but rather when the OpenGL implementation validates the requested state changes.

To change this behavior, it is possible to ask OpenGL to operate synchronously with regards to generating debug output. To do this, call **glEnable()** with the GL_DEBUG_OUTPUT_SYNCHRONOUS parameter. This is disabled by default, although some implementations may force all debug output to be synchronous in a debug context, for example. However, it's generally a good idea to turn synchronous debug output on if you want to rely on it for catching errors.

Filtering Messages

Messages are filtered before they are sent to your callback function. When you create a debug context, by default, only medium- and high-severity messages are sent to your callback function. You can enable and disable various types of messages, filter messages by severity, and even turn individual messages on and off using their identifiers. To do this, use **glDebugMessageControl()**.

---

void **glDebugMessageControl**(GLenum *source*, GLenum *type*,
                                GLenum *severity*, GLsizei *count*,
                                const GLuint * *ids*,
                                Glboolean *enabled*);

Establishes a message filter that is applied to subsequently generated messages. If *enabled* is GL_TRUE, then generated messages matching the filter formed by *source*, *type*, *severity*, and the list of messages whose identifiers are stored in *ids* will be sent to the active debug output callback. If *enabled* is GL_FALSE, then those messages will be discarded.

source must be GL_DONT_CARE or one of the defined message severities, GL_DEBUG_SOURCE_API, GL_DEBUG_SOURCE_WINDOW_SYSTEM, GL_DEBUG_SOURCE_SHADER_COMPILER, GL_DEBUG_SOURCE_THIRD_PARTY, GL_DEBUG_SOURCE_APPLICATION, or GL_DEBUG_SOURCE_OTHER.

type must be GL_DONT_CARE or one of the defined message types, GL_DEBUG_TYPE_ERROR, GL_DEBUG_TYPE_DEPRECATED_BEHAVIOR, GL_DEBUG_TYPE_UNDEFINED_BEHAVIOR, GL_DEBUG_TYPE_PERFORMANCE, GL_DEBUG_TYPE_PORTABILITY, GL_DEBUG_TYPE_MARKER, GL_DEBUG_TYPE_PUSH_GROUP, or GL_DEBUG_TYPE_POP_GROUP.

severity must be GL_DONT_CARE or one of the defined message severities, GL_DEBUG_SEVERITY_HIGH, GL_DEBUG_SEVERITY_MEDIUM, GL_DEBUG_SEVERITY_LOW, or GL_DEBUG_SEVERITY_NOTIFICATION.

count contains a count of the number of message identifiers stored in the array whose address is given by *ids*. If *count* is nonzero, then *ids* is the address of an array of message identifiers that will be used to filter messages.

If *source* is GL_DONT_CARE, then the source of the messages will not be used when forming the filter. That is, messages from any source will be considered to match the filter. Likewise, if either *type* or *severity* is GL_DONT_CARE, then the type or severity of the message will not be included in the filter, respectively, and messages of any type or severity will be considered to match the filter. If *count* is nonzero, then it indicates the number of items in the array *ids*, allowing messages to be filtered by their unique identifiers. Example H.4 shows a couple of examples of how to build filters to enable and disable certain classes of debug message.

Example H.4   Creating Debug Message Filters

```
// Enable all messages generated by the application
glDebugMessageControl(GL_DEBUG_SOURCE_APPLICATION,  // Application messages
                GL_DONT_CARE,      // Don't care about type
                GL_DONT_CARE,      // Don't care about severity
                0, NULL,           // No unique identifiers
                GL_TRUE);          // Enable them

// Enable all high severity messages
glDebugMessageControl(GL_DONT_CARE,       // Don't care about origin
                GL_DONT_CARE,       // Don't care about type
                GL_DEBUG_SEVERITY_HIGH, // High severity messages
                0, NULL,            // No identifiers
                GL_TRUE);           // Enable

// Disable all low severity messages
glDebugMessageControl(GL_DONT_CARE,       // Don't care about origin
                GL_DONT_CARE,       // Don't care about type
                GL_DEBUG_SEVERITY_LOW,   // Low severity messages
```

```
                    0, NULL,                 // No identifiers
                    GL_FALSE);

    // Enable a couple of messages by identifiers
    static const GLuint messages[] = { 0x1234, 0x1337 };
    glDebugMessageControl(GL_DONT_CARE,      // Don't care about origin
                    GL_DONT_CARE,            // Don't care about type
                    GL_DONT_CARE,            // Don't care about severity
                    2, messages,             // 2 ids in "messages"
                    GL_TRUE);
```

Application-Generated Messages

There are two sources of message that are reserved for the application or its
helper libraries and tools. These two sources are
GL_DEBUG_SOURCE_APPLICATION, which is intended to be used by the
application for its own messages, and
GL_DEBUG_SOURCE_THIRD_PARTY, which is intended for use by
third-party libraries such as middleware or by tools such as debuggers and
profilers. Messages with these two source identifiers should never be
generated by an OpenGL implementation. Instead they may be injected
into the debug output stream by the application, library, or tool. To do
this, call **glDebugMessageInsert**(), whose prototype is as follows:

---

void **glDebugMessageInsert**(GLenum *source*, GLenum *type*,
                           GLuint *id*, GLenum *severity*,
                           GLint *length*, const GLchar * *buf*);

Insert a message into the context's debug message stream. The text
message contained in *buf* is sent to the context's debug message callback
function along with the *source*, *type*, *id*, and *severity* as specified. If *length*
is greater than or equal to zero, it is considered to be the length of the
string contained in *buf*. Otherwise, *buf* is treated as the address of a
NUL-terminated string.

When you call **glDebugMessageInsert**() the message contained in *buf* is
sent directly to the context's callback function (which might be inside
your application or inside a debugging or profiling tool). The values you
pass in *source*, *type*, *id*, and *severity* are passed as specified to the callback
function. In general, you should use GL_DEBUG_SOURCE_APPLICATION
for messages generated by your application (or
GL_DEBUG_SOURCE_THIRD_PARTY if you are writing a tool or utility
library). Example H.5 shows an example of sending a message via the
glDebugMessageInsert() function.

Example H.5   Sending Application-Generated Debug Messages

```
// Create a debug context and make it current
MakeContextCurrent(CreateDebugContext());

// Get some information about the context
const GLchar * vendor = (const GLchar *)glGetString(GL_VENDOR);
const GLchar * renderer = (const GLchar *)glGetString(GL_RENDERER);
const GLchar * version = (const GLchar *)glGetString(GL_VERSION);

// Assemble a message
std::string message = std::string("Created debug context with ") +
                      std::string(vendor) + std::string(" ") +
                      std::string(renderer) +
                      std::string(". The OpenGL version is ") +
                      std::string(version) + std::string(".");

// Send the message to the debug output log
glDebugMessageInsert(GL_DEBUG_SOURCE_APPLICATION,
                     GL_DEBUG_TYPE_MARKER,
                     0x4752415A,
                     GL_DEBUG_SEVERITY_NOTIFICATION,
                     -1,
                     message.c_str());
```

The result of executing this code on a debug context with the example implementation of the debug callback function given in Example H.3 is shown below.

```
Debug Message: SOURCE(0x824A), TYPE(0x8268),
ID(0x4752415A), SEVERITY(0x826B), "Created
debug context with NVIDIA Corporation GeForce
GTX 560 SE/PCIe/SSE2. The OpenGL version is
4.3.0."
```

Debug Groups

In a large, complex application, you may have many subsystems rendering various parts of the scene. For example, you may render the world, dynamic and animated objects, special effects and particle systems, user interfaces, or post processing. At any given moment, it is likely that you'll be concentrating your attention on just one of these elements. You may be debugging issues or concentrating on performance. It is likely that you'll want to turn on very verbose debug message reporting for the sections of code you're working on while leaving debug messages only at their most concise levels for code that you've already debugged. To do this, you will need to turn certain categories of messages on and off and to restore the debug log to its original state, you would need to query the current state of the debug context to determine whether certain types of messages are enabled or disabled.

Rather than trying to implement all of this yourself, you can rely on OpenGL's *debug groups*, which is a stack-based system of filters that allows you to push the current debug state onto an internal stack managed by OpenGL, modify the state, and then return to a previously saved state by popping it of the stack. The functions to do this are **glPushDebugGroup()** and **glPopDebugGroup()**.

---

void **glPushDebugGroup**(GLenum *source*, GLuint *id*,
                                      GLint *length*, const GLchar * *message*);

void **glPopDebugGroup**();

---

glPushDebugGroup() pushes the current state of the debug output filter onto the debug group stack and injects *message* into the current debug output message stream with the *type* GL_DEBUG_TYPE_PUSH_GROUP, *severity* GL_DEBUG_SEVERITY_NOTIFICATION, and the *source* and *id* as specified. If *length* is greater than or equal to zero, then it is considered to be the length of the string in *message*, otherwise *message* is treated as a NUL-terminated string.

glPopDebugGroup() removes the debug state from the top of the debug group stack and injects a debug message into the debug message output stream with *type* GL_DEBUG_TYPE_POP_GROUP and all other parameters sourced from the corresponding group that was popped from the stack.

For both functions, *source* must be either GL_DEBUG_SOURCE_APPLICATION or GL_DEBUG_SOURCE_THIRD_PARTY.

In addition to allowing the current state of the debug output filters to be saved and restored, pushing and popping the debug group also generates messages to the debug output callback function. This function, often implemented inside tools and debuggers, can track the current depth of the debug group stack and apply formatting changes to the displayed output such as coloring or indentation.

Each implementation has a maximum depth of the debug group stack. This depth must be at least 64 groups, but you can find the actual maximum by calling **glGetIntegerv()** with the parameter GL_MAX_DEBUG_GROUP_STACK_DEPTH. If you attempt to push more than this number of debug groups onto the stack, then **glPushDebugGroup()** will generate a GL_STACK_OVERFLOW error. Likewise, if you try to pop an item from an empty stack, then **glPopDebugGroup()** will generate a GL_STACK_UNDERFLOW error.

Naming Objects

When OpenGL generates debugging messages, it will sometimes make reference to objects such as textures, buffers, or framebuffers. In a complex application, there may be hundreds or thousands of textures and buffers in existence at any given time. Each of these objects has a unique identifier that was assigned by OpenGL's **glGenTextures()**, **glGenBuffers()**, or other name-generation functions and those names may have no bearing on what the application intends to use them for. It is possible to name the objects by giving them labels. If you give an object a label, then when a reference to it appears in a debug message, OpenGL will use the object's label rather than (or as well as) its number. To give an object a label, use **glObjectLabel()** or **glObjectPtrLabel()**.

---

void **glObjectLabel**(GLenum *identifier*, GLuint *name*,
               GLsizei *length*, const GLchar * *label*);

void **glObjectPtrLabel**(void * *ptr*, GLsizei *length*,
                  const GLchar * *label*);

---

glObjectLabel() and **glObjectPtrLabel()** allow objects owned by OpenGL to be labeled for the purpose of identification during debugging. Labeling objects allows them to be referenced by name rather than number in debug messages. **glObjectLabel()** is provided to label objects represented by names within the namespace *identifier*, whereas **glObjectPtrLabel()** is provided to label objects that are represented as pointers by OpenGL (such as sync objects).

If *length* is greater than or equal to zero, then it is interpreted as the length of the string pointed to by *label*. Otherwise, *label* is considered to point to a NUL-terminated string that will be used to label the object.

When you apply a label to an object then the label is stored with the object by OpenGL. When it is referred to in a debug message, OpenGL can then use the label you provided rather than just using the numerical name directly. You can also retrieve the label of the object by calling **glGetObjectLabel()** or **glGetObjectPtrLabel()**.

> void **glGetObjectLabel**(GLenum *identifier*, GLuint *name*,
> GLsizei *bufsize*, GLsizei * *length*,
> GLchar * *label*);
>
> void **glGetObjectPtrLabel**(void * *ptr*, GLsizei *bufsize*,
> GLsizei * *length*, GLchar * *label*);

glGetObjectLabel() and **glGetObjectPtrLabel**() retrieve the labels that have previously been assigned to objects by the **glObjectLabel**() or **glObjectPtrLabel**() functions, respectively. For **glGetObjectLabel**(), *name* and *identifier* provide the numeric name of an object and the namespace from which it was allocated. For **glGetObjectPtrLabel**(), *ptr* is the pointer variable that is provided by OpenGL.

For both **glObjectLabel**() and **glGetObjectLabel**(), *name* is the numerical name of the object that was provided by OpenGL through a call to **glGenTextures**(), **glGenBuffers**(), or other object name-generation functions. Because names for different object types are allocated from different namespaces, the *identifier* parameter is provided to allow you to tell OpenGL which namespace *name* resides in. *identifier* must be one of the following tokens:

- GL_BUFFER indicates that *name* is the name of a buffer object generated by **glGenBuffers**().

- GL_SHADER indicates that *name* is the name of a shader object generated by **glCreateShader**().

- GL_PROGRAM indicates that *name* is the name of a program object generated by **glCreateProgram**().

- GL_QUERY indicates that *name* is the name of a query object generated by **glGenQueries**().

- GL_PROGRAM_PIPELINE indicates that *name* is the name of a program pipeline object generated by **glGenProgramPipelines**().

- GL_SAMPLER indicates that *name* is the name of a sampler object generated by **glGenSamplers**().

The maximum length of a label that can be applied to an object is given by the value of the implementation-dependent constant GL_MAX_LABEL_LENGTH. One potential use of object labels, for example, is to modify your texture-loading code such that the generated texture objects are labeled with the filename of the texture. Then, if there's a problem with a particular texture, a tool might be able to cross reference the texture object with the file that it was loaded from to verify that the data ended up in the right place.

Profiling

Once your application is close to its final state, you may wish to turn your attention to performance tuning. One of the most important aspects of performance tuning is not the modifications you make to your code to make it run faster, but the measurements and experiments you make to determine what you should do to your code to achieve your desired performance goals. This is known as *performance profiling*.

Performance measurement techniques generally fall into two[1] categories; the first is tool-assisted profiling and the second involves actually making changes to your code to measure its execution time.

Profiling Tools

Perhaps the most powerful way to profile your application is to use an external profiling and debugging tool. This type of tool *hooks* OpenGL on a running system and intercepts the function calls that your application makes. The simplest tools merely take a log of the function calls, perhaps gathering statistics or other information about them. Some of these tools may even allow you to play back the resulting trace and replicate the execution of your application in a standalone environment. More advanced tools allow you to inspect data that flows between the application and OpenGL, to time execution of various elements of the scene and even to modify the application's behavior as it executes by disabling parts of the OpenGL pipeline, replacing shaders or textures with alternatives, and so on.

One such application is AMD's GPUPerfStudio 2, a screenshot of which is shown in Figure H.1.[2]

In Figure H.1, GPUPerfStudio 2 is being used to examine the application's call trace generated by the Unigine Heaven 3.0 benchmark, which makes advanced use of modern OpenGL. A screenshot of the application is shown in Figure H.2.[3] The application makes use of advanced graphics features including tessellation, instancing, and off-screen rendering, and renders effects such as reflections and volumetric lighting effects. GPUPerfStudio 2 is able to capture the OpenGL calls made by the benchmark and measure their execution time. On some GPUs, it is even

---

1. Not including "try a bunch of stuff and see what happens".

2. Figure H.1 courtesy of AMD.

3. Figure H.2 is of Unigine Heaven DX11 benchmark developed by Unigine Corp.: http://unigine.com/ . Used by permission.

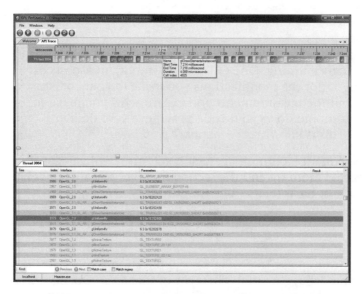

Figure H.1 AMD's GPUPerfStudio2 profiling Unigine Heaven 3.0

Figure H.2 Screenshot of Unigine Heaven 3.0

able to measure the amount of time various parts of the OpenGL pipeline (such as the texture processor, tessellation engine, blending unit, etc.) spend on individual commands. The tool will tell you if you are making too many draw commands, which ones are the most expensive, and what the GPU spends its time on for each one. Profiling tools such as GPUPerfStudio 2 are an invaluable resource for performance tuning and debugging OpenGL applications.

In-Application Profiling

It is possible for your application to measure its own performance. A naïve approach is to simply measure the amount of time taken for a particular piece of code to execute by reading the system time or just measuring framerate (besides, framerate is a fairly poor measure of application performance). However, assuming your application is efficiently written, the goal is for the graphics processor to be the bottleneck, and therefore you are interested in the amount of time it takes to process parts of your scene.

You can make these measurements yourself. In fact, some tools may use very similar mechanisms to measure GPU performance by injecting equivalent sequences of commands into your application's rendering thread. OpenGL provides two types of *timer queries* for this purpose. The two types of query are an elapsed time query and an instantaneous time query. The first operates very similarly to an occlusion query as described in "Occlusion Query" in Chapter 4.

Elapsed Time Queries

Elapsed time queries use the GPU's internal counters to measure the amount of time it spends processing OpenGL commands. As with occlusion queries, you wrap one or more rendering commands in a timer query and then read the results of the query back into the application, ideally at a later time so as to not force the GPU to finish rendering that may be in the pipeline.

To start an elapsed time query, call **glBeginQuery()** with the *target* parameter set to GL_TIME_ELAPSED and with *id* set to the name of a query object retrieved from a call to **glGenQueries()**. To end the query, call **glEndQuery()** again with the *target* parameter set to GL_TIME_ELAPSED. Once the query has ended, retrieve the result by calling **glGetQueryObjectuiv()** with the name of the query object in *id* and the *pname* parameter set to GL_QUERY_RESULT. The resulting value is the time, measured in *nanoseconds* to execute the commands between the calls to **glBeginQuery()** and **glEndQuery()**. You should be aware that a nanosecond is an extremely small amount of time. One unsigned integer is large enough to count roughly four seconds worth of nanoseconds, after which it will roll over and start from zero again. If you expect your timer queries to last a very long time (such as the duration of several tens or hundreds of frames), you might want to use **glGetQueryObjectui64v()**, which retrieves the result as a 64-bit number.[4]

An example of using an elapsed time query is shown in Example H.6.

Example H.6   Using an Elapsed Time Query

```
GLuint timer_query;
GLuint nanoseconds;

// Generate the timer query
glGenQueries(1, &timer_query);

// Set up some state... (not relevant to the timer query)
glEnable(GL_DEPTH_TEST);
glDepthFunc(GL_LEQUAL);

glEnable(GL_BLEND);
glBlendFunc(GL_SRC_ALPHA, GL_ONE_MINUS_SRC_ALPHA);

glBindVertexArray(vao);

// Begin the query
glBeginQuery(GL_TIME_ELAPSED, timer_query);

// Draw some geometry
glDrawArraysInstanced(GL_TRIANGLES, 0, 1337, 1234);

// End the query
glEndQuery(GL_TIME_ELAPSED);

// Go do something time consuming so as to not stall
// the OpenGL pipeline
do_something_that_takes_ages();

// Now retrieve the timer result
glGetQueryObjectuiv(timer_query, &nanoseconds);
```

Instantaneous Timer Queries

Instantaneous timer queries also use the query object mechanism to retrieve times measured in nanoseconds from the GPU. However, as they are essentially snapshots of the GPU clock, they don't have a duration and are never "current", and so cannot be used with **glBeginQuery()** or **glEndQuery()**. Instead, you use the **glQueryCounter()** function to issue a timestamp query.

---

4. 64-bits worth of nanoseconds should allow you to count until the end of the universe.

> void **glQueryCounter**(GLuint *id*, GLenum *target*);
>
> Issues a timestamp query into the OpenGL command queue using the query object whose name is *id*. *target* must be *GL_TIMESTAMP*.

When **glQueryCounter()** is called, OpenGL inserts a command into the GPU's queue to record its current time into the query object as soon as it comes across it. It may still take some time to get to the timestamp query, and so your application should perform meaningful work before retrieving the result of the query. Again, to get the result of the query object, call **glGetQueryObjectuiv()**. Once you have instantaneous timestamps taken at various parts of your scene, you can take deltas between them to determine how long each part of the scene took, *in GPU time* and have some idea what is making the application expensive to execute and where you should focus your energy as you try to make it run faster.

Buffer Object Layouts

This appendix describes ways to deterministically lay out buffers that are shared between multiple readers or writers. It has the following major sections:

- "Using Standard Layout Qualifiers"
- "The **std140** Layout Rules"
- "The **std430** Layout Rules"

Using Standard Layout Qualifiers

When you group a number of variables in a uniform buffer or shader storage buffer, and want to read or write their values outside a shader, you need to know the offset of each one. You can query these offsets, but for large collections of uniforms this process requires many queries and is cumbersome. As an alternative, the standard layout qualifiers request that the GLSL shader compiler organize the variables according to a set of rules, where you can predictably compute the offset of any member in the block.

In order to qualify a block to use the `std140` layout, you need to add a `layout` directive to its declaration, as demonstrated below:

```
layout (std140) uniform UniformBlock {
    // declared variables
};
```

This `std140` qualification also works for shader storage buffer objects. The layout qualifier `std430` is available only for shader storage buffer objects, and is shown below:

```
layout (std430) buffer BufferBlock {
    // declared variables
};
```

To use these, the offset of a member in the block is the accumulated total of the alignment and sizes of the previous members in the block (those declared before the variable in question), bumped up to the alignment of the member. The starting offset of the first member is always zero.

The `std140` Layout Rules

The set of rules shown in Table I.1 are used by the GLSL compiler to place members in an std140-qualified uniform block. This feature is available only with GLSL Version 1.40 or greater.

Table I.1   `std140` Layout Rules

Variable Type	Variable Size and Alignment
Scalar `bool`, `int`, `uint`, `float` and `double`	Both the size and alignment are the size of the scalar in basic machine types (e.g., sizeof(GLfloat)).
Two-component vectors (e.g., `ivec2`)	Both the size and alignment are twice the size of the underlying scalar type.
Three-component vectors (e.g., `vec3`) and Four-component vectors (e.g., `vec4`)	Both the size and alignment are four times the size of the underlying scalar type.

Table I.1   (continued)   `std140` Layout Rules

Variable Type	Variable Size and Alignment
An array of scalars or vectors	The size of each element in the array will be the size of the element type, rounded up to a multiple of the size of a `vec4`. This is also the array's alignment. The array's size will be this rounded-up element's size times the number of elements in the array.
A column-major matrix or an array of column-major matrices of size C columns and R rows	Same layout as an array of N vectors each with R components, where N is the total number of columns present.
A row-major matrix or an array of row-major matrices with R rows and C columns	Same layout as an array of N vectors each with C components, where N is the total number of rows present.
A single-structure definition, or an array of structures	Structure alignment will be the alignment for the biggest structure member, according to the previous rules, rounded up to a multiple of the size of a `vec4`. Each structure will start on this alignment, and its size will be the space needed by its members, according to the previous rules, rounded up to a multiple of the structure alignment.

The `std430` Layout Rules

The set of rules shown in Table I.2 are used by the GLSL compiler to place members in an `std430`-qualified uniform block. This feature is available only with GLSL Version 4.30 or greater.

Table I.2   `std430` Layout Rules

Variable Type	Variable Size and Alignment
Scalar `bool`, `int`, `uint`, `float` and `double`	Both the size and alignment are the size of the scalar in basic machine types (e.g., sizeof(GLfloat)).
Two-component vectors (e.g., `ivec2`)	Both the size and alignment are twice the size of the underlying scalar type.
Three-component vectors (e.g., `vec3`) and Four-component vectors (e.g., `vec4`)	Both the size and alignment are four times the size of the underlying scalar type. However, this is true only when the member is not part of an array or nested structure.

Table I.2   (continued)   `std430` Layout Rules

Variable Type	Variable Size and Alignment
An array of scalars or vectors	The size of each element in the array will be the same size of the element type, where three-component vectors *are not* rounded up to the size of four-component vectors. This is also the array's alignment. The array's size will be the element's size times the number of elements in the array.
A column-major matrix or an array of column-major matrices of size C columns and R rows	Same layout as an array of N vectors each with R components, where N is the total number of columns present.
A row-major matrix or an array of row-major matrices with R rows and C columns	Same layout as an array of N vectors each with C components, where N is the total number of rows present.
A single-structure definition or an array of structures	Structure alignment is the same as the alignment for the biggest structure member, where three-component vectors *are not* rounded up to the size of four-component vectors. Each structure will start on this alignment, and its size will be the space needed by its members, according to the previous rules, rounded up to a multiple of the structure alignment.

Glossary

affine transformation   A transformation that preserves straight lines and the ratio of distances of points lying on lines.

aliasing   Artifacts created by *undersampling* a scene, typically caused by assigning one point sample per pixel, where there are edges or patterns in the scene of higher frequency than the pixels. This results in jagged edges (*jaggies*), moiré patterns, and scintillation. See *antialiasing*.

alpha   The fourth color component. The alpha component is never displayed directly, and is typically used to control blending of colors. By convention, OpenGL alpha corresponds to the notion of opacity, rather than transparency, meaning that an alpha value of 1.0 implies complete opacity, and an alpha value of 0.0 complete transparency.

alpha value   See *alpha*.

ambient   Ambient light is light not directly associated with a light source, and is distributed uniformly throughout space, with light falling upon a surface approaching from all directions. The light is reflected from the object independent of surface location and orientation, with equal intensity in all directions.

amplication   The process of a geometry shader creating more geometry than was passed to it.

animation   Generating repeated renderings of a scene, with smoothly changing viewpoint and object positions, quickly enough so that the illusion of motion is achieved. OpenGL animation is almost always done using double-buffering.

anisotropic filtering   A texture-filtering technique that improves image quality by sampling the texture using independent texture-interpolation rates for each texture dimension.

antialiasing   Rendering techniques that reduce *aliasing*. These techniques include sampling at a higher frequency, assigning pixel colors based on the fraction of the pixel's area covered by the primitive being rendered, removing high-frequency components in the scene, and integrating or averaging the area of the scene covered by a pixel, as in *area sampling*. See *antialiasing*.

API   See *application programming interface*.

application programming interface   A library of functions and subroutines that an application makes calls into. OpenGL is an example of an application programming interface.

area sampling   Deciding what color to color a pixel based on looking at the entire content of the scene covered by the pixel. This is as opposed to *point sampling*.

array textures   Array textures are texture objects that contain multiple layers or slices that are treated as one associated block of data.

atomic counter   A counter object usable in all of OpenGL's shader stages that is updated atomically. See *atomic operation*.

atomic operation   In the context of concurrent (multithreaded) programming, an operation that is always completed without interruption.

attenuation   The property of light that describes how a light's intensity diminishes over distance.

back faces   See *faces*.

barycentric coordinates   A coordinate system where a point is represented as a weighted sum of two or more reference points. Varying a barycentric coordinate between zero and one in each component moves it within its domain.

Bernstein polynomials   A family of polynomial equations named after Sergei Natanovich Bernstein that are used in evaluating Bézier curves. The polynomials are defined as follows:

$$b_{n,m}(x) = \binom{n}{m} x^n (1-x)^{n-m}$$

where $\binom{n}{m}$ is a *binomial coefficient*.

billboard   Usually a texture-mapped quadrilateral that is oriented to be perpendicular to the viewer. Often billboards are used to approximate complex geometry at a distance.

binding an object   Attaching an object to the OpenGL context, commonly through a function that starts with the word *bind*, such as **glBindTexture()**, **glBindBuffer()**, or **glBindSampler()**.

binomial coefficient   The coefficients of the terms in the expansion of the polynomial $(1 + x)^n$. Binomial coefficients are often described using the notation $\binom{n}{k}$, where

$$\binom{n}{k} = \frac{n!}{k!(n-k)!}$$

where $n!$ is the *factorial* of n.

binormal   A vector perpendicular to both a surface tangent vector and the surface normal vector. These three mutually orthogonal vectors can form the basis of a local coordinate system, including a *surface-local coordinate space*.

bit   A short form for "binary digit". A state variable having only two possible values: 0 or 1. Binary numbers are constructions of one or more bits.

bit depth   The number of bits available for a particular component, limiting the set of values that can be stored in the component.

bitplane   A rectangular array of bits mapped one-to-one with pixels. The framebuffer can be considered a stack of bitplanes.

blending   Reduction of two color components to one component, usually as a linear interpolation between the two components.

buffer   A group of bitplanes that store a single component, such as depth or green. Sometimes the red, green, blue, and alpha buffers together are referred to as the color buffer, rather than the color buffers.

buffer object   A buffer located in the OpenGL's server memory. Vertex and pixel data, uniform variables, and element-array indices may be stored in buffer objects.

buffer objects   Objects representing linear allocations of memory that may be used to store data.

buffer ping-ponging   A technique—mostly used for GPGPU—where two equally sized buffers are used accumulating results. For a particular frame, one buffer holds current results and is read from, and the other buffer is written to updating those results. For the next frame, the buffers' roles are swapped (ping-ponged).

bump map   See *normal map*.

bump mapping   Broadly, this is adding the appearance of bumps through lighting effects even though the surface being rendered is flat. This is commonly done using a *normal map* to light a flat surface as if it were shaped as dictated by the normal map, giving lighting as if bumps existed on the surface, even though there is no geometry describing the bumps.

byte swapping   The process of exchanging the ordering of bytes in a (usually integer) variable type (i.e., `int`, `short`, etc.).

C   The programming language of Unix kernel hackers.

C++   Most common programming language for programming computer graphics.

cascading style sheet   A presentation mechanism for specifying the look and layout of Web pages.

client   The computer from which OpenGL commands are issued. The client may be the same computer that the OpenGL server is running on (see *server*), or it may be a different machine connected via a network (assuming the OpenGL implementation supports network rendering).

clip   See *clipping*.

clip coordinates   The coordinate system that follows transformation by the projection matrix and precedes perspective division. View-volume clipping is done in clip coordinates.

clipping   Elimination of the portion of a geometric primitive that's outside the half-space defined by a clipping plane. Points are simply rejected if outside. The portion of a line or triangle that's outside the half-space is eliminated, and additional vertices are generated as necessary to complete the primitive within the clipping half-space. Geometric primitives are always clipped against the six half-spaces defined by the left, right, bottom, top, near, and far planes of the view volume. Applications can optionally perform application-specific clipping through use of clip distances, `gl_ClipDistance[]`.

clipping region   The intersection of all the half-spaces defined by the clipping planes. See *clipping*.

CMYK   Cyan, Magenta, Yellow, Black. A *color space* often used in printing.

color space   A model for describing colors, often as vectors within a three- or four-dimensional domain such as the *RGB color space*.

compatibility profile   The profile of OpenGL that still supports all legacy functionality. It is primarily intended to allow the continued development of older applications. See also *core profile*.

components   Individual scalar values in a color or direction vector. They can be integer or floating-point values. Usually, for colors, a component value of zero represents the minimum value or intensity, and a component value of one represents the maximum value or intensity, although other ranges are sometimes used. Because component values are interpreted in a normalized range, they are specified independent of actual resolution. For example, the RGB triple (1,1,1) is white, regardless of whether the color buffers store 4, 8, or 12 bits each. Out-of-range components are typically clamped to the normalized range, not truncated or otherwise interpreted. For example, the RGB triple (1.4,1.5,0.9) is clamped to (1.0,1.0,0.9) before it's used to update the color buffer. Red, green, blue, alpha, and depth are always treated as components, never as indices.

compressed texture   A texture image which is stored in a *compressed* form. Compressed textures benefit from requiring less memory, and using texture-cache memory more efficiently.

compression   Reducing the storage requirements of data by changing its representation in memory.

compression ratio   The ratio of the amount of storage required for some compressed data relative to the size of the original, uncompressed data.

compute shader   A shader that is executed as the result of a compute dispatch command. A single invocation of a compute shader represents one *work item* and a group of invocations forms a *local workgroup*. A number of local workgroups form a *global workgroup*.

concave   A polygon that is not convex. See *convex*.

conditional rendering   A technique of impliclitly using occlusion queries to determine if a sequence of OpenGL rendering commands should be executed based on their visibility (as predicated by depth testing).

constructor   A function used for initializing an object. In GLSL, constructors are used to both initialze new objects (e.g., `vec4`), but also convert between types.

context   A complete set of OpenGL state variables. Note that framebuffer contents are not part of OpenGL state, but that the configuration of the framebuffer (and any associated renderbuffers) is.

control texture   A texture that tells the shader where an effect should be done, or that otherwise controls how and where an effect is done, rather than simply being an image. This is likely to be a single-component texture.

convex   A polygon is convex if no straight line in the plane of the polygon intersects the polygon's edge more than twice.

convex hull   The smallest convex region enclosing a specified group of points. In two dimensions, the convex hull is found conceptually by stretching a rubber band around the points so that all of the points lie within the band.

convolution   A mathematical function that combines two functions such that evaluating the combined function at a point returns the area of the overlap of the two input functions. Convolutions in graphics are usually used in image processing operations.

convolution filter   In image processing, a two-dimensional array of values which are used in a convolution operation on the pixels of an image.

convolution kernel   See *convolution filter*.

coordinate system   In *n*-dimensional space, a set of *n* linearly independent basis vectors anchored to a point (called the origin). A group of coordinates specifies a point in space (or a vector from the origin) by indicating how far to travel along each vector to reach the point (or tip of the vector).

core profile   The modern, streamlined profile of OpenGL that should be used for new application development. See also *compatibility profile*.

cracking   Gaps that appear between edges of adjoining, filled geometric primitives. Cracking can occur during tessellation when the tessellation levels of two adjoining edges are not equal.

cube map   A type of texture that has a multiple of six square faces that may be used to provide environment maps and other effects in OpenGL.

culling   Removing objects that shouldn't be or don't need to be rendered. They can be geometric primitives outside the view frustum, the nonvisible front or back face of a polygon, a fragment outside the viewport, etc.

current   The state used to describe when an OpenGL object is active, either for use or modification. For instance, a texture is made current by calling **glBindTexture()**, after which time, it can be modified, such as changing its minification filter.

debug context   An OpenGL context that automatically reports errors to simplify debugging of OpenGL applications.

decal   A method of calculating color values during texture application, where the texture colors replace the fragment colors or, if alpha blending is enabled, the texture colors are blended with the fragment colors, using only the alpha value.

default framebuffer   The framebuffer object with name zero that's created for every OpenGL application. Its color buffer is the only one that can be displayed to the physical screen.

deprecated   The identification of a function entry point, or feature exposed as a token passed into a function call, that is slated for potential removal in future versions of an *API* or language. Use of the feature is still legal, but will suffer from reduced support and interaction with new features.

depreciation model   The plan used for the identification and potential removal of features from the OpenGL library. The depreciation model was introduced with Version 3.0, and the first features were removed from the API in Version 3.1.

depth   Generally refers to the *z* window coordinate. See *depth value*.

depth buffer   Memory that stores the depth value at every pixel. To perform hidden-surface removal, the depth buffer records the depth value of the object that lies closest to the observer at every pixel. The depth value of every new fragment uses the recorded value for depth comparison and must pass the comparison test before being rendered.

depth range   The portion of the *z* direction (range of *z* coordinates) that will be rendered for a scene. OpenGL takes a near and far parameter to describe this range. Goes hand-in-hand with your *viewport*.

depth testing   Comparison of a fragment's depth coordinate against that stored in the *depth buffer*. The result of this test may then be used to control further rendering—say to discard the fragment, or to control how the stencil buffer is updated.

depth texture   A texture map composed of *depth values*—as compared to colors—often used in generating shadows.

depth value   The depth coordinate of a fragment, or a value stored in the depth buffer.

destination-blending factor   The coefficient associated with the color stored in the frame buffer used for blending.

diffuse   Diffuse lighting and reflection account for the direction of a light source. The intensity of light striking a surface varies with the angle between the orientation of the object and the direction of the light source. A diffuse material scatters that light evenly in all directions.

directional light source   See *infinite light source*.

displacement mapping   Use of a texture or other data source to move the vertices of a tessellated object along the surface normal to give the appearance of a bumpy finish.

display   The device used to show the image to the user, usually a computer monitor, projector, or television. Also refers to the final framebuffer into which a computer image is rendered.

display callback   A function that is called by an application framework whenever it is time to render a new frame of animation.

dithering   A technique (no longer used on modern graphics displays) for increasing the perceived range of colors in an image at the cost of spatial resolution. Adjacent pixels are assigned differing color values; when viewed from a distance, these colors seem to blend into a single intermediate color. The technique is similar to the half-toning used in black-and-white publications to achieve shades of gray.

double buffering   OpenGL contexts supporting both front and back color buffers are double-buffered. Smooth animation is accomplished by rendering into only the back buffer (which isn't displayed), and then causing the front and back buffers to be swapped. See **glutSwapBuffers**() in Appendix A.

dual-source blending   A blending mode where the fragment shader outputs two colors: one to be used as the source color in blending, and the other as one of the blending factors (either soruce or destination).

dynamically uniform   In GLSL, a dynamically uniform expression is one where each shader invocation evaluating that expression will generate the same value as a result.

emission   The color of an object that is self-illuminating or self-radiating. The intensity of an emissive material is not attributed to any external light source.

environment map   A texture used to color surfaces to make them appear to be more integrated into their environment.

environment mapping   The application of an environment map.

event loop   In event-based applications, the event loop is a loop in the program that continuously checks for the arrival of new events and decides how to handle them.

exponent   Part of a floating-point number, the power of two to which the *mantissa* is raised after normalization.

eye coordinates   The coordinate system that follows transformation by the model-view matrix, and precedes transformation by the projection matrix. Lighting and application-specific clipping are done in eye coordinates.

eye space   See *eye coordinates*.

faces   Each polygon has two faces: a front face and a back face. Only one face is ever visible in the window at a time. Whether the front or back face is visible is effectively determined after the polygon is projected onto the window. After this projection, if the polygon's edges are directed clockwise, one of the faces is visible; if directed counterclockwise, the other face is visible. Whether clockwise corresponds to front or back (and counterclockwise corresponds to back or front) is determined by the OpenGL programmer.

factorial   For nonnegative integers, the factorial of n (denoted as $n!$) is the product of the integer values from n to 1, inclusive.

far plane   One of the six clipping planes of the viewing frustum. The far plane, is the clipping plane farthest from the eye and perpendicular to the line-of-sight.

feedback   Modes of operation for OpenGL, where the results of rendering operations, such as transformation of data by a vertex shader, are returned to the application.

filtering   The process of combining pixels or texels to obtain a higher or lower resolution version of an input image or texture.

fixed-function pipeline   A version of the graphics pipeline that contained processing stages whose operation were controlled by a fixed number of parameters that the application could configure. Programmable pipelines, like the current OpenGL pipeline, that allowed more flexibilty in operation have replaced the fixed-function versions.

flat shading   Refers to a primitive colored with a single, constant color across its extent, rather than smoothly interpolated colors across the primitive. See *Gouraud shading*.

fonts Groups of graphical character representations generally used to display strings of text. The characters may be roman letters, mathematical symbols, Asian ideograms, Egyptian hieroglyphics, and so on.

fractional Brownian motion A procedural-texturing technique to produce randomized noise textures.

fragment Fragments are generated by the rasterization of primitives. Each fragment corresponds to a single pixel and includes color, depth, and sometimes texture-coordinate values.

fragment discard The execution of the `discard;` keyword in a fragment shader is known as fragment discard. It causes the fragment to have no effect on the framebuffer, including depth, stencil, and any enabled color attachments.

fragment shader The shader that is executed as a result of rasterization. One invocation of the fragment shader is executed for each fragment that is rasterized.

fragment shading The process of executing a fragment shader.

framebuffer All the buffers of a given window or context. Sometimes includes all the pixel memory of the graphics hardware accelerator.

framebuffer attachment A connection point in a framebuffer object that makes an association between allocated image storage (which might be a texture map level, a renderbuffer, pixel buffer object, or any of the other types of object storage in OpenGL), and a rendering target, such as a color buffer, the depth buffer, or the stencil buffer.

framebuffer object The OpenGL object that stores all of the associated render buffers for a framebuffer.

framebuffer rendering loop The condition where a framebuffer attachment is both simultaneously being written and read. This situation is undesirable, and should be avoided.

Freeglut An open-source implemetation of the OpenGL Utility Toolkit written by Pawel W. Olszta and others that is an up-to-date version of the original GLUT library by Mark Kilgard.

frequency clamping A technique used during procedural texturing to represent complex functions in a simpler form.

front faces See *faces*.

front facing   The classification of a polygon's vertex ordering. When the screen-space projection of a polygon's vertices is oriented such that traveling around the vertices in the order they were submitted to OpenGL results in a counterclockwise traversal (by definition, **glFrontFace()** controls which faces are front facing).

frustum   The view volume warped by perspective division.

function overloading   The technique of modern programming lanugages where functions with the same name accept different numbers of parameters or data types.

gamma correction   A function applied to colors stored in the framebuffer to correct for the nonlinear response of the eye (and sometimes of the monitor) to linear changes in color-intensity values.

gamut   The subset of all possible colors that can be displayed in a certain *color space*.

geometric model   The object-coordinate vertices and parameters that describe an object. Note that OpenGL doesn't define a syntax for geometric models, but rather a syntax and semantics for the rendering of geometric models.

geometric object   See *geometric model*.

geometric primitive   A point, a line, or a triangle.

global illumination   A rendering technique that illumates a scene using all available light sources, including reflections. This technique is generally not possible in rasterization-based systems.

global workgroup   The complete set of work items that are dispatched by a single call to **glDispatchCompute()**. The global workgroup is comprised of an integer number of local workgroups in the x, y, and z dimensions.

GLSL   OpenGL Shading Language

GLUT   the OpenGL Utility Toolkit

GLX   The window system interface for OpenGL on the X Window System.

Gouraud shading   Smooth interpolation of colors across a polygon or line segment. Colors are assigned at vertices and linearly interpolated across the primitive to produce a relatively smooth variation in color. Also called smooth shading.

GPGPU   The short name for General-Purpose computing on GPUs, which is the field of techniques attempting to do general computation (algorithms that you would normally execute on a CPU) on graphics processors.

GPU   graphics processing unit

gradient noise   Another name for *Perlin noise*.

gradient vector   A vector directed along the directional-derivative of a function.

graphics processing   The tasks involved in producing graphical images such as vertex processing, clipping, rasterization, tessellation, and shading.

graphics processing unit   A term used to describe the subsection of a computer system comprising one or more integrated circuits that are at least partially dedicated for the generation of graphical images.

half space   A plane divides space into two half spaces.

halo   An illumination effect that simulates light shining behind an object that produces a halo-like appearance around the object's silhouette.

hidden-line removal   A technique to determine which portions of a wireframe object should be visible. The lines that comprise the wireframe are considered to be edges of opaque surfaces, which may obscure other edges that are farther away from the viewer.

hidden-surface removal   A technique to determine which portions of an opaque, shaded object should be visible, and which portions should be obscured. A test of the depth coordinate, using the depth buffer for storage, is a common method of hidden-surface removal.

homogeneous coordinate   A set of $n + 1$ coordinates used to represent points in n-dimensional projective space. Points in projective space can be thought of as points in Euclidean space together with some points at infinity. The coordinates are homogeneous because a scaling of each of the coordinates by the same nonzero constant doesn't alter the point that the coordinates refer to. Homogeneous coordinates are useful in the calculations of projective geometry, and thus in computer graphics, where scenes must be projected onto a window.

image   A rectangular array of pixels, either in client memory or in the framebuffer.

image plane   Another name for the clipping plane of the viewing frustum that is closest to the eye. The geometry of the scene is projected onto the image plane, and displayed in the application's window.

image-based lighting   An illumination technique that uses an image of the light falling on an object to illuminate the object, as compared to directly computing the illumation using analytical means.

immutable   The state of being unmodifiable. Applied to textures, it means that the parameters of the texture (*width*, *height*, and *storage format*) cannot be changed.

impostor   A simplified model of a complex geometric object, often using a single, texture-mapped polygon.

infinite light source   A directional source of illumination. The radiating light from an infinite light source strikes all objects as parallel rays.

input-patch vertex   The input vertices that form a patch primitive. After processing by the vertex shader, these are passed to the tessellation control shader where they may be used as control points in the representation of a high-order-surface.

instance id   An identifier available in vertex shaders for identifying a unique group of primitives. In GLSL, the instance id is provided in the monotonically increasing variable `gl_InstanceID`.

instanced rendering   Drawing multiple copies of the same set of geometry, varying a unique identifier for each copy of the geometry. See *instance id*.

interface block   The grouping of shader variables between two successive shader stages.

interleaved   A method of storing vertex arrays by which heterogeneous types of data (i.e., vertex, normals, texture coordinates, etc.) are grouped for faster retrieval.

internal fomat   The storage format used by OpenGL for storing a texture map. A texture's internal format is often different than the format of the pixels passed to OpenGL.

interpolation   Calculation of values (such as color or depth) for interior pixels, given the values at the boundaries (such as at the vertices of a polygon or a line).

invocation   A single execution of a shader. In tessellation control shaders, it represents a single control point. In geometry shaders, it represents a single instance of the shader when instancing is turned on. In compute shaders, a single invocation is created for each *work item*.

IRIS GL   Silicon Graphics' proprietary graphics library, developed from 1982 through 1992. OpenGL was designed with IRIS GL as a starting point.

jaggies   Artifacts of aliased rendering. The edges of primitives that are rendered with aliasing are jagged, rather than smooth. A near-horizontal aliased line, for example, is rendered as a set of horizontal lines on adjacent pixel rows, rather than as a smooth, continuous line.

lacunarity   A multipler that determines how quickly the freqeuncy increases for each successive octave for Perlin noise.

layout qualifier   A declaration associated with the inputs, outputs, or variables in a shader that describe how they are laid out in memory, or what the logical configuration of that shader is to be.

lens flare   An illumination effect that simulates the light scattered through a lens.

level of detail   The process of creating multiple copies of an object or image with different levels of resolution. See *mipmap*.

light probe   A device for capturing the illumination of a scene. A common physical light probe is a reflective hemisphere.

light probe image   The image collected by a *light probe*.

lighting   The process of computing the color of a vertex based on current lights, material properties, and lighting-model modes.

line   A straight region of finite width between two vertices. (Unlike mathematical lines, OpenGL lines have finite width and length.) Each segment of a strip of lines is itself a line.

local light source   A source of illumination that has a position instead of a direction. The radiating light from a local light source emanates from that position. Other names for a local light source are point light source or positional light source. A spotlight is a special kind of local light source.

local viewer   The mode of the Phong lighting model that more accurately simulates how specular highlights shine on objects.

local workgroup   The local scope of a workgroup that has access to the same set of shared local variables.

logical operation   Boolean mathematical operations between the incoming fragment's RGBA color or color-index values and the RGBA color or color-index values already stored at the corresponding location in the framebuffer. Examples of logical operations include AND, OR, XOR, NAND, and INVERT.

lossless compression   Any method of compressing data where the original data may be retrieved without any loss of information.

lossy compression   Any method of compressing data where some of the original information is discarded in order to improve the compression ratio.

low-pass filtering   Taking a scene and keeping the low-frequency components (slower spatial variation) while discarding the high-frequency components. This is one way to avoid *undersampling*, by bringing the highest frequency present down to the level that sampling will be done.

luminance   The perceived brightness of a surface. Often refers to a weighted average of red, green, and blue color values that indicates the perceived brightness of the combination.

machine word   A unit of processing as seen by computer systems—usually represented by a single register in a processor. For example, 32-bit systems generally have a 32-bit machine word and 32-bit wide registers.

mantissa   Part of a floating-point number, represents the numeric quantity that is subsequently normalized and raised to the power of two represented by the *exponent*.

material   A surface property used in computing the illumination of a surface.

matrix   A two-dimensional array of values. OpenGL matrices are all 4×4, though when stored in client memory they're treated as 1×16 single-dimension arrays.

mipmap   A reduced resolution version of a texture map, used to texture a geometric primitive whose screen resolution differs from the resolution of the source texture map.

models   Sets of geometric primitives representing objects, often including texture coordinate (and textures), normals, and other properties.

modulate   A method of calculating color values during texture application by which the texture and the fragment colors are combined.

monitor   The device that displays the image in the framebuffer.

multifractal   A procedural-texturing technique that varies the fractal dimension of the noise function based on an object's location.

multisampling   The process of generating or producing multiple samples per pixel.

multitexturing   The process of applying several texture images to a single primitive. The images are applied one after another, in a pipeline of texturing operations.

mutable   Capable of being modified, usually in reference to a texture map. See *immutable*.

name   In OpenGL, a name is an unsigned integer representing an instance of an object (texture or buffer, for example).

NDCs   Normalized Device Coordinates.

near plane   One of the six clipping planes of the viewing frustum. The near plane, which is also called the *image plane* is the clipping plane closest to the eye and perpendicular to the line-of-sight.

network   A connection between two or more computers that enables each to transfer data to and from the others.

noise   A repeatable pseudo-random deviance as a function of an input location, used to modify surface colors and geometries to give a less than perfect look, such as to make stains, clouds, turbulence, wood grain, etc., that are not based on rigid, detectable patterns.

nonconvex   A polygon is nonconvex if a line exists in the plane of the polygon that intersects the polygon more than twice. See *concave*.

normal   The short form for a *surface normal*, and a synonym for perpendicular.

normal map   A map saying for each location on a surface how much an apparent surface *normal* should deviate from the true surface normal. This is typically used when *bump mapping*. Usually, the normal is stored as a relative vector for a *surface-local coordinate space* where the vector (0,0,1) is assumed to be the base surface normal.

normal texture   A *normal map* stored as a texture.

normal vector See *normal*.

normalize To change the length of a vector to have some canonical form, usually to have a length 1.0. The GLSL built-in `normalize` does this. To normalize a normal vector, divide each of the components by the square root of the sum of their squares. Then, if the normal is thought of as a vector from the origin to the point (nx', ny', nz'), this vector has unit length.

$$factor = \sqrt{nx^2 + ny^2 + nz^2}$$
$$nx' = nx/factor$$
$$ny' = ny/factor$$
$$nz' = nz/factor$$

normalized See *normalize*; after normalizing, a vector is normalized.

normalized-device coordinates The coordinate space used to represent positions after division by the homogeneous clip coordinate before transformation into window coordinates by the viewport transform.

normalized value A normalized value is one that lies between an assumed range—for OpenGL, almost always meaning having a vector length or absolute value of 1.0. See *normalize*.

NURBS Non-Uniform Rational B-Spline. A common way to specify parametric curves and surfaces.

object An object-coordinate model that's rendered as a collection of primitives.

object coordinates Coordinate system prior to any OpenGL transformation.

occlusion query A mechanism for determining if geometry is visible by using the depth buffer (but not modifying its values).

octave The name given to the relationship of two functions when one function's frequency is twice the other function's frequency.

off-screen rendering The process of drawing into a framebuffer that is not directly displayed to the visible screen.

The OpenGL Shading Language The language used for authoring shader program. Also commonly known as GLSL.

orthographic   Nonperspective (or parallel) projection, as in some engineering drawings, with no foreshortening.

output-patch vertex   A vertex generated by the tessellation control shader. These vertices generally form the control mesh of a patch.

overloading   As in C++, creating multiple functions with the same name but with different parameters, allowing a compiler to generate different signatures for the functions and call the correct version based on its use.

pack   The process of converting pixel colors from a buffer into the format requested by the application.

padding a structure   The addition of members (often unused) to a structure—normally at the end—in order to ensure that it is a specific size, or will be aligned on a specific boundary.

pass-through shader   A shader that performs no substantial work other than to pass its inputs to its output.

patch   A high order surface representation made up of a number of control points. Patches are used as the input to a tessellation control shader, which executes once for each control point in the patch and may generate a set of data for the patch to be used by the fixed-function tessellator or the subsequent tessellation evaluation shader.

Perlin noise   A form of *noise* invented by Ken Perlin designed to be effective while not too computationally difficult for real-time rendering.

perspective correction   An additional calculation for texture coordinates to fix texturing artifacts for a textured geometric rendered in a perspective projection.

perspective division   The division of x, y, and z by w, carried out in clip coordinates.

Phong reflection model   An illumination model used for simulating lighting effects in computer-generated images.

Phong shading   The coloring of pixels using the Phong reflection model evaluated at every pixel of a geometric primitive. This is in comparison to evaluating the Phong reflective model at the vertices, and interpolating the computed colors across the geometric primitive.

ping-pong buffers   A GPGPU technique of writing values to a buffer (usually a texture map) that is immediately rebound as a texture map to be read from to do a subsequent computation. Effectively, you can consider the buffer written-to, and subsequently read-from as being a collection of temporary values. Ping-ponging buffers is usually done using framebuffer objects.

pixel   Short for "picture element". The bits at location (x, y) of all the bitplanes in the framebuffer constitute the single pixel (x, y). In an image in client memory, a pixel is one group of elements. In OpenGL window coordinates, each pixel corresponds to a 1.0×1.0 screen area. The coordinates of the lower left corner of the pixel are (x, y), and of the upper right corner are $(x + 1, y + 1)$.

point   An exact location in space, which is rendered as a finite-diameter dot.

point fade threshold   The minimum value used in point rasterization where point-antialiasing effects are disabled.

point light source   See *local light source*.

point sampling   Finding the color of a scene at specific points of zero size. For example, deciding what color to turn a pixel based on the color of the scene at the pixel's center, or based on a finite number of point samples within the pixel, as opposed to looking at the entire area the pixel covers (see *area sampling*).

polygon   A near-planar surface bounded by edges specified by vertices. Each triangle of a triangle mesh is a polygon, as is each quadrilateral of a quadrilateral mesh.

polygon offset   A technique to modify depth-buffer values of a polygon when additional geometric primitives are drawn with identical geometric coordinates.

positional light source   See *local light source*.

primitive assembler   A component in graphics hardware that groups vertices into points, lines, or triangles ready for rendering. The primitive assembler may also perform tasks such as perspective division and the viewport transform.

primitive generator   See *primitive assembler*.

procedural shading   Using shaders to create a surface texture, primarily algorithmically (procedurally) rather than by doing texture lookups. While side tables or maps may be stored and looked up as textures, the bulk of the resources to create the desired effect come from computation rather from a stored image.

procedural texture shader   A shader that helps perform *procedural shading*.

procedural texturing   See *procedural shading*.

programmable blending   The blending of colors under shader control, as compared to OpenGL's fixed-function blending operations.

programmable graphics pipeline   The mode of operation where the processing of vertices, fragments, and their associated data (e.g., texture coordinates) is under the control of shader programs specified by the programmer.

projection matrix   The 4×4 matrix that transforms points, lines, polygons, and raster positions from eye coordinates to clip coordinates.

projective texturing   A texture-mapping technique that simualtes projecting an image onto the objects in a scene.

protocol   A standard for interchanging messages between computer systems. Some implementations of OpenGL use a protocol for communicating between the client (usually the application) and the server (usually the machine rendering OpenGL).

proxy texture   A placeholder for a texture image, which is used to determine if there are enough resources to support a texture image of a given size and internal format resolution.

pulse train   A sequence of pulses—usually equally spaced—used in procedural shading techniques.

quadrilateral   A polygon with four edges.

race condition   A situation in multithreaded-application execution in which two or more threads compete for the same resource, such as a counter. The results of computations during a race condition are unpredictable.

rasterization   Converts a projected point, line, or polygon, or the pixels of a bitmap or image, to fragments, each corresponding to a pixel in the framebuffer. Note that all primitives are rasterized, not just points, lines, and polygons.

rasterizer The fixed function unit that converts a primitive (point, line, or triangle) into a sequence of fragments ready for shading. The rasterizer performs rasterization.

ray tracing A family of algorithms that produce images or other outputs by calculating the path of rays through media.

rectangle A quadrilateral whose alternate edges are parallel to each other in object coordinates.

render-to-texture A technique where the storage for a texture map is used as a destination for rendering (i.e., a renderbuffer). Render-to-texture enables a more efficient method for updating texture maps than rendering into the color buffer, and copy the results into texture memory, saving the copy operation.

renderbuffer An allocation of memory in the OpenGL server for the storage of pixel values. Renderbuffers are used as a destination for rendering, as well as able to be as texture maps without requiring a copy of the renderbuffer's data.

renderer An OpenGL implementation in Apple Computer's Mac OS X operating system. Since a computer may have multiple graphics-capable facilities (e.g., multiple graphics cards or a software implementation), there may be multiple renderers supported on a Mac OS X machine.

rendering The process of taking a representation of a scene in memory and generating an image of that scene.

rendering pipeline The sequence of independent functions that together implement rendering. This may be a set of both fixed-function and programmable units.

resident texture A texture image that is cached in special, high-performance texture memory. If an OpenGL implementation does not have special, high-performance texture memory, then all texture images are deemed resident textures.

resolved The process of combining pixel sample values (usually by a weighted, linear combination) to the final pixel color.

RGB color space The three-dimensional color space commonly used for computer graphic images, with one channel for each of the red, green, and blue components. Other commonly used color spaces are CMKY (in printing) and YUV (in video processing).

RGBA Red, Green, Blue, Alpha.

RGBA mode   An OpenGL context is in RGBA mode if its color buffers store red, green, blue, and alpha color components, rather than color indices.

sample   A subpixel entity used for multisampled antialiasing. A pixel can store color (and potentially depth and stencil) data for multiple samples. Before the final pixel is rendered on the screen, samples are *resolved* into the final pixel color.

sample shader   A fragment shader that's executed per pixel sample location, allowing much finer-grain determination of a pixel's color.

sampler object   An OpenGL object representing the state used to fetch texture values from a texture map.

sampler variables   Variables used in shaders to represent references to texture or sampler units.

samples   Independent color elements that make up a multisampled pixel or texel. See also *multisampling*.

sampling   See *point sampling*.

scissor box   The rectangular region defining where the scissor test will be applied to fragments. See *scissoring*.

scissoring   A fragment clipping test. Fragments outside of a rectangular scissor region are rejected.

second-source blending   Blending that uses both the first and second outputs from the fragment shader in the calculation of the final fragment data.

selector   Part of the OpenGL state that stores the unit to be used for subsequent operations on indexed state. For example, the active texture unit is a selector.

server   The computer on which OpenGL commands are executed. This might differ from the computer from which commands are issued. See *client*.

shader   Executable programs that take as input data produced by one stage of a pipeline (such as vertices, primitives, or fragments) and produce a different type of data ready for consumption by the subsequent stage in the pipeline.

shader plumbing   The administrative work involved in executing shaders. This will include setting the values of uniforms, setting input and output primitive types, defining interfaces, and so on.

shader program   A set of instructions written in a graphics shading language (the OpenGL Shading Language, also called GLSL) that control the processing of graphics primitives.

shader stage   A logical part of the shading pipeline that executes a particular type of shader. A shader stage may not be a physically separate execution unit in the OpenGL implementation; for example, a hardware implementation may execute both vertex and geometry shaders on the same execution engine.

shader storage buffer objects   Render-time sizeable GLSL buffer objects that can be read and written from within a shader.

shader variable   A variable declared and used in a shader.

shading   The process of interpolating color within the interior of a polygon, or between the vertices of a line, during rasterization.

shadow map   A texture map that contains information relating to the locations of shadows within a scene.

shadow mapping   A texture-mapping technique employing *shadow maps*, to render geometric objects while simulating shadowing in the scene.

shadow sampler   A sampler type that performs a comparison between the sampled texels and a provided reference value, returning a value between 0.0 and 1.0 to indicate whether the fetched texel satisfies the comparison condition. Commonly used in shadow mapping algorithms.

shadow texture   See *shadow map*.

shared exponent   A numeric representation of a multicomponent floating-point vector where components of the vector are packed together into a single quantity containing a mantissa per component, but with a single exponent value shared across all components.

shininess   The exponent associated with specular reflection and lighting. Shininess controls the degree with which the specular highlight decays.

singular matrix   A matrix that has no inverse. Geometrically, such a matrix represents a transformation that collapses points along at least one line to a single point.

sky box   A representative piece of geometry—usually a cube—that contains encompasses all other geometry in the scene, and is usually texture mapped to look like the sky.

slice   An element of an array texture.

smooth shading   See *Gouraud shading*.

source-blending factor   The coefficient associated with the source color (i.e., the color output from the fragment shader) used in blending computations.

specular   Specular lighting and reflection incorporate reflection off shiny objects and the position of the viewer. Maximum specular reflectance occurs when the angle between the viewer and the direction of the reflected light is zero. A specular material scatters light with greatest intensity in the direction of the reflection, and its brightness decays, based upon the exponential value shininess.

spotlight   A special type of local light source that has a direction (where it points to) as well as a position. A spotlight simulates a cone of light, which may have a fall-off in intensity, based upon distance from the center of the cone.

sprite   A screen-aligned graphics primitive. Sprites are usually represented as either a single vertex that is expanded to cover many pixels around the transformed vertex, or as a quadrilateral its vertices specified so that it is perpendicular to the viewing direction (or put another way, parallel to the image plane).

sRGB color space   An RGB color space standard specified by the International Electrotechnical Commission (IEC) that matches the color intensity outputs of monitors and printers better than a linear RGB space. The sRGB approximately corresponds to gamma correcting RGB (but not alpha) values using a gamma value of 2.2. See IEC standard 61966-2-1 for all of the gory details.

state   All of the variables that make up a part of an OpenGL context. For example, texture, blending, and vertex attribute setup are considered state.

stencil buffer   Memory (bitplanes) that is used for additional per-fragment testing, along with the depth buffer. The stencil test may be used for masking regions, capping solid geometry, and overlapping translucent polygons.

stencil testing   Testing the value contained in the stencil buffer against the current stencil reference value to determine if and how the fragment should be written to the framebuffer.

stereo   Enhanced three-dimensional perception of a rendered image by computing separate images for each eye. Stereo requires special hardware, such as two synchronized monitors or special glasses, to alternate viewed frames for each eye. Some implementations of OpenGL support stereo by including both left and right buffers for color data.

stipple   A one- or two-dimensional binary pattern that defeats the generation of fragments where its value is zero. Line stipples are one-dimensional and are applied relative to the start of a line. Polygon stipples are two-dimensional and are applied with a fixed orientation to the window.

subpixel   The logical division of a physical pixel into subregions. See *sample*.

supersampling   Performing full per-sample rendering for multiple samples per pixel, and then coloring the pixel based on the average of the colors found for each sample in the pixel.

surface normal   A surface normal vector at some pointis a vector pointing in the direction perpendicular to the surface at that point. A three-component normal vector can define theangular orientation of a plane, but not its position.

surface-local coordinate space   A coordinate system relative to a surface, where no matter the true orientation of the surface, the surface is taken to be the *xy* plane, and the normal to the surface is (0,0,1).

surface-local coordinates   Coordinates relative to a *surface-local coordinate space*.

swizzle   Rearranging the components of a vector—for example, a texel or vertex into a desired order.

tangent space   The space of vectors tangent to a point. In general, tangent space is the plane perpendicular to the *normal vector* at a vertex.

temporal aliasing   Aliasing artifacts that vary with time.

tessellated   A patch is said to be tessellated after it has been broken down into many primitives—often quads or triangles.

tessellation control shader   A shader that executes in the tessellation control stage and accepts as input the control points of a patch and produces inner- and outer-tessellation factors for the patch and per-patch parameters for consumption by the tessellation evaluation shader.

tessellation coordinates The generated *barycentric coordinates* within the *tessellation domain* produced by the fixed-function tessellator and provided to the *tessellation evaluation shader*.

tessellation domain The domain over which a high-order-surface is tessellated. This includes quad, triangle, and isoline domains.

tessellation evaluation shader A shader that executes once per tessellation output-patch vertex produced by the fixed-function tessellator.

tessellation level factor See *tessellation levels*.

tessellation levels There are two tessellation levels associated with a single patch primitive and that are generated by the *tessellation control shader*. The *inner* tessellation factor controls by how much the interior of a patch is tessellated. Additionally, each outer edge of the patch has an associated *outer* tessellation factor that controls by how much that edge is tessellated.

tessellation output patch vertices The output vertices produced by the tessellation control shader.

tessellation shaders Collectively the tessellation control and tessellation evaluation shaders.

texel A texture element. A texel is obtained from texture memory and represents the color of the texture to be applied to a corresponding fragment.

texture comparison mode A mode of texture mapping that evaluates a comparison when sampling a texture map, as compared to directly returning the sampled texel value.

texture coordinates The coordinates used to fetch data from a texture map.

texture filter A color-smoothing operation applied when a texture map is sampled.

texture map See *textures*.

texture mapping The process of applying an image (the texture) to a primitive. Texture mapping is often used to add realism to a scene. For example, you can apply a picture of a building facade to a polygon representing a wall.

texture object   A named cache that stores texture data, such as the image array, associated mipmaps, and associated texture parameter values: width, height, border width, internal format, resolution of components, minification and magnification filters, wrapping modes, border color, and texture priority.

texture sampler   A variable used in a shader to sample from a texture.

texture streaming   A technique where texture maps are updated at a periodic frequency (e.g., one per frame).

texture swizzle   See *swizzle*.

texture targets   Often used in place of a texture type, the texture targets include 1D, 2D, 3D, cube map, array forms, and so on.

texture unit   When multitexturing, as part of an overall multiple pass application of texture images, a texture unit controls one processing step for a single texture image. A texture unit maintains the texturing state for one texturing pass, including the texture image, filter, environment, coordinate generation, and matrix stack. Multi-texturing consists of a chain of texture units.

texture view   A technique that interprets a single texture map's data in different formats.

textures   One- or two-dimensional images that are used to modify the color of fragments produced by rasterization.

transform feedback object   The OpenGL object that contains post-transform (e.g., after vertex-, tessellation-, or geometry shading) data.

transformation matrices   Matrices that are used to transform vertices from one coordinate space to another.

transformations   The warping of spaces. In OpenGL, transformations are limited to projective transformations that include anything that can be represented by a 4×4 matrix. Such transformations include rotations, translations, (nonuniform) scalings along the coordinate axes, perspective transformations, and combinations of these.

triangle   A polygon with three edges. Triangles are always convex.

turbulence   A form of procedurally-generated noise that includes sharp creases and cusps in the output image.

typed array   A JavaScript construct for storing binary-typed data in a JavaScript arrays. It's required for use with WebGL.

undersampling Choosing pixel colors to display by *point sampling* at intervals further apart than the detail in the scene to render. More formally, it is sampling at less than double the frequency of the highest frequencies present in the scene. Point sampling always under samples edges, since edges are step functions containing arbitrarily high frequencies. This results in *aliasing*.

uniform buffer object A type of buffer object that encapsulates a set of uniform variables, making access and update of that collection of uniform variables much faster with less function call overhead.

uniform variable A type of variable used in vertex or fragment shaders that doesn't change its value across a set of primitives (either a single primitive, or the collection of primitives specified by a single draw call).

unit square A square that has a side length of one.

unpack The process of converting pixels supplied by an application to OpenGL's internal format.

Utah teapot The quintessential computer-graphics object. The Utah teapot was originally modeled by Martin Newell at the University of Utah.

value noise A function-based noise generation technique.

vector A multidimensional number often used to represent position, velocity, or direction.

vertex A point in three-dimensional space.

vertex array A block of vertex data (vertex coordinates, texture coordinates, surface normals, RGBA colors, color indices, and edge flags) may be stored in an array and then used to specify multiple geometric primitives through the execution of a single OpenGL command.

vertex-array object An object representing the state of a set of vertex arrays.

vertex-attribute array An array of data that will be used to form the inputs to the vertex shader.

vertex shader A shader that consumes as input vertices supplied by the application and produces vertices for consumption by the subsequent stage (tessellation control, geometry, or rasterization).

vertex winding   The order of vertices that will be used to determine whether a polygon is front facing or back facing.

view volume   The volume in clip coordinates whose coordinates satisfy the following three conditions:

$$-w < x < w$$
$$-w < y < w$$
$$-w < z < w$$

Geometric primitives that extend outside this volume are clipped.

viewing model   The conceptual model used for transforming three-dimensional coordinates into two-dimensional screen coordinates.

viewpoint   The origin of either the eye- or the clip-coordinate system, depending on context. (For example, when discussing lighting, the viewpoint is the origin of the eye-coordinate system. When discussing projection, the viewpoint is the origin of the clip-coordinate system.) With a typical projection matrix, the eye-coordinate and clip-coordinate origins are at the same location.

viewport   A rectangular collection of pixels on the screen through which the rendered scene will be seen. Goes hand-in-hand with depth-range parameters (see *depth range*).

voxel   An *el*ement of a *vol*ume. See also *texel* and *pixel*.

winding   See *vertex winding*.

window   A subregion of the framebuffer, usually rectangular, whose pixels all have the same buffer configuration. An OpenGL context renders to a single window at a time.

window aligned   When referring to line segments or polygon edges, implies that these are parallel to the window boundaries. (In OpenGL, the window is rectangular, with horizontal and vertical edges.) When referring to a polygon pattern, implies that the pattern is fixed relative to the window origin.

window coordinates   The pixel coordinate system of a window.

wireframe   A representation of an object that contains line segments only. Typically, the line segments indicate polygon edges.

word aligned   A memory address is said to be word aligned if it is an integer multiple of the machine word size.

work item A single item of work within a workgroup. Also known as an *invocation*.

workgroup A group of work items that collectively operate on data. See also global workgroup and local workgroup.

X Window System A window system used by many of the machines on which OpenGL is implemented. GLX is the name of the OpenGL extension to the X Window System. (See Appendix F.)

z-buffer See *depth buffer*.

z-buffering See *depth testing*.

Index

abs(), 692
acos(), 689
acosh(), 690
adjacency primitives, 511, 516–523
aliasing, 178, 442
all(), 705
alpha, 25, 143, 166
alpha value, 166
ambient light, 361, 363
amplification
  geometry, 527
analytic integration, 452
anisotropic filtering, 330
antialiasing, 153, 442–459
any(), 705
application programming
  interface, 2
area sampling, 453
array textures, 262
arrays, 44
asin(), 689
asinh(), 690
atan(), 689
atanh(), 690
atomic counter, 604–608, 624, 629
atomic operation, 577
  on image variables, 578
atomicAdd(), 588, 724
atomicAnd(), 588, 724
atomicCompSwap(), 588, 725

atomicCounter(), 723
atomicCounterDecrement(), 723
atomicCounterIncrement(), 723
atomicExchange(), 588, 725
atomicMax(), 588, 724
atomicMin(), 588, 724
atomicOr(), 588, 725
atomicXor(), 588, 725
attenuation, 368

barrier, 599
  memory, 599
barrier(), 734
barycentric coordinates, 493
Bernstein polynomials, 503
Bézier patches, 500
billboard, 525
binding an object, 17
binomial coefficient, 503
binormal, 435
bit depth, 143
bitCount(), 707
bitfieldExtract(), 706
bitfieldInsert(), 706
bitfieldReverse(), 707
bitplane, 148
blending, 14, 166, 616
buffer
  pixel unpack, 280
  shader storage, 575

buffer objects, 11
buffer ping-ponging, 181
built-in variables
    compute shader, 630
    geometry shader, 561
bump map, 441
bump mapping, 433–442
byte swapping, 289

cache, 596
    coherency, 596
    hierarchy, 596
callback
    function, 868
callback(), 869
cascading style sheet, 662
ceil(), 693
CGL
    CGLChoosePixelFormat(),
        851
    CGLCreateContext(), 852
    CGLDescribeRenderer(), 851
    CGLDestroyPixelFormat(), 851
    CGLDestroyRendererInfo(), 851
    CGLQueryRendererInfo(), 851
    CGLSetCurrentContext(), 852
ChoosePixelFormat(), 846
clamp(), 694
client, 3
clip, 211
clip coordinates, 213
clipping, 13, 206
    frustum, 211
    user, 237, 238
clipping region, 11
coherent, 598
communication, 632
compatibility profile, 842
components, 42
compressed texture, 260
compression, 179
compression ratio, 326
compute shader, 36, 623–649
conditional rendering, 176

constructor, 40
constructors, 39
context, 15
    debug, 866
control texture, 414
controlling polygon rendering, 90
convex, 90
convolution, 453
convolution filter, 453
convolution kernel, 453
coordinate system, 205
coordinate systems, 208
core profile, 15
cos(), 688
cosh(), 689
cracking, 505
CreateDIBitmap(), 847
CreateDIBSection(), 847
cross(), 700
cube map, 262, 559
culling
    frustum, 211
    in a geometry shader, 527
current, 18

deadlock, 601
Debug
    Groups, 875
debug context, 865, 866
debug message, 869
debug output, 868
default framebuffer, 145
degrees(), 688
DeleteObject(), 847
deprecated, 658
depth buffer, 146, 375, 400
depth coordinate, 209
depth fighting, 404
depth range, 208, 236
depth testing, 13
depth texture, 400
depth value, 13
DescribePixelFormat(), 846
determinant(), 703

dFdx(), 729
dFdy(), 729
diffuse light, 361
directional light, 365
dispatch, 627
  indirect, 628
displacement mapping, 487, 507
display, 4
display callback, 15
display(), 8, 9, 15, 18, 28–30,
    651
distance(), 700
dithering, 171
dot(), 700
double buffering, 146
dual-source blending, 168
dynamically uniform, 297

edge detection, 643
emission, 384
emissive lighting, 380
EmitStreamVertex(), 733
EmitVertex(), 733
end
  of the universe, 882
EndPrimitive(), 733
EndStreamPrimitive(), 733
environment map, 313, 559
environment mapping, 313
equal(), 704
event loop, 8
exp(), 690
exp2(), 691
exponent, 274
eye coordinates, 209, 232, 382
eye space, 208, 209, 382

faceforward(), 701
faces, 90
factorial, 503
far plane, 211, 227, 236
feedback, 206, 239
feedback buffer objects, 239
fence, 589

filtering, 203
  debug messages, 872
  linear, 330
findLSB(), 707
findMSB(), 707
fixed-function pipeline, 34
flat shading, 153
floatBitsToInt(), 696
floatBitsToUint(), 696
floor(), 692
fma(), 697
fonts, 842
fract(), 693
fractional brownian motion, 463
fragment, 3, 144
fragment discard, 13
fragment shader, 3, 4, 35
fragment shading, 13
fragment tests
  early, 604
framebuffer, 4, 145
framebuffer attachment, 183
framebuffer object, 145
framebuffer rendering loop, 351
frequency clamping, 457
frexp(), 697
front facing, 91
frustum, 210
  clipping, 211
  culling, 211
function overloading, 296
fwidth(), 729

gamut, 143
GdiFlush(), 847
geometric model, xli
geometric object, 173
geometric primitive, 2
geometry shader, 35, 509
geometry shaders, 562
GetVersion(), 846
GetVersionEx(), 846
gl.h, 836
gl3.h, 836

glActiveSampler(), 294
glActiveShaderProgram(), 83
glActiveTexture(), 265, 294,
    303–305, 571
glAttachShader(), 74, 625, 647
glBeginConditionalRender(),
    176, 177
glBeginQuery(), 173, 174, 881, 882
glBeginQueryIndexed(), 538
glBeginTransformFeedback(),
    250–252
glBind*(), 18, 181
glBindAttribLocation(), 436
glBindBuffer(), 18–20, 63, 69, 94,
    242, 891
glBindBufferBase(), 63, 64, 241, 242
glBindBufferRange(), 63, 64,
    242–244
glBindFragDataLocation(), 194, 195
glBindFragDataLocationIndexed(),
    194, 195
glBindFramebuffer(), 181, 182, 191
glBindImageTexture(), 570, 571
glBindProgramPipeline(), 82
glBindRenderbuffer(), 184, 185
glBindSampler(), 293, 891
glBindTexture(), 264–266, 293,
    303–305, 309, 356, 571,
    891, 894
glBindTransformFeedback(), 240
glBindVertexArray(), 8, 17, 18, 29
glBlendColor(), 168, 169
glBlendEquation(), 170, 609
glBlendEquationi(), 170
glBlendEquationSeparate(), 170
glBlendEquationSeparatei(), 170
glBlendFunc(), 167, 168, 171, 198,
    200, 609
glBlendFunci(), 167,
    168, 198
glBlendFuncSeparate(), 167, 168,
    171, 198
glBlendFuncSeparatei(), 167, 168,
    198

glBlitFramebuffer(), 203
glBufferData(), 11, 21, 22, 63, 69,
    95, 97, 99–103, 108, 242, 243,
    357, 602
glBufferSubData(), 97–101, 103,
    242, 602
glCheckFramebufferStatus(), 190,
    191, 557
glClampColor(), 203
glClear(), 8, 28, 29, 147, 190
glClearBuffer(), 192
glClearBuffer*(), 190
glClearBufferData(), 98, 99
glClearBufferfi(), 190, 192
glClearBufferfv(), 192
glClearBufferiv(), 192
glClearBufferSubData(), 98, 99
glClearColor(), 29, 147, 190
glClearDepth(), 147, 190
glClearDepthf(), 147
glClearStencil(), 147
glClientWaitSync(), 590, 591, 593
glColorMask(), 147, 148
glColorMaski(), 148
glCommand{sifd}(), xlvi
glCompileShader(), 73, 511,
    624, 647
glCompressedTexImage1D(), 327
glCompressedTexImage2D(), 327
glCompressedTexImage3D(), 327,
    328
glCompressedTexSubImage1D(),
    328
glCompressedTexSubImage2D(),
    328
glCompressedTexSubImage3D(),
    329
glCopyBufferSubData(), 99–101,
    602
glCopyTexImage*(), 196, 197
glCopyTexImage1D(), 281, 282
glCopyTexImage2D(), 281, 282
glCopyTexSubImage*(), 196, 197
glCopyTexSubImage1D(), 282

glCopyTexSubImage2D(), 282
glCopyTexSubImage3D(),
    282
glcorearb.h, 9, 836
glCreateProgram(), 73, 76, 878
glCreateShader(), 72, 76, 510, 511,
    624, 627, 647, 878
glCreateShaderProgramv(), 81
glCullFace(), 91, 92, 160
glDebugMessageCallback(), 868, 869
glDebugMessageControl(), 872
glDebugMessageInsert(), 874
glDeleteBuffers(), 20
glDeleteFramebuffers(), 182, 183
glDeleteProgram(), 75, 76
glDeleteProgramPipelines(), 82
glDeleteQueries(), 174, 176
glDeleteRenderbuffers(), 184
glDeleteSamplers(), 295
glDeleteShader(), 74, 75
glDeleteSync(), 591
glDeleteTextures(), 266
glDeleteTransformFeedbacks(), 241
glDeleteVertexArrays(), 17, 18
glDepthFunc(), 163
glDepthMask(), 148
glDepthRange(), 236
glDepthRangeArrayv(), 551, 555
glDepthRangef(), 236
glDepthRangeIndexed(), 550, 551
glDetachShader(), 74
glDisable(), 31, 92, 125, 156, 157,
    160, 169–172, 871
glDisablei(), 170, 197
glDisableVertexAttribArray(), 28,
    112, 129
glDispatchCompute(), 627, 628,
    630, 632, 648, 899
glDispatchComputeIndirect(), 628,
    629, 632, 648
glDrawArrays(), 11, 30, 115–119,
    128, 135, 487, 518, 539, 540,
    628, 639
glDrawArraysIndirect(), 117–119,
    121, 122, 628
glDrawArraysInstanced(), 117, 118,
    128, 129, 132, 135, 136, 139,
    541, 549
glDrawArraysInstancedBase
    Instance(), 135
glDrawBuffer(), 115, 196
glDrawBuffers(), 115, 191, 192, 196
glDrawElements(), 93, 115–118,
    120, 125, 128, 129, 135, 518,
    522
glDrawElementsBaseVertex(), 116,
    117, 121, 128, 129, 135, 136
glDrawElementsIndirect(), 118, 119,
    121, 122
glDrawElementsInstanced(), 117,
    128, 129, 139, 549
glDrawElementsInstancedBase
    Instance(), 135
glDrawElementsInstancedBase
    Vertex(), 117, 119, 128, 129,
    139
glDrawElementsInstancedBaseVertex
    BaseInstance(), 135, 136
glDrawRangeElements(), 117, 806
glDrawRangeElementsBaseVertex(),
    117
glDrawTransformFeedback(), 540,
    548
glDrawTransformFeedback
    Instanced(), 540, 541
glDrawTransformFeedbackStream(),
    540, 541, 546, 547
glDrawTransformFeedbackStream
    Instanced(), 541
glEnable(), 31, 91, 92, 125, 154–158,
    160, 163, 164, 166, 170–172,
    179, 180, 316, 511, 871, 872
glEnablei(), 170, 197
glEnableVertexAttribArray(), 27, 28,
    112, 113, 116, 129, 130
glEndConditionalRender(), 176, 177
glEndQuery(), 173–175, 881, 882
glEndQueryIndexed(), 539

glEndTransformFeedback(), 252, 540
GLEW
  glewInit(), 9, 15, 837
glew.h, 837
glext.h, 9, 836, 837
glFenceSync(), 589, 591–593
glFinish(), 31, 106, 841, 847
glFlush(), 30, 31, 590, 842
glFlushMappedBufferRange(),
  105–107
glFramebufferParameteri(), 183
glFramebufferRenderbuffer(), 187,
  188
glFramebufferTexture(), 351, 352
glFramebufferTexture1D(), 351, 352
glFramebufferTexture2D(), 351, 352
glFramebufferTexture3D(), 351, 352,
  354
glFramebufferTextureLayer(), 354,
  557
glFrontFace(), 91, 899
glGenBuffers(), 19, 20, 92–94, 356,
  877, 878
glGenerateMipmap(), 337
glGenFramebuffers(), 181–183
glGenProgramPipelines(), 82, 878
glGenQueries(), 173, 174, 176, 539,
  878, 881
glGenRenderbuffers(), 183, 184, 188
glGenSamplers(), 292, 293, 295, 878
glGenTextures(), 264–266, 319, 352,
  354, 356, 570, 877, 878
glGenTransformFeedbacks(), 240
glGenVertexArrays(), 17, 18
glGet*(), 745
glGetActiveAtomicCounter
  Bufferiv(), 738
glGetActiveAttrib(), 738, 784, 785
glGetActiveSubroutineName(), 738
glGetActiveSubroutineUniformiv(),
  738
glGetActiveSubroutineUniform
  Name(), 738
glGetActiveUniform(), 304, 738, 784

glGetActiveUniformBlockiv(), 63,
  739
glGetActiveUniformBlockName(),
  739
glGetActiveUniformName(), 739
glGetActiveUniformsiv(), 65, 739,
  786, 787, 792
glGetAttachedShaders(), 739, 783
glGetAttribLocation(), 129, 739, 784
glGetBooleani_v(), 739, 770, 798
glGetBooleanv(), 739, 745, 755, 770,
  778, 779, 799, 807, 827
glGetBufferParameteri64v(), 739
glGetBufferParameteriv(), 739
glGetBufferPointerv(), 739, 750
glGetBufferSubData(), 100, 101,
  242, 532, 602, 739
glGetCompressedTexImage(), 739
glGetDebugMessageLog(), 739
glGetDoublei_v(), 740, 751
glGetDoublev(), 740, 745
glGetError(), 591, 738, 740, 827
glGetFloati_v(), 740, 751
glGetFloatv(), 740, 745, 746,
  753–755, 769, 770, 804–806,
  825
glGetFragDataIndex(), 195, 740
glGetFragDataLocation(), 195, 740
glGetFramebufferAttachment
  Parameteriv(), 740
glGetFramebufferParameteriv(), 740
glGetInteger64i_v(), 740, 748, 786,
  799–801
glGetInteger64v(), 740, 820, 825
glGetIntegeri_v(), 740, 748, 755,
  767, 769, 786, 798–801, 816
glGetIntegerv(), 154, 157, 160, 527,
  533, 549, 555, 559, 593, 634,
  738, 740, 745, 746, 748, 749,
  751–754, 756, 757, 766–772,
  775, 778–780, 783, 786,
  799–801, 803–827, 847, 876
glGetInternalformati64v(), 740
glGetInternalformativ(), 740, 826

glGetMultisamplefv(), 154, 741, 827
glGetObjectLabel(), 741, 748, 750, 761, 765, 772, 777, 781, 782, 784, 797, 799, 802, 877, 878
glGetObjectPtrLabel(), 741, 877, 878
glGetPointerv(), 741
glGetProgramBinary(), 741, 784
glGetProgramInfoLog(), 75, 741, 783
glGetProgramInterfaceiv(), 741
glGetProgramiv(), 74, 629, 630, 741, 783–786, 788–790
glGetProgramPipelineInfoLog(), 741
glGetProgramPipelineiv(), 741
glGetProgramResourceIndex(), 741
glGetProgramResourceiv(), 742
glGetProgramResourceLocation(), 741
glGetProgramResourceLocation Index(), 742
glGetProgramResourceName(), 742
glGetProgramStageiv(), 742, 789, 790
glGetQuery*(), 176
glGetQueryIndexediv(), 742
glGetQueryiv(), 742, 825, 827
glGetQueryObjecti64v(), 742
glGetQueryObjectiv(), 175, 742, 797
glGetQueryObjectui64v(), 742, 882
glGetQueryObjectuiv(), 175, 539, 742, 797, 881, 883
glGetRenderbufferParameteriv(), 742
glGetSamplerParameterfv(), 742
glGetSamplerParameterIiv(), 743
glGetSamplerParameterIuiv(), 743
glGetSamplerParameteriv(), 742
glGetShaderInfoLog(), 73, 743, 781
glGetShaderiv(), 73, 743, 781
glGetShaderPrecisionFormat(), 743
glGetShaderSource(), 743, 781
glGetString(), 738, 743, 808
glGetStringi(), 743, 808, 847
glGetSubroutineIndex(), 79, 743

glGetSubroutineUniformLocation(), 79, 743
glGetSynciv(), 589, 590, 743, 802
glGetTexImage(), 93, 287, 288, 291, 602, 743, 757, 758
glGetTexLevelParameterfv(), 743
glGetTexLevelParameteriv(), 743
glGetTexParameter*(), 759–761
glGetTexParameterfv(), 744, 760
glGetTexParameterIiv(), 744
glGetTexParameterIuiv(), 744
glGetTexParameteriv(), 744, 760, 761
glGetTransformFeedbackVarying(), 744
glGetUniform*(), 784
glGetUniformBlockIndex(), 63, 744
glGetUniformdv(), 744
glGetUniformfv(), 744
glGetUniformIndices(), 65, 744
glGetUniformiv(), 744
glGetUniformLocation(), 47, 569, 744, 784
glGetUniformSubroutineuiv(), 744
glGetUniformuiv(), 744
glGetVertexAttribdv(), 745
glGetVertexAttribfv(), 745, 797
glGetVertexAttribIiv(), 745
glGetVertexAttribIuiv(), 745
glGetVertexAttribiv(), 745
glGetVertexAttribLdv(), 745
glGetVertexAttribPointerv(), 745
glHint(), 178, 179
glInvalidateBufferData(), 107, 108
glInvalidateBufferSubData(), 107, 108
glInvalidateFramebuffer(), 192, 193, 354, 355
glInvalidateSubFramebuffer(), 192, 193, 354, 355
glInvalidateTexImage(), 355
glInvalidateTexSubImage(), 355
glIsBuffer(), 20
glIsEnabled(), 32, 157, 161, 738,

745, 749, 751, 753–756, 767–769, 797, 827
glIsEnabledi(), 197, 767, 769
glIsFramebuffer(), 182, 183
glIsProgram(), 76
glIsQuery(), 174
glIsRenderbuffer(), 184
glIsSampler(), 293
glIsShader(), 76
glIsSync(), 592
glIsTexture(), 265, 266
glIsTransformFeedback(), 240
glIsVertexArray(), 18
glLineWidth(), 88
glLinkProgram(), 47, 61, 64, 74, 245, 537, 625, 627, 647
glLogicOp(), 172
glMapBuffer(), 61, 101–104, 132, 532, 807
glMapBufferRange(), 104–106, 591
glMemoryBarrier(), 601, 603
glMinSampleShading(), 155, 156
glMultiDrawArrays(), 119, 120
glMultiDrawArraysIndirect(), 121, 122
glMultiDrawElements(), 119–121
glMultiDrawElementsBaseVertex(), 119, 121
glMultiDrawElementsIndirect(), 121, 122
global illumination, 384
glObjectLabel(), 877, 878
glObjectPtrLabel(), 877, 878
glPatchParameterfv(), 496, 501
glPatchParameteri(), 487–489, 500
glPauseTransformFeedback(), 251, 252
glPixelStore*(), 669
glPixelStoref(), 288
glPixelStorei(), 288
glPointParameter(), 350
glPointParameterf(), 350
glPointParameteri(), 350
glPointSize(), 87, 88

glPolygonMode(), 90, 91, 164
glPolygonOffset(), 164–166
glPopDebugGroup(), 870, 876, 877
glPrimitiveRestartIndex(), 125
glProgramParameteri(), 81
glProgramUniform(), 83
glProgramUniform*(), 83
glProgramUniformMatrix(), 83
glProgramUniformMatrix*(), 83
glProvokingVertex(), 524
glPushDebugGroup(), 870, 876, 877
glQueryCounter(), 882, 883
glReadBuffer(), 191, 196, 197, 201
glReadPixels(), 93, 196, 197, 200–202, 282
glRenderbufferStorage(), 185, 186
glRenderbufferStorageMultisample(), 185, 186
glResumeTransformFeedback(), 251, 252
glSampleCoverage(), 158
glSampleMaski(), 158, 159
glSamplerParameterf(), 294, 338
glSamplerParameterfv(), 294
glSamplerParameteri(), 294, 318, 338, 339
glSamplerParameteriv(), 294
glSamplerParameterI{i ui}v(), 294
glSamplerParameter{fi}(), 294
glSamplerParameter{fi}v(), 294
glScissor(), 157
glScissorArrayv(), 555
glScissorIndexed(), 554, 555
glScissorIndexedv(), 554
glShaderSource(), 72, 511, 627, 647
GLSL, 23, 34–84
  .length(), 44
  #version, 23, 36
  arrays, 44
  barrier(), 489, 634, 635, 644
  blocks, 60
  bool, 40
  boolean types, 38
  buffer block, 49

GLSL *continued*
  buffer blocks, 69
  buffer, 46, 49, 60, 62, 636
  centroid, 730
  clamp(), 445
  column_major, 62
  const, 46, 54
  constructors, 39
  control flow, 52
  conversions, 39
  defined, 57, 58
  dFdx(), 450, 459
  dFdy(), 450, 459
  discard, 88
  dmat4, 111
  do-while loop, 52
  double, 39, 40, 49, 111
  dvec2, 111
  dvec3, 111
  dvec4, 111
  extensions, 59
  false, 39, 695, 696
  flat, 424, 730
  float, 39, 40, 49, 113, 426
  floating-point types, 38
  for loop, 52
  functions, 52
  fwidth(), 450, 453, 458, 459
  groupMemoryBarrier(), 636
  if-else statement, 51
  image, 564
  implicit conversions, 39
  in blocks, 70
  in, 37, 46, 54, 60, 155, 451, 491
  inout, 54
  int, 40, 49, 110, 426
  integer types, 38
  interface block, 60
  invariant, 55
  isolines, 497
  ivec2, 110
  ivec3, 110
  ivec4, 110

  layout, 194, 489, 490, 497, 498,
    500, 502, 886
  length(), 44, 45, 69
  location, 194
  mat4, 113
  matrix, 40, 42
  memoryBarrier(), 635, 636
  memoryBarrierAtomicCounter(),
    635
  memoryBarrierBuffer(), 635
  memoryBarrierImage(), 635
  memoryBarrierShared(), 635
  mix(), 445, 481
  noperspective, 730
  operator precedence, 49
  operators, 49
  out blocks, 70
  out, 37, 46, 54, 60, 194, 417, 424,
    490, 491, 497
  packed, 62
  parameter qualifiers, 53
  precise qualifier, 55
  precise, 507
  preprocessor, 56–59
    #extension, 59
    #if,#else,#endif, 57
    #version, 23, 36
    __FILE__, 58
    __LINE__, 58
    __VERSION__, 58
  quads, 497, 500, 502, 505
  row_major, 62
  sample, 154, 155
  shared storage, 49
  shared, 46, 49, 62
  smoothstep(), 418, 426, 427, 445,
    449, 451, 459
  std140, 62
  std430, 62
  step(), 448
  storage qualifiers, 45
  structures, 43
  subroutines, 76
  switch statement, 51

GLSL *continued*
    triangles, 497
    true, 39, 695, 696, 705
    uint, 40, 49, 110
    uniform block, 61–69
    uniform, 37, 46, 47, 49, 60, 62,
        235, 363, 366, 368, 380
    uvec2, 110
    uvec3, 110
    uvec4, 110
    vec2, 113
    vec3, 113, 115, 452, 480
    vec4, 37, 113, 115, 425, 426, 502,
        577, 893
    component names, 42
    vectors, 40, 42
    while loop, 52
glStencilFunc(), 148, 159
glStencilFuncSeparate(), 159, 160
glStencilMask(), 148
glStencilMaskSeparate(), 148
glStencilOp(), 159, 160
glStencilOpSeparate(), 160
glTexBuffer(), 319, 357
glTexBufferRange(), 320
glTexImage*D(), 602
glTexImage1D(), 268–270, 279, 282
glTexImage2D(), 94, 268–270, 282,
    357, 570
glTexImage2DMultisample(),
    268–270
glTexImage3D(), 268–270, 279, 291,
    292, 307
glTexImage3DMultisample(),
    268–270
glTexParameterf(), 295, 338
glTexParameterfv(), 295
glTexParameteri(), 295, 302, 318,
    319, 408
glTexParameterIiv(), 295
glTexParameterIuiv(), 295
glTexParameteriv(), 295, 302
glTexParameterI{i ui}v(), 295
glTexParameter{fi}(), 295

glTexParameter{fi}v(), 295
glTexStorage1D(), 266, 267, 270,
    327
glTexStorage2D(), 266, 267, 270,
    285, 310, 322, 327, 337, 339,
    356, 357
glTexStorage2DMultisample(), 267,
    268
glTexStorage3D(), 266–268, 270,
    307, 327, 570
glTexStorage3DMultisample(), 267,
    268
glTexSubImage*D(), 602
glTexSubImage1D(), 278
glTexSubImage2D(), 267, 270, 274,
    278–281, 285, 288, 290, 310,
    337, 356
glTexSubImage3D(), 278, 291, 292
glTextureView(), 322
glTransformFeedbackVaryings(),
    244, 245, 536, 537
glUniform(), 48
glUniform*(), 9, 47, 48, 83
glUniform1i(), 304, 305, 356, 564,
    569
glUniform2f(), 9
glUniform2fv(), 9
glUniform3fv(), 9
glUniformBlockBinding(), 64
glUniformMatrix(), 48
glUniformMatrix*(), 47, 48, 83
glUniformMatrix4fv(), 554
glUniformSubroutinesuiv(), 80
glUnmapBuffer(), 102–106
glUseProgram(), 75, 81–83, 627,
    629, 648, 667
glUseProgramStages(), 82
GLUT, 8
    glutCreateWindow(), 15, 181,
        652, 653, 654, 837
    glutDisplayFunc(), 15, 16, 655,
        658
    glutGetProcAddress(), 654, 655,
        836

GLUT *continued*
  glutIdleFunc(), 658
  glutInit(), 15, 652
  glutInitContextFlags(), 652, 866
  glutInitContextProfile(), 15, 23, 652
  glutInitContextVersion(), 15, 652
  glutInitDisplayMode(), 15, 181, 652
  glutInitWindowPosition(), 652
  glutInitWindowSize(), 15, 652
  glutKeyboardFunc(), 656
  glutKeyboardUpFunc(), 656
  glutMainLoop(), 16, 654, 658
  glutPassiveMotionEvent(), 657
  glutPostRedisplay(), 655, 657
  glutReshapeFunc(), 656
  glutSwapBuffers(), 146, 896
glVertexAttrib(), 113
glVertexAttrib*(), 113–115
glVertexAttrib4(), 113
glVertexAttrib4N(), 114
glVertexAttrib4N*(), 26
glVertexAttrib4Nub(), 114
glVertexAttribDivisor(), 129, 130, 139
glVertexAttribI(), 114
glVertexAttribI*(), 114
glVertexAttribI4(), 114
glVertexAttribIPointer(), 110, 114
glVertexAttribL(), 114
glVertexAttribL*(), 114
glVertexAttribLPointer(), 111
glVertexAttribN*(), 149
glVertexAttribPointer(), 26, 27, 30, 93, 108–113, 129, 130, 149
glViewport(), 236, 656
glViewportArrayv(), 551, 555
glViewportIndexedf(), 550, 551, 554
glViewportIndexedfv(), 550, 551
glWaitSync(), 593, 825
GLX
  glXChooseFBConfig(), 839
  glXChooseVisual(), 840

glXCopyContext(), 841
glXCreateContext(), 841
glXCreateContextAttribsARB(), 840, 867
glXCreateGLXPixmap(), 840
glXCreateNewContext(), 840
glXCreatePbuffer(), 840
glXCreatePixmap(), 840
glXCreateWindow(), 840
glXDestroyContext(), 841
glXDestroyGLXPixmap(), 842
glXDestroyPbuffer(), 842
glXDestroyPixmap(), 842
glXDestroyWindow(), 842
glXGetClientString(), 839
glXGetConfig(), 840
glXGetCurrentContext(), 841
glXGetCurrentDisplay(), 841
glXGetCurrentDrawable(), 841
glXGetCurrentReadDrawable(), 841
glXGetFBConfigAttrib(), 839
glXGetProcAddress(), 840
glXGetSelectedEvent(), 841
glXGetVisualFromFBConfig(), 839
glXIsDirect(), 840
glXMakeContextCurrent(), 840
glXMakeCurrent(), 841
glXQueryContext(), 841
glXQueryExtension(), 839
glXQueryExtensionsString(), 839
glXQueryServerString(), 839
glXQueryVersion(), 839
glXSelectEvent(), 841
glXSwapBuffers(), 842
glXUseXFont(), 842
glXWaitGL(), 841, 847
glXWaitX(), 841, 842, 847
glxext.h, 840
gl_ClipDistance, 238
GL_CLIP_PLANE0, 239
Gouraud shading, 153
GPGPU, 181, 194
GPU, 4

gradient vector, 450
gradient, 450
graphics processing unit, 4
greaterThan(), 704
greaterThanEqual(), 704
groupMemoryBarrier(), 735

half space, 89
halo, 384
hemispherical lighting, 384
hidden-line removal, 164
hidden-surface removal, 145
homogeneous clip coordinates, 209
homogeneous coordinate, 206
homogeneous coordinates, 209,
    215, 216

image processing, 642
image, xli
image-based lighting, 389
imageAtomicAdd(), 582, 727
imageAtomicAnd(), 582, 728
imageAtomicCompSwap(), 583, 729
imageAtomicExchange(), 582, 583,
    728
imageAtomicMax(), 582, 728
imageAtomicMin(), 582, 728
imageAtomicOr(), 582, 728
imageAtomicXor(), 582, 728
imageLoad(), 572, 727
imageSize(), 573, 574, 727
imageStore(), 573, 727
immutable, 267
impostor, 558
imulExtended(), 706
init(), 7, 8, 15–17, 24, 25, 27, 29,
    147, 663, 664, 837
input-patch vertex, 489
instanced rendering, 85
instancing
    geometry shader, 548–550
intBitsToFloat(), 696
interface block, 60, 514, 516
interpolateAtCentroid(), 730

interpolateAtOffset(), 730, 731
interpolateAtSample(), 730
interpolation, 153
invariance, 54
inverse(), 703
inversesqrt(), 691
invocation, 55
invocation
    compute shader, 625
isinf(), 696
isnan(), 696

jaggies, 178

lacunarity, 466
layered rendering, 525, 550–559
layout qualifier, 24, 511, 566, 626
ldexp(), 697
length(), 700
lens flare, 384
lessThan(), 704
lessThanEqual(), 704
level of detail, 333, 340
light probe, 389
lighting, 70
    ambient, 363
    directional, 365
    emissive, 380
    hemispherical, 384
    image based, 389
    material properties, 379
    multiple lights, 376
    point lights, 368
    spherical harmonics, 395
    spotlight, 370
    two sided, 381
linked list, 610
LoadImage.h, 283
LoadShaders(), 8, 22, 23, 76, 664,
    665, 667
LoadShaders.h, 22
local viewer, 383
log(), 691
log2(), 691

logical operation, 171
lossless compression, 326
lossy compression, 326
low-pass filtering, 449
luminance, 43

Mac OS X
   NSOpenGLContext(), 854
   NSOpenGLPixelFormat(), 854
   NSOpenGLView(), 854
magnification, 329
mantissa, 274
material, 70
matrix, xlii, 214
matrix
   column major, 234
   multiplication, 214
   OpenGL, 232
   row major, 234
matrixCompMult(), 702
max(), 694
memory
   read only, 598
memoryBarrier(), 735
memoryBarrierAtomicCounter(),
   735
memoryBarrierBuffer(), 735
memoryBarrierImage(), 735
memoryBarrierShared(), 735
min(), 693, 694
minification, 329
   magnification, 335
mipmap, 262
mipmaps, 332
mix(), 695
mod(), 693
model coordinates, 209
modeling transformation, 207
models, 4
modf(), 693
modulate, 362
monitor, 181
multisampling, 146, 153, 262
mutex, 585

nanosecond, 881
near plane, 211, 227, 236
network, 3
noise, 459–483
   gradient noise, 464
   granite, 478
   marble, 477
   octave, 463
   turbulence, 475
   value noise, 462
   wood, 478
noise1(), 732
noise2(), 732
noise3(), 732
noise4(), 732
normal, 362
normal vectors
   transforming, 831
normal map, 441
normal maps, 441
normalize(), 701
normalized device coordinates, 209
normalized homogeneous
   coordinates, 208
normalized value, 149
normalized-device coordinates, 22
not(), 705
notEqual(), 705

object, xli
   label, 877
object coordinates, 209
occlusion query, 173
octave, 463
off-screen rendering, 181
opaque types, 38
optimization
   loop hoisting, 594
orthographic projection, 230
orthographic viewing model, 212
orthographic, 212
outerProduct(), 702
overloading, 40

pack, 97
packDouble2x32(), 699
packHalf2x16(), 699
packSnorm2x16(), 698
packSnorm4x8(), 698
packUnorm2x16(), 698
packUnorm4x8(), 698
pass-through shader, 12, 501
patch, 12, 485, 486
performance profiling, 879
Perlin noise, 460
perspective correction, 730
perspective division, 213
perspective projection, 207, 210,
    227
Phong reflection model, 376
Phong shading, 376
pixel, 4
point fade threshold, 350
point lighting, 368
point sampling, 444
point sprites, 346
point, 4
polygon culling, 91
polygon faces, 91
polygon offset, 404
polygon, 90
pow(), 690
primitive generator, 487
procedural shading, 412
procedural texture shader, 412
procedural texturing, 412–433
    brick, 419
    lattice, 431
    regular patterns, 414
    toy ball, 422
programmable blending, 609
projective texturing, 342, 408
protocol, 3
proxy texture, 260, 276

quadrilateral, 299
queries
    timer, 881

race condition, 645
radians(), 688
rasterization, 3
rasterization
    disabling, 511
rasterizer, 152, 153
ray tracing, 4
readonly, 598
reflect(), 701
refract(), 701
renderbuffer, 145, 181
renderer, 851
rendering pipeline, 10
rendering, 4
resolved, 154
restrict, 595
restricted pointer, 595
RGB color space, 25, 143
RGBA mode, 29
RGBA, 143
rotation, 224
round(), 692
roundEven(), 693

sample shader, 155
sample, 153
sampler, 629
    object, 292
sampler variables, 262
samples, 35
scaling, 221
scissor box, 157
scissoring, 157
selector, 265
separate shader objects, 81
server, 3
SetPixelFormat(), 846
shader, 3
    compiling, 627
    compute, 36, 623–649
    fragment, 35
    geometry, 35, 510
    subroutines, 76
    tessellation, 35, 510

vertex, 35
shader plumbing, 8
shader program, 8
shader stage, 4
shader storage buffer object, 69
shader storage buffer, 46
shader variable, 23
shading, xliii
shadow coordinates, 406
shadow map, 400
shadow mapping, 400
shadow sampler, 317
shadow texture, 402
shared exponent, 274
shared variables, 633
sign(), 692
sin(), 688
sinh(), 689
sky box, 312
slice, 261, 262
smoothstep(), 695
sorting, 616
spaces
   clip space, 209
   eye space, 209
   eye, 383
   model space, 209
   object space, 209
specular light, 362
spherical harmonic lighting, 395
spotlight, 370
sprite, 88
sqrt(), 691
sRGB color space, 143, 274
state, 4, 29
stencil buffer, 146
stencil testing, 13
step(), 695
stereo, 146
stipple, 163
storage qualifiers, 45
structures, 43
subpixel, 146
subroutines, 76

supersampling, 445
surface-local coordinate space, 434
surface-local coordinates, 434
SwapBuffers(), 847
sync object, 589
synchronization, 577, 634

tan(), 688
tangent space, 435
tanh(), 690
temporal aliasing, 444
tessellated, 12
tessellation
   control shaders, 488–491
      bypassing, 495
      gl_in variable, 490
      gl_out variable, 490
      other variables, 491
      pass-through, 495
   cracking along shared edges, 506
   displacement mapping, 507
   domains
      isolines, 493
      quads, 491–493
      selecting, 497
      triangles, 493–495
   evaluation shaders, 496–510
      coordinate spacing options, 498
      gl_in variable, 499
      gl_out variable, 500
      other variables, 500
   patches, 487, 488
   primitive winding, 497
   tessellation coordinates, 498
   view-dependent, 504–506
tessellation control shader, 486
tessellation coordinates, 487
tessellation domain, 485
tessellation evaluation shader, 486
tessellation level factor, 489
tessellation output patch vertices,
   488
tessellation shader, 35, 514
tessellation shaders, 486

texelFetch(), 321, 714
texelFetchOffset(), 714
texels, 261
texture
  array, 262
  buffer, 319–321, 572
  compressed, 326–329
  cube map, 559
  gathering texels, 345
  immutable storage, 357
  proxy, 276, 277
  rectangle, 263
  target, 263
  unit, 262
  view, 321–325
  writing to, 574
texture comparison mode, 402
texture coordinates, 153, 261
texture map, 14, 149
texture mapping, 8, 149
texture object, 261
texture sampler, 262
texture streaming, 339
texture swizzle, 302
texture targets, 262
texture unit, 262
texture view, 322
texture(), 296, 309, 317, 318, 711
textureGather(), 345, 721
textureGatherOffset(), 721, 722
textureGatherOffsets(), 722
textureGrad(), 341, 717
textureGradOffset(), 346, 718
textureLod(), 340, 712
textureLodOffset(), 715
textureOffset(), 341, 342, 713
textureProj(), 342, 343, 712
textureProjGrad(), 346, 719
textureProjGradOffset(), 346, 719,
    720
textureProjLod(), 346, 716
textureProjLodOffset(), 346, 716
textureProjOffset(), 346, 715
textureQueryLevels(), 344, 711

textureQueryLod(), 343, 710
textures
  binding to image units, 569
textureSize(), 344, 709, 710
timeout, 590
transform feedback, 239, 532–548
  objects, 239
  particle system example, 252
  starting and stopping, 250
  varyings, 244
transform feedback object, 239
transformation matrices, 12, 831
transformation matrix
  projection
    orthographic, 230
    perspective, 227
  rotation, 224
  scaling, 221
  translation, 219
transformations
  model-view, 209
  modeling, 207
  normals, 231
  orthographic projection, 230
  perspective projection, 207, 210,
    227
  rotation, 224
  scaling, 221
  translation, 219
  viewing, 207
  viewport, 209
translation, 219
transparency
  order independent, 609
transparent types, 38
transpose(), 702, 703
trunc(), 692
turbulence, 475
txtureProj(), 342
typed array, 667

uaddCarry(), 705
uintBitsToFloat(), 696
umulExtended(), 706

uniform block, 61–69, 629
uniform buffer object, 61
uniform variable, 46
unit square, 491
universe
  end of, 882
unpackDouble2x32(), 699
unpackHalf2x16(), 699
unpackSnorm2x16(), 698
unpackSnorm4x8(), 698
unpackUnorm2x16(), 698
unpackUnorm4x8(), 698
user clipping, 238
usubBorrow(), 706
Utah teapot, 500

vector, 7, 214
vertex shader, 4, 35
vertex winding, 497
vertex, 11
vertex-array object, 17
vertex-attribute array, 26
vglLoadImage(), 277, 283–286
vglLoadTexture(), 286
vglUnloadImage(), 284, 286
viewing frustum, 210
viewing model, 206
viewing transformation, 207
viewpoint, 156
viewport, 13
  index, 555
    multiple, 550–559
  transform, 209
vmath::frustum(), 229
vmath::lookAt(), 229
vmath::ortho(), 231
vmath::rotate(), 227
vmath::scale(), 224
vmath::translate(), 220
volatile, 595
voxel, 307

WebGL
  InitShaders(), 666, 667
  onload(), 668
  setupWebGL(), 663
WGL
  wglCopyContext(), 847
  wglCreateContext(), 846, 867
  wglCreateContextAttribsARB(),
    846, 866, 867
  wglCreateLayerContext(), 846
  wglDescribeLayerPlane(), 846
  wglDestroyContext(), 847
  wglGetCurrentContext(), 847
  wglGetCurrentDC(), 847
  wglGetLayerPaletteEntries(), 848
  wglGetProcAddress(), 846, 847,
    867
  wglMakeCurrent(), 847
  wglRealizeLayerPalette(), 848
  wglSetLayerPaletteEntries(), 848
  wglShareLists(), 847
  wglSwapLayerBuffers(), 847
  wglUseFontBitmaps(), 848
  wglUseFontOutlines(), 848
winding, 91
window coordinates, 209
window system, 866, 867
windows.h, 846
wingdi.h, 846
wireframe, 165, 525
workgroup, 625, 630
world coordinates, 209
writeonly, 598

X Window System, 3

z precision, 237
z-buffer, 146
z-buffering, 13

FREE
Online Edition

 Safari
Books Online

Your purchase of **OpenGL® Programming Guide: The Official Guide to Learning OpenGL®, Version 4.3, Eighth Edition,** includes access to a free online edition for 45 days through the Safari Books Online subscription service. Nearly every Addison-Wesley Professional book is available online through **Safari Books Online**, along with thousands of books and videos from publishers such as Cisco Press, Exam Cram, IBM Press, O'Reilly Media, Prentice Hall, Que, Sams, and VMware Press.

Safari Books Online is a digital library providing searchable, on-demand access to thousands of technology, digital media, and professional development books and videos from leading publishers. With one monthly or yearly subscription price, you get unlimited access to learning tools and information on topics including mobile app and software development, tips and tricks on using your favorite gadgets, networking, project management, graphic design, and much more.

Activate your FREE Online Edition at informit.com/safarifree

STEP 1: Enter the coupon code: YGEYQZG.

STEP 2: New Safari users, complete the brief registration form.
Safari subscribers, just log in.

If you have difficulty registering on Safari or accessing the online edition,
please e-mail customer-service@safaribooksonline.com

 Addison Wesley   AdobePress   ALPHA   Cisco Press   Press FINANCIAL TIMES   IBM Press   Microsoft Press   New Riders O'REILLY

 Peachpit Press   PRENTICE HALL   que   Redbooks   SAMS   SAS Publishing vmware PRESS   WILEY   wrox